CAVORTING WITH CANNIBALS

AN EXPLORATION OF VANUATU

By Rick Williamson

THE NARRATIVE PRESS
TRUE FIRST-PERSON HISTORICAL ACCOUNTS

Dedication
To my parents, Derek and Doreen, and to those selfless people I met during my travels who shared their material comforts, their friendship, and the very essence of their previously shrouded beliefs.

Acknowledgments
A special thanks to, Air Vanuatu, Van Air, Ralph Regenvanu, Vanuatu's Cultural Centre, Vanuatu's National Tourism Office, The Great Outdoors (Arthur Ellis Ltd), and Murray Crabb of Murray Crabb Photo Services.

Mr. Williamsons' first trip to the Solomon Islands was in March 1993. The events in the chapters "Beginners Luck" and "Stone Age Meets the Clone Age" take place during September 1997. The chapter "Crossing the Cultural Divide" takes place during June 1998. "Where Spirits Dwell" and "Winea" take place during May 1999. "Moral Obligation" and "Rough Justice" take place during June 2000. And "Disgruntled Devotion" takes place during May 2001.

The Narrative Press
P.O. Box 2487, Santa Barbara, California 93120 U.S.A.
Telephone: (800) 315-9005 Web: www.narrativepress.com

ISBN 1-58976-236-3 (Paperback)

Produced in the United States of America

CONTENTS

Chapter One

INTRODUCTION

I've always had an instinctive love for the outdoors and cherish being able to experience the escapism of exploring remote areas of unparalleled beauty, contacting and gaining a deeper understanding of fascinating primitive peoples. Sometimes I've gained total acceptance from isolated tribes and ended up documenting the lives and the beliefs of my newfound friends as one of the clan rather than as an interested observer. To gain an intimate and factual insight into their unique way of life, whenever it's possible, I cross the cultural divide and live exactly as they do. It hasn't always been easy, and the numerous rewards have usually been earned by climbing a sometimes unforgiving learning curve that's filled with personal sacrifice and unwelcome suffering.

Whenever I'm on an expedition and trying to achieve a risky objective, making my own decisions has always been paramount. The option of being able to resign at any time to ensure my safe return is the ultimate reason—one of the main reasons—why I've always travelled alone. Solo exploration is often dangerous and has been a huge compromise, but it's opened a lot of otherwise closed doors. There are countless times when I've wished that I had someone to share my privileged experiences with, but if I had a travelling companion those precious moments might never have eventuated.

In an ever-decreasing world, observing primitive peoples who have never been documented before has become a rarity. Explorers, propounding missionaries, anthropologists, scientists, and those who are trying to reap the bounty of nature's hidden resources have ventured into all but a few remote tracts of unexplored jungle where a few inaccessible clans have managed to cling to their primeval purity by vigorously avoiding or repelling outsiders. It's a sad reflection on humanity that only a few of what we wrongly label as "lost tribes" remain. They are anything but lost, and most of them purposely choose to remain hidden in their secluded environments. It's inevitable that with the passage of time they will eventually succumb to our ignorance and arrogance. I feel it's important to bring their knowledge to us before modern man's destructiveness infringes upon their fragile ecosystems and their vulnerable societies because history has proved our treatment of indigenous peoples is despicable.

During my first expedition as a photojournalist I walked across Vanuatu's largest island and found myself thrust into a unique and often precarious position when I was the only man on the planet who was able to document a cannibalistic pygmy tribe living deep in the jungle amidst the rugged heart of Espiritu Santo. With a village name like Winea, which translates into "to eat man," it's hardly surprising I was the first to record their complex culture. After I undertook a full initiation into a neighbouring clan that shared the same language and customs as Winea's inhabitants, the circumstances demanded that if I wanted to study these fascinating people, I had to place myself completely at their mercy by returning alone. Irrespective of my intuition, expelling fear and doubt and shedding my morals and beliefs became a necessity each time I immersed myself into their sometimes cruel and unsympathetic society. They live in a timeless world that's filled with complex traditions that were totally devoid of compassion or compromise for my lack of understanding, especially if I accidentally breached one of the numerous tribal laws.

Uninterrupted nature will always contain a harsh element. Primitive tribes are often associated with violence and brutal customs, yet when they aren't performing barbaric rites, they're generally a beautiful and selfless people whose whole morality is bound in vigorously guarding their environment and their beliefs. Whenever I've lived with primitive people, I've found their social behaviour differs from the mannerisms of many civilized societies. Acts that are violent or dominate others are very rarely motivated by greed or by unprovoked aggression.

Most primitive societies are comprised of deeply spiritual peoples dedicated to nurturing and appeasing their ancestral spirits so that once they join them, they will be well positioned in the afterlife. Their beliefs are often shrouded in intense secrecy, and some will argue that the deepest and darkest secrets of any veiled culture should remain just that, hidden from the rest of humanity, and accessible only to those who worship its philosophy. Undoubtedly the copyright of any religion must belong to the culture that nurtures its principles. But history is at a phase where many previously isolated ethnic groups are being subjected to enforced hybridisation and exposed to external influences they are unable to control when the rapidly encroaching outside world erodes their primeval beliefs. Where myths, traditions, and the very essence of a people's purpose and being are passed on by word of mouth from their early ancestors to each successive generation, it's paramount that a written and photographic reference remains for future generations.

All of the knowledge I've reaped from these unique peoples and the right to share it with others has been gifted or hard earned. Absolutely nothing has been pried from the weak willed or stolen by shrewd interrogation. If I did that with some of the tribes I've lived with, it wouldn't only be devious, it would be extremely reckless and dangerous because the repercussions for misplacing the most sacred of knowledge into the hands of those who haven't undertaken the necessary rites of passage, or don't have the right cultural awareness, are often dire. Death is sometimes the penalty for both the bearer and the recipient if the beneficiary hasn't first gained the acceptance and approval of the supreme beings that reside in the spiritual realm.

When we acquire new and interesting anthropological information, when the most sacred of beliefs and rituals are shared in an impartial and sensitive manner, we should learn from them. By putting the information into perspective, it may give us a much deeper understanding of the evolutionary process, of cultural diversity, and of the remaining living roots of mankind's heritage. Primitive peoples can provide us with a unique insight into the human condition. Maybe the study of primitive societies will enhance our understanding of how we relate to each other in a naturally violent world and enable us to see more clearly into our own future.

Over the past decade, I've found that exploration can be a lot easier than you'd otherwise presume, but at times the hardships and dangers are far worse than anything you've ever imagined. I've also learnt that the reality of life amongst primitive peoples can be a far cry from the word pictures that are depicted by writers who have portrayed an idealistic image, or what is shown in carefully edited documentaries that are dictated to by economic profit. The first casualty of profit is often the truth, and the truth is often avoided by those who are afraid of being ridiculed for showing or writing about something we can't comprehend. Sometimes the author or producer's main priority is to please an accepting audience who might otherwise be repulsed by the reality. This book isn't written by an expert, and it was never intended to be a heart-warming literary ray of sunshine. It conveys a "warts and all" account of my experiences, be they enlightening, inexplicable, or barbaric. I've included events and rituals that I didn't witness myself that were someone else's interpretation of what they believe was the truth to provide a clearer picture of what I did see, and so we have a better understanding of how primitive peoples see themselves.

Chapter Two

HUMBLE HERITAGE

It wasn't until I was in my mid-thirties that my father, Derek, and his brother Les, told me they'd weathered experiences that would leave anyone who has a hint of adventurous blood flowing through their veins in awe. When adventure inevitably became my profession, in their typically humble and causal manner they both mentioned they'd taken part in expeditions that were involved in historical firsts. They were born into the end of an enviable and never to be repeated era that was filled with iron willed explorers who often overcame daunting odds to achieve their objectives. If an adventurer tried to emulate their astounding feats nowadays, under the same conditions, using the same simplistic equipment, they would find it hard to match their predecessor's incredible stamina and astonishing perseverance. These were the last of the pioneers who embodied the true spirit of adventure. They often reached their goals after they'd endured epic struggles and at a time when rescue airlifts, satellite navigation, modern survival equipment, and accurate weather predictions were still in their infancy or unthinkable luxuries.

Derek got his first taste of exploration beyond the fringes of northern civilization in the vast and desolate white upon white landscape of the Canadian Arctic. In 1956, when he was twenty years old, he travelled to Yellowknife as an integral member of a fifteen-man advance party after he was handpicked to work in the demanding polar climate under the employment of an American mining company called Consolidated Goldmines. Back then Yellowknife was just a few crude huts scattered around a tiny settlement that served as the Arctic's last civilized outpost. It was from there that he ventured north to help with mining and exploration, and although the work was often dangerous, it was exciting and varied. His resilience and versatility made him a vital asset to any expedition, and after he proved his worth, he was leased out to the American government to help their scientists track the Nautilus, which was the world's first nuclear powered submarine. The Nautilus began its historic journey from Point Barrow in Alaska, and after it wove through the North West Passage beneath the thick ice, it emerged in the Greenland Sea on the fifth of August 1958. When he helped the scientists follow the submarine from above by dogsled, Derek was dressed in traditional Eskimo boots, called *mutlaks*, and clothing that was lined with wolverine fur.

Whenever he worked outside in extreme conditions, he insulated his body from the mind-numbing cold by rubbing seal blubber in the fleshy webs between his fingers and toes, behind his ears, and over any skin that was exposed to the elements. Then he bound his fingers and toes together with tape to trap every bit of precious body heat. No matter how careful he was he constantly suffered from frostbite. Once the temperature started to plummet, Derek and his companions always kept a close watch on each other's faces for any patches of frozen, pale skin. When they kneaded their nipped flesh with their fingertips, the blood surged back into the afflicted tissue with a rush of blinding pain that was so intense it sometimes had the strongest of men screaming in agony.

During one expedition the mercury plunged to a nerve rattling and warmth sucking minus seventy-two degrees. In such steely conditions, even the most basic activities became life threatening as simply breathing heavily ran the risk of instantly freezing their lung tissue. Every torturous breath seared Derek's lungs, then literally froze with a soft cracking sound as it was exhaled into the frigid air. On one of his trips across the ice, the cold was so brittle that when he stood up after riding on the back of the dog sledge, his mutlaks snapped in half.

In times of severe weather, rather than run the risk of freezing their flesh the instant it was exposed to the bitter cold and ending up like the proverbial brass monkey, the men were forced to defecate and urinate themselves. Their excrement froze and rattled around inside their pants, and their frozen urine painfully cut into their skin like acidic shards of glass, especially when they were working or running behind the dog teams. While they were out on the ice, day after day crept by until sometimes months had passed without them taking a wash or enjoying the luxury of fresh clothing. When the freezing conditions were so severe that heating water to take a wash was unrealistic and simply too dangerous, the enforced lack of personal hygiene led to boils, chaffing, rashes, and other painful ailments. Although he smelt like a broken sewer, after a few weeks Derek's senses become oblivious to the overpowering stench of his body odour.

Like all of the natural inhabitants that live in the barren arctic, at times he became dependant on the environment and was forced to hunt bears and other game to survive. The mental strain of constantly suffering from frostbite and the hardships they endured while they lived out on the ice took their toll on even the hardiest of men. A few of his companions perished when the eternal cold drove them so insane they lost all self-control. One of his close friends was pushed beyond the brink of logical reasoning by the uncompromising arctic and ended his misery by blowing his head off with a stick of dynamite. Another flicked his eye out when he fell on a shard of ice while they were running behind the dog team, and spent three agonizing weeks sledging across the ice before they made it back to base. He had to wait six months before the next Bristol freighter dropped of supplies and flew him back to civilization to be treated.

When Derek and a companion were told to take a dog team and look for survivors after a plane carrying medical staff went down in the vast desert of snow and ice, their unsuccessful expedition had a grisly ending. They were determined to locate the wreckage, but after an extensive search, they failed to find any sign of the plane. Despite the atrocious conditions, a few of the passengers managed to survive the crash. Their extreme circumstances drove them to extreme measures when they were faced with two unenviable options. They could either suffer from lingering starvation in the hope that a rescue team came to their aid before they perished or cannibalise a young nurse who'd died in the crash. They chose the latter, which kept them alive until another search party saved them.

It was Derek's experiences with the Inuit Eskimos that held me spellbound rather than the hardship he suffered when he was out on the ice. Some of the Inuit had never seen a white man until he made contact with them. The primitive Eskimos were nature unto itself and had a close affinity with their severe surroundings that Derek could never hope to fully understand. Millennia of evolving in the brutal arctic had equipped them with an uncanny knowledge of the ice and its movements that even seasoned veterans of the polar region could never match. Some of the Inuit's customs were just as harsh as their uncompromising environment. They were indifferent towards any Europeans that were associated with mining, and sometimes weeks ticked by without them uttering a single word to Derek, which worsened the bouts of loneliness he occasionally suffered from. But over time and with patience, he eventually befriended several remote clans who were living in dome-shaped igloos made from compressed blocks of snow.

Once he'd gained their trust the Inuit gave him a unique insight into their primal existence. During one of his visits, when he was invited to witness an Eskimo birth, the huskies tethered alongside the igloo barked and howled with excitement when they smelt the woman's water breaking. The restless dogs had good reason to serenade the arrival of the infant. Once the child was delivered, a woman who acted as a midwife led one of the dogs inside to lick the mother's legs and genitals clean of the warm blood and steaming afterbirth. New life nurtures life in such extreme conditions. Millennia of adaptation had instilled in the Inuit that absolutely nothing was to be wasted. In such a severe ecosystem, where the prospect of hunger constantly lingers on the horizon until the next successful hunt, the howling dogs were fed the child's afterbirth.

During another visit, he discovered the corpse of a stillborn child that had been buried alongside an igloo. The Eskimo's ravenous huskies had unearthed the body and were midway through their gruesome meal. An already grim task, the type that numbed his already freezing senses, was made even more terrible when he had to wrestle the grisly remains from the snarling dogs.

The Arctic was as captivating as it was brutal, and he fondly recalls the rugged beauty of the ever-changing snow and ice and the sheer excitement of surviving many memorable adventures and challenges, which at the time were paled by the exuberance and optimism of his youth. He relished the lasting friendships and watching the aurora borealis's flaming dance cast eerie flares of light into the sky.

After three years of polar life, Derek left the Arctic, and in what must have been a gargantuan contrast of environments, he worked in the steamy jungles of the Brazilian Amazon. While he was in transit to the tropics, he stopped off at Fort Resolution and stayed at Consolidated Goldmines, aptly named Tramp Miner Hotel. The years of isolation and the numerous hardships they endured in the merciless and freezing climate sometimes took a heavy toll on the mental health of even the hardest of men. They normally embraced civilization with mammoth drinking binges that usually lasted for days. It's said the arctic is a make or break place where the weak can become tough, but the toughest can become weak. While most men became stronger and left the icy wilderness with treasured memories, for some the arctic had been to humbling. They carried festering mental wounds that were inflicted by years of polar remoteness, from enduring eternally dark winters, and from suffering the agony of constant frostbite. The mental torment that preyed on the weak willed had an ugly habit of surfacing when a drunken taste of reality amplified the enormity of having to return to the brutal arctic conditions. While they were under the influence of alcohol, the sobering prospect of having to face the strain of living on the ice again became so overwhelming that some of them opted for suicide. The company was forced to take preventative measures to stop the distraught men from jumping to their deaths and had bricked up all of the windows in the hotel that were above ground floor.

While he was on leave from Consolidated Mines, a chance meeting in Canada with a deeply religious geologist led to a free trip and the opportunity to begin another adventure in a region with an equally daunting reputation. He travelled by canoe to deep in the Amazon rainforest where he built huts for catholic missionaries. As well as constructing the buildings, he portaged gifts of pots and pans and other enticing goods through the jungle, which the missionaries used to entice the Jivaro Indians so they could convert them to Christianity.

The Jivaro were fearsome headhunters who were renowned for the practice of shrinking human heads. The early explorers who travelled through the Amazon basin called it "the green hell" after they encountered sprawling jungle, malaria, wilting heat, venomous creatures, and hostile cannibalistic Indians. Because of the numerous dangers, a red security rope surrounded the worker's compound, and they were given strict orders never to stray beyond the confines of the border unless they were told to. Any excursions that were made into the rainforest were always carried out by at least three men. When two of Derek's audacious companions violated the rules, they were never seen again. The dog tags the men were made to wear were never found, and it was feared their heads ended up as shrunken trophies that hung from the rafters in the hut of a Jivaro headhunter. When Derek travelled up the highway of rivers and tributaries by dugout canoe, he sometimes caught a fleeting glimpse of the primitive Jivaro as they faded into the gloom of the jungle. On one occasion he was within ten meters of a band of fierce looking headhunters, and that was the closest he ever came to making contact with the reclusive natives before they quickly vanished into the weave of rainforest.

Derek's older brother, Les, was twenty-five years old when he participated in another historical first. During 1957, a unique merging of cultures culminated in a way that will never be repeated in mankind's history when Russia and America, the world's two superpowers, strived to be the first to send a satellite into space to orbit the earth. Australia's parched interior set the scene where modern man in his most advanced state of technology and science entered the realm of natural man in his most primitive existence. Les was one of thirty handpicked volunteers who were chosen after rigorous psychological and medical tests to spend a year in one of nature's most inhospitable regions, the Gibson Desert, to establish the Giles weather station. With Woomera rocket range nearing completion, the countdown was on for Giles weather station to be established so that its computers, which were imperative to register the satellites annual geophysical orbit, would be ready for the launch of the American's rocket.

The government kept the project hidden under a shroud of secrecy and neither confirmed nor denied any knowledge of the men they sortied across the arid desert in a decrepit Bristol freighter. The Landrover, tents, fuel, and enough basic supplies to sustain the men for three months that filled the plane left barely enough room for the passengers. Two hardy surveyors who'd already made an arduous overland journey, virtually in the famed footsteps of the legendary explorers Wills and Burke, had cleared the stunted mulga scrub and made a crude runway. Oil from a leaking engine streaked across Les's window as the plane skimmed above the arid wilderness. Everyone nervously searched for smoke from the surveyor's signal fires, which as well as showing the wind direction, indicated the whereabouts of the makeshift airstrip. No one had predicted the aborigines inhabiting the desolate wasteland would also have fires burning during the heat of the day. Several anxious passes were made before the relieved pilot and passengers sighted the surveyors waving arms.

A successful landing on the unpacked sand would be where the passengers and equipment exited the aircraft unscathed. The air force had purposely provided an aging plane, as they expected the dilapidated Bristol freighter to sustain irreparable damage during the landing that would cripple the aircraft and prevent its return flight. When it touched down amidst a cloud of blinding dust the hulking plane and the weight of its cargo drove the tyres into the soft sand and thrust it into an abrupt and precarious nosedive. The tail momentarily lurched into the air, and then slammed into the desert when the plane shuddered to a halt to end a safe but nerve-racking landing.

The nomadic hunter-gatherer aborigines living in the area were terrified by the unexpected intrusion on their lives. For thousands of years and for countless generations, their extreme geographical isolation had quarantined them from the unfathomable world that lay beyond their tribal boundaries. To ensure the sudden disruption didn't have a detrimental effect on the Stone Age natives, an aboriginal protector was appointed to safeguard their welfare. The construction crew had been given strict instructions not to violate any aspect of the aborigine's lives.

Once the gear was unloaded from the plane and a camp was set up, the first priority was to drill for precious water, which is the most crucial element of desert survival. Seventeen wells were sunk before drinkable water was found as salt tainted most of the water tables. The aboriginal protector had told the workers that if ever they got lost in the desert and were found by the natives, if nothing else, they needed to remember the word *kapi*, which means water, because the aborigines would no doubt give them some to save their lives.

As they toiled away in the repressive heat and built the weather station, the workers knew the aborigines were keeping a vigilant watch on the hive of strange activity. But the discreet onlookers blended so perfectly with the terracotta desert and the stunted mulga scrub that they remained undetected by the construction crew's searching eyes.

Up until the arrival of the white man, the animals indigenous to the area had little fear of humans. The aborigines were extremely selective when they hunted game and left most of the animals undisturbed. As a consequence, the kangaroos, emus, turkeys, and other tasty game that fell prey to the camp rifle were hunted with relative ease. It didn't take long for the inquisitive dingoes that skulked around the weather station to associate the camp with food when they caught the scent of roasting meat. Before the workers left their tents each morning they pounded a petrol drum with a stick to chase the scavenging dogs away. The foraging dingoes became so persistent that the cook was forced to hang any meat out of reach of the animal's ravenous jaws.

Whenever Les had any free time, he wandered off into the desert to fossick amongst the profusion of flora and fauna that he found so interesting or to simply enjoying the solitude of the pristine landscape. He loved to sketch, and while he was drawing the local wildlife, he would often hear an aboriginal *cooee* call when one native shouted to another and it floated through the incessant chatter of the huge flocks of galahs and budgerigars. Les could sense he was being watched and could almost feel the stare of their curious primal eyes. The inquisitive aborigines always stayed out of his sight, but they never stayed out of his mind.

The native's interest eventually overshadowed their apprehension and a naked hunter who looked unsure of himself gingerly appeared from behind a clump of mulga scrub. The universal recognition of Les's smile and relaxed mannerisms hastened the aborigines uncertain approach. With a wave of his hand, which he did with his palm facing downwards, he motioned the alien white man to follow him back to his camp. Les's tent back at the weather station seemed palatial when he compared it to the aborigine's meagre campsite. A haphazard shelter constructed from an untidy heap of mulga scrub, with an entrance that was barely big enough for a human to crawl through, offered the natives their only protection from the elements. The simple and easily constructed shelter suited the aborigine's nomadic lifestyle. Because they were such an integral part of the landscape, they had an intimate knowledge of all of nature. By observing the behaviour of animals, the aborigines were able to accurately predict the arrival of an impending dust storm and knew beforehand when they'd need to shelter in the makeshift humpy. During fine weather they slept under the canopy of the stars. To stay warm throughout the cold desert nights, they scraped holes in the sand to accommodate their hips and shoulders and filled them with hot embers. Then they covered the depression with sand to make a crude but warm bed. Whenever they slept in the open they curled up alongside a small fire. Most of them rolled into the flames while they slept, and were covered in the marks of old burns as well as the ritualistic scars that adorned their bodies.

Due to the severe environment, the aborigines Les visited were a peaceful people who enjoyed a harmonious relationship with their neighbouring clans. Their continued survival demanded interdependence, unity, and respect not only towards one another, but also towards all of nature. Unlike the aborigines in Northern Arnheimland, intertribal conflict never occurred, because merely surviving from day to day was struggle enough without the added strain of violence. Most of the nomadic clans were comprised of no more than five to seven members. They felt that having any lesser or larger amount of people in their group would drastically reduce their chances of survival. Their only material possessions were *woomeras* (a throwing stick that's used to launch a spear), spears, clubs, boomerangs, and hunting dogs. Nothing was seen to belong to an individual. And although an object may have been crafted by a single member of a clan, everything was shared rather than borrowed. Only nature could claim ownership, because she provided the raw materials that were vital to life.

Civilization's concept of modesty had yet to attach itself to the aborigine's nakedness. They never felt embarrassed when they urinated or defecated in front of others as answering the call of nature in public was perfectly natural. It never registered that emptying their bowels in the company of a white man could be seen as an offensive act. Les noticed that the aborigine's faeces were almost powdery due to their diet and the small amounts of water they drank. The supple natives replaced our paper work by standing on one leg after they passed a bowel motion, then they wiped themselves clean with the sole of their foot.

Les developed a close rapport with the aborigines, and with hunting and gathering being the mainstay of their existence, they sometimes took him out into the desert to secure game. Just like their prey the aborigines depended on the land, and just like their prey they had a profound knowledge of the weather and how it influenced animal behaviour. Being totally at one with nature, and having amassed a wealth of inherent wisdom, they had evolved into highly skilled and extremely patient predators. Their children were taught at an incredibly early age how to hunt, to mimic animal behaviour, and to move as and with the land rather than through it. They played games that taught them to draw animal tracks in the sand so that identifying the footprints of target species became second nature. From the time they were able to cast a stick into flight they became proficient at throwing a boomerang. The weapon always flew in a circular motion, but never returned back to the thrower. Birds were killed with a heavy boomerang that was thrown into the middle of a flock and usually resulted in a high success rate. A smaller more accurate boomerang was used for rabbits and other small ground dwellers.

If kangaroos were being hunted, a spear-toting hunter led the way and the others walked behind him in single file, while Les was made to follow in the distance. The aborigines never washed and were always covered in kangaroo fat and blood to mask their scent. They found the smell of Les's clean body repugnant and thought his offensive odour would forewarn any game of their silent approach. When the natives entered the hunting ground, everyone stopped talking and communicated by used hand signals that were both slow and discrete. Once game was sighted the lead hunter minimised his movements by slowly pointing at his quarry with his chin. His movements were so precise and so instinctive that he would usually stalk to within about ten metres of an unsuspecting animal. The *woomera* is a flat piece of wood with a peg bound to one end, and in the hands of an expert, it's a formidable weapon used to throw a two-metre long spear. A hunter always aimed at the hindquarters of a kangaroo, as it offered the largest target. The spears were made so that the spearhead snapped off in the marsupial's limb then if the animal escaped its injured leg stiffened and splayed, which made it easy for the expert trackers to return with their hunting dogs and run it down. A fully-grown kangaroo possesses incredibly powerful hind legs armed with sharp claws that can easily disembowel a human. To avoid the animal's dangerous feet, the natives always crept up from behind a wounded animal, jumped on its tail, and clubbed the hapless marsupial to death with a *nullah nullah* (a wooden club).

After a successful kill, the hunter always carried a ligament from a kangaroo's hind leg in his mouth to keep the tissue moist until he got back to his campsite and used it to bind another spearhead to a shaft. If a female was killed while she was carrying a Joey in her pouch, the children kept the young kangaroo as a plaything until they were hungry, then killed it and roasted it whole over a fire.

The women also hunted, but only for small game, which they normally did by using a stick as a primitive stethoscope to listen for rabbits that were nestled in the sanctity of their burrows. Whenever a female with a litter was captured, only the kittens were eaten and the mature animal was released to breed again to ensure a continued abundance of game.

Because the hunter was a clan's main provider, he always ate first to maintain his strength and good health. Children were next in the pecking order as they represented the future generation and the continuance of a bloodline. The women followed, and then the elderly finally dined on whatever remained. Females suffered such a poor social standing due to their limited input towards the tribe's general welfare.

Just as Derek had with the Eskimos, Les developed such a close relationship with the aborigines that he was invited to witness a child being born. With an uncanny sense of woman's intuition a pregnant aborigine knew before her first contraction when she was about to give birth. She prepared for the delivery by digging a hole in the sand, then once her water broke she squatted over the scrape while an elderly woman acting as a midwife massaged her from behind. The baby was quietly delivered without any fuss or complaint, then the mother buried her infant so that only its head was exposed to give it some relief from the droning clouds of flies that feasted on the embryonic fluids that covered its body. Then just as the Eskimos had done, the midwife used a hunting dog to lick the mother's thighs and crotch clean of blood and mucous, before she fed the dog the afterbirth.

As the months slipped by and Les became more familiar with their customs, he would wander into their camp when he saw the glow of a blazing fire lighting up the night to watch them perform a mystical rite that coincided with the cycle of each new moon. Dance sticks clashed and the men sung, while a few of the other males broke out into a highly animated dance. The women added to the primitive melody by flapping their arms against their sides and simultaneously slapping their cupped hands over their genitals to produce a unique type of farting sound from both their armpits and groin. It was during one of these rituals that Les witnessed how the aborigines maintained their tribal law and order. A death was never thought to have occurred from natural causes unless an obvious physical injury was responsible. Whenever someone died, sorcery was always thought to have been the cause, and the clans from the surrounding area gathered to apprehend the offender by evoking their ancestral spirits during a divination rite. The men gathered in a circle around a roaring fire, while the women sat about five metres behind them in neat rows. To the aborigines nothing is inanimate, and when the men passed a sacred stone around the circle they held it to their noses and quietly sniffed, then they rubbed it in a circle across their chests. Then a hallowed hush fell over the crowd as the headman connected with the supernatural realm and asked for divine guidance from his ancestral spirits. Once he received the judgement from his mystical forefathers and he pointed to the guilty party, the offender was filled with an impending sense of doom and, under a sentence of eternal banishment, wandered off into the desert to die.

The elderly and infirm members of a clan who'd succumbed to the ravages of time imposed the same sentence upon themselves. Rather than remaining a burden to a tribes continued existence, in an act of absolute selflessness, they wandered off into the wasteland knowing that they would never return. Their family never tried to intervene or objected to the self-imposed euthanasia. They had no reason to because the suicidal elders were about to enter a beautiful supernatural realm that was filled with millennia of ancestral spirits.

The aborigines eventually succumbed to curiosity, and a few of them who were fascinated by the weather station's strange equipment sheepishly wandered in from the desert and crowded around the cook, who was having trouble starting the camp's fickle generator. Just as he pulled on the starter chord and the troublesome motor spluttered to life, an inquisitive native from the spellbound aboriginal audience touched an uninsulated spark plug. Twenty thousand volts of western culture shock surged through the terrified aborigine, who let rip with a bloodcurdling scream that echoed around the whole camp. The workers came running from all directions to see what the commotion was about and ended up in hysterics when they found out why the aborigine had streaked out of the tent and was still screaming as he bolted across the desert at full steam. He didn't stop running and kept shrinking in size until he wilted into a speck on the distant horizon.

While Les found it hard to comprehend the science and advanced technology that powered the weather station's computers, grasping the mental capacity of the aborigines proved to be equally difficult. Complex electronics and the discovery of the silicon chip led to modern man's evolution of computers, while millennia of evolving in an intimate relationship with the environment and each other had developed the aborigine's cerebral software. The Internet can send information around the globe in seconds, but by using their highly developed telepathy the aborigines' mind power exhibited equally incomprehensible feats. When a native used sign language to tell Les that the aboriginal protector's dog had just died and the protector drove up to the camp several hours later, Les was stunned when the protector told him that without any warning his dog had suddenly passed away while he was travelling along in his Landrover. Les noticed the aborigines were like intuitive animals before an earthquake and always became uneasy several hours before supplies were about to be airdropped. The perceptive natives constantly looked up to the sky when they somehow sensed that the plane was about to arrive.

On the fourth of October 1957, history was in the making while Les sealed the windows of the hut that housed the computers to keep out the ever-present dust and sand. When a computer automatically whirled to life and lights started flashing and a series of beeps sounded, Les sensed that something important had just happened and rushed outside to find Sir William Penny, the famed rocket scientist who'd worked on the atomic bomb with Oppenhiemer. Penny verified that the computer had registered that the space race was over and that humanity had entered the beginning of the Space Age. The Soviet Union had just launched Sputnik 1 into orbit and beaten the Americans in their quest to be the first to fly into space.

Of all the primitive peoples, Aborigines probably have one of the most intimate connections with the environment and are as much a part of the landscape as the rocks and cliffs that are adorned with their totemic designs and art. Their close affinity with all of nature extends to the cosmos, which is why the nomadic clans never got lost in the sometimes featureless landscape. They looked to the heavens and used the stars for navigation. On the first night of the Sputnik's orbit, the ever-observant aborigines lives were suddenly thrown into total chaos when they peered up at the clear sky. Aircraft had never flown over this remote region of desert at night, and since the beginning of time, their legends had never told of a bright light that passed through the night sky every ninety minutes. Some of them were convinced a new star was being born, while most of the others, who were shaking with fear, were adamant the satellite was an ominous omen from the gods and a prelude to Armageddon. Only a thorough explanation to the superstitious natives from the protector, who they'd grown to trust, laid their fears to rest.

A year had almost slipped by, and as it was almost time for Les to return to civilization, he was eager to spend as much time as possible with his primitive friends. He entered an aborigine camp in the still of early morning, just as the rising sun burnt the chill off the desert's dawn breath. The headman offered him a charred piece of fire roasted lizard, then pulled a glowing stick from the fire and used the embers to singe his hair and beard to a length he was happy with. Once he was satisfied with his personal grooming he motioned to Les to follow him to a nearby *billabong* for a drink of stale water. Although it tasted foul, it was much quicker and easier than using grass to sponge up the moisture that gets trapped in the forks of trees then wringing it into their mouths.

The soft-spoken aborigines had never tried to teach Les their language, so the elder motioned for Les to follow him back to his camp, where he scrawled a spiral in the sand, then drew a straight line from its centre. Each circle the line intersected represented the number of day's walks it would take to reach their new campsite. When they gathered their meagre possessions, the headman left a few hunting spears for any other clans who might use the camp to acknowledge his people's interdependency and close affiliation with the other transient tribes in the area. With the rest of his people in tow, the free spirited aborigines silently walked into a shimmering sea of heatwaves to find a new campsite somewhere in the liquid horizon. It was a fitting way to end Les's last moments with these incredibly resilient peoples.

There were incredible parallels and amazing contrasts between the adventures that Derek and Les enjoyed, such as the historical firsts, the harsh polar ice and the unforgiving desert, and a space rocket and a nuclear powered submarine, but it was the similarities between the primitive peoples that had fascinated me. Derek and Les had been extremely fortunate to experience life amongst indigenous peoples who hadn't yet endured the social dislocations that were about to be imposed upon them by the intrusion of biased Western ways. In a relatively short time span, both the Eskimos and the aborigines suffered bitter prejudices and unwarranted hostilities that were inflicted by modern man. Their enforced cultural limbo led to mental illness, alcoholism, suicide, drug abuse, horrendous homicide rates, and the virtual demoralization of what had for millennia been a self-sufficient and proud peoples.

Whether I liked it or not, it seemed my fate was sealed. Irrespective of what path I chose to take in life, the trail would inevitably collide with another less travelled road. With the genetics I'd inherited, it was inevitable that at some stage I'd be compelled to step off the beaten track, to follow in the footsteps of my adventurous relatives and blaze a few trails of my own.

Chapter Three

CULTURE SHOCK

Travel never really entered my thoughts until a few days after my thirtieth birthday. Neither did daring to try and replicate my relatives' adventurous exploits, simply because I never knew the full extent of their travels. When I caught up with like-minded friends living a bohemian, surfing orientated lifestyle in Australia, it squashed my travel bug. I was single, free spirited and carefree, and had a great time surfing perfect swells along the east coast, snorkelling with sharks on the Great Barrier Reef, and riding up through the outback on a dirt bike. Australia had been great and had definitely opened up my eyes, but not with iris popping intensity. The pages of *National Geographic* and the other cultural magazines I'd read had already taken me there long before my passport was stamped. While I walked through the streets of Cairns to book a flight home, I'd decided that travel was a great educator, but I could take it or leave it, and that New Zealand had everything that I ever needed to keep me satisfied—or so I thought.

When I decided to fly to the Solomon Islands for a week instead of returning to my building business back in New Zealand, it was a decision that was about to impact on my whole unsophisticated world overview. Without a religious bone in my body, life had been simplistic, generous, and enjoyable. Things were either black or white, and I either believed or disbelieved. The nearest I'd ever come to purposely experiencing anything even remotely spiritual was when I connected with the ocean while I rode along a wave or stepped off the world into a primeval Eden to hunt in the mountains. Yet beyond any of my wildest expectations, the Solomons would be the adventurous catalyst that sent me spiralling into a daunting but fascinating spiritual abyss. Over the next nine years I clawed up the face of that chasm, sometimes until my fingers bled, and emerged at the top with a much different and much clearer perspective of life.

The Solomons' largest island, Guadalcanal, was a world away from anything I'd ever experienced; so was absorbing the emotive and unfamiliar intensity of arriving in a distant land that had such a huge initial impact on my senses. Culture shock overwhelmed my limited experiences as a traveller and changed my whole perception of travel during the bus ride to Honiara when I witnessed Melanesians etching out their simple subsistence lifestyles. The bustling capitol's alliance with the western world gave it a dishevelled third world appearance as it merged from its primitive past into a modern society. The crude shanties lining the back streets cast a sombre mood over the depressing rubbish strewn slums. They looked dismal and alien compared to the organic leaf huts that seemed so much a part of nature. The rusting buildings that had been corroded by time appeared melancholy, whereas the aged leaf huts on the outskirts of town that begged for repair reeked of character as they tumbled back to where they had came from. They were just buildings, and I'd never bothered to be philosophical about anything in life, yet for some inexplicable reason I was totally captivated by anything that was related to the primitive aspect of the Solomons' culture.

To a tourist who's visiting the Solomons for the first time, some of the islanders with fierce Melanesian features can look imposing. But even the meanest looking locals lived up to the islands' sociable reputation of being "the happy isles" by initiating friendly greetings while I ambled around the streets to get the feel of the place. It was incredibly easy to befriend a local amongst peoples who were once considered the most dangerous headhunters in the pacific. Within minutes of meeting Badley, I jumped at the offer to visit his relatives who lived in a traditional village fifty kilometres up the coast. Badley was in his early twenties, sure of himself, and like so many unemployed youths milling around Honiara, he slowly revealed an opportunistic outlook, which led to our friendship being brief and one-sided. Late that afternoon, we sat on the back of a truck that kicked up a pale cloud of blinding dust as it sped along a crushed coral road that followed the coastline.

When we pulled up at Veravaolu village, the towering mango trees and feathery coconut palms shading its six leaf huts gave the hamlet a serene and welcoming look. Its friendly inhabitants offered me a warm greeting, then told us that just beyond the wall of jungle that crowded around the edge of the hamlet, bush fires that had ravaged their gardens were still smouldering. To add fuel to the fading fires, an epidemic of debilitating malaria had cast its cruel kiss of death over Veravaolu's inhabitants. My naïve western mindset had me instantly thinking that due to their unenviable situation, I'd be the opportunity and they'd be the opportunists. This couldn't have been further from the truth. In a humbling gesture of overwhelming hospitality, from the moment we first walked into the village, even though I was a total stranger, these selfless people were prepared to share the very best of what little they had until nothing remained.

It was a harsh introduction to the realities of rural village life, unlike my introduction to twenty-five-year old Luko, which blossomed from our first handshake into a strong and lifelong friendship. I threw my pack down and joined a small crowd of anxious onlookers that had gathered on his veranda. Luko's already wild looking features exaggerated the look of concern on his face. He slapped at a mosquito on his wiry body, scratched at the lice in his huge halo of frizzy hair, and then placed a cold compress on his son's burning forehead. The small child's teeth chattered like a pair of clattering castanets as he wallowed in a pool of his own sweat. With nothing to offer but moral support, I held his hand as malaria took a firm grip of his exhausted and frail looking body. The little battler went toe to toe with the sickness, and thankfully he emerged from his fever several hours later as the victor.

It was hard to imagine what ran through the villagers' minds while outwardly they remained so cheerful. They had every reason to feel pessimistic, but kept on smiling and remained indifferent to their run of bad luck. Not one of the villagers grumbled about the dire state of their lives. Instead they maintained a carefree outlook and enjoyed the ride along life's unpredictable flow. When I asked Luko why everyone remained so positive, he said, "It is our *kastom*," and told me how his beliefs teach that complaint shaves the edge of a people's confidence, and to look for beauty in everything, no matter how grim the reality is. It set an enviable precedence on a lifestyle I was keen to learn about.

Europeans drive along the road that runs past Veravaolu everyday, but only one other white man had ever stayed in the village. Unfortunately we didn't possess like-minded attitudes, as he spent most of his time staggering around in a hazy alcoholic stupor, abusing the villagers and trying to pick fights, which hardly helped to bridge the gap and destroy any bias or apprehension that existed between our vastly different cultures. Now that they had their own tourist who willingly answered a barrage of questions they would never dream of asking other Europeans, I became a popular novelty. Luko invited me to stay with his family, and each night I sat on his hardwood deck and hung on every one of his fascinating words while the villagers listened intently to mine. I learnt about strange voodoo-like customs, black magic that terrified the villagers, and barbaric rituals their forefathers practised to appease their gods. While Luko talked about the *Ramos* and the *Vele*, who are potent magicians that kill with their supernatural powers, it created an eerie hush amongst the previously animated listeners when he explained how the spiritual mercenaries murder one of their own relatives to enhance their mystical powers. Although they wore western clothing, and most of the villagers in their twenties have had a secondary school education, their unflappable belief in mythical creatures and evil sorcerers had surfaced only weeks before my arrival, when a small child mysteriously died, supposedly at the hands of a *Vele*.

It felt surprisingly natural as I slotted into the slow pace of village life, and the days quickly passed by. Although I'd spent most of my youth in the mountains back in New Zealand, I didn't know much about surviving in a tropical rainforest, so I eagerly soaked up every drop of information Luko shared from his seemingly bottomless pool of inherent knowledge. Each day presented something new and interesting. When we hiked through the jungle to start replanting Luko's decimated garden, we passed freshly exhumed graves that were scattered around the path we followed. They were a grim reminder of Guadalcanal's bloody past when the allied and American forces fought the invading Japanese during World War II. A group of Japanese veterans and their despondent families had recently hired Luko to locate the missing remains of their comrades and loved ones so that they could be properly laid to rest in Japan. The looming threat of attack, and suffering from exhaustion and energy sapping diseases, meant many of the dead soldiers were quickly buried in shallow graves. These graves sometimes yield human fertiliser when the villagers are digging in the garden. And as well as leaving some of their dead behind, both armies littered the area with a minefield of unexploded shells. Whenever the villagers burn off a plot of jungle to prepare a new garden, they always make a hasty retreat to escape the exploding ammunition that's sometimes detonated by the flames.

We got up an hour before sunrise one morning to avoid the oppressive heat, and climbed up a sheer ridge at the back of the village so that Luko could further my knowledge of how to survive in the jungle. Before we reached the top of the ridge and headed deeper into the rainforest, he insisted that I wear a necklace made from sacred leaves to offer me protection from a legendary Japanese ghost that several villagers had glimpsed over the years. I felt the Asian spirit who haunted the islands' rugged interior was of a more earthly origin and probably more alive than dead. Like most of the other villagers, I had every reason to suspect that an old soldier had somehow managed to survive the war. To all but the most superstitious villagers, it was obvious a mortal was responsible for the numerous wounds thirty-year-old Patrik had suffered two years earlier. While Patrik wandered up through the jungle to gather medicinal leaves, without provocation or any warning, the Asian suddenly materialized from the gloom of the rainforest and attacked him. Although he was gaunt and aged, the aggressive soldier launched a vicious assault before he fled back to his ghostly realm. Patrik limped back to the village bloodied and bruised. The villagers were shocked by his injuries, and the majority of them are still adamant that human rather than supernatural forces were responsible for his wounds.

Other parts of the Solomons' have dispelled the superstitious myths surrounding legendary Asian ghosts. In an incredible display of patriotism, a Japanese soldier obeyed his orders of never to surrender and survived in the jungles of an island in the western province for decades. By living off of his wits, the jungles pantry, and stealing from villagers' gardens, he resiliently endured time, disease, and the elements. When a mob of villagers managed to capture the elusive Asian, he was completely naked and his years of isolation had affected him both physically and mentally. His unkempt hair scraped the back of his knees, while decades of solitude had cruelly robbed him of the ability to speak. The hard-nosed soldier eventually managed to tell a Japanese interpreter that surrender wasn't an option unless the emperor himself declared that Japan had lost the war. The poor man was horrified when he was told that the leader of his country had been dead for years and that the Solomons were now self-governed.

Of all the things we could have talked about on the veranda each night, the conversation shifted to cannibalism. And of all things, eating human flesh put Luko and I on common ground as, during intertribal conflict, both of our ancestors had dined on two-legged meat. While no one has ended up as mystery mince in New Zealand for over a century, when Luko's father was a small boy travelling through Malaita Island, Luko witnessed firsthand what he believes was an act of cannibalism. On all of the islands throughout the Solomons, the Malaitans have been labelled with the stigma of having quick and volatile tempers, especially the isolated primitive clans who live in central and north Malaita. Several remote tribes have been so successful in maintaining their primeval purity that they're still stark naked, and only married women wear a small T-piece of beaten bark to cover their genitals. Luko's father remembered being absolutely terrified when three Kwaio warriors who were armed with bows and machetes were arguing with another villager about twenty metres from where he was standing. The heated discussion erupted into a savage outburst of violence that was filled with a terrible blood curdling scream and aggressive cries when machetes flashed and the lone man was ruthlessly hacked to death. Luko's father and his older companion were so terrified that they literally shook with fear, especially when the victors butchered their victim and then flung the dismembered body over their shoulders. As they casually wandered off, they were licking up the victim's blood as it trickled down their arms.

After I heard Luko's story, I went and talked with several elderly priests from the Melanesian Brotherhood who had tried to spread the gospel throughout Malaita. They said venturing into Kwaio territory to contact the isolated tribes had been a hellish experience that they never wanted to have to repeat. Most of them were greeted with death threats and a volley of arrows that hissed around their heads. Every one of them had made a hasty retreat to safer ground and forgot about trying to convert the heathen natives. But not all of the Kwaio despised outsiders, and a few of the evangelists had contacted other pagan tribes who were naked but were peaceful and welcoming. I didn't doubt Luko's story as headhunting and cannibalism were said to be so rife throughout Malaita and several other islands that the Solomons were reputedly the most hazardous destination in the Pacific. It wasn't until the early 1940s that district commissioners who were appointed by the British government managed to curb the rampant cannibalism that the warring clans practised.

Luko and the others were pleasantly surprised when I told them Maori blood from my mother's side of the family courses through my veins. They were happy I wasn't a true white man and said that was the reason I was so different from the other tourists they'd met. Everyone fell silent when I shared my forefather's fondness for dining on human flesh. The captives that they brought back after raiding an enemy tribe were destined for the *hangi* (earth oven) and had their arms and legs broken to prevent them from escaping while their captors kept them well fed and fattened them up like livestock. When the prisoners were about to become the main course for a *hakari* (gathering for a feast), death was a merciful escape that was usually inflicted with a swift blow to the head from a *mere* (fighting club). Some of the tribes had a novel way of knowing when human flesh was cooked to perfection: by leaving the head exposed while the rest of the corpse cooked in the smouldering *hangi* pit. Although it seems unlikely that the eyes would have actually popped out of their sockets, it was said that when they did the meat was tender.

My Maori grandmother's generation were well and truly civilized, unlike Luko's Malaitan grandfather who dined on human flesh numerous times. He lived in a brutal era, when paranoid warriors slept with their bows and knives tied to their hands so that they were always ready to face the constant threat of being attacked by an enemy clan. When he fought with a warring tribe and his clan was victorious, they usually dragged several captives back to their village. Their fate was so horrendous that the prisoners would sometimes defecate themselves with fear. Luko's grandfather used a bamboo knife to cut holes through the palms of their hands and through their Achilles heels, then he threaded vines through the wounds and tied the victim to a tree. If a female was about to be cannibalised, she had a breast severed, and if it was a male he watched in horror as he said goodbye to his genitals. The detached organs were forced into the screaming victim's mouth, which was then gagged with a vine to muffle their cries. Then the villagers lined up in single file, in a pecking order that was determined by their social status. After the chief sliced the best cut of meat from the still conscious victim with a bamboo knife, he barbecued the twitching muscle over a fire that blazed alongside their terrified captive. The patriarch's barbaric ringing of the dinner bell invited each villager to follow his lead, and in what must have been a horribly grotesque way to die, they ate the victim alive.

When the villagers in our area evolved from being cannibals to Christians in the space of a few generations, it didn't subdue their tendency to solve problems with violence. Luko warned me that I always needed to be careful and not to trust anyone. Past grievances that simmered beneath the surface between headstrong youths from the nearby villages could quickly reach boiling point, and on one occasion they did. It didn't take much of a catalyst for already strained relationships to quickly flare into vicious full-on brawls between hereditary enemies as old rivals from the headhunting days still treat each other with suspicion. There was plenty of domestic violence as well, and right outside our door, when most nights a Malaitan in the neighbouring hut beat his screaming wife and daughter while we shook our heads in disgust, then minded our own business and carried on talking as if nothing had happened. Six months earlier, two Malaitans felled a tree across the road not far from Veravaolu, and then they waited to ambush their employer, who was a New Zealander that managed a copra plantation. Because Europeans are equated with money, when he got out of his truck to shift the tree, they hacked him to death with their machetes and stole a paltry four hundred Solomon dollars.

I knew it would be virtually impossible to reason with the adolescents and adults that roamed around at night in an agitated stupor while they were drunk on meths and dry bomb (home brew). Due to the rising social problems that are associated with alcohol, the government has banned drinking alcohol in public. The drunks were as big a danger to themselves as they were to me. If meths is drunk over a lengthy period of time it leads to partial and even full blindness and a host of other health problems. Dry bomb lives up to its name by killing drinkers who are impatient by literally blowing them up until they suffer an agonising and lingering death.

The potent brew is made by mixing fruit with yeast and sugar in a bucket of water. If it isn't left to stand for long enough and the yeast is still fermenting, it creates a lethal concoction that bloats the drinker's stomach until they look nine months pregnant and die.

Despite the social problems, the positives outweighed the negative aspects of tasting a true slice of village life. Most of the Solomon Islanders were an affable and hospitable peoples. I quickly learnt a western outlook didn't always belong and that Luko and my other newfound friends would watch my back. As our friendship grew stronger, he said several times that I was different from the other whites he'd spent time with. I certainly felt different. In the short space of a week, the desire to live in one comfortable world no longer existed, and whether I liked it or not, the Solomons was no longer just a country on a map, Veravaolu had become an alluring place that was firmly etched into my mind. I knew within myself that this brief encounter with a fascinating and totally alien culture was about to shape my future. I left most of my possessions behind, and during the flight back to New Zealand, I vowed never take for granted the life of abundance that I was returning to.

Chapter Four

LEARNING TO WALK

To enhance my understanding of primitive cultures, I read through a mountain of fascinating books and revelled in the compelling stories written by legendary explorers who encountered hostile natives, endured months of uncertainty, and succumbed to tropical diseases while they travelled through vast tracts of uncharted territory. As I turned each page, I became increasingly restless, and after only several months of being back in New Zealand, I was winging my way back up to the Solomons.

Luko's basic leaf hut felt even more like home when I returned to find several of Veravaolu's newborn children had been named after members of my family, and instead of being treated as a visitor or a tourist, I was welcomed back as one of Luko's clan. To get a genuine insight into village life, I had to shrug off some of my values and western society's individualistic mindset. Although essential items belong to an individual, in general, unimportant possessions are readily lent out or are borrowed by members of a clan's extended family. When some of my things began to circulate within the community, it helped to reinforce my relationship with individuals, cemented our mutual obligations when someone borrowed something from me, and made me more readily accepted. My close-knit family in New Zealand had always worked as a team, so adopting the what's-mine-is-yours attitude came naturally.

As the days turned into weeks, my already strong sense of belonging blossomed into total acceptance when Luko sealed our rock solid friendship by announcing to the village I was his *wantok*, and extended his selfless values and the ethic of sharing by gifting me a beautiful piece of land that overlooked the nearby lagoon. It was a moving gesture, but I graciously declined the offer to build myself a leaf hut and to start clearing my own garden. I intended to have a passing rather than a permanent impact on the villagers' lives.

Life as an honorary member of an extended family isn't without its pitfalls. If a distant relative urgently requires financial help, the moral obligations of a *wantok* include lending money that will probably never be repaid. Tightfisted villagers who refuse to help their needy *wantoks* live in shame and are usually treated as social outcasts. If an enterprising islander starts up a business, he often faces huge social pressures because numerous blood relatives randomly taking free goods from a *wantok* is a recipe for financial disaster and inevitable bankruptcy. The Chinese community and the other immigrants quickly capitalised on the pitfalls of the *wantok* system and established chains of stores in Honiara. I was lucky that no one ever tried to profit from my newfound status, but it did invite already close companions to become even more intimate. The grown men and boys who'd previously made slight body contact during our conversations started holding my hand as we walked and talked. I've definitely got all of my hormones, and when it first happened my heterosexual mindset involuntarily clenched my anus so tight that the muscles around my rectum started throbbing, even though the bonding was one of true friendship rather than a homosexual advance.

The massive learning curve I so eagerly climbed slowly flattened out as the villagers patiently taught me how to speak Pidgin English, furthered my ability to survive in the jungle, and shared more of their beliefs. Although we differed biologically and our circuits weren't wired the same mentally, as my tolerance levels grew, coping with an alien diet and adapting to the tropical climate came naturally. But it felt as if it would take an eternity to understand *kastom*, the Pidgin word that's used to describe the Solomon Islanders' pagan religions. From all of the facets of the villagers' lives that I tried to learn, the complexities of *kastom* were by far the hardest to understand. Kastom encompasses all aspects of life, whether they're earthbound or in the supernatural. When I tried to get a deeper insight into the spiritual side of village life, even my most complicated questions were answered with the most simplistic reply. Without further explanation, the villagers always answered, "It is *kastom*."

When I visited Ullawa, which is Luko's home island, it did little to enhance my understanding of the Melanesian's mindset and beliefs. The only means of travel was sailing for three rough days on a rusty old copra boat laden with livestock, seasick passengers, and bags of sickly sweet smelling copra. Months can pass before the arrival of the next boat, so as a consequence, very few outsiders ever visit the island.

While I was the only European living amongst two and a half thousand Ullawans, I visited *tabu* (sacred or forbidden) caves that housed sacred ancestral skulls which had never been seen before by a white man, and lived in animist villages that worship the shark and the snake. The villagers' primitive beliefs belied their civilized appearance, but even after I spent time with them, the real essence of their closely guarded religion still remained a mystery, and the more I learnt about *kastom* the less I knew. When I returned back to New Zealand my head was filled with more questions than answers.

I returned yet again and hunted wild pigs with a spear, dived in the lagoon at night and caught huge turtles with Luko, and continued my integration with an alien culture. The brief but fulfilling trip created a real thirst for adventure, and although I was hardly an expert, I was no mug either. I had sufficiently found my feet and felt confident enough to satisfy my craving for real exploration by contacting the primitive Kwaio people the next time that I returned.

Chapter Five

GIANTS AND PYGMIES

When I returned to Veravaolu several months later and started making plans to visit the Kwaio, nearly everyone questioned the logic of why I would put myself at risk to satisfy my lust for exploration. Luko was undeterred by everyone's concern and shared my adventurous spirit, but warned that gaining acceptance where even Solomon Islanders are despised and the white man is hated would be difficult. Because the Malaitans have a bad reputation for fleecing Europeans we decided to try and find a guide on neutral ground. It proved to be virtually impossible as no one was prepared to contact the isolated tribes, but they were more than willing to visit the more accessible clans in other parts of Malaita. I wanted something challenging and hardcore and, more important, to spend time with a people who were truly primitive. As a last resort, Luko suggested I should try and contact Kulum, who claimed to be a Malaitan land chief and lived at White River, a scruffy settlement on the outskirts of Honiara. His chiefly status could oil the hinges to otherwise closed doors. But Luko warned me to tread carefully as Kulum had a fearsome reputation and liked nothing better than living up to it. When I eventually tracked him down and he agreed to act as a guide, he cast an edgy mood over our conversation. For a middle-aged man with his intimidating appearance and such a cruel reputation, that he feared the Kwaio reinforced how very real the hazards were. So did the barbed tone of the stern warning he gave me. His words couldn't have been any more candid when he said, "Maybe we will sell our lives. Unless you do exactly as I tell you in the villages, I will fucking kill you myself." From the threatening look on his cheerless and heavily tattooed face, he obviously wasn't joking. His Mohawk haircut and solid build gave him a menacing almost barbarous look that suited his sour personality. That didn't faze me, but there was something in his soulless eyes that was unnerving. They brimmed with hatred and had the flatness of a hardened man who'd seen and done it all.

I knew within minutes of taking Kulum to Veravaolu to finalise our travel plans that I'd made a dismal mistake. From the instant he somehow managed to get his hands on a duty-free bottle of rum I'd gifted Luko, all hell started to break loose. I was grateful he'd bypassed the other more practical items I'd given Luko and his family, but it was small consolation as compromising my nagging intuition proved to be a disastrous and stupid blunder. By the time he'd single-handedly emptied the whole forty-ounce bottle down his throat, he'd transformed the previously tranquil village into a frightened hub of tautly stretched nerves. Most of the villagers wisely grabbed their children and fled into the sanctity of their huts. I joined them and looked on in horror when Kulum brandished a machete and started threatening everyone with extinction. He went on the rampage, and in a mindless orgy of violence, he started chasing and hacking up the villagers' scampering pigs and squawking chickens until, thankfully, the full effect of the rum snuck up and he collapsed into an unconscious heap. We loaded him onto the back of a passing truck and instructed the driver to drop him off in Honiara. My foolish error in judgement and ignoring my instincts not only cost me my own self-respect, I had to pay compensation to the villagers for putting everyone's lives at risk.

I found out afterwards that Kulum had earned his formidable reputation when he was sentenced to life imprisonment for committing a double murder. No one ever dared to cross him after he answered another inmate's threats with the blade of a knife. He sliced him from belly button to brisket, pulled out his intestines, then reached up into his ribcage and ripped out his beating heart. Despite the severity of his crimes, he was granted a full reprieve, and when I saw him later he told me that his relatives had used *kastom* magic to set him free.

Our run of luck went from bad to worse when Luko collapsed from a serious attack of malaria and I keeled over with a hellish fever that was laced with chronic diarrhoea and bouts of recurrent vomiting. Because of the severity of my illness, the concerned villagers called in a *kastom* man who was renowned for his black magic but was also a traditional healer. First he anointed my quivering body with lime, and then he spat a mouthful of chewed ginger into my ears, over my face, and on my stomach. His simplistic healing ritual drove out the evil spirits that had invaded my soul, while the western medicines I took drove out the sickness. I made a speedy recovery, but Luko wasn't so lucky. He'd succumbed to a vicious strain of malaria that demanded weeks of slow recuperation.

Luko had been just as excited as I was about visiting the Kwaio, so while he recovered, I decided to explore Guadalcanal. I'd read a book by D. C. Horton called *The Happy Isles*, which gives the British district commissioner's detailed account of how he discovered a remote pygmy tribe hidden in the heart of the island. During the early twentieth century, when Horton ventured through Guadalcanal's rugged terrain, he contacted the diminutive highlanders by edging along a cliff that had kept the secluded tribe quarantined from the rest of the world for millennia. No one from around our area had ever heard of them, so I travelled to Honiara with twenty-two-year-old Johno to hopefully find out if the pygmies still existed. Johno was always good company, and although a recent bout of malaria had left him thin-faced and emaciated his body, it hadn't robbed him of his good sense of humour.

The bustling central market seemed like the best place to begin. We started at opposite ends and slowly worked our way through the crowd. My questions about "the small people" were answered with creased frowns, shrugged shoulders, and strange looks that implied that I must be mad. Several islanders muttered "*Kokomora*," gave me a sideways glance, and then doubled over with laughter. Word quickly spread from stall to stall about the crazy white guy who was looking for *kokomora*. When Johno and I met in the middle and he shared why we were the brunt of a massive joke, we both burst into hysterical laughter. The more sophisticated natives view the *kokomora* as a figment of overactive imaginations, but to those who still live a primitive and superstitious existence, the mythical dwarfs covered in long shaggy hair are very real. The creatures are said to possess superhuman strength and are thought to be so heinous and so savage that simply mentioning the word *kokomora* instils fear into natives that live in remote villages deep in the jungle. Trying to solve the enigma of a junior Bigfoot that has managed to elude mankind for millennia wasn't part of our plan. Although it's possible new species of bipedal apes are yet to be discovered in remote tracts of jungle, my objective wasn't to prove that folklore was based on fact. I was looking for a much closer and, hopefully, much friendlier version of primate.

When no one seemed to know anything about the pygmy's whereabouts, it seemed their evolution might have run its course to extinction. Then a lanky islander in his mid-twenties with a gaunt face and tightly cropped hair shouldered his way through the crowd. He stretched out his arm, said "Matty," and introduced himself with a firm handshake. Matty panned gold for a living from the network of rivers and isolated streams that course through Guadalcanal's jagged mountains and never came into town unless he had gold to sell. It seemed we'd both struck it rich and had made a lucky find when he said he knew how to find the pygmies. He offered to guide us there when he returned to his village in several days' time. When he suggested we could walk across Guadalcanal and visit the primitive Moro people living on the south coast, although he'd never been there himself, it made much more sense than backtracking from the pygmy village.

We left the market and ended up in a government office that could give us advise on visiting the Moro people. A totally bored looking elderly administrator offered a negative response to our volley of questions by saying, "The Moro are rebellious and dangerous. Leave them alone. I can't tell you not to go there, but if you do you probably won't be welcome and can expect a volatile reception."

On the way back to Veravaolu, we called into Kakambona village to visit a few of our *wantoks*. Our already fruitful day kept on producing more good luck when we were told a small band of Moro followers lived in the hills behind Kakambona. There were a few hours of light left, so we quickly set off on a forty-minute walk along a narrow trail. An indifferent chief in his late fifties, looking anything but fierce and primitive dressed in western clothing, reluctantly welcomed us into a small hamlet nestled in a clearing alongside a small stream. When I told him we hoped to visit chief Moro, the suspicious chief questioned our motives from every angle until he was satisfied beyond all doubt that we weren't missionaries or in any way associated with the government. We gave him all the right answers, and after we made friendly small talk, his guarded attitude finally softened and he agreed to help us.

He changed into a *kabilato* (a loincloth made from beaten bark) and disappeared into a small hut that we were forbidden to enter. A warble of dramatic song floated out to our curious ears, then it tapered off to a monotone chant that came to such an abrupt halt, it filled the air with an almost jarring silence. He placed three strips of shell money on a *tabu* rock, and then projected his telepathic thoughts across the jagged mountains and down to the coast to forewarn Moro of our arrival. Before he placed the shell money in my hand, he warned us to abide by *kastom* and to make sure we followed the correct protocol when we arrived at the entrance to Moro's village. If we placed a few token gifts on the ground and laid the strips of shell money on top of them, it would increase our chances of being accepted.

The next two days passed swiftly as I eagerly made the final preparations for what I considered to be my first real expedition. Luko's malaria ravaged body looked too weak and emaciated to struggle across the road bordering Veravaolu, yet alone climb across the island's mountainous spine. It typified his caring manner when he insisted that his twenty-five-year-old half-brother, Francis, join Johno and I for a bit of added protection.

We met Matty at the market, grabbed a few supplies, and jumped on the back of a pickup. Once we turned off the main road, we bucked and slid inland on the back of a four-wheel drive Toyota over a deeply rutted and badly washed out track. Our white-knuckled ride ended when the Toyota slewed sideways across a foaming river and clawed up a small bank to Matty's village. An Australian company that was goldmining upstream had transformed the normally clear flowing body of water into an ugly chocolate-coloured undrinkable disgrace. This was more than just a river; it was the very lifeblood of the people's existence, so I casually introduced myself as a New Zealander to avoid taking the brunt of the villager's anger.

The leaf huts scattered along the river were built from an untidy and gloomy looking mixture of modern and traditional materials. Most of the villagers were dressed in soiled ill-fitting clothes, and only a few of them voiced their disgust at the state of their water or bothered to ask if I was an Australian. The good-natured chief invited us into his hut to share a meal of steaming taro and kumara, and offered Johno and Francis a handful of beetle nuts. They slipped a mildly narcotic acorn-sized kernel into their mouths and started chewing. The nut comes from the areca palm and produces a feeling of wellbeing and slight euphoria. To give their mellow high a bit of a boost, they dipped a stick into a container filled with lime and stuck it into the corner of their mouths. Their saliva turned bright red, and each time they stopped chewing, they sent a globule of oily spittle sliding across the dirt floor and added a new streak to the crosshatch of pale red stains that were already splattered around the hut.

As the day was drawing to a close, I sat outside and watched the soft light of the sinking sun highlight the ridges and shaded valleys that lay ahead of us with a golden hue. Then in the early evening, the setting just kept getting better as the rising silvery moon momentarily balanced on the tip of a distant peak and cast a subtle glow over a group of villagers who were serenading us with bamboo panpipes. We sat around a blazing fire and enjoyed the serene atmosphere until a middle-aged and hopelessly drunk native staggered out of the small crowd. He seemed harmless enough and was grinning from ear to ear when he hung over my shoulder and slapped me on the back. When the normally cheerful chief sprang to his feet and roared at the drunk to leave me alone the melodious singing and music came to an abrupt halt and was replaced with an uneasy silence. While a villager tried to tear him off my shoulder and I was readying myself for the inevitable fight, before I could move out of the way, a full-on brawl erupted and, amidst chaotic screams and pained groans, the *wantok's* from the two opposing families beat one another to a bloody pulp. I hardly slept at all that night while I listened to sporadic fighting and obnoxious taunts that continued into the early hours of the morning.

We were up early and away at dawn the next morning. Matty set a blistering pace along a well-worn path that twisted through a forest of towering trees while, overhead, the rising sun vainly tried its best to fight and burn its way through the dense canopy. Any native whose life is ruled by primitive beliefs and superstition believes the spectral gloom of the rainforest is the haunt of malevolent ghosts and evil spirits. When Matty was adamant we needed to rush from village to village because giants roamed the mountains, I figured he was winding me up after the *kokomora* incident, but from his deadly serious expression and his apprehensive tone, it was obvious the six to seven foot tall giants he spoke of were nothing to laugh about.

Incredulous sightings of elusive apelike creatures have been made around the globe by those who stand to profit from their claims, yet what may lend credibility to their existence is that some of the world's greatest and most respected explorers believe they have glimpsed the evasive ape-man. Although extensive searches have failed to supply enough concrete evidence to satisfy science, they actually exist; to the villagers living in Guadalcanal's interior, Bigfoot isn't an inexplicable mystery, giants are a definite reality. Burning the bones of freshwater fish is strictly forbidden, as the odour is believed to throw the giants taste buds into a frenzy. They are said to possess such an incredible sense of smell that they are drawn to the source of the enticing aroma from kilometres away. Unlike some of their legendary counterparts, the Solomon Islands' version of Sasquatch has no fear of man. A woman was reputedly kidnapped while she returned from her garden and was held captive by the creatures for two years. She managed to escape and returned to her hamlet in a crazed state with a child that looked more like a hairy Neanderthal than a human being. In other parts of the world, villagers in remote locations who live in close proximity to the mythical creatures often have similar tales of females being abducted. Later, when I was in Vanuatu, I spoke with two men who worked for the malaria board in Honiara. They claimed to have contacted all of the remote villages throughout Guadalcanal while they dispensed medicines. They said the demented woman and her grossly deformed child actually existed, but they knew nothing of the pygmies.

As we raced through the picturesque mountains, the demanding terrain threw a variety of challenges at us. Before we made the sometimes chest-deep river crossings, to reduce our chances of becoming an unwilling organ donor, we carefully scanned the surface for crocodiles. The narrow ledges we clung to, which had dizzying drop-offs, demanded absolute concentration and unwavering nerves. Rock hopping up sheer-walled riverbeds in a huge catchment area required attentiveness from both above and below. We constantly scanned the sky and looked for any cloudbursts or distant rain before we committed ourselves to entering the gorges. To survive one of the flash floods which sometimes surge along the rivers while we were in the bowels of a steep canyon would take nothing short of a miracle.

As dusk was gathering the last rays of light and we entered the sanctity of an unreceptive and dismal looking hamlet, I had a gut feeling that Matty had made a detour to avoid travelling through country he thought was inhabited by the fabled giants and had taken us the long way. Bare breasted women who were uninterested by our presence wore cloth skirts, and nearly all of the impassive looking men were dressed in *kabliatos*. Only a few of the villagers were wearing scruffy western clothing. An old man with sun-withered skin who was smoking a clay pipe had ugly raised scars that ran in parallel lines across his bony chest. In the eyes of the villagers, the geriatric was a living legend, and an incredibly brave one. Here was an old man who'd been attacked by a giant that, during their desperate struggle, had raked its massive hands across his ribcage before the man broke free and ran for his life. In remote jungles where new species are still being discovered, anything is possible, but I couldn't help but think of the damage a good-sized crocodile can inflict with its claws.

Towards the end of the following day, I narrowly escaped what could've resulted in a serious injury or a messy death. Matty set an energy-sapping pace with little rest, and in wilting heat, through a seemingly endless succession of ridges and valleys until we stood at the bottom of a sheer fifty-metre rock face. It wasn't the only way up, but it was the quickest way to reach our destination in the rapidly fading light. There were plenty of strong roots and firm handholds that made reaching the top a reasonably safe and simple climb. Then just as I was pulling myself up and over the lip, rocks began falling and a gaping crack opened up as the edge of the cliff crumbled from beneath me. It was an act of fate and a chance in a million that when I somersaulted backwards my foot hooked under a sturdy root. For a split second, the bottom dropped out of my world until I slammed into the cliff with a winding thud that left me breathless and hanging upside down by my ankle. I groaned and gasped, then clawed my way back up my leg, to where Francis's outstretched arm pulled me to safety. Apart from an ugly bruise on my throbbing shin I was unscathed, and as I peered back down the face to the rocks below, I shook my head in disbelief. I'd been incredibly lucky and kept counting my blessings for the whole of the time it took me to limp to three huts perched on a knoll above a gin clear river.

Throughout the night and into the small hours, listening to the pained moans of an ailing old man in the next hut stabbed at my sympathy and wrenched at my heart so much that it was impossible to sleep. He whimpered in agony and tried his best to suppress his suffering with stifled groans. After hours of torment, his resolve finally folded and he let rip with a blood-curdling scream. His mournful wife quietly wept at his side while he clung to the last spark of his mortality. The dying old man had that glassy look of death in his eyes when he'd refused what limited help we could offer. Instead of letting me try to alleviate his pain with modern medicines, he turned to his pagan beliefs and chose to rely solely on traditional remedies.

The next morning, with only an hour's walk separating us from the pygmy village, Matty sent a messenger, up a mist filled valley ahead of us, to forewarn them that we were on our way. We waited a while to let him put plenty of distance between us, then splashed in his wake along a shingle riverbed, until with my curious mind in a mania of anticipation, we made a short climb up a near vertical, ankle grabbing, sticky clay bank. We clambered back through the ages, through a surreal time warp that took my awed senses into an incredible picture of timeless tradition. Even the air had a primal tang to it. The potent stench of piles of pig shit that were scattered everywhere and the excrement from the snarling dogs and other animals roaming around mingled with the earthy odour that comes with humans living a primitive existence.

An unusually high flash flood that killed three villagers had swept away the original site, but apart from the new location, little had changed since Horton's visit. Melanesian missionaries had visited the last village, but no white man had ever set foot here. The instant several small children cast their wide eyes on me, they started shaking and cried out with fright. A naked boy thrust his sobbing face into his mother's grass skirt, nervously sneaked another quick look, and then let out a piercing scream. He began running on the spot and reached up to his mother who picked him up and buried his shaking head in her bare breasts. While his heaving chest gasped for air, tears streamed down the terrified child's contorted face.

Apart from the few shocked children giving me a wide berth, the rest of the villagers received us with an exceptionally warm and incredibly sincere welcome. The baldheaded chief, with drooping, apologetic looking eyes and a snowy beard, wore a bailer shell necklace as a mark of his authority. He embraced all of us with a handshake that was as comforting and as affectionate as a hug from a loved one. It wasn't the primitive aura created by the dank rainforest crowding the remote hamlets edge or the pygmy's simplistic existence that had the biggest initial impact, it was the childlike innocence these people radiated. They possessed an almost naïve purity that was borne from being alienated from the struggles the outside world faces. The politics and prejudices of mankind held no place or had yet to impact on such a remote environment, and our mutual curiosity, and the way they embraced us and each other, wasn't only enlightening, it was deeply moving.

Compared to Veravaolu, the village was incredibly primitive as very little had been absorbed from the outside world. Dishevelled looking animals that were crawling with a plague of fleas and lice moved freely about the village and in and out of the huts, which they shared with their owners. Even though Francis had travelled throughout other primitive areas in the Solomons, he was visibly stunned by the squalid conditions and when he saw that most of the villagers were afflicted with some type of tropical sickness. A teenage girl who was suffering from the worst case of ringworm I'd ever seen was white from head to toe and dazed by misery. The fungus had attacked every square inch of her skin and made her morose and apathetic. Although Francis and Johno were revolted by the disgusting lack of hygiene, I was surprised when they both politely refused the offerings of food we were gifted as a welcoming gesture as they both knew it would be taken as an insult. The rancid smelling pork that was swimming in a bowl of suspect looking jet-black bush cabbage, which crawled with hordes of blowflies, repulsed even their cast iron stomachs.

I could tell from the shell jewellery hanging around everyone's necks, several brand new grass skirts, and the clean loincloths some of the men wore that it was obvious they'd spruced themselves up for our arrival. To show respect, we shed our clothes and tied on the *kabilatos* the chief handed us before we followed him to the *kastom* house (sacred men's hut). Several disgruntled pigs squealed and scoffed in annoyance when they were chased outside the dank and musty smelling hut. The pigs are bred as a form of currency, for bride price, and for sacrifice during rituals. They were as tame as the friendliest pet dog, and soon came trotting back to us. While we sat and talked outside in the sun, one of the villagers slowly brushed his hand across the back of a contented looking piglet that was comfortably nestled in his lap. Each time he plucked a plump blood gorged lice from amongst the bristle he slipped it into his mouth. Before he swallowed them down with a noisy gulp, they exploded with a soft clicking sound when he crunched them between his teeth.

I faced an expected barrage of questions in Pidgin English about where I came from and how I lived. When I was asked how I felt about the uninvited missionaries who had tried to exploit their naivety and convert them to Christianity, I tried my best to remain impartial. Religion was the one aspect of life from any culture of which I didn't have any real understanding. The only thing I could tell them with any type of certainty was that cultural differences have fuelled mindless hatred and petty jealousies since the beginning of humanity. They nodded when I said in the world beyond their tribal boundaries, religious wars have taken more lives than the church has saved, but so has the pagan beliefs of warring tribes who were similar to themselves. Then I told them if a total stranger waltzed into my life and deprived me of everything I believed in and valued, even though I'm not a spiritual person, it would be as devastating as being denied of everything that nurtured my physical wellbeing. The chief stared at me and smiled, then with a look of understanding on his face, he reached out and clasped my hand. The others greeted my words with a murmur of approval. In spite of their unsophisticated outlook, they were hardly vulnerable. Propounding missionaries had failed miserably to convince these fiercely independent people to abandon their animist beliefs. Instead of worshiping a book of alien words, total reverence belonged to the snake and to practising the same pagan rites their forefathers had used.

I failed to see how the small isolated clan could possibly benefit from Christianity, because apart from medicines and a better understanding of basic hygiene, they wanted for nothing. Each consecutive generation had experimented and figured out how to successfully etch a demanding existence out of the mountains. Their hand to mouth subsistence lifestyle had stifled their greed and suppressed their need to be ambitious so that they were a people who were simply content with thriving on and worshiping life itself. To diminish their beliefs would mean they would have to readapt to alien pressures, and the repercussions of those foreign demands would have a massive impact on the pygmies for the rest of their lives and on each successive generation. Clothes harbouring disfiguring skin diseases held no place amongst these immodest people. When they were left alone, even with all of their obvious faults, they were in their own little peaceful world and more than happy in it.

It was refreshing to know the pygmies still existed, yet saddening to discover that only a handful remained. Some of them were small in stature but only two of the men had the unmistakable features of a genuine pygmy. Their intermarriage with the surrounding clans had all but decimated their bloodline and ensured that within the next generation their true genetics would be lost forever.

I knew virtually nothing about the pygmies when we left the next day. I could have stayed and learnt more from them, but I had no desire or right to probe and intrude upon such a contented peoples. Simply spending time with them had been satisfying enough. When I overheard Johno saying, "This fucking village is a stinking pile of pig and dog shit that no one should have to live in," I knew it was time to leave. Although I didn't make any startling discoveries, this had been the perfect introduction to a truly primitive peoples. In such a safe and friendly environment, there had been no need to constantly look over my shoulder or to worry about how I'd be received. According to Matty, a recent earthquake had made the track we'd hoped to follow down to the coast to visit Moro dangerous and impassable. I knew it was an excuse. Like the other villages throughout the interior, the pygmies believed in and lived in fear of giants. I could sense their dread of the creatures washing over the others. The giants, the phobia of devils lurking in the jungle, and the pygmies' suspect food no doubt swayed the others' decision that we should head back to Veravaolu.

The two men from the malaria board, who I later met in Vanuatu, thought they'd visited all of the inland tribes. They shook their heads in disbelief and were amazed when I showed them the few photos I took of the pygmies. Others who saw the prints and were familiar with inland clans also voiced their surprise when they found out that the stunted highlanders still existed. It was strange, as I didn't feel any sense of achievement whatsoever from doing what anyone else who was willing to traipse behind a guide could have done. The adventurous and elemental aspect of venturing into a wild looking horizon had been awesome, but it was the minuscule insight I gained into the primitive mindset that I valued the most.

Chapter Six

MORO AND MADNESS

I spent the next few weeks taking it easy at Veravaolu with an enjoyable routine of spear fishing in the lagoon, doing a little bit of work in the garden, and relaxing on the beach. Luko slowly regained his strength until he was his usual cheerful and dangerously fit self again, and although he'd finally shrugged off the last of his lingering bout of malaria, he started looking queasy at the thought of flying across the island to Marau Sound with Francis and me to finish our visit to the Moro people. Christmas was almost upon us, and at this time of the year, there were plenty of high-spirited revellers making an early start to their unruly end of year celebrations. I hoped by leaving for the airport at four o'clock the following morning we would reduce our chances of being targeted by the inevitable mobs of inebriated troublemakers.

Our headlights probed through the quiet of the early morning darkness and picked out gangs of drunken youths who had nothing better to do than roam the roads and look for trouble as they waited for their next victim to come hurtling past. The nervous taxi driver was worried that a rock would be thrown by some meths crazed maniac and come smashing through his windscreen, so he jammed the accelerator flat to the floor and slid sideways around the corners as he raced towards Honiara. We arrived at the airport in one piece, having endured little more than a bombardment of drunken taunts and harmless yelling.

That this was Luko's first flight and he was already a bundle of frayed nerves made no difference to Francis or to me. This was way too good an opportunity to pass up on. We couldn't help ourselves and both gave him hell. After we checked in our packs, I slipped a baggage label over both my wrists and wrote my name on each tag. When Luko said, "What are those for?" there was a slight tremble in his voice. I answered in a serious tone and said, "It's standard practice, mate, when you fly over the mountains in a small plane. If we crash, it makes it easier for the rescuers to piece your scattered body parts together." He answered me with a flood of profanity in his native tongue, then made a nervous trip to the toilet.

For the first half of the flight, when the Cessna started doing a few impromptu aerobatics in the turbulent thermals, Luko's chest began heaving in time with his panting breath and small beads of sweat formed on his forehead and top lip. He was rigid with fear, and only his lips moved while they continually mumbled a hilarious mixture of Ullawan and English profanity in answer to our endless stream of snide and lame comments like, "Is that smoke coming from the tail?" "Holy shit! The engines on fire!" "Where's all that oil coming from?" and "That shouldn't be loose." When I finally managed to coax him to take a quick look out the window, the first thing he noticed was a patch of bare canvas on one of the plane's bald tyres. It was all too much for him, and while I was buckled over with raucous laughter, his terrified eyes remained riveted on his white knuckles as he gripped the seat in front of him. As we safely touched down on Marau's grass airstrip, it brought an end to our cruel taunts and an end to his nervous misery. If Luko was given half the chance, with his wicked sense of humour, he would've done exactly the same to us.

Before we started the fifty-kilometre walk up the coast, a small crowd of curious bystanders each took their turn to feed us highly exaggerated tales of what to expect when we visited Moro. Thirty-metre long snakes with girths as round as the belly of a bullock obeyed Moro's every command and were trained to devour insolent guests. Gigantic man-eating crocodiles guarded the entrance to the village, and like the snakes, they made short work of any unwelcome visitors. Most of the onlookers claimed they could reach the village on the outskirts of Avu Avu in only three to four hours, and even those who had a perception of time could stretch their legs miles further than the truth by completing what would take us a full day in a leisurely two hours. And when we did get there, Moro could be a devious and evil man, whose magical *kastom* powers surpassed those of a *vele*.

When we shouldered our packs and headed north along a black sand beach that stretched into a thin black line on the horizon, the gullible natives were so engrossed in their overstated folk stories they carried on sharing them with each other. Due to the region's often unkind and unpredictable microclimate the locals have aptly christened the expanse of shoreline "the weather coast." Within minutes of setting off, we walked into slanting sheets of blinding rain whose blissful drops helped to cool down the stifling humidity's almost physical presence. Then as quickly as it appeared, the tropical deluge ceased, the dark clouds dispersed, and the sun's fiery orb transformed the black sand into an oppressive inferno. It didn't take long for the overpowering heat to squeeze a continuous flow of perspiration from our every pore. When kind-hearted islanders who were living in the sparsely populated villages dotted along the coastline greeted us with green drinking coconuts, we relished every refreshing mouthful of the cool effervescent juice. After we'd walked about twenty kilometres, heavy inland rain transformed the numerous rivers and creeks tumbling down from the interior to the ocean into muddy torrents that threatened to pluck us off of our feet.

From the look of the blisters on Luko's and Francis's broad flat feet and the way their stride was shortened to a painful hobble, walking on the scorching sand without shoes to Avu Avu must have been the equivalent of hiking on a smouldering hot plate. Although they'd been barefoot since birth, even their leathery soles wilted from the intense heat that radiated off of the black sand. I tested it with my thin white skin to see what they'd suffered and swore aloud the instant the searing heat burnt the palm of my hand. Luko and Francis looked at me and smiled and kept bearing their pain in total silence.

When we were only minutes away from Moro's village, I could see a distinct nervousness slowly creeping over the faces of Luko and Francis. Their superstitious natures no doubt questioned how much of the exaggerated tales we were fed along the coast were in fact reality. The small amount of factual information I knew about Moro justified their apprehension. Moro's legendary rise to fame took place while he slept back in 1953, when his angered ancestral spirits entered his dream world and told him that he had to resurrect his people's vanishing traditions. He was the chosen one and was destined to appease the irate gods by creating an impenetrable traditional stronghold. The church, the government, and any other institutions that were trying to erode his age-old beliefs were to be fought at all costs. Moro took his role as a cultural warrior very seriously and led a rebellion against any faction of society that he figured would be detrimental to his cause. His contemptuous attitude towards bureaucracy, and his deep-seated hatred of a rapidly growing, almost militant Christian culture, eventually landed him in jail. But instead of suppressing his objectives, the short but well publicised jail sentence raised his profile to celebrity status along the coast. Hordes of disillusioned Christians who wanted to return to their animist beliefs shunned their western clothing and alien values in exchange for loincloths and grass skirts as they flocked to join his movement.

When we placed ten kilos of rice, the three strips of shell money, and an assortment of other small gifts at the village entrance, Moro, the living legend, was as drunk as a mutant chicken. After all of the hype, meeting the great chief Moro, who looked to be well into his sixties, proved to be a disappointing anticlimax. What was left of his soiled loincloth resembled a tattered windblown flag, and lime-coloured pus filled the corners of his crusty bloodshot eyes. When Luko caught a pungent whiff of Moro's body odour, he quietly muttered, "Shit, he stinks. We should throw the dirty bastard in the river." I whispered back, "Think of the poor fish, mate. He'd probably pollute the water." The air was so thick with his heady aroma that I could almost taste Moro's vile stench.

Although he was a drunken mess and a physical wreck, history had proved Moro's deceptively frail and ragged appearance belied his bold nature. We knew from his reputation he was a hard-hearted character, and we needed to tread carefully. Two of his burly bodyguards wearing resentful expressions sized us up as he slurred that telepathy had forewarned him of our arrival. In a drunken garble he repeated over and over that because of our observance of *kastom* we were welcome to stay in the village. He rocked backwards and forwards on his unsteady feet, then slowly bent down and picked up our three strips of shell money, which he exchanged for five of his own. As he went to put them in my hand, he staggered back a few paces, recomposed himself, then tottered forward again. He carefully lined me up, gave me the traditional currency, and said if ever we visited again, they were our customary passport to instant acceptance.

With his head hung low and his inebriated legs lurching from side to side, Moro led us to our hut and then asked me to buy him a beer from a tiny leaf hut that doubled as a store. I paid for another one and with the bottle cradled tightly against his skeletal chest, in a grave tone, he began laying down the law by literally spitting out a short list of rules we were to abide by. As he told us a new *kastom* house was definitely off limits, flecks of spittle rained in our faces, while white foam formed in the corners of his slobbering mouth. Members of the English monarchy, the Solomons' prime minister, and other dignitaries had been invited to the sacred dwelling's grand opening in one month's time to view the antiquities, ancient weapons, and *tabu* fetishes that are stored inside. He asked me if Queen Elizabeth liked taro with her roast pork and if Prince Phillip would mind drinking lukewarm beer. We were never to walk beneath a woman's grass skirt that was hanging out to dry, and being positioned lower than a female was forbidden as in this patriarchal society subservient women must always remain lower than males. I strained my ears to hear his last slurred instructions, which were to never raise our voices in the village unless we were warning others of danger and that treating the villagers with respect was paramount.

He took a long swig of beer, wiped his mouth with the back of his hand, and then warned us to take the next piece of advice very seriously. Only a week before our arrival, while a woman was taking her daily wash in a pool at the base of a waterfall just several minutes' walk from the village, a wild boar leapt to its death from the top of the falls and landed in a mangled heap on the rocks beside her. The shocked woman was even more horrified when she noticed that something had already mutilated the pig with what looked like puncture wounds and claw marks. She could feel that something was watching her and instinctively looked to the top of the waterfall where she saw a wild-eyed giant leering down at her through a fringe of brown shaggy hair. She started shaking with fear, and for a brief moment, the bewildered woman gazed in disbelief, her eyes dilated by sheer terror and her mouth agape, before she ran in a blind panic back to the village. Although a week had passed when we saw her, she was still visibly shaken by the traumatic encounter. Moro advised us to carry a torch or a lighted stick if we walked around the village at night as an edgy air was still slowly dissipating, and the jittery villagers were armed with bows, machetes, and spears and still had itchy trigger fingers. He said without hesitation that any unidentified silhouette would be shot on sight, so we took serious heed of the threat that what was left of us would be questioned afterwards. If I started grunting like a wild animal and was walking around in low light, my six-foot one-inch frame and mop of shaggy hair could easily be mistaken for a mythical boar-slaying giant.

We were completely taken by surprise when, without any warning or reason, Moro catapulted through the air and suddenly broke out into a wild dance. His skinny arms and legs flailed and jerked without rhythm or grace as he grinned from ear to ear and slurred an incoherent tune. So as not to cause any offence, we initially choked back our amusement, until his lunatic antics were too much for us and we doubled over with side-splitting laughter. The impromptu jig came to an equally sudden halt. Moro regained his chiefly composure, staggered towards his leaf hut, and waved for two nubile village maidens with full voluptuous breasts to join him.

Although the villagers were reasonably friendly, we could sense they were a little bit indifferent and suspicious of us. A young and inexperienced evangelist who was hell bent on rescuing Moro and his flock from their primitive world of darkness and heathenism had visited the village the day before our arrival. He'd acted more like a mercenary than a missionary, and his fire and brimstone attitude no doubt contributed to why the villager's greeted us, and outsiders in general, in an unresponsive manner. The way he'd waved the bible while he quoted scriptures at the top of his voice not only breached village protocol, it was a huge insult to the native's morality. After Moro's men finished beating him to a bloody pulp, they abruptly showed him the door. The Christian exited the traditional safe haven horizontally and twice as quickly as he entered, when they literally threw him onto the trail bordering the village.

It was a very different chief that visited us the next morning. He was sober, but he still hadn't washed and looked a disgrace to the species. He had an air of arrogance, and a chiefly aloofness that changed him from the initial drunken disappointment of the previous day to a man that demanded instant respect. When Luko asked if anyone sold beetle nut, in a barbed tone Moro ordered a cheerful looking adolescent to take us to his plantation. After a five-minute walk from the village, Francis and Luko ogled in disbelief at the great clusters of nuts hanging from an impressive forest of areca palms. They were in beetle nut heaven. The offer to fill our empty pockets from the addict's nirvana quickly turned from controlled excitement into a wild picking frenzy. Each of my carefully aimed swats with a bamboo pole sent a hail of nuts thudding around our feet. After each brief sprinkling, the others reminded me of squirrels readying for winter as they gathered our narcotic bounty into neat piles.

Of all the creatures that can inflict a nightmare of pain or death in the Solomons, one of my pet hates is the fire ant. I'd noticed that Luko was grinning and flinching when he'd poured the last handful of nuts into my ripped pockets. After months of living in the villages, what was left of my torn shorts looked like a tattered rag. An already hot and cloudless dawn had forewarned me that we were in for another uncomfortably humid day, and although I love mushrooms I didn't want them sprouting in my crotch, so to reduce my chances of catching an irritating fungal infection in my sweaty groin, I'd passed on wearing any underpants. The reason for the massive smirk on Luko's face transformed my features into a shocked grimace, when I realized this was the ultimate payback for giving him hell during the flight to Marau Sound. I was suddenly hit with an almost indescribable agony when thousands of red-hot needles started searing into my hypersensitive testicles. Hordes of barely visible fire ants swarmed over my tender wrinkled spuds and inflicted venomous bites that were so torturous even the strongest of men would've been reduced to a blithering idiot. For a fleeting moment the intensity of the pain paralysed my reflexes, then my instincts returned and I wrenched my shorts down while Luko and Francis screamed with laughter. While tears of joy rolled down Luko's cheeks he screeched, "That's where they get their name from, bro. Because before you enjoy a good chew you have to beat all nuts." I was too busy swearing and frantically brushing the vicious little monsters from my burning testicles and smarting penis to even think about his quick-witted remark.

When I waddled back to the village a group of women and girls walked past us in single file with woven baskets that were laden with food and beetle nuts tucked under their arms. They gave me permission to take their photo, but two men who were carrying a sacrificial pig which grunted in annoyance as it swung upside down from a sapling they carried on their shoulders thought otherwise and yelled at me to put my camera away. Moro was furious when he heard me being reprimanded and raced to the doorway of his hut, then scuttled across to where I was standing. He screamed a venomous warning that watching or photographing the sacred shark calling that was about to take place was *tabu*.

To witness the ritual first hand would have been an incredible experience, but I had to settle for listening to one of the villager's share what had happened several hours later. Moro had waded into the tepid lagoon until the water lapped his waist, then he gazed out to sea and for several minutes, he cast the sound of a loud chant across the lagoon. While everyone else patiently waited for their totemic creature to rise from the depths of the ocean, they maintained a hallowed silence. Then about fifty metres from the shore a fin broke the glassy surface of the lagoon with an almost silent swirl as a fully-grown shark appeared and slowly cruised up to Moro, who handfed the docile fish pieces of sacrificial pork. As well as being personified with a human spirit, the *kastom* shark is believed to have a supernatural link with Moro's youngest son. If the fish scrapes itself on the reef, a graze is said to mysteriously appear on the child in exactly the same place as the shark was injured. The rite ended when the contents were emptied from the woven baskets into the ocean to appease the spirit that's embodied within the shark.

The next uneventful day slipped past quickly. Then on Christmas Eve, while the three of us were sitting outside with our backs propped against the wall of our hut, I was thinking the villagers were so intent on safeguarding their *kastom* that no matter how much time we spent here, we'd only ever sample the edges of true village life. I could feel the tensions from the past that were created by outsiders and the mythical giants still hanging in the air. It was unfair to make comparisons, but the atmosphere in the Moro village was caustic at times and a stark contrast from the bristling smiles and the carefree mood we'd experienced at the pygmy hamlet. Only minutes later, a self-assured, lean and fit looking man in his mid-thirties sat down beside us. While he greeted each of us with a firm handshake, he introduced himself in perfect English and said his name was Fred Laku. Fred had those mischievous eyes that showed he had a personality which brimmed with an irrepressible zest for life. His outgoing nature and witty conversation made him incredibly easy to befriend, and when he offered to take us hunting crocodiles and provide us accommodation at a nearby hamlet, it was obvious the three of us all shared the same gut feeling about leaving the Moro village when we virtually answered yes in unison.

We spent a perfect Christmas day relaxing at Bubuvua village, which is nestled on the palm-fringed shores of tranquil Lake Lauvi. It felt heavenly being amongst newfound friends who were even happier to play the genial hosts than we were to be the appreciative guests. Since I'd gone feral, I'd walked off ten kilos of weight and began drooling when I saw the smorgasbord Bubuvua's easy-going inhabitants started to lay out in front of us. We politely ate like well-mannered ravenous pigs, and massacred a succulent Christmas platter of roast pork, fish, eel, rice, and vegetables.

Bubuvua translates to "the place to watch crocodiles," but Fred isn't content with being a spectator. Right along the weather coast, his prowess as a hunter is legendary, and stories abound of him wrestling the carnivorous creatures with his bare hands and single-handedly killing huge crocs with just a machete. I couldn't decide if he was incredibly brave or belonged in a tight fitting jacket in a padded room. When pigs and huge bullocks that feed too close to the water often fall prey to the prehistoric predators, matching your biceps and wits against the immense power of the world's largest reptile definitely has kamikaze overtones. The locals warned us to be careful as one of the creatures has a taste for human flesh. Only six months ago, a teenage boy was attacked by a croc while he was swimming in the shallows. The boy's father raced to his son's frantic screams for help and after a violent struggle, he managed to wrench the boy free from the crushing jaws of a small croc. Fortunately it only required a mass of stitches to patch up one relatively unscathed but very shaken youth. The boy was extremely lucky to have been taken by a smaller reptile as saltwater crocodiles can reach lengths of seven metres.

Luko had a brainwave, and decided shooting or spearing a croc wasn't only non-productive, it was way too easy. He figured if we were going to risk an arm and a leg or whatever else could fit inside the gaping jaw of a fully-grown crocodile, we should capitalize on the hunt. His idea of catching a live croc, smuggling it back on the plane in a rice sack, then fattening up the reptile back at Veravaolu to charge tourists to visit a Solomon Islands' man-eater was put to the vote. When everyone readily agreed with the exhilarating and entrepreneurial plan, it called for an immediate change of strategy. We would arm ourselves with dive torches and machetes just in case things turned ugly and paddle across the murky water at night in dugout canoes and capture our quarry by hand.

The following day, to familiarise ourselves with the four-square kilometre lake we took two canoes and paddled around its slime coated perimeter. The first croc we saw lay motionless and semi submerged beneath the surface and looked more like a harmless floating log than an amphibious carnivore basking in the sun. The deception was almost perfect until, with a sudden flick of its huge tail, the massive reptile slid into the depths of the lake. We paddled further around the lake edge and enjoyed its primeval atmosphere until Fred stalled the canoe to point out an island that was made from a messy weave of reeds and was somehow defying all logic by drifting into the wind. An ancient *kastom* story that Fred couldn't remember suggests the bizarre phenomenon has occurred for centuries. According to Fred an Australian scientist had used diving tanks and braved the crocodile infested waters to search for a more plausible explanation than a superstitious tale, but at the end of his study when he couldn't rationalize the islands' peculiar movements, the baffled scientist was dumfounded.

As the day drew to a close and we took to the water again, the setting sun detonated the vocal chords of every noisemaking insect and creature around and in the lake's grimy water. In the rapidly fading light we watched graceful flocks of birds skim only a few feet above the water as they headed across the lake to roost. Fireflies flitted and dived around our heads as they put on an impressive light show in an attempt to attract a mate, while our torches attracted whining clouds of bloodthirsty mosquitoes.

Fred's expertise automatically put him and hopefully our catch at the helm, Luko took the middle, and I squeezed behind him into our cramped and unstable dugout. Francis enjoyed the luxurious legroom of sharing another three man canoe with a young boy. With only a few inches of freeboard separating us from the jaws of our quarry, I felt as vulnerable as Luko looked when Fred said "Let's try and keep it quiet, unless you have to scream for help if a croc grabs hold of you." While Fred and Luko expertly sliced their paddles through the water, I used a half coconut shell to constantly bail out the steady stream of water seeping into our leaking canoe. The picturesque wildlife haven where shags and herons dived for fish, and wild pigs fed on the shores, underwent an eerie transformation once it became entombed in darkness. Our dugout quietly knifed through the grimy water into a haunting world where a wild imagination could easily travel beyond the reaches of time into the realm of living dinosaurs.

No matter where we went a symphony of baleful bleating echoed around the reed-choked shores. The incessant chorus of immature crocs calling for their parents meant we were in for an eventful night. Although the vocal juveniles were entertaining, it was their silent guardians that were cause for concern, especially when Fred whispered, "There you go, Luko, this one's the perfect size for the tourists." About twenty metres away, our diving torches stabbed through the pitch-black darkness and picked out two glowing eyes. Ever so slowly and with silent strokes, Fred sent us drifting towards a huge reptile that was about the same length as our canoe. Luko muttered in a voice that trembled with apprehension, "When I said I wanted to fatten up a croc, I didn't mean with me! This is frightening the shit out of me. Back up!" From where we were sitting in the low-slung dugout, the scant ten meters between us and the rows of menacing looking teeth felt like ten inches. Just as the last word rolled off the tip of my tongue when I jokingly said in a hushed voice, "Can't see you stuffing that big brute into our rice sack," an arc of spray burst into the air. With an astounding surge of strength, the massive creature thrashed the water into foam with its powerful tail and exploded into a dive. It was a strange sensation being in absolute awe, yet amidst the fury of the same moment being filled with a terrible sense of dread. Fred yelled, "Keep your hands inside the canoe!" while our eyes nervously scanned the water lapping the dugout. We swore aloud in three different languages and gripped the side of the unstable canoe while we shuffled our weight as a counterbalance each time the dugout threatened to capsize in the croc's wake.

For the next couple of hours, we mesmerised numerous sets of reflective eyes as the fading beam of the torch reduced to a pallid glow. When we quietly drifted to within arm's reach of a small crocodile, Fred expertly plucked it from the water with lightning quick reflexes, bound its jaws, and crammed the writhing creature into our rice sack.

The water boiled again twenty meters from the start of the track leading up to the village when another gigantic croc made a hasty retreat. After we slid up onto the beach, to me it was an act of total lunacy when Fred decided to take his evening bath while we watched from the safety of the shore. If splashing and washing in waist deep water wasn't bad enough, he swam to within metres of where the croc had just disappeared. We sat there shaking our heads in disbelief, and half expected a silent but deadly V-shaped wake and an armour-plated monstrosity with cavernous jaws to wrench him under the surface. His reckless actions removed all doubt: When after witnessing firsthand how incredibly quick and frightening huge crocs were, I used to think he was mad to even consider wrestling the creatures with his bare hands, but from his behaviour, I now definitely knew he was.

On New Year's Eve, absolutely nothing could persuade Luko to venture back onto the lake. Francis and I decided croc spotting from a dugout would be a memorable way to see in the New Year, so beneath an angry looking sky, just the two of us paddled across the lake after dark. Apart from when he had to fly for the first time, I'd never seen Luko frightened by anything. No matter how daunting the situation was, he'd always remained calm and collected, yet getting up close and personal with crocodiles had absolutely terrified him.

For me, the sole purpose of this outing was to explore the different states of my mind, rather than the lake's begrimed waters. It was a chance to learn to confront intimidation and involuntary emotional responses in a situation where I had no control over the outcome, and a chance to try and embrace the shudder of fear I felt when we were only metres away from a potential man-eater. While we listened to the deep-throated territorial roar of mature reptiles, and the warning hiss of massive crocs that were so close we could almost smell their fetid breath, it provided the perfect circumstances for learning to eject an intense feeling of dread from my senses. For several hours, we pushed our luck to the extreme and managed to get away with a few uncomfortably close encounters that left us tingling with exhilaration. Then thunder clapped, lightning flashed, and the heavens opened up with a ferocity that only the tropics can generate. Each stroke of our furiously paddling arms nudged our craft through a thick curtain of blinding rain as we powered towards a foul smelling and dismal looking swamp. We hissed up onto a bed of reeds, and when the atrocious weather eventually subsided, the thunderous rain was replaced with a thick and stifling humidity. With all of our repellent washed off, the whirling clouds of demonic mosquitoes that choked the sticky air quickly zeroed in on every available piece of our exposed flesh. I never want to have to hear such a loud and menacing drone again or to see such an inconceivable number of the insects and experience the burning sensation of being bitten by so many. Each time I slapped the back of my neck, it painted my palm red with blood. Unbeknown to us, most of the villagers had recently recovered from a malaria epidemic. Antimalarials aren't one hundred percent effective so there was a strong likelihood we'd succumb to the disease, and we did.

Fred and Luko had a much happier New Year's Eve. As a rule I don't ever ply alcohol into Islanders because once they get drunk, it's normally an open invitation for trouble. But I knew my friends could hold their drink without getting violent and didn't have any reservations about buying a case of Fosters beer from Avu Avu store to celebrate changing the calendar. We were soaked to the skin, itching like crazy, and eager to raise a few toasts to life and living in the New Year, but we returned to find that Fred and Luko and all of the beer had mysteriously vanished.

The next morning, after we followed a trail of empty beer cans we found Luko sprawled amongst the vegetation on the side of the track to the airport. He reeked of vomit, complained that he had a terrible hangover, and was shivering from head to toe with malaria again. A few hours later, apart from giving the rice bag a bit of a rustle the croc nestled in Luko's lap didn't seem to mind the flight back to Honiara.

After I spent several days feeling horribly sick at Veravaolu from what would later turn into recurrent bouts of malaria, I decided it was time to head home. I thought I'd mastered culture shock, and it came as a huge surprise when I found myself going through the transition of having to readapt to life back in New Zealand. Although it's a paradise, returning to what initially felt like an impatient consumer society and a world that's been poisoned by blatant greed, left me feeling a little disjointed from what had previously seemed a satisfying and wholesome environment. It was a good experience because it gave me a small taste of how indigenous peoples must feel when they're influenced by an alien culture.

Now that the Solomon Islanders had taught me how to remain relatively comfortable in an alien and potentially dangerous environment, the jungle's numerous hazards were predictable and for the most part preventable. Out of everything that I'd learnt, it was the better understanding of its people's philosophy on life that I valued the most. Despite all of my newfound skills, I knew I was still a boy in a man's underpants, with a lot to learn about human nature and true exploration. The experience I gained from the Solomon Islanders and Guadalcanal's pristine rainforest was invaluable. Besides the added confidence, it instilled me with a heightened respect for all of nature, furthered my love for life in the wilderness, and transformed me into an incurable nomad. It wasn't long before I started making plans to travel alone to Irian Jaya, which is one of the planets last great frontiers, where I hoped to search for some of the earth's most reclusive tribes in some of the world's most inhospitable jungles.

In the years that followed, I received letters from Luko which kept me updated on the grim civil war that was to rage in the Solomons. He believed land disputes were the catalyst, and when the Malaitan Eagle Force's bloody battle against Guadalcanal's Isatabu Freedom Movement and the Guadalcanal Revolutionary Army escalated, it had a lasting and devastating impact on Veravaolu's inhabitants. A Malaitan landing craft that was aptly named *The Mover*, crept into a lagoon at Araligo, further up the coast, while a hijacked fishing boat spewed soldiers onto the beach at Visale Mission. Then in an act of hate-filled carnage, burnt Veravaolu to the ground and attacked the villagers. Luko and his family were forced to flee into the sanctuary of the jungle, where to this day they are still holed up in basic shelters. So far they've managed to survive amidst a spate of murders and mindless brutality by living off of their wits and from whatever they can reap from the surrounding rainforest. There are kind people who I'd befriended that changed their outlook to transform their tradition of hospitality into hostility when they fought for the Malatians, and like so many others who I'd once considered friends, now they are the much-despised enemy of my *wantoks*. According to the media, as a consequence of the civil unrest, the level of violent crime in Honiara has escalated to epidemic proportions, and Guadalcanal is teetering on the brink of anarchy. With the instinctive tendency to revert back to the traditional means of settling disputes with warfare, even travelling along the remote weather coast is unthinkable as the whole region is considered way too volatile. Because of the feuding tribes who appear to be unable to grasp the concept of peace, and with lawlessness being such a popular pastime amongst Honiara's despondent and impressionable youths, the Solomons has well and truly lost its innocence.

Chapter Seven

CAVORTING WITH CANNIBALS

After several months of anticipation and careful planning, I looked through the tiny window of an Indonesian aeroplane as it bucked and shuddered in the turbulent tropical thermals, and watched Irian Jaya, one of the earth's most daunting yet beautifully diverse destinations, quietly slipping beneath us. Even from the sky the endless realm of rainforest that blanketed the world's largest tropical island left me in awe. Despite lying two degrees south of the equator, I marvelled at the improbable snow capped peaks that towered over glaciers and fed rivers which snaked through a sea of emerald treetops. Some of the serpentine rivers ran down into inhospitable malarial swamps, while others merged with a shimmering ocean that was fringed with dazzling white sand beaches. We slowly descended over vast and unexplored tracts of jungle where cannibalistic tribes who had never been contacted by outsiders were still living amongst the trees.

I was mesmerised by this land of mystery and its immense contrasts and couldn't wait to touch down in a country that isn't only menacing, but also menaced. For over a century, the western half of New Guinea was governed by the Netherlands as a part of the Dutch East Indies. Then amidst huge controversy in 1963, the United Nations handed the province and its goldmine of natural resources over to Indonesia, who had gained independence in 1949. For the hundreds of thousands of animist aborigines scattered throughout Irian Jaya's wilderness areas, the transition to Indonesian rule has been anything but smooth. The primitive peoples, who are renowned for intertribal warfare and acts of cannibalism, now live under the constant threat of being attacked by the militant Indonesian government as they try to unify hundreds of diverse and isolated societies into a contemporary Indonesian province. The Indonesians' attempts to modernize a fifty thousand year old Melanesian culture in a few decades by using wanton violence to merge two ways of life that couldn't be more diametrically opposed in their beliefs and objectives has failed miserably and has made the natives feel as if they are being held as prisoners in their own land.

The tribes who used to fight each other have ignored their past grievances and have amalgamated to become freedom fighters. Remote clans, armed with spears, bone daggers, and poisoned arrows, have united to form the Free Papua Movement and are engaging in guerrilla warfare against the ruthless Indonesian military in an attempt to cling to their land, their culture, and to push for independence. Unlike the Indonesian's concept of goal driven conflict, where their objective is to dominate others, tribal war in Irian Jaya is a practiced art form. Most tribal battles are stringently controlled and are fought to appease ancestral spirits, to retain law and order, to conserve land, and as I later found out first hand, for self and cultural preservation. The missionaries, mercenaries, and misfits who are synonymous with New Guinea and Irian Jaya, who have taken an aggressive stance against both the land and its inhabitants, have fuelled further discontent and created a burning bitterness in some areas that is sometimes directed towards uninvited outsiders.

Because tourists have been kidnapped and killed in the past by anti-Indonesian forces in an attempt to bring their shocking plight to the attention of the outside world, officialdom keeps close tabs on every traveller's whereabouts. When I took the full brunt of a totally bored looking Indonesian officer's frustration while I applied for a *surat jalan* (travel permit), it wasn't the ideal welcome to Sentani on Irian Jaya's northern coast. I was hoping to springboard from the steamy swamps in the Asmat region, and then head deeper into the interior to make contact with the cannibalistic Korowai who reside in one hundred feet high tree houses. It seemed as though months of planning were about to come crashing down around my ears when the soldier shook his head and said, "Runway no good. Plane no land. You no go Asmat." I thought for a few seconds, then said, "If it's okay, I'll walk down from Wamena. I love exercise." The bombastic soldier raised his abrupt voice a couple of octaves and slammed one of his animated hands on the counter when he barked, "Korowai too dangerous! They eat you! What wrong with you? You deaf! You no go Asmat!" After five persistent minutes of getting nowhere with my carefully selected words and a tactful approach, he made it more than clear that nothing was going to sway his decision. He was the king of his own small bureaucratic world and his word was law. When the soldier's naturally scarce patience finally wore thin and he roared, "What broody wrong with you! All travel to Asmat stopped!" his riled exclamation severed any chance I had of contacting the Korowai. I later heard unconfirmed rumours that the military had recently strafed several Asmat villages. After I listened to a lot of verbal mud slinging, it was eventually agreed on that I could visit the Dani, living in the Bailem Valley up in the highlands, and the rattan hoop wearing Yali, who inhabit the sparsely populated Jayawijaya Mountains east of the Bailem Valley.

I wasn't too disappointed because from what I'd read while I was in New Zealand, the highlands sounded fascinating. When westerners first discovered the Grand Bailem Valley in 1938, they exposed the huge basin to the world as a mystical Shangri La. The inaccessible highlands were previously thought to be uninhabited, but for millennia they had been home to thousands of agriculturalist Dani tribesmen who were preoccupied with war and with breeding pigs for bride price to accumulate numerous wives and as a form of wealth to achieve elevated status amongst their peers as bigmen. It wasn't until 1945, when a plane crashed and its survivors were rescued from the isolated valley, that tales of savage cannibalistic tribes created sensational world news and sent a stampede of exploiters, explorers, and evangelists into the pristine and often volatile region.

Nearly sixty years after outsiders had first ventured into the region, my flight up to the highlands in a decrepit propeller-driven Fokker plane revealed the same unforgiving terrain that previous adventurers had sighted. Deep chasms and sweeping valleys that were choked with a profusion of lush vegetation folded the spellbinding landscape into an explorer's paradise. We soared up the mountains, then dropped through a wall of thick cloud into a clear blue sky, where below us, blade-like ridges spilled down from the surrounding hills into a stunning sixty kilometre long valley blanketed in coarse sun bleached grass. Dome shaped huts that were thatched with grass were scattered about in fenced off clusters. Irrigation ditches separated a patchwork of sweet potato plantations that stretched for acres. Right across the valley, wispy clouds of bluish white smoke climbed skywards from numerous cooking fires and burning brush that had been cleared to plant new gardens. Small dark figures travelled along a network of narrow pathways, while others toiled in their gardens. After a rough landing, the aging plane ground to a shuddering halt, and once the aircraft's doors swung open, we were enveloped by the freshness of the cool mountain air.

I clanked down the metal steps and headed across to the tiny airport terminal, where I was greeted by registered guides who quoted exorbitant prices as they hit on new arrivals. As soon as I grabbed my pack off the baggage counter, I went outside and was plagued by annoying hawkers during the five-minute walk into Wamena. The highlands' only metropolis had the typical rawness of third world Indonesia and the feel of a frontier town that had stagnated yet was trying its best to grow into something bigger. Vile smelling open sewers that lined the streets flowed past tired looking dishevelled buildings in various stages of decay. The virtually naked natives who were milling around the town mingled with an array of people from differing ethnic backgrounds. The government's transmigration schemes have transformed Wamena into a cultural melting pot. Their offer of escapism from Indonesia's other hopelessly overpopulated islands to a land of wealth and promise has fallen well short of most of the immigrants' expectations. Wamena isn't too bad, but many of the immigrants live in the clutches of abject poverty in ramshackle settlements or in sombre camps that have been carved out of the jungle, where they are barely able to grow enough crops to provide for their disillusioned families let alone make any sort of a decent living.

While I looked for somewhere to stay, during a moment of weakness I bought a dogtooth necklace from one of the Dani hawkers who were thrusting and rattling their wares in front of my face. When I left the main road and cut down a narrow side street to find a backpackers' lodge, the babbling hawkers kept jostling with one another to stay at my side. Their excited burble of, "You buy! You buy!" carried on long after I'd patiently told them in Indonesian that I wasn't interested. I tried a less subtle approach, and with a huge smile on my face, I said, "for Christ's sake fuck off ya parasites." Everyone caught the gist of what I meant, but rather than take offence, they burst out laughing and followed me across a lawn to a small store that was attached to a corrugated iron shack.

The amused storekeeper smirked to himself, then in almost perfect English told me to come inside. Before I had a chance to ask if I could use his toilet, he opened the side door to the store and barked at the hawkers to back off. As he shook my hand he said, "All of the tourists complain about them. I'm Ano." Ano looked to be about twenty-five-years old, and his round and friendly face was obviously Melanesian, but it lacked any distinctive features that linked him to one particular tribe. When a persistent hawker waved a bone dagger over the shop counter, I said, "I know the poor bastards are only trying to make a living, but look at them. They're like bloody leeches. The only way to get rid of them is to burn them off." Ano's mother seemed to appear from nowhere, and beneath her gentle looking exterior and the wide smile she flashed me lurked a fearsome temper. She was armed with a broom and jarred the hawker's enthusiasm to an abrupt halt when he received an unexpected mouthful of bristle. Then she yelled abuse at the top of her lungs, gave the persistent boy another swift swat in the face, and marched the hawkers off the property.

Besides letting me use their toilet, the typically warm Melanesian hospitality I was shown quickly extended to the heartening offer to stay with them and use one of their beds for as long as I wished. Over the next few days, Ano's light-hearted manner, and having the same earthy sense of humour, made it easy for us to become firm friends. He was free of any responsibilities and jumped at the offer to travel with me into Yali country. Throughout his youth he'd often visited his relative who lived in a traditional Dani village and had even witnessed several bloody tribal battles, but he'd spent most of his life in town and had never travelled beyond the Bailem Valley to visit other clans. As well as speaking English, he was fluent in Indonesian and several other native dialects, which was an unexpected bonus as his translating skills would prove to be invaluable.

Ano suggested that instead of hiring an expensive guide, for the fraction of the cost, we could travel with a Yali he knew who was about to return to his village. He arranged for me to meet him that afternoon. From the instant I saw Api, something in my gut warned me to think twice about hiring him. He was a tiny, restless looking man who didn't seem to be at ease with himself yet alone with others. It showed in his shifty and arrogant looking eyes when he muttered he would act as a guide and porter if we were ready to leave in two days' time. When I asked him about the Yali's fierce reputation, it didn't make my decision to use him any easier. He replied in Indonesian that his people wouldn't hesitate to kill us if we stole a pig or created problems, but since the government had banned cannibalism, they probably wouldn't eat us. This was small consolation. Because of my doubts, at the very least I normally would've gone on a day trek together to ensure we were compatible, but Ano felt the language barrier and Api's limited contact with Europeans were probably responsible for his aloof attitude.

We were up early the next morning and walked into town behind a bare breasted Dani woman who was hunched over beneath the crippling weight of the vegetables she carried in a string bag that hung from the top of her head. When she dropped her load alongside a foul-smelling open sewer and wiped the sweat from her creased brow, Ano said, "You watch this. It's disgusting." She waded into the filthy drain and brushed aside the raw sewage and vile smelling scum floating on the surface, then washed her crisp looking bag of vegetables in the disease-ridden water.

We followed her to the market where she was about to sell her vegetables and joined a growing line of customers who haggled with an Indonesian trader as he sliced off cuts of meat from a side of beef that was hanging alongside the entrance to the market. The carcass was black with a crosshatch of feeding flies, and when it came to our turn to buy a couple of juicy steaks for dinner, only a pile of soup bones remained. As we went from store to store, it took us a while to find rice that wasn't crawling with weevils, and even changing my money into smaller denominations at the bank to pay for extra porters, firewood, accommodation, and other items we might need during our travels proved fruitless. An elderly teller, who instead of a nose bone wore a ballpoint pen through his pierced nasal septa, shrugged his shoulders, said the bank had run out of smaller notes, and suggested we try a store.

The minor setbacks were part and parcel of the frontier town's rugged no frills character. When we came out of a store and watched a Dani being beaten over the head with a bottle of black market whisky, it added to Wamena's already wild atmosphere. Prohibition has created a thriving business for the Indonesian bootleggers who smuggle liquor up to the highlands. The Dani had traded a camera that obviously wasn't his for a contraband bottle of alcohol, and when the camera's irate owner found out, he snatched the full bottle from the Dani's hand and with a bone shattering blow, smashed it over his head. The Dani collapsed in a quivering heap and let out a slow groan as blood poured from a deep gash in his horribly injured scalp. When I said to Ano, "He didn't even get the cap off the bottle, but it still went straight to his head and made him legless," he simply smiled, shrugged his shoulders, and kept on walking as if the violent outburst was a part of everyday life.

A clear day dawned for the start of our expedition once the usual early morning fog floated across the valley and was burnt off by the rising sun. Although Api's surprisingly quick pace and our leg buckling loads of food, tobacco, salt, and other gifts made the hike up from the valley floor strenuous, I was so captivated by the stunning scenery that I was oblivious to the laborious climb. While we followed a path that had been worn bare by centuries of tribal traffic, it was easy to let my mind drift back to when the valley was first discovered, to a time when the hostile natives would've dictated how and where we'd travel through what was once perilous country. Although the Indonesians have forced the Dani to adopt a more peaceful outlook, and there was the odd glint of corrugated iron from some of the surrounding ridge tops, the highlands still felt wild and primitive.

As we climbed higher and deeper into the mountains, we watched villagers using simplistic digging sticks and some who were using shovels work their cleverly engineered terraced gardens, which seemed to defy gravity as they clung to near vertical hillsides. Bare breasted women with protruding bellies, who wore skirts made of coiled plant fibres that somehow hung from below their wide hips, stooped beneath the painfully heavy loads of sweet potatoes they carried. As they walked past they greeted us with a smile and said, "*wa wa.*" The wide smiling men who were practically naked except for their gourd penis sheaths, called *holim*, offered us the same friendly greeting. Most of the men wore a mixture of soot and pig fat smeared over their chests and shoulders in a crude attempt to ward off the highland chill. Their hair had been pulled and rubbed into tight ringlets that shined from a heavy coating of soot and pig grease, and as they walked past, I caught a heady whiff of the pungent smell of wood smoke, animal fat, and the layers of unwashed sweat that wafted from their bodies. My first impressions of the highlands were a far cry from the romantic visions most people have of them being a dangerous destination that's filled with barbaric and cannibalistic headhunters. In general the Dani's primal features were soft and open, and they were a cheerful people who were quick to smile and offer a friendly greeting.

Most of the villages we passed through were enclosed by stonewalls which had been painstakingly built by hand to prevent the native's precious pigs from straying. The way several ancient looking hamlets had been strategically placed to dominate the surrounding landscape and their defensive construction, showed the paranoia the villagers must have felt when intertribal conflict used to be rampant. At the end of a toilsome and tiring day the friendly inhabitants of our destined village offered us a warm greeting. While Ano went to find another much needed porter, I dug out my camera and my one luxury item, toilet paper, and wandered off into the jungle to relieve my rumbling stomach.

As I picked my way back to he hamlet, I was looking downwards and pushing through a patch of knee high grass. The instant I looked up, I screeched to an abrupt halt and was shocked to see a Dani warrior standing directly in front of me with his bow aimed at my midriff. He wore an iridescent headdress, a cowry shell breastplate to deflect enemy arrows, and a pig tusk nose bone to imitate a ferocious wild boar and to instil fear in the enemy. Once I got over the initial jolt, his imposing presence was as fascinating as it was frightening. I smiled and thought to myself that he had to be kidding and said "*wa wa*" and waited for him to answer. He maintained his unnerving silence, and kept glaring at me as he shifted his body into an even more aggressive stance. I stood rooted to the spot for what seemed like an eternity, and wondered what the hell I'd done to rile him. With the luxury of hindsight, smiling again, then raising my camera and clicking off a shot definitely wasn't the smartest move I could've made. It spread a look of rage across his already menacing features, and I figured he definitely wasn't joking when he pulled his bow to what I thought was full draw. I looked directly into his wild eyes and shuddered when I heard the twang as he released the bamboo bowstring. It sounded as loud as rolling thunder, and in that split second, when I'd expected his arrow to slice into my flesh, it felt as if I'd been struck by lightning. My sense of dread turned to utter relief when I realized the arrow hadn't been nocked to the string and was never meant to have been.

The torrent of profanity that flew from my mouth had the same impact on the Dani that the sound of his plucked bowstring had on my stunned senses. Ano had taught me a few choice words from the Dani lingo, so I shook off my jangled nerves by telling the equally shocked warrior that he was unnaturally close with his mother. For a brief moment, we looked at each other in total silence, then when he couldn't hold back any longer his grimace turned into a smile, and we both burst into hysterical laughter. I paid him for the photo, then traded for his nose bone as a memento of the heart-stopping moment.

When I found Ano, he laughed so hard and so long that tears streamed down his flushed cheeks. The rest of the hamlet erupted into joyous whoops, rapturous howls, and almost screeched themselves hoarse over Ano's practical joke.

After walking hard and fast all day, we'd worked up a mean hunger. We cooked a meal of rice and sweet potatoes and shared it with a small group of curious Dani who were crowded into a crude hut that seemed to be the only shelter that was shared by both sexes. I should've known better and wasn't thinking when I stopped eating and pulled out my false two front teeth to get at an annoying grain of rice that was stuck at the back of my mouth. From the way everyone reacted you would've thought I'd just ripped my head off of my shoulders. A small boy screamed and started bawling while his mother shrieked and started shaking as she swept him into her arms. The poor Dani were petrified and jumped back with their mouths agape and their faces contorted into looks of sheer horror. A wizened old man covered in battle scars from arrow and dagger wounds gasped so hard that he started choking and sprayed the mouthful of rice he was eating into the air. There wasn't much that the terrified old man hadn't been witness to during his tumultuous life. He'd dined on human flesh numerous times and he'd mediated with the supernatural, but he'd never witnessed sorcery this powerful. When Ano had jumped to the defence of an innocent man who was being harassed by the Indonesian military, a soldier had knocked out his front teeth. He worsened the already panic-stricken situation by telling the frantic crowd I was a devil who was about to implant my teeth into his gums. I turned to Ano and said, " Don't say that, mate! Look at how upset that old guy is. Tell them the truth and put them out of their misery before things get ugly." Once the old man was over his initial fright, he'd grabbed a knife to either protect himself or to do battle with the toothless demon. It demanded a rapid explanation because Ano's idea of a harmless joke could so easily have backfired at my expense. He quickly laid everyone's fears to rest by explaining that the white man's dentistry was responsible for my potent magic. To the superstitious Dani, I'd just performed an inexplicable act of magic that defied their primitive logic, so to help reassure them that I wasn't from the spirit world I let them pass my teeth around one another. Their fear turned to intense curiosity, and then to ecstatic fits of laughter when the old man held my teeth up to his mouth. The excitable women screamed with delight, while the men expressed their joy by flicking their penis gourds with a fingernail.

Although the Dani were still naïve when it came to comprehending certain aspects of western science and technology, they knew how to handle money, and some of them were quick to try and fleece tourists. The Indonesians attitude of treating travellers as a commercial commodity has rubbed off on the Dani and tainted their otherwise unselfish mindset. I had to pay for firewood, to take photos, and for our accommodation. It even cost me to look inside a *honay*, which is a men's hut, to see how they sleep before we stretched out on the dirt floor of a disused hut. The domelike structure crawled with annoying fleas and lice and definitely wasn't built for comfort. For anyone who wasn't used to it, trying to sleep on a raised wooden platform above a warming fire guaranteed an uncomfortable and sleepless night amidst a toxic fog of gagging smoke.

Antagonism between the sexes has moulded the patriarchal Dani society. Females have virtually no social status whatsoever and sleep with their children and pigs in separate huts from the men. When I questioned a Dani chief about the way women are treated he told me, "Women bleed (menstruate) and are dirty; pigs are also filthy animals that live in shit. The two belong together." How the women ever manage to sleep and resist the urge to constantly scratch at the bites that are inflicted by the hordes of parasites living on the pigs is beyond comprehension, as a plague of fleas instantly feasted on my blood when I was shown inside a women's hut. We were lucky our hut was insect free, and after a tiring day I slipped into a sound sleep.

We were away at dawn the next morning, and while we followed a well-defined path from village to village, a woman pulled alongside us wearing a string bag called a *noken*, which is woven from the bark of a tree. She carried her *noken* like all Dani women do, hanging from the top of her head with the bag draped over her shoulders and falling down to the small of her back. When I heard a grunt, I had a closer look, and through the open weave I could see her newborn child cuddling a tiny piglet. In the more remote regions, pigs are so highly prized that if the runt of a litter appears to be undernourished, it's breastfeed by a lactating woman. A traditional Dani woman very rarely removes her *noken*, as it wards off evil spirits and keeps malevolent ancestral ghosts at bay.

One of the hamlets we briefly stopped at was in mourning. Two grieving women were caked from head to toe with white mud that had dried and cracked to give them a ghoulish almost inhuman appearance, which is what they wanted as they were hiding beneath their pallid disguise to confuse the departing spirit of their deceased relative in case it decided to return to the village and haunt its family.

A few of the isolated villages we visited shared horrific stories of how they'd endured unprovoked attacks from the Indonesian military. At first everyone remained tight-lipped when I asked if they'd been witness to the brutality and killings as they were fearful of retribution. But once they realized we weren't affiliated with the government and were sympathetic to their dreadful plight, they started to voice their anger. The cold-blooded extermination of Irian Jaya's indigenous peoples has been veiled from the outside world by their geographical remoteness. No one is ever charged for the atrocities or is ever made accountable because theirs is a silent and secretive genocide. When President Suharto's government ordered that Irian Jaya's savages must be modernised, a Dani chief was made to wear clothes by the Indonesian army to signify his status. The military decided that by dressing him in black bellbottom trousers and a black shirt, he would set an enviable example to the other Dani the luxuries they would receive if they chose to became sophisticated Indonesians. His initial protests were met with appalling violence when several women and children were tied up with rope then thrown into a nearby river where they all drowned. Then to really emphasize that the self-righteous military wouldn't take no for an answer, several babies were bayoneted. As if that wasn't enough, to reinforce the brutal message, the chief's wife and daughter were thrown out of a hovering helicopter. When they fell to their deaths at the feet of the horrified onlookers the soldiers felt they had finally done an adequate amount of killing to sway the despondent chief's thinking.

The days had turned to passing weeks before the Indonesians returned to make sure the Stone Age chief was still fully clothed. In the meantime, he was so fearful that his people would face further punishment if he touched any of his clothing that he defecated and urinated in his pants for a full month. Their perpetrators disgusted the Dani so much that they decided if that's the way the filthy Indonesians lived they could keep it, and instead of taking a step forward towards making the province truly Indonesian, the soldiers' cruelty caused the scathing Dani warriors to despise and rebel against the government.

It was great to get back into the jungle and clear my mind of the senseless violence and hatred those unfortunate people had been subjected to. Api's legs have been genetically geared to suit the demanding terrain that we tackled, and despite his small stature, he handled his hefty load surprisingly well. Being burdened with the added weight didn't hamper the blistering pace he set, which stayed the same if he was climbing a sheer ridge or charging down a greasy slope. My gut feeling about Api was slowly proving to be right, when throughout the day he'd arrogantly ignored our repeated requests for him to slow down to a more comfortable speed. Ano and I were hardly slouches, and had no problem digging deeper and upping our already quick tempo to match his tireless legs.

Night falls rapidly in the tropics, and we were just about ready to collapse as well at the end of another exhausting day. As dusk cast a damp mist over the highlands, even the crudest of the primitive huts that were scattered around a grassy knoll looked plush and inviting. Hospitality is at the very core of Dani culture, and as usual, the friendly villagers made us more than welcome. While we were boiling a pot of rice, a short muscular youth in his early twenties with a badly swollen eye and a relaxed manner squatted beside us and introduced himself. Natan was the son of the chief and had such a likeable personality that Ano and I almost jumped at his offer to join us as a porter. When Ano asked him about his bruised eye he began to fidget nervously and seemed a bit evasive. He said it was nothing and was from a scuffle earlier in the day. It was hard to imagine someone with such an affable nature and such a placid looking face being involved in any sort of conflict, but his tattered jean shorts looked as if they'd definitely seen a few wars. His testicles dangled beneath the ragged crotch of his pants, and each futile attempt he made to flick them back into his excuse for shorts had us in hysterics. They kept flopping out one side of his pants, then the other, time and again, until he let rip with a hearty laugh and gave up trying to cover them.

It was impossible not to notice Natan's aging mother's badly mutilated hand when she generously gifted each of us several steaming sweet potatoes. Death had taken four of Natan's siblings, and for each one a finger had been cut off so that only the thumb remained on his mother's left hand. His father had inflicted a brutally painful anaesthetic, which he administered by repeatedly punching her upper arm until the limb was numb before he amputated the first two joints of her finger with a stone adze. Sometimes a more gentle method is used to deaden the arm, and it's anaesthetized by striking the funny bone. A young female from the deceased's family normally endures the agonizing surgery to appease the ghost of the departed. The men sometimes express their sorrow in the same manner, but normally choose to slice off a portion of their ear, as a warrior's fingers must remain intact so that he can draw his bow. The amputated body parts are burnt on a funeral pyre when the corpse is cremated to show the deceased they will be missed and will still be loved when they are in the spirit world. Nowadays the rapidly encroaching church and the militant Indonesians have virtually eradicated amputations from occurring during a funeral rite.

When I asked Natan if I could look at the bow and arrows he'd carried into the hut, he willingly obliged and was especially eager to share his knowledge when I told him I was an avid archer. All of the highland tribes use basic D shaped bows that are crafted from black palm and other hardwoods. The weapons they use for hunting large game and for warfare can be up to six feet long and have a heavy draw weight, whereas the bows that are used to hunt birds, fish, and other small game are much shorter and easier to draw. Their bowstrings are normally fashioned from a flat strip of bamboo or rattan about ten millimetres wide. In some areas an intricate weave of rattan is bound around the tip of the bow to prevent the string from slipping down the limb, but there are numerous clans who don't bother. Because of the flat string the arrows are devoid of a cut nock, and are always sliced square, directly below a stipule to give them added strength and to ensure a tight fit against the flat surface of the string.

Irian Jaya's arrows rate as some of the most beautiful in the world, and Natan's were no exception. A diverse array of arrows averaging one hundred and thirty centimetres in length are crafted for specific tasks. The arrows that are used for fighting, fishing, hunting, and exchange at ceremonies all vary. They are all devoid of fletching, and the dried wild cane shafts are tipped with an assortment of arrowheads made of human bone, which is believed to harbour a deadly spirit, animal bone, bamboo, black palm and other hardwoods. The arrows that are used for warfare have fearsome looking barbed arrowheads that are normally decorated with elaborate carving.

Retribution for a family member who is slain by an opposing clan is known as payback, and is deemed as a necessity to appease the gods and ancestral spirits and to avenge the ghost of the murdered relative. Ornately barbed arrows that are used to kill an enemy are decorated with beautiful carvings and weave that deliver death with an attached message. The unique designs are functional as well as being a visual garnish and act as a signature to ensure the victim's family know which tribe and which individual to target for payback. Before the government and the missionaries banned warfare, Natan's clan were no strangers to intertribal conflict. The clashes were planned carefully and were normally carried out in open valleys, where the fighting occurred in spurts over a full day of battle rather than in an all-out skirmish. Once enough enemies had been slain to appease the spirits, towards the end of what was normally a well-disciplined battle, the warriors taunted each other with insults instead of trying to draw more blood with their bone daggers or well-aimed spears and arrows. These days ambush is the most common and preferred method of killing an enemy.

Over the next couple of days, we briefly visited several hamlets that had been impoverished and disillusioned from their integration with one-eyed evangelists. Wherever remote primitive peoples exist, others are waiting in the wings to exploit them to suit their own desires instead of catering for the inhabitant's immediate needs. The downtrodden natives living in isolated Christian villages that had been abandoned by transitory missionaries were clothed in filthy tattered rags that not only harboured disfiguring skin diseases, they hid the people's true identity. Compared to the traditional villages, the squalor and the indelible sense of misery that hung in the air from where the church had caused cultural sufferance was depressing. The Dani asked exorbitant prices for accommodation and firewood so they, in turn, could purchase more material goods. We gave the Christian hamlets a wide berth and slept in the jungle in basic shelters or spent the night in more hospitable villages.

As each day passed, Api kept reassuring us that replenishing our dwindling supplies at Angguruk mission wouldn't be a problem. We were heading there in a roundabout way and had gifted most of our food to the isolated villages to reciprocate their hospitality and to give them a change of diet. While Ano and I were revelling in the escapism and the adventure, the others were becoming increasingly quiet and moody. The further we ventured into the jungle, the more anxious and reserved Natan became. Api became more and more unsociable and at times he was so blatantly arrogant that it was a waste of time trying to talk to him. Late one afternoon, as we churned and toiled through a swamp that was studded with beautiful tree ferns, trying to keep up with him became almost impossible. The only way we managed to keep his indefatigable legs in sight was by running, and when we finally caught up with him he looked unwell and I felt uneasy. Then the day went from bad to worse when a suspicious looking villager joined our ranks. Jale was middle-aged, wore western cloth-ing, and while we rested in a village then moved on, he'd simply picked up part of our supplies and included himself as a member of our expedi-tion. His volley of probing questions, the scornful expression he wore, and his swing shift temperament put me on edge. It wasn't unusual for natives that were travelling from village to village to happily help us carry our supplies without being asked, but this time there'd been a misunderstand-ing where I thought Ano had asked Jale along, whereas Ano figured I'd hired him.

For some strange reason Jale seemed to get a great deal of sadistic pleasure from telling us that just a few days ago, a Dani had been decapi-tated in the shelter where we were planning to spend the night. A bamboo knife had been used to hack off his head, which had been left alongside the body to show it was a payback killing. When Natan heard Jale talking about the murder, he pricked up his anxious ears and grimaced, then he quietly regained his composure. It was obvious that the further we trav-elled away from his tribal boundaries, the more he was out of his comfort zone. When I asked him what was wrong, he calmly mentioned his family was involved in a heated payback dispute. Once he explained his situa-tion, it was easy to understand why he'd endangered himself. One of his family required funding for urgent medical care and working as a porter was his only means of earning money. The way he selflessly hung his life by a thin thread to help his ailing relative was admirable, but our welfare was paramount. When Ano reassured me that my grave concern for Natan's wellbeing was justified, I took Natan aside and offered to pay him double and to give him a generous bonus. Then I told him he should head back to his village in the morning so as not to compromise everybody's safety. In a humbling gesture, he graciously declined the offer and added that he would work for the agreed amount. He reassured me that we weren't at risk, because his enemies would only have him in their sights. After we discussed his predicament, he decided to stay with us for another two days' walk, then head home as it would be to risky for him to carry on into dangerous enemy territory.

As the day drew to a close Ano and I became increasingly wary of Jale. One minute he was sullen and calm, then in a flash, his unpredictable mood would swing into an almost quivering rage. By the time we reached the primitive shelter, because of his hostile mannerisms, we'd agreed to keep a careful watch on each other's backs. We became even more anx-ious when he began noisily chopping firewood with our machete. At the end of each vigorous swing, he let out a short sharp grunt, gave Natan a dirty look that had evil intent plastered all over it, then started cutting again. I waited and timed my approach until he put the knife on the ground before I grabbed the machete and started cutting kindling. Although I found his limited English hard to understand at the best of times, I did my best to humour him while I made small talk. Without any warning or provocation, his erratic conversation suddenly turned into a flurry of abuse. Eleven hours of trekking over demanding terrain and slog-ging through energy sapping mud at Api's cracking pace had taken its toll on all of us. It had been a long, hard day and we were all bone tired, but Jale's swing shift mannerisms went way beyond irritable fatigue. He was obviously suffering from some type of mental disorder, because when I quietly asked him how long he intended to travel with us, he started ranting and raving, then he exploded. Ano stopped making repairs to the ramshackle bivouac, walked behind Jale, and acknowledged with a nod of his head that he was prepared for the worst. The twilight had ended and entombed the jungle in an almost pitch black darkness when Jale muttered, "Kill you bastards," mumbled he was heading east, and then without any type of light to find his way he stormed off into the gloomy rainforest towards the west.

With the ugly aura of the brutal murder still lingering in our primitive shelter and Jale's parting threat still rolling around our minds, a growing nervousness washed over us. We quickly plugged any gaps in the vegetation that lined the thin walls of the hut to prevent any arrows passing through, and then barricaded ourselves in with sticks and logs. Irrespective of what we did, we were incredibly vulnerable if Jale decided to carry out his threats. It was impossible to see if someone was sneaking through the darkness to attack us. Not that it mattered because an incendiary arrow would quickly turn our bivvy into a deadly inferno.

The fundamental rule for self-preservation whenever you're living or travelling amongst potentially volatile clans is to remain neutral during times of conflict. Jale had directed his death threat at all of us, which left me with no other option than to fight if I had to. I despise any type of violence, but I won't hesitate to defend myself if a peaceable solution isn't an option in a hostile situation. We armed ourselves with machetes, knives, and crudely carved clubs and braced ourselves for a possible attack. Then we lit a smouldering fire in the centre of the damp mud floor, and until it crackled to life, a heavy smog of eye watering smoke that was so thick we could almost chew on it filled our cramped shelter. When the noxious air slowly cleared, the orange flames provided a kind of mental solace as well as a hot meal and warmth. Api looked as though he was coming down with some type of illness so we all agreed that he should take the last watch.

While we sat and waited, hour after nervous hour crept by until, shortly after midnight, I floated in the netherworld between consciousness and slumber. No matter how hard I tried to stay hyper vigilant, an irrepressible enemy, drooping eyelids and sleep, subdued my senses. I knew Ano was keeping watch, so I briefly succumbed to fatigue and allowed myself to nod off. A bloodcurdling scream, the kind that sets your heart thumping so hard that it hurts, sent a fight or flight impulse racing through my startled senses. I grappled for my weapon and as I flashed my eyes around the hut's gloomy interior, I expected to have to fight for my life. It was a huge relief to see in the flickering glow of the fire that Api had rolled into the flames as he slept and barbecued his foot, and that all of our heads were still intact. The shelter was alive with a nervous tension, and like everyone else, I stayed wide-awake until daybreak.

In dawn's gathering light, birds of paradise flittered high amongst the treetops and put on an impressive display with their beautiful iridescent plumage while the other waking creatures of the forest heralded the start of the new day. Once the sun crept over the horizon and cast enough light for us to find our way through the jungle, we quickly broke camp and took off at full gallop. The further we distanced ourselves from the shelter, the more relieved we all felt. The rainforest offered us a feeling of sanctity, and our trek gave the day a new purpose. After about an hour, most of us had stopped glancing over our shoulders when the tough terrain demanded our total concentration. We climbed up sheer faces and dropped down into deep valleys that were dotted with white limestone cliffs, then we had to clamber back up through harsh mountain passes that taxed our sleep-deprived systems. Api had always streaked ahead of us, but now his inexhaustible legs were starting to fail him. Since midday he'd struggled to keep up, even when we slowed the pace to a crawl to match his listless gait. Natan was leading the way, and when I looked back to check on Api's progress I was just in time to watch him sway, stagger a few steps, and then collapse in a shivering heap when malaria chalked up another victim.

Api crawled inside my warm sleeping bag, and like most hardy primitive peoples, he endured his pain in silence and with an almost impassive calm. A dose of quinine helped to relieve his suffering as wave after wave of brain-rattling chills wracked his body. He was drenched in sweat and clearly exhausted, yet half an hour later, he somehow managed to drag himself from the sleeping bag and swagger off into the jungle. Several minutes later, he returned with a handful of leaves from a stinging nettle tree, then lifted his shirt and rubbed the venomous vegetation all over his abdomen. When I brushed one of the leaves against my arm out of curiosity, a searing red welt with the flaming itch of a thousand mosquito bites left me shaking my head in disbelief. Api's trembling stomach must have been aflame with the fires of hell and burned so intensely the only way he could relieve the excruciating pain was to keep moving. I'd suffered numerous bouts of malaria after I returned from the Solomons and knew exactly how he felt. In an incredible display of resilience and stamina he led us to a crude shelter, made from a tangle of sticks that were covered in clumps of damp moss. Those two tiresome hours of grinding slog must have felt like two weeks of drawn out agony. Once the sun started sinking behind the mountains, at such a high altitude it quickly became bitterly cold. I gave Api my sleeping bag, curled around a fire, and felt too tired to care about the freezing conditions when I fell into a deep and blissful sleep.

Chapter Eight

SELFLESS ASPIRATIONS

Most payback disputes are complicated and prolonged affairs that can be temporarily settled by appeasing the gods with the death of an enemy, but they will most likely never be resolved due to the perpetual nature of clan retribution. Even with the government's ban on intertribal warfare, inbred tensions still simmer between traditional enemies whose differences are still cooling, and whose enraged tempers still haven't calmed enough for rival clans to come to an amicable truce. Natan was on the threshold of dangerous territory, where a brutal death from a bloody ambush most likely awaited him if he risked travelling further. He shook our hands, then cantered off into the dawn mist towards the sanctity of his own village with more than enough money to pay for his ailing relative's treatment.

Two days later, after we'd tackled a variety of terrain and had just enough food left for another measly serving, we made the calf-burning climb up the sheer face to Angguruk mission. Although we were tired and hungry, Ano had proved to be a great travelling companion who was made of granite. No matter what the conditions were like, he remained easygoing and never complained once, whereas Api had become increasingly arrogant and bull headed. There was no reasoning with him, especially once we entered Yali country.

Like all of the other villages that had succumbed to Christianity, Angguruk had a cheerless and demoralized air about it. The mission looked alien and seemed out of place in such a remote and primitive hinterland. When Gerrit Kuijt, who was a Dutch protestant missionary, built Angguruk in 1967, to the cannibalistic Yali living in the area, the mission was definitely an unwelcome slur on the rugged landscape. Not long after we'd arrived, while Ano and I rested in the warm sun, an old Yali warrior called Paru, who had a slight build and a sharp mind, told us about the settlement's violent past. When I learnt about the surge of discontent Kuijt had created, it quickly explained Api's loathsome attitude towards me and anyone else with a light skin tone.

Right from the start of his unwelcome arrival into the volatile region, Kuijt established a shocking rapport with the Yali. He preached in a forceful rather than a thoughtful manner and as well as spreading the gospel, his obnoxious visits to the surrounding hamlets introduced a fatal flu epidemic. The outbreak spread like wildfire and killed a frightful number of natives whose immune systems were devoid of any resistance to introduced diseases. Word filtered back to Angguruk that any white man who entered the Yali's territory would be killed on sight and cannibalised. Kuijt was undeterred by the threats and carried on preaching with his fire and brimstone attitude. The Yali were incensed by his deplorable efforts to undermine their culture, and at times he was forced to hold off the agitated natives with a shotgun while a hail of arrows rained around him. The Yali had already decided who would receive the tastiest morsels of his flesh when they murdered him and roasted his body in their cooking fires. When the bitter hostilities reached boiling point, Kuijt took his annual leave and left the volatile area under the control of one of his native converts.

The Yali were quick to capitalize on his absence and came charging down from the surrounding hillsides in a shrieking rage and turned the mission into a bloody battleground. From the thirteen of Kuijt's devout followers who were massacred, those who died instantly were lucky. While Kuijt was away on leave, three of the Christians had sexually abused several Yali women, and when the warriors singled them out, they severed their genitals, then hung the organs from a post to enforce the traditional penalty for rape or adultery. Although the Yali had avenged their dead and appeased the spirits, their victory was to be short-lived. The ruthless Indonesian pacification patrols who were sent to quell the violence carried out their so-called pacification by going on indiscriminate killing sprees in the Yali villages and didn't care that the Christian's insensitive actions had been the catalyst for the Yali's act of vengeance.

All the Yali wanted was to be left alone, but their pleas and threats kept falling on either unsympathetic or deaf ears. In 1968, they gained worldwide notoriety when they fell prey to another fanatical evangelist, and they, in turn, preyed upon him. Two years earlier an Australian missionary called Stan Dale had ventured into Yali country to thrust his unwanted gospel upon the pagan natives. He had a contemptuous attitude towards their customs and went from village to village with a band of equally passionate followers. Over seventy varieties of sweet potato flourish throughout Irian Jaya, and of these, there are different strains that are only ever consumed during certain rites. The Yali believe if the sacred vegetables are eaten to satisfy a hunger rather than to appease a spirit, they will die a horrific death from supernatural causes. At one of the hamlets Dale visited, in a pitiful display of arrogance, he lit a bonfire and fuelled the flames with the native's most hallowed fetishes. Then he dug their most revered sweet potatoes from their gardens, roasted them in the coals, and ate his fill. His boundless arrogance continued when he boasted that the only repercussion he would suffer from eating the sacred food was indigestion. While he carried out the despicable acts in front of a crowd of stunned Yali, his faithful followers triumphantly sang hymns and quoted scriptures from the bible. The enraged chief decided he'd seen more than enough disrespect and destruction and ordered his people to attack. The Christians were forced to flee and were lucky to escape with their lives as the scathing Yali sent a volley of arrows hissing through the air.

The Yali were hell bent on seeking vengeance, and during an open-air sermon, they attacked and killed two of Dale's belligerent Melanesian preachers. Dale returned with a posse of Indonesian soldiers in the hope of recovering his clerics' bodies, but he was to late; they'd already been eaten. The military and the evangelist were greeted with a volley of arrows, and when five barbed arrows plunged into Dale's body, the Yali were bewildered when he somehow managed to stagger to safety after being hit so many times, and were even more dismayed when he made a full recovery.

Dale's wounds may have healed, but the Yali's were still festering. Their ancestral spirits demanded appeasement with the spilling of the missionary's blood, but the warriors were apprehensive and wondered if the white man's god had made Dale immortal, as was the Jesus he spoke of. They figured this was the only way he could've survived five arrow wounds. The next time they encountered the evangelist, they were determined to put his mortality to the test.

The overzealous preacher returned to spread the good word in 1968, but this time he had an American missionary called Phil Masters, three Dani, and a Yali porter with him. As soon as they saw the Christians, the infuriated warriors launched an attack. Their hate-filled war cries echoed around the hills until Dale and his companions frightened them off by throwing Chinese firecrackers at them. The Yali were amassing for another attack when the heavens opened up and thunder and lightning sent them scurrying to their huts. When the torrential rain sluiced down all night, they wondered if this was another display of power from the white man's god, and if maybe Dale really was immortal. They feared their own gods would be frowning in disgust and getting ready to inflict sickness and other catastrophes upon them if they didn't provide the spirits with the white man's sacrificial blood. No matter what happened, the Yali were adamant that tomorrow would be the day of reckoning and that the persistent missionaries who were still holed up in the valley would die.

As the warriors moved in for the kill the next morning, their blood curdling cries filled the air. Dale ordered a retreat, and the Christians escaped over a spindly suspension bridge that stretched across a foaming river. When the three Dani feared for their lives and started hacking the bridge away with their machetes, this would've saved them but it also would've guaranteed certain death for the next white man who entered the region. Masters and Dale decided to burn their own bridges when they ordered the Dani to leave the crossing intact, and told them their faith in God and the spirit of Jesus would protect them. Dale was the first to feel a barbed arrowhead slice into his flesh. When more of the deadly arrows found their mark and he defiantly pulled them from his body, some of the stunned Yali reeled in horror, while others looked on in total disbelief and wondered if maybe Dale wasn't of flesh and blood. They discovered he was mortal after all when he fell to his knees, collapsed to the ground, and gasped his last breath. Masters decided to stay behind and face the onslaught while the three Dani and the Yali porter escaped into the nearby jungle. In an incredible display of reckless courage and blind faith, he stood his ground and let a flurry of arrows slip into his body.

An air of uncertainty prevailed amongst the triumphant warriors. They were afraid the missionaries would rise from the dead just as Jesus had done, so after they butchered the corpses, the body parts were scattered around the jungle. When the Yali returned the following morning and the dismembered limbs had failed to resurrect themselves, the jubilant warriors gathered the flesh and celebrated with a cannibal feast.

While I was in the Solomons, I was amazed at how events that occurred decades ago were recalled with a freshness and in exact detail as if they had just happened. The stories were retold with excitement, joy, remorse, or whatever emotion matched the mood of the tale when it actually took place. Irian Jaya's primitive peoples shared the same vivid memory recall. Api had just cause to despise outsiders and to treat them with deep-seated suspicion or even blatant hatred. If anyone was put in his shoes, even after decades of holistic healing, the most forgiving person would find it difficult not to harbour a small amount of contempt.

I tried to imagine how Api and his people must have felt. Imagine having an inseparable bond with the environment, your religion, and your fellow man, and an unquestionable belief that all of nature and the supernatural realm are entwined. Then imagine having your total world overview condemned so that your strong sense of purpose with life and the certainty with what lies beyond death now amounts to nothing. Foreign languages are introduced when your native tongue is your only means of being able to truly express yourself. The missionaries change your appearance and even give you another name. But what they fail to give you is a choice. In numerous cases, only the scriptures are translated into native tongues. The repercussions of swapping beliefs and embracing an alien way of life are learnt firsthand by primitive peoples who are thrust from the Stone Age into the Clone Age without adequate guidance or preparation. My philosophy on life is live and let live if people's actions aren't at the expense of others, but I had to question on what basis the evangelists who infiltrated the Yali were chosen. It seemed a penchant for violence and insensitivity were necessary qualifications. The commandment of love thy neighbour seemed to have been replaced with an eye for an eye and a tooth for a tooth. Well meaning missionaries can enhance a community if the villagers willingly embrace Christianity, but evangelists with little understanding or appreciation of others' cultures can also do irreparable damage.

Later that evening, we barely had enough food left to satisfy our three ravenous appetites let alone two of Angguruk's mischievous teenagers who were drooling over our paltry meal. While we shared the last of what little we had with our sheepish guests, Api confidently reassured us that restocking with food wasn't an issue.

The reason for the adolescents' sly mannerisms became obvious the following morning when we visited the mission store, where the stocktaking could literally be done on the fingers of one hand. Only one kilogram of rice, two small cans of corned beef, and one packet of noodles sat on the dust-covered shelves. The storekeeper had understandably earmarked the last of the food for his own family until another shipment of freight was delivered on the next missionary flight. No one seemed to know for sure when the plane would arrive as the weather changes rapidly in the highlands and can wreak havoc on flight schedules. Aircraft are sometimes grounded for days and end up with a huge backlog of loads to distribute. With our supplies exhausted, if we wanted to contact the Yali, our most sensible option was to move on to Api's village in the morning, where, he boasted, there were lush gardens and an abundance of food.

The next morning Api became even more aloof and erratic. When he was talking to a callus looking villager, I was pretty sure I'd heard him say knife, kill, and money while they looked in my direction. Because my grasp of Indonesian is limited, I may have misinterpreted their conversation, but even if I had, he knew I was carrying cash, so I paid him for his services on neutral ground before we reached his village later in the afternoon. It put Ano and I on edge, and we agreed to keep a close watch on each other's backs.

We had a light lunch when a Dani family gifted us a small bowl of rice each, and then we climbed the sheer face that towers over Angguruk and headed deeper into the mountains. Several hours later, when we dropped down into a sweltering valley, rain and lots of it was desperately needed to revitalize the arid landscape. It was incredible. A few hours' walk had taken us into another climatic zone, where deep cracks parted the parched earth and the dehydrated plantations we passed were yielding poor crops. Two naked and badly malnourished children who were covered with boils from dietary deficiencies, dug for vegetables in the exhausted soil. Their arms and legs were pathetically thin and exaggerated their horribly swollen torsos. Burdening peoples who were battling to survive themselves wasn't an option, so I suggested to Ano that we should go back to Angguruk. Api waved me ahead and insisted we should carry on, and then he bragged that two extra mouths wouldn't be an imposition on his village's ample supply of food. I didn't believe a word because these sorry looking gardens belonged to his village, but as we were almost there Ano and I agreed to carry on.

I led the way and carefully balanced along the trunk of a gigantic tree that had conveniently fallen across a narrow ravine. Then we walked through a patch of jungle into reasonably open country that was mantled with fern and scrub, and as I rounded a curve in the trail, I was so startled by the iris-popping sight of a tiny Yali woman who was hiding amongst the vegetation on the side of the track that I swore out aloud. Before me stood the heart wrenching reality of trying to live a subsistence lifestyle in a drought-ridden landscape. The ravages of time, disease, and hunger had transformed her morose face into an almost inhuman looking mask. A few tufts of what hair dotted her crusty scalp were covered by a *noken* that hung down to her atrophied buttocks. What was left of her shrivelled breasts hung from her bony chest, and crumpled folds of leathery skin mutilated her distended abdomen. Her arms and legs were skin and bone, her knees were hideously calloused, and she carried herself on feet that were way too big for her emaciated body. Although I was smiling when

Ano took a photo of me sitting alongside her, I was filled with pity and sadness when we moved on.

From the moment we entered Api's village we were greeted by gloomy faces and surly stares. Without so much as a handshake, a good-bye, or an introduction to his chief, Api disappeared and we never saw him again. These people were incredibly destitute, and from what we could see, they had little to smile about. Most of the downtrodden Yali were afflicted with various diseases and were all clad in filthy and ragged clothes that were in keeping with the vile state of the village. I'd never witnessed such appalling conditions or felt such a malignant atmosphere. We were taken to an empty sleeping hut whose interior was lined with mould and filth which was so vile that as soon as we were alone, Ano and I looked at each other with screwed up faces and shook our heads from side to side in disgust. While we briefly sat inside, even breathing the rank air seemed like a major health hazard. From the frigid looks we were getting from a small crowd of villagers who'd gathered in the doorway, it was obvious they resented our presence. We grabbed our belongings and asked the chief to return the money I'd already paid for our nauseating accommodation, and asked if we could buy some sweet potatoes. His face soured, and he refused both of our requests. When I stood my ground and demanded my money back, the glaring villagers who'd gathered at his side were clearly spoiling for a fight, but I persisted until the argumentative leader finally softened and reluctantly returned the money.

Once we were away from the village, I jokingly said to Ano, "Don't worry, mate. Worse things have happened. At least they didn't eat us." He laughed and said, "We're not out of the shit yet. There's not much food around here. Maybe they will." Not long after we'd left Wamena, he'd quickly developed an intuitive liking for life in the wilderness. His attitude to the minor hindrance was so laidback that he was almost horizontal.

Two teenage twins who looked more like African pygmies than Yali, caught up with us along the craggy trail we followed and offered to guide us to a traditional Yali village for a small fee. The boys had only led us one hundred metres down the path when the sound of running feet made us stop and look over our shoulders. A panting messenger told the teenagers their chief was furious when he was told they were helping us, and they were to go back to the village to face his wrath.

We didn't even bother to question each other as to whether we should press on and pulled out our map to get our bearings. When I was in Wamena, a Dani guide who was familiar with the area had scrawled *makan orang*, which is the Indonesian phrase for "to eat man," across parts of our map. According to him, several decades earlier this would've been dangerous cannibal country. Ano doubted that outsiders would ever feature on the village menu nowadays, but felt that isolated clans still secretly dined on the flesh of their slain enemies. Some of his friends who'd travelled to remote areas, especially to down in the Asmat, came back to Wamena with tales of cannibalism and of clan warfare. We felt confident we'd be better received at a more traditional village once we made it clear to the chief that we only wanted to visit for a few days, and pressed on until dusk forced us to stop and build a basic shelter for the night.

Our growing hunger took the edge off of a beautiful sunrise the next morning and fuelled our desire to find another village. We followed a well-used track over rugged terrain until we stood at the bottom of an almost vertical ridge. Ano said, "That could mean trouble," as he pointed to a pillar of grey smoke that belched into the sky from a Yali hamlet that was perched on the top of the ridge. As we stood in silence for a brief moment, although it was highly unlikely, I wondered if the settlement had been attacked and torched. Then I turned to Ano and said, "It could be a bit dodgy, mate, but it could be a bloody great cooking fire filled with pork and kumara." When we started clambering up the trail, Ano said, "And us if we're unlucky."

Any apprehension we had during the arduous climb to the top of the ridge was quickly outshined by interest when a pint-sized warrior wearing a pig tusk nose bone, a metre long gourd penis sheath, and a woven skull-cap, welcomed us into the small hamlet. He greeted us by saying "*wahe*," the Yali word for hello, and as he led us to the chief, the coils of rattan covering him from beneath his pectorals to the top of his thighs rattled in unison with each of his steps. Everyone wore traditional dress and from the look of their primitive surroundings, still worshiped their pagan gods. Instead of wearing a pig tusk through their noses, a few of the men wore a piece of bamboo that splayed their nostrils into an uncomfortable looking sneer. The miniscule reed skirts all of the bare breasted females wore seemed to defy gravity as they clung to their lower hips. Everybody was visibly stunned by our presence and treated us with the genuine curiosity of a peoples who have had limited contact with outsiders

The chief was a tiny and proud looking man, with a staunch attitude that gave me the impression he was always ready and willing to fight. He'd obviously been involved in his fair share of intertribal conflict. His battle-scarred body was adorned with the puckered scars of old arrow and dagger wounds, and there was a shrewdness in his eyes and a look on his angular face that warned he had a zero threshold for tolerating anything that angered him. I couldn't help but feel his hospitality could just as easily turn to hostility when he offered to let us spend the night in a hut and provide us with a hearty meal of sweet potatoes.

A ten-year-old girl had suddenly died from unknown causes and because the villagers were fearful of a possible epidemic, they'd burnt her family's hut to the ground to curb the spread of any diseases. While her family was busy making the final preparations for her funeral rite, Ano warned that emotions would probably be running high during the girl's cremation. The chief had told us that only one other European had stayed in the hamlet for just one night, and that was three years ago. Because outsiders were still treated with suspicion, we both agreed that our presence would be an undesirable imposition while the Yali were in mourning and decided to leave first thing in the morning after a good nights sleep.

Our plans to depart at first light were put on hold the next day when the chief welcomed us to stay for the funeral rite. Such a poignant and personal moment didn't belong to us, so we decided to leave just before the girl's body was cremated. The sun had almost reached its zenith when impressive looking warriors wearing bailer and cowry shell necklaces looked unimpressed by our presence at the start of the ritual. Most of the men were armed with bows and arrows that clattered against their rattan-hooped skirts. Animal bones and palm spines pierced the fleshy nostril flanges and the tips of a few of the older women's noses. Although this was a fantastic opportunity to get some great photos, I didn't want to capitalize on the villagers' grief, so just before were about to leave, I approached the chief and asked if I could take a shot of him only. Even this far off the beaten track the white man equated to a source of easily obtained money. The chief said for twenty thousand rupiah I could capture all of the villagers on film, and he threw in an ancient stone adze that was hanging from the rafters of his hut. I'd just secured a bargain compared to what the Dani had charged me to take photos, but a gnawing suspicion made me reluctant to point my camera at anyone. When the chief told me it was no problem, it still didn't sit well with me, but in such emotive circumstances I wasn't in a position to question his decision.

It was impossible to remain inconspicuous when I asked several villagers if they were happy to be photographed, and I gingerly started snapping away with my camera. A malevolent looking warrior who was wielding a bow motioned for me to take his photo, and just as I clicked the shutter he sent an arrow hissing dangerously close to my head. Another warrior repeated the same unnerving performance, only this time his arrow whistled even closer to the top of my tingling scalp. As the atmosphere became charged with aggression and tension, Ano looked how I felt, deeply concerned that this was turning out to be much more than a harmless photo shoot. Those anxious moments escalated into a feeling of immense dread when an old crone spoke to the chief in such a heated tone that it incited an emotive response from the already agitated villagers. They went berserk and hurled a flurry of insults at us that came in a heated and menacing burble. While the scheming chief stroked his chin, I hoped like hell he wasn't thinking about digging two more cremation pits, or who would enjoy the best cuts of steak from our bodies. It was definitely time to leave before the mounting rage and contempt exploded into violence. I asked Ano to tell the chief I was getting his money, and then I went and grabbed our gear from our hut.

When I gave the chief his money, he scowled and looked down at the amount in his hands as if it had insulted his intelligence and then glared at me. I knew serious trouble was brewing when his rising anger reached boiling point, and on his cue, the whole village erupted. The women shrieked venomous abuse and the men screamed taunts and threats as they charged towards us. My legs felt strangely hollow and my churning stomach tied itself in a tight knot, while on the surface I made sure I remained composed. I looked to Ano and when I saw his chocolate complexion was drained of its colour, I said, "Stay calm, mate. These guys are like a pack of wild dogs. If they sense fear, they'll move in for the kill." Ano said through his quivering lips, "If we die, I hope it's quickly." A highly-strung warrior went berserk as he waved an arrow from his half drawn bow in my face. There was a crazed core of rage in his hysterical threats that said there would be no reasoning with him. Most of the barbed arrowheads that were pointed in our direction were bound with a toxic rattan, so that if the Yali failed to place a fatal shot, we were guaranteed of suffering an agonizing infection. Either option didn't brighten up what appeared to be our rapidly shortening lives. While the tension kept mounting towards a possibly fatal crescendo, Ano told me that instead of the agreed price, the devious chief was demanding twenty thousand rupiah for every photo. I told Ano to translate as quickly as the words spilled from my smiling lips that I didn't have enough money, and could only afford to pay another thirty thousand for all of the shots.

The feverish villagers looked disappointed when after several tense minutes, more money and no doubt the thought of having their village strafed by the Indonesian military if we were killed smoothed things over long enough for us to make our escape. During a hectic getaway, our limbs flailed wildly as we flew down to the bottom of the sheer ridge that flanked the village in reckless leaps and semi-controlled bounds. I peered back over our shoulders, and saw two Yali quickly making their way down the slope. They had to clasp their rattan skirts while they ran, which gave us a slight edge. We dropped out of sight into a small gut, nervously glanced at each other, both swore, and then ran as fast our legs would carry us. If they were going to catch us, they'd have to be quick because instead of hiding in the cover of the jungle where we risked being hunted like wild animals, we were going to give them a good run for their money. When the furious warriors started hurling abuse, it quickened our already scorching pace.

We didn't stop running, and in what can only be described as a nightmare journey, the Yali trailed us all the way back to Angguruk. As we slumped to the ground and recovered in the doorway of the mission, we were both physically and mentally exhausted. When I glanced back up the steep face we'd just clambered down, I was amazed when I saw the persistent Yali heading down the hill towards us. After having wondered during the mad dash to save our lives if trying to flee from the super fit Yali was futile, when they walked over and told Ano they'd only chased us because we'd forgotten to pay the chief for accommodation, I burst out laughing and willingly met their demands when they asked for the money.

I was ridden with guilt and asked them to tell the chief we apologised for creating an uproar at the girl's funeral and hoped that the unfortunate incident wouldn't reflect on how he treated future visitors. Although we weren't the instigators of the hostility, just our presence had been enough to disrupt the ritual. Once the litres of adrenaline eventually burnt off, the reality of the heart-thumping experience started to sink in. Ano felt we'd been incredibly lucky, and warned that if the Yali had caught up with us in the jungle, the outcome might not have been so happy or as passive.

Later that afternoon, the sound of a Cessna's droning engine reverberated off the walls of the valley and announced the much-awaited arrival of the plane. The aircraft literally dropped from the sky and jerked to an abrupt halt on the short airstrip that had been built on the grass-covered plateau. An appreciative crowd of hungry onlookers greeted the sacks of desperately needed food with joyous whoops and excited cheers. We decided to fly back to Wamena, and after a short briefing on where the first aid kit and axe were in case we had to smash our way out after a crash, we taxied to the top of the crude landing strip. The Cessna vibrated violently and the engine screamed as it provided the necessary thrust and catapulted us off the end of the precarious runway. The missionary plane banked steeply then kept circling around the deep valley until we gained enough altitude to clear the mountains.

After going feral in Irian Jaya's alluring wilderness, Wamena felt like a bustling metropolis. Its civilisation and consumerism felt vulgar and uncivilised, and the open sewers, the hawkers, and the shabby buildings with rusting rooves seemed squalid after trekking through some of the planet's most pristine and striking terrain. Food and more food had been our number one priority during our conversation on the flight, yet we both settled for sitting on the side of the road and gorging on a large packet of crackers topped with mushed banana until there wasn't a single crumb left.

I had four days to spare before I flew to Bali, so Ano and I carried ten kilograms of rice and an assortment of other useful gifts back up to Natan's village. Not knowing if he'd made it back safely weighed heavily on my conscience, and I felt a huge sense of relief when he came out of his hut wearing a big grin and I saw that he still had everything intact. When I told him I'd been unable to buy a decent bow, he led me to a hut from which a weather-beaten old man emerged holding a beautiful black palm bow and cluster of aged arrows. Although he only wanted thirty thousand rupiah I gave him sixty as they were the best I'd seen during my travels throughout the highlands and were still a bargain at twice the asking price. It was hard to return to Wamena the next day. Even though I still really knew very little about the customs and culture of the primitive peoples that live in the stunning highlands, the time I spent with them had been truly special. A few of the older members of Natan's clan had dined on human flesh, but they were hardly fearsome cannibals who should be avoided. They were some of the most friendly and hospitable peoples you could hope to meet anywhere.

Just like Dale and Masters, we'd compromised our safety by venturing to the remote Yali villages and making arrogant uninvited contact. The overbearing and violent outsiders who'd visited previously had planted the seeds of mistrust that have geminated and grown into an instinctive hatred. I felt sad for the Yali. We obviously bore the brunt of their frustration at having been forced to fight to cling to what remains of their diminishing traditions. The missionaries who are trying to spread their fundamentalist beliefs and the Indonesians who are trying to civilise them have kept nurturing this distrust, and although I thought my motives for visiting Irian Jaya's suppressed primitive peoples were harmless, they were just as selfish as the other intruders. To have experienced escapism in such a beautiful environment and to have felt true vulnerability during our trek was priceless. But it was seeing firsthand how it will take many successive generations of outsiders treating indigenous peoples with respect before primitive man's alliance with the outside world will grow into a trusting relationship again that had the greatest impact on me.

Our adventurous journey had left an indelible mark on both of us. Not long after I left Ano, he bravely tried to bring to light the plight of his people and the other persecuted Melanesian tribes by defiantly flying the flag of independence for Irian Jaya's indigenous peoples. His dissident attitude earned him two years in an Indonesian prison, and while the military incarcerated him, he suffered numerous severe and brutal beatings. I met my selfish objectives, but only time will tell if Ano and the thousands like him will achieve their selfless aspirations.

Chapter Nine

GUARDIANS OF THE JUNGLE

After I'd stepped off of the civilized world and revelled in the primitive aspects of Irian Jaya, the detrimental effects of globalisation and the inevitable onslaught of development and change seemed to have ruined the character of traditional Bali. The throngs of foreigners who are seeking an island idyll have transformed Bali into another casualty of the Indonesians' lust for the tourist dollar. For a brief moment, the chaotic atmosphere at Kuta made my head spin, but once I quickly became acclimatised, I lapped up the mystical intrigue of its dynamic Hindu culture, the frenetic cremation rituals, the intense religious life, and the ancient temples that are stylised with distinctive Balinese art. I spent a few days surfing the perfect waves that rolled onto sun-bleached beaches that were swarming with tourists, and kicked back on the beaches at dusk to soak up the beauty of the postcard image sunsets.

When I'd finished relaxing in Kuta, I left its crowds, its persistent hawkers, and its hectic pace to visit the deeply spiritual and primitive Mentawai peoples who live on Siberut Island, which lies one hundred kilometres off the west coast of Sumatra. After a whirlwind journey up through the archipelago by bus and ferries, the hustle and bustle of Jakarta's millions of inhabitants almost swept me off my feet. I spent my first night in Indonesia's capital sleeping on the floor of a bus station with a cheerful group of vagrant locals, then the next day, I took a walk through the city. Several hours of dodging the congested traffic, breathing the fumes, witnessing the pollution, and being awed by Jakarta's gross overpopulation was long enough to satisfy my curiosity.

I carried on to Padang, and from there I sailed in a decrepit but seaworthy freighter and shared a small sweltering cabin with an amorous German couple who completely ignored my presence while they romped and frolicked in numerous passionate embraces over the next couple of days. If I wasn't robbed of sleep by listening to the constant wail of the ships throbbing engine or from the way the graceless tub kept rolling in the heavy swell, I had to endure the energetic Germans' exhibitionist panting and moaning throughout most of the night. On the final day of our voyage, the fierce winds dropped and the turbulent ocean became a sheet of velvety glass. I was awake at dawn and went up to the deck to catch my first glimpse of Siberut just as the crimson glow of the rising sun lit up the horizon. While I gazed across a becalmed sea, the first few rays of the sun gradually highlighted the rainforest covering the island until it resembled an emerald-coloured jewel set in the sparkling Indian Ocean.

Before I could head into the interior of the 4,500 square kilometre island from Muara, which is Siberut's main port, I needed to secure a travel permit to keep the vigilant Indonesian military satisfied. They were using the same barbaric tactics on the Mentawai that they used on Irian Jaya's indigenous peoples and stipulated that anyone who visited the Mentawai had to be accompanied by a guide. The friendly locals told me to hire Parmenson, who is a leading member of the Association of the Indigenous People of Mentawai and the best guide on the island. When I eventually found him, for a man in his early twenties he looked aged beyond his years and emotionally shattered. He had a slight build and was quick to tell me that his constant concern over the uncertain future the Mentawai faced had disheartened him, made him lose his appetite, and was taking a heavy toll on his health.

About an hour after I met Parmenson, we were sitting in a dugout canoe with its prow slightly raised by the outboard motor that pushed us along the artery of swollen rivers flowing down from the interior. We navigated the chocolate-coloured rivers with ease, then when we trekked inland, to avoid constantly slogging through an energy-sapping quagmire of mud, we balanced along a highway of greasy logs until we reached firmer ground deeper in the rainforest. We were lucky that we enjoyed the luxury of hiking through the steamy leech infested jungle in the dry season. During the monsoon season, travelling through the waterlogged island can be a daunting struggle through a sea of sludge.

I didn't have much time left on my visa, so I had to decline Parmenson's offer to visit a remote clan who are rarely contacted by outsiders. The last time he stayed with them, they were in mourning, and to empower the deceased's spirit, they sat underneath a funeral pyre and wallowed in the body fluids as they dripped down from the corpse. Parmenson said he cringed when he saw them eating sago while the fetid juices trickled onto their virtually naked bodies. I had to opt for a closer village which had still retained its customs and was occasionally visited by tourists. We trekked through the sweltering jungle and entered a hamlet that was neatly laid out within a square of interconnecting roads that were bordered with well-kept gardens and towering palm trees. It was refreshing to see that it had managed to escape the onslaught of the insensitive Indonesian bureaucracy.

We climbed up a notched pole to the veranda of a thatch hut and were greeted by a terrible moan that came from the front room. A young woman let out a hideous scream that trailed off to a groan, and then she cried out again and begged for someone to come and put an end to her suffering. Her family was gathered on the hardwood porch, where they patiently waited with solemn faces and bowed heads for four shaman to arrive. They were hoping that the medicine men who were about to unite their healing powers would combine the supernatural energy they evoked and drive away the evil spirits that were causing her sickness.

The last thing I expected was for them to eye me up like ravenous vultures and then swoop in on what they thought were easy pickings. They tugged at my watch and shamelessly asked for tobacco, while only metres away their relative shrieked and whimpered from her terrible pain. Every society spawns black sheep who are the exception to the rule. It was easy to read between the lines when Parmenson shook his head in disgust and without saying a word motioned for me to shoulder my pack. I offered the family my condolences and followed him to another hut on the other side of the village.

Before we reached the next hut, Parmenson stopped and talked to the four impressive looking shaman who were going to help the ailing woman. They were serene looking men, with tranquil personalities, who gave me the impression they were totally devoid of any self-importance. All of them wore a wide red, white, and blue bead headband from which feathers and the stems of plants protruded. The headbands covered their long hair, which was tied into a bun and dangled down the back of their necks. Magical leaves and small fetishes hung from their thick bead necklaces and from the red and white armbands and yellow and red bead bracelets they wore. Their bodies were decorated with a mass of ritualistic tattoos that help to ward off evil spirits during healing rituals. Each of the photogenic shaman carried the ingredients for the healing ritual in a quiver that was filled with mysterious fetishes and curative plants.

The Mentawai are an incredibly placid and deeply spiritual race whose whole morality is bound in worshiping all of nature. They are revered throughout Indonesia for the poison arrows they use for hunting, for mediating with the supernatural, for their belief in spiritual healing and their ability to restore health with herbs and plants. To ensure their constant wellbeing, they must maintain a harmonious relationship with all of the elements. The traditional name for a Mentawai shaman is a *sikerie*, and his main priority is to remain in daily contact with the supernatural, which he does by chanting incantations and by dancing and singing to spirits. It was easy to see why the Mentawai hold the *sikeirei* in such high esteem. Here were mere mortals who entered the other world to manipulate its overwhelming forces, and after they faced its darkness and grappled with its demons, they returned from the dangers unscathed. *Sikeirei* who possess the knowledge to enter into a trance and successfully battle the other reality command huge respect. One of the shaman enhanced his mystical appearance when he smiled and flashed a set of jagged teeth that had been ritualistically chiselled to a point. The *sikeirei* allowed me to quickly take their photo, then they went to the ailing woman and kept using their magic chants and administering their medicines well into the night until she died.

The serene atmosphere that filled the next hut we climbed up to couldn't have been more of a contrast from the troubled mood that surrounded the family we'd just visited. Parmenson introduced me to Hermoni, who was a gentle looking middle-aged man and a gracious host that had that special aura of mystique I'd hoped to find. He possessed a contagious air of peace and had a quiet dignity that befitted his role as a shaman. He reeked of inner calm, of harmony with others, with himself, and with all of nature. None of his actions were rushed when he offered us a warm and genuine greeting. Hermoni's bare breasted wife showed us the same becalmed respect when she welcomed us to sleep in their hut. The rows of monkey, pig, and deer skulls that glared down at us from the rafters were one of the main reasons I'd travelled to the island. Since my early childhood, taking game with a bow had been one of my favourite pastimes, and if the opportunity arose, I hoped to accompany the Mentawai archers on a traditional hunt. Most of the monkey skulls wore beards of decorative grass that helped to soften the grotesque look of their large hollow eye sockets and the snarl of their fanged teeth. The bony orbits were more than just trophies from a successful hunt. They allowed the souls of living animals to reunite with the dead and receive offerings to appease the spirits before the Mentawai go hunting.

That evening, when Hermoni served us a meal of domesticated pork and sago palm flour that had been roasted over a fire, the pork was tender but it had a unique and unusual flavour I'd never tasted before. Later that night, when I went to go to the toilet I was told to either head into the jungle or to squat over a gap in the deck at the rear of the hut. Most of the villagers prefer the latter. The village pigs were waiting below with open, salivating mouths, and didn't waste any time consuming my shit the instant that it hit the ground. Although the village sewerage system is extremely efficient at recycling wastes, it has one unwelcome side effect. Any hunter or pig farmer knows that if a pig is fed tuna, the pork becomes tainted and tastes of fish, which explained the strong taste of the methane marinated pork we'd eaten.

When we visited another longhouse the following day and dined on monkey head and entrails soup, consuming the primate required us to keep other things down as well as the stomach churning meal. Because the headman had taken the animal with a bow, everyone who dined on the primate had to appease the spirits by refraining from sexual intercourse.

Parmenson knew my days with the Mentawai were numbered, so he didn't waste any time trying to organise a bow hunt. When Hermoni agreed to take me on a monkey hunt, I was ecstatic but remained quietly enthusiastic when Parmenson told me mentioning the pursuit of game is strictly forbidden. The Mentawai enjoy the simplicity of a primitive lifestyle, but their lives are complicated and filled with constant ritual and endless taboos which define their animist beliefs. When the preparations are being made for a hunt, bathing and sex are prohibited, as is drinking coconut milk or water unless the fluids are first boiled. If these prerequisites are ignored, it's believed the poison that's used to anoint the arrows will be rendered useless. Once the necessary rituals had been performed and I saw Hermoni waiting by his hut with his bow, we'd act oblivious to the fact we were heading into the jungle to hunt for wild boar, deer, birds, frogs, or monkeys, because if we spoke of our obvious intentions, we'd incur the wrath of the benevolent spirits who haunt the rainforest.

Every living creature holds a special place in the natives' lives. They believe all feral animals are the domesticated counterparts of their spiritual brothers that reside in the supernatural world. A strict ritual precedes the killing of any animal, as taking the life of any creature is believed to free its spirit, which in turn will offer protection to the village. Sacrificial chickens are held in high esteem by the shaman, who pull out the bird's intestines and use them during a divination rite to predict the future. If the prophecy produces a bad omen, a second bird is killed and another rite is performed to reconfirm the unfavourable reading.

Although the Mentawai practice low-level agriculture, unlike most of Indonesia's primitive peoples, they have remained predominantly hunter-gatherers. They prefer to use a bow to harvest game and fashion their weapons from the heart of the black palm due to its strength and flexibility. Their beautifully crafted bows are extremely reliable, and in the right hands, are surprisingly accurate. But it's the poisoned arrows that have made Siberut's hunters famous. The poison is made from three key ingredients. Leaves from the *raggi* tree are ground into a paste and reduced to a liquid, a cutting from the *urat* tree is crushed until it oozes a white juice, then these fluids are combined with pulped green chillies to form a lethal toxin that's capable of killing most large game. The arrow shafts are made from a member of the rattan family called *osibiau* and are tipped with arrowheads that are made from the *ariribuk* tree and have spirals carved along their length to facilitate the poison. The arrowheads are normally given five coats of the toxin with a brush that's made from monkey hair before they are considered potent enough to use on game. A small notch is carved around the tip of the arrowhead so it breaks off in the animal's flesh to ensure that a good supply of the circulatory stimulant enters its bloodstream and causes a quick and humane death.

The children are taught from an early age how to make their own bows and arrows and accompany the adults into the jungle to learn how to hunt, are shown which foods and medicines to gather, and become skilled at living from the land. By the time they reach adolescence, they are already expert hunters and trackers and can survive in an environment where the uninitiated would perish.

While I patiently waited to go hunting, the precious days seemed to race by as I watched the villagers refine sago palm into flour, make perfumes from plants to repel evil spirits, and expertly weave baskets from rattan. Whenever I observed these tranquil peoples, it quickly became obvious that the Mentawai don't cut time into small measures and that maintaining an eternal kinship with the spirits dictated the villagers' sedate pace of life.

My patience came to the fore one morning, when just before dawn, as the village roosters rubbed the sleep from their eyes and routinely heralded the start of a new day, I followed Parmenson and Hermoni into the jungle. A team of eager hunting dogs trotted in front of us and ploughed their noses along the forest floor as they ground scented or momentarily stopped and raised their snouts to try and catch a telltale whiff of our quarry that might still be hanging in the humid air. Four species of monkey inhabit Siberut's rainforest. The Langur, the Pigtailed Langur, and the Macaque are all fair game, but the Kloss Gibbon doesn't have a tail and is thought to share too many similarities with humans for it to be included on the village menu. Although the poisoned arrows are lethal on larger game, for some reason they're less potent on monkeys, so dogs are used to capture and finish off the primates that aren't mortally wounded.

I marvelled at Hermoni's natural affinity with his environment as we followed a narrow trail that carved its way through a profusion of luxurious vegetation. The thick equatorial heat wrung sweat from every pore in my body as we climbed slight ridges and dropped into shallow gullies for the next hour, while Hermoni somehow managed to remain free of perspiration. He signalled a halt several times and pointed to the tracks in the ground where animals had recently crossed or followed the trail. His keen eyes saw and read the marks with ease, and at times he tasted the air like a scenting dog and somehow managed to detect the faintest of smells long before I got a definite whiff of passing game. When he stopped to dig out a vicious looking thorn from his foot, I couldn't help but envy his bare feet. They were much better suited to the boggy terrain than my cumbersome boots, which slithered hopelessly as they struggled to find a decent grip in the greasy mud.

We walked for hours and tried our best to stay in silent step with Hermoni's quiet footsteps, which were as fluid and as hushed as a passing shadow that slipped through the trees. While we briefly rested on a fallen log and I was wiping the rivulets of salty sweat from my eyes, when the dogs cocked their heads Hermoni stopped talking and listened. Then without any sense of urgency he slowly stood up and pulled his unstrung bow from a slit in the coconut fibre rope that held his bamboo quiver over his shoulder. While Hermoni strung his bow, Parmenson held the quiver and showed me the numerous arrow tips that had been retrieved from successful kills then inserted into the bottom of the quiver as a status symbol and to show the spirits the hunt had been a success. The Mentawai create their bowstrings from narrow strips of the same inner bark that they use to make their loincloths. These are twisted together, anointed with sap from the *unam* tree, and then dried under tension in direct sunlight to create an incredibly strong string. Once he'd finished stringing his bow, Hermoni motioned for us to quietly move on. When we stalked through clouds of mosquitoes that swarmed around our heads in an annoying drone, I thought of the woman I'd heard moaning on her deathbed and constantly swatted at the deadly insects.

We crossed a crystal clear stream then skirted the edge of a reasonably clear ridge until the faint sound of a screeching and babbling troop of monkeys drifted to us on a light breeze as it gently slipped through the trees. How Hermoni had ever managed to pick up the muffled sound in such thick jungle from where we'd stopped to rest on the log was beyond me. I've always prided myself in having good hearing during a hunt, yet I'd strained my ears and heard nothing. When Hermoni told me he'd heard the monkeys, I wondered if his senses were much keener than mine or if a lifetime of being able to discriminate an individual noise from the numerous sounds of the jungle had made his hearing seem sharper. Hermoni's prowess as a hunter amidst the crowded weave of rainforest was incredible when quietly and ever so slowly, we edged our way to the base of a towering tree, and then he nocked an arrow. A mass of dense growth shielded a group of primates who noisily chattered away high up in the canopy. Each time Hermoni drew his bow, I craned my neck, then watched him slowly slacken his draw when with a crackle of leaves the animals kept moving into cover about twenty-five metres above us. Several anxious minutes ticked by without him getting a clear shot, then pandemonium erupted when a jabber of piercing shrieks seemed to suck every particle of our anxious silence from the jungle. The expert gymnasts swung and leapt from tree to tree as their frantic warning cries echoed across the forest. Then the deafening pitch of their agitated alarm calls faded into the distance as they vanished into the safety of far off treetops.

As we returned home empty-handed, a strange yet pleasant sensation washed over me. Maybe it was the envoys of soft light filtering through the canopy that were casting shifting patterns of dappled light on the lush vegetation or the soothing babble of the nearby creek and being serenaded by a gentle breeze that rustled the trees. Whatever it was, for some reason I felt an inexplicable inner calm, a newfound awareness, and an indescribable sense of wellbeing. Perhaps it was Hermoni's inner peace and his Zen-like presence rubbing off on me while I was amidst the soothing cathedral of rainforest, because I'm definitely not a deep or spiritual person. I was having a bit of a pensive moment when my Mentawai guru paused, reached into his quiver, and pulled out a can of coke then tore back the tab and muttered, "The real thing." I couldn't believe my ears and eyes and laughed hysterically to myself as I came back to reality with a massive thud.

Now that the hunt was over and we hadn't arrowed any meat, the women from Hermoni's clan could resume fishing. There would be no enforced restrictions to appease the gods, and no one would beat the python skin drums to challenge the other clans to better the spoils of our hunt. Yet to me, the hunt had been a huge success. Merely observing the Mentawai shaman, the guardian of the jungle, had been satisfying enough. Practitioners of archery in western society often relate the concentration that's required to proficiently shoot a bow as being a deeply spiritual experience. For the self-reliant Mentawai who depend upon their archery skills for survival, it definitely is.

During the long bus trip back to Bali, a Mentawai bow and a quiver full of poisoned arrows that I'd bought were lying on the floor beside me. Patience and courtesy aren't one of the Indonesian bus driver's most obvious virtues. Our driver seemed to have learned how to handle a bus at the school of kamikaze and sat on his horn and yelled abuse during several near misses with other traffic, even when he was clearly in the wrong. After we unexpectedly screeched to a whiplash inducing halt for a truck that had right of way, I looked down in sheer horror when the cap flew off the end of the quiver and the deadly arrows shot forward in all directions. I cringed and swore as the lethal missiles hurtled under seats and rattled down the isle of the bus. For a moment I had visions of rotting away in a rat and cockroach infested Indonesian prison cell for committing multiple manslaughter, but fortunately the arrows miraculously missed everyone on the crowded bus.

In recent times, Indonesia's Department of Social Affairs has been anything but sociable. The sacredness of the Mentawai culture has received profane treatment from the government division, who are preparing a civilization and development plan that threatens to obliterate the native's way of life. The government's recent declaration will be a slow death sentence for the Mentawai when they replace their loincloths and grass skirts with clothing, and modern education will replace their age-old teachings. Ownership of the forest is clearly defined amongst individual clans, yet the unsympathetic officialdom plans to shift every last village to resettlement sites that will no doubt be brutally supervised. This type of social humiliation and oppression will inevitably lead to a total loss of identity, to a loss of the natives' sense of purpose, to mental illness, to becoming detribalised misfits on their own island, and to a possible collapse into poverty as was the case with many American and Brazilian Indian tribes when the once free roaming peoples were confined to reservations. The Mentawai's passive resistance and their protests to the enforced changes have been answered with violent military policing. If the government goes ahead with their plans to transmigrate over ten thousand families to the island as a labour force for the oil palm plantations they are going to establish on Siberut, this will lead to the further loss of land and will drive another nail in the natives' coffin with their inevitable integration and absorption of unwelcome external influences.

Anyone who has been conditioned since birth to live in a consumer society would find it hard to even start to comprehend the Mentawai's spirituality, their mindset, and their reverence for all of nature. With only a few diminishing hunting societies remaining throughout the world, humanity has to question who has the monopoly on common sense and compassion and the motives of those who are so resolute in their quest to take away harmless indigenous peoples' right to choose a meaningful and dignified future for themselves. How can any living creature accept the injustice of being punished merely because it chooses to live an instinctive life? When those instincts are suppressed, any animal will inevitably begin to despise its new characteristics and over time, will begin to self-destruct because of what it has been forced to become.

Chapter Ten

BEGINNER'S LUCK

The two months that I travelled around Indonesia, and the time I spent with other remote primitive tribes, had long-term repercussions. It was almost as if something primeval from within the very core of my soul had been awakened. I constantly fought a yearning to return to less complicated environments where indigenous peoples still clung to their innocence and to their beliefs. The constant temptation to leap off the treadmill that turns the tainted world civilization has devised, to further explore and experience the other timeless and mystical world of primitive man, made me more and more restless with the passing of each day.

Up until now my course in life had been relatively smooth, well-planned sailing, and my building business had been satisfying and creative. My travels had changed my whole outlook, and building began to take on a new and tiresome slant where transforming a bare piece of land into an architecturally designed work of art had lost its buzz. When I had an article and photos that covered my experiences in Irian Jaya published, it came as an unexpected and pleasant surprise. It was enough to make me shut up shop and buy a few new tools for a different trade. I bought an idiot-proof single lens reflex Canon camera, a notebook and pens, and decided that recording the rapidly fading remnants of humanity's heritage would help to justify my selfish motives for contacting remote tribes. With absolutely no training or background that even remotely lent towards photography or journalism, I became an adventurer and a photojournalist. Life's predictable and well-laid path suddenly became exhilarating and erratic, and so that I would have total freedom, I put any intentions I had of finding a wife and starting a family on temporary hold.

I'd stopped over in Vanuatu several times on the way back from the Solomons and had vowed that one day I'd return to explore the archipelago's beautiful outer islands and live amongst the primitive peoples. Once I started delving into the country's remarkable history, I quickly realised that this was the perfect place to embark on my new career. Vanuatu consists of a Y shaped chain of islands that run in a north-south direction across the Pacific Ocean, and lies eight hundred kilometres west of Fiji, 230 kilometres north east of New Caledonia, and 170 kilometres south of its nearest neighbour, the Solomon Islands. Before Vanuatu gained independence in 1980, the archipelago was called the New Hebrides and was a jointly governed British and French condominium. When the word *Vanuatu* is translated into English, depending on which language is being used, it means "our land," or "the country that stands up." Vanuatu also stands out due to its tremendous cultural, geographical, and religious diversity. Around 105 different dialects are spoken, and each island has its own artistic styles and unique cultural ethics, which the people are trying to faithfully conserve in their original form.

Vanuatu's geography is as diverse as its fascinating cultures, and as a consequence, the archipelago is filled with vast and abrupt contrasts. The cathedral silence of a dense rainforest can be broken by a cannonade of sound then coated with ash that erupts from the bowels of a volcano. Powdery white sand beaches that are fringed by tranquil sparkling blue lagoons merge with rocky shores that have been shaped by millennia of raging surf. In places, the exceptional beauty of the land is far from gentle, and in many respects, its people haven't enjoyed a gentle transition from the past into the twenty-first century. During the nineteenth century, the Melanesians experienced immense disruption from the church, from blackbirders, from colonial settlers, and worst of all, from introduced diseases. Depopulation occurred at an alarming rate. In 1800, Vanuatu housed an estimated one million inhabitants, yet only one year later, measles had decimated a staggering one third of the entire population. By the turn of the nineteenth century, less than one hundred thousand people remained, and in 1935, only a dismal forty-five thousand natives were thought to have survived the devastating epidemics. After being physically emaciated, they faced another foreign scourge when a steady stream of evangelists started eroding their age-old traditions and beliefs.

Nowadays, fish, beef, copra, kava, and cocoa are Vanuatu's principal exports, but the countries biggest asset is its hospitable and wide smiling people. Vanuatu's population is predominantly Melanesian, and the indigenous inhabitants are jointly known as Ni-Vanuatu. Tourism remains the largest earner of foreign income, but very few visitors ever venture to the remote outer islands.

There is only a limited amount of literature that covers the archipelago's post-modern history. A few anthropologists and interested missionaries managed to document Vanuatu's fascinating past during a time when warring cannibalistic tribes practised human sacrifice, sorcery was rampant, and life revolved around composite and hallowed rituals. The more I read about Vanuatu, the more entranced I became. I purposely avoided islands that have been documented by anthropologists and decided to walk across rugged Espiritu Santo (also known as Santo), Vanuatu's largest island, to hopefully make contact with the archipelago's most geographically isolated and most primitive inhabitants. It was a decision that would change my life forever. When I read that black magic is at the very core of Santo's primal religions, it further enhanced the island's mystique, and so did learning that there was absolutely no literature available which covered the customs that are practised by the remote clans inhabiting the highlands. It offered the perfect destination for a fledgling photojournalist, where I'd investigate the true Vanuatu of old and where maybe startling discoveries still lay hidden in the depths of the jungle or in the minds of its peoples.

It was ironic that fifteen years before I travelled to Santo, Luganville, which is the island's only town, had very nearly become our temporary family home. When my father was a construction foreman for a multinational company, we were making preparations to move there so that he could oversee various building projects, then at the last minute, the firm he was working for terminated their contract—and for good reason. Political unrest had been brewing on the island for decades, so in 1963, chief Jimmy Stevens and chief Buluk established a political party that they hoped would lead the island to becoming independent from the troubled condominium and jointly formed what was to become the *nagriamel* movement. They named their party after two leaves called the *nagria* and the *namele*, which are sacred to the island's indigenous inhabitants. The faction's prime objectives were to restore the supremacy of traditional customs and to reclaim all undeveloped land that had been purchased by the Europeans and the other expatriate settlers. When Stevens and some of his radical followers illegally occupied land that was under foreign ownership, they earned themselves a brief jail sentence. Once word of Stevens incarceration and what his party stood for started spreading like wildfire, he became a hero, especially amongst the primitive clans that lived in the jungle. Over the following years, while Santo's political turmoil simmered, the *nagriamel* movement kept growing financially and in numbers. After they failed to win an election that they'd expected to swoop in a landslide victory, Stevens and his incensed followers began planning immediate retribution for what they felt was rightfully theirs. On the 27th of May 1980, Stevens commanded an army that was comprised mainly of bushmen wearing loincloths who were armed with bows and arrows and staged a coup that later became known as the coconut rebellion. They easily overran Luganville and proclaimed independence from the British and French condominium. Stevens named the new country Vemarana. But his victory was to be short lived because six days prior to Vanuatu's legal independence, French and British troops flooded the island. The military took a passive stance and looked on while businesses were looted and civil unrest erupted. The government called in Papua New Guinea's Kumul soldiers, who are renowned for their hardline approach, to rapidly quash the rebellion and to restore law and order. On the 1st of September 1980, Stevens was arrested and earned himself a fourteen and a half year jail sentence. It took a further month for the Papuan soldiers to sweep through the jungle and quell the pockets of Stevens' fanatical primitive followers who refused to lay down their bows and arrows. The coup resulted in only one ironic fatality when Stevens' son was shot by troops. Due to the coconut rebellion and Vanuatu's political instability, the construction project my father was to be involved in was cancelled.

The day after I arrived at Port Vila, which is the capital of Vanuatu, I met with the director of Vanuatu's cultural centre and museum. Ralph Regenvanu looked about thirty years old, had dreadlocks that hung halfway down his back, and kindly supplied me with a letter of introduction to one of his field workers who I hoped would act as a guide. In return, I agreed to supply him with any interesting photos that I secured to help chronicle the island's history. Although I was extremely grateful of the best help he could offer, realistically the letter was of little value because none of the field workers had ever ventured up to the ridge-top hamlets despite the island being only 4,010 square kilometres in size. After I spoke with several staff from the cultural centre, it seemed incredible that there was absolutely nothing in their archives which documented the customs of the peoples living in the heart of the mountainous island.

While I purchased my tickets to fly to Santo, the manager of the domestic airline, Van Air, told me he'd heard rumours about a legendary cannibalistic pygmy tribe, small and elusive men who lived in the heart of Santo's rainforests. If I could find a conch shell nestled in a sacred banyan tree and blow a couple of blasts, if I was lucky, the pygmies would emerge from the jungle to greet me. I'd read that the pygmies did actually exist in the highlands but had become extinct, so instead of rubbishing some of the obviously exaggerated stories I heard, I felt there might be an element of truth to them and became even more determined to cross the island.

Several days after I arrived in Vanuatu, I flew to Santo and landed just as dusk was quickly enveloping Luganville airport in darkness. I had to smile at the irony when from the fleet of taxis that were ferrying customers into town, I chose a driver who'd been a close friend and ally of Jimmy Stevens. In an assertive tone and with a firm handshake, he introduced himself as John Noel, and then he threw my well-travelled pack onto the back of his battered pickup. John loved to talk, and as we rattled along the road into town when his friendly conversation extended to an offer to stay with his family, I had no idea that I'd just fallen down the long drop toilet and climbed out with a mouthful of diamonds.

Besides his bushy shock of frizzy hair, John's small middle-aged frame carried a huge reputation as a politician and as a hard-nosed chief, who would later become the paramount chief for all of Santo. He was quick to tell me that his political status spread far afield, even to the reclusive villages hidden in the remote highlands. Over time I was to learn that most expatriate businessmen and urban settlers considered his political views as extremely dangerous and his no nonsense demeanour as being unstable rather than self-confident. The Ni-Vanuatu either scorned or revered his leadership of the peoples who are hell bent on a return to total ownership of the island to those who are indigenous to Santo. Like Stevens, John was no stranger to the police and had been imprisoned for inciting politically motivated riots. He became a close friend, but he was the sort of man I'd hate to become my enemy. Politics and religion can be emotive topics that sometimes form divisions between those who might otherwise be good friends, so I quickly made it known that I remained neutral regarding his political aspirations and swayed the conversation towards the island's isolated tribes.

When we arrived at John's western style home and I met his wife, Missy, and his four children, I was treated as one of the family. Once we'd finished making small talk, I showed John the photos I'd taken in the Solomons and Irian Jaya. They added credibility to my ability as an adventurer, but once he was fully aware of my intentions, he delivered a stern warning not to underestimate the islands harsh terrain or the volatile natives living in the highlands. He sounded concerned when he said this wasn't the Solomons or Irian Jaya, and I could expect an indifferent reception from the isolated clans living in the mountains, who are called "man bush" by Vanuatu's more sophisticated inhabitants. The few trampers, tourists, and adventurers that rarely trekked into the mountains normally followed the scenic Jordan River and stuck to the lowlands. Ni-Vanuatu are renowned for their cheerful natures and warm hospitality but the highlanders were a breed alone. Violent intertribal skirmishes still occurred, and I was to always ask before I even considered taking a photo. I took heed of his warnings and mentioned I was never filled with overblown optimism or had any expectations when I made a rude incision into the lives of primitive peoples. My already inflated spirits soared sky high when he offered to find me a guide who wasn't afraid to take me across the island.

I knew that delving into the lives of those who are separated from outsiders by natural barriers such as rugged mountains and dangerous rivers, or by emotional barriers that had been created by ancient traditions, warfare, and suspicion, would always involve an element of risk. From what John had told me, the highlanders isolation had shaped their hardy character and made them impervious to the degradation and the debilitating influences that had been forced upon the archipelago in the name of Christ and civilization. He reinforced his warning one more time but needn't have bothered. From what he'd already said it was obvious that a peoples who were dominated by the struggle for survival in an uncompromising environment would almost certainly be naturally tough and have no qualms about using violence to repel unwelcome visitors.

The next day, John delivered a guide as promised, but unfortunately his first choice was laid low with malaria. When we drove down a rutted track to the back of a ramshackle settlement called Pepsi and met Remmy, John's second choice would've been my last. Remmy was half asleep when he walked out into the acute tropical glare from a dim leaf hut. While his pupils slowly adjusted to the blinding light, he blinked and shielded his eyes, and whenever he glanced from John's dark skin to my European complexion, it seemed to have the same effect on his persona. When his wide smile kept changing to a frown and a grimace, my little voice cupped its hand and whispered a warning in my ear that Remmy shared the same racist mannerisms as Api had in Irian Jaya. He also had his same diminutive build, but with features that had a hint of pygmy genetics.

As soon as I learnt Remmy was in town looking after his sick mother, I declined his enthusiastic offer to work as a guide. The last thing I wanted to do was drag a son away from his ailing mother while she lay violently ill in hospital. Although I sensed he was nothing but trouble, my normally firm resole softened, and I let compassion overrule commonsense when he mentioned that working for me would help to pay his mother's mounting medical fees. There wasn't anyone else John knew of who was able to walk across the island, so Remmy and I made plans to meet at the market after lunch, and then catch a truck to Natchara village where his family lived.

    While I walked around and waited for Remmy, Luganville had the look and feel of a frontier town that's taking its own good time to grow into something a little more forward thinking while it slowly gets a facelift. It hardly gleamed with beauty, but it was a comfortable and snug-fitting place to live, just like a favourite jumper that's worn full of holes but you can't bear to throw away even though it's in desperate need of repair in the odd place. The weary looking, unkempt buildings lining the main street, screaming out for a fresh coat of paint, and the rotting rooves and rusty reinforcing jutting out from unfinished projects created a sub-missive, almost remorseful air, as did the rust ridden Nissen huts and the other decaying buildings that were erected during World War II.

    The war had a massive impact on Santo, when in 1942, Luganville was transformed into a makeshift army base capable of housing one hundred thousand servicemen. The American and allied forces desperately needed a southern stronghold to repel the Japanese army if they succeeded in taking the Solomons, so vast amounts of military equipment were transported to the island, roads were cut, and the once sleepy hollow was transformed into a bustling military base. Only one Japanese bomb ever landed on Santo, and despite the region being such a prime target, the poorly aimed missile claimed one victim, a grazing cow. It was a cruel act of fate when after the military survived the botched attack from the air without any loss of life, the American troopship, the President Coolidge, sunk after it hit mines that the Americans had laid in Segond channel and five soldiers died.

    When the Japanese finally surrendered and the bloody conflict ended, the military put their equipment up for sale instead of taking it back to America. Buyers swarmed from around the pacific to secure a bargain, yet they hardly made a dent in the vast amounts of equipment. The condominium government thought they were being shrewd when they held out on the military and offered nothing for the goods in the hope they would be left and forgotten. But the Americans' patience wore thin, and when they became tired of waiting, they bulldozed everything into the ocean at the aptly named Million Dollar Point, much to the horror of Luganville's stunned inhabitants and the tight fisted government who thought they were about to get a massive windfall. Nowadays both Million Dollar Point and the President Coolidge are a Mecca for divers from around the world.

    While I passed the time buying several gifts for Natchara's chief and window shopped in the Chinese stores until Remmy arrived at the market, my thoughts were focused on what lay up in the mountains thousands of feet above the wrecks that lay on the floor of the ocean. We arrived at Natchara not long after sunset, just as a radiant full moon rose above a backdrop of silhouetted jungle and washed the path winding through the leaf hut village with a soft glow. Throughout all of Vanuatu, it's customary for a new visitor to be introduced to the chief, so Remmy led me straight to his patriarch. He wore a cloth loincloth and was a kind, aged man, with warm eyes and a soft broad smile. When I gifted him a small bundle of kava roots, he reciprocated with a true mark of hospitality and friendship when he told Remmy to formally welcome me with a kava drinking ceremony.

Kava is an acrid tasting, muddy looking brew that's made from the roots of the piper methysticum shrub. The word kava loosely translates to "intoxicating drink," and Vanuatu stakes claim to having the most potent strains of root in the world. Throughout most of the archipelago, kava plays an integral role in daily life when nearly every evening men congregate in the *nakamal*, which is a sacred men's hut that's reserved for drinking, and normally houses *tabu* fetishes and objects of worship. Women are strictly forbidden from ever entering the *nakamal*. Not only is the drinking of the analgesic and anaesthetic brew seen as a chance to relax and socialize at the end of the day, the Ni-Vanuatu believe that while they are under the influence of kava it creates a supernatural link with their ancestral spirits, during which time they receive guidance and messages and warnings from their kindred ghosts. As well as providing mental solace, when it's taken in moderation, the drink has many beneficial medicinal properties. Yet when it's drunk in excess, impotency, lethargy, skin problems, and photosensitivity of the eyes towards sunlight are unwanted side effects. To refuse an offer to drink kava is to refuse friendship and is the ultimate insult to a host. Besides sealing casual alliances, a kava drinking ceremony is normally a vital part of important rituals or any other special occasion. A solemn and respectful atmosphere always prevails whenever the brew is imbibed and conversations are kept to low murmur, because any loud noises or frivolous actions are deeply frowned upon.

We left the chief's hut and walked in the moonlight to the village *nakamal* where a smoke blackened hurricane lamp cast a pool of soft light across its murky interior. Ten men were already sitting in a tidy circle, and in a dim corner, a moaning adolescent who was curled up in the foetal position was soaked with sweat and shivering from a blazing fever. Most of the men started cramming kava that had been cut into small chips into their mouths until their cheeks bulged. Their teeth were coated with a generous fuzz of green and yellow plaque, and a few of them coughed and gently choked as they furiously chewed the root into pulpy cuds. Once they'd finished they placed their cuds on a lap lap leaf (similar to a banana leaf) in the centre of the circle. Everyone became sombre and reverent when the cuds were placed in a cloth bag and Remmy added a carefully measured amount of water, then viciously wrung the mixture into a bowl.

I'd spent months travelling around Fiji and whenever I lived in the villages, I spent most nights drinking kava with the locals. On Rabi Island, I'd drunk with the immigrant Banaban's on a marathon binge that lasted from six in the evening till four the following morning. Apart from feeling inebriated and lacklustre the following day, I'd suffered no ill side effects and assumed that Vanuatu's kava would be the same. Remmy gave a short speech to officially welcome me to the village in a low and serious tone, and then etiquette dictated that the highest-ranking person drank first from half of a coconut shell that had been fashioned into a cup. An even deadlier hush fell over the already quiet room when I was passed a shell that was brimming with kava. The hut was alive with interest, and all eyes were focused on me as I raised the shell to my mouth and quaffed down the coppery, acrid tasting concoction in one hit. Everyone's lips curled into a smile while mine went numb as the potent brew started coursing through my body. My welcome was complete, and more importantly, I'd passed the credibility test that proved my friendship was genuine by drinking the villagers saliva.

By the time we'd all drank three shells, everyone sat with their heads bowed in a silent state of subdued euphoria. Remmy reached over and gently grabbed my arm, then he looked at me through drooping eyelids that had partially covered his glazed eyes and slurred that because the kava was exceptionally strong no one in the *nakamal* could drink six shells. When he kept offering one drink after another, I'd knocked back the previous five merely to be sociable, and had to force down the sixth shell. It wasn't until I ate a second piece of taro from the communal plate that the mind-numbing brew snuck up and suddenly grabbed me. The room began to spin violently, the ground wavered wildly, and my reeling senses became hopelessly bewildered.

The reason for the previous look of awe on the villager's faces suddenly became apparent when my mind spiralled through layer after layer of my subconscious into a bizarre and unfamiliar void. When my vision doubled, Remmy and his unsteady clone split into two and started teetering from side to side. Every languid cell of my body seemed to turn to lead. I tried to move but my cumbersome limbs were trapped in a nauseating world, where everything seemed surreal and my actions were in slow motion. As lumps of vomit rose to the top of my throat, it was obvious I going to be violently sick, but not in front of my attentive audience, and not in the sacred *nakamal*. It took a Herculean effort to pull myself up the wall of the hut but falling out the door onto the damp grass was easy. I just made it outside when what seemed like gallons of vomit erupted from my churning stomach. In between gasping for breath and coughing and panting, I vomited again and again until I dry retched. I rolled onto my back and looked up at the full moon bouncing across the sky like a giant luminous beach ball. Then the silver orb split into two and became the piercing eyes of a giant celestial demon who cast a scornful glare at my stupidity. I felt as though I'd lost my turgid mind and was unable to find my feet, so I rolled around on the ground in a paralytic stupor until the heady brew sent me into a deep sleep.

When I awoke from the sleep of the dead the next morning, my mouth swung open before I'd even thought about prising my crusty eyes apart. I vomited numerous times until I'd completely emptied my stomach, then I started bringing up a foul tasting yellow bile. All of my get up and go had gotten up and gone during the night, and never in all of my life had I felt so lethargic and hung over. I was an absolute wreck and doubted I'd be capable of remaining upright or walking properly, let alone making the sixty-five kilometre two-day trek that Remmy was excitedly talking about. Linduri village was holding a *lafaet* (a *kastom* feast) and a three-day *kastom* dance to commemorate the death of a woman, which Remmy felt would make a great story. After I finished retching, I told him he would probably honour the death of a photojournalist as well if I tried to move. I stood up on my unsteady legs, noticed my hands were shaking uncontrollably, vomited again, and then, to try and regain some semblance of self-esteem, I staggered behind Remmy towards the main road.

He'd obviously lied about his profound knowledge of the trails that wind through the mountains and about his grasp of the numerous languages that are used by the clans living in the interior. When he insisted that, for added safety, we definitely needed three in our party, I thought about what lengths I'd go to if I was trying to help my sick mother and agreed to another guide. A scruffy villager, who looked about fifty years old and sat with his back against the base of a tree, whooped and laughed in approval when Remmy explained why I was throwing up again. Once he stopped laughing, Wintae introduced himself, suddenly became serious, and in a dramatic tone, he asked if I was afraid of contracting dengue fever or malaria or tackling long and arduous days in rugged terrain. I told him they were the least of my worries because I was half dead anyway, then I vomited again, which brought on another fit of laughter and his offer to act as a guide. Wintae's patient looking face, laid back personality, and his good sense of humour made him instantly likeable. From the state of his derelict looking body, it was easy to believe his claim of having never drunk anything but kava for the last thirty-five years. Deep and painful looking splits parted the flesh of his cracked heels and as we talked, when he kept habitually scratching his shins each scrape of his fingernails sent a flurry of skin flaking from his scaly legs. His toenails were in a terrible state of decay due to his kava addiction and had just about rotted away.

I was a physical wreck, but I dug my heels in and decided to try and stagger to Linduri for my first story. No matter how hard I tried, I couldn't walk in a straight line as I slowly snaked down the road until Wintae mercifully relieved me of my pack. When I belly flopped into the first river that we crossed, it didn't help to revive my flagging state of mind or my waning stamina. The wall of dense jungle flanking the road wore a choking tangle of American vine that stretched for miles. It left a horrible scar on the landscape and was first introduced by the American forces to provide camouflage for their military bases. In the ideal climate, the fast growing creeper quickly ran rampant and has ensnarled vast tracts of Santo's rainforest.

We followed the road until it petered out to a trail that wound along the coast and cut through copra plantations and pockets of bush. It became painfully obvious when we started heading inland and the sun started disappearing over the horizon that reaching our destined village before nightfall was going to be a race against the clock. I felt violently ill and exhausted from pushing myself beyond what I thought were the limits of my endurance, but by concentrating on each individual step and thinking of what my father endures I managed to dig deeper. He's stricken with Parkinson's disease and is well into his sixties, but he's bravely fought the ailment by running marathons. Despite his obvious discomfort he's always crossed the finish line and completed his last marathon in a respectable four hours and eight minutes. Although my life hardly depended on reaching Linduri in time for the *lafaet*, I tore a leaf out of his inspirational book and told myself that failing to reach the village wasn't an option.

In the last of the rapidly fading light we leapt from foothold to foothold down a sheer ridge then dropped into a gloomy stream that was hemmed in by the canopy of a dense jungle. In a matter of minutes, day abruptly turned to night, and we suddenly found ourselves groping our way through pitch-black darkness as we splashed along the boulder-strewn riverbed. After we eventually climbed out of the waterway, a welcome moon illuminated the climb up a slippery clay slope to Sulemaori village. Once the old men wearing *mul muls* (cloth loincloths) and the topless women dressed in wrap around skirts finished their genuine and warm greeting by hugging me, I collapsed on a bamboo slat bed and instantly succumbed to a fatigue induced sleep.

The fried pig gut they gave us for breakfast the next morning hardly helped to settle my still churning stomach. Although the shaking in my hands had reduced to a slight tremor, I still felt drained and desperately wanted to lie down and go back to sleep, but we pressed on and by mid-afternoon, we'd reached Naramach village. The black clouds of droning flies that relentlessly swarmed around our heads exaggerated the sorry state of the impoverished and disease ridden hamlet. Primitive men clad in *mul muls* and women, wearing only a cluster of *nagria* leaves that covered their crotches and the cleft of their buttocks, cradled infants who were covered in weeping sores and deep ulcers. Malaria, dysentery, and an assorted other ailments that caused debilitating health problems were rife. It was a saddening sight, and although no one appeared to be suffering from serious malnutrition, these were a people who were clearly struggling with grave medical problems. Despite their poverty, they made us welcome and offered us the best of what little they had.

It's hard to adequately reciprocate the generosity that's shown by those who are battling against impossible odds themselves and have every reason to view guests as an unwanted addition to their burdens. Fortunately my education allowed me to return their kindness with priceless reassurance when the villagers asked if I was afraid to die on the eve of the new millennium. Ever since a self-proclaimed minister who'd created his own bogus church had prophesised the day of Armageddon, for most of the primitive natives an impending sense of doom had hung in the air. The preacher told them God had appeared on the screen of his computer to warn him that the world was going to succumb to a horrendous flood on New Year's Eve. One of the villagers who'd seen a computer in Luganville had been astonished by its complex workings and told the others from what he'd seen there could be no doubt that the prophecy must be true. The evangelist preached that he was chosen to be the modern day Noah and warned that he alone possessed the gift to rescue the native's souls at the time of reckoning. He threatened the impressionable villagers with a one-way trip to hell unless they joined his flock and made outrageously high donations to his church. For the past ten years he'd ruthlessly cast a shadow of fear over Naramach and had embezzled what little money the villagers made from cutting copra and selling kava, while they struggled to buy basic medicines. It sickened my already nauseated stomach and was heart wrenching and infuriating to think that one devious man held so much power over the amiable villagers.

Like all religions, Christianity adapts when it comes into contact with other cultures. People sometimes change a religion to meet their own ends and to understand it on their own terms, but God sure as hell wouldn't approve of the minister's deceitful motives. I spent a good hour laying everyone's fears to rest until they seemed convinced that we wouldn't be harmed when the world slipped into the next millennium.

Several villagers who were travelling to the dance joined our ranks, and when we reached the coast, the full tide meant more than just a tricky climb around the rocks for one of the men. *Kastom* dictated that no saltwater could touch his body because if it did, malicious spirits would inflict a violent illness upon his newborn child. To avoid the spray from the pounding surf, he clawed his way across the cliff face with the skills of a seasoned mountaineer that would've done Sir Edmund Hillary proud. I felt a huge sense of relief when, just before dusk, we crossed a wide expanse of boulders that had been washed down from the mountains in a recent flash flood. Linduri was only minutes away, and we'd made it just in time for the start of the three-day celebration.

Chapter Eleven

WE'RE NOT LOST!

Just as we entered Linduri, from the throng of over one hundred bobbing heads came a deep assertive voice which bellowed to the milling crowd that drinking or fighting wouldn't be tolerated. The chief cast his baritone words over the hordes of dancers and reiterated his command with a warning that anyone who foolishly broke the *tabu* would be severely dealt with. Most of the youths had already defied his stern ruling and were staggering around in varying states of drunkenness. The crates of beer, the cheap wine, and the spirits that were delivered by a cargo boat had obviously primed many of the dancers. Others had resorted to drinking methylated spirits, aftershave, and the spirits that are used to fuel lanterns. A few had even stooped to getting hammered on a repulsive broth they made from boiling either old tyres or dry cell batteries. In a situation like this, I knew the drunken youths were a ticking time bomb and that trouble was inevitable. Being the only European amongst so many natives didn't faze me, but knowing they couldn't hold their drink was slightly unnerving as there was no reassurance that Remmy or Wintae would come to my aid if things got ugly. They were becoming increasingly aloof, and within minutes of arriving in the village, without saying a word they'd both disappeared, no doubt to satisfy Wintae's kava addiction.

The chief gave us our own sleeping hut from where I enjoyed a comfortable front row seat on a hardwood veranda only twenty metres away from the *nasara* (dance ground). I sat with my back against a wall and watched a beautiful full moon rise over a backdrop of jagged mountains as the celestial spotlight cast a pallid light over the crowd of animated dancers. In the middle of the *nasara*, a slab of wood with a small opening chopped out of its centre covered a one metre deep hole. A nucleus of men who were dripping with sweat surrounded the slat of timber and sung with a feverish gusto while they pounded out a deep resonating beat on the wood with a two metres long bamboo dance sticks called *boe*. A circle of singing women who encased the men shuffled their feet and swayed their hips in gentle unison, while the rest of the village swirled in a dizzying ring around the inner core. Their scuffing feet kicked up a choking fog of dust that hung in the air in a dirty brown halo. At the end of each song any *boe* sticks that were split at their bases from the constant pounding, hissed through the air as they were hurled like javelins over the dancers heads.

A teenage girl with demure eyes and huge breasts invited me to join the vibrant, almost maniacal throng. I felt it might lead to trouble and hesitated at first, but so as not to insult the memory of the dead woman I reluctantly agreed. When I entered the suffocating haze, all of my senses were embalmed by the tone of the primitive music as it reverberated from what sounded like the very bowels of the earth. The hypnotic rhythm of the *boe* combined with the impassioned singing to create an intoxicating, almost haunting atmosphere. I quickly became one with the beat and fell into step with the mass of gyrating bodies. The sound of the pounding *boe* sticks became a potent and seductive force, as were the young girls who cheekily pinched me as they whirled past. They were offering much more than just the opportunity to dance and unwittingly painted a bullseye on my wellbeing. Several drunken adolescents who noticed the girls' sexual advances expressed their jealousy by linking hands and slamming into me as hard as they could when they danced by. I ignored the assault and got lost in the crowd but my anonymity was short-lived, and when the boys quickly found me again they repeated the battering from behind. I quietly slipped away none the worse for wear and sat against the side of our hut. When a *boe* stick hummed through the dusty air and speared the earth between my feet and others bounced off the wall of the hut, I was forced to retreat into the safety of the doorway.

With seemingly endless amounts of energy, the villagers kept up the tireless dancing for hours until the inevitable happened. Their emotions seemed to be running out of control, and then as I'd anticipated, the crowd's excited whoops and joyous yelling turned to angry screaming and pained cries when a chaotic full-on brawl erupted. *Boe* sticks whistled through the air as they were swung like oversized baseball bats and clubbed skulls and cracked ribs. An unlucky boy who looked about sixteen was hammered to the ground and set upon by a small mob who ruthlessly beat him to a bloody pulp. A fighting maul of bodies crashed into the side of the hut with their arms and legs flailing as furious punches and sickening kicks landed bone-crunching blows. Mothers screamed, scratched, and punched, while they fought and pulled attackers off of their family members. Anyone who was within arm's reach was fair game. A disorientated youth who'd been spun around by a blow to his temple, lunged through the doorway with his head down and threw a punch. I instinctively slipped the wayward jab and sprung back out of harm's way. When the boy raised his head to take another shot, he quickly pulled his punch and apologised the instant he saw who I was.

Once the commotion died down, the dancing resumed as if nothing had happened. Small pockets of sporadic fighting flared and simmered until the dancing ceased at dawn. I was absolutely shattered and stretched out on a woven mat to snatch a desperately needed few hours sleep just as Wintae and Remmy stumbled into the hut, crashed to the floor, and fell into a kava-induced slumber.

After I awoke from a sound sleep and asked the locals about the pygmies. They fed me incredulous rumours and bizarre stories. The superstitious villagers spoke of three-foot high beings who looked like devils with long flowing beards, pointed teeth, and matted hair that draped to their ankles. Some of them said ferocious creatures lived deep in the interior that ran around naked and had a voracious appetite for human flesh. The

Mentawai on Siberut Island had chiselled their teeth to a point, as do some of Africa's pygmies, so I didn't rubbish part of the exaggerated descriptions. Late in the afternoon the chief made everyone involved in the fighting line up in front of the whole village. When each offender was made to stand before him and receive their punishment, the instigators copped a heavy fine of twenty thousand vatu, and a stern warning that tribal law would stretch to beyond paying compensation if anyone disrespectfully disrupted the dance with more violence. With the last of the alcohol gone and the threat of a more ruthless form of policing hanging over any potential offenders, I looked forward to a more peaceful night.

Fresh bundles of *boe* sticks were being stacked near the *nasara* when the din of an outboard motor caught everyone's attention. A twelve-foot aluminium dinghy rode the crest of a wave onto the beach, and then a jovial European with a rotund belly and smiling eyes jumped out and inspected his damaged boat. He was a scientist who'd travelled around the islands for over thirty years to measure the seismic movement of the mountains. A large wave had creased the bow of his small craft while he sailed from Malakula Island to take new readings on Santo. From the state of his crumpled dinghy, I was amazed he'd made it this far. Our conversation quickly drifted to his experiences with remote tribes thirty years ago. While he was at Malakula, he'd feared for his life several times during frightening encounters with rarely visited clans, and although he'd never ventured up to Santo's highlands, he'd heard numerous rumours that the inhabitants vigorously repelled outsiders. I wasn't interested in taking timid footsteps along the coast and wondering what lay hidden in the mountains, but I took serious heed of his warning to treat the region with extreme caution. When I mentioned braving the unpredictable ocean in a small dinghy seemed far more reckless than venturing into the jungle, he shrugged his shoulders and downplayed the dangers. The only time he really felt threatened was when tiger sharks were mating and the aggressive males sometimes attacked his frail craft.

That night, an air of peace prevailed when we danced right through to dawn again. The following afternoon, the enticing aroma of food being cooked in hot stones wafted across the village. Everyone was invited to the *lafaet* for the deceased woman, where we recharged our systems for another night of celebrating by eating our fill of roast beef and chicken, the last of the village rice, and a doughy dish made from pulverised taro called *lap lap*.

We had another night of wild and energetic dancing, and although Wintae and Remmy had agreed to start walking across the island first thing in the morning, we all partied with the villagers into the small hours. I was caked in dust and grime from hours of dancing when I slumped onto the floor of our hut at about three a.m. to catch a few hours of precious sleep before we headed inland. When I awoke, I had a haunting feeling of déjà vu and my mind raced back to what had happened with Api at Irian Jaya, when, for no apparent reason apart from maybe the raging hangover he appeared to be suffering from after drinking methylated spirits all night, Remmy seemed to despise the very sight of me. Back at Natchara, he'd reassured me that Linduri could easily cater to our needs, but it turned out that the barren village store had nothing to offer. The intermittent cargo ships had failed to arrive and drop off more provisions, and the unexpected influx of visitors quickly depleted the tiny store's already dwindling supplies. It cast a grim shadow over our journey because all we had between us was one small packet of cabin biscuits that I'd bought in Luganville, and they'd been partially eaten by a rat.

To even consider travelling inland without adequate provisions was reckless enough, but to cross the island with the threat of a mutiny hanging over my head was asking for trouble. I confronted Remmy in a quiet but assertive tone and asked him about his spiteful attitude. He readily admitted to hating the white man ever since he'd watched two drunken Europeans fornicate like dogs in front of his family while they were picnicking at Champagne Beach. I agreed that the tourists' actions were disrespectful, then jokingly mentioned I'd get stage fright getting it on in front of an audience and imitated how certain parts of my anatomy would react to a crowd of onlookers. His stoic features gradually softened, he managed a faint smile, then he apologised by slipping his curled index finger between my fingers, which we pulled apart to make a loud clicking sound. Throughout Vanuatu, the handshake is mostly used to indicate joy when men joke or to signify that all is well between two people. Remmy felt confident that we could live off the land and buy food from the villages we passed through so we agreed to carry on as we'd planned. After an all night drinking binge, Wintae's recumbent body would've blissfully snored the day away if we hadn't given him a good shake. He rubbed his bloodshot eyes, scratched his head, and then looked at our pitiful packet of biscuits when I told him it was all the food we had. He muttered "No problem," then said we should get moving as we had a hard day ahead of us.

After we wearily waved goodbye to a small crowd of onlookers, we rock hopped up the boulder-strewn Vakola River. Wintae wore a cheap pair of jandals, yet he still clambered up and over large greasy boulders with ease. We spent hour after hour leaping from boulder to boulder, which was much quicker and easier than trying to travel through the jungle because on each side of the river, sheer ridges covered in impenetrable rainforest ran down from a rugged mountainous spine. The further we ventured inland, the happier Winate became. If he wasn't whistling a happy tune he sang *kastom* songs at the top of his voice and seemed to draw energy and become stimulated from some type of soulful connection he had with our beautiful surroundings. Several hours later, he fell silent, suddenly came to a halt, and raised his machete into the air. Then he pointed the knife in different directions and scratched his head when he seemed unsure of the way. Once he got his bearings, he happily nodded to himself, started singing again, and we carried on climbing over the jumble of rocks to a nearby trail. We clawed our way up a vertical incline, then followed a virtually nonexistent track that clung to the side of a huge face which led us away from the river up to a sheer and windblown ridge.

Rock hopping up the riverbed had been a breeze compared to the torturous terrain we were following. When we eventually dropped back down into the boulder-choked river, it offered our burning legs a much welcomed rest. By mid-afternoon, we'd nearly reached the headwaters tumbling down from Vanuatu's highest mountain. Directly ahead of us, Mount Tambewassana's impressive cloud snagged summit dominated an already looming landscape. When Wintae was unsure of the way and started looking for a familiar landmark, he went through the motions of scratching his head and raising his machete again. We sat down and waited for five minutes while he boulder hopped upstream. When his drawn out yodel called us forward, after ten hours of gruelling slog since we'd left Linduri, we stood at the start of a trail that was buried beneath a small landslide. Remmy's inherent beliefs made picking our way through the jungle way too dangerous for him because the small spirit devil called Damate roamed the mountains. Damate is covered in long scraggly hair, has black skin and razor sharp claws. If we left the track, Remmy was adamant that Damate would feel our presence, hunt us down, and use his menacing fangs and supernatural strength to tear us mere mortals apart before he gorged on our flesh and drank our blood. No matter how translucent or whimsical others' beliefs may seem, I've always treated them with the utmost respect. We had no other choice but to backtrack and made a demanding climb up to a stand of coconut palms where we made camp in the rapidly fading light.

A few evil-tempered wild bulls that roamed around the area had recently charged and tried to gore several natives, and from the piles of fresh dung that were scattered around our campsite, it looked as though they were probably still in our valley. We lit a blazing fire next to the crude mattresses we made from palm fronds to keep the aggressive animals at bay and our bodies warm at night. Then we staved off our growing hunger by eating the succulent flesh of green coconuts and sharing out our packet of cabin biscuits. Remmy was in mourning for one hundred days due to the recent death of his younger brother so he spat out a mouthful of coconut meat into his hands, and then rubbed it into the fringe of the dreadlocks he was wearing for one year to show respect to his brother. The greasy coconut flesh is believed to make the twists of hair grow faster. Wintae chewed a mouthful of sharp tasting kava to satisfy his daily addiction then sieved the cud through the natural matting that grows at the base of coconut leaves. When I shifted away from the fires in the middle of the night to escape the gagging smoke and slept barefoot in the grass it sent out an open invitation for the resident leeches to use my legs and feet as a smorgasbord.

We awoke the next morning to the sound of birdsong and the distant rumble of the river as it tumbled through the gorge way below us. The patches of heavy mist that lingered in the valleys slowly lifted and coiled with the rising thermals then vaporised in the sun's warming rays. We had a light breakfast of coconut flesh and wild *pablemous* (similar to grapefruit), which hardly provided us with the energy we needed for another punishing day. Wintae led us inland and set a deceptively quick pace with his gangly gait. When he angled off the track, we followed and began a slow slog up a side trail that went straight up a sheer five hundred metres high face. Remmy sighed with disappointment and shook his head in disgust when after a hard climb, we discovered a vertical bluff capped the rear of the peak. Wintae scratched his lice infested head and shrugged his shoulders, looked bewildered and apologetic, and then he pointed to the coast with his machete. When I shook my head in disbelief and said, "You're joking, mate," in his calm and matter of fact manner, Wintae replied, "We must go back to Naramach, then head for Vatea. Some small men live there." It was foolhardy enough travelling inland without adequate food, but to do so without knowing the way was nothing short of kamikaze. In terrain this rough, I needed a lot more than just a map, a compass, and a burning curiosity to keep me going. I decided my only sensible option was to head back to Naramach and hopefully find another guide.

We climbed back down to the river, and after we'd walked downstream for half an hour, we spied a wild fowl drinking its fill. The bird was totally oblivious to our presence, and slipped into a shallow pool where it dipped its head and breast under the surface and shook water through its iridescent plumage. Without saying a word, Remmy instinctively switched into predator mode and crept towards the tasty looking bird while it was preoccupied with preening its feathers. He moved at a crouch, with silent and carefully measured steps, to behind a huge boulder, where he patiently waited until the moment was right, then flew through the air and pounced on the waterlogged fowl. Wintae plucked the wing and tail feathers from the squawking rooster and bound its feet together with a vine to prevent the hapless bird from flying off. As Remmy stroked and hugged the shaking fowl, he said, "It's got beautiful grass (feathers). I want to take him home." I said, "Don't get to attached mate," and licked my lips while Wintae imitated wringing the bird's neck. Realistically we had no more right to live or eat than the wild fowl, and like the rooster, we to would've been scavengers of the rainforest if we'd continued inland. Its tasty flesh would give a new lease of life to our plunging energy levels, but we agreed to only eat the bird as a last resort.

We retraced our steps part of the way, then followed a trail back to Naramach and entered the destitute village just as the rapidly sinking sun pulled down the last rays of light. Remmy and Wintae were both unwell and were adamant that sinister forces were the cause of their illness. They sought the healing powers of a wizened old *kastom* woman, who stooped over the remnants of a cooking fire and performed a simplistic divination rite by singing and chanting into a pile of ash. After a brief moment of silence, she declared the rat that'd partially eaten our cabin biscuits had been a devil and its evil spirit had become embodied in their souls, then she told them to eat a small mouthful of the ash to exorcise the fiend from their ailing bodies. Later that evening, after a hearty meal of boiled taro, it was sheer bliss to be able to stretch out on a springy bamboo slat bed with a full belly. The old woman sat several meters away form us alongside a blazing fire and began gently rocking back and forwards while the lilt of her aged voice lulled us to sleep with a beautifully sung, soothing melody.

Because of the very nature of my work, I knew, to get an honest insight into the lives of primitive peoples, the job would call for numerous sacrifices, be they mental or physical, which civilized readers would find inconceivable. I decided there could be no half measures and that I would embrace everything the natives considered normal no matter how repulsive they were so long as I didn't do anything that I would be ashamed of later in life.

When I awoke to a breakfast that smelt like gastronomic suicide, it was hardly the healthiest way to start the day. The steaming yams that were piled high on a rusty tin plate looked appetising, but the rank odour coming from the pieces of rancid pork made me cringe. Pork is considered a delicacy and was the very best the villagers could offer. So as not to disrespect their hospitality or cast shame on Remmy and Wintae for bringing me to the village, I ate my fill. By swallowing bite-sized chunks and clenching my nostrils together, I managed to coerce the ripe smelling meat down my throat without heaving. Then I thanked everyone for the food and quickly went for a walk and hid behind a mango tree about fifty meters from the village. As soon as I placed my hands on my knees, I vomited until I dry retched, to the delight of the cannibalistic village pigs who greedily consumed what I'd failed to keep down. It's always amazed me how quickly I become indifferent to conditions that I know are teeming with a plethora of vile bacteria. To any sane person, my actions would seem insane and reckless, but if I was to maintain the respect of the village, and of Remmy and Wintae, I had to eat the vile meat.

Back at the village, I sat alongside Wintae and watched him scrape layers of dead skin off his kava-ravaged legs with our machete. He used the point of the knife to dig slithers of mud from the bloodied splits in his heels then he cut me a piece of succulent looking ripe pawpaw. I said, "Thanks, Wintae, but that bit's yours, mate," and then I asked him to clean the blade before he cut me another slice. He gave me one of his redeeming smiles and thought he was being hygienic when he wiped the knife under the soiled armpit of his shirt and sliced off another portion of the fruit.

Although I offered to pay them well, not even the staunchest of Naramach's men were willing to guide me into the highlands. As a last resort, I asked Remmy and Wintae if they wanted to head inland again, to which Wintae calmly replied, "No problem. I know the jungle like the back of my hand."

We packed our gear and followed a well-defined trail over demanding terrain that even had Wintae's tireless legs stopping to rest as we toiled up abrupt inclines. When we came across an area covered with secondary growth and pockmarked with the diggings of an ancient village site, we gave the graves of chiefs that were fenced off a wide berth. Remmy explained that any animals wandering across the burial sites are said to be possessed by the chief's spirit. If a hunter unwittingly kills such an animal, he's doomed to die a horrific death from some divine form of intervention.

After we'd almost finished one of the numerous strenuous climbs, Wintae motioned for us to stop just short of the top of a peak. He chanted towards the heavens for several minutes while Remmy and I maintained a reverent silence. Fifty metres further up the track, he stopped again, took off his small pack, and climbed halfway up a large tree. Its trunk had grown around old knives, a rusted tin mug, and other personal possessions of the dead when their mourning relatives had embedded them in the timber decades ago. Wintae pounded out a tune on a *tam tam* (bamboo slit drum) that was hanging from a branch and sang a *kastom* song at the top of his voice to announce our presence to the spirits of the dead. It was almost as if he'd summonsed the gathering clouds when they suddenly darkened the sun and blotted out the blue sky. When the weather steadily worsened and a swirling mist and biting rain soaked us to the skin, Remmy grew increasingly nervous. He turned to me and said, "The spirits of our *bubu* (ancestors or grandparents) can feel you. Come, we must make *kastom*." He looked worried and warned me that my presence had angered the ancestral ghosts who were unleashing their wrath by creating the foul weather.

A short walk up the track, we stopped again, but this time it was Remmy's turn to make *kastom*. He cleared tufts of overgrown vegetation from the base of a small boulder while he mumbled an ancient chant, then he gave me a *tabu* leaf and told me to place it on top of a stone called *Levu Levu*, which means "the rock that weeps." The leaf was an offering to appease the gods so that they'd protect me from Damate. Remmy reassured me that although the spirits were angered by the colour of my white skin, they'd battered me with rain and shrouded me in mist to hide me from the pint-sized devil. When the clouds unfurled, the rain stopped, and the mist began clearing, Remmy said, "*Levu Levu* is protecting you. Dry the rock and see for yourself." I wiped the rock dry with my shirt and felt an overwhelming sensation like a short but sharp electric shock that sent a cold shiver up my spine when the boulder inexplicably began to weep fluid. A mass of goose bumps started appearing all over my skin, and it felt as if a ghost had just stomped on my grave. Even after I wiped the rock dry several times, long after the rain had ceased to fall, the ancestors kept acknowledging our presence with a steady trickle of tear-like drops which kept leaching from the sacred stone.

While we trudged through a mantle of thick rainforest and I asked Remmy why, of all the things that were in a jungle, a stone should become *tabu*, his explanation made it easy to see why his ancestral spirits were embodied in a rock. In the midst of the jungle's ever changing biomass, with its profusion of life and death, spirits didn't alter over time and in the eyes of his primitive forefathers neither did stone. Compared to the rate that the surrounding rainforest grows and dies, the effect the elements and centuries of time has on a sturdy rock are normally subtle.

When Wintae led us to the top of a blustery peak, the bewitching vista was the same in every direction. A confusing maze of luscious rainforest creased by treacherous descents and energy sapping hills lay ahead of us. Wintae's urgent pace didn't give us much time to soak up the captivating beauty of the mountains and by late in the afternoon, we trailed several minutes behind him. We thought the worst when we heard a pained cry in the distance, and threw off our packs and sprinted through the jungle to catch up to his distraught wailing. He sat in the door of a leaf hut, uninjured and hugging an old woman who was his distant relative. Tears were streaming down his face to express his sorrow and to show respect to the woman and to her recently deceased husband. When I burst onto the scene, the terrified old crone screamed with fright and her body began to shudder. Her daughter shrieked, then shook with fear while she hugged her suckling infant even tighter to her trembling chest. The petrified women were both naked except for a scanty covering of *nagria* leaves, and my unwelcome intrusion horrified them so much that they fled into the murky interior of Marama village's only leaf hut. I didn't want to add terror to their mournful moment, so I quickly slipped out of sight and waited for Wintae to come out of the hut.

Wintae cried with the women for about half an hour, then we carried on and dropped down a steep pitch into a valley that followed the banks of a narrow, slow flowing river. A sapling with a weave of *tabu* leaves tied to its top had been speared into the riverbank to claim ownership of a crystal clear pool that had been dammed with rocks and *lap lap* leaves. It also warned that fishing for the teeming schools of small but tasty looking fish was strictly forbidden. We sidled along the banks to where the stream gushed from a much larger river, and then we left the side stream and followed the flow of the Jordan River. There was only half an hour of light left when we entered Vatea village, where apart from the ragged clothing hanging out to dry, the untidy cluster of huts showed little sign of life. When two villagers wearing grimy and tattered garments gingerly emerged from their doorways, they were reserved and hesitant, and I understood why when they told us that two French tourists who'd visited them three years ago had treated them disrespectfully by refusing the food they offered and to drink kava. The way their hospitality was snubbed had left a lasting impression. As they led us to a hut, I overheard Wintae telling them, "This white man is different to the others. He respects *kastom* and eats and drinks like a black man."

Although I was starving, my normally cast iron stomach had trouble trying to keep down a steaming bowl of fish that had been caught by squeezing toxic wild kava into the dammed up pool. The finger-sized fish had been boiled whole, with their guts still intact until they disintegrated into a brown, foul smelling, fetid tasting soup whose nauseating taste was on a par with the rancid pork at Naramach. The villagers quickly warmed to our presence when I thanked them for the meal and we shared several shells of freshly chewed kava. I wasn't disappointed to hear that Vatea's stunted inhabitants had left several days earlier to work the gardens they'd planted in another area, as western influence had stamped its dishevelling mark on the hamlet. Wintae drank shell after shell of kava well into the night, and just as I was starting to nod off, I heard him asking our hosts if they knew anything about the pygmies. Several villagers who'd followed the Jordan River to Big Bay on the other side of the island had met what they called dwarfs travelling along the river. The promising conversation faded into quiet when the effect of the kava sent me drifting off into a deep and blissful slumber.

The new day was dawning when I awoke to a stodgy breakfast of fire-roasted taro that Wintae had cooked several hours earlier. It wasn't until we'd left the village and had been following the river for almost an hour that Wintae realised he'd forgotten to bring the taro the villagers had gifted us. Several hours later, from somewhere within the bowels of the island, he scratched his head to decide where he'd gone wrong again and went through the familiar motions of looking unsure while he raised and pointed his machete from side to side. This was virgin territory for all of us, and following a well-worn wild bullock trail was an easy mistake that anyone could have made. We wrestled with the loud torrent of the Jordan River and crossed its foaming surge to find that Wintae had been following the wrong side of the river. We pressed on, then as he rounded a bend in the river Wintae screeched to a sudden halt. A dishevelled looking archer wearing a tattered *mul mul* was standing on the edge of a flat rock overhanging the river. He had grey hair, a grim face, and his bow was partially drawn as he slowly trailed a fish meandering in a tranquil stretch of water. The instant the withered native glimpsed us out of the corner of his eye he calmly turned and, probably without having any malicious intent, drew a bead on us from across the river. Our profane response to his bitter stare and to looking down the end of an arrow turned the air blue. He held our anxious gaze for a few seconds then slowly lowered his bow. When I asked him if I could take his photo, I got a gruff refusal, so we quickly moved on.

The lack of adequate nutrition, eating the rotten pork, and the demanding terrain were starting to take their toll my health. We used well-aimed sticks and knocked wild *pablemous* from the top of a fruit laden tree to try and satisfy my lingering hunger. It was just before midday when Wintae managed to find the base of a neck-craning trail on the edge of the Jordan River that Vatea's inhabitants had told us would lead to the remote tribes living in the highlands.

Remmy and Wintae both looked troubled as they grappled for roots and firm handholds to slowly pull themselves up the seemingly endless face. While I was staying with John Noel, he'd spoken of a massive precipice that soared up from the Jordan River, and from his description, I was pretty sure this was the same place. During the coconut rebellion, when the soldiers from Papua New Guinea were trying to mop up the last of Jimmy Stevens' rebellious followers, they'd refused to make the almost vertical climb. It was just as well, because Stevens' primitive supporters were hiding amongst the trees halfway up the hill, and were ready to rain down a hail of arrows if the Papuans tried to scale the sheer wall of jungle. I learnt later that the natural barrier is also a spiritual blockade. Around 1970, a devastating earthquake killed every inhabitant of Vonumatui village, which had been built near the edge of the drop off. Ever since the catastrophe, a mysterious bright light is said to glow through the jungle at the site of the demolished village. The superstitious highlanders are adamant that Damate created the upheaval and refuse to go anywhere near the *tabu* face. They call the rise Mount Lappemarau and blame the diminutive devil for the eerie nighttime glow. There are certain species of fireflies that congregate in large numbers to emit a synchronous glow which may well have been responsible for the mystifying lights. The legend attached to the area and knowing any error in judgement while they made the vertical climb would almost certainly result in a serious injury was no doubt the cause of Remmy and Wintae's apprehension.

Once we reached the top, after all of our minor setbacks, we were finally heading through the jungle towards the heart of the island. We balanced along a tangle of greasy roots paving a trail that followed a razorback ridge, then when the roots gave way to mud, a cool steady drizzle turned the undulating track into a leech-infested quagmire. For the next six hours we put all of our faith in Wintae's suspect navigation as we blindly trekked through the mountains. By the end of the day, his kava-emaciated feet had become a split and bloodied mess, but the cheap Jandals he'd bought from a Chinese store had somehow managed to hold together.

Dusk was approaching when he got a vacant look on his face and he stopped and pointed his machete skywards. He was clearly disorientated but hardly distraught when he predictably started scratching his head. As I stared into a dense wall of brooding jungle that hemmed in the faint trail I said, "We're lost, aren't we?" Without any warning my simple statement sent Remmy into such a fierce rage that I could see the blood pumping through his temples. Then when I tried to calm the situation by telling him not to worry and that worse things could happen than being lost, the veins pulsing up the side of his neck seemed to double in size and he screamed, "We're not! You must never fucking say that! Fucking never!" Then he vented his anger further with another much stronger string of foul language.

Through my ignorance I'd just committed an innocent yet heinous breach of *kastom*. Now that Damate knew we were lost in the gloomy depths of the jungle, the pint-sized devil had us completely at his mercy. Unless Remmy took urgent action to fend off Damate, we were guaranteed to suffer an agonizing death. He stormed off into the jungle, then returned ten minutes later with three lily stigma that were covered with yellow pollen. Then he remedied our dilemma by anointing a cross on the top of our heads with the plants' dusty granules so that his ancestral spirits would thwart Damate's attack and offer us guidance at the same time. I used my map and compass to get a general idea of where we were the tried and true way. Not that it mattered, because from some of the high vantage points we climbed we could see Mount Tambewassana away in the distance.

The swathe of opaque cloud cloaking the numerous mountain ranges had reduced the setting sun to a cold and insipid glow. Our search for a village had proved futile, so in the remaining light, we quickly set up a makeshift camp. Remmy shied away from me and protectively hugged his tasty looking fowl close to his chest when I suggested we should kill and eat the bird. I only had a little bit of water left in my drink bottle, so Win-tae resorted to satisfying his daily vice by eating and somehow managing to keep down bitter tasting kava roots. In the time that we'd spent together, I'd never seen a single drop of pure water go past his lips. We made ourselves a meagre meal of coconut flesh, a *pablemous* each, and bush cabbage which we steamed inside a piece of bamboo, but it didn't help to stave off the hunger pangs that stabbed at our grumbling stomachs. When we curled up on a bed of damp fern alongside a blazing fire, we were shaken awake throughout a fitful night's sleep by the bitterly cold conditions of our crude elevated camp.

Chapter Twelve

THE STONE AGE MEETS THE CLONE AGE

When the rising sun shed light over the highlands and gave warmth to our cold bodies, the eye catching views were the same in every direction. We were enveloped by an endless succession of sharp ridges and plunging valleys that resembled a mapmaker's nightmare. The dramatic landscape and not knowing where we were heading added to the air of mystery and to the excitement of trying to discover if the legendary pygmies still existed. I felt comfortably cradled in a botanical paradise rather than captured by the islands unyielding geography, and although I was tired and hungry, I still revelled in every minute of our weary travel through the challenging landscape. Late in the afternoon, Wintae climbed a towering tree, yodelled several times from up in the canopy, and patiently waited for a reply, but only his shrill echo answered. An hour later our spirits soared when we intersected what looked to be a well-used track. We careened down the steep trail, then clambered skywards to where an elevated view gave me a chance to scan the mountains with my telephoto lens in the hope of seeing a telltale clearing amongst the sprawling canopy of the forest. I slowly panned the landscape, then stopped when several kilometres away, on a lofty grass covered knoll, faint wisps of smoke rising from two leaf huts dissipated into a mantle of rapidly descending cloud and mist. As we traipsed towards the tiny hamlet, a bitter wind drove sheets of blinding rain in our faces. When the rain stopped and a thick mist raced down the hillsides and engulfed us in a ghoulish wreath that limited our visibility to about ten metres, I could see Remmy and Wintae were growing more and more anxious. They were probably afraid that Damate was responsible for the abrupt change in weather, so I led the way down a steep ridge.

When an old woman raised her head, assumedly to greet a fellow villager, and she saw me emerge from the dense wall of mist, her features contorted into a look of total shock and utter disbelief. The white tridacna shell nosepiece she wore through her pierced nasal septa matched the widened whites of her fear filled eyes. She was rooted to the spot and shook from head to toe until her fear suddenly turned to self-preservation and she threw her heavy load of taro to the ground, shrieked in terror, then fled into the sanctuary of the jungle as fast as her trembling legs could carry her. I learnt later that her name was Vetrivu, she was over seventy years old, and had never ventured beyond the geographical isolation of her tribal boundaries. By worshiping the doctrines of her primitive culture while her people were quarantined in the remote highlands, she'd preserved her virtual Stone Age purity and had witnessed more in the first few years of her life than most westerners would in their entire lifetime. Although she'd watched the most barbaric of acts during composite rituals, she'd never seen a white man.

I was no stranger to the quandary that's sometimes involved with making first contact with primitive peoples. The emotive dilemma of each initial encounter remains deeply etched into my memory banks. To have my mind buzzing with awe and to experience the feeling of excitement in every fibre of my body while the poor natives are usually aquiver with fear isn't an experience that's easily forgotten. Those brief encounters had changed me forever. When I materialized like an alien spectre from the veil of low cloud, it had literally been a haunting experience for Vetrivu. To her, I wasn't a European or of flesh and blood. I was either Damate, who is normally black but can sometimes appear in the guise of a white spirit, or, as I later found out, due to the belief that when she dies her spirit will turn white, I was an ancestral ghost.

Vetrivu's fading screams were replaced with the sound of running feet and agitated shouts that chilled the core of my spine. When five men clad in *mul muls* came charging out of the mist, it was our turn to experience the type of fear that has to felt before it can be understood. Some of them were armed with bows, while others held tightly gripped machetes at their sides. All of the fearsome looking warriors gave me the impression they were about to attack us. I told myself to remain calm and clear-headed and not to reveal my true emotions, which is an unthinkable luxury when primitive people confront you during a volatile situation. When Remmy gingerly moved forward and explained we were walking across the island, the gut wrenching emotion of looking at the receiving end of a drawn arrow started to fade when the arrows aimed at my chest were slowly lowered. The hostility suddenly changed into hospitality when Ravae, the village chief, spoke to Remmy in Bislama and told him we could stay in a hut for one night only as his people's strict tribal law demanded that I must leave tomorrow at first light. I swore under my breath and let out a massive sigh of relief as we followed the muscular warriors, who would tower above pygmies, down to a hamlet comprised of four large leaf huts.

As we walked past the huts to a *nakamal* that looked as if it had been ravaged during a cyclone, children whose features were masked in sheer terror began screaming while several older women adorned with nose bones shrieked and trembled with fear. All of the men wore *mul muls*, and the bare breasted women were clad in *nagria* leaves. Their scanty attire offered them little protection against the extremes of mountain weather. Like the millennia of violent geographical upheaval that had shaped the rugged island, they were a resilient people who had obviously evolved to become hardened to the rigours of their environment. The naked toddlers who hugged their shoulders to stave off the cold, who tearfully sprinted into their mothers shaking arms, looked extremely vulnerable to the elements. When Ravae led us into the decrepit *nakamal*, it looked as though it was about to collapse, but its skeletal timbers defiantly held the black palm walls and the thatched sago palm roof together. A group of curious men and wary boys who followed behind us spilled into the hut. They were much darker than their costal counterparts and wore intimidating black expressions that mirrored the tone of their ebony skin.

While the *nakamal* hummed with quiet chatter and brimmed with interest, I readily answered a barrage of questions that were asked in a harsh and abrupt manner. At first I thought everyone was being obnoxious until Remmy told me their abrasive tone was the way the men normally spoke to one another. There was something about Ravae's intense gaze and his broad shouldered physique that commanded instant respect. He wore a beard and had the quiet dignity of a natural leader who seemed at ease with himself and others. His lithe yet muscular body bore a ritualistic scar in the middle of his well-built chest, and like the rest of the men and some of the older boys, circular ceremonial scars were dotted around his upper arms. All of them had two vertical rows of scars on their abdomens, and single dotted lines of tattoos graced the faces of several older villagers. While Wintae and Ravae chatted, the chief kept nodding then turning from Wintae and staring at me. At first it was a little unnerving until Wintae's easygoing manner had him smiling and laughing and his piercing gaze started to gradually soften.

The eleven men who crowded around me expressed a variety of emotions, but their instinctive blend of curiosity and antagonism created an uncomfortable and unpredictable mood. When I showed them the photos of myself living with other tribes, it proved to be a great icebreaker and helped to relax the rigid atmosphere. Everyone was fascinated and in absolute awe that I'd spent months with other tribes who existed as they did. They excitedly fingered the photos and whooped and yelled until a wide-eyed boy yelped, "Damate!" and threw the shot of me and the emaciated Yali woman to the ground. To anyone with a primitive mindset she could easily be mistaken for a devil, and it took a while to reassure everyone that the miserable looking woman was a withered mortal. Once they settled down again they pawed at the shots and noisily discussed the similarities between themselves and the tribes I'd visited. The photos of the pygmies I'd taken in the Solomons generated a universal reaction when the men suddenly looked astonished, carefully studied the photos, and then mentioned the word *winea*.

Before the men and boy started chewing freshly cut kava chips for a traditional welcoming ceremony, they cleared their airways by spitting and by blowing snot around our feet. Even though I knew food wasn't consumed until after kava is drunk, I mentioned to Ravae that we were starving. He motioned for me to eat from a cast iron cooking pot, and when he shifted it to in front of my feet, about a dozen cockroaches that were hiding beneath the saucepan scurried for cover. I lifted the lid and cringed when the nauseating odour of rotting meat assaulted my senses, but my hunger sharpened my appetite and dulled the thought of committing hygiene suicide again when I reached in with my fingers, and despite the rancid taste I ate my fill of rice and decaying beef.

The filthy teeth of those who were chewing kava made me wince and my repulsed stomach churn. A doctor in Luganville had warned me of the dangers of drinking chewed kava in the rural areas or anywhere that dental care was nonexistent. Although the government has banned the practice, in the remote regions, the restrictions bureaucracy have imposed are seen as inconsequential and are blatantly ignored. The risk of catching hepatitis, tuberculosis, and a host of other fatal diseases from saliva and bleeding gums was worrisome. I spat and blew my nostrils clean, then I grabbed a handful of chips and slowly chewed a small mouthful of the vile tasting kava until my lips went numb. When I added my pathetic looking cud to the growing pile of munched up root and Remmy boasted that I'd drunk six shells of potent kava at Natchara, either my sheer stupidity or my drinking ability spread a smile across everyone's faces. Once Ravae had noisily gulped down the first shell, anyone who was standing near him or walked past him stooped over like a question mark to show him their respect. He handed me a welcoming drink, then I downed the saliva-greased brew in one hit. Although *kastom* demanded that we must leave in the morning, the necessary rite we'd just performed went way beyond swapping body fluids. It had kindled our temporary friendship.

Whenever I casually looked back at Ravae, I could feel his intense gaze burning into the very core of my soul when his unshifting and quizzical stare remained riveted on my every move. Then he became introverted and distant as shell after shell of the enlightening brew opened up his mind and a portal that united him with the supernatural realm. After half an hour of staring blankly at the ground in a drunken stupor, his inebriated look suddenly changed to one of revelation when he announced that his ancestral spirits had spoken to him. *Kastom* had just dictated over all logic when he said in a solemn voice that I wasn't an uninvited stranger, I was the reincarnation of his dead grandfather's spirit. He christened me Tavua, (*Ta* means "man," *vua* means from "the jungle"), then everyone acknowledged his startling announcement by repeating my new name over and over. Remmy and Wintae looked at each other in astonishment while they shook their heads from side to side to express their disbelief.

The isolated hamlet felt anything but remote when Ravae added that it had just become my new home. There was a sudden change in everyone's attitude, and their previous reluctance to make any kind of physical contact with me no longer existed when for the first time, the fascinated villagers explored the body of a much-despised white man, of a hated *disale*. They were overcome by intense interest, and numerous hands started feeling the texture of my hair, fondled my chest, stroked my skin, and squeezed my athletic body. "*Tamamasa Tavua, tamamasa Tavua*," ("Everything is good Tavua, everything is good Tavua."), rang around the hut while I let the men enjoy the novelty of touching a *disale*. Ravae seemed pleased with himself when he stood up, said goodnight, and disappeared into the darkness with all of the highlanders following behind him. Although I was taking antibiotics, a leech bite on my ankle had become badly infected from hours of wading through rivers and stagnant pools. The sore had quickly turned septic, and pus oozed from a gaping hole while I dressed the wound in the firelight. When I stretched out on a woven sleeping mat that was laid over a thin layer of *lap lap* leaves, I felt exhausted, elated, and extremely privileged. I slipped into a deep sleep while in a nearby hut the men were singing and dancing to the beat of throbbing *tam tams*.

During the night I was too comatose from the kava to feel the cockroaches that feasted on the remnants of unwashed food covering my hands and lips. The next morning I avoided touching any tender patches of red skin that they'd munched on, especially my throbbing thumb, which resembled a huge welt. Luckily the rats screeching and scurrying along the rafters hadn't chewed on my food-scented flesh. The scavenging rodents sometimes gnaw at the callus on the soles of sleeping villagers' feet. Ordinarily I would've washed before I slept as I've seen the horribly mutilated face of an infant who'd been attacked in a rat infested hut, but my mind whirled from the dizzying kava and the dramatic announcement Ravae had made after he'd mediated with his ancestral spirits. Due to the actions of the unscrupulous white men that first visited Vanuatu, throughout the highlands Europeans are synonymous with death, disease, disrespect, and deception. To have gained any type of acceptance from an uncompromising peoples who saw the white man as a devil, a ghost, or as a despicable *disale*, was unthinkable.

I felt physically drained by too many shells of kava but mentally invigorated by my newfound status, and while almost everyone was working in their gardens, I enjoyed the peace and solitude of the virtually empty village. Remmy and Wintae were still sleeping off one shell too many when I rolled off my mat and wearily stepped outside. An intense yet approachable looking man in his mid-twenties who'd been patiently waiting by the hut with a roasted taro said, "Here is your breakfast, Tavua. My name is Gramma." For such a powerfully built man who carried himself as if he feared nothing, he spoke with a soft, melodious voice. Although his basic command of English was hardly perfect, it came as an unexpected surprise, especially when he told me he'd spent several months in Luganville and had grasped the basics from an English-speaking friend.

We sat in the sun while I chewed on the doughy taro, and by using a mixture of broken English and Bislama, Gramma explained that the name of the village was Vanakanakarea, and it shared the same language and customs with Winea, Porea, Nakurekum, Matai Lono, Vunasuli, Tapuimoli, and Vavoru. All of these highland villages hate the white man, and if the highlanders are forewarned that *disales* are approaching, the uninvited travellers are normally greeted with bows, *nul nuls* (fighting clubs), and machetes. If the visitors were extremely lucky, they're invited to stay for one night, but of the few outsiders who have visited the highlands, most of them were forced to leave immediately. I wasn't the first Caucasian to stay at Vanakanakarea. An adventurous missionary had also been allowed to spend the night, but his refusal to drink kava and share a meal with the villagers had inflicted a scathing insult, so the next day he was forced to leave. Ni-Vanuatu are welcome so long as they ask absolutely nothing about *kastom*. Those who foolishly delve into the high-lander's beliefs or create problems are beaten to a bloody pulp without exception, and then physically thrown from the village. If a guest commits a severe breach of *kastom*, they're killed. After our wild reception, it came as no surprise to learn that intertribal conflict still occurs. The coastal dwellers from Matantas have been the highlander's traditional enemy for centuries. Some of them have moved inland to Navele village and had recently stolen kava the highlanders had planted on land they own down in the lowlands, and it was only because of an already tense atmosphere that we'd been greeted with drawn bows.

Gramma guessed at least half of the highlanders had been into Lugan-ville at some stage of their lives to sell kava, to purchase rice and other luxuries, or to simply satisfy their curiosity. I later befriended a man in his mid-twenties called Tutino who'd been to town four times. When he saw tourists walking around the main street for the first time, he was so terri-fied he trembled with fear, and thought that the gathering of so many Damates signalled the world was about to end. Despite his apprehension, he'd greeted me with a wide smile when we first met. Once I got to know him better, no matter how many times I told him I was a *disale*, he was adamant that I was a Damate, or an ancestral ghost in disguise. It made me realise how powerful and consuming the spirits of their *bubu* were to these people. There were those who must surely see me as being a *disale* after having seen tourists and expatriates living in town, but their absolute belief in *kastom* ensured they didn't.

The softness left Gramma's voice when he dropped his facade and spoke in as brutal a tone as the others did when he explained that just as it was in the Solomons, *kastom* can't be categorized into individual facets of life. *Kastom* encompasses every aspect of the supernatural and natural realms. The books I'd read about the contact the colonials previously had with the natives in Vanuatu had a saddening history that describes the exploiters and the exploited. Gramma warned that I needed to exercise sensitivity and extreme caution, because simply asking about and receiv-ing *kastom* is seen to be stealing a vital part of tradition. Under tribal law, the penalty to both a careless informant and the recipient of the most sacred of customs is death. With the approval of ancestral spirits, closely guarded knowledge could be gifted at the discretion of an individual but only if it was reciprocated with a gift, and only if the informant was posi-tive that his people's wellbeing wasn't at risk. Without being able to learn anything about the highlander's beliefs in advance, timely fate had inter-vened before I naively had the opportunity to ask any dangerous ques-tions. By the end of the day, Gramma and I had become firm friends and formed a close bond that would one day save my life.

That evening, as a heavy mist started to sag over the ranges, Ravae returned to the village lathered in sweat and caked in mud from running over crippling terrain for almost a full day to visit hundreds of ancestral skulls hidden in a sacred cave. He'd chanted to the collection of bones, chewed *tabu* leaves, and then drunk *tabu* kava to create a link with the spirit world. Although there was no need for him to question the integrity of his descendants, the spirits had reconfirmed that Tavua was his grandfather's reincarnation. Ravae had carried a sacred banana plant back from the hallowed site, and in the last of the fading light, I planted it alongside the *nakamal*. The simplistic ceremony sealed my status in the village with a rite called the *essengo*. Ravae had an obligation to dutifully clear any weeds from around the plant and to nurture its growth until I returned to eat the first fruit it bore. Then after we performed a kava ceremony together, I would either gift him a pig, a fowl, or a woven mat to conclude the rite, after which anyone else was allowed to eat the fruit. Each time Ravae walked past the plant during my absence, it would remind him of Tavua and fill his mind with good thoughts about me that warmed his heart.

By performing the basic ritual, I'd unwittingly become part of a ruthless society whose peoples were impossible to predict and even harder to understand. Although it's a lot easier for a native to think like the white man than it is for a *disale* to think like a man bush, they made it clear that they wouldn't allow any type of compromise if I errantly breached a tribal law because I was unaware of their beliefs. I'd entered a timeless world that isn't divided by the past and the present. Neither believing nor disbelieving in god and being born and conditioned to live in a modern society limited my span of thought and made it hard for me to understand things that were way beyond my limited comprehension of the supernatural world.

Without any way of knowing the repercussions, I'd treated the essengo way too lightly. I couldn't ask about the significance of the ritual until after I'd undertaken the ceremony. Although it formed a bond as strong as brotherhood, if I failed to return before one year had passed to culminate the rite, it would result in dire consequences. If I arrived beyond that date, the instant Ravae saw me he would shoot me with his bow or attack me with a weapon of his choice. *Kastom* demanded at the very least my blood must flow and my bones must break. If I retaliated, it guaranteed my death. And even if I did manage to somehow survive my injuries, what was left of me would be carried to the edge of the village to fend for myself under a sentence of eternal banishment. But if I successfully reciprocated the *essengo*, the kinship between us would be so close that it meant if ever we went into battle, we'd willingly sacrifice our own lives to save one another.

The next day, when Ravae offered me a full initiation into his clan, I was stunned and honoured and sensed I would be placing myself in an extraordinary once-in-a-lifetime position. No outsider had ever been presented such a rare and daunting opportunity. Here was more than just a chance to genuinely christen my *kastom* name. I could gain a rare insight into the very roots of humanity's heritage, from a primitive peoples that had never been documented. As an adventurer and photojournalist, I knew I would profit by becoming a member of this rich and diverse culture, but at what price? I knew it would mean compromising my ethics and beliefs, but irrespective of how I felt, there was a moral obligation that virtually made the decision for me. I chose to take the plunge, but as an interested participant in a unique and privileged position rather than as a testosterone overloaded Rambo cloned with an amateur Margaret Mead. The only incentive to become a member of the highlanders' fascinating society was so that I could gather priceless anthropological information that might benefit academics who were better qualified than myself.

Over the next few days, I spent each evening in the *nakamal* with Ravae and Gramma and hung on their every word while I took notes as they shared millennia of history and inherent customs. Until I'd undertaken my initiation, *kastom* limited the amount of information they could share, and only then would I fully appreciate the implications of becoming a fully-fledged member of the clan. For an illiterate people who pass on their history by word of mouth, they recalled events that occurred centuries ago with vividness, passion, and incredible ease.

The early explorers planted the seeds of mistrust in the highlands when the Spanish explorer, Pedro Ferdinand de Quiros, first discovered Espiritu Santo in 1606. From the time the Spaniards set foot on the island, they faced numerous dangers after already enduring months of hardship at sea. They ended up in bloody battles with the natives and succumbed to fish poisoning and malaria, which created a growing discontentment amongst his travel-weary men. One exceptionally blood thirsty member of Quiros's crew shot a native, then cut off his head and foot and hung the mutilated body from the limb of a tree. The chiefs were enraged by the brutal actions of the white man, and as a consequence, the ferocity of the skirmishes became so intense that the disgruntled and diseased Spaniards abandoned the island.

Then came the whalers whose visits to the islands seldom ended peacefully. Blackbirders followed to steal the natives' bodies, and then the missionaries vied to steal their souls. Finally the colonists arrived to take their lands. The highlanders initial hatred of Europeans stemmed from the unscrupulous blackbirders. While the blackbirders were recruiting their human merchandise from Santo, sometimes they anchored their slave ships offshore and ignited sticks of dynamite. When the explosions reverberated off the mountain ranges and rolled down the valleys, the inquisitive natives, who'd never heard such a sound, were drawn to the source of the blast. Some of the more remote highland clans walked for days to satisfy their curiosity. Many of them were either tricked into visiting the ship or were forced aboard by gunpoint. Then they were shipped abroad to work in the sugarcane fields at Queensland in Australia or at Fiji, where the work was cruel and the hours were long for ridiculously small wages. The unsanitary and inhuman living conditions onboard the blackbirding ships and at the plantations led to dreadfully high mortality rates. Once the islanders became wise to the atrocities, they greeted returning ships with violence, and bloody skirmishes became increasingly frequent.

The natives sometimes toiled for years to obtain a single axe or a rifle which proved to be a poisoned form of payment. Before guns were introduced, warring tribes had merely irritated each other with their bows and other primitive weapons. The healthy equilibrium they'd maintained over the number of enemies they killed and cannibalised had been self-imposed by fighting with simplistic armaments. Although arming tribes with rifles resulted in the bloody massacres of opposing clans, by far the most deadly and despicable thing the Europeans ever did was purposely introducing microbes by returning infected natives to their villages in retribution to previous attacks on the blackbirders. Because the Ni-Vanuatu were devoid of any immunity to the introduced diseases, the scourge of fatal epidemics led to rapid depopulation throughout the island. The only obvious positives that came from blackbirding was when new crops were introduced. Although the plantation owners carefully searched the slaves who were returning to Vanuatu to ensure they didn't take any seeds back with them, one of them concealed corn seeds in his rectum when he came back from Australia, and another native smuggled *tarovit* (Fijian taro) from Fiji, which became welcome additions to the villager's diet.

Early missionaries who possessed unshakeable fortitude and questionable motives further ignited the Ni-Vanuatu's bias towards the white man. At times the evangelists became reckless and were driven by a fanatical courage that did little to help merge two cultures that couldn't be more diametrically opposed in their beliefs. When it came to converting the natives, the Christians had a long and hard road to hoe. The most formidable barrier between differing societies is a lack of understanding, failing to have an appreciation of each other's philosophy on life. In order to break down the heathen's beliefs, those who first assessed the situation by cross-examining the villagers about their secretive religions endangered their lives by breaching *kastom* and were sometimes killed instantly. Evangelists didn't dare enter the highlands. To the natives, anyone with white skin was either akin to being a blackbirder, Damate, an ancestral ghost, or a Christian who was trying to steal or destroy *kastom*. Any single minded missionary who was foolish enough to enter Middle Bush (the highlands) was guaranteed a swift death.

The last cannibal feast that featured a cleric on the menu occurred in the early 1960s, when a missionary who was guided by a converted native climbed up from the coast to Hapuna village near the base of Mount Tambewessana. A hail of arrows, spears, and swinging *nul nuls* killed the preacher the moment he set foot in the village. The non-smoking, clean living Christian's untainted meat was cooked in hot stones and enjoyed by everyone, except for those who ate his leathery feet. Some of the naïve cannibals who suffered from aching jaws and indigestion thought his boots were a part of his anatomy. They eventually managed to eat the boots after they recooked them numerous times and cut them up into small pieces. Nowadays Hapuna village is nonexistent as all of its inhabitants reside in coastal villages. Like all of the other white men who'd invaded the natives' lives, I also hoped to gain something from them. I sought hidden truths, but not by educated lying or by shrewd deception. If I wanted to safely document the highlanders' beliefs, from what Gramma and Ravae had told me, exercising boundless patience and extreme care would be paramount.

Theft, rampant black magic, land disputes, breaching tribal law, and adultery are the main catalysts of conflict in Middle Bush. Each night, ten men joined us in the *nakamal* to drink kava and to plan an attack on Navele village. Now that I'd performed the *essengo*, there was no way that I could avoid joining the warriors because *kastom* demanded that I had to fight our enemies. Gramma casually swung a *nul nul* at my head as he mentioned I had to join the band of men in warfare. When I instinctively blocked his arm that swung the club, and half-heartedly put him in a painful shoulder lock, it shed an uncomfortable hush over the *nakamal*. During my youth, I'd studied several martial arts and had become a proficient fighter. I absolutely hate any kind of violence, but whether I liked it or not, if I wanted to gain total acceptance, the fight was also mine. When Gramma grabbed a machete and slowly stabbed at my stomach to see how I'd react, I easily placed enough painful torsion on his elbow to make him drop the knife. Ravae looked exceptionally proud of my fighting prowess, because valour and the ability to fight are admirable traits in the highlands. The men began smiling and nodding their heads in approval, then they started discussing my potential as a warrior. After a barrage of relentless coercing, I was cornered with no way out but to show the eager villagers a combination of twenty basic but effective jujitsu holds, locks, strikes, and throws. Although the men were skilled with their traditional weapons, even after I gave them slow and patient instruction, their primitive minds found it hard to emulate even the most simplistic locks and arm bars. It pleased me no end, as the last thing I wanted was to teach them how to injure or maim others. I told Ravae my badly infected ankle required immediate treatment, and when he saw the puss filled mess, he agreed that if I chose to use modern medicines, I should leave for Luganville in the morning.

I was up early the following day and walked down a steep hill for five minutes to get from Vanakanakarea to a neighbouring hamlet comprised of six tidy looking huts called Nukurekum. The instant Vetrivu saw me approaching, instead of making her early morning trek to her garden, she screamed out "Aweeey! Aweeey!," then she crossed her hands in front of her flaccid breasts and shuffled her creaking bones back into Nukurekum's *nakamal*. I quietly peered through the doorway into the hut's gloomy interior to get a proper look at where I would be living when I returned. Once my eyes adjusted to the light, I could see Vetrivu cringing in a corner. The ill-fitting and badly wrinkled skin on her face was pulled taught by her wide fear-filled eyes while the poor woman shook from head to toe. In spite of the relatively small size of the island, I was amazed at how little had been absorbed from the outside world. A few old bottles filled with salt, pots, axes, machetes, plastic bowls, and a kerosene lamp were the only modern goods I could see. The odd pair of Jandals, brightly coloured bead necklaces, and several watches that were worn by natives who couldn't tell the time did little to taint the hamlet's primeval atmosphere.

Gramma's middle-aged mother, Voemanu, looked photogenic with her short greying hair, her tattooed face, and her shell nosebone and seemed approachable as she entered the hut to reassure her mother, Vetrivu, that I wasn't dangerous and meant her no harm. Voemanu's flabby yet robust physique and her wicked sense of sarcastic humour set her apart from the others. There was something about her endearing wit and strong personality that made her instantly likeable. I asked Gramma to see if it was okay to take her photo, and when she agreed, her husband Peta, who is the second most powerful *kastom* man in the highlands, also stood in the shot.

From the instant I laid eyes on Peta, I knew I'd have to tread very carefully around him. His imposing stature, his arrogant bearing, and his zero tolerance for even the slightest breach of *kastom*, belied his kind heart and caring nature. I tried my best to explain to them how photography worked, but when I pointed the camera at Voemanu, she looked frightened and seemed uncertain of what was about to happen. She yelped "Wiiii!" and made a hasty retreat to behind the hut. Like a few of the others who were laughing, I thought she was joking and began running on the spot to make out I was about to chase her. Without any explanation as to what I'd done wrong or even a harsh word of warning, Peta nocked an arrow into his bow and began screaming abuse in my face. I could tell from the look of hatred in his eyes that the threat was very real. Gramma said something in his native tongue to his father, which thankfully diffused the tense situation, then he took me aside and warned that I'd come within a gnat's whisker of being shot, and to never, ever, treat anyone with disrespect. If ever I upset his mother again, the next time he had no choice but to help Peta to kill me. The last thing I'd wanted to do was to offend Peta and Voemanu, so I quickly offered them a sincere apology, as when I returned to share their hut they were to be my *kastom* parents. Ravae had granted me permission to write an article that would set my photojournalism career in motion, so Gramma organised a few willing villagers to pose for a roll of contrived photos.

Before I left with Remmy and Wintae, Ravae promised to name his next born son Tavua and gifted me a woven mat to signify that we were true *kastom* brothers. Physically the mat was mine, but spiritually it belonged to *yumi* (you and me), and symbolized that we shared an inseparable kinship. To reciprocate the honour he'd bestowed upon me, I gave him a bracelet a Mentawai shaman had gifted me, which was the only item I had that I really cherished. It was a magical and unforgettable moment when we said our goodbyes, and I disappeared into the jungle to the sound of the villagers singing a farewell and calling out my name. As we followed the trail down to the lowlands, Ravae's last words kept ringing in my ears. When I'd cautiously asked him about the whereabouts of the legendary pygmy tribe, he'd merely smiled and replied, "When you return next year, alone." At first I felt a real sense of achievement after we eventually crossed the island, but then I put it into perspective by thinking that to the inhabitants of Middle Bush, traversing the torturous terrain and indulging in what we consider adventurous activities is a part of their everyday life.

Our exit from the village had been timely. Away from the legal sanctions of the civilized world, hostility and violence were the penalties chosen to settle the score with their long-established foes. The following day,

Ravae and ten warriors armed themselves with traditional weapons and two muskets (rifles), then went to the Lappe River to seek retribution. But when the old rivals faced off against one another, the highlanders had badly underestimated the number of their lawless opponents and were grossly outnumbered by forty men from Navale village who stood on the opposite bank and were spoiling for a fight. Gramma's quick thinking conquered the enemy without a battle and abruptly ended what could have been a virtual massacre. Two wayward rifle shots drowned out the taunts and screams of abuse, and three poorly aimed arrows hissed harmlessly through the air before he threw a well-aimed rock at Navele's paramount chief. The chief screamed in pain and dropped like a stone when the razor edged rock struck him in the temple. Blood was pumping down the face of the unconscious chief when Navele's shocked warriors made an instant retreat and carried him back to their village. The women thought their beloved patriarch was dying and began to wail and grieve as if they were in mourning, but their tears and sadness were wasted on the seriously wounded chief who eventually made a full recovery. Centuries of animosity were laid to rest and the longtime enemies became honoured friends when the highlanders received compensation from Navele, and sealed a truce with a kava ceremony to temporarily heal the rift between the warring tribes.

Chapter Thirteen

CROSSING THE CULTURAL DIVIDE

I knew that from amongst the confusion of Santo's unyielding wilderness, and from amidst the mists that shrouded the remote peaks, I was about to unravel the mystery surrounding the cannibalistic pygmies' existence. I also knew that by sheer good and bad luck, I'd stumbled upon a rarity in an ever-decreasing world. Back in New Zealand I managed to get my first article as a photojournalist published when I sold a story that covered trekking across Santo. My adrenaline bottling vocation slowly started to click into place when *The Great Outdoors*, the southern hemisphere's largest camping and adventure company, kindly offered me product sponsorship, and Air Vanuatu and Van Air both gave me free airline tickets so that I could return to their captivating islands. I kept to myself anything about my travels that would even remotely upset my loved ones in New Zealand. My decision to return to both the hostilities and the charm of a society that was filled with soul-devouring evil spirits and brutal peoples was surprisingly easy. Without any written language to document their own culture, there was no one else who could catalogue the living library of unique highland clans while they still enjoyed a freedom other persecuted tribes have lost forever. I eliminated all of the preventable hurdles as best I could by liberating my fears and embracing my doubts and focused all of my energy on the potential hazards and the massive task I'd undertaken.

A few weeks before I flew back to Vanuatu, a spate of civil unrest made headline news when riots broke out in Port Vila and on Santo. John Noel had instigated the uprising on Santo. He led over one thousand unruly followers, but many of them were using his political motives as an excuse to cause mindless mayhem while they went on the rampage through the main street of Luganville. He demanded the closure of every business, placed a curfew on the expatriates, and threatened to kill the police and their families if they intervened on the short-lived rebellion. Once law and order was eventually restored and the police captured John, he was given a two-week prison sentence. I arrived a few days after his release and used his network of contacts to send a message up to Middle Bush to forewarn the villagers that I was heading inland.

While I shopped in Luganville, I ran into Garae, a staunch looking thirty-year-old *kastom* man from Vanakanakarea. The massive loads of firewood he constantly carried on his shoulders had transformed his trapezius muscles into calloused chords of thick muscle. His bull neck was way out of proportion with the rest of his lithe body and enhanced the wild-eyed cannibalistic look that belied his good nature. He'd ventured into town to sell kava and invited me to head back to Middle Bush with him that afternoon. We spent three hours bouncing inland on the back of a pickup over badly rutted, potholed roads. And after walking through the jungle until dusk, we spent the night at Malories village.

The next morning, as the sun was still rising, Garae's wide, flat feet led us to the edge of the Jordan River. When I first glimpsed a native sitting on a rock downstream, from a distance, the silhouette of his well-developed body made him look huge, but as we drew closer and his dimensions gained perspective, he started growing smaller and smaller. Inwardly I was bursting with overwhelming excitement, but outwardly I divorced myself from expressing any exuberant emotion when Garae pointed to a pygmy patiently waiting for us on the jungle-fringed river-bank.

Unlike the exaggerated descriptions I had been given of his legendary counterparts, Busa sported a short beard, had tightly cropped hair, and stood no more than four feet nine inches tall. In spite of his small stature, he possessed a quiet dignity and had the noble look of a born leader who commanded instant respect. I was in absolute awe and was totally fascinated and drawn to every aspect of his tiny Herculean frame. Although I didn't realise it at the time, the patriarch of the legendary pygmy tribe was standing in front of me. By rearing and slaughtering sacrificial fowl and pigs, he'd achieved the elevated status of becoming the paramount chief for all of the highlands. Garae had merely told me that above all else, Busa was to be treated with the utmost respect. That couldn't have been any easier. After I introduced myself to Busa, he made it known in no uncertain terms that I was the first European to spend any length of time in the highlands. Then in an assertive tone, he made it crystal clear that he saw me for what I was and said that even if I was a reincarnation of an ancestral spirit, I was still a *disale*. Although he had absolute respect for the spirits of *bubu*, and for Ravae's judgement, as far as he was concerned, I was still physically a white man. If I broke the most fickle of customs or showed the slightest disrespect, I would incur his personal wrath or face punishment under brutal tribal law. From the harsh look in his eyes, he obviously meant every word as he mimicked with his machete how he would cut off my testicles and penis. After he'd forced me to dine on my own organs, he would be shoot me with his bow, then roast and eat me.

Mother nature had been in one of her fickle moods when we started heading inland. When I looked up to amongst Vanuatu's highest peaks, dark sheets of water were sluicing down and seemed to merge the earth and sky into one ominous wetness. Unrelenting torrential rain had transformed a section of normally lazy flowing river into a raging torrent. To constantly ford the violent surge of water would've been kamikaze, so we entered the highlands through what was virgin territory for me. When a gigantic five-metre boulder with a groove running from its top to bottom stood before us Busa pointed to the rock and said, "Tavua, you must climb to the top and piss." While Garae solemnly nodded in agreement, the thought of choking on a mouthful of my own genitals if I failed to comply sent me scurrying to the top of the stone. I hoped the attentive audience below wouldn't give me stage fright, and after a bit of grunting, I forced myself to urinate down the groove to chase away Pulminero, the spirit devil. Millennia ago, Pulminero had pulled the massive boulder to the top of a mountain with a *kastom* rope that had been woven from pandanus leaves. When the spirit of *bubu* saw what Pulminero was doing, they overwhelmed him and snapped the rope, which sent the massive rock crashing back down to the riverbed. Anyone who passes through the region for the first time must empty their bladder down the groove in the boulder to spite and drive away Pulminero, otherwise he rains huge rocks down on them.

After we finally finished the heart-thumping climb up to Nukurekum and I entered the hamlet, several older women were still intimidated by my presence. Once they got over the initial shock of seeing a *disale* again, they were as receptive as the rest of the villagers who greeted me with wide smiles and open hearts. The joy I felt from receiving such a warm welcome was quickly forgotten when I noticed a small girl was bent double and clutching her abdomen to ease her pain. The highlanders are extremely indulgent towards their children, but they won't tolerate even the slightest lack of discipline. Her father had whipped her with either a stick or a length of bamboo until blood flowed, but when it hadn't been a harsh enough punishment to quell her insolent attitude, he used a bamboo knife to make numerous cuts across her torso.

Busa maintained his regal aloofness around the others, but in a sociable and accessible way. From the way the villagers treated him, I could tell they saw him as being much more than just their patriarch and as much more than just a man. To them their diminutive leader was a symbol of greatness and a demigod. He told me in a formidable tone that tomorrow he was heading deeper into the mountains to return to his village, and made the same brutal threat of cannibalising me as he pointed to my crotch. I knew better than to ask about his clan and hoped that the villagers would tell me when they were ready.

Poor Vetrivu shuddered at the very sight of me when I made myself at home in her hut at Nukurekum. Even though she was my *kastom bubu*, it didn't help to curb her fear of living with an ancestral ghost. Fortunately the sixteen metres long by seven metres wide leaf hut allowed plenty of room for me to distance myself from her. She sat on her sleeping mat in a dark corner with her knees pulled tightly to her chest and with her head buried between her knees. While she gently rocked back and forth, she was so distraught she couldn't bear to look at me and kept mumbling and groaning.

Throughout the highlands, communal living is the norm. A man bush who lives alone is seen to be inadequate. To be complete, he can't just survive on food and water; he must be happy and communicate with others, because when you talk and laugh you *"hearem gud"* (feel good). Social intercourse is an extremely important part of daily life. We enjoyed the luxury of living as one extended family that had just four permanent residents, including myself, who permanently slept in our hut. Over the next few days a steady stream of friends and relatives visited to gossip, to share meals, and to check out the *disale*. I'd often awake to find a total stranger was sitting at the end of my sleeping mat and quietly staring at the white man bush novelty.

Our hut was more than just a shelter and a consoling home, it served as a symbol of culture by doubling as Nukurekum's *nakamal*. As well as providing me with basic creature comforts, the hut also posed a threat to my very existence. When Ravae and Gramma shared generations of inherent *kastom*, I recorded every intricate detail, then out of necessity, I carefully memorized everything over and over as if I was studying for an exam. Even doing something that seemed harmless, like entering a hut through the wrong door, could incur severe repercussions. There was so much crucial information for me to remember. If I mistakenly walked in the women's entrance, slept on a brother's mat, used his wooden stool, walked past a sister if I grew a beard, sat on her bed, or entered or left a hut during a healing ritual, it could result in varying forms of punishment. The fine of a fowl, a mat, or a pig is sometimes eclipsed by the death sentence if the circumstances demanded it. It was so confusing, as some of the *tabus* blatantly contradicted the ethic of sharing and that gifted goods belonged to both the bearer and the recipient. I constantly kept my wits about me and carefully queried if I had even the slightest element of doubt about breaching a *tabu*.

Both sexes mingle freely inside a hut and can move throughout each other's designated zones. Men enjoy totally occupancy whereas women may only sleep in the rear. I also had to take careful note of the outside of every hut. The rear gable is barged with black palm and fringed with sago palm leaves, which acts as a signpost for the women's door. The front of a hut is much blander, with a flat wall that rises up to a short eave. Males can only enter and exit through the front entrance as using the rear door is *tabu*. All front doors are heavy and solid and painstakingly carved from a single slab of timber. They are always barely wide enough for a man who is stooping to pass through—and for good reason. When Taute (the *kastom* god) made the first men and women for all of Santo, he created two couples that resided at nearby Matai Lono village, which is Ravae's hamlet. Go, Sari, chief Kasus and his wife, Waibetbet, lived in a volatile era and soon had many enemies. Cannibalism and warfare became so rampant that Kasus cast a spell to cause the death of any male who entered the rear of a hut. Even their enemies who worshiped different forms of *kastom* feared they would die a horrific death if they broke the *tabu*. They were so afraid of spiritual retribution that any warriors who were attacking a hut always entered through the narrow doorway in single file, which gave the occupants a fighting chance. The *tabu* ensured clans were never slaughtered to extinction and is still observed nowadays.

Our hut was a typical highland dwelling that was basic yet functional and reasonably strong. Decades of tribal traffic had compacted the mud floor to the consistency of concrete. The walls are lined with bamboo that had been split and sun-dried, then woven into matting with a horizontal and vertical chequered pattern. A thatch made from sago palm leaves clad the roof and kept out even the strongest of rain. The *nakamal* is divided into two by a centre post which carries a tree trunk that's used as a sturdy ridgepole. On each side of the centre post, one metre from its base, a pole splays upwards at an angle to support the roof's under purlins. The firewood rack is supported by the centre post, and the cooking fire is cleverly positioned directly below it so the rising heat ensures a continuos supply of dry wood. Shiny soot blackened rafters run down to pole top plates supported by intermittent forked posts. The thatch roof normally needs replacing after about ten years and the walls last about fifteen, but the existing framework is never replaced unless it's absolutely necessary, for the posts are sometimes gravestones for the dead.

By sheer good fortune, apart from Busa, I lived with the most influential and knowledgeable people in all of the highlands. Peta and Busa shared the same unsurpassable knowledge of *kastom*, and had both instilled their wealth of understanding into Gramma. Busa is the spiritual father to all of the highlanders and was especially fond of Gramma. He treated him like his own son and discussed at length any matters of importance with him, where he both sought and valued his opinion. I was extremely lucky to have performed the *essengo* with Ravae, who is also feared and respected for his prowess as a *kastom* man throughout Middle Bush.

The timeless days quickly slipped by and blended into timeless weeks. There was so much to learn each night when Gramma and Ravae filled my mind with more and more *kastom*. Not once did I ever ask a probing question. I figured by sitting quietly and listening intently, I would gain more respect and, therefore, a much quicker understanding. Whenever they started teaching me, both of them adopted a solemn and deeply reverent tone. One night, when they said we were in for a lengthy session, I got comfortable when they started sharing a steady stream of customs and *tabus*. This is the exact order that they gifted their *kastom* to me. Only the chief bears the burdens of rank. All other men are deemed as equal and must be treated as such as their personal wealth and social status are immaterial. Theft never occurs from within a clan. If something is stolen, it's believed a passing Ni-Vanuatu, Damate, or black magic is responsible. In this patriarchal society women are inferior, and I was to always speak to them in a firm and ruling voice. Physical affection is never expressed towards a wife. The concept of kissing, holding hands, or hugging a spouse is unthinkable, but a father can openly hug his daughter while she is still a child. Beating a wife or daughter is acceptable and expected so long as blood is never drawn. In certain instances if blood is made to flow unnecessarily, a man must stand before his chief to receive a fine of a fowl, a mat, or a pig. If ever a woman with a "strong head" spoke to me in a disrespectful manner, I had to strike her without hesitation or lose face in front of the other men. Women have such a low social standing that, unlike the men, they have no designated areas to perform *kastom*. If a woman wishes to perform a ritual that belongs solely to the female domain, it is simply carried out wherever it's felt appropriate. All rites that are unique to females are closely guarded and performed under a veil of secrecy as men have no knowledge of and are forbidden to view women's *kastom*.

Once I'd completed my initiation, Ravae wanted me to take a wife so I could continue my bloodline. It came as a huge relief when he told me homosexuality is despised and that if anyone was caught indulging in a same sex relationship, they would be beaten to a bloody pulp. Sexual intercourse is only ever performed in the missionary position, otherwise its believed a woman will never fall pregnant. Both partners must keep their eyes closed while they indulge in any type of sex as seeing the fully developed genitals of the opposite sex is strictly *tabu*. Men had absolutely no idea what foreplay was or that a woman could achieve an orgasm. Penetration is forbidden while a wife is pregnant, so she performs oral sex to satisfy her husband's needs. Other than when it's an integral part of a ritual, sex is strictly forbidden out of wedlock. Anyone who's at the mercy of their hormones and foolishly breaks this *kastom* pays severely. In most instances, the offender is hacked up with a bush knife, shot with a bow, or stoned or clubbed to death. Those that are spared the death sentence suffer broken and bloodied limbs, and males have their genitals severed. These brutal penalties ensure overpopulation never becomes a problem and that food sources aren't stressed or depleted. After the birth of a child, a three-year abstinence from intercourse must be observed to ensure the infant gains the full benefit and nurturing of its mothers milk. I often saw children as old as four and five suckling a mother's breast. No doubt the period of grace also tests the newborn's development as the highlands have a high child mortality rate. Once a man feels he has enough children, he may simply abstain from sex, or his wife is given a *tabu* leaf to chew that renders her sterile. Man bush has an intimate knowledge of the natural pharmacy of remedies that grow in the jungle, but millennia of testing for medicinal plants has failed to find a similar leaf which makes men infertile.

When Ravae and Gramma started talking about marriage, I had to listen and translate carefully because it's such a complicated affair. Once a suitor has chosen his prospective bride, if he has an unwed sister, and the bride has a single brother, the groom's sister must marry the bride's brother to strengthen the alliance between the two families. Throughout Vanuatu, pigs, money, and gifts are used as the currency for bride price. Ravae told me I'd need to purchase or raise ten pigs to buy a wife, but if I was unable to provide the animals, then eighty thousand vatu would suffice. The dowry is payable to the bride's parents as a social rather than an economic transaction, and although females are held in low esteem, from what I was told, paying bride price to a bride's family is a public expression that the groom recognises and appreciates his wife's womanhood. Gramma didn't have any pigs or money when he chose his wife, so as an alternative, *kastom* demanded that his first-born girl would be given to his wife's parents when she reached three to four years of age. The child can never return to its parent's village, but the parents can freely visit their daughter at the grandparent's hamlet. When Gramma's daughter Voemabu was gifted to her grandparents, they immediately put her to work.

Gramma and his wife, Petakara, were so saddened by the loss of their child, they cried for one full week, which is the length of time *kastom* requires the parents to express their grief. An only son who can't raise the bride price may marry a girl from another hamlet by selling himself. This very rarely ever happens as he's banished from his village for life to strengthen the manpower of his new clan. He can never return to his original home, but his family and friends can visit him in his wife's village.

Life's priorities are well defined and have a definite order. An unshakable faith in *kastom* is the ultimate as it encompasses every aspect of our earthly and otherworldly existence. A garden provides sustenance to nurture friends and family. Land is viewed as being as equally important as a garden and is inseparable from man, who is an integral part of the landscape. Water is vital to all of life. A hut provides shelter from the elements, from enemies, and from evil spirits. Pigs are required to secure a wife, to become a chief through sacrificial slaughter, for ritual, and to pay fines. A wife produces children, she works hard in the garden, and in her spare time, she makes mats that are used for sleeping, for rituals, and as a form of currency. Children are the future and ensure a clan's continuance, which guarantees *kastom* will always be worshiped by successive generations. Mats double as currency and provide solace when they're slept on. Fowl provide food and are used for sacrifice and for payment of fines. And last on the list of life's priorities, a man is incomplete unless he plants kava.

My mentors became deeply serious when they touched on the subject of respect. Any visitors who are welcomed into the village must be treated with the utmost courtesy. If we have little, the needs of others must selflessly come before our own. They must be given the very best of what we can offer, and we must treat them as a loved one, as a brother or a sister. Even the despicable *disale* must be graced with our generosity until he leaves us. Those who disrespect our hospitality and religion must be beaten or, depending on the severity of their contempt, killed without hesitation. If I failed to inflict injury on an enemy or someone who abuses our hospitality and beliefs, I would receive the same bloody punishment as we must stand together to appease Taute with vengeance. The wealth of hospitality we so readily provided could just as quickly turn to savage hostility.

I must respect all of sacred nature as the earth and the land won't respect us if we misuse its fruitful bounty. We are the earth, for our ancestors are buried in and nurture the same soil that grows our food, which nurtures us while we exist in a timeless world. Because the highlanders share the same *kastom*, we are all brothers and sisters because our tribal land contains the remains of the first forefathers that Taute created, and their spirits and the land sustains all of us. Boundaries stake claim to clan land, but in reality, we are only the earth's guardians, as are the bodies of our *bubu* who are laid to rest in the soil and therefore make us one with the land. Man is such an integral part of the land that the two are firmly entwined with an inseparable bond.

To maintain a healthy equilibrium between our physical being, our soul, and our spirit, we must constantly appease Taute so that he will continually battle evil and help to protect us. To live without trying to maintain a harmonious relationship with the entire universe is simply to exist, for we can't function as a complete whole if our emotions and environment are in constant turmoil. The cool refreshing breeze that drifts up the mountains and whispers to the leaves, the shimmering waters of the fish-filled rivers, the warming rays of the rising sun which cast growth throughout the land, and the soothing sounds of the rainforest are all sacred in the minds of man bush. Unlike the *disale*, land isn't treated as a sellable commodity by a true Ni-Vanuatu, for to sell the holy land that beats in tune with our hearts is to part with our very selves. As I listened intently to Ravae's every word, he said, "Tavua, why does the white man spoil the land?" I said, "There are many greedy *disale* who don't love the earth as a brother. They have no respect and treat nature as an enemy that they need to conquer and control. Sometimes the *disale* treats other men the same." Then Ravae said, "Tavua, when I go to Luganville, I see the *disale* is wise. He makes trucks, radios, and aeroplanes. Things man bush cannot understand. The more I see, the less I like. Luganville is too busy. It makes my head spin and my body slack. Tavua, the more our people learn from the wise *disale*, the more stupid we will become."

Complaint injures the soul. I must never under any circumstances moan about anything. Even during times of sickness, no matter how much I was suffering, I was to never cry out in pain. Outwardly expressing discomfort would display weakness, my clan would be shamed, the ever-present devils would capitalize on my feeble constitution, and worst of all, I'd be open to attack from Damate.

I was hardly entering a society that was filled with total harmony and boundless peace. The highlander's realm is touched by mystery, where the mystical and inexplicable are tangible and comprehensible. Black magic moulds the daily life of man bush in an imperfect world that is often filled with turmoil and whose ideals are far from perfect. Irrespective of what caused an ailment, devils are always held responsible for every type of sickness and are to blame for every death. The villagers are aware that mosquitoes carry malaria and dengue, but evil spirits are believed to cause the insects to inflict the diseases. Disputes are frequent amongst a people who, although they are absolutely selfless, possess an almost insane jealousy of others who prosper like I'd never experienced anywhere in the world. Being a *disale* with expensive boots, an expensive looking backpack, and my other western goods made me extremely vulnerable.

It was vital that I finished the last scrap of food from my plate when I visited other villages to prevent the leftovers from being used to cast a spell that could bring me bad luck or even cause my death. An enemy can be a traditional foe, someone who I thought was a close friend, or anyone that shares our *kastom* from a neighbouring or distant village. If I got involved in a dispute and my enemy survived a physical attack, it would normally guarantee a continuous quarrel with my adversary. Spiritual conflict is rampant throughout Middle Bush, and malevolent and sickness-bearing demons are constantly being evoked to settle the score with an enemy or to kill a foe. Nothing is safe from an attack, and even a garden that bears poor crops is believed to have succumbed to a rival's spell. It wasn't only humans that I had to be wary of because devils and powerful *kastom* men can become embodied in animals, in fish, and in birds. Dogs are the most feared, followed by a cat, a nighthawk (owl), and a fowl. The unmistakable screech of a nighthawk flying overhead is a sign of impending doom, and if the bird's ghoulish call is heard outside or if the bird flies over a hut, venturing outside is *tabu* until daylight. No one ever dares to leave the sanctity of the hut, even to go to go to the toilet. If I needed to relieve myself, I was to go in the corner of the hut rather than dashing outside, which would result in my certain death when the spirit within the nighthawk attacked me.

When I left the *nakamal*, I was overloaded with information, but Gramma and Ravae told me I still knew nothing and had a lot to learn. While the days passed by and the highlanders kept cramming my head full of profound and complex *kastom*, having to carefully watch the actions of others and live off of my wits was hardly relaxing. It was the practical side of the learning curve that I enjoyed the most when I was taught how to reap the goldmine of natural resources from the jungle. I was shown how man bush hunts with a primitive bow and shot birds, fish, and a small pig while I learnt to creep through the jungle as he does when he moves with the land. Although the highlanders rear pigs, bullocks, and chickens, horticulture is the mainstay of their existence. A variety of vegetables are grown, but taro is the main staple, and to supplement our normally bland diet, we gathered nuts and edible plants from the rainforest. We speared eels in the rivers and garnished their flesh with salt that we made by refining ash from the black palm. I was taught by using the most basic of implements how to enjoy a rich and simplistic existence, but I was devoid of any responsibilities and faced none of the pressures a subsistence lifestyle places on the villagers. Life in the mountains is hardly carefree. It requires a disciplined work ethic if enough crops are to be planted and harvested to ensure the highlanders survive.

Early one morning, as torrential rain pounded a wake up call on the thatch roof and I rubbed the sleep from my eyes, Ravae told me I'd been sufficiently prepared, and it was time for my initiation. I quietly followed him up to Vanakanakarea's *nakamal* and knew I would gain more respect by simply submitting to what was expected of me. When I shed my clothes, I also discarded my western mindset, and when I bared my body in a *mul mul* that was held in place with a sacred *navola* vine, I decided to expose my whole being to the rite. The men from several villages looked on while Gramma and Ravae anointed my body with bright orange streaks of pigment from the *ol* nut, and with ground charcoal mixed with saliva to form a paste called *vavara*. Ravae explained that by painting my white skin with the black mixture, Taute would see that I had the heart and spirit of a true man bush who had been born with the Caucasian skin of a despicable *disale*. All of the other men stood back when Ravae placed a laurel of *tabu mele mele* leaves atop of my head, and then tied the leaves around my biceps. The leaves are considered so sacred that only a chief can handle them while they are being placed on an initiate's body. Then he tied on a *mele mele* necklace to ensure that when I left this enclave of traditional life, the spirits of our *bubu* and Taute would provide me with two potent bodyguards who would watch over me wherever I travelled.

When Ravae gave me a large coconut shell cup filled with an incredibly potent kava which is only ever drunk during *tabu* ceremonies, a hallowed hush—the type that shows immense respect during a sacred ritual—cast a deadly quiet over the *nakamal*. This time I was swapping cultures as well as saliva when I knocked back the foul tasting kava in one hit. While my senses start to reel, each of the men took their turn to drink a shell of the intoxicating brew. The incessant rain had forced the women to shelter outside under the eaves of the *nakamal*. If they witnessed my preparation, they would commit a huge breach of *kastom* which incurs a brutal penalty. Only when the men were fully satisfied with my physical transformation were the women called inside. If the weather had been kinder, we would've gone outside and performed the rest of the rite on the *nasara*.

Without any drama or mystical fanfare, Ravae took centre stage and looked to the heavens while he sang to Taute and started beating out a tune on a bamboo *tam tam*. The women and young girls went and stood in a line behind him and began singing and gently shuffling from side to side. As I fell into step with the throng of dancing men and boys when they started circling Ravae, I felt the hypnotic rhythm of the primal music become persistent and monotone. Each thud of the throbbing *tam tam* sounded like a pulsating heart that was beating a new life into my spirit and into my soul. As the potent kava kicked in and my head started to spin, it surged through my veins and opened up a hidden vortex in the unexplored recesses of my brain. I opened my mind, my soul—my everything—to the voices of *bubu* and to all of the highlands phantom deities, but I heard and felt nothing. We danced on and on in a tireless and dizzying trance for several hours as one swirling animal, while sweat dripped from our invigorated systems and the air seemed to shiver with tension. It was probably psychosomatic, and from the biorhythm of my body being manipulated by the primal beat and the feverish dancing, but I definitely felt a newfound awareness as the intoxicating atmosphere dissipated and the throb of the *tam tam* finally ceased. When Ravae spoke an ancient chant, I slowly repeated his words and gave thanks to Taute and to our ancestral spirits. Then we drank another shell of kava again, but this time I poured a small portion of the brew onto the sanctified ground of the *nakamal*, which equated to spilling the blood of a sacrificial pig onto the earth as an offering to invite the almighty Taute and the spirits of *bubu* to enter my soul.

Once the kava rite was over, I remained stoic when Ravae stood before me holding a thorn from a sago palm that had been burnt and rolled in ash in one of his hands and a burning splinter in the other. I was surprised and relieved when he pushed the thorn into his own flesh then set it alight. It glowed a bright red as it seared into his muscle, and after it festered and formed a scab the wound would heal into the *bulu* scar. Mutilating the flesh with scarification to appease the supernatural forces plays an important role in Middle Bush *kastom*. Ravae explained the significance of the rite, and told me he'd aroused Taute's compassion by enduring the pain and that, in return, Taute would empower the *bulu* so that it wards off evil spirits and Damate when Ravae travelled through the jungle. The highlanders believe they are vulnerable to an attack from a devil when they're walking alone.

A boy receives his first *bulu* when he's about five to seven years old and has a minimum of five holes burnt into the flesh on the outside of his biceps. If a child can withstand the pain, he sometimes has over thirty thorns burning into his flesh. A spirit that will help to protect the child from evil spirits enters each wound, so the more *bulus* he receives, the more resilient he becomes to the devils that roam the jungle. On the day of the *bulu* rite, he joins a group of boys who are also about to be subjected to the ritual. After they receive their *bulus*, they're lowered into a hole that's about two metres deep and is long enough for them to lie in. There they live in isolation for ten days to go through a form of rebirth and to advance their spiritual growth. It's *tabu* for the children to leave the pits for any reason, and during their confinement, they survive solely on wild yams that have been cooked inside bamboo. When they leave the holes, those who are sexually mature enough have sex with a widow, while those who haven't developed enough physically simulate the act. Young girls also receive the *bulu*.

During the initial part of the healing phase, the sores normally become ulcerated and weep pus and blood. Both a fowl and a pig are believed to share the same blood as man. When the *bulus* become infected, either a pig or a fowl has its throat slit and the gushing blood is directed into the wounds as a primitive transfusion to replace the blood the child has lost. Once the blood dries, it is *tabu* to wash it off. When the boys become men, dotted lines whose designs are entirely up to the individual are tattooed on the face or forehead by using soot and a thorn from an orange tree to further enhance the potency of the *bulu*. Although I was physically approaching middle age, I was still a boy in a man's loincloth when it came to enhancing my body and mind with spiritual powers. Ravae told me as I grew from a *disale* into a fully-fledged man bush, when the time was right, I'd get my *bulu*. My initiation was far from over when we celebrated with a *lafaet* and drank numerous shells of kava. In the morning I still had to prove my manhood and worth.

Throughout all of Vanuatu, killing a wild pig with a spear has never played a role in a child's initiation—but then neither has smearing a thirty-five-year-old white man with black paste to make the spirits think he's a Ni-Vanuatu. Ravae decided I would have to kill a pig after I'd told him about other primitive cultures and about how the Dani initiates in Irian Jaya dine on wild pork. A small pocket of wild pigs live in a valley close to the village, but these animals are only ever hunted when meat is needed for the most sacred of rites. Ravae told me the reason very little game exists in the highlands dates back millennia, to when Taute created Go and

Sari, the first man and woman, and he gave them a fowl and a pig. They'd worked hard all day while they cleared the jungle to make a garden and were furious when they returned home and found that the animals had defecated throughout their leaf hut. After they cleaned up the mess, without realizing the consequences, they told the animals to leave the mountains forever. The animals decided to spite the humans for eternity and left the highlands to inhabit the lowlands, which left only a few wild pigs and fowl living in Middle Bush.

The next morning I was awake long before the village roosters threw back their heads and announced the start of another brilliant day. I sat outside with Garae and watched a slither of crimson splay across the horizon as the rising sun slowly energized and warmed the early morning thermals that gently lifted the mist carpeting the chain of valleys below us. Once the beautiful sunrise was over, Garae looked to the heavens to seek the guidance of Taute and the spirits of his *bubu*. He pursed his lips around the Tavue, a sacred conch shell, and blew a short sharp blast. Its volley of flat echo reverberated into past ages and called upon the supernatural powers of his ancestors. I filled my lungs with the invigorating and cool mountain air and followed suit. Then we both threw a sacred *oktre* leaf to the ground and stepped over the leaves to remove any chance of our quarry sighting or smelling us as we hunted through the rainforest. While we rubbed wild kava over our machetes, which we would later tie to sturdy saplings to form a spear, we both asked Taute to empower our weapons and for his divine guidance. Like most aspects of the highlanders life, the success of a hunt depends entirely on mediating with the supernatural. Because I was single, I didn't have to worry about observing the *tabu* of sexual abstinence the night before a hunt. If a hunter violates the *tabu* and isn't carrying a full load of semen, his angered *bubu* will hex him with an unsuccessful hunt, and the dogs will be torn apart by their quarry.

Not one of the seven hunting dogs would take any notice of my commands, which made it impossible for me to hunt alone. Most of the ill-tempered pack were just as happy to bail and maul me as they were to attack a pig. Garae's dog, Bobi, was especially vicious due to a custom that's performed on most dogs in the villages. For the ritual to be effective, the owner must be alone with his dog, then he rubs a *tabu* leaf over its muzzle and chants a spell which transforms the canine into a savage watchdog. To avoid being attacked by a dog, it's essential to remember its name and call it out whenever you approach a hamlet because this temporarily renders the black magic useless and at the same time it pacifies the savage canine. Although Garae had castrated Bobi to prevent him from straying, it hadn't quelled the mongrel's naturally aggressive nature, so I made sure I kept well away from its snarling jaws. After we'd chewed a mouthful of *oktre* leaf, we both fed each of the dogs that were milling around our feet a small cud to enhance their hunting prowess and to make them invisible and scentless. They'd been through the rite many times before and started whining and yapping to one another when we followed a trail down to the lowlands.

After nine hours of trekking and having travelled through what's considered prime hunting territory, it was obvious the dogs hadn't hunted pigs for a long time. Although we saw plenty of signs, their lacklustre performance was disappointing. At the end of a long and fruitless day, we built a makeshift shelter and spent a fitful night sleeping alongside a fire.

The next day we were up before the sun, and after a breakfast of *orata* nuts and fish that we shot from a nearby river with a bow, we set off again. We ran behind the dog's frenzied trail while they chased after pigs for several sweat-soaked hours, but due to their lack of hunting fitness and the demanding terrain, they failed to hold or bail any animals. When we followed a well-used pig run, the recent imprint of passing animals and patches of freshly nosed earth looked promising. Our finder started whining and took off with its nose to the ground when it tasted a whiff of fresh scent, then all of the other dogs scurried after him. Just as we climbed to the top of a slow sloping ridge, they opened up with a chorus of excited barking. Garae screamed out, "*sook, sook, sook, sook,*" at the top of his voice to encourage the already frenzied dogs. To watch a highlander stalk with a bow is to witness sheer poetry in motion. Man bush becomes one with the rainforest and moves with an effortless silence, but hunting with dogs is a total contrast, where all caution and stealth and cunning is thrown to the wind. When a hunter shouts either "*sook, sook,*" or "*cous, cous,*" he believes he's empowering the dogs with supernatural strength. Garae led the way as we jumped, sidestepped, flailed, and bulldozed through the jungle. As we sprinted towards the deafening fracas, it sounded like all hell was breaking loose, then Garae added to the racket by screaming more encouragement to the frantic dogs. I heard a piercing yelp and a deep guttural scoff when the pig hammered one of the dogs. Then another more high-pitched shriek urged us forward as another dog took what sounded like a hard a hit. The whole jungle seemed to be crashing down when yelling more encouragement as we approached the bail had the inevitable effect and the pig made a noisy bid for freedom.

We raced through a confusing tangle of rainforest and arrived at what looked like the scene of a riot. Two of the dogs had been massacred by a good-sized boar and were lying amongst a flattened ring of vegetation. One of them had a shattered foreleg that dangled from a strip of skin, and blood pumped from a deep gash in its throat that it wasn't going to survive, so I drove my spear into its heart and mercifully ended its suffering. The other hapless dog had collapsed on its side after its intestines trailed along the ground from a huge rip in its belly. When it gasped its last breath then died with a silent shudder, there was no time for sadness or compassion. We took off in hot pursuit of the remaining dogs, but this time when the boar broke from the bail, Garae wisely called them in. Apart from a few nicks, superficial pokes, and one badly ripped muzzle, the panting team were relatively unscathed.

Living with nature is never permeated with an atmosphere of absolute nirvana. Something must always give its life, and when it does, absolutely nothing is wasted. We sliced off the best cuts of meat from the two dead dogs and headed back to camp, where we packed the succulent flesh inside green bamboo and roasted it to perfection in the red-hot coals of a fire. I was determined that nothing was going to stop me from killing a pig to prove my credibility and worth as a man bush, even if it meant having to stalk a pig by myself.

With our systems refuelled, and feeling refreshed, we followed the fresh-faced dogs into virgin territory. Nearly an hour ticked by before our finder put his sensitive nose to good use and started whining again. The tan mongrel dropped into a wide gut and scampered along a pig run with two younger dogs in tow. A few minutes passed, then two older dogs who were well past their prime left our side when they heard the other dog's hysterical barking fading into the distance. We slid down to the bottom of the gully and chased the faint yapping through reasonably flat and open jungle. During our reckless pursuit the searing heat sent rivulets of sweat into my eyes and my heart thumped wildly against my ribs while we slid under windfalls and clambered over logs in a desperate struggle to keep the dogs within earshot.

When we stopped at the top of a small knoll, after the exertion of the chase, it was almost impossible to hear the dogs above the sound of our own deep breathing. A muffled bark was enough to inject a few ounces of energizing adrenaline into our jaded systems. This time when we arrived at the bail, the divine guidance of our ancestral spirits had provided us with better luck. A good-sized sow chomped and scoffed at the bailing dogs from amongst the tangled mass of roots of a gigantic banyan tree. Instead of moving in for a hold, as they had with the boar, for some reason the apathetic dogs danced around the base of the tree. The natives have a healthy respect for what can be a ferocious and dangerous quarry, so they very rarely tip and stick a pig. I tried to get a clear shot at the holed up animal with my spear, but it was impossible. When the sow broke from cover, I hurled the spear at full force over the back of one of the dogs and hit the fleeing pig just behind the shoulder. We sprinted behind the dogs for one hundred metres and found the sow lying on her side. She kicked and clawed the air with her hooves, then she gave a final quiver as the last traces of life left her body. Garae was ecstatic, and I was both relieved and elated as I stood hunched over with my hands on my knees and drew long deep breaths. I don't know if it was the strenuous chase or the massive surge of emotion I experienced from having successfully made the gigantic leap across a colossal cultural divide that had sapped my energy.

The dogs were made to drink some of the pig's blood, to empower them with the sow's *rapee* (spirit) for the next hunt. We cupped our hands inside the sow's abdominal cavity and scooped up large handfuls of blood, then smeared it all over the dogs. They always beat the hunters back to the village, and the blood-covered canines indicate that the hunt was a success, which lets the villagers know they can start preparing the cooking fires in anticipation of a welcome meal of roast pork. If the blood is washed off when they swim across a river or by rain, the villagers sniff a dog's coat or cup their hands around its muzzle and smell for blood. If a boar is killed, its testicles are removed, they're slit open, and then a *tabu* leaf is inserted into the cut. One of the bollocks is held in front of the face of the strongest dog and moved from left to right, then up and down. If the dog follows the movement, the testicle is thrown in front of its muzzle, and if it catches and consumes it, the dog becomes empowered with such a sharpened sense of smell for the next hunt that it's believed to be capable of detecting the scent of a pig from miles away.

We rubbed the pig's blood over our machetes to empower the knives with the animal's *rapee* for the next kill, and then we gave thanks to the slain sow. To conclude the hunt and express our gratitude to Taute, we performed the *bobo* ceremony by whooping and yelling while we kicked the base of a tree. Garae tucked sacred leaves into his *mul mul* and behind his ears, then ended the rite in a much more solemn and dignified manner by dancing and singing to the spirits of his *bubu*.

Chapter Fourteen

HORRIFIC SACRED INHERITANCE

Now that I'd completed my initiation, I viewed my newfound world through different eyes. Although the hamlets that share our beliefs were hardly a haven of peace and harmony or secretive utopias hidden in the heart of the island, when the villagers aren't following the dogma of their inherent beliefs, in general they are a gracious and selfless people. But in the back of my mind lingered the constant thought that their affable manner could be eclipsed by barbarism and brutal violence in a heartbeat. Instead of life becoming more simplistic, the villagers filled my head with more and more *kastom* until my cranium was bulging at the seams from information overload. Physically I was ready for whatever I had to face, but nothing on this earth could buffer or prepare me for the mental shock I endured as I learnt about the more horrific rites I'd become akin to. I was surprised and saddened when I fully appreciated, but would never fully understand, the sheltered world I now lived in. As much as I wanted to, I couldn't afford to be weak or afraid because an infallible inner strength and rapid personal growth were a must for a *disale* to survive in Middle Bush.

When Ravae began making immediate plans for me to clear a garden and to find me a bride, irrespective of the consequences, I graciously declined both. Crops don't simply flourish of their own accord. The spirits are appeased in the hope they will reciprocate with a bountiful harvest. To clear one of the near vertical slopes where the villagers plant a new garden would require a lot of time-consuming and backbreaking work. That aspect didn't bother me. It was the gruesome rituals that are associated with having a wife and a garden that I shied away from. When the jungle is being felled, making an early start is paramount since you must leave the village before someone passes by your leaf hut. If an early riser sharing the same religion travels past the hut before it's vacated, singing a hallowed chant into the ash of any fire in the hut lifts the *tabu*. But if a passer-by has alien beliefs, then all plans for working in the garden must cease, and the gardener must remain in the village until nightfall. No one ever breaches this *tabu*, as failing to observe the restriction results in poor crops.

Before taro, yam, pumpkin, cucumber, *tarovit, kumala* (kumara), *manioc, shut shut*, beans, sugarcane and bananas are planted in a garden, the spirits are appeased with the ultimate sacrifice. In the remote regions, ten men are chosen to fornicate with a village maiden. When she's ready to give birth, she's taken to the new garden and squats over a hole, into which she delivers her child. Then the infant is buried alive. A newborn's heart is seen as the penultimate offering to Taute as it contains the most potent *rapee* of any living object.

The planting of a new crop involves careful timing. Apart from immediately after a cyclone or any other natural disaster, planting normally occurs when wild cane is in flower, otherwise a garden will yield a poor harvest. If a garden suddenly becomes infertile for no obvious reason, black magic is always to blame. To rectify the situation, Ravae or any other chief visits the cave that houses the ancestral skulls, then sings to the spirits of his *bubu* and into a leaf on a cutting from the *oktre* tree. Only a chief has the right to enter the sacred shrine, anyone else who foolishly enters the catacomb is sentenced to death. The *tabu* branch is then planted in the garden to cleanse the soil of all evil.

Menstruating women are strictly prohibited from entering a garden or from cooking food. It's feared their *"rabis blood"* (rubbish blood) will severely inhibit a plot's production and will taint any food they come into contact with.

A garden is normally weeded three times before the first harvest is ready, and depending on the climatic conditions and the size of a plot, it will normally supply crops for anywhere from three months to one year. While a garden's bounty is being reaped, another plot of land is always being cleared and burnt off. Once all of the crops have been harvested, a garden is deemed fallow and reverts back to jungle for at least five years before it's cleared and replanted again. A surplus of crops is always grown to feed friends and visitors, to gift to those with a poor harvest, and to forestall famine during times of natural disaster. If there is an overabundance of vegetables, the glut is left to rot in the ground. When food is in short supply, if a newborn infant is available, the child is sacrificed to empower an already established but struggling crop. Modern science has proved beyond all doubt that plants respond to outside stimulation such as music, a loving touch, or to soothing talk. The thought of nurturing my plantation with human fertilizer made the decision to pass on a wife and a garden an easy one.

Because the continuance of a man's bloodline is paramount, Ravae felt that at thirty-five years of age, I should have at least one son to look after me in my old age. In stark contrast to western society's nuclear family, the highlanders place a huge emphasis on being part of an extended family. Irrespective of our lineage, we all cherished each other as brothers and sisters, so if I did take a bride, which was expected of me, and if I produced a child, during my absence the infant would enjoy the nurturing and guidance from many fathers, mothers, and siblings. The children live in a world that isn't rigidly separated from adult activities, and incredibly, an infant is given its first machete when it's three years old to help clear and plant their own small garden. During the early years of its development, a child may have witnessed the most repulsive of acts during barbaric rituals. As a consequence, they possess a maturity that stretches way beyond their years, yet they still maintain a childlike demeanour. Because they adapt to life gradually, through learning by example, their constant participation in everyday survival gives them a strong sense of self-reliance at a young age, whereas western youths remain dependant until they are subjected to an almost abrupt change in their development. Sadly, some highland children have their lives cut short and never get to develop at all.

When a child grows into a man, he's rooted to his ancestral earth, but an unmarried woman is a free spirit who may leave her birthplace to reside with a husband in another village. Though it's rare nowadays, polygamy is an acceptable practice, where wives are more prized for their childbearing potential and for their labour than as sexual objects. Ravae warned that as he'd only taken one bride, I must also have just one wife. If she fell pregnant, she would have to deliver our child in solitude, then sever the umbilical chord with a bamboo knife. The mother and child remain in isolation for five days, during which time she is forbidden to cleanse herself and her infant of any blood or body fluids. If either of them succumbs to sickness, the mother is given *tabu* leaves to clean both herself and her newborn, but they must remain incarcerated in the hut for another five days of solitary confinement. During this time the placenta has been left in the corner of the hut to decay in the tropical heat. If the mother and child exit the hut after the first five days of the child's birth, the placenta must remain inside for another five days. I'm not a fussy eater, but the thought of committing cannibalism hardly sends my tastebuds into frenzy. Along with the men and women from my immediate family, we would divide the fetid ten-day-old afterbirth into equal portions, then eat it raw. Those who have eaten rotten placenta say the nauseating meal made their head spin, and was similar to getting drunk on the *disale's* whisky. The human appetiser is then followed by a much more palatable meal when the family holds a *lafaet*, where either a fowl, a pig, or a bullock is killed. To celebrate the new addition to the clan, the feast always finishes with a kava ceremony.

If I produced twins or a handicapped child from a possible union, it would result in my worst nightmare, as both suffer the same horrific fate. One twin is seen to belong to Taute, while the other belongs to Damate. A *kastom* man holds a divination rite to decide which child was spawned by the devil, then the unwanted evil child is placed in the corner of the hut and suffers a slow and agonising death from starvation. A handicapped child is seen as a totally useless commodity that will place an unwelcome burden on a clan's wellbeing. Because a family must live complete lives to be able to properly appease the spirits, their welfare can't be jeopardized, so the handicapped child also dies from hunger in the hut's corner and is then buried outside. It's extremely rare for a child to be born out of wedlock. Without a father to cater for its spiritual and physical growth, a fatherless child is reviled because none of the extended family want to foster the development of a bastard. The despised child is buried alive at birth and always outside of the hut.

Throughout all of Vanuatu an albino is believed to be the direct offspring of the devil. Their constantly flickering pink eyes, which are sensitive to glare from the heavens where Taute resides, are seen to be always shying away from the *kastom* god and looking to perform evil deeds. In

Middle Bush, albinos are instantly killed at birth by whatever means the mother chooses to use. The preferred method is to club the child to death with a *nul nul*. Although there are none in Middle Bush, a half-caste child would be a "*rabis pikinini*" (rubbish child), yet it would still be accepted by the community. In the highlands, a child with a heritage that's tainted with *disale* blood would always be viewed with suspicion, but never be treated as a total outcast. When I suggested to Ravae I wouldn't always be around to provide for a child, and I might not be present to eat a portion of placenta after its birth, I felt a huge sense of relief when he agreed I should remain a bachelor. I'm a real romantic and could never enter a loveless relationship. For man bush, marriage isn't an act that fulfils the love between two individuals; the bonding of sexes is more of a communal act of togetherness. But that's not to say that spouses don't care deeply for one another.

In a world where the passage of time is irrelevant, I needed endless amounts of patience to document even the most insignificant of customs. Information was fed to me at the villager's leisure, and while some of them freely shared their religion because of my initiation, others expected gifts. It wasn't so that the informant could profit, it was to follow strict tribal protocol. While *kastom* can be sold in some of the other islands throughout Vanuatu, in Middle Bush, copyright is extremely important. By learning the essence of a custom without providing any obvious benefit to the bearer, I would be seen as a thief and as a consequence, I'd probably be killed. The wealth of free knowledge I received about black magic was priceless. Right throughout Vanuatu the *kastom* men who use sorcery to kill or disrupt the lives of others are known as *nakaimas*. All *kastom* men in Middle Bush are *nakaimas*, but in the highlanders language, the malevolent sorcerers are known as *matia*.

Just as the Christians believe that Adam gave mankind a raw deal after eating an apple, evil abounds everywhere in man bush's archaic world thanks to the first men. When Taute first created two men and two women for the whole of Santo, the couples paired off and married. One wife thrived on doing nothing but evil deeds, while the other was filled with boundless love and compassion. Kasus, the husband of the wicked wife shared his spouse's penchant for disrupting harmony and being immoral. He wasn't satisfied with having just one woman and lusted after the wife of Go, the other man bush. While Kasus was out hunting for pigeons with Go, the two men spied a hawk that was flying back to feed its young. They followed the bird and watched it disappear into a yawning crevice that dropped deep into the bowels of the earth. Kasus was the more domineering of the two men. He tied Go to a *kastom* rope and lowered him down into the hole to capture the young hawks. When Go was out of sight, Kasus cut the rope in half, and listened to Go's screams turn to silence as he fell into a bone-crunching heap at the bottom of the chasm. Kasus left him for dead, and when he returned to the village, he lied to Go's bride and told her how his dear friend had tragically slipped into the abyss and died. Unbeknown to Kasus, who was enjoying the fruits of both of the women's loins, Go had miraculously survived the fall and kept himself alive by eating the young hawks, but after being trapped for weeks, he was on the brink of dying from starvation. Damate entered his delirious dreams and told him that if ants bit his flesh, he must shut his eyes and that crying out in pain was forbidden. If Go saw a hawk soaring overhead, he was to stand still with his eyes closed. Both an army of swarming ants and the bird entered his dream. Despite the intense pain he endured during the subconscious encounter, he obeyed the devil's commands. When he awoke, he was overjoyed to find that an *orisina* tree had grown up to the sky. He made the easy climb back up to ground level, and then he returned to the village and hid in the garden, where he stayed until he'd eaten the last of the bananas. While the others were in the hut, he quietly crept up and swung open the door. In his usual overbearing manner, Kasus ordered his first wife to go and see what had opened the door. When she ventured outside, Go cut off her head with a *jaike* (stone axe). Several minutes passed, then Kasus ordered his remaining wife to see what was taking the other woman so long. Go decapitated her as well, then he did the same to Kasus when he stepped outside. From that point in time, because he'd murdered his wife and members of his own bloodline, in return for having fed the devil with their sacrificial blood, Damate gave Go the ability to manipulate supernatural forces. Damate was proud of his new disciple's achievements and made Go the first *nakaimas*. In doing so, it meant that for the rest of eternity, a good man could also be evil.

Every aspect of mortal life is directly related to the inescapable influences of both good and evil spirits. *Kastom* men are an essential part of maintaining the community's social and spiritual wellbeing, for they control or encourage the actions of supernatural forces. Their magic commands huge respect as it's incredibly powerful and dangerous. Whenever they practise rites that evoke and repel the supernatural, it requires the observance of strict *tabus* and exactness to prevent the devils from turning and attacking the *kastom* man who induced them. Malevolent spirits invade the souls of the villagers out of malice, in retribution from conflict within a family or with another clan or enemy, for the blatant breaking of a *tabu*, or as tribal punishment.

Constricting prisons and physical policing are unnecessary due to the social value the revered *kastom* men have in Middle Bush society. Fear and awe of the powers that Damate, Taute, and the spirits of *bubu* possess ensures that most villagers rigorously adhere to traditional customs and to tribal law. *Kastom* men sometimes hold public displays of the strength and power they possess in the hope of never having to use them to maintain harmony. In extreme cases where a serious breach of etiquette has occurred, a chief or sorcerer will summon devils to inflict the death a penalty. Not only is the guilty party the recipient of the punishment, in the eyes of the community, breaching *kastom* casts a shadow of disgrace and shame over the offender's family. When all of society's mortality is hinged on appeasing the spirits to ensure a good place in the afterlife, an individual's conduct is ideally confined to acting in a socially acceptable manner that will enhance a community's wellbeing. But it isn't.

Men who wear a beard are always viewed with suspicion, as this is the mark of a *nakaimas*. Unless the cause is absolutely obvious, all of life's misfortunes are blamed on demons or black magic. The superstitious villagers are even suspicious of explicable and rational dilemmas. To become a *kastom* man defies all of the highlander's ethics, yet Middle Bush's dogma deems the practice as normal and acceptable, and the sorcerers are held in high esteem. To become a *matia*, a man must murder one of his relatives then eat their raw heart and drink their warm blood, which is the start of a closely guarded apprenticeship. Ravae became one of the highlands' most feared and powerful *kastom* men by getting an ancient human bone that contains a benign spirit, then inserting into his chest. The bone was from the little finger of one of the most dangerous sorcerers that ever existed. Ravae wrapped the bone in a *tabu* leaf, made a cut in his chest, then he sealed the bone into his muscle by cauterising the wound with a burning stick. Because he is empowered by such a powerful force, he can easily become embodied into the living flesh of other animals, and he even possesses the ability to fly.

Those who mysteriously disappear from a village do so for good reason. It's common knowledge that after a *nakaimas* commits a murder, he utilizes a victim's body parts for black magic and to further enhance his powers. Outsiders are always told that missing members of the community have succumbed to malaria or died from natural causes. Of all the ways to die from sorcery, the villagers are terrified of having their gut removed and leaves inserted into their abdominal cavity, which then miraculously heals. For the next five days, the victim appears normal to everyone, even though they are actually a lucid zombie, then on the sixth day they suddenly die.

Most men possess a profound knowledge of how to create poison. Whenever I visited other villages, a welcoming drink of kava always preceded a meal. Gramma warned that if my body ever started shaking while I reached for food, the spirits of *bubu* from within the kava were warning me that my murderous hosts were trying to poison me. If I failed to take heed and still ate the offering, after I drank the kava it would cause me to involuntarily vomit out the deadly food. The same would happen if I drank poisoned kava. My two spiritual bodyguards would protect my wellbeing by making me throw up. I'd entered the heart of the spiritual beast when I'd agreed to return to this unique society as an initiate.

The physical aspect of adopting a primitive lifestyle was equally worrisome. All of my life I've been extremely health conscious and a fitness fanatic, but nothing could prepare my body for the type of punishment it suffered. It wasn't *if* I became sick, it was *when* and how badly. If I wanted to gain total acceptance while I lived with primitive tribes, I was forced to break all of the common sense rules that guarded my wellbeing and commit some form of hygiene suicide everyday. From what I observed, it seems that compared to western society, infectious diseases are more prevalent than degenerative ailments. Despite the poor hygiene conditions, even the old and frail-looking are generally much fitter and stronger than those of a similar age in industrial civilizations.

Food that's first chewed by a mother who then feeds it to her infant transmits germs which invariably provide the child with an immunity against diseases. I was still going through the often painful and draining process of receiving my primitive vaccinations by contracting the assortment of tropical ailments that lingered in our hut. Slimy patches of spittle and bacteria-infested snot dotted most of our floor. To blend with the others, I spat and expelled snot inside the huts whenever they did, but no matter how hard I tried, I could never match the staccato that most of the men were capable of when they sent three globules of spittle spiralling to the earth to my one. The other microbes and organisms that I picked up, as well as the globules of spit that dotted their mud floors, also helped to build up my antibodies.

Fowl and dogs were always trying to sneak inside our hut. The scavenging dogs skulked inside to look for scraps of food, and if they were lucky, they tipped the lid off of a pot and quickly lapped up the food before they were discovered. Everyone in the village knew when a dog had been caught with its snout in a cooking pot. Screams of "*kesa*" ("get out") were usually followed by the pained yelping of the dog as it received a swift kick or a thrashing with the flat side of a machete. We still ate any food that remained in the pot, and in leaner times, we ate the dog as well.

Most nights' food is shared from a large communal pot. Voemanu would sometimes pinch the ever-present snot that dangled from the noses of children, then flick it from her fingers before she reached into the saucepan with the same hand to offer me a portion of food. When the word "*grease*" (dirty) was mentioned in relation to the old plates we sometimes used, I knew they were going to be a health trap. A grime-covered rag hanging from the centre post would be used to wipe my plate clean if it hadn't been washed before the food was served. The living conditions are extremely basic but far from squalid. Most villagers bathe daily in the nearby rivers, and what little plates and utensils they use are normally washed. The huts are swept and cleaned frequently, and the highlanders are aware that personal cleanliness is relative to good health.

Due to the lack of game in Middle Bush, meat is a luxury that the villagers may not get to eat for months. To dine without meat is to "*kai kai dri*." While eating a nice big juicy piece of steak installs a sense of fullness and wellbeing afterwards, I shuddered if a village bullock was killed to top up a barren pantry. The bulk of the meat was wrapped in *lap lap* leaves then roasted in hot stones. This was recooked numerous times and often smelt so vile when it started to rot that I could barely get past the repulsive odour to put it in my mouth. Sometimes the smell of rotting flesh filled the hut for weeks. Parts of the bullock were cooked inside bamboo, and up to six weeks could pass before the fat stained bamboo would be pulled from the rafters of the hut, split open, and the contents consumed. The only way I could keep down the stomach-churning meat was to swallow the pieces whole without chewing them. No one in their right mind would willingly jeopardise their health by committing this type of gastronomic suicide, especially in such a remote location. But if I refused to share in the best of what my family offered, the consequences would've no doubt been dire and painful, and I'd be treated like a social outcast or possibly banished forever. Although the rotten meat made me violently ill, there are much worse meals. During certain rites, meat is hung in the searing sun until it seethes with maggots and oozes dripping juices, which are caught in a bowl. Then the nauseating concoction of maggots and fetid fluids are mopped up as gravy with a piece of taro, and the rotten meat is eaten raw. Everyone must brave the repulsive feast, and when they do, vomiting is *tabu*. No one ever explained why the vile meal features on the village menu. The necessary rite is simply deemed as an important part of *kastom*. Because cannibalism, becoming a *nakaimas*, and several other rites forbid vomiting, it's possible the ceremony is performed to harden the villagers' already cast iron stomachs for these sacred occasions.

It wasn't only the diet that took its toll on my health. Merely sleeping in our hut gradually wore down my resilience and stamina. Most nights, Peta's insatiable thirst for strong kava kept our hut brimming with hardcore drinkers. We'd sit around a warming fire and chew down a mountain of kava chips until our jaws ached and until a muddy lake of brew lapped the lip of a ten-litre bowl. The mind-bending concoction is only ever drunk fresh, and the gritty remnants covering the bottom of a bowl, which are called *makas* are always discarded. As far as I was concerned, the more men that shared our bowl the better. Although I enjoyed the relaxant and beneficial health properties of drinking a few shells each night, trying to keep pace with the others was a nightmare, especially if we drank a potent strain of root. Whenever we did, the instant the coppery tasting brew slid down my throat, a cold shiver shot down my spine. My blood felt as though it had slowed to a virtual halt, but at the same time had warmed up a few degrees. The circumference of my physical world became no larger than the confining walls of the hut. Once I was intoxicated, I'd sit in a trance and blankly stare at the bamboo walls and the mud floor. If the brew was really strong, it expanded my consciousness to another dimension, and the more I drank, the more vivid my dreams were. My nightmare fantasies were so real and so dramatic that I'd awake lathered in sweat and breathing heavily, having wrestled with the reality of the dream in my sleep.

If Peta had toiled in the garden or chopped firewood during the day, we were usually in for a big night, where we made short work of the first bowl. When only a few of us shared a full bowl, hearing, "*mas flatem*," ("must finish it") sent a shudder down my back before we'd even started drinking. Sometimes we'd begin a session by knocking back a shell of "blood," which also made me cringe as it's on a par with hitting the top shelf. A shell of water is mixed with a generous wad of masticated root and then sieved into another shell of kava. If I was handed an old tin army mug that had been filled to the top, it had the same effect. I nicknamed the rusty cup "bulldozer" because it flattened me and all of my senses. After three bulldozers, I always fell into a hypnotic stupor and hallucinated with double vision. A solemn and relaxing silence prevailed after a few rounds as everyone slipped into another plane of reality to connect the link to the spirit world. Either a stony silence or the quiet hum of subdued chatter was often broken by the sound of gushing vomit. Some would make it to the door in time, while others would erupt copious amounts of vile smelling spew at the end of my sleeping mat, which was normally positioned a few metres from the bowl. On a really huge night we binged until everyone threw up, then we all resumed drinking again. As well as acting as an appetite suppressant, kava helped to numb the discomforts associated with sleeping in the hut.

When it's time to sleep, sometimes the fires are stoked so much that a dense fog of noxious smoke fills the poorly ventilated huts with pollution that's worse than any urban smog, and as a consequence, most of the villagers end up suffering from respiratory complaints. Although everyone sleeps on the floor on a woven mat that is laid on top of *lap lap* leaves, it offers little respite from the eye watering cloud. It was during times of sickness that the smoke was at its worst. Peta created a dense smog to confuse any sickness bearing devils who might be trying to invade our souls while we slept.

I always found it easier to doze off to the rustle of foraging cockroaches after a few shells of kava. After I finished eating or had handled food, thoroughly washing the smell from my body was a must. Even then I'd awake to find I was crawling with the annoying insects. If I placed a piece of *kote* bark alongside my mat, I would be free of the hideous creatures until I fell asleep. Cockroaches have a fatal attraction to the strong smelling bark, which is lethal to their hardy systems, but for some reason, throughout the night they always found using my skin as a smorgasbord much more appealing. I always resisted the urge to scratch the stinging bites they inflicted, as they liked feeding on weeping sores.

Sleep is always intermittent, even after overindulging in a few shells of stupefying kava, because of the symphony of farting, loud coughing, and the drone of snoring that always reverberates around the hut. Once the fires die down, the resident rats come out of hiding and start scurrying across the rafters. Sometimes their screeching and the high-pitched chatter from their fighting was so loud it woke the whole hut up. While they foraged for scraps, our pots clanked and rattled until someone swore and threw anything within arm's reach at the scavenging rodents. The tropical days were usually hot and steamy, but the highland nights are deceptively cold. Because I slept without any type of blanket as the others did, the biting chill normally shook me awake at leat two or three times a night. I'd breath life back into the warming fire, and huddle the comforting flames until I was warm enough to go back to sleep again. Sometimes the creaking sound of our door being opened would wake me up and a complete stranger would acknowledge me with a nod and a handshake. Then he'd squat on his haunches in front of my fire with his hands held towards the flames and patiently wait for his shivering to stop. I'd awake in the morning to find the man bush who'd slept alongside me on another sleeping mat was a distant relative.

Not once did I ever rise feeling fresh and invigorated after a good night's sleep. If we binged on kava, the following morning I always remained lethargic and hung over for the first few hours. I'd often start the day off with a pounding smoke induced headache until the fresh mountain air rejuvenated my clogged senses. I always relished getting out into the jungle or working in the garden. Nearly all of the plots cling to almost vertical hillsides, where simply remaining upright requires careful concentration and excellent coordination. Most mornings, after a breakfast of fire-roasted taro, we left for the gardens at around seven o'clock. Merely travelling to most of the plantations requires a strenuous hike over the intimidating landscape. We drew strength from Taute by singing, by yelling the long drawn out *kel* call, and by whistling to no set pattern as we cheerfully walked along. Working in the garden absorbs most of the villagers' time and energy, so to lighten the heavy workload, a carefree and jovial atmosphere always abounds. Whenever we shouted the *kel* call, which was often, and it echoed around the valleys, we were empowering one another with the spirits of our *bubu*. The long hours we spent toiling in the garden were usually under a blistering sun that tired even the strongest of man bush. Towards the end of a hard day, the women sing to Taute to recharge their jaded and aching bodies, while the men sometimes take a single shell of kava to draw strength from their ancestral spirits.

Irrespective of the weather conditions, the women tend to their crops almost every day. Males work at their leisure and normally visit the garden every other day, but this varies and depends entirely on a clan's immediate needs. At the end of an arduous day, both sexes carry crippling loads of vegetables back to the village. The women normally hoist impossibly heavy loads of taro onto their backs in bags woven from plant fibres, which they hang from their heads. To prevent the plaited handles from painfully cutting into their scalp, they place a pad of folded *lap lap* leaves on the top of their heads. Males always carry lighter loads than the women, but they are still heavy and are strung from each end of a sturdy sapling that's carried across one shoulder. Even without the added burden of a heavy load, in the extreme topography, the climbs from any of the gardens back up to the hamlets are demanding. The men dig their heels in without complaint, whereas the women relieve the pain of the torturous climbs by rolling their tongues and softly cooing like a pigeon to call upon Taute for added strength. A mother who is nursing her child bears the additional burden of carrying her infant in a cloth sling so as it can suckle her breast. It always amazed me when I watched children as young as three years old carry a small load of crops as far as their still developing legs would carry them. Most of the infants over fours years of age make it all the way back to the village. Whenever we visited the garden, I loved the hard but satisfying work and the good-humoured atmosphere

Somewhere from within my fatigued body, a lingering tropical ailment was about to sneak up and pounce, and with the passing of each day, I could feel it growing stronger. One morning, I knew something was drastically wrong when I struggled to keep up with Gramma's quick pace during the walk down to his garden. The worst of the steep declines were behind us and we'd almost reached the garden when Gramma screeched to a sudden halt. A wild dog with its head lowered in an aggressive posture and its snout curled back to bare its fearsome looking teeth held its ground in the middle of the trail. I quickly glanced at Gramma and noticed his whole body was shaking. When he unexpectedly screamed a string of profanity at the dog, I followed suit and called the crazed animal everything under the sun. The canine showed no fear whatsoever and answered us with a series of growls, then drew back its lips and bared more of its savage looking fangs. While I wondered if its strange actions were a result of it being infected with rabies or some other illness, Gramma knew otherwise. The spirits of *bubu* had made his body shake to warn him that a *nakaimas* had fed the dog a small cud of *tabu* leaf so that Damate would become embodied in the animal. Our flurry of profane insults were to appease Taute and to call for his protection, because receiving a bite from a possessed dog guarantees certain death. We had two options: try and kill the dog with our machetes or run. If we failed to slay the animal at close quarters with our knives, we would suffer a horrific death when Damate entered our souls.

Gramma screamed, "Run, Tavua!" then he wheeled around and sprinted back up the trail as fast as his well-muscled legs would carry him. I followed in his swift footsteps and managed to stay right behind him until we hit the sheer inclines. Although I was already weak with sickness, I ignored the pain and jogged where walking was normally a marathon effort. When I reached the hamlet, I collapsed in an exhausted and quivering heap. While I gasped for breath, I reassured Gramma that I hadn't stopped along the way to avoid having to submit to a painful exorcism ritual. His inherent fear of the devil and the massive surge of adrenaline energised him so much that he'd sprinted most of the way back to Nukurekum. He was in the *nakamal* performing the necessary rite to safeguard us and to protect the village while I was still struggling up the steep slopes. First he sang into a smouldering fire, and then he frantically kicked pieces of glowing wood aside and scooped up handfuls of warm ash. He scattered them around the hut, around the village, and on the track leading up to the hamlet. To be doubly sure he sprayed mouthfuls of water in the same places to repel any evil spirits. While I lay on my back with my hands over my pounding forehead, for added protection, Gramma spat water over me just in case Damate had caught up and invaded my soul when I'd lagged behind.

That night it wasn't the devil who made me ill. It was microscopic protozoan that were responsible for my rapid decline in health when I quietly succumbed to a hellish bout of malaria. Fortunately, everyone else slept while the fever violently shook my body from head to toe. Although the upper reaches of the highlands are free of the disease bearing insects, mosquitoes thrive in the humid climate of the lower gardens, and as a consequence, malaria is prevalent throughout the villages. Damate can assume every form except that of a coloured Ni-Vanuatu, and he always preys first on the weak and insipid. After our close encounter with the possessed dog, I knew the hamlet would be thrown into turmoil if I showed any sign of sickness. My better judgement forced me to leave immediately as battling malaria was bad enough without compounding my suffering by having to endure the torment of an exorcism ritual. I was too sick to ignore my instincts and decided contacting the pygmies would have to wait. After I medicated myself, I told Gramma it was time for me to head back to civilization.

If Gramma hadn't helped me down through the highlands and carried my largest pack for me, I definitely would've crumpled into a shattered heap on the side of the trail. I don't know how I did it, but I managed to hide the worst of my sickness while we trekked down to the lowlands. That hike was agony and pushed my stamina into the realm of a cruel and torturous exhaustion. The Jordan River was in full flood, so to avoid crossing the dangerous surge numerous times, we made a safe but demanding detour through the undulating jungle. An unbearable pain in my head made each crippling step a nightmare. At the end of the day when we entered a small and secluded hamlet, I'd hit the wall. Gramma and our hosts were deeply offended when I slept alone in another empty hut, but I had to as something was trying to smash its way out of my head with a ten-pound sledgehammer. I lay on the floor trembling and delirious and muffled my pained moans with my hand while I waited for an exhaustion-induced sleep to put an end to my misery.

The next morning, Gramma refused to help carry one of my packs as punishment for spending the night away from where our hosts had offered us sleeping mats. My array of photography equipment, plus a minimum of basic survival gear necessitated carrying an eighty-five and forty-five litre pack. There wasn't any malice or contempt in Gramma's actions, I'd breached *kastom*, and he was letting me off lightly—or so he thought. We said our goodbyes on the bank of the Jordan River, from where I followed its flow to the nearest road. I was on the verge of collapsing and staggered from side to side when I waded out of the river and lay down at the start of the road. I rested for an hour to try and regain some semblance of composure, then I dragged myself to my feet and pushed on. I had my head down and focused every ounce of my concentration on each of my sluggish steps. When I rounded a bend in the narrow road, the last thing I expected or wanted to see was a bullock pawing the ground. It snorted a threat from its flared nostrils and gave its massive head a shake just before it charged. I dove to one side as the mountain of beef bore down on me, and landed on my shoulder to cradle and protect my precious photography equipment. As the enraged bull spun around, I sprung to my feet and exploded into flight like a sprinter out of the starting blocks. I heard the sound of pounding hooves bearing down on me and looked over my shoulder just as the thick rope swinging from the animal's neck jerked the bull to a violent halt. I burst out laughing when I saw that the stroppy beast was tethered to a sturdy tree, then I swore at the bull and muttered, "I must be fucking mad. I'd have to be to willingly put myself through so much shit." I grit my teeth and pressed on to the nearest village, where I caught a ride on the back of a truck to the Lappe River.

To find a flash flood had swept away a friend's leaf hut as I stumbled to the edge of the river was soul destroying. My heart sunk to the pit of my stomach, my head spun, and my frail legs buckled while I backtracked to a nearby hut. I was eternally grateful when the occupants offered me a meal of freshly speared fish, let me sleep on a bamboo slat bed, and nursed me back to health for a few days. I lay delirious on the back of a pickup that took me into Luganville, where it took another four days in hospital, then bed rest at John Noel's before I was well enough to book a flight to another island.

Chapter Fifteen

WHERE SPIRITS DWELL

I returned to Nukurekum nearly a year later to find one of the jungle's nameless fevers had swept through the highlands. A recent cyclone had cut a destructive path through the mountains that destroyed most of the crops and had left an inevitable outbreak of disease in its wake. Almost everyone had succumbed to the debilitating epidemic. When I entered our hut Vetrivu shrieked, then quietly groaned until the initial shock of seeing a *disale* subsided. Peta looked like hell and dragged his emaciated body from his sleeping mat as he tried his best to offer a warm welcome.

It was hardly the perfect start to another stint in Middle Bush, especially when only minutes after I arrived, Peta began shaking violently from a bout of malaria. Voemanu padded across the mud floor, locked both doors to the hut, and stoked the fire. The flames crackled and danced into the air and filled the hut with a blinding smog of smoke to confuse Damate when he was driven from Peta's soul. Peta slowly sat up, waded through the smoke, and then tried to thrust his quivering hands into the fire. Although he was burning with fever, I knew from experience that he felt as if ice was flowing through his freezing veins. The chattering teeth, the chills, and the goose bumps covering his skin contradicted the sheen of sweat and the inferno of delirium gripping his body. Voemanu screamed then threw her arms around Peta and quickly wrenched him away from the flames. Then she gently eased him onto his back, straddled his trembling body, and sat down on his thighs. She drew phlegm from her throat and rained globules of spittle down onto his sweat soaked torso. While she viciously massaged the spit into his stomach, the stifling smoke was so thick that I coughed and gagged as tears streamed down my cheeks. Peta gasped and tried his utmost not to utter a pained moan when Voemanu summonsed all of her strength and drove her thumbs into his belly button. She scooped a handful of ash from the fire and sung into it, and then used it to anoint Peta's forehead, chest, wrists, knees, and ankles. Only when she'd finished looking to the heavens and singing a chant to Taute and Peta had curled up into a ball on his sleeping mat, did I race outside and suck in a long cool mouthful of fresh air. The penalty for anyone who enters or leaves a hut during a healing ceremony is death at the ghostly hands of the sickness bearing demons. This *tabu* is never broken, as everyone who was in the hut during the rite also suffers the same fate.

Over the next few days, numerous healing rituals took place as several *kastom* men went from hut to hut, and with an earthy practicality, they exorcised the evil spirits who were responsible for the epidemic. There was no dramatic theatre or mysticism attached to any of the hallowed rites. Anyone who'd succumbed to the sickness had to observe a *tabu* that prevented them from eating *pablemous*, coconut, sugarcane, and bush cabbage. It also prohibited them from washing themselves until they fully recovered. The heady smell of rank body odour hovered around all of the ailing villagers. A multitude of remedies are prescribed to heal different forms of sickness. Sometimes sacred leaves are held over a fire, then the smoking vegetation is rubbed over a patient's body. Other illnesses are treated with a mildly toxic broth that's made by mixing wild kava with boiling water. Before a patient drinks the curative potion, they sing into the poisonous brew and ask Taute to expel the demons from their body. Bark from the *pasa* tree is also boiled and used in the same manner. After a villager drinks any type of broth, they must undergo the rest of the healing rite where they are spat on, massaged, and painfully prodded in the navel with both thumbs. Of all the *tabus* that are placed on those who are suffering from an illness, the restrictions that are sometimes imposed on the intake of fluids are the most detrimental. Days can pass before a seriously ill patient is allowed to drink water.

For a sick infant, the primitive remedies can be much harsher. Sometimes pain is treated with pain. Anyone who possesses the knowledge can carry out a healing rite, but only a *kastom* man can perform the *kova* rite on a child. It's up to the parents to decide when the child will undergo the ritual, but as a rule, an infant is normally subjected to the harrowing rite the first time it falls ill after its third birthday. On the morning of the *kova* the patient is forbidden to eat any type of food. Most operations are performed in the afternoon with a bamboo knife that is used to cut away pinches of skin in two vertical rows up the child's torso. If the infant is seriously ill, it can take as many as twenty incisions to bleed out the evil spirits. The stomach becomes so tender that for up to one week after the *kova*, a child can only walk by hunching over, as standing upright is too painful. In most instances a fowl is bled into the wounds to replace the lost blood, then the cuts are covered with a poultice of curative leaves.

When I succumbed to a nameless fever, Peta had become so ill that he looked as though he was on the verge of entering the spirit world forever. Because of his potent *rapee*, he normally performed our healing rituals, but as he barely had enough strength left to move, I asked Ravae's brother, Ravu, who is well known throughout the highlands for his prowess as a *kastom* man to exorcise my demons. His powerful middle-aged body, his hypnotic eyes, and his flowing beard gave him an intuitive look that suited his reputation. It was known to all that he was comfortable stepping into the supernatural world, to totally immerse himself into its reality to manipulate both its soothing and its sadistic forces. From the first time we met I was mesmerised by his mystical appearance and found myself drawn to his charismatic personality. By asking Ravu to heal me, I sealed our already firm friendship.

Only two weeks after my fresh-faced return, I felt exhausted and lethargic, yet I was grateful to have survived the debilitating sickness. While I sat outside our hut and recuperated in the warm sunshine, I heard

Petekara crying out aloud as she fought the excruciating headache that starts off the illness. She no doubt thought that apart from Peta, we were alone in the hamlet and relieved the pain with a long groan. Gramma had been working in the garden and caught the tail end of her moan just as he arrived back at the hut. His untimely return earned his wife a loud slap in the face and a flurry of verbal abuse for shaming the family with her noisy suffering.

The vicious fever was hard on the elderly, and the news that an old woman from another village had died travelled like wild fire throughout Middle Bush. During my absence, Gramma had spent three months completing a Red Cross course in Luganville and had asked me to help him set up a basic clinic, so while I was back in New Zealand I started a charity called The Vanuatu Child Aid Foundation. After a lot of letter writing and numerous phone calls, I managed to drum up a two thousand dollar grant to supply him with medicines. His basic knowledge of administering medication may well have saved the old woman's life, but like most of the villagers, she defiantly chose *kastom* medicine over the *disale's* magic pills, and sadly, she paid the ultimate price. When another dose of fever crept up and hit me again, I was way too sick to even think about attending her funeral.

Her body was given a simple funeral rite. How the deceased is farewelled depends on their social status. To punctuate the death of a fellow man bush, all of the villagers, whether they are directly related or not express genuine grief and sorrow. A chief is given the most hallowed send off from one of two rites. Its up to the immediate family to decide which ceremony is the most suitable. The corpse is laid flat on the firewood rack, directly above the cooking fire inside the hut. From first light until the sun reaches its zenith, the mourning relatives sit beneath the cadaver and wallow in the body fluids as they drip down from their decaying relative. Then they step outside into the midday sun and sunbathe until the fetid juices have dried into a crusty membrane. They do this for ten consecutive days, during which time it's *tabu* to wash off the deceased's body fluids. Then the head is severed from the body and stored with the hordes of other ancestral skulls in the sacred cave. At most wakes in western society, we charge our glasses and drink a toast to the dead. In Middle Bush, the send off is much more personal, they literally drink the dearly departed after the rest of his remains are cremated. The deceased's ashes are mixed with water and are drunk by all of the relatives, which ends the macabre ritual, and empowers the family with the chief's *rapee*.

The alternative funeral rite for a chief has such a strong *tabu* that if anyone who doesn't share the same beliefs views the body they are killed on sight. The cadaver is smoked on a platform in the deceased's hut for one hundred days. All of the relatives sit beneath the corpse for the first five days, and wail and cry while they hold *nagria* leaves. Over the following ninety-five days, only the men sit beneath the cadaver, which they do each night while they chew and drink kava. When they make the brew, the root must be chewed as pounding the root into a pulp is forbidden. Either a length of dried wild cane or an arrow is placed in one of the cadaver's hands and set alight. It's tantamount that the flame never burns out, and painful measures are taken to ensure that it's constantly transferred to another shaft during the mourning period. At the end of the one hundred days, the head is severed and placed with the other ancestral skulls. What remains of the mummified body is buried either alongside the central post inside the hut, or outside alongside the dwelling. Both of the funeral rites for a chief finish off with a huge feast.

Apart from chiefs, all other highlanders are laid to rest in the same manner. Although *kastom* men are revered and respected, they are also given the same send off as everyone else. The deceased is laid out on a woven mat inside their hut, then the mourning relatives sit around the body and hold *nagria* leaves while they continually wail and shed tears for three full days. Then the corpse is decapitated, and the rest of the remains are either buried inside or outside of the hut. For the next ten days, a feast is held where everyone must dine at the same time. When the food is eaten, it's skewered with sticks as it must never come into contact with the mourner's hands. At the end of the *lafaet* the deceased's spirit flies skywards, up to the realm of the supernatural, to a beautiful heaven where they will never marry. No one is damned to hell, as it doesn't exist. Everyone goes from the physical world to a nirvana filled with boundless love and eternal harmony where no one wants for anything. A small sacred bird is said to sing outside the leaf hut to mark the passing of the villager's spirit. A spirit can only return once of its own free will in the form of a white ghost. After that, the spirit can only ever return to the earth again when it's evoked to combat devils and mortals, and then it will have no size, shape, or form. As well as going to heaven, the spirits become embodied in all of nature, and there are potent spirits whose sole purpose is to inhabit specific objects. If a villager who missed the funeral returns to the hamlet of a dead relative, even after a long period of absence, they must cry for at least one hour to show respect to the deceased's spirit and to the family.

Not only had a cyclone wreaked havoc on Middle Bush during my absence, the inevitable winds of development and change had also swept through the highlands. During the cold nights, some of the villagers had started wearing ragged and filthy clothes to stave off the highland chill. Ravae looked absolutely ridiculous wearing a frilly woman's blouse which was two sizes to small for him.

While Gramma completed the Red Cross course in Luganville, the protestant mission had lured him to Christianity. For someone with such a firm belief in *kastom* to have embraced an alien religion stunned and disappointed me. Although only a handful of converts attended the Sunday service in a new leaf hut at Vanakanakarea that doubled as a church and a school, it signalled the beginning of the end of a dogma that had managed to elude hybridisation with outside influences for millennia. A European missionary from another denomination who visited Middle Bush had been sent packing, but Gramma had somehow convinced the chiefs that the education and the medicines the Protestants had promised would enhance their lives. The church was making plans in Luganville for a Ni-Vanuatu minister cum teacher to come and live with the highlanders. It was difficult to remain impartial while a culture which I thought I could only ever dream of finding was succumbing to Christianity. I knew better than to try and intervene and focused on documenting as much as I could while *kastom* still defined daily life.

I'd managed to unwittingly smuggle an ancient three-piece takedown recurve bow into the country when the customs officer at the airport had naturally assumed that the tube housing the aluminium arrows was part of my photography equipment. When I queried later, I was told that modern bows are considered too dangerous, and only primitive bows are allowed into Vanuatu. I figured my bow would prove to be invaluable in topping up the village pantry if we ventured down to the lowlands to hunt game. Each time I strung it, it had the same hilarious effect on the hordes of curious villagers who traipsed to our hamlet to see Tavua's amazing bow. Whenever an arrow hissed through the air into a black palm target most of the lively onlookers reacted in the same shocked manner. First the astounded spectator's eyes bulged and their tongues poked out, then they looked to one another and began whooping and jumping with joy. They'd seen a rifle in action, but loosing an arrow had the same impact as if I'd let rip with a scud missile for the first time. Everyone's exhilaration turned to ecstasy when I told them to feel free to use the bow whenever they liked.

The bow and arrow may be one of man's most simplistic weapons, but it has been instrumental in shaping Santo's fascinating history. To man bush, the bow is much more than just a weapon. It's a spiritual object that possesses great power, which at times is the focal point of barbaric and life threatening rituals. A weapon that's so basic in its concept is also an integral part of the highlander's complex philosophy on life.

During times of sickness, I always kept my ear to the jungle grapevine because the news of the death of a son or daughter not only brought sorrow and despair, it's a time that's fraught with immense danger. The day after a child has passed away, its grieving father has the option of arming himself with either a spear or a bow, and of the two, the bow is always the preferred weapon. Then for one full day he stalks the village in search of victims. Absolutely no one is spared from being targeted with his barbed arrows, and even unsuspecting visitors are fair game. No one dares to leave the sanctity of their barricaded huts as deaths sometimes occur during this grim ritual.

Peta's health had deteriorated so much that he looked as though he was about to take a one-way journey along the path to heaven's door. Each day that his condition worsened, my thoughts shifted to Gramma. If Peta died, because he's the second most powerful *kastom* man throughout the highlands, there was a strong possibility that Gramma might follow his father into the supernatural realm. To gain the full strength of his father's *rapee*, a son may choose to first carry out a ritual before the corpse undergoes any other funeral rites. This is only ever performed when a man who is on his way to the hereafter possessed the strongest of spiritual power while he was a mortal. The body is laid flat on its back in a hole approximately two and a half metres deep. From the first dusk of the man's death until the following dawn, the son lays face up on top of his father's corpse. If the cadaver embraces his offspring by wrapping its arms around his son's chest, the he receives all of his father's *rapee*. But if during the night, the deceased pushes his offspring aside, then the son exits the hole on daybreak without having been empowered by any of his father's *rapee*. Even if the son inherits his father's powers, he does so at great risk as he must then look death in the eye. Either his uncle, who is the first choice, or any another male villager stands ten to fifteen metres away and is armed with a bow and arrow. The grieving son uses a *nul nul* to defend himself and must try to parry away a barbed arrow which is aimed at his heart and fired from full draw.

Every death is treated with suspicion, but if it's blatantly apparent that black magic is to blame, the chief of the deceased's bloodline drinks a shell of sacred kava, then he visits the ancestral skulls. After a closely guarded rite, the spirits of *bubu* divulge the killer's identity, and the chief tells the mourning family who was responsible for the death. *Kastom* demands that the relatives who are seeking retribution must first allow the murderer to flee into the jungle immediately after they inform him that the spirits have passed sentence. The mourners vent their initial anger by attacking the murderer's house with axes, which gives him and his family time to escape before the dwelling is burnt to the ground. The murder's family are allowed to seek refuge in another village, but nowhere is safe for the offender, who is banished from his village. He's ruthlessly hunted for one full cycle of the moon, and if the avenging family are given half a chance, they shoot the killer full of arrow holes or club him to death with a *nul nul*. If the murderer manages to survive his sentence, when he returns to the village, all is forgotten and he's fully forgiven. Those who so desperately wanted to execute him help to build his family another hut, and he's welcomed back to the village and treated as a *kastom* brother.

Because I'm an avid archer, I was especially interested in the way the villagers make their bows. Since its initial development, the bow has enabled primitive man to become one of the earth's most efficient hunters. To complete the crafting of a bow in Middle Bush, this is a necessity. Most bows are fashioned from a carefully chosen limb from the *natora* tree. Due to its year round development, the tight grain of the *natora* is typical of tropical trees in that it doesn't produce growth rings. Bowyers use either a bush knife, a piece of broken glass, or a sharpened pig tusk to sculpt a D-shaped bow, which is relatively flat on its back and rounded across the belly. When it's finished, the bow is greased with chewed coconut flesh to improve its moisture resistance. The first arrow that's shot from a newly crafted bow always hisses towards a hunter's quarry. A smear of the victim's blood is rubbed into a small notch which is cut into the bow to empower the weapon with the animal's *rapee*. If the first arrow fails to harvest any game, the bow is rendered useless and ends up as firewood.

Bowstrings are made from the inner bark of the banyan tree. Strips of the slimy bark are hung in the rafters directly above the cooking fire, where one week is normally long enough to sufficiently dry them out. A surprisingly strong cordage is made by rolling the bark up and down the thigh with the palm of the hand, and then stretching it between two men while one of them twists it tight. Instead of using wax to keep a string supple, a cut is made in the trunk of a *moure* tree and the string is rubbed across the bleeding resin.

Arrows are fashioned from dried wild cane and tipped with arrowheads that are carved from rock hard, black palm, and *telepau*, which is another species of hardwood. An archer very rarely carries any more than four arrows during a hunt, and no quivers are used as the arrows are simply gripped alongside the bow. Unlike the arrows that are used in modern bows, the shafts are extremely long for the draw, which puts their centre of gravity in a better position during the release and also helps to improve their accuracy. The highlander's shooting technique is one hundred percent instinctive. They don't have any definite nocking points or use an arrow rest. The arrows are shot off of the hand, and are gripped onto the string between the thumb and top two fingers. It's extremely rare for an archer to hold his bow at full draw. The weapon is partially drawn, the shot is anticipated, and then the bow is drawn and released in virtually one fluid motion. When you take into account how primitive their shooting methods are, a proficient archer uses his bow with astounding accuracy.

I'd only been back in the highlands for several weeks, yet I felt drained and noticed when I was shaving in a small hand mirror how tired and unwell I looked. Peta's staunch belief in the curative powers of *kastom* ensured he stubbornly refused to take any *disale* medicine. The traditional healing he so passionately used left him looking horribly gaunt and more and more emaciated with the passing of each day. Although Taute and the spirits of *bubu* were being far from kind to us, no one dwelled on our plight or found fault in the gods. While I'd battled my fever, I survived solely on *tarovit* and water and it hadn't taken long for the inadequate diet to take its toll. Once I recovered, I welcomed the addition of bush cabbage, which had been *tabu* during my illness. When Garae unexpectedly gave me a bowl of steaming rice, I was so emaciated that I relished every single grain. There were other crops that had survived the hurricane which the villagers could have served me, but I never once questioned what was offered in case there was an underlying reason. It would've been so easy to flee back to the creature comforts of civilization, but apart from a more nutritious diet, I wanted for nothing. Weeks of unrelenting rain had transformed the normally clear rivers into thundering stretches of dirty brown water that were impossible to fish. These were lean and testing times, but no one was going to die of starvation as the cyclone had left us with a plentiful supply of *tarovit* and taro. Instead of becoming preoccupied with food, I focused all of my depleted energy on the positive aspects of life, and on its simplest pleasures. I savoured the warmth of a comforting fire, of being enveloped in contagious laughter, of enjoying a mellow kava induced glow, and of simply wallowing in the beautiful and serene atmosphere of the highlands. The resilience and uncomplaining outlook of man bush washed over me. I took a leaf out of their book and chose to look and feel like hell while I experienced these fascinating people's highs and lows, instead of being fresh faced and unenlightened in my own comfortable society.

When I was given a small portion from the last of the fire roasted village cats, it did little to satisfy my craving for protein. Gramma used a novel way to skin the feline. He made a small incision in the pelt with a slither of bamboo, inserted a hollow piece of bamboo into the cut, and then blew for all he was worth so that the skin pumped up like a balloon and separated from the carcass.

Unless you've been violently ill and have had to survive on a basic diet, it's probably hard to imagine how dining on rat could be sheer culinary bliss, but it was. Unlike the repulsive and disease ridden grey rodents which scavenge in the towns, Middle Bush vermin are clean animals that made my mouth water each time one of them scurried across the rafters. The rats that scampered around the villages come in two colours. One type is brown with a white belly, and the other is jet-black. Either a bow or a traditional trap is used to kill the succulent creatures, which are quick and easy to prepare. First the fur is singed off and the skin is scraped with a bamboo knife. Then the rodent is gutted, the skin is peeled off the tail, and finally the feet are cut off. The villagers deem them *tabu* and said it's because "the rat walks in his own shit." The appetising smell of a rat roasting over the red-hot coals of a cooking fire was definitely on a par with the enticing odour of a sizzling Sunday roast and sent my taste buds into multiple orgasms. To my meat-deprived body, the vermin tasted better than my favourite, chicken breast stuffed with apricots, and of all the food types, roast rat is definitely the children's favourite dish.

I found it incredibly easy to form a close rapport with the good-natured children. The highlander's strong sense of unity and their deep family devotion has a flow-on effect, and because the children receive such boundless love, they in turn are wholly dedicated to each other. Not once did I ever see a violent or really venomous argument between young siblings. If they weren't grooming my hair for lice as a sign of friendship and affection, they marvelled at its wavy texture and compared it to everyone else's tightly cropped wiry feeling tresses. Once they were over their initial fear of my skin tone, they revelled in being allowed to touch a *disale* and spent ages curiously running their fingers over my body.

Late one afternoon I couldn't help myself and decided to have a bit of fun with a group of quick-witted kids who were noisily milling around my feet. They suddenly became quiet when I told them I was about to perform *disale* magic. Every one of them stared up at me with wide, inquisitive eyes and hung on my every move. As I built up to the climax of the act by chanting and singing in English, just as a *kastom* man would while he performed black magic, I could see the anticipation mounting in their eyes. I cupped my hands closed and held them up to the face of Jonli, chief Busa's cheeky ten-year-old nephew. First I shook them left and right, and then I moved them up and down. From the priceless look on Jonli's face, I could tell that he was absolutely fascinated by the performance. It was obvious his curiosity had gotten the better of him so I told him to sneak a peek inside my hands. Just as he went to pry my fingers open, I quickly tore my hands apart and simultaneously let rip with a loud fart. The startled children paused for a second, then every one of them erupted into hysterics. A few of the boys jumped up and down in a squatting position with their clenched fists hanging at their sides. While they roared with laughter, they clicked their heels together in midair. The girls doubled up and clutched at their stomachs while tears of joy welled up in their eyes, especially when I let out another noisy gush of flatulence when a small boy obediently pulled my finger.

When they eventually stopped giggling, I called for silence again and turned my back to prepare for the grand finale. I pulled my false teeth out so they stood out like buck teeth, tucked my hair behind my ears, and blew out my cheeks. Then I pulled out my ears with my hands, widened my eyes, and spun around and faced the crowd while I made a deep guttural moan. In a blend of total chaos and hilarity, some of the panicked children tripped over one another as they screamed and ran for their lives from the devil, while once they got over the initial shock, the others literally rolled around with laughter. For the rest of the day I was asked over and over to make my "monkey face" for both the adults and the children. When poor Vetrivu saw my contorted features, she shrieked and shook and was convinced that I was Damate when I pulled my teeth out.

Not all of the children were there to marvel at Tavua's magic. Gramma's three years old son, Tutino, had collapsed from a fever. We all shared his parents' anguish, but did so in silence and without outwardly exuding any concern for fear of Damate sensing our weakness. Although he was still seriously unwell himself, Peta used his potent *rapee* to perform a healing ritual on his grandson and to empower a broth he made by boiling *tabu* leaves. Petakara spat mouthfuls of the steaming fluid into her son's down turned mouth. The poor child screamed in protest and began writhing in pain when his frail body was washed from head to toe with the piping hot brew. For the next two days we were all deeply concerned when his condition steadily worsened. When he became delirious and slipped in and out of consciousness, I feared the worst, but the resilient child slowly recovered after Gramma combined numerous healing rituals with modern medicine.

Tutino's recovery instilled a sense of joy in all our hearts. Gramma was so happy he decided it was time to party—and big time. I had double reason to celebrate that night as we whirled around the fire to throbbing *tam tams*. Back in Luganville telephones could dial directly around the world, and here in the highlands, news also travelled from hamlet to hamlet at astounding speed. I figured it was just a matter of time until curiosity got the better of the pygmies and that sooner or later one of them would trek across the mountains to come and check out my bow. One of them did, and he'd also come to celebrate Tutino's recovery. Even without a shared interest in archery, Atison and I would've no doubt become close friends. He resembled his African counterparts facially, and shared their love of dance. His jovial eyes, his gregarious personality, and his constant raucous laugh stood him head and shoulders above the sweat-soaked throng of dancing bodies. Atison looked at me and yelled, "Tavua, tomorrow we go hunting," while he stomped the bare earth, then twirled around in a dizzying circle. After I nodded a yes, I stumbled over to a wall and rested. I was buzzing from both the invitation and from drinking way too much kava. When another shell of the brain-rattling concoction was thrust into my hands, as soon as I knocked it back, everything became surreal. I bounced off the walls of the hut, staggered over to a sleeping mat, and fell to the ground. Despite the noisy singing and the ebb and flow of the persistent *tam tam*, I curled up into the foetal position and instantly succumbed to a kava induced slumber.

When I groggily awoke in a hung over stupor the next morning to the sound of Atison expertly blowing life back into the remnants of last nights fire, it was hardly the perfect way to start a hunt. Although my system had become much more tolerant to kava, I regretted drinking the last shell. Atison transformed a few glowing embers into a blazing inferno, then he pushed several taro into the flames. We picked our way through a maze of bodies strewn across the floor, and stepped outside to perform the *bobo* ceremony. While I lived amongst the hunter-gardeners, of all the ways that we obtained food, hunting is the one I enjoyed the most. I loved walking through the jungle and the psychological feeling of wellbeing that eating fresh meat instilled. After a filling breakfast of taro, we wound our way down the steep greasy slopes towards the lowlands. Voemanu and Vetrivu gossiped as they walked behind us for half an hour, then they dropped off the side of the trail and followed another path to their gardens. When the terrain slowly levelled out, weeks of continuos rain had transformed the track into a leech-infested ankle-grabbing bog.

We squelched off the muddy trail into an undulating expanse of reasonably open jungle where there were good numbers of pigeons and flying foxes (fruit bats). I relished the opportunity to see what Atison could do with his primitive bow as millennia of evolution have moulded him into the perfect jungle dweller and into an expert hunter. At six feet one inch tall, I towered over his tiny body, which was much better suited to travelling through the island's luxurious rainforest than mine. I fell into silent step behind his wide flat feet while he quietly led the way and was spellbound when I watched him transform from an affable carefree soul into a grim-faced hunter. We spent the next half an hour stalking through the lush forest until the gentle cooing of a nearby pigeon brought us to a halt. When Atison expertly mimicked the bird's call by softly chopping his throat with the edge of his hand, the pigeon responded with a noisy whoosh of its feathers as it flapped to the top of a nearby tree. How he picked out its iridescent plumage amongst the weave of leaves and branches was beyond me and the reach of his arrow when it struck a tangle of growth that shielded most of his target. The unscathed pigeon erupted into flight with a flurry of feathers and raced across the valley.

For the next couple of hours that we silently moved through the jungle, luck was on our quarry's side. Several arrows rattled through the branches as they narrowly missed plump pigeons that were gorging on berries or drinking the sweet nectar from the flowering trees. While we were walking to a nearby river, Atison pointed skywards to a flying fox as it eerily flapped overhead and quietly said in an excited voice, *"Tavua, garae, garae!"* ("Tavua, flying fox, flying fox!") Just as we arrived at the water's edge, an *isio* bird warbled its melodious tune. Because we were standing face to face, the bird's cries were over Atison's left shoulder and my right. It was a good luck sign for my little pygmy friend, but as far as superstitious man bush is concerned, it was an omen of impending doom for me. For the next uneventful hour, we stalked downstream by crossing back and forth through the river's foaming waters. The only wildlife we saw were small inquisitive birds that peered down at us from amidst the foliage of towering trees and beautiful multicoloured lizards that basked in the sun to energize their slow metabolisms. Whenever we approached the reptiles, they nervously scurried off amongst the leaf litter or scuttled up trees.

While we were quietly walking around a bend in the riverbank, Atison suddenly stopped mid-stride, and then crouched down ever so slowly. His keen eyes had instantly zeroed in on a flying fox that was fast asleep and hanging from a branch in a *bulacho* tree about fifty metres away. When he quietly crept forward, his silent footfalls were as fluid as the waters that tumbled over a small precipice below us. A smile spread across my face as I watched him move effortlessly and with a oneness with his surroundings that was borne from spending a lifetime in the rainforest. Each flex of his muscles and his every thought were purely instinctive when he made narrowing the gap to seven metres from the dozing flying fox look easy. His muscles danced and knotted beneath his ebony skin when he stretched the limbs of his bow to full draw. As the divine guidance of his ancestors sent the arrow hissing through the air, the unsuspecting bat never awoke when one of the three prongs on the arrowhead humanely sliced through its head.

To say Atison was happy is a gross understatement. My little friend was absolutely ecstatic. His shinning eyes brimmed with bliss as he started whooping and wildly flailing his arms. He shouted, *"Oh, Tavua! Now we will eat well my brother,"* then he ran towards the tree he'd shot the bat from, kicked its trunk with the sole of his foot to express his joy, and roared with booming laughter. As he gave thanks to the bat and rubbed its blood into a small notch in his bow, he was still grinning from ear to ear.

For the next fifteen minutes, Atison danced and smirked and gazed up to the heavens as he sang a thanks to Taute. I fell into step alongside him and broke out into a wild dance to appease the spirits and to share in his euphoric happiness. His overwhelming joy was infectious, and I laughed so hard and for so long that I ended up rolling around on the ground in hysterics. Here in the depths of the jungle, away from the fickleness of what lay beyond our tribal boundaries, we were in our own little world and more than happy in it.

We gathered succulent *meme* stalks and bush cabbage as a side salad to go with our meal of flying fox and headed for Poroua, a sacred waterfall, where we decided to roast our kill. While we were pushing through a patch of knee-high grass, a slight movement caught the corner of my eye.

A large brown pacific boa calmly slithered through the grass and instead of quietly slipping away as I'd normally expect, it kept moving alongside us. I immediately started salivating at the thought of all that protein enriched flesh and grabbed a sturdy stick and whacked the reptile across its head. The dazed creature twisted and coiled until I grabbed it by its tail and lashed it across a rock. As soon as Atison saw me holding the writhing snake, his lips started to quiver, then the rest of his tiny body began to shake. He had every reason to be frightened because not only does Damate sometimes appear in the guise of a snake, unbeknown to me, I'd just committed a huge breach of tribal law by killing it at the base of the sacred waterfall.

I knew Atison was terrified of snakes and although I tried to reassure him it was harmless, I did little to quell his superstitious fears. When I thoughtlessly asked him to drape the snake across his shoulders and pose for a photo alongside a rock face that was blanketed with an impressive plume of tumbling water, it came as a surprise when he agreed. It typified his generous nature, and in hindsight, its something I deeply regret. Not because of the repercussions, but because I'd selfishly held a good photo in higher esteem than his beliefs. Just as I cranked off the last shot, a grinding shudder shook the ground with a deafening roar that was on a par with rolling thunder. Due to the weeks of incessant rain my first thoughts were that we were about to get hammered by a flash flood so I screamed out "Run!" to Atison, but I needn't have bothered. He'd already scrambled across the face of the waterfall and clawed over a fern covered bank before the words of warning had started spilling from my mouth. By the time I grabbed my precious camera and tripod and cradled them as a mother would protect her child, it was too late. Large chunks of rock exploded from the face of the waterfall and began raining all around me. I was standing in the middle of a pool, and the way the water erupted from the hail of boulders amplified the sudden ferocity of the landslide. When apart from the sound of the cascading waterfall everything fell silent, we looked at each other and burst into nervous laughter. It was a great feeling to be able to stand there and joke about how incredibly lucky we were to have walked away unscathed.

While Atison started a fire and singed the fur off the flying fox, I looked at the snake through ravenous eyes. The protein that my body so desperately craved and the alarming amount of weight I'd lost from the fever made the thought of sinking my teeth into the snake's rejuvenating flesh more and more appealing. When I threw the snake into the glowing coals, if Atison had informed me of the repercussions or if I was aware that I was breaking a *tabu*, it would've been left to rot amongst the jungles detritus. If it was anyone else, they wouldn't have hesitated to tell me I was about to breach one of the numerous tribal laws. Although he was very much his own man, Atison treated me with an almost subservient respect. Sometimes primitive peoples can be difficult to understand, but it still doesn't explain why he never warned me not to eat the snake's forbidden flesh as reptiles that inhabit a *tabu* place are never eaten. Snakes that are caught in the jungle are fair game, but due to the villagers' inherent fear of Damate, and because it's quite common for them to fall ill when they dine on snake, most highlanders won't eat them. The devil is always to blame for the illness, which is treated by chewing a *tabu* leaf that drives out his malicious spirit. Because every garden is sacred, snakes that inhabit a plantation are never eaten. This serves a double purpose as they help to control the rats which live off of taro and other crops.

A geologist would probably have a rational explanation as to what had caused the rock face to explode. Maybe after the constant deluge of rain, the searing heat of the tropical sun had combined with the forces of nature to loosen the rocks, or maybe a tremor had caused the landslide. Atison knew otherwise. He believed that supernatural rather than natural powers had made angered spirits shower the rocks all around us. To kill a snake in a consecrated spot was bad enough, but now that I'd eaten it, I'd become possessed by the devil. During the walk back to Nukurekum, Atison became grim faced and fell into an uncharacteristic silence.

When he dutifully broke the news of my having killed and eaten the snake, the villagers were horrified. Once I fully understood the consequences of my sumptuous meal, it was a huge relief to see that Busa hadn't paid us a visit. As small consolation, it meant I wasn't about to be shot and cannibalised for my honest mistake. Peta was still gravely ill and barely able to move, so with a sense of urgency, he sent a runner to get Ravu. Everyone gave me a wide berth. They were all adamant that I was no longer human and of flesh and blood. I was a devil. When I ate the succulent serving of snake, Damate had become embodied in my spirit and my soul.

Ravu was mortified by my actions and started making immediate preparations for an exorcism to restore harmony to my physical and spiritual wellbeing by purging the demon from my body. He rushed out the door, sped down to his garden, and returned just as the sun had slipped beneath the horizon. When I watched him chewing yellow two-day kava, I shuddered. Ravu told me that I had to wear a *mul mul*, which I quickly threw on. Then, to help nullify the effects of the *tabu* root, I raided the nearest cooking pot and gorged myself on as much bush cabbage and taro as my stomach could hold. After Ravu finished preparing the brew, he filled a huge cup made from a coconut shell to the brim. He then led me to my sleeping mat, where I gulped down mouthful after mouthful of the vile tasting concoction until I finished the shell in one hit. When the acrid brew made me retch, I grit my teeth and fought the urge to vomit. The fires had been stoked so much that a stifling cloud of smoke choked the air as Ravu started singing to Taute. From the healing rituals I'd previously endured, I knew the rite would involve a certain amount of discomfort. I felt a huge sense of relief when the kava kicked and helped to dull the pain when Ravu used all of his brute strength to flay my naked back with a branch of wild kava. The kava was so overwhelming that my vision doubled, my whole body started shaking violently, and my mind spiralled into a dimension that distorted any rational thinking. I collapsed in a quivering heap and again wanted to throw up, but I fought the feeling of nausea in my churning stomach. The floor began to gently rock and the hut reeled as my brain started spinning around inside my skull. I felt as if I was floating when Ravu straddled my body, then sat on my hips and started spitting large globules of phlegm in my face and on my torso. Even though it hurt like hell when he kept viciously grabbing my stomach to rub in the spit, I refused to wince or show any signs of weakness as regaining the villager's full respect was paramount. A wave of nauseating pain swept through my body when he used all of his strength and drove his thumbs deep into my navel. The sound of his monotone chanting was the last thing my traumatized senses registered when I mercifully drifted into unconsciousness.

For the next two days (how the kava derived its name) I was rendered paralytic in an unfamiliar world that was filled with oblivion and the most hellish nightmares imaginable. I was so helpless that I couldn't even brush off the cockroaches feeding on my unwashed hands and lips. When I awoke and I nervously clutched at my stomach and testicles, it was a huge relief to find that the evil spirits hadn't been bled from my torso—and an even bigger relief to feel that my manhood was still intact. If Busa had been around to inflict the sentence he threatened me with if I breached tribal law, he probably would've sliced off my genitals. Now that I was a mere mortal again, I hoped I wouldn't have to face any further punishment from him. My damp *mul mul* reeked of urine, and I was still shaking from head to toe. Apart from the bluish-grey skin on my swollen lips and fingers, pissing myself in my sleep, and having to blow a cockroach from my nostril when I awoke, I'd gotten off extremely lightly. Voemanu shrieked with horror when she saw me snort the insect from my nose. The Dani in Irian Jaya believe that evil spirits are sometimes expelled through their nostrils, and Voemanu was also convinced that she'd just seen a devil and rushed outside to find Ravu. When she returned with him, he performed another less painful ritual to purify my tarnished soul.

When Gramma saw me lying comatose on my mat and found out why, he was scathing. He didn't hold back when I awoke, and told me I'd shamed everyone from my bloodline and from my totem, which is the flying fox. In a heated flurry of abuse, he said it was okay for me to eat a bat, but a snake had never been a part of my lineage and that I must never dine on the reptile in a *tabu* place again. He told me I was lucky, that he'd had the clever foresight to send a message to Winea that said my breach of *kastom* had already been dealt with, which no doubt saved me from facing a more brutal reprimand from Busa. Now that my soul was cleansed, thankfully the shame I cast over my clan and everyone belonging to the flying fox had been lifted.

Once he cooled off, Gramma sat on a log next to my mat and said, "Tavua, it is hard if you don't know about *kastom*. I will tell you more about your bloodline." The close affinity man bush has with his totem stretches beyond the realm of most primitive peoples in that although the bond is sacred, the highlanders' intimate relationship with their given totem allows them to eat it. In the past, each of the eight villages originally worshiped a single totemic object that was unique to their bloodline. Because each clan is descended from a common ancestor who was akin to their totem, it enhances a feeling of unity and belonging and helps to form a strong social and spiritual bond between the members of a village. This is why many villagers share the same name. When an infant reaches three to four years of age, it receives its true *kastom* name from a namesake who shares the same totem. The child's namesake gifts either a pig, a fowl, or a mat to the infant. The parents also receive a similar gift, then christen their offspring with a kava ceremony. When cannibalism and warfare were rampant, the eight villages worshiped the Taro, pig, flying fox, spider, fire, water, wild taro, and the owl as totemic objects. Nowadays the christening rite is seen as a vital vehicle for strengthening the peaceful alliances with other villages, and as a consequence, there are now members of different clans who share the same totem.

Gramma shared the *kastom* story which tells of how the flying fox bloodline originated. One night, a bat flew into the hut of an unmarried woman. When he saw she was alone, the bat fornicated with her and as a result of the union, she gave birth to a son, the first male of the flying fox clan. The highlanders call the variety of black palm that is devoid of needles *wuluwulu garae*. One day a man was walking through the jungle when he heard a small girl crying. He climbed up to the top of a ridge where *wuluwulu garae* always grow, and there, nestled in the fronds of a black palm, he found a small girl who had been abandoned by the devil. He held her in his arms and shouted, *"Wono garae"* ("You are of the flying fox"), as the palm shares the same name as the bat. The totemic children married each other and formed the true bloodline of the flying fox.

Whenever a highlander passes through a village sharing the same *kastom*, taking food from a vacant hut is welcomed and expected. Because I'm of the flying fox, I helped myself, but I always left a small branch from the *arabous* tree above the front door so the occupants knew that the food wasn't stolen and from which bloodline the hungry visitor belonged to. No matter how much you've previously eaten, failing to share a portion of food from every hut you visit is an insult to the host.

Both Gramma and Busa are of the taro. While a woman worked in her garden she heard a baby crying from inside a taro plant. She rescued the infant and reared the child as if it were her own, who, in turn, produced the bloodline for taro. This is why taro became the staple food for all of the highlands.

Our totems are linked to the supernatural, as is everything during our life on earth. Even the cockroaches that feasted on my lips while I lay comatose from the exorcism are closely linked to Damate, which explains Voemanu's horror when I expelled one of the insects from my nostril. Most of the huts are virtually free of the pests, but there are those that suffer from heavy infestations which are believed to be cursed. Gramma told me that nowadays the pygmy village was clean of the scourge of cockroaches, but in the past the remote hamlet was crawling with the vile insects. Busa's mother, Notsan, had inherited the curse from her own mother, then the instant Notsan died all the cockroaches mysteriously vanished.

Up until 1994, Ravae's hut was alive with the insects. Damate had shifted the plague from the pygmy hamlet by hexing Vatious, Ravae's grandmother. The infestation was so bad that cockroaches continually rained down from the rafters and made trying to eat or drink a nightmare. The villagers spent more time picking the pests from their food than they did eating. In the end, Vatious had resigned herself to consuming the vile insects as well. When she passed away, the hordes of cockroaches suddenly and inexplicably disappeared from the hut.

Vatious had passed the plague of repulsive insects onto her relative, Voemaburu, who lives in the hut next to us with her son Jonli, her sister Estala, and Malon, her brother in law. Though they were nothing but civil to us, by highland standards, they were the neighbours from hell. Voemaburu and Estala are a rarity in Middle Bush society, where screaming, swearing, and disputing over petty items is deeply frowned upon. They constantly argued. Things got so bad that Voemaburu's sister, Simi, moved to Vanakanakarea after Voemaburu chased her with a machete and threatened her with extinction. If Voemaburu had caught her, she probably would've been hacked to pieces. If they weren't quarrelling, a continuous tangle of chatter drifted across to our hut. Peta calls them *tongan* (noisy) and often yelled out to our droning neighbours to shut up. Especially when they get up at four o'clock every morning to either argue or engage in a never-ending flurry of deep conversation. When I shouted out that they all had mouths that were big enough for two sets of teeth and to shut up, everyone in our hut went into hysterics. In spite of the reputation they carried, they were nothing but friendly and were always kind to me. The bickering was of no consequence to my wellbeing, but what did bother me was the curse of cockroaches that Voemaburu had been damned with, as up until Vatious's death, Nukurekum had been virtually free of the annoying pests.

Voemaburu is by far the most primitive looking woman I've seen anywhere in Vanuatu and bears a striking resemblance to an Australian aborigine. It's interesting because in the north of Santo, a village uses a boomerang called the *tihok* which is believed to be indigenous to Vanuatu. The diversity of both physical and facial features throughout Middle Bush is astounding. Ethnologists who studied skeletal remains from the highlands could easily assume the pygmies and the taller villagers never shared the same bloodline, whereas in fact, they are closely related. Unlike some indigenous peoples who closely resemble one another, the highlanders are as diverse in their appearance as individuals are in some European cultures.

Chapter Sixteen

WINEA

From deep in the highlands Atison had relayed a message across the mountains to Nakurekum. My little pygmy friend had finally oiled the hinges to the closed door I'd been so patiently waiting to open. It had taken three years to hear Garae's blissful words, "Tavua, Atison has sent for you. Ravu will take you to Winea tomorrow." I was bursting with excitement when he added that Atison had also made arrangements for me to go pig hunting with two pygmy archers. My body trembled, not from the mounting anticipation, but from the dwindling effects of the two-day kava. I was slowly recovering but the harsh exorcism had taken a heavy toll on my health. The wild shaking in my hands had healed to a slight tremor, and the chronic diarrhoea and my quivering body were little more than a slight nuisance. I'd waited so long for Garae's fantastic news that nothing was going to stop me from visiting Winea. Garae's son, Lono, had followed him into our hut and had a badly infected eye that kept discharging a steady flow of tears down his cheek. Garae gently prised Lono's puss filled eyelids apart, inspected the infection, and spat a huge globule of saliva into the bloodshot eye. Lono blinked hard, smiled at his father, and thanked him for driving the devil from his eye as a bead of spit slowly slid down his face.

I'd formed a close friendship with Ravu and looked forward to travelling with him, but not until he first became his own patient. Late that evening as we sat around my fire, I caught the heady whiff of his rotting flesh when he unwrapped a bandage of leaves from around his finger. He wiped the blade of my Duel pig-hunting knife clean on his grime covered *mul mul*, then with the precise skill of a surgeon he pushed its razor sharp edge through the vile smelling wound and carefully sliced away the top layer of his badly infected finger. I helped him with his primitive surgery by using bamboo tongs to hold a coconut shell cup that was filled with boiling coconut oil over the embers. When the oil spat onto the back of my hand, the string of profanity I muttered when a red welt appeared on my skin spread a smile across Ravu's tired looking face. He dipped a piece of fibrous coconut husk into the smoking oil then dripped the hot fluid onto the open wound. His head swung from side to side, he screwed his eyes tightly shut, and he grit his teeth while he fought the pain in total silence. It must have been sheer agony. The type of torment that over-whelms your mind with white hot flashes of pain that are so severe they block out all other thoughts. He endured the torture of applying the searing oil several times until the steaming fluid completely covered his wound, and throughout the excruciating ordeal he never once uttered a single sound.

A bamboo knife is normally used to cut away the evil spirit that was responsible for his puss filled mess, but Ravu was so impressed with the sharpness of my knife that he decided its keen edge would be more effective at driving away the devil. Voemanu finished off his treatment with a healing ritual, then she tied *tabu* vines around his wrist and bicep to act as a spiritual blockade and to hopefully prevent the sickness from spreading throughout the rest of his body. He guzzled down an extra strong shell of medicinal kava, and within minutes he was fast asleep.

When I awoke the next morning, Ravu had been up before the sun and was roasting taro in the embers of my fire. He looked tired and barely well enough to walk, let alone cross the physically demanding mountains that lay ahead of us. I looked down at my trembling hands, then to his drained complexion, and felt we'd both share the same level of fitness when we started squelching along the trail.

The tiresome slog through the waterlogged terrain taxed our already weary bodies. For someone who looked dead on his feet, Ravu possessed a resilient mindset and an incredible stamina that seemed to be impervious to pain. When we reached the Lappe River, fording its foaming waters at the normal crossing would've been suicidal. The rainforest had lived up to its name, and weeks of unrelenting heavy rain had transformed a normally gentle flowing river into a boiling surge. We traipsed downstream to find a quieter stretch of water, but even then we had to make a hazardous crossing. While we sidled along the riverbank to the base of a sheer climb, Ravu told me the *kastom* story that explains why the Lappe River usually has a gentle current. The first time the Jordan River flowed down to the sea, the unfriendly ocean pushed it back up to the mountains. The same thing happened to the Lappe River the first time it tumbled down from the highlands. This enraged the much more powerful Jordan River, who boasted to the Lappe River that next time, it would overwhelm the ocean. It unleashed all of its power in one thunderous roar and sluiced into a submissive sea. The victorious Jordan River yelled to the Lappe River to come down from Middle Bush, but the Lappe River was still wary of the gigantic sea and flowed quietly into the becalmed ocean. This is the reason why the Jordan River sometimes rumbles, whereas the Lappe River nearly always murmurs down to the coast from the valleys surrounding Santo peak.

As Ravu craned his neck and looked up at a daunting almost vertical climb, he said, "*Tavua, kevoro. Yumi mas go first time*" ("Tavua, let's go. We must walk quickly"). *Kastom* required us to scale the massive face as quickly as was humanly possible, without resting until we reached the halfway point, where in the past, a sentry was always posted. When I tried to stay in step with Ravu's blistering pace, it became a torturous grind that made my entire body beg for rest. By the time we finally rested against a tree that had a weathered conch shell nestled in a fork in its lower branches, my protesting leg muscles were ablaze, my pulse raced, and my burning lungs gasped for air. For someone who was unwell, Ravu's fitness and incredible recovery rate were mind-boggling. He casually wiped the sweat from his eyes, smirked at my deep breathing, then rolled a cigarette and commented on how exceptionally strong I was for a *disale*.

From this lofty vantage point it was easy to see how a sentinel could cast a watchful eye over the canopy of interlocking treetops to across to the valleys and basins in search of approaching enemies. The warning blast he blew on the *tavue* shell (conch shell) if he saw any rival warriors alerted Winea's inhabitants and gave them plenty of time to prepare for an impending attack. With a village name like Winea, which translates into "to eat man" due to the pygmies' penchant for dining on human flesh, it came as no surprise when, according to Busa, I was about to be the first white man to walk into the village for nearly a century. When he was a young boy, blood feuds were an institution, and the enemy clans living in close proximity treated the ridge-top hamlet with permanent suspicion and antagonism. In spite of their small stature, the pygmies commanded huge respect throughout the rugged interior. They also evoked so much fear that no one ever dared to wander into their territory unannounced, as to do so invited certain death from a hail of barbed arrows.

The pygmies' cannibalistic tendencies nearly led to Winea's demise when warring clans from the surrounding valleys, who were tired of living in constant fear and were fuelled with vengeance from previous killings, united to deliver the ultimate retribution. Under the veil of darkness, a swarm of heavily armed warriors made the arduous climb up to the remote hamlet. One of them crept ahead and expertly dispatched Winea's inattentive sentry with a well-placed arrow. The *tavue* shell never blasted a warning to the pygmies, and the next time its echo reverberated throughout the rainforest, its flat pitch would be heard by the ghosts of the dead.

A virtual massacre ensued during the ambush, when volley after volley of arrows hissed through the air then sliced into human flesh. Unlike the other paybacks, where only enough blood was spilled to appease the spirits, this time absolutely no one was going to be spared. Several lucky pygmies who saw the futility of trying to retaliate while they were so grossly outnumbered fled into the sanctity of the gloomy jungle. Those who were captured and held in a bamboo cage died a cruel and horrific death. The shouts of the triumphant warriors were entwined with the tormented cries of the incarcerated pygmies when the barbaric victors started a fire beneath the cage, roasted the pygmies alive, and then dined on their flesh.

The handful of men and women who survived the brutal attack managed to rebuild Winea, then, in a cruel twist of fate, they succumbed to a tuberculosis epidemic that swept through the highlands. Busa and his resilient people endured the disease by chewing medicinal leaves and using healing rituals.

With the pygmies' daunting reputation in the back of my mind and the last of the intimidating climb below us, I marvelled at the captivating views and the raw beauty that surrounded Winea. It seemed ironic that the archipelago's smallest people should command the islands highest inhabited peak. From this lofty position, the cunningly placed village, which is comprised of two huts, would appear to be a strategic safe haven that's nestled in the clouds, but the hamlet's bloody history has proved just how vulnerable the pygmy's were to an attack. Dense rainforest covers the surrounding mountains and valleys, but Winea's knoll is stripped bare of jungle and mantled in mud and short grass. I felt jaded just thinking about how the villagers make the exhausting climb up and down the sheer face everyday to reach their gardens.

When Busa came out of his hut holding his bow, I took serious heed of his harsh warning to wear a *mul mul* the next time I entered the village and knew he wasn't joking when he said that no matter how hungry I was, he would kill and cannibalise me if I ever breached tribal law again by eating a snake at a *tabu* site. Then he put his bow aside, smiled, and asked me if the snake tasted good. Once his chiefly duties were over, he greeted me as a long lost brother would. This was a very different paramount chief to the one I'd previously mixed with. He was more open and much friendlier, but beneath the welcoming smile, there lingered a regal aloofness that demanded I treat him with respect. Atison stepped outside and was followed by two other pygmy men in their early thirties. When Silas and Matai introduced themselves, they were more emotive and much more cheerful than their taller counterparts from the other villages that shared our beliefs. They were completely devoid of any inhibition and had no fear whatsoever of my skin tone. When they both welcomed me with a tight hug, Matai made clicking noises with his tongue and looked up at me with a genuine and affectionate smile.

I could see my bow was making them wild with excitement, so before we entered Busa's hut for the customary drink of welcoming kava, I offered to give them a quick archery exhibition. When I loosed off several arrows in front of an astounded audience, I couldn't help but laugh, but it was nothing compared to watching them shoot the bow, which was an unforgettable and hilarious experience. We all roared with laughter when the diminutive archers broke out into an overly expressive and joyous jig after they fired each arrow. The way they poked their tongues out and their eyes bulged was too much for me. I literally fell over laughing and tears of joy rolled down my cheeks.

Although my pint-sized friends were all heart and couldn't have offered me a warmer greeting, their fierce reputation is justified. While Matai and Silas chewed our kava, Busa shared Winea's fascinating history with me. Even if Christianity eventually overwhelmed *kastom*, as the paramount chief, Busa must eat anyone he kills to appease Taute. During the 1950s and up until the1960s, cannibalism often occurred as a result of intertribal conflict. To travel through the highlands unarmed was unthinkable because the threat of an ambush lurked behind every tree and attacks from enemy clans were commonplace. Several decades later, the skirmishes became less frequent, but even now fighting still occurs, and traditional enemies are viewed with suspicion and contempt. Though it's extremely rare, nowadays cannibalism still occurs when an enemy is slain, but the consumption of human flesh remains a highly secretive practise as the government banned cannibalism in the mid-1980s. Because word travels so quickly in the highlands, to avoid government retribution, the death of a victim is blamed on natural causes or on Damate. If any outsiders ask of the whereabouts of a missing person, a more plausible and peaceful explanation is offered as to how they died.

Busa's father, Calico Mia, provided the meat for the last cannibal feast that gained notoriety throughout the highlands. After he made a solo one-hour trek to Nambamba village, he shot and killed three men with his bow. To have faced the enemy village alone is a tribute to his prowess as a warrior and showed just how incredibly brave he was and why his exploits will always remain legendary. In an amazing display of stamina, he spent the rest of the day carrying the bodies back to Winea by himself. The preparation of a corpse for a feast involves strict ritual and the observance of strict *tabus*. All three cadavers were tied to poles then they were stood upright in front of Calico Mia's hut. To reap his victim's *rapee*, he placed his hand on each of their hearts, then no one else could touch the bodies for one full day. Unlike most of the other islands throughout Vanuatu, where only the men ate the dead, the women willingly joined in the grisly meal. Vetrivu fondly recalls dining on the flesh of Calico Mia's victims after the corpses were cooked whole in hot stones. To obtain their full *rapee*, Calico Mia ate their hearts, and then he smashed a hole in each of the skulls and ate the brains. While the bodies were staked out, an exceptionally strong sun had caused the rapidly decaying flesh to start smelling. *Kastom* dictates that a clan must eat everything their hardened systems can digest until the whole carcass is finished. Busa remembers the feast vividly, and in a matter of fact tone said that by the time only three skeletons remained, the vile meat reeked, had turned dark, and tasted so repulsive he almost vomited. Irrespective of how putrid the flesh is, if anyone failed to keep the gruesome meal down, they would've suffered a horrific death from the victim's regurgitated spirit. This *tabu* also prevented any indiscriminate slaughter, as killing the enemy was always measured and with definite purpose, which ensured a clan was never annihilated to extinction.

Busa is proud of his cannibalistic tendencies, not because he has a penchant for violence, but because it's such an integral part of *kastom*. Instinctively carrying on his father's legacy as a revered warrior has elevated his prowess as a fighter to legendary status throughout Middle Bush. Although I tower over Busa and weigh ninety kilos, his size ten feet are wider than mine, his hands are the same size, and his powerful calves, thighs, and biceps roughly mirror my athletic measurements. His pocket dynamo physique belies his incredible Herculean strength. To have the stamina to carry a fully-grown man who was dying from malaria over his shoulders all the way to an aid post in the lowlands for lifesaving treatment in just one day is an amazing testament to his staggering endurance. And to have the skill to fight off two much larger men who launched a surprise attack, and clubbed him to the ground three times with their *nul nuls*, is equally remarkable. In spite of a severe wound on his forehead, he still managed to find his feet a fourth time and knocked both men out cold with his bare fists. Gramma told me that when he travelled with him through the lowlands, a stick had stabbed right through Busa's calf muscle. Without so much as a grimace, Busa pulled the stick out, treated the injury with herbal *kastom* medicines, and covered the gaping wound with *lap lap* leaves, which he bound with a vine. Then he carried on walking as if nothing had happened and made the torturous hike all the way up to Winea without complaint.

Although Busa is swift to inflict tribal justice or retribution, natural aggression isn't a part of his character. He exudes an effortless inner calm and has the inborn attributes of a chief who leads by setting an enviable example. For someone who's illiterate and has a primitive mindset, he's a remarkably intelligent, deep thinking, and fair man who willingly listens to others before he makes his own decisions. He strives to maintain harmony and a spiritual balance throughout the highlands, but foolishly cross him or disrespect *kastom* and he will kill you in a heartbeat, as the helicopter that landed on the grassy knoll directly above the village found out. The sheer arrogance and stupidity of landing a helicopter in a primitive people's backyard when they have yet to make contact with outsiders is beyond me. Just the chaotic noise and the downdraught had the terrified women crying with fright. They were to afraid to even think about looking outside and cringed with fear in the corner of their huts while Busa and the other men raced towards the chopper's deafening roar with their bows. If the women had seen the devil fall from the sky and the Damate's within the demons belly, such a horrific sight would've completely overwhelmed them. Its terrified passengers tried to explain they were geologists who meant no harm and were extremely lucky to have escaped with their lives when the helicopter made a quick exit, as the pygmy warriors were intent on drawing blood over the unwelcome and ear-splitting intrusion. Such an insensitive invasion left a lasting impact on the two remaining pygmy women. The news that a *disale* was coming to Winea had terrified them so much that they fled to a hut nestled alongside their gardens because neither of them has seen a white man.

Ravu told me how he'd watched a helicopter "fall down" beside the Lappe River. He charged through the jungle to the hovering chopper and was convinced that its pilot and passenger were about to steal gold from the river. He threw a rock at the chopper's canopy and narrowly missed the pilot, who wisely took off at high speed. Ravau wished he'd had his bow or, better still, a musket to kill the thieves. Gramma had mentioned that the villagers had seen a helicopter land on several occasions, and for some reason thought they were Australians who were trying to steal gold. If the highlanders ever catch them, they've already planned how they will kill the thieves.

When Busa said "That's enough storying for now Tavua. We will drink kava and sleep," it was disappointing as I could've listened to him talk for hours. Even though we were in an incredibly remote location and night had fallen, Atison barricaded the hut doors. To enter or exit a hut while Busa is drinking kava is forbidden. It's believed those who blatantly breach the *tabu* will become involved in some type of physical conflict in the immediate future that will result in their violent death. If someone mistakenly enters the hut, Busa must stop drinking to reduce the chances of the unintentional offender dying. In our compromised states of health, Ravu and I quickly succumbed to the effect of the potent kava. Not long after we stretched out on our sleeping mats, we both drifted off to sleep.

It wasn't the bout of simultaneous diarrhoea and vomiting which made me feel uneasy when I rushed into the nearby jungle at three in the morning. Although I was fully focused on being violently ill, I could sense with an incredible clarity a supernatural presence from the unearthly world that I presumed would always lay beyond the reach of my thoughts and comprehension. Winea mirrored my own village in ever way but without the intrusion of western clothing or an alien religion, yet here, even to a *disale*, the spirits were tangible. Alone and in the dark, I experienced a strange and newfound perception. I didn't feel a sense of dread, or fear, it was more of a nervous awareness that was tinged with curiosity. While I'd participated in rituals, or drank copious amounts of kava, I'd never engaged in direct personal communion with the ever-present supernatural, although there had been times when I thought I'd felt a subtle spiritual presence. The heavy mist cloaking the chilly peak had enhanced the eerie mood, but I wondered if maybe during my initiation my consciousness had in fact expanded its horizons, as when I later told Busa about my weird experience with the paranormal, he merely nodded his head with an expression that said I now shared a deeper understanding of how man bush perceives the universe. As well as being nestled in the heart of the rugged island, Winea is the pulsating spiritual heart of the island.

If a highlander is murdered anywhere on Santo, their spirit travels to the knoll above the hamlet to "sing out" a plaintive scream as a warning. In the past, this gave the pygmies time to make plans for retribution or to ready themselves for a possible attack. Anyone who has travelled beyond Winea, deeper into the island's interior, claims to hear ghostly sounds. The jungle is said to be alive with spirits, where babies cry, men shout, and even the sound of the *tavue* shell reverberates through the rainforest. Every noise that's associated with village life can be clearly heard. To say to one another "What was that?" while you listen to the ghouls is *tabu*. Silence is essential, or cloud descends and thunder booms, and then the jungle envelops the trail just before the noisy spectres kill their mortal intruders. Only Busa and Garae have ever ventured into the ghostly realm, as all of the other superstitious highlanders give the haunted region of jungle a wide berth. Throughout Middle Bush, its common knowledge that Winea and the surrounding area is home to both friendly and evil eternal beings from past generations.

The next morning, the flat echo of the *tavue* shell reverberating around the valleys stirred me from a deep sleep. Ravu lay shivering on his mat and lathered in sweat from either one of the jungle's numerous fevers or from the infection having spread from his badly infected finger. Busa spat, prodded, and chanted while he sat atop of Ravu's hips during a brief healing ritual. It was obvious that Ravu wasn't going anywhere in his sorry state, so I stepped outside half awake and blurry eyed and joined Matai and Silas in a *bobo* ceremony to ready ourselves for the hunt. While

Busa and Atison headed for another village, I followed Matai and Silas into the predawn darkness. As we walked through misty patches of low cloud, I noticed the tiny archers, who were dwarfed by their large and powerful bows, were so confident that the spirits would shed good luck on our hunt they only carried three arrows each.

Winea has a similar *kastom* story to Nukurekum as to why a long walk lay ahead of us to reach our hunting ground. At the turn of the twentieth century, one of Winea's warriors had killed and eaten a hunter from an enemy clan who had been tracking a wild pig. In a fit of rage, his brother, who was a *kastom* man, used black magic to banish every wild pig that roamed the highlands down to the steamy lowlands.

As the rising sun tried to vainly sear its way through a veil of dark ominous cloud, sheets of rain sluiced down from the heavens. Back at Nukurekum, I'd been praised for my agility when I travelled through the jungle, but I almost felt cumbersome and like a lumbering giant as I struggled to keep up with the nimble pygmies. They were quick and light on their bare feet and surprisingly strong for their size. With an astounding yet natural agility, they clambered over greasy logs and slippery slime covered rocks and casually leapt from one foothold to another down muddy slopes that were almost vertical. Whenever it was possible, we jogged through the difficult terrain, but I was more mentally tired from concentrating than I was physically fatigued when we stopped four hours later to dine on *nakavika* berries and edible fungus.

A dull sun was well past its zenith when we reached our hunting ground. This was virgin territory for me, with rugged contours that stretched through a vast tract of jungle. We wound through the trees at a swift pace along a well-worn pig run to an empty wallow, then we pressed on to a nearby patch of rooting where a boar had nosed the soft earth in search of worms and grubs. If there was a prize for tracking game at the fastest speed, these pint-sized hunters would win hands down. Their eyes instinctively searched everywhere for a tell tale mark, for disturbed vegetation, and to see how much of a broken spider web had been repaired to indicate how long it had been since an animal had recently passed by. We squelched along the game trail at a trot, then slowed to a walk when the water-filled tracks we were following still retained their sharp edges. Silas led the way as we quietly trailed the prints to a gigantic banyan tree where the animals sometimes bed down amongst the tangled mass of huge buttress roots. Our painstaking stalk proved fruitless when we peered amongst the weave of roots to find that the pig had moved on.

After a luckless day, when dusk fell, we kept a huge fire blazing to keep Damate and the other phantoms that prowled the jungle at bay. We dined on the pith of a palm, on *orota* nuts, and on bush cabbage cooked inside green bamboo, but it did little to quell my still churning stomach. The dismal weather had soaked us to the skin, and we were all feeling the cold when we stretched out on a bed of *lap lap* leaves and soft tree fronds alongside a comforting fire. Throughout a fitful night, we all awoke shivering and took turns to stoke the fire and hug its flames until the rising sun gave warmth to our chilled bodies.

After a light breakfast of nuts, which we washed down by cutting a liana vine and drinking its gush of fluid, Matai led us through a light drizzle. Running in wet pants had chaffed my crotch red raw, and overnight the tender rash had turned into a weeping mess that was painfully reminding me of every step that I took. We twisted through the jungle along a pig run, and then snaked down a ridge to the wallow we'd previously visited. The imprint of bristle we'd initially seen, from where a large pig had recently used the mud bath, had washed away, and with no other fresh sign in the area, we moved on.

By late in the afternoon, we'd covered a lot of country without coming across any game. When the persistent rain finally stopped and we found the fresh marks of a small boar, Silas tracked the wandering pig with the skills of a bloodhound. He trailed the marks along a gentle sloping ridge that ran down into a messy fern-filled gully. As the sun ended its daily voyage into the horizon, a shroud of descending mist clouded the cool air and left a damp sheen on our skin. Because of the rapidly fading light, I could feel the sense of urgency when Silas bent over and parted the fern to look for signs. A muffled grunt and a rustle in the fern about thirty metres away brought us to an abrupt halt. Silas nocked an arrow and switched into predator mode. He become one with the jungle and responded to its every sound and its every movement. With his senses heightened, his lithe body seemed to almost flow along the pig run in virtual silence. I held back with Matai and watched and shared in each of his carefully placed footsteps. He stopped mid-stride several times with his foot poised above the ground. He held the motionless pose when the fern became still, then carried on when it started shaking and the pig began rooting and feeding again. He silently crept forward until he'd expertly narrowed the gap to about eight metres, then he slowly rose from a crouch, shuffled slightly to get better positioned, and pulled his bow to full draw. As the deadly arrow hissed through the air, Silas was almost right behind it. The startled boar scoffed in annoyance when the black palm arrowhead punched its way through its thick hide and sliced into several vital organs.

It had been a textbook shot, but the mortally wounded pig instinctively spun around and fled on a surge of adrenalin. I'd never witnessed anything like it when Silas exploded after the animal and literally flew through the air, pouncing on the hapless pig to end the hunt. He no doubt knew that tracking an animal in total darkness amongst country this rough would've been virtually impossible.

My pygmy friends went ballistic when they performed the *bobo*, and as usual, I burst out laughing when I shared in their frenzy of boisterous bliss. We were all famished and dining on the pig's fire roasted heart, kidneys, and liver helped to dull the razor-edged hunger pangs that were slicing at my already upset stomach. The glow of contentment from having a full belly after a successful hunt and having a warm soothing fire to sleep next to enhanced our cheerful mood when we chatted late into the night.

There were smiles all round the following day when we made the arduous trek back to Winea and divvied out the pork. It was a little disappointing to find that the two pygmy women had failed to return, but it was great to meet Busa's son, Sakele, who had returned after visiting the west coast and to see that Ravu was back on his feet after shaking off his fever. Ravu and I were still unwell, so the next day we both took a well earned and much needed day of rest.

I was surprised to learn while we rested our weary bodies that most of Nukurekum's and Vanakanakarea's inhabitants originated from Winea. Centuries ago, a cataclysmic cyclone all but flattened the pygmy village, and after they survived the disastrous hurricane, many of Winea's occupants decided to shift from the exposed knoll and built new villages on the outlying ridge tops. Over the years their integration with neighbouring clans led to intermarriage, which has ensured the pygmies are destined to follow evolution's course through to extinction. Busa took a wife who is almost six feet tall from another village, and as a consequence, Sakele towers over him. I would never have thought that Ravae, Peta, Vetrivu, Voemanu, Ravu, Gramma, and numerous others were born at Winea. Physically they share little of the pygmy's characteristics, but their bloodlines have evolved from the pygmy gene pool.

After we hiked back to Nukurekum, several hours later, Matai entered our hut clutching his hand. It was covered with banana leaves, and when he unwrapped them, one of his fingers flopped limply below his shaking hand. He'd slashed it with his machete while he was cutting firewood, and he said, "*String himi no gud*" ("the string is no good"), as he pointed to where a cut tendon had rendered the finger useless. To stem the flow of blood, he'd wrung the sap from a wild kava shrub into the gaping wound, and although the bleeding had stopped, the deep cut needed stitching. While Gramma dressed the wound, I urged Matai to head to the coast for some proper treatment, but he was adamant that he would use *kastom* medicine to heal his injury. He shrugged his shoulders, then laughed aloud and told me that if he lost his finger, he still had two good thumbs and seven "number one" (good) fingers left.

That same night, even though the topic was nothing to laugh about, listening to a group of men discussing the renewed problems they were having with their archenemies from Matantas was almost comical. It was difficult to tell the difference between their highly exaggerated anger and their real hatred while the highly emotive conversation raged. As they vented their anger to one another, most of the speakers' tones climbed then collapsed from a whisper to a shout, in what appeared to be undulating verbal battles that were delivered with riotous enthusiasm and drama. To an outside observer, it would have seemed the men were locked in a heated argument rather than casually discussing a problem.

Whenever the highlanders travel to Luganville to sell kava and purchase a few basic goods, there is always a slight element of danger. Once their business is conducted, they normally return to the relatively safe haven of Middle Bush as soon as possible. Mantantas has remained traditional enemy territory for centuries. The hatred between the coastal tribe and man bush originally stemmed from the "*sol wota*" (salt water) people's jealousy over the vast amounts of land the highlanders occupy. The melodramatic discussion was about the men from Matantas who'd recently beaten a highlander from another village to a bloody pulp while he was in Luganville. Most of the villagers have tales of engaging in bloody conflict when they've been in town, as the slightest provocation usually erupts into a full-on brawl. Ravu chased a mob of men from Matantas down the main street when they threatened to kill him. He was brandishing his machete and was disappointed when the fleeing men outran him, otherwise blood would've flowed for sure. Gramma broke his hand and arm fighting off two men who he eventually managed to beat to the ground. For us to venture anywhere near Matantas is virtually out of the question unless we're accompanied by a horde of highlanders. Word of the beating quickly spread through Middle Bush, and it was made known that anyone who ventured into town needed to exercise caution.

Peta's battle with an unrelenting bout of malaria had been raging for weeks, and because of the *tabu* that prevented him from washing, he absolutely reeked of rancid body odour. The numerous healing rituals he'd substituted for the lifesaving quinine that Gramma offered him were proving to be ineffective against the deadly disease. Besides using medicinal leaves and calling upon the supernatural, eating goat meat is believed to cure malaria. When Gramma asked me to join him on a wild goat hunt the following morning, I would've shamed myself if I refused to help my *kastom* father and agreed to go even though my groin was weeping puss. When he mentioned "*yumi go longwea small*" ("we will go a fairly long way"), I knew we were going to have to work really hard for our meat. Especially in this type of unforgiving country, and especially when *kastom* required us to capture the nimble goats alive and with our bare hands.

We were away early the next day and although keeping up with Gramma's surefootedness in the rugged jungle was painful, it was soon forgotten when the burning in my lungs eclipsed the discomfort I felt in my inflamed and bleeding groin. While I ran after him in jagged terrain that was more suited to fleet footed goats than unarmed hunters, my heart pounded so hard I could feel it beating a tune on my eardrums. I slowed down to a fast walk to track Gramma, who'd taken off in hot pursuit after a mob of feeding goats that had fled when a vigilant nanny stamped her foot and snorted a warning. In an incredible display of fitness, he caught up with the tiring animals as they ran uphill and managed to wrestle a medium-sized billy to the ground. About twenty minutes later, after I followed the sound of his *olau* call, which let me know where he was and that the hunt had been a success, I found him hanging on to the goat under the shadow of a giant wild taro plant.

Gramma was ecstatic and said, "Number one, Tavu! Number one! Here you hold him," so I grappled with the belligerent animal while he wiped the stream of sweat from his eyes. He prepared himself for the *bobo* rite by gathering *ori* leaves and tucking them into the side of his *mul mul*. Then he used a leafy branch from the *asparo* tree to make a wreath, and after he tied it around his head, without any warning, he suddenly exploded into a frenzy of wild emotion. The startled goat started thrashing around and tried its best to escape as Gramma landed a flurry of bruising kicks into the nearest tree and whooped and screamed to vent his joy. For the next half an hour he sang and danced to give thanks to Taute. *Kastom* required us to carry the goat back alive and untied, as it's believed tethering the limbs together stems the flow of *tabu* blood and destroys the medicinal qualities of the meat. We took turns carrying the irate goat, which bleated and thrashed about on our shoulders during most of the gruelling walk back to the village.

After we'd made the climb back up to Nukurekum, to preserve the meats curative properties, Gramma put a noose around the goat's neck and then hung the hapless animal from a sturdy tree limb. When the struggling goat stopped frantically kicking the air and gave a final shudder, he slit its throat, gave thanks to Taute again, and smeared its blood all over his body to gain the goat's *rapee*. Any flesh from below the knee of a captured goat is *tabu* and can only be eaten by the hunter. The meat must be roasted over the fire, and by dining on the sacred flesh, the hunter empowers his legs with the animal's *rapee* and its stamina for the next chase. I was exhausted yet elated after the long and toilsome day. By capturing a live goat, Gramma had gained immense respect as a hunter and Peta had plenty of medicinal meat.

When I awoke the next morning and looked around me, I needed to escape from escapism and to take a short break away from the constant sickness and the confines of communal living. I wanted a bit of time to myself so I armed myself with my bow and quietly slipped away into the jungle. When I returned late in the afternoon with a wild dog, the cooking fires were stoked, and we all enjoyed a hearty meal of the canine's tender flesh when it was roasted to perfection amidst a pile of smoking hot stones.

Peta made a slow but steady recovery, and once he was well enough, I was asked to perform an *essengo* rite with him and with Ravu. The simplistic rituals and the gestures behind them bestowed me with an immense amount of honour. They meant I held a permanent place in the hearts and souls of Ravu and Peta and that I'd formed an inseparable alliance with two of the highlands' most respected and most powerful men. If anyone ever held any contempt towards me, now they would have to think long and hard before they inflicted any type of malice on their *disale* brother.

Over the next few days, I felt within myself that it was definitely time to leave. Peta's illness had worn out his patience as well as emaciating his normally muscular body. He became increasingly irritable and appeared to be suffering from a type of post-fever depression. His swing shift moods were uncharacteristic, as he'd always been sociable and totally selfless. When I followed him and Voemanu to the garden after he'd invited me to take a few photos, it nearly ended in disaster. For no apparent reason, when I raised my camera, he screamed abuse and threatened to cut me up with his machete. Although I'd done nothing wrong, I offered a sincere apology to both him and Voemanu for having upset my *kastom* father. Gramma was with me and whispered, "You go, Tavu, now. Before he kills you!" I took heed and put plenty of distance between Peta and myself before things got ugly.

According to Gramma, I'd been incredibly lucky, as a year earlier Peta had the ability to cause an animal's death merely by yelling. Numerous villagers claim to have witnessed the phenomenon, where pigs, fowl, a bullock, and even a nighthawk that was flying overhead were killed instantly when his lethal shouts evoked a potent ancestral spirit whose sole purpose is to take life. Peta was so worried that he might misuse his power in anger to kill a fellow villager—or even worse, a family member—that he performed a rite which exorcised the spirit and its deadly powers from his soul forever. I could foresee serious if not fatal problems arising. If I got on the wrong side of Peta, I knew the repercussions would involve at the very least the spilling of my blood, so I decided to leave the next morning.

Matai and Gramma followed me to Luganville to sell some of their kava. During the short time that we became separated while we shopped and talked to old friends, four men from Matantas confronted Matai when he was alone. He knew he was no match for his burly opponents and used his brains instead of his tiny brawn and wisely ran for his life. When we eventually regrouped and went looking for the men, they were nowhere to be found.

My search for a new pair of innersoles for my boots left me doubled over in hysterics. The only place that sold them was a chemist, and when I told the woman behind the counter I was after a size twelve, she acknowledged my request with a nod and handed me a large tube of haemorrhoid cream. Because of the way I waddled into the shop due to my still healing crotch, she mistakenly thought I'd said arsehole instead of innersole. From the way I had to painfully walk with my legs bowed, it felt as if that part of me needed replacing, but it still puzzles me as to how she knew what a size twelve looked like, and how much cream was needed to heal it.

I spent a couple of days resting at John Noel's, then I continued working on another island, where, in spite of taking careful precautions, I succumbed to what the doctors thought was a hellish bout of malaria. I was violently ill, and after months of rehabilitation, I was lucky to regain my full health. Unbeknown to me, the next time I returned to Middle Bush, the lingering aftereffects of the deadly disease would also become life threatening.

Chapter Seventeen

MORAL OBLIGATION

Very few people could even start to relate to the mental resilience that was required to voluntarily return to Middle Bush. I still kept all of the negative experiences I'd previously endured close to my chest and said absolutely nothing to my friends and family about the highlander's present-day penchant for violence. Rather than depicting their lives through rose-coloured glasses, I concentrated on their turbulent past to help generate enough morbid interest to sell my work and portrayed a realistic image of just how difficult life is for man bush. Despite the closely guarded truth, Busa had given me strict instructions to write that cannibalism had ceased long ago in the highlands. Although it ran against my grain and morals, it was of no real consequence to anyone, so I reluctantly worded the articles as he requested. Every attempt I'd made to try and open the door to the highlands so that academics who were better qualified than me could study man bush had failed miserably. Busa had stated emphatically that there was no way he would allow any outsiders, including Ni- Vanuatu from the cultural centre, to accompany me when I returned. Those who were foolish enough to flout his decision would be killed on sight. Even though I'd eventually bounced back health wise, meeting the moral obligation to return and further study the highlanders required a lot of serious soul searching. That the responsibility rested solely on my shoulders didn't make the decision any easier to go back to where my kind, the *disale*, is absolutely hated. I believe in creating my own destiny, but to embrace what appeared to be my fate called for further personal growth and the ability to adequately control my anxieties while I lived with constant uncertainty. I needed to generate an immense inner strength where instead of grappling with stress and fear, I was able to relax and almost revel in the face of danger. I couldn't have chosen to live in a more contrasting and exhilarating society to my own than that of Middle Bush when I decided to return.

As usual, John Noel was fronting another social quandary when I arrived on his doorstep. Throughout all of Vanuatu *nakaimas* from Ambrym Island are feared and despised because they blatantly misuse black magic for personal gain or to commit serious crime. John had called an emergency meeting after four "man Ambrym" had exhumed the corpses from fresh graves and eaten their hearts. In the days that followed, other people living in the area started dying. Rumour abounded that they were all victims of the *nakaimas*, and rampant gossip spread that corpses were being found and leaves had replaced the organs which normally occupied their stomach cavities. After an emotive witch-hunt, those who were believed to be responsible were arrested and jailed. Each morning when the police officers checked on the four prisoners, they'd mysteriously disappeared without a trace, but were later recaptured at the homes of their friends who lived in Luganville. The judicial system decided that imprisonment was futile against the supernatural powers of the *nakaimas*, so a revered *kastom* man from Maewo Island was called for, as their powers surpass those of black magicians from Ambrym. With virtually the whole town in tow, John led the agitated crowd through the main street as they marched the accused murderers to the wharf. Before the criminals were literally thrown on a departing ship, the *kastom* man from Maewo cursed them to a brutal death if ever they set foot on Santo again.

The debilitating bout of malaria I'd previously survived not only required physical healing, as the incapacitating disease had also damaged me mentally. When I filled in the departure card before the flight back to New Zealand, I was shocked to read that, like a dyslexic, I'd jumbled the letters of my name. Whenever I tried to memorise past events, it proved to be equally frustrating because I constantly had to refer to my notes and diary. It took three patient months of recovery before I could write a legible article.

During my absence, an immense wind that carried social and economic change had swept through Middle Bush with the force of a cyclone when kava prices had skyrocketed to an incredible twelve hundred vatu per kilo. A mood that was reminiscent of a gold rush surged through the islands. John Noel became a kava agent and made an easy one hundred thousand vatu per tonne, at a time when he was buying two tonnes a week. In Vanuatu, that's huge money compared to the average weekly wage of three and a half thousand vatu.

Before the price of kava escalated, the more sophisticated coastal and urban inhabitants had looked down upon man bush. Many viewed them as being impoverished, unhygienic, and savage heathens. But now, those whose main source of income came from the hard toil of selling copra suddenly envied their primitive counterparts. Because of their substantial kava plantations, man bush was on a roll, but knew that some of the civilized Ni-Vanuatu either mocked or despised them behind their backs. Some of the more boisterous natives literally walked down Luganville's main street scorning and laughing at the expatriate businessmen, the industrious Chinese traders, the Ni-Vanuatu who laboriously worked on copra plantations, or those who were employed to do other menial tasks. Young boys who'd previously never had any real concept of the value of money became instant millionaires by selling their entire crop of kava. The bars in Luganville overflowed with men wearing *mul muls* who squandered more money on alcohol than they could have previously hoped to have ever made in an entire lifetime. There was no shortage of shrewd city shysters who were quick to capitalize on the kava boom by asking the hopelessly inebriated natives for huge amounts of money that they never intended repaying.

For some of the natives, the shock of earning such vast amounts of money completely overwhelmed them. A previously destitute old man from south Santo started shaking when the bank teller pushed a pile of notes towards him. First he began crying over his newfound affluence, then his tears turned to emotive screams of disbelief. The poor man was so emotional, he couldn't come to terms with his sudden wealth and he left his money sitting on the counter and ran away. It took a lot of soothing talk from his son to calm him down before they returned to gather his riches. Another elderly villager from Pentecost Island fainted and fell on the floor of the bank when he saw the massive wad of notes he was about to receive. The boom lasted for a year, then the government foolishly sold plants to America, Hawaii, and Mexico, who went on to establish a niche for themselves in what had previously been a relatively uncompetitive market. With a bit of foresight, the government may well have done better to retain ownership of some of the world's most potent plants and marketed not only the kava, but also the cultural significance of the plant.

Whereas some primitive peoples veered into a downward spiral of extravagant spending and quickly frittered away their instant wealth, Busa kept a clear and sharp business head. When man bush accumulated millions of vatu, he called all of the chiefs together, and it was unanimously agreed that the archipelago's most remote and primitive peoples, who still zealously repelled outsiders, would jointly invest their profits as a down payment on a new Toyota pickup that was to be used as a taxi. They also chose a driver who moved to Luganville so as he could obtain his license. It was incredible, as many elderly, and especially the very young members of some clans had never seen a white man before my arrival, let alone had shares in a truck. I once witnessed how an old woman who'd never ventured down from the mountains before reacted when she saw a vehicle for the first time. She was hysterical and was terrified of the monster that had swallowed the villagers who were comfortably seated inside. She curled up into a quivering ball and rocked back and forwards while tears streamed down her cheeks until one of the amused onlookers explained there was nothing to be afraid of.

Other communities purchased vehicles, only to find that once their kava plantations were depleted, they couldn't meet the repayments and the banks ended up repossessing them. Santo's rough roads soon took their toll and incurred frequent maintenance costs that financially crippled those who had just managed to meet each instalment. Because they were unable to fund replacement parts, many of the vehicles became a useless commodity that didn't warrant any further repayments, and the banks ended up recovering what was left of them.

It took a while for me to get my head around the initial realization that one of the world's most primitive peoples were now the proud owners of a brand-spanking new Toyota. Other dramatic changes had also occurred during my absence. As I travelled inland with Ravu on the back of a brand new white pickup with "Winea" painted on its side, I was dismayed when he told me the protestant mission service had placed a teacher and his wife at Vanakanakarea's school, and as a consequence, even more villagers were wearing a mottled mix of traditional and ragged western clothing. I shuddered when I thought of the once proud looking warriors emerging from their huts to greet me with an impoverished and downtrodden appearance, and again when Ravu told me about the other changes that had taken place. All of the children wore clothing when they attended school, and the Christians had stopped working on Sundays to observe the Sabbath and pay their respects in church to Jesus and to God. About thirty worshipers, some travelling vast distances through the jungle, attended each service. The teacher's wife was so afraid of man bush that she fled back to Luganville. When the teacher took a break to visit his wife, he borrowed the school's only calculator. The villagers viewed this as blatant theft, and even though it obviously wasn't, they made it known that if he ever returned he would be killed on sight.

Another replacement teacher, Stephan Vavanaru, from Lalaolo village in southwest Santo filled the precarious void. Like his predecessor, he found the first few months extremely difficult. The constant fear of being killed and the stress of worrying about his wife took its toll and quickly frayed his nerves. The strain of living with constant anxiety became too much for his petrified wife, so she fled back to the coast. Stephan put all his faith in God and stayed behind to forge ahead with the unenviable task of trying to put a halt to the barbaric rituals while he tried to convert and educate the highlanders.

Ravu used a mixture of Bislama and broken English when he said, "Tavua, two *disales* stop on top close up die finish." As we bounced and juddered along the potholed and badly rutted road, he told me what else had happened while I was away. If it wasn't for Stephan's persistent teachings, two American missionaries in their mid-twenties would have met their untimely deaths. A grossly overweight woman and a reed thin man made the arduous trek up to Nukurekum with a Ni-Vanuatu guide. By the time the unfit woman staggered up to the village she was so exhausted the two men had to support her under their arms to prevent her from collapsing. Gale force winds blew driving rain into their faces and washed away the tears that were streaming down the distraught woman's cheeks. Although she was a physical and emotional wreck, her troubles had only just begun because the evangelists couldn't have picked a worse time to invade the villagers' lives. About one hundred and fifty visitors were celebrating the opening of a new cookhouse that Peta had just built, and while a *lafaet* was in full swing, bottles of whisky and rum were being passed around. To wander into Nukurekum unannounced can be a harrowing experience for a *disale* at the best of times, but to be greeted by hordes of high-spirited warriors who were drunk on alcohol spelt a recipe for disaster, especially when the evangelists interrupted them when *kastom* was being made.

Gramma shook his head in disgust while Ravu and the rest of the outraged highlanders shook their fists at the contemptuous *disales* who were disturbing a ritual. Just the mere sight of the Christians provoked chants from the enraged crowd of "*Killem! Killem! Killem finis!*" ("Beat them! Beat them! Kill them!). The violent taunts grew louder and more fervent as the angered warriors worked themselves into a frenzy. When several men screamed above the chanting crowd that they were going to kill and cannibalise the missionaries, then feed their bones to the dogs, the panic-stricken woman fainted. Gramma was disgusted when her tearful male companion hunched over and held his shaking legs while he urinated and defecated himself with fear. When the woman regained her unsteady feet, the three clerics begged not to be killed. Dusk was falling and the heavens had opened up with a steady deluge of rain. The blubbering woman pleaded for shelter and groaned that she thought she was about to die from exhaustion. Her plea for help fell on indifferent ears and Gramma said to her, "That would be good. It will save us killing you and give the dogs something to eat." He meant every word, and told them to go and sleep in the jungle with the devils, while a string of death threats from the furious crowd reduced the missionaries to blithering wrecks.

It's ironic that if it wasn't for Christianity's impact, the evangelists would've definitely been beaten until their blood flowed and their bones were broken. With the drunken crowd already in a volatile mood, so many men indulging in an act of violence towards a *disale* would no doubt have escalated into mass hysteria and probably incited the highlanders to beat them to death. Gramma and Peta decided to let them live, and allowed them to stay in the *"haos blong kava"* (the kava house), which is used to dry kava only thirty metres from the *nakamal*. Gramma softened and gifted each of the Christians a fire-roasted taro, then warned them that if they were still around in the morning, it would be the last time they saw the sun rise. They listened to taunts, threats, and blood curdling screams that were intended to instil terror into them throughout what must have been a long and horrific night. As soon as dawn cast enough light for the evangelists to follow the trail, they fled for their lives back down to the lowlands.

Midway through our bone-jarring journey, when Ravu asked about the gifts, I had no idea what he was referring to until he told me I was supposed to reciprocate the *essengo* rite I'd performed with Peta by gifting him saucepans and knives. Ravu probably figured I would remember the rite I'd performed with him as well, but I didn't. Although I'd mentioned the ritual in my notes, there was no way I would ever normally forget about something as vitally important as reciprocating an *essengo*, so it wasn't surprising I hadn't bothered to write it down in my diary. But I had forgotten, and without getting into any details, I told Ravu that because of unusual circumstances where I'd had problems changing a foreign bank draft due to strife in the Solomons, I didn't get a chance to buy the items that would prevent me from being beaten to a bloody pulp. I banged on the roof of the truck and was about to jump off as we pulled to a halt and start walking back towards Luganville when Ravu said, *"Yumi brothers, Tavua. No problem"* ("We are brothers, Tavua. No problem"), and suggested that weeks could pass before I might get the opportunity to travel up to Nukurekum with another villager. In the highlands' primitive society, if a man fails to keep his word, it can hold his very existence in the balance, and although it was hardly a persuasive argument for risking my life, I trusted his judgment, and like the rest of the villagers, I always valued his opinion. He couldn't speak for Peta, but as far as he was concerned, the monetary equivalent or sending the goods up to Nukurekum when I returned to civilization would suffice.

The next day Ravu looked how I felt as we entered the village, unsure if he'd made the right judgment call and deeply concerned. Peta had regained his muscular physique, and his cheerful temperament had returned with a vengeance, but the instant he realized I'd arrived without the gifts for the *essengo*, his smile faded and I knew I had a serious problem. The *essengo* was a profound demonstration of friendship and of trust. Now that I'd abused that friendship and violated the trust that had been gifted to me, I'd hurt Peta's feelings and had infuriated the gods. If I'd offered a litany of excuses, not only would it have been futile, it would've worsened my situation, for what I'd done was inexcusable. When a deadly hush fell over the hut, it seemed my worst fears were about to be confirmed. Vetrivu sneered and spat, and then looked away. Voemanu spat in disgust, as if to get rid of the bad taste I left in her mouth, and turned her back on me. She didn't do it because of what was about to happen, but because I'd disgraced my clan and my *kastom* family. Gramma glared at me and shook his head in disapproval, and then he quietly spoke to Peta in his native tongue. Ravu remained stoic and silent. I hoped like hell that Peta didn't nock a barbed arrow when he reached for his bow, and shuddered when he did. There was no hatred behind his cold-blooded expression or behind the look of disgust in his eyes. He was both my *kastom* father and my brother, who loved me like a son and a sibling. His intentions of drawing blood with the bow, then smashing my bones were totally void of malice, because conforming to the doctrines of his sometimes-violent religion motivated his decision and actions.

If I retaliated, it guaranteed certain death, so I looked Peta squarely in the eyes and hoped he'd lower the arrow to wound an arm or a leg instead of keeping it aimed at my face. I remained calm and dignified TO look human and like Peta's *kastom* son and brother rather than a terrified *disale* who would be much easier to shoot. My strong friendship with Gramma undoubtedly saved me from being seriously injured or killed. To question Peta's authority was unthinkable, yet Gramma bravely stood between us and risked his own life. It wasn't so much what he did, but the way that he did it, when in a strong tone, but using submissive body language, he calmly suggested to Peta that as I was his son, maybe I could give him the monetary equivalent of the gifts. There was absolutely no doubt in my mind that Christianity's dogma had influenced Peta's thinking when he agreed. Gramma was now a minister of the church, and if this had happened during an earlier visit, he would've willingly helped his father to shoot and beat me till blood flowed and bones broke to appease Taute.

The huge risk I'd just taken outweighed any possible rewards I could ever have hoped to reap from documenting the highlanders. I apologised and went outside for some fresh air and to regain my composure. My conscience took over where Peta had stopped short, and I beat myself up for forgetting such a crucial gift. Once the adrenaline had slowly burnt off from my initial fight or flight response, I returned inside ten minutes later to find the hut was vacant and spent my first night back in Middle Bush alone.

Ravae paid me a visit early the next morning and told me that last year, after he drank several shells of kava, he'd entered a deep trance and the spirits of *bubu* had spoken to him. The voices of his ancestors called out from an abstract world and told him that he must go and sleep because Tavua was dying. During a vivid dream, he saw me battling for my life as I lay in a hospital bed and knew if he didn't help me I was going to die. When he awoke, he ran through the jungle to the *tabu* cave, where he sat in front of the ancestral skulls and called for all of the spirits of *bubu* to heal me. I was dumbfounded as only a few people new of my illness. There was a remote possibility that word may have travelled up to Middle Bush, but it was highly unlikely.

In Middle Bush, society life is generally orderly, but it's always unpredictable and everything is taken on face value. There's no place for ifs, buts, or maybes. Timid actions and absent-minded decisions don't belong. My breach of *tabu* had cast a gloomy shadow over my trustworthiness. It had taken a long time to build a strong rapport with my *kastom* family, and more importantly, to gain their respect. By failing to reciprocate the *essengo*, I'd unwittingly pulled a foundation block out which caused all of my hard earned work to come crashing down to a useless pile of rubble. My family was ashamed of me, for I was a man who'd shunned our values and who'd shunned being a soul mate with Peta. Some serious damage control needed to swing into swift action.

My number one priority was to find Gramma and mend our strained friendship. After a lot of searching, I eventually found him clearing the weeds from his garden. I said nothing as I listened to his flood of expected abuse which ended with how lucky I was to still be alive. Once he'd finished venting his anger, I explained my temporary memory loss and decided to deal my ace card. Up until now, no one was aware that at great personal risk, I'd obtained the medicines for his leaf hut aid post illegally. The health authorities in New Zealand had asked who was qualified to administer the prescription medicines I'd asked them to supply. At the time there was no one, as Gramma had yet to complete a Red Cross course, so they justifiably gave a firm no regarding any involvement. Gramma may be virtually naked, but he's far from stupid when it comes to running his bush clinic. A more compassionate medical professional who could relate to the remote location and the severity of tropical diseases shared my opinion that getting something into them was a much better option than them dying, if non lethal quantities of medicine were administered. I asked Gramma if he would risk possible imprisonment in a foreign country to help *disales* who'd threatened to kill him. His apologetic expression and the sympathetic tone of his voice when he said, "Tavua kevoro," ("Tavua, lets go"), answered my question.

We raced back up to Nukurekum to find that none of the others had returned, and from what they'd taken with them, it looked as if they were planning to stay away for a few days. Without telling me where we were going, Gramma led us through several villages, then down into a sweeping valley filled with an ocean of unspoilt rainforest. He stopped on the side of a claggy track to sharpen his machete on *viki*, a sacred stone that's inhabited by the spirit of a *bubu*, whose sole purpose is to provide knives with a razor sharp edge. A short climb up the other side of the basin led us to a scruffy leaf hut nestled alongside one of Peta's gardens. I followed Gramma inside, to where a few of the villagers were crowded around a cooking pot filled with steaming taro. For the next ten lingering minutes that I patiently sat alongside Gramma, apart from the sound of slurping and chewing, an uncomfortable silence filled the hut. It was so painfully quiet that even the sound of their ungracious eating seemed to blare in my eardrums. Gramma waited until everyone had finished their meal, then he stood up and delivered a long and drawn out speech in his native tongue. His opening line visibly dazed Peta, Voemanu, and Vetrivu, and from then they hung on his every word. Garae and his two sons listened intently and were surprised when Gramma explained my illness. When they heard how I'd also provided the medicines at personal risk, a look of remorse spread across everybody's faces.

They rose to their feet and started saying, "Tamamasa Tavua. Tamamasa." (*"Everything is good Tavua. Everything is good."*) Peta wore a saddened expression as he shook my hand. Violence may be an integral part of *kastom*, but his compassionate apology came straight from the heart. His emotions were so profuse and so intense it was almost as if I could reach out and physically touch them. I hoped Busa would accept the unfortunate turn of events just as peacefully as Peta did, when in lieu of the saucepan and knives, I healed our rift by handing him five thousand vatu. Probably the single most important thing I'd learnt in Middle Bush was never to say "no," "I won't," "I can't," or "you can't." By explaining why a request wasn't possible, or why I couldn't or hadn't done something, rather than bluntly saying no first, I gained respect. To do a good deed without emphasising how others would benefit from your actions also earns esteem. Because I'd provided the medicines without mentioning the risks I took, it stood me in good stead. But I'd still breached *kastom*, and in the back of my mind, I knew the spirits would demand some form of recompense.

In the afternoon we all traipsed back to our respective villages. A father is always pleased with the birth of a son, but he is deeply disappointed when a daughter is delivered. The daughter will inevitably marry into another clan, but a the sone will almost always remain rooted to his ancestral land and support his parents in their old age. Garae was especially proud of Vira. In an astounding display of strength that stretched way beyond his seven years of age, he carried a sugar sack full of coconuts all the way back to Vanakanakarea without resting. Even poor old Vetrivu hauled a reasonably heavy load of taro up the sheer hills.

Peta carried the heaviest load of all. He was weighed down by the burden of feeling guilty and traipsed back to Nukurekum without uttering a word. His emotive self-reproach softened the normally harsh pitch in his voice to a much gentler tone when he took me aside to say that in one week we would go and hunt for wild bullock so that I could enjoy fresh meat. Then the day after the hunt, he would kill one of his finest fowl, gift me a mat, and prepare a *lafaet* for a *tamamasa* ceremony in my honour. As a mark of deep respect, he would also instruct the villagers to perform a *kimpeti* dance. Such a flattering gesture is rarely bestowed upon another villager, yet alone a *disale*. My intuition warned me that his good deeds would come with a price, and that somewhere along the line I had to pay penance to the spirits for breaching *tabu*. Although I didn't know it, Ravu began writing out the invoices for spiritual restitution when he returned from Winea and asked me to go bow fishing the following morning. After the recent tension, relaxing in the jungle with an affable and good-natured friend sounded like the perfect tonic.

The next day started with a serene and beautiful sunrise. When we were halfway to our destined stretch of river, I veered off the trail with Gramma and Petekara and climbed up to a nearby hamlet to wait for Ravu. While I was standing outside a hut, I saw him jogging along the track below us and yelled out in a gruff voice "Hey, Damate," then I jokingly drew a bead on him with a bow I'd been admiring. He laughed and then mimicked shooting back and screamed a blood curdling war cry. An hour later we joined him on the bank of a crystal clear stream. To ensure the rivers remain well stocked, only a bow, spear, spear gun, or a line are used to fish. Set nets are *tabu*, but the highlanders sometimes use a sackshaped net made from the woven bark of the tanamara tree, called a *koru*. To use the koru, the fishermen face upstream and place their feet inside the front of the basket while two woven ropes at the top of the opening are held by one hand. They use their free hand to dislodge rocks and then sweep across where the rock originally lay to chase fish into the net.

Gramma and Petekara speared *naura* (crayfish) and small fish with a simplistic spear gun called a *saribonebone*, which was cleverly fashioned from umbrella wire and a thick rubber band. I stalked downstream along the riverbank with Ravu and carefully scanned the shallows for small fish called *nangoro* that grow no bigger than the length of a man's hand. While Ravu enjoyed a cigarette and softly sang *kastom* songs, his hawk eyes soon picked out fish that were feeding in the shallows. He moved with the poise and grace of a heron and with actions that were as fluid as the gentle flowing water. Before each shot, as he anticipated the right moment, he slowly rocked back and forth ever so slightly. Each time a *nangoro* flapped on the end of a well-aimed arrow, he raced from the water's edge to kick a tree, then he whooped with joy and yelled a thanks to Taute.

I relished the peaceful atmosphere, and my recent troubles faded into insignificance while I wallowed in the serenity of the sublime rainforest and listened to the babble of the stream. When the river tumbled over a thirty-metre high waterfall into a foaming pool, Ravu cut me a length of wild cane and told me if I liked an unmarried woman, to call out her name and throw the reed into the pool. If the cane sank she would find me irresistible and welcome a marriage proposal, but if the reed floated it prophesised a doomed relationship. After a few months of marriage, the unhappy bride would run away and find another husband. My wild cane circled around on the top of an eddy then sank like a stone.

Ravu seemed terrified when I caught a small frog that was croaking in a patch of reeds. To see one of the highlands' fiercest warriors absolutely petrified of someone handling a tiny amphibian doubled me over in hysterical laughter. Because there was no cultural significance fuelling his phobia, I opened my cupped hands to show him how harmless the frog was. He reeled in horror, shot me a black look, and muttered something in his native tongue. Ordinarily he would have laughed at the way he reacted, but when I looked up after I released the frog, his carefree mood had changed, and drastically.

His darkening mood worsened when his favourite arrow split when it hit a rock. He glared at me as if I was to blame, and then he tore a strip of cloth from his *mul mul* and tied the shaft together. The previously relaxed atmosphere became tense and was filled with uncertainty. Ravu's happy features had transformed into a look of loathing, and such a deep hatred filled his eyes that I was sure there was no way this was over a stupid frog. The highlander's unpredictable mindset made situations like this extremely dangerous. I had no idea what to expect and no clue as to what was going on. When we built a blazing fire to roast a few fish and *tarovit*, Ravu looked like he was ready to explode. As I stood and watched crackling palm fronds send a plume of bluish smoke skyward, he casually picked up an arrow from the ground then flew into a rage. He thrust the barbed arrowhead to within millimetres of my eyes, and with an unnerving fury he said, "Busa said it is up to me if I kill you, Tavua." His venomous tone caused Petekara to turn her back and bow her head. She knew what was about to happen. Gramma seemed to be bracing himself for an expected outburst of violence. I knew if I'd unknowingly breached a *tabu* that Ravu's unflappable belief in *kastom* allowed little room for compromise, because he was a man who acted on principle rather than on impulse.

When he told me in a venomous tone that he'd expected me to respond in the same way to his *essengo* as I did to Peta's, by giving him five thousand vatu, I blurted out twice that I had no recollection of the ritual and emphasized that my close shave with Peta had failed to jolt my memory which was still returning. Because of Ravu's brutal reputation, I knew he wouldn't have any qualms about killing me, and since the first time I'd set foot in the highlands, I felt I was definitely about to die. When I looked into Ravu's scathing eyes his rising anger seemed to have pushed any chance of a peaceful resolution past the point of no return. He quietly glared at me for several agonizing minutes, while I came to the sickening realization that at the first sign of violence, I would fight to the death. Back in the village I didn't stand a chance, but here in the jungle, at least I would have a good head start to run for my life if I overwhelmed my attackers. When he finally said, *"Tavua fashion blong bubu rabis"* ("Tavua the fashion of my ancestors is rubbish"), they were the sweetest words I could have hoped to hear. I was amazed that even his unshakable faith in *kastom* had begun to erode and agreed to provide him with a small backpack and a watch instead of giving him money or a traditional form of payment. The volatile atmosphere subsided, but when I sat down to eat, it felt as if my whole body was trembling. The thought of almost having to maim or even kill my close friends made me feel strangely hollow. There wasn't any noticeable shaking in my hands, only a very slight tremor which I easily hid, but inside, I was recovering from the confrontation big time. If I'd faced a total stranger, I wouldn't have felt so emotional, but these were more than just close friends. They were family.

During the walk back up to Nukurekum, Ravu vented his simmering anger. He told me I was a brother, and an incredibly lucky one at that, as he would've killed any other *disale*. If this was a year earlier when he knew little of Sari (Jesus), because I'd reciprocated the *essengo* with Peta, but not him, only my death could adequately appease Taute and the sprits of *bubu*. He really got the phlegm off his chest, and spat out that the next *disale* to enter Middle Bush must die. If a helicopter falls down from the sky, he will kill everyone then burn the chopper. If the government officials who were taking a census ever come back, he will shoot them all through the heart with his bow. He looked at the healed knuckles he'd broken by repeatedly punching a visitor who'd made a derogatory remark about Vepeta, his lovely wife, and kept saying, "*Mus killem finis*" ("*They must die*"). Several villagers had told me that during a fight, Ravu had clubbed a man so hard with his *nul nul* that his victim's brains had hung over his forehead. I knew I'd been extremely lucky to have walked away unscathed.

The thought of leaving for good crossed my mind more than once during the climb up to Nukurekum. When I got back to the village, to get rid of any negative thoughts, I started kidding around with Garae's children who were playing outside our hut. Vira stood between my legs on a raised bamboo seat, and while I pushed him backwards then quickly caught him at the last minute and said, "Just saved you," it sent him into raptures. Just as Garae returned from his garden, when I pushed Vira, his foot slipped and he flailed backwards onto the hard ground. As a trickle of blood flowed from a cut on the child's back, Garae barked, "Rabis fashion" in my face, and for a moment, I wondered if he was going to start hacking into me with his machete. I was definitely having one of those days and quickly apologised for what was an obvious accident.

Humour is a great sedative, so as dawn was breaking the next morning, amidst a friendly and jovial atmosphere, I hiked to a communal garden to help plant kava. Later in the day, when we were walking back to the village, I slipped on a jumble of greasy rocks and split my forehead open. My bleeding brow and the pinkeye I was suffering from in my left eye made Voemanu shriek with laughter the instant I walked into our hut. She closed one eye, held her forehead, and kept mimicking falling onto a rock. Each repeat performance was greeted with the same ecstatic laughter, although deep down everyone was concerned for my wellbeing. Anyone suffering from a minor ailment usually became the brunt of numerous jokes, whereas a serious illness caused grave anxiety, which the villagers always kept to themselves.

The next day, when we were pulling kava deep in the mountains alongside the Lavasuli River, the numerous cockroach bites dotting my stomach sent a wave of laughter through the amused villagers. During the night, Rat, who's one of the peskier village dogs, had slowly pushed the creaky door to our hut open with his snout. Peta had everyone in fits of laughter by re-enacting how I'd sworn at Rat and called him Damate and a *nakaimas* as I chased the dog around the village like a demented lunatic. Even the simplest of acts could incite riotous laughter.

Collectively working together eases the toil of pulling kava. Most crops are located considerable distances from the hamlets, and can only be reached after a hard slog over crippling terrain. When I was paired off with Atison, who'd paid me a visit, it brightened my life up no end. To pull kava, first a pointed sapling is driven into the base of the shrub to loosen the roots. It normally takes two men to push down on the pole to prise them from the soil, then they use their bare hands to wrench the whole shrub out of the ground. Atison was a tough little nut power to weight wise, but he obviously couldn't match the strength of my ninety-kilogram frame. Each time we wrenched a head of kava from the rocky ground, he whooped and yelled, "*Tavua, yu bulldozer blong mi*" ("Tavua, you are my bulldozer"). To help make light work of a tiring task, we sang loudly to Taute, constantly jibed each other, and cracked crude jokes when we were sure the women were out of earshot.

Once we'd gathered enough kava, all of the men rallied together and scrubbed the roots clean in the river with fibrous segments of inner coconut husk. Kava and tribal land are a crucial part of the link between man and the supernatural. Whenever freshly pulled kava is about to be washed in a river, it always rains. From an already sombre sky, the spirits of *bubu* acknowledged our presence by showering us with a brief downpour just as we started cleaning a mountain of roots.

To give us strength for the hard carry back to Nukurekum, we each drank two small bamboo cupfuls of kava. Two of Peta's domesticated pigs that had tagged along trotted beside us like loyal dogs. The slog through the jagged rainforest drew on every ounce of my strength and stamina, and the sturdy sapling I carried with heavy bundles of kava tied to each end pressed painfully into my shoulder. Even Ravu kept pausing to catch his breath and to rest his normally tireless legs as we toiled up each steep slope. Vepeta carried a sizeable cooking stone on top of her already iris-popping load. Rivers of perspiration ran down her back while she cooed to Taute and asked for more stamina to trudge up the muscle burning climbs. I had a real soft spot for Vepeta, her lovely nature and quick smile warmed my heart whenever the harsh realities of highland life taxed my nerves. Her capacity to work long hours in the garden, then carry ridiculously heavy loads back to her hamlet was mind-boggling.

Over the next relaxing week, my mental bruises had faded, there hadn't been any more anxious moments, and I wallowed in a balm of serenity and contentment. I felt a huge sense of relief when Busa passed through the village and left my manhood intact. For someone who'd threatened me with extinction in the past, his verbal reprimand over failing to reciprocate the *essengos* was fairly tame. The gut feeling I had that he would definitely punish me for flouting such a hallowed ritual started not long after he left, when the whole village became painfully aloof. Peta warned me to sleep well, because in the morning when the others carried bags of dried kava down to the lowlands, we were to hunt wild bullock with a spear. Then when I returned, I was to visit Winea.

It was easy to see how the villagers would reason that if I remembered other important information, then I should surely be able to remember the two rites. I tried to tell them I'd studied my notes to make to sure I didn't breach any *tabu*, but it didn't seem to register. For all of its simplicity, the *essengo* is so meaningful and so deeply spiritual, that if I mentioned the spirits of *bubu* hadn't forewarned me of my blunder, I would be seen to have a feeble relationship with the supernatural, which would alienate me even further.

We were up at daybreak, and after munching through a doughy taro, I stepped outside to perform the *bobo* rite, and as I'd anticipated, to pay penance. The early morning mist slowly rolled up the valley walls as we raced down greasy mud caked slopes towards the lowlands. Neither sickness nor age had robbed the spring from Peta's step, and for a man in his mid-fifties, he moved with incredible speed. Gramma glided over the rough ground with ease, and Pilip and Davit, who were both carefree adolescents, revelled in jumping from foothold to foothold. On the near vertical faces where I lacked their nimbleness, I struggled to keep up with the reckless pace. When we stopped to chew and drink kava it provided a welcome rest until our journey started to resemble a pub-crawl. After four drink stops, and slamming back eight bamboo cups filled with medium-strength kava, I wasn't completely hammered but I was well on the way. I knew I was being made to run the gauntlet and accepted each drink Peta thrust into my hands without question.

As we jogged through the jungle, I could tell from the distant rumble that the Jordan River was running dangerously high. While I questioned my sanity to even think about entering the fierce surge when I was intoxicated, Gramma said, "No problem" as we made the first of several crossings. Instead of fighting against the gushing torrent of a river as the inexperienced white man tends to do, man bush literally goes with the flow as he does with all of nature. At one tricky section, Davit and Pilip bounced across the bottom and let the swift current sweep them one hundred metres down stream. The exuberance of their youth robbed them of any fear, and they yelled and laughed as they stood dripping wet on the opposite bank. I fully expected the turbulent water to pluck me off my feet. Instead of looking down at the foaming river, I focused directly ahead so as the water boiling around my legs didn't disorientate my inebriated sense of balance. I threw myself into the first relatively calm section we crossed to revive my numbed senses.

During the strenuous climb up to our hunting ground, the wilting heat soon had us dripping with copious amounts of sweat. It only took several minutes to transform our machetes into lethal spears by tying them to sturdy saplings with the roots of a native fig tree. The herds of cattle roaming the area had recently churned the waterlogged earth into an ankle grabbing bog, but for an uneventful hour we carefully picked our way through the mantle of lavish rainforest and relished its shade while we carefully avoided the numerous *piko* trees armed with flesh tearing thorns. We climbed higher, up to a sizeable plateau, where a pile of warm dung and the tell-tale rustle of vegetation brought us to a halt. The crackle of snapping twigs tightened our nerves, and the sound of hooves squelching in the soft mud followed by a halfhearted bellow sharpened our wits. I lingered behind with Pilip and Davit and watched Gramma and Peta expertly stalk in on our quarry. A gigantic *nambanka* tree gave them perfect cover until they were within striking distance of a sizable herd. They singled out a heifer grazing on the edge of the mob and slowly crept closer. With their crude weapons at the ready, they patiently waited for the right moment, then with perfect timing they instinctively sent their spears flying simultaneously. One struck the animal in the top of the neck and the other found its mark just behind the heifer's front leg.

From the chaotic racket of thundering hooves and saplings breaking with a sharp crack when the cattle exploded into flight, it sounded as if the whole jungle was being bulldozed down. The mortally wounded bullock quickly gained a healthy lead on us as it fled downhill towards the river. We literally took off in hot pursuit and wiped at the sweat stinging our eyes as we charged through the steamy jungle. We flailed through the rainforest for at least a kilometre, and twisted and swerved between the hordes of *piko* trees studded with organic barbed wire until the exhausted heifer noisily ploughed to the ground. *Kastom* prevented us from mercifully ending the bullock's life because it would release its precious spirit. We gasped for air as we stood over the hapless animal and watched it draw its last breath before it gave a final shudder. Gramma and Peta rubbed blood over their machetes to embody them with the heifer's *rapee* for the next hunt, then after they finished performing a short *bobo* rite, they began butchering the bullock. While they were cutting up the meat, they kept glaring in my direction. It wasn't the most comforting feeling to be on the receiving end of their menacing stares, especially when those who are trying to intimidate you have a penchant for violence and are dripping with blood.

Pilip carried the head on his shoulder, Davit placed a light cut of meat on top of his head, and we lifted painfully heavy loads threaded over each end of a stout branch onto our shoulders. No one sung an impassioned thanks to Taute and hardly spoke a word as we traipsed back down to the river to find a campsite. I was being chastised with a wall of silence and the blackest of looks. We stopped at a stretch of dry riverbed that was strewn with uncomfortable looking rocks and started making camp. Even though I knew they had no intentions of sleeping there, as I started cutting *lap lap* leaves for the beds, out of the corner of my eye I caught Gramma and Peta grinning to one another. Peta shouldered his load, then headed for a clear patch of white sand beach alongside the river. Before we made camp, everyone had a brief but well-earned rest. While hordes of buzzing flies started feasting on our piles of bloodied meat, Pilip and Davit kept themselves amused by splattering the insects with well-aimed rocks, and each time they plastered a fly across the beef, they celebrated the kill with a quick victory jig.

We made crude but comfortable beds by topping an underlay of *lap lap* leaves with a thick mattress of *oauk* branches. A few ribs and bits of offal sizzled over the flames of the fires that blazed alongside our beds, and the rest of the beef slowly cooked in parcels of *lap lap* leaves beneath a pile of smoking hot river stones. When darkness entombed our make-shift campsite, we used the subtle glow of burning dried bamboo to find small fish and crayfish swimming in a nearby pool so that we could chop them with our machetes.

When a rock from a cooking fire exploded and showered me with shards of smoking rock, everyone except me reacted with a volley of shouts and roared with laughter. I jumped up and down, and ignored the *tabu* of never complaining as I howled with pain and furiously brushed the burning embers from my smouldering clothes. My profane response and what must have looked like an impromptu Indian rain dance somehow transformed the sullen mood into a light-hearted drinking session, where copious amounts of kava flowed to toast the successful hunt. Peta kept charging our empty bamboo cups until we both vomited.

While we lay side by side on our adjacent beds, Gramma pointed to three stars which according to folklore represent a jubilant hunter returning to his hamlet after a successful hunt. My kava impaired vision turned the hazy constellations into a white blur of two lucky hunters heading for home. After our gruelling day, I was bone tired and quickly drifted off to sleep under a twinkling star studded sky. Despite the strong kava, a bitting chill kept shaking me awake throughout the night. Each time I sat up to hug the fire, there was Peta, sitting on his haunches and continually stoking the flames to ensure I stayed reasonably warm. When an angry looking sky threatened us with rain, he said if the heavens opened up, we would be hunched over and miserable and shaking like a drenched wild fowl with his head tucked down during a storm. The day had been strenuous, and the kava we drank at camp had been potent, yet Peta stayed awake and fuelled the fire until daybreak. His warm-hearted gesture was a sign of affection, and after the way I'd been treated, much more comforting than the flames of his fire.

The next morning I awoke crusty eyed and lethargic and had to feign a smile when Peta kept enforcing my punishment by bombarding my hung over system with more kava. The hearty breakfast of roast beef he gave me was the last thing I needed as it enhanced the debilitating effects of the energy-sapping brew. We shouldered our heavy loads of meat and started the long, hard climb back up to the highlands, to where the rugged peaks were wreathed in ominous black cloud and thick grey walls of rain sluiced down. When we kept stopping along the trail to guzzle more kava, this stretched way beyond the normal amounts of brew we sometimes drank to empower our spirits as we travelled through the jungle. I had to keep suppressing the urge to vomit, and by the time we reached the base of the harsh climb up to Nukurekum, my resilience had been pushed to its absolute limits. My every fibre was totally shattered and all I wanted to do was collapse on the side of the trail, curl up, and go to sleep.

Busa was conveniently sitting on the edge of the swollen stream that swirled past the start of the climb. Although it was the middle of the day, he was plastered on kava, no doubt to receive divine guidance from the sprits of his *bubu* as to how he should punish me. He grabbed his machete then threatened to kill and eat me, and just as the last words of his stern warning left his lips, a huge arc of vomit gushed from his mouth. He broke the following silence by offering me several rounds of mind numbing kava, which I was obliged to accept and which clouded my already hazy vision until it was on the verge of doubling. When Peta started complaining about his aching back and shoulders, it didn't take x-ray vision to see through the translucent façade as Peta never ever moans about anything. Irrespective of the obvious sham, the opportunity to regain everyone's respect was being handed to me on a platter, and right in front of Busa.

I picked up both mine and Peta's cumbersome loads and started the daunting climb up to the village. I slogged upwards in a drunken swagger, through slanting torrents of rain and through the rivulets of water cascading down the sheer greasy trail. Each one of my laborious steps became the sole focus of my entire universe. As my pounding heart thumped against my chest, it felt like battery acid was pumping through my muscles. My lungs burned and begged me to stop for a rest before they burst, but I kept going and staggered into the village ahead of everyone else, having pushed through a newfound agony to conquer the terrain and the debilitating kava.

Voemanu's eyes widened with disbelief, and she shrieked "Weeeee!" when I asked her where she wanted me to dump the meat. I was gasping for breath, and with my lungs puffing like bellows, I blasted new life into the remnants of the fire smouldering alongside my sleeping mat. Half an hour later, Busa squatted beside me and held his outstretched hands towards the warming flames. He looked at the bruises that were starting to appear on my throbbing shoulders, smiled, and then gave an acknowledging look of approval. His one word, "Surprised," said it all. The stain had been removed from my respectability, but I was too weak and too unwell to wallow in the afterglow of having gained total acceptance again.

Chapter Eighteen

ROUGH JUSTICE

The following day, possibly as a reward for the arduous manner in which I regained everyone's respect, Busa invited me to document a rarely practised divination ritual called the *tuvetuveseri*. When Jonli was practising with his bow, he'd accidentally killed Gramma's most prized rooster with a wayward arrow. Everyone had assumed a wild dog or some other predator had taken the bird, and its disappearance was forgotten until word filtered back to Gramma that Jonli had shot it. To teach him a lesson, Gramma took the boy's brand new machete and hid it in the jungle. Although he intended to return the knife in one week's time, and despite the uproar it created, Gramma decided it would teach Jonli the importance of facing the consequences of his actions.

Only stones which have heated food in a cooking fire can be used for the ritual. Busa carefully selected two rocks that fitted into the palm of his hand, then he carried them outside to the *nasara*. He used one of them to drive two short stakes of wild cane into the ground about one hundred millimetres apart and wrapped four wild kava leaves around the base of each stake. Then he held two wild yam leaves on top of one another and pushed them over the stakes until they were lying flat on the ground and sprinkled ash from the cooking fire on top of the leaves. The process was repeated three more times until eight leaves were pushed over the cane, then he looked to the heavens and quietly sang a chant to Taute and to the spirits of his *bubu*. He thumped the ground with a rock and circled it around the stakes four times, then he carefully balanced two pieces of charcoal from the same cooking fire on the top of each stake and told Gramma and Jonli to stand and face one another.

No one uttered a sound as we patiently scanned the sky for half an hour until Gramma broke the lingering silence by pointing to an eagle that was gliding on the thermals. As the bird wheeled directly over our heads, Jonli did the same. A hallowed hush prevailed while Jonli and Gramma remained standing and Busa sat cross-legged with his hands resting on his knees, entering a trance and listening for divine guidance from the spirits. Busa turned to Gramma to pass his sentence and declared that Gramma had hidden the knife and must return it to Jonli, but because the boy had shot his finest rooster, he wouldn't receive a fine or be ordered to pay compensation. Busa and Gramma finished the rite by drinking a shell of kava.

If two adults were involved in the dispute, they would've rekindled their friendship with a kava ceremony and replacing the plaintiff's fowl with another rooster would've sufficed as reparation. Theft of a pig or an item of similar value is so improbable that it's treated as seriously as murder. At the very least, tribal law requires the offending party to replace the lost property with the equivalent of the original article. Such a heinous offence normally incurs the death penalty by way of retribution. Either black magic or violence is used, which explains why the divination ritual is such a rarity. According to Gramma, for me to have witnessed the ceremony had been a huge privilege as only Peta and Busa possess the powers to perform the rite. To reciprocate the honour Busa had bestowed upon me, and for letting me document *kastom*, I gave him my leather belt. I knew he'd been quietly admiring it from the first time he saw it.

Instead of working in the garden with everyone else, I decided to have a lazy day and hung around the deserted village with Gramma. It was great to be able to completely unwind, to bounce jokes off of one another, and to rest my jaded body. We made a tasty lunch of roast beef and *kumala*, and just as we were getting ready to eat, the ever-vigilant dogs barked a frenzied warning that strangers were approaching. I peered outside and saw two Ni-Vanuatu walking towards our hut, and although one of them was a total stranger, because he'd accompanied a highlander who'd moved down to the lowlands, he was guaranteed a warm reception. While his friend stopped to urinate in the bushes, the first-time visitor strolled past the dogs and placed his life in jeopardy by simply placing his foot over the doorway of our hut before we had a chance to offer him a welcome. A stranger is forbidden to go inside a hut until he has been asked to enter, but to do so in a hut which is also a *nakamal* is sacrilege. Gramma frowned and became tense, then after giving it some thought he decided to overlook the serious breach of protocol. To express our offer of friendship, we gave our affable guests a customary token of food. Gramma began chewing a welcome drink of kava and I made small talk with the hungry travellers while they gulped down a plateful of steaming *kumala*. Kapie, who'd errantly barged into the hut, looked to be in his mid-twenties and had a likeable carefree nature. His lively personality literally proved to be his downfall when, without meaning any disrespect, he jokingly said with a smile on his face that drinking chewed kava was "*fashion blong pig*" ("The fashion of a pig"). *Kastom* makes no leeway for ignorance or for scornful comments. Gramma calmly turned to me and in a cold unruffled voice, said, "*Killem Damate!*" ("Kill the devil!") His primitive logic saw Kapie's scathing remark as being on a par with coming straight from the mouth of the devil, and even worse, as someone who scorned our beliefs.

Kapie's companion knew what was about to happen and sprung to his feet, making a hasty beeline for the door. Irrespective of my morals, I was the first to avenge the disrespect that had been shown to our spirits. As Kapie slowly stood up, his look of bewilderment became a grimace when I leapt through the air and slammed a front kick into his temple. In Middle Bush society, if you hesitate during a skirmish, in most cases you'll either be the quick, the seriously injured, or end up dead. I have an incurable addiction to breathing and knew there was no reasoning with Gramma and that if I tried to intervene, I would receive the same brutal treatment. When we launched into a brutal frenzy of kicks and punches. Plenty of blood was already flowing, but I knew bones must break so I reached down and snapped one of Kapie's fingers. I hoped it would end the violence, but as I looked on, Gramma systematically delivered a hail of sickening bone crunching blows and yelled, "*Killem Tavua! Killem!*" Taute needed further appeasement, so I nudged Gramma aside to better line up our moaning victim's thigh and delivered a loud slapping kick that inflicted little pain.

Gramma still hadn't finished. He muttered a string of obscenities when he lifted his foot in the air and stomped on Kapie's outstretched arm, which broke with a loud snap. I felt relieved when Kapie's screaming trailed off to a groan and the nauseating assault was over. He was unable to stand and began whimpering like a wounded animal as he crawled towards the door, so we grabbed a leg each and dragged his quivering body to the edge of the village. Although geographically the archipelago covers six hundred and eighty thousand square kilometres of ocean, in reality, Vanuatu is an extremely small place when it comes to gossip. If word of my involvement in the violent attack leaked to the other islands, not only could it be detrimental to my work, it would probably be hazardous to my health—especially when I visited other racist tribes who would despise a white man who had helped to beat up a native. When I quickly explained the situation to Gramma, he could see the value in keeping the lid closed on the assault. I let Kapie know in no uncertain terms that if he ever breathed a word of what happened to anyone, especially to the police, we would hunt him down and kill him. Gramma kicked him in the head and told him to give his lowland friend the same warning, and then to hasten his delayed response, he gave him another solid kick in the stomach. Although Kapi was semiconscious, he groaned over and over that he wouldn't tell a soul and would say he'd fallen over a bank. The pain must have been unbearable when we lifted him by his arms and legs and threw him down the slope at the village entrance. From the sound of his screaming as we watched him roll down the hill, it was. We yelled that he belonged in the jungle with the devils and walked back inside and finished our lunch.

To be part of a warm welcome that, without any intentional provocation, had suddenly exploded into appalling violence made me realize how lucky I'd been in the past. Christianity's impact wasn't as marked as I thought, and I wondered if maybe the way I was treated was the exception to the brutal rule. I'd witnessed plenty of assaults at *lafaets*, but because I hate violence, I've always remained a spectator. It was easy to maintain my self-respect when I thought about the beating. We'd simply performed a violent ritual to ensure others respected our values and our protocol. The assault wasn't personal or vengeful, it was brazen tribal justice where there was no room to consider the victim's feelings. Because it's deemed as normal in this society, I had no reason to be ashamed of what I'd done and divorced myself from any feelings of guilt. Simply refusing an offer of food or making a derogatory remark about another man's wife receives the same callous treatment. I was grateful when Gramma agreed to tell only Busa and Peta about the attack, as the last thing I wanted was a violent reputation.

My eagerly awaited trip to Winea was postponed when, that night, Busa unexpectedly decided to head down to the lowlands, which also meant Peta had to reschedule the *tamamasa* ceremony for one week's time. With the passing of each day, the sickening stench of rotting beef began to fill our hut. The ripe beef was recooked over and over until I could barely get past the vile smell to force it down my throat. It's ironic that the villagers no doubt thought I would revel in the luxury of enjoying meat on a regular basis, and for the first few days, I looked forward to a sumptuous piece of fresh beef. But it didn't take long for the meat to start rotting and for the stomach-churning meals to take their toll on my health.

Now that I'd shown I had the fighting spirit of a man bush, and that I would resort to violence to protect and enforce our beliefs, Gramma and I formed an inseparable kinship that elevated my standing to a level of acceptance I would otherwise never have achieved. One afternoon I noticed a slight nervousness in his voice when he told me to grab my camera and follow him. After a ten-minute walk from Nukurekum, he stopped and checked in every direction to make sure no one had followed us, then we stepped about twenty metres off the side of the trail, where he carefully parted the overgrown vegetation around the base of a *namele* palm. He checked again to make sure we didn't have any company, then pulled out an almost rectangular stone and lovingly cradled the rock as a father would a frail newborn child. A shallow depression had been carved into the top, and just below that, a groove had been etched around the rock's entire circumference. According to legend, Molilelei, who was an ancient chief Taute created from an *oro* tree, had shaped the sacred fetish millennia ago.

An enormous honour and a gargantuan amount of trust had just been bestowed upon me. Before I could view the rock, Gramma needed Peta's and Busa's unanimous consent, as they are the guardians and the only other men who are still alive that have ever viewed Sulevous, which translates to "the stone that is used for kava." Molilelei's potent spirit resides within Sulevous and is evoked whenever a man with immense *rapee* sacrifices pigs to become a chief. To achieve the elevated status of paramount chief, Busa first sacrificed fifty roosters. When he and Peta killed ten sacrificial boars with curved tusks, they both used Sulevous. During this most hallowed of rites, no one else must view the stone and only those who have used its potent supernatural powers are present. The stone is placed at the base of the *nakamal's* centre post, where the ancient remains of previous chiefs are buried. Busa was the only other person that was present when Peta became a chief. He milked *tabu* kava into a coconut shell which was placed on the top of the stone, then they drank the brew while they were holding a *namele* leaf. Peta went outside to the *nasara* and touched each of his tethered pigs on the forehead, first with the *namele* leaf and then with his *nul nul*. Instead of clubbing the animals to death with his *nul nul*, which is the norm during a pig kill, he stuck them with a knife. When the blood flowed onto the sanctified ground of the *nasara*, he not only reaped Molilelei's *rapee*, he became embodied with the spiritual power of every chief who had used the stone. One of the pigs was gifted to Busa as payment for preparing the *tabu* kava. During the feast that followed, Peta's immediate relatives were forbidden to dine on the flesh of the sacrificial animals, whereas those from outside of his bloodline enjoyed a huge *lafaet*, where the pigs took pride of place on the menu. The members of his bloodline also dined on pork, but from another batch of pigs that Peta killed for them.

The economic burden of attaining chiefdom equates to a hefty mortgage in a civilized society, especially when the sacred stone is used, as every highlander and every distant relative living in the lowlands is invited to the feast. Peta and Busa had over three hundred hungry mouths to feed. Copious amounts of kava flow and mountains of food are consumed during a celebration that normally lasts for one week. The responsibility rests solely on an aspiring chief's shoulders to rear ten pigs with curved tusks and to supply all of his guests with food and kava, but to do so is a physical impossibility. To maintain political and social stability, no matter how affluent a man is, *kastom* forbids him to purchase sacrificial pigs with money. That way, anyone who doesn't possess the respectability or doesn't have the full support of the villagers can't buy his leadership, and only those who are willing to face the responsibilities of incurring a huge debt ever succeed. The only way a man can become a patriarch is by becoming deeply indebted to the members of his bloodline, who loan him extra pigs, supply crops, and provide labour for the *lafaet*. It takes him years to settle his debts with the equivalent amount of crops and the same number of pigs, which he must rear with the help of his immediate family. In the past, to secure himself a good place in the afterlife, a chief would sometimes sacrifice as many as twenty pigs. At times the highlanders are an insanely jealous people, but chiefdom is never envied, only deeply respected. For a people who are already living a demanding and often precarious subsistence lifestyle, becoming a chief is considered to be a lot of backbreaking, long-term work, with few fringe benefits during life as a mortal.

Tabu rocks also play an important role in everyday life. Stones which are personified with ancestral spirits are strategically hidden around the village perimeter to act as supernatural guardians. If anything untoward happens in a hamlet during its inhabitant's absence, the magical rocks cry out like a child and warn that all isn't well when the villager returns. Sometimes the spirits of *bubu* speak directly to the village elders and identify the offender. If a serious crime has been committed, the perpetrator is usually killed on sight or the *tabu* stones will inflict a curse, and the culprit's death is delivered in the guise of an accident or illness.

That evening, after being allowed to photograph the *tabu* rock, I decided to push the trust I'd been shown to its extreme limits. While I worked on Malakula Island, I managed to take the most *tabu* of photos. Some of the staff at Port Vila's cultural centre were amazed that I'd been able to take shots of a primitive Small Nambas villager holding an ancestral skull. I had to be careful as simply showing the prints to man bush could evoke an unwelcome response. They had warned me several times that they would kill anyone who ever tried to photograph the skulls of their forefathers. I felt confident the time was right, as being able to photograph the stone fetish had proved the highlanders' appreciated the vital importance of documenting even the most sacred aspects of their culture for future generations. I waited until a group of men gathered in our *naka-mal* to drink kava, then I pulled out one of the shots. The instant Gramma's younger brother, Maiken, cast his eyes on the skull, he became both entranced and traumatized. His eyes nervously darted across the forbidden image for several minutes, and then with a sudden jerk, he threw the print to the ground as if it had given him an unexpected electric shock. In the urban areas, Ni-Vans viewed the photos with a relatively unemotional and morbid curiosity, but in Middle Bush, where ancestral skulls are lovingly worshiped and held in the highest esteem, the photo was viewed with either stark terror or the utmost reverence. Ravu held the print, looked back at me, and then gazed intently into the shot for ages. Everyone was in awe, not only that I'd taken the photo, but also that the Small Nambas and their ancestral spirits had allowed me to live for capturing such a hallowed object on film. The instant that Make, Busa's younger but much taller brother, joined a hub of men mulling over the photos, he suddenly stopped slapping his head in a vain attempt to kill his annoying infestation of lice. He became mesmerised by the sacrosanct shot and stood there for several minutes with his mouth agape. Until I laid the women's fears to rest, they literally jumped back with fright and were terrified that they faced certain death from viewing even a photo of such a powerful and hallowed object.

The next day, Peta began making preparations for a huge *tamamasa* ceremony. The size of the *lafaet* is relative to the respect a man has earned from those who are attending the feast and to the amount of esteem that is being bestowed upon the person who is being honoured. So as not to place any unnecessary burden upon Peta, I asked Gramma to try and persuade him to tone down the rite. Peta agreed to keep the feast relatively small, but still sacrificed his finest fowl, which he roasted in the *unamoru* (heated cooking stones) along with a mountain of taro and other readily available foods.

When the sun had reached its zenith, I grabbed a long wooden pestle called the *bonatolo* and joined Ravu and Peta around the *rova*. The large oblong wooden plate is used to make and serve *nalot*, which is a tasty dish that's made from pulverised taro. Vigorously pounding the taro into dough is part of an important and energetic ritual that lets everyone know the *lafaet* is about to begin. Our frenzied hammering became so intense that sweat coursed down our bodies and dripped into the steaming taro. While Ravu and I stopped to rest our aching muscles, Peta pounded out a pulsating tune called the *kore*. The resounding thud lets everyone know that *nalot* is being pounded and calls anyone within earshot to join the *lafaet*. Once the taro was softened, a doughy base which is about fifty millimetres thick was spread over the whole of the dish, and then a topping of coconut oil that had been boiled and refined into sweet golden crumbs garnished the *nalot*. Ravu cut out a small square in the centre, filled the void with coconut oil, and then poured the rich oil over the entire creation. The completed dish is called *kira lacona*, and after Ravu cut it into squares, he kept spitting on the edge of his oil-covered hand and pushed it along all of the cuts to separate each portion.

Several other dishes completed our traditional smorgasbord. Busy groups of women made *tuluk* by wrapping grated manioc around pieces of decaying beef, then slowly baking the small parcels inside *lap lap* leaves that they buried amongst the cooking stones. They also made *ori*, which is manioc that's prepared in a similar fashion but without the sickly filling. Once the *ori* was cooked, the rubbery segments were placed on wooden plates and covered with succulent coconut milk.

Thirty villagers filed into the *nakamal*, which by highland standards was a relatively small crowd. Five chiefs stood in a row, and each of them was holding a full shell of kava. When Peta walked to the centre of the hut, it caused an instant hush to fall over the drone of subdued chatter. He launched into a touching speech and told the crowd his past grievances with Tavua were buried. Now that we were true *kastom* brothers, he had nothing but absolute respect for me, and his material possessions were no longer his own, they belonged to both of us, as did any of life's burdens or problems that we might face. The crowd was visibly moved by the last of his affectionate words when he said if we entered battle together, he valued my life more than his own and without hesitation, he would willingly sacrifice his own mortality to ensure that I lived. The gifting of a pig, a mat, or a fowl at any time is a mark of inseparable kinship and of huge respect, but to have a fowl sacrificed, and then a mat gifted during the *tamamasa* ceremony is one of the biggest honours a villager can bestow upon another man. When it was my turn to speak, I reciprocated by saying that what was mine was also his and added it would be an honour to travel to the spirit world having sacrificed my life during battle for a brother with such powerful *rapee*. Peta handed me a shell of kava, which I gulped down in one hit, and then he refilled the shell and did likewise. Each chief took his turn to say a few words that focused on bestowing me with deep respect, to which I offered a similar reply. I shared kava from each of their shells, and in doing so, we formed an inseparable bond. My status in Middle Bush had just soared to a height that should have been way beyond the reach of a *disale*. To have such a close alliance with Peta, the second most powerful man in the highlands, put me in a position that every man bush would envy.

Once the formalities were over, it was time to party. Before we attacked the mountain of food, we drank shell after shell of kava, and although kava is a natural hunger suppressant, it did little to curb the villagers' voracious appetites. Make's ability to gorge gluttonous amounts of food is legendary throughout the highlands. At a food stall in Luganville, he once consumed five large servings of rice and beef in a single sitting. While I was helping Ravu clear a new garden, when we stopped for a brief lunchbreak, he ate eighteen large bananas with ease. The selfless villagers are anything but greedy, but during a *lafaet*, they have seemingly insatiable appetites. I slowly munched through the generous portions of food that were piled in front of me until my stomach ached and it felt as though my bulging intestines were about to rupture.

Any pig kill or a *lafaet* where *kastom* has been made is always followed by a dance, and it didn't take long for impromptu singing and festive dancing to break out. The monotonous thump of the *tam tam* and the hollow sound of *bolo* sticks (one metre long portions of bamboo) pounding the ground soon had everyone stomping and twirling around the *nakamal*. A group of small boys warbled a shrill tune with shell whistles made from the *mele* nut. Their cheeks gently puckered each time they blew into an opening at the end of the shell and as they delicately lifted their fingers over holes that are drilled into each side of the tiny instrument. Like most of the drunken men, I staggered outside and vomited numerous times. It was four in the morning when I finally collapsed in an exhausted heap on my sleeping mat to snatch a few hours of sleep before the *kimpeti* dance started.

It felt as though I'd just drifted off to sleep when Peta shook me awake and told me to put on a *mul mul* and wait in the village. I stepped outside to revive my sluggish senses with some fresh air just as everyone disappeared over the hill to Vanakanakarea. The *kimpeti* is traditionally a welcome dance, but after careful communion with the spirits and getting their approval, Peta adapted *kastom's* slightly flexible rules to suit his own needs. When he returned with the others and slowly walked down the steep slope from Vanakanakarea, his evocative voice sang of welcoming me into his heart. A chief from another village who carried a large portion of a *wiaer* tree stopped every few paces to quietly chant, and then shook the mushroom of foliage above his head before he started walking again. The bright cloth of the men's *mul muls*, the purple flowers behind some of the women's ears, and the stripes and squiggles the young boys had smeared on their faces with the bright orange pigment from the *ol* nut added a vibrant splash of colour. Most of the men wore *tabu* leaves which they'd tucked into the side of their loincloths. By the time the keyed up crowd of dancers entered the *nasara*, their emotions were running high. Peta launched into a few lines of fervent song, and then after his brief cue, the other men joined his singing with voices that were charged with passion. The feverish nucleus of men pounded the earth in perfect unison with two metre long *lauma* sticks (bamboo dance sticks), while I fell into step with a swirling throng of women and children and ran around the core of men until a thick sheen of sweat was dripping from all of our bodies. During the brief moments of rest, to let us catch our breath, the *wiaer* tree pounded the ground while the chief sang a haunting melody.

It was two in the afternoon when Peta led us into the *nakamal* for another kava ceremony that turned out to be a primer for another mammoth drinking session. It was two in the morning when I fell onto my sleeping mat in a drunken and worn out heap, while the others carried on with their tireless drinking binge until dawn.

The hard living and the detrimental effects of dining on rotten meat for weeks were taking a heavy toll on my health. Committing hygiene suicide had turned my complexion a jaundiced yellow colour, and my normally bright eyes were dulled and had discoloured whites. I decided to follow Gramma when he headed to Luganville the following day so I could visit a doctor and then return later.

It's ironic that the most stunning stretch of the Jordan River is also where the river's most violent piece of history took place. We waded through its waters and along its banks, in the hope of reaching the road back to civilization before nightfall. As I watched swallows gracefully darting amongst a gorge whose beautifully slotted contours flow from one ribbed layer to the next, it was easy to forget the violent forces of nature that carved such a striking sight are equalled by the small canyon's turbulent past. Each time we pass through the chasm, the villagers share my awe—but for a different reason. They splash through the one hundred metre long canyon as quickly as possible because they believe the portion of river they call *lococoma* is inhabited by Damate. Centuries ago, the waters rushing through the canyon ran red when scores of warriors were massacred in one of the island's bloodiest battles. When Peta was a child, the villagers always travelled through the gorge in single file and held onto the shoulders of the person in front of them. If they failed to observe this *tabu*, it was believed the native lagging at the rear would be whisked away by Damate and vanish into thin air. Nowadays only a few of the elderly villagers abide by the *tabu*.

Gramma agreed to pose for a few quick photos about thirty metres from the end of the canyon. Before I even had a chance to grab my camera, a huge boulder that could easily have killed us slammed into the water between us with so much force that it sent a plume of spray into the air. We were both standing midstream and instinctively looked up to see where the rock had come from. It was an eerie experience, as no other debris, not even a lone leaf or solitary pebble fell over the sandstone walls, and there hadn't been the sound of crashing vegetation or anything else to forewarn us. Gramma turned to me and yelled, *"Damate mo Pulminero himi hearem yu Tavua!"* ("Damate and Pulminero the spirit devil feel your presence, Tavua!") He swore at the devils, then ploughed through the water at full speed, with me following in his wake until we splashed out of the gorge to safe ground. The rock had slammed into the water with such a sudden and frightening impact, that both of us were shaking when we stopped running. When we looked at each other, there was no nervous laughter, only a stunned silence while we regained our composure.

After what had just happened, I felt now was a good time to tell Gramma about the hideously graphic dreams I'd been having since my initiation. During the last night of each of my visits to the highlands, in vivid technicolour, I saw myself standing helpless and rooted to the spot not by fear, but by an overwhelming demonic force. As I screamed a mute warning, I witnessed a black devil slowly murdering my immediate family back in New Zealand, one by one, and in the most horrific and inhuman ways imaginable. Gramma told me my faith in *kastom* and Taute must remain strong, and then he rubbed wild kava leaves over my body and then over himself to drive out the devil. He warned me that Damate and the other malevolent spirits of the jungle were attacking my soul. Since my early childhood, even though I'm not a spiritual person, the Maori blood flowing through my veins provided me with an inherent but subtle awareness of the spirit world. I'd been a part of tangible events that defied science and logic, but I never questioned or tried to rationalize them. To my mother and I, they were simply an unquestionable part of Maoridom that we kept to ourselves. For the first time, I experienced a chilling fear like I'd never felt in my entire life. It froze my blood, literally made me shiver, and raised goose bumps on my arms and legs. I felt so uneasy, that the pristine river meandering through the luscious rainforest suddenly seemed sinister and uninviting.

Chapter Nineteen

DISGRUNTLED DEVOTION

Nearly a year had slipped by before I returned to Middle Bush, and in that time the highlanders' timeless world had been subjected to further change. They'd been rushed through the ages to keep pace with the white man's spirituality, learned his morals and picked up his vices. Their desire to experience the better way of life the church promised, their ailments that were induced by old age, an uncertain future, and spiritual disillusionment had caused a small exodus of Middle Bush villagers to live in the lowlands. They weren't living in harmony with *kastom* any more, which meant they could never be at peace with themselves.

Before Gramma and I climbed up to Nukurekum, we visited a tiny hamlet, comprised of two huts which Busa had built, thirty minutes' walk from the Jordan River. They were in a serene setting surrounded by luxuriant jungle and provided him with a perfect base when he visited the lowlands. But the tranquil atmosphere Matantas who were raiding his crops and stealing from the huts and from nearby villages. Busa was disappointed that the wayward bullets that had been fired at the fleeing criminals had failed to kill anyone or at least managed to draw blood. He'd called an urgent meeting, as such a heinous crime demanded swift retribution. Each villager held the floor and had his input as to how the problem should be rectified. Like all dilemmas, the issue was discussed at monotonous length, only to be repeated over and over until the speaker had fully voiced his opinion. When Busa asked for my thoughts, I also repeated several times that if we had to resort to violence, which seemed to be the general consensus of the previous speakers, we shouldn't shoot to kill. Busa graciously thanked everyone, and after a short but careful deliberation, he gave his final verdict. After listening to hours of passionate discussion, his ruling was to shoot to kill on sight. There could be no second chances or warning shots as the thieves had blatantly chosen to ignore his previous warnings.

The highlands' judicial system is ruthless, yet fair to those who live within the boundaries of tribal law. Individual chiefs deal with trivial matters, and black magic or clan retribution is used to kill those who commit serious crimes. If an offender fails to pay compensation to heal a rift, several chiefs hold a court, and the guilty villager is sentenced to pay a fine to the plaintiff of a pig, a mat, or a fowl. Then if the criminal still fails to compensate his victim, an additional hefty fine of twenty thousand vatu is imposed. Although it very rarely happens, if the fine still isn't paid, then the villager is sentenced to death, and the spirits are called upon to inflict the severe sentence.

There were enough trigger-happy highlanders living in the lowlands to take care of the problem, so the next day we headed back up to Nukurekum. While I was pushing through a low patch of thick vegetation, I stumbled onto my hands and knees and felt a sharp nip, then a searing pain in my neck. Gramma took a look at the angry welt and thought that maybe a scorpion had stung me, but although it was painful, I felt something less toxic was responsible. He rubbed the milky sap from the stem of a *krismas* plant over the red swelling, which seemed to help nullify the venom of whatever had stung me and provide some welcome relief. If a *melpat* (centipede) was thought to have inflicted the bite, the cure would probably have done little to alleviate the insect's agonizing bite. The highlanders break ten twigs across the top of their head and sing to Taute.

We arrived at Nukurekum just at dusk, and once my eyes adjusted to the twilight darkness of the interior of our hut, I could see Vetrivu cowering in the corner. I was amazed when, for a brief moment, she still thought I was Damate until Voemanu calmed her down. Vetrivu may have clung to her old values during my absence, but there were those who were taking a gigantic leap of faith across the ages and across a gaping spiritual divide to embrace Christianity. The church's attempts to modernize the village seemed to have peaked without any real impact. Apart from a volleyball court outside our hut, the surroundings were still extremely primitive. Little had changed physically, but mentally, the highlanders were in a state of upheaval and discontent.

On my first Sunday morning back in Middle Bush, a bell tolled from Vanakanakarea to call everyone to church. A growing flock was small consolation to the frazzled nerves of the protestant teacher cum preacher, as the mental strain of living in constant fear had finally eroded the last of his crumbling resolve. He planned to resign at the end of the year and had recommended to his superiors that no replacement should be sent to fill the vacant position. When I traipsed behind Ravu and most of the other villagers up the hill to Vanakanakarea, it came as no surprise to see the teacher was taking a brief break from the stresses of his challenging position, but I was aghast to see Atison dressed in full religious garb while he nervously stood at the pulpit. He kept fretfully wringing his hands and his anxiety made him cough as he struggled to read quotes from a protestant bible written in Bislama. His ability to have learnt the basics of reading in only a few short months was incredible.

Due to my beliefs, the dull sermon failed to keep me interested, so I focused on the way the restless and disjointed congregation was reacting. A constant murmur of garbled chatter continued while Atison stumbled through reading a passage from the bible. Because I was completely impartial to the villagers' religious decisions, it made it easy to make the comparison between Christianity and *kastom*. Ravu and I joked with one another throughout the service, but to do something as unthinkable or as disrespectful during a ritual would incur a brutal penalty. Atison's eyes were confused and empty when he looked to the heavens to lead a hymn and were missing the spark and the smiling shine they radiated during *kastom* rituals. Rather than projecting with pride and commitment, he swallowed the words of his song. His voice lacked the passion and the enthusiasm that's associated with singing or dancing during a primitive ritual, and the apathetic hymn didn't have the fervour and the doubtless understanding of a *kastom* song.

While an uninterested crowd listened to Gramma's closing sermon, he was a very different person to the one I'd known when he preached to the bored parishioners. His normally humble nature was horribly eclipsed by self-importance as he belted out the sermon. It was almost as if, under this roof, he enjoyed an elevated standing in the community, where he could impose his intelligence and superiority to gain prestige amongst the illiterate villagers. But once the sermon was over, he became the Gramma I admired again.

It was so easy to see how the more impressionable villagers could start to merge the two faiths. Both religions believe in the power of gods, spirits, sacred fetishes, sorcery, prayer, and devils. And both beliefs had practiced the ultimate sacrifice. Man bush believed that the *disale* god had sacrificed the blood of his own son to appease mankind, while they offer human blood to appease the gods. When they compared the bible to *kastom*, many beliefs and, more importantly, several placenames were the same. Having the Jordan River flowing through Santo became an important catalyst to converting even the staunchest of pagans. The early missionaries twisted stories from the scriptures to suit their own personal goals and to increase their following. Around the middle of the nineteenth century, the evangelist's manipulative tales filtered up to the highlands and are still being passed on to each successive generation. They told the natives that Noah first built the ark atop of Mount Tambewassana, and after it rained for forty days and nights, when the ship floated past the highlands, Noah left the *natangora* (sago palm) so that they could use its leaves to rethatch their rooves once the flooding subsided. Nowadays, Supemalau village in south Santo believe Noah's legacy remains in the form of a boat shaped rock which is perched atop of a nearby mountain. The self-imposed guardians of the deity trek up to the rock each day for worship and to keep it cleared of the ever-encroaching vegetation.

While everyone milled around outside after the service, I asked why outsiders are still vigorously repelled, but the *disale's* Christianity had been allowed into the highlands. Ravae spoke first and told me education and medicines were the sole incentive. The lowlanders enjoy the benefits of good healthcare and are becoming more knowledgeable when it comes to dealing with alien influences. By using what they have learnt wisely and cautiously, it seems to be benefiting the community. When *kastom* healing fails, modern pharmaceuticals save lives. But, he told me, he feels deeply saddened by having to inevitably compromise a part of *kastom* for the material returns of the *disale* church. Once future generations are better educated, they will enjoy a deeper understanding of their own future if the government invades the highlands for land or for its natural resources. Cultivating kava to get cash is hard work. Those who gain employment in town will bring a better business sense and more affluence into the highlands, but before the introduction of the church, there was no need for a steady income or to have an understanding of how to handle finances. Now, what little money the people have is spent on clothes and schooling, while they struggle to pay off their Toyota pickup. Having so many children in one area is placing demands on the region's resources, and the villagers have to venture further into the jungle for various items that would otherwise remain plentiful. Bigger bundles of already crippling loads of firewood are being carried from farther distances to comply with the highlanders' stringent conservation laws. Ravae was disillusioned by the compromises man bush has had to make.

For the first time in his life, Gramma feels guilt, and he's almost ashamed of introducing Christianity now that the hospital supplies the medicines he so desperately sought. He feels the new beliefs he's implanted have flourished into a cancerous growth that is slowly destroying everyone's previously happy mindset. Without *kastom*, he would feel empty, and he's concerned that its void will be filled with a hollow purpose he'll never be able to grasp. Now it feels as if working in the garden is only to eat rather than to appease and call upon the spirits and Taute while he sings and yells. The toil of gardening seems much harder and the results are less satisfying. Even planting and pulling kava feels different, as now it's mainly grown for money. His heart and soul tell him he must revert back to *kastom*. He's confused about what he's done, as the repercussions are far worse than he could ever have imagined.

Peta felt angry, sad, worried, and betrayed by the church's lack of compromise for *kastom's* beliefs. He feels that without the dignity and respect *kastom* instils in a man, he can never be complete.

No one could understand why the pastors take money from struggling and destitute villagers who clearly have little. More importantly, no one could fathom why the ministers allow the highlanders to walk past their hut without inviting them in to share food as man bush always does. To them it was a heinous breach of *kastom*. Above all else, they asked me why the church only offered the bible. They wanted to know why there aren't other books which offer them well-informed choices. Because the white man's religion condemns other factions who worship the same god, they couldn't understand the hypocrisy, and they asked me why anyone should be damned to hell for being an atheist, as every highlander will go to Taute's heaven after they die. To answer their question of whether they would burn amidst hell's eternal fires if they returned to *kastom*, I told them that an estimated scant twenty percent of New Zealanders attend a Christian church and that if the rest of us are going to hell, many who are good and loving people with enviable morals, it's going to be standing room only.

From deep within the eyes of the old reflected a sad resignation that despite their attempts to faithfully adhere to *kastom*, for future generations, things will never be the same. Outsiders will still be vigorously repelled, but with Christianity's seed germinating in Middle Bush, many view the alien religion that belongs to the unscrupulous *disale* as an impending omen of an unwanted and uncertain future, filled with false hopes and broken promises. But worst of all, they know it will eventually lead to the loss of *kastom* and their inherent spiritual identity. Rather than Christianity filling the villagers' hearts with love and joy, the majority of them felt discontented and unhappy.

In the past, the Ni-Vanuatu missionaries who tried to enter the highlands have always been told to leave immediately, despite them telling me otherwise in front of their flock in Luganville. An Australian pastor was allowed to spend two nights at Nukurekum during my absence, but only because he belongs to the protestant mission service. Most of the European evangelists who have tried to spread the gospel have been instantly threatened with violence.

The desire for European goods and the need for a steady income had broken down the cast iron morals that have resiliently withstood development and change for centuries. *Kastom* was starting to develop a few chinks in its armour. When chief Susurobo from nearby Vunasuli village led four Ni-Vanuatu members of the Christian Fellowship church through Nukurekum, the previously relaxed atmosphere instantly soured into a mood of discontent. A middle-aged minister hailing from Ambrym Island reeked of narrow-minded arrogance as he strutted towards me like a cocky village rooster. While his tired looking companions pressed on, when he walked past me he barked in a venomous tone, "I will talk to you later!" Then he flashed a conceited sneer, spat at the ground, and wearily traipsed after the others. I had absolutely no idea what motivated the missionary to target me and didn't give the rude greeting a second thought until later in the day when a heated conversation erupted inside our *nakamal*.

Only his god knows what motivated the Christian Fellowship's pastor to tell all of Vunasuli village that Tavua was a *giavman* (liar) who was stealing *kastom* for his own financial gain. Whatever the reason was, it wasn't a very Christian action that spawned close fellowship. Peta and Gramma knew this wasn't true as I'd shown them a letter that Ralph Regenvanu from the museum and cultural centre had given me, which mentioned copies of my slides and articles would be stored in the archives as a reference for future generations. A note that was attached to the letter showed a copy had been faxed to the Sanma provincial office, who I was supposed to register with before and after each trip to the highlands, as the cultural centre held fears for my safety. I decided not to clock in and out with the authorities because I'd willingly chosen to enter Middle Bush at my own risk, and irrespective of what happened to me, I didn't want the highlanders to suffer any repercussions. Several animated villagers in the *nakamal* started waving their arms furiously and vented their anger with harsh raised voices as they pointed in my direction. I was totally oblivious as to what was going on and felt uneasy, and with good reason, for if this had been my first visit to Middle Bush, my family would've killed me for stealing *kastom*, without question and without remorse. Peta and Gramma both swore and shot me angered looks as they charged out the door. With a sense of urgency they sprinted up the hill towards Vunasuli village yelling, "*Tamamasa Tavua. Tamamasa Tavua*" ("Everything is alright, Tavua. Everything is alright, Tavua.")

Not only was the impending acceptance of the Christian Fellowship another crushing blow to traditional life, it could just as easily have driven the last nail in my coffin. Without so much as a second thought for their own safety, Gramma and Peta charged into Vunasuli and bailed up the minister on my behalf. If the pastor labelled me a liar, all of Nukurekum's inhabitants shared the same despicable insult. My *kastom* brothers read the missionary the riot act and told him if so much as one more scathing remark was directed at Tavua, blood would flow here and now. The stunned but still obnoxious pastor said, "That's enough," and offered his hand. He has no idea how close his arrogant remark brought him to a sudden and violent death, and luck stayed on his side when he demanded that Peta and Gramma give him my full name. To curb a possible outbreak of inter-clan violence, they drew on all of their self-restraint, and it was only because the obnoxious evangelist was the guest of Vunasuli's chief that they returned to Nukurekum.

The Christian Fellowship dangled a massive material carrot under the nose of Vunasuli's inhabitants when they promised to build them a guesthouse where they could charge tourists to stay alongside the Lappe River. The Christians told them the National Tourism Office would fund the project and that the guesthouse would be gifted to Vunasuli if they reciprocated by allowing a church to be erected in their village. How and why I ever became involved is still a mystery, but once I learnt what had happened, I was scathing. Not once have I ever held any personal contempt towards missionaries, but that had just changed. Rather than the organization, I held the pastor personally responsible for putting my life at risk. I told Gramma and Peta I wanted to give him more than my name, and grabbed a *nul nul* and headed out the door. Whether he was a respected man of the cloth or not, *kastom* demanded that I beat him to a pulp, or so I thought. Because a chief had brought him to Middle Bush as a guest, no one had the right to intervene until *kastom* had been breached. Although the minister had disrespected our protocol, now that Peta and I were one kindred spirit, Peta had confronted the Christian to protect his beloved brother Tavua. I was relieved that violence wasn't necessary, but made it known that if the missionary violated a *tabu*, he was mine.

The mere thought of culturally insensitive tourists tramping through the villages worried me. For a country that has so much to offer to travellers, Vanuatu would be committing tourism suicide, because deaths would be inevitable. The other chiefs quickly made it clear that if sightseers so much as looked at them wrongly, they would be hacked to death with machetes. Busa remained calm and said it was Vunasuli's land and any decision lay with them, but he put out a message that if any tourist breached even the smallest of *tabus*, they would have either their breasts or testicles cut off. The organs were to be fed to the victims while they were still alive, they would mercifully be shot with a bow and arrow, and then he would celebrate every death with a cannibal feast. If a tourist even pointed a camera at anyone from Nukurekum, Gramma threatened to slice all of them up with his bush knife. He was furious and imposed immediate sanctions on Vunasuli and made it known that no matter how dire any of their health problems were, none of them would have access to the medicines in his leaf hut clinic or receive any type of treatment. Despite the obvious friction the Christian Fellowship was creating, in the name of the Lord, they arrogantly started making plans to mark out a site for the proposed guesthouse and walked around with big smiles plastered across their smug faces now that their church was gathering momentum in the highlands.

When I travelled back to Port Vila later on, I couldn't find anyone associated with the National Tourism Office or any other tourism related agency who had any knowledge of the minister or of his plans to build a guesthouse in Middle Bush. I warned them that if they were approached to help with any form of marketing, not to offer any assistance if the project eventuated, as it would undoubtedly result in the injury of a luckless and probably innocent tourist.

Several days later, Garae was deep in the jungle and about to end a long and hard day of cutting firewood when a wayward swing of his machete hacked into his big toe. The keen edge of his freshly sharpened knife sliced the underside of his toe from the tip to the back where the toenail begins. He wrung sap from the stalk of a wild kava shrub into the gaping wound to stem the gush of blood and scraped kava bark into the cut to relieve the pain during the strenuous one-hour trek back to the village. When Gramma carefully unwrapped the bandage of leaves that covered Garae's shaking foot, the flap of flesh clearly needed stitching. Garae refused my offer to stitch the gash together and held his shaking leg still while Gramma rinsed the cut clean. Then Garae slit a fowl's throat and let the blood pour into the wound to replace the blood he'd lost. The three of us had planned to visit Winea in the morning, and in spite of his injury, after a strong drink of relaxing kava, Garae told us not to leave without him.

Even walking must have hurt, but during the trek to Winea the next day, Garae divorced himself from the pain as we trotted along at a brisk pace through the steamy rainforest then dropped down to the Lappe River. We'd taped the corner of a rice bag over his heavily bandaged toe, and by the time we'd reached the river, it had filled with blood. Up until now, holding a grudge against the minister seemed like a waste of my emotions, but when I looked away from Garae's bloodied toe, I kept seeing red when I watched the missionaries crudely marking out the profile of the proposed guesthouse with rocks on the river flats below us. While we listened to them laughing and whooping several hundred metres away, Gramma snarled that they won't be so happy when he kills the first tourist who visits the nearby *tabu* waterfall. Garae's venomous tone belied his composed look when he said, "They can visit, but they'll have a real good look at the water when I hack them up with my machete, then drown them in the pool."

The way Garae scaled the face up to Winea without rest or complaint typifies the resilience of man bush. Even though I was fit and healthy, I couldn't keep up with his blistering pace, and by the time I'd caught up to him and Gramma at the halfway point, I was gasping for breath. Gramma had fully recovered, and Garae had found and cut three tubes of bamboo that were full of water. When I took a swig, as soon as the first rancid mouthful hit the bottom of my stomach, I vomited. My light-hearted flood of profanity had Garae quickly apologising for not sampling the fluid first, and he offered me what was left in his sweet tasting tube. Three quarters of the way up the hill, we shouldered heavy loads of firewood that had been left on the side of the track and dumped the wood just below the village, where I put on my *mul mul* before we entered Winea.

No one had told the last of the pygmy women that Tavua was about to pay them a visit. When Eten and Vivi saw a *disale* for the first time, they hurled the half-finished mats they were weaving into the air and shrieked in horror. Then they sprang to their feet and scurried into the nearest hut as fast as their stumpy little legs would carry them. Silas and Matai strode across the *nasara* to greet me and roared with laughter at the terrified women's response. They hugged my waist, tugged at my *mul mul*, and expressed their approval of my loincloth with a loud yell. When we entered their hut to drink kava and to eat the customary offering of food, the two women shrieked with fright and scampered out the rear door.

After a hearty meal of taro, Sakele and Matai gave their muscular stomachs a pat, then they leapt over the *lap lap* leaf plates and grabbed an arm each and started gnawing on my biceps. They took an imaginary bite and started chewing slowly, then they burst out laughing and gave my muscles a firm squeeze. Sakele urged me to eat another helping of taro and said, "Tavua, another couple of weeks of good food will make your belly fat and greasy like a bullocks. Number one for eating." He jokingly licked his lips and gave me a look that said I would make good eating.

Silas rubbed his hand over my stubble, then told me that if I didn't shave, after another month of growth I'd be ready for a beard cutting ceremony. From the first hair that sprouts on an adolescent's chin, the years leading up to a boy growing a full beard are greatly anticipated. Although a child may act and carry himself like a man, this is the long-awaited, true coming of age. When a beard is shaved for the first time, it's the relished rite of passage into adulthood, and the single most important moment in a male's life. The cutting of the facial growth is entrusted to an initiate's uncle, but if he doesn't have an uncle, any male from the same bloodline is chosen. For each snip of beard that falls away, the feathers from a live fowl and the bristle from a live pig are also trimmed until the youth is clean-shaven. When the boy gifts a mat and receives a reciprocal mat from whomever cut the beard, it's a proud moment in his life, for he is now a man who is deemed ready to take a wife if he chooses. This is normally followed by a huge *lafaet* and a *kastom* dance, but this is entirely up to the initiate's family.

We'd travelled to Winea to help with a communal working bee that Busa had organised to clear a site for a new *nakamal*. Matai and Silas beamed with pride when they told me to grab the shovel and the wheelbarrow at the back of the leaf hut. My pygmy friends gloated over their new acquisitions with the same amount of pride as the owner of a new Ferrari would. The others toiled away using traditional methods and used digging sticks to break up clumps of earth that were loaded onto a tray made from the sturdy bark of a *woru* tree. After I'd pushed the barrow, when I dragged the bark across the rough ground like a draught horse, it was hard work. By late in the afternoon, Peta, Ravu, and a dozen other villagers had trekked across the mountains to lend a hand.

Later that evening, déjà vu reared its ugly head. While Garae sat alongside me drinking a broth of boiled leaves to treat his toe, I lay on my mat feeling nauseous from a raging inferno that burned inside my stomach. Ravu performed a healing and a divination rite, then told me the others had drank clean water from their bamboo because Damate had said, "*Himi who yea?*" ("Who is this disale?") when he saw my white skin and had poisoned me. Ravu told me that if he hadn't exorcised the devil from my spirit, I would've definitely died.

Not long after midnight, when I staggered outside into a solid wall of fog, I was too sick to make it to the nearby jungle so I vomited and emptied my screaming bowels alongside the hut. I also sensed the same unsettling feeling that I wasn't alone as I had during my last visit to Winea. When Peta stepped outside at dawn into the unusually thick mist and mentioned that someone had died, I apologised for going to the toilet so close to the hut and told him once I felt better, I would clean up the mess. Everyone burst out laughing and told me he wasn't referring to the smell. The mist was an omen, which forewarned someone of great importance had just passed away. His prediction was confirmed four days later when we received a message that a lowland chief had died on the day the fog had enveloped Winea.

In spite of my illness, I worked as hard as I could so as not to shame my bloodline, until Sakele dug up a shard of bone, which brought our work to an immediate halt. Because he was unsure of its origin, he reverently buried the remains at the base of a tree in case the bone belonged to one of his ancestors. At the end of what had been a torturous day, while we were drinking kava, Matai gifted me a badly rusted two-inch long metal spike. Years of cutting sugarcane in Queensland had yielded a black-birded villager from Winea the unbelievably miserable payment of one nail. The children from each successive generation were shown the nail as testament to how untrustworthy the devious *disale* is. Maybe Matai felt I'd earned the corroded nail by working while I was unwell, just as his forefather had when he slaved away for the insulting payment. Whatever his reason was for insisting I have the nail, the next day I really earned it when we travelled back to Nukurekum.

Before we left, when everyone from the hamlet jointly gifted me a sleeping mat, Busa emphasised that it belonged to "*yumi,*" (to all of us), and now it was more than just a mat, it was a bed we could all share and was a reminder for me to never forget Winea's inhabitants. Each time I looked at the gift, it would ensure I remembered them forever. My total acceptance did little to quell the fear I instilled in the two pygmy women, because no amount of coaxing from the others could convince them to have their photo taken. Everyone gathered at the edge of the village to perform a *wos tulleningo* ritual in my honour, and for the next half an hour, they sang a beautiful melody and kept shouting throughout the farewell rite, "Oh Tavua. We are very sad that you are leaving us." To return the display of eternal friendship and the esteem they bestowed upon me, I kept yelling back up the steep slope that I was equally sorry to be leaving. The trip back to Nukurekum was a hellish nightmare, and when exhaustion kept forcing me to stop, Gramma and Garae looked on in silence with unsympathetic and unemotional stares. By the end of the trek, I was barely able to walk and staggered into the village wondering how much more abuse my body could take.

The following afternoon, Atison tripped and plunged over a vertical bank when he was pushing Vanakankarea's wheelbarrow while it was fully laden with bottles of water. Short of flashing lights, blaring sirens, and rescue helicopters, all of the drama associated with a major road crash swept everyone off their feet and had them running to the scene of the accident. Atison was lucky and survived the fall relatively unscathed, but the prized wheelbarrow was a mangled wreck that was still lying at the bottom of the precipice. The villagers were like analytical police officers as they each took their turn to re-enact the accident and to deduct how a normally surefooted Atison must have fallen.

Because of the severity of my illness, I decided it was time to head back to civilization and all its material comforts as my ailing body needed to undergo medical tests and professional treatment to return me back to full health. Garae's toe had turned into a horrible puss-filled mess that desperately needed proper treatment, so he joined Ravu, Busa, and Gramma when they followed me back to Luganville. While we walked around town, I left myself barely enough money to travel back to New Zealand and spent the balance of my funds on essential goods for the villagers. Later in the day, while I rested at John Noel's, Busa and Ravu unexpectedly arrived with a gift of food and said they didn't want to "spoil" me by using all of my money. They crossed their arms across their chests and said "*Tamamasa Tavua*," as a mark of profound respect. The simple gesture has immense meaning in Middle Bush culture and signified the spirit of our friendship will always be embodied in their hearts. That special moment will stick with me for an eternity. Not because of their typically selfless gesture of bringing me food and making sure I was okay, but because it was a fitting way not to say goodbye, but to part with Busa while he remained a mortal. For sadly, it was the last time I would see him.

Chapter Twenty

DEATH AND DESTRUCTION

Exactly where Santo's pygmies originated from, and how they evolved in the isolated heart of the island will always remain an unsolved enigma. The diminutive highlanders lived relatively contented lives for millennia before they faced the social turmoil that was created by the introduction of alien beliefs and unfamiliar morals. Like so many other primitive peoples, they are about to follow evolution's path right through to extinction, and Busa's death marked the end of an era. He was the last of the cannibalistic pygmy chiefs to rule the rugged highlands, and now, with only four men and two women remaining who are true genetic pygmy's, due to their intermarriage with taller villagers, within the next generation, the last of the small mountain dwellers will be lost forever.

Whenever I travel as an adventurer, to avoid being disappointed by the outcome of an unsuccessful expedition, I never have any expectations. It's just as well, because my next trip to Santo proved to be an absolute disaster. The first night that I spent with John Noel and his family, thunder shook the house and lightning flashed through the rain-drenched panes of glass during a violent electrical storm. During my absence, John had become the paramount chief for all of Santo, but he'd also become seriously ill and was so delirious that he teetered along the fragile line that divides life from death. He was convinced he'd been poisoned by a *nakaimas*, and when he wasn't groaning, he screamed that he was being attacked by the devil. His son, George, armed himself with a rifle and ran outside into a shrieking wind that drove thick sheets of rain into his face. He started firing into the air to ward off the evil spirits that were attacking his father and to chase away the *nakaimas* John thought he could hear outside his window. The claps of thunder were so close and so loud that his volley of shots were completely muffled by nature's ear-splitting din.

Earlier in the year, a hurricane had carved a destructive path through the highlands and left a mass of destroyed property and ruined gardens in its wake. The devastating cyclone caused as much spiritual mayhem as it did physical damage. Busa had been on the brink of death, and with their patriarch nearing his untimely demise, *kastom* dictated over all logic amongst man bush. They were adamant Mother Nature hadn't unleashed her destructive forces of her own accord and that Damate had wreaked havoc on Middle Bush due to Busa's weakening spirit.

Busa had looked jaded and unwell when we said our final goodbyes. His normally washboard torso had lost its muscular definition and had become smooth and bloated. When his health started deteriorating, the doctors at Luganville were baffled by the cause of his condition and couldn't do anything to relieve his suffering. After he returned to his village, Busa died in his sleep, as did four other men who were afflicted with the same illness.

Damate immediately capitalized on the loss of his most potent mortal adversary, and not long after, another brutal hurricane bombarded the highlands while the villagers were still recovering from the onslaught of the previous cyclone. The belligerent demon claimed another life when a ten-year-old boy was swept to his death in a flash flood that surged along the Jordan River. When the torrent of foaming water burst its banks, the highlanders' Toyota was washed away and badly damaged.

In what was to be the first of a few unusual quirks of fate, while I walked down Luganville's main street, I was stopped by a total stranger. He called me Tavua, said he knew of my initiation, and warned that there were highlanders who held me directly responsible for the spate of recent catastrophes. Before my initiation, *kastom* had never been gifted to a *disale*, and because so much *tabu* knowledge had been passed on to Tavua, the gods had been angered.

The news of Busa's death in early May of 2001 left me dazed and deeply saddened. My run of bad luck seemed to be changing when I met Sakele and several other highlanders who were in town to buy rice and flour due to a shortage of food in Middle Bush. *Kastom* demanded that I cry and wail in front of Sakele for at least an hour to show him respect for his tragic loss and to show respect to Busa's spirit. Although I always had nothing but absolute respect for Busa, because we never had a close friendship, the initial impact of the saddening news had surprised me. I'd witnessed death and had mourned before, but even when members of my genetic family had died I'd never felt anything like this. It was as if a giant syringe had been inserted into the top of my skull and sucked the life and the enthusiasm out of me. I felt strangely hollow and experienced a huge sense of loss. In the wake of my emotionally fatigued state of mind, my numbed senses were drained of any other reaction when I swore aloud in front of Sakele without thinking. It was totally uncharacteristic of me when I said, "I'm really fucking sorry to hear about Busa." My profane language and my lack of tears had inflicted a huge insult to not only Sakele, but to all of Busa's immediate family. Because of the uncertain reception that awaited me, I declined the offer to travel back up to Middle Bush with him and the other highlanders.

I was disappointed when I heard that Gramma had received a message I sent asking him to meet me at John Noel's and he didn't arrive as we'd planned. Without his reassurance that it was safe for me to travel up to the highlands, I reluctantly decided that returning back to New Zealand was my only sensible and safe option. It was totally out of character for Gramma not to turn up at John's, and after the harrowing moments I'd already faced while I lived with the highlanders, the risk of being poisoned or killed was too great if they did in fact hold me responsible for their run of bad luck, so I flew back to Port Vila.

With two days to spare before I could fly home, I stayed with my close friend Simeon Tovovur and lived with his wife and family in a one bedroom flat at Freshwater, a suburb on the outskirts of town that's filled with weary-looking western style houses. Several days before my arrival, an angry lynch mob who were seeking vengeance for the recent deaths of four locals had chased a *kastom* man through the streets and beat him to a bloody pulp. The *nakaimas* literally had to run for his life and sought refuge in the cluster of shops at the end of Freshwater, only to have every door slammed in his bruised face. The resentful crowd held a traditional court to decide his fate and armed the judge and the jury with a rifle to deliver the expected death penalty if the *kastom* man's guilt was proven beyond all doubt. Without having any concrete evidence, the disgusted locals reluctantly released the *nakaimas* at the end of their self-constituted but fair trial.

In what must be the ultimate act of irony, I flew home only a week after I arrived in Vanuatu having unknowingly contracted a waterborne parasite called giardiasis while I stayed at Freshwater. Not long after our plane took off and we climbed above a thin veil of white cloud, I gazed across the horizon towards Santo and was deeply moved by the thought that the irreplaceable Busa, who'd been cast from an ancient mould that would never shape another man like him, was dead. The pygmies derived their name from the Greek word pygme, which is a measure meaning half an arms length. The impact Busa's demise will have on the highlands' unique culture is immeasurable. This tiny man's death left a colossal void in a fascinating society that had managed to survive for millennia. From a *disale* point of view, I'd lost the race against time to document all that I could about the last of the great pygmy chiefs, but for Busa, who now resides with Taute and the eternal spirits of his *bubu*, time never runs out.

Chapter Twenty-One

PRIMEVAL EDEN'S DEMISE

Now that my previous experiences in Middle Bush, Santo, had successfully bridged the gap between innocence and insight, an inexplicable driving force kept urging me to delve deeper into the highlanders' fascinating culture. Perseverance has always been one of my family's virtues, but simple inner strength and determination to travel back to Middle Bush hardly justified risking an unsafe return. I sent a letter to Gramma via John Noel explaining that nature was solely responsible for the recent catastrophes, not human error or diabolical forces. Several months later, when I received a positive reply, it gave me a good enough reason to return to Vanuatu. The chiefs had been shown my letter and after careful deliberation, they unanimously decided that not only was I welcome to return, but I could also start organizing the necessary preparations to film a documentary for Blue Planet Productions, who were seeking National Geographic Television as co-producers, so long as I returned alone.

I couldn't get back to Vanuatu quick enough, and when I followed Gramma up to a small plateau about twenty minutes' walk from the Jordan River, the warm reception I received at Lusunatu village quelled any previous doubts I had about returning. There were plenty of smiling and familiar faces, and rekindling my friendship with Gramma had never felt better. It was only because Voemanu had suddenly become ill that he'd been unable to meet me at John Noel's. According to Gramma, there'd been a gross misunderstanding, as the informant who'd warned me that the highlanders felt I was to blame for their spate of bad luck turned out to be a lowlander who was jealous of the material gains man bush stood to reap if the proposed documentary went ahead. Although there were a few villagers in Middle Bush who held me responsible for disrupting their spiritual wellbeing, and for Damate unleashing his demonic forces, Gramma felt that I wouldn't be killed by them to appease Taute.

Over the years, I'd learnt, whenever dealing with primitive peoples, to expect the unexpected, and I wasn't the least bit surprised when Gramma told me other problems had arisen. Winea's women feared that not only would their images be captured on film, but so would their spirits. Gossip which had been fuelled by superstition and primitive rationale had spread like wildfire through the villages. Someone had started a rumour that a video camera stole a person's *rapee*, and if they somehow managed to survive, they would suffer horrific physical deformities. Then to compound the numerous difficulties I already faced with trying to shoot the documentary, the lowlanders made it known that if any film crew passed through their region, they would be greeted with violence. They gave me a typically warm greeting and told me I was always welcome anytime, but jealousy, that wasted emotion, had reared its ugly green-eyed head when they warned me in no uncertain terms that because they weren't being paid anything for the documentary, the crew who was to shoot up until I entered the highlands had better stay in Luganville.

Up in the mountains, the villagers had become so divided, that if filming proceeded, bloodshed was inevitable—and because I would be the only cameraman, I'd be targeted first. Although the chiefs welcomed the documentary as they appreciated the immense value of having a visual reference of how they had lived for future generations, if it went ahead, my death wasn't a probability, it was a certainty. I quickly reassured Gramma that I had no intentions of making the documentary, as the last thing I wanted was to cause a rift between the clans in Middle Bush and to put myself and my *kastom* family at risk.

That night, while we sat and drank kava, Gramma told me "Tavua" had become a household name in the isolated hamlets throughout the highlands. Stories about the *disale* who'd become a man bush were being told way beyond our tribal boundaries, right down to the coastal areas. Many of the natives were questioning how a white man could keep returning and survive in a region where most Ni-Vanuatu feared to tread. It appeared my influence would no longer become transitory like I'd originally hoped when Gramma said the legend of Tavua would be told around the fires and in the *nakamals* to successive generations.

I've never been interested in recognition or being a glory hunter, and the next day, I found that even in the jungle fame comes at a price. We hiked beneath the blistering midday sun for half an hour to Natori village, where I met an aged lowlander called Toflan, and his family, who treated me like a celebrity and started preparing a welcome ceremony. When I helped them pound a pile of roasted taro into *nalot*, the stifling humidity wrung sweat from my every pore. Gramma did his bit by chewing kava and scowled "*Cus himi balasa*" ("I'm surprised by how strong the kava is") when he put a cud on a *lap lap* leaf covered in a mounting pile of root. Balasa is top shelf root, and drinking it during the heat of the day is usually a recipe for disaster. Once we started drinking, Toflan kept lining them up until I'd guzzled down four large shells that were filled to the brim with what NASA could probably have used as rocket fuel. It didn't take long for my senses to be blasted into orbit, and although Toflan and Gramma drank from a shell that was half the size I was given, as the ceremony was in my honour, to refuse the offer of kava would've been in poor taste. From the moment we met, Toflan had treated me like a hero, and because the brew was for Tavua, the *disale* who'd knocked back six extra strong shells at Natchara then walked to Linduri over the next couple of days, he no doubt felt that four would hardly touch the sides.

The following morning, after Gramma had reassured me again that once it became known the documentary was shelved, I wouldn't be poisoned or killed, when we started heading up to Middle Bush, it felt like one of Damate's disciples was trying his best to smash his way out of my pulsating head with a jackhammer. The frequent toilet stops I made were a front so that I could vomit in seclusion, because if there were a few highlanders who still despised me, I needed to radiate strength and confidence. Apart from the Jordan River having changed its course in a few places and coming across a bit of scattered debris, it wasn't until we ventured inland that I fully appreciated just how cataclysmic the cyclones had been. What had previously been a treasured jewel that wound its way through a lush tropical paradise was now a dishevelled mess. Nature had ravaged the river with her own unimaginably destructive forces when the thundering waters had reshaped their own flow and thrown huge piles of cumbersome boulders up onto the banks. Uprooted trees were wedged into crevices and massive chunks of riverbank and large pieces of canyon wall had fallen into the riverbed. When we reached an area where rock hopping used to be a necessity, tonnes of silt and sand carpeted what was now a smooth and flat expanse alongside the river. It was humbling to see how nature could wage war on itself on such a saddening and devastating scale. I could understand how the highlanders' primitive rationale could embody their worst fears and why they thought because they lovingly worship nature, such brutal forces could only be the work of Damate.

Although Gramma was carrying five empty backpacks that the villagers had asked for, and a few of his own personal items, he charged up gruelling slopes with his usual astounding ease. Petekara carried a traditional string bag that hung from her forehead and bulged at the seams from a hefty load, and she also carried her four-week-old daughter in a cloth sling she draped over her shoulder. Throughout the day, her child never cried once and either suckled a breast or contentedly slept for the whole of our journey up to Nukurekum. I was weighed down with two packs that contained the basic necessities and my usual array of photographic equipment. The kava had poisoned my system and my body begged for rest as I struggled to keep up with the others. By late in the day, I was too unwell to disguise my discomfort, and all I could do was suffer in silence until we made the final slog up to the village.

My *kastom* family put my mind at ease when they gave me a warm welcome, but I could still feel a bit of tension in the air when I handed out the gifts. To be given five packs and two watches equated to winning a lottery in western society, and although they were obviously grateful, Ravae, Ravu, Peta, and Gramma showed little emotion when they received the goods. Gramma stated in a flat tone that he was extremely lucky. Ravu said *"Tamamasa Tavua"* with his arms folded across his chest, and Ravae offered a small thank you. Peta shook my hand and patiently placed his seventy-five-litre pack alongside him without bothering to even look at it. The other pack was for Sakele to show respect and to express my sorrow to his family over Busa's death. Sakele filled the poignant void Busa had left and was now the new chief of Winea, but Peta had been elected as the paramount chief of the highlands due to his profound knowledge of *kastom* and his social standing as a highly respected chief. Instead of maintaining a regal air of chiefly aloofness as Busa had done most of the time, Peta had never been so friendly and talkative. When I told him I had no desire to film the documentary, he immediately picked up his pack and started playing with the zips and tried to work out what each compartment was for. He marvelled at the attached storm cover he found in the top pocket just as a teenager would do while he figured out the workings of his first car or some other prized possession. Then he ignored any chiefly self-restraint, shouldered the pack, and proudly wore it for all to see while we chatted away.

Anyone who was opposed to the documentary turned their back on me, or spat on the ground in disgust as they walked past, until word raced along the jungle grapevine that the filming was canned. There was no need for me to try and keep up my healthy facade now that everyone knew the documentary wasn't going ahead, so I left Peta, and while I was lying down in Gramma's hut, I couldn't help but wonder if the excruciating pain in my head was due to something more sinister than a hellish kava induced hangover. The hordes of screaming children who were playing soccer outside robbed me of the merciful sleep that I hoped would help me escape from my unbearable headache. More kava was the last thing I needed when Gramma summonsed me to a welcome ceremony in Peta's *nakamal*. After I drank one shell and gave a short speech to reciprocate Peta's formal greeting, I excused myself from the small crowd and collapsed on a sleeping mat, where I quietly moaned in agony until the kava thankfully sent me to sleep.

The next morning when I awoke to a normal headache and less severe vomiting, it erased any negative thoughts I had about my health. I suddenly made a miraculous recovery when Peta offered to treat what was nothing more than a nuisance with *kastom*, as his primeval prescription for a headache had nearly claimed Vetrivu's life. He'd armed himself with a miniature bow and an arrow fashioned from a sago palm spine that was tipped with a shard of broken glass. When he shot the pulsating "rope" (vein) running past Vetrivu's temple that was filled with the "*rabis blood*" (dirty blood) which carried the evil spirits to her head, the rate at which the demons had been expelled from the severed artery had horrified Gramma. Blood spurted in unison with each beat of Vetrivu's racing heart and arced across the bare earth until the range of each jet of fluid slowly diminished to a steady trickle down the side of her pallid face. She became weak and collapsed into a pool of her own blood that had stained the earth dark red. It looked as though Damate was about to claim another victim, so an alternative healing ritual was used, and it wasn't until poor Vetrivu was given a thorough dousing with water that she regained her senses. If a *kastom* man feels it's necessary, sometimes he will remove the "*rabis blood*" from an infected or ailing body part by plugging it full of miniscule arrow holes.

Gramma was unwell from eating too much rotten beef and although the treatment he was about to receive from Peta wasn't as graphic as Vetrivu's, the medication was equally as cruel. There are only a few courageous men in Middle Bush who will drink the broth which is used to cure that type of sickness. Most villagers resort to a more forgiving type of treatment. Voemanu prepared the potion by rubbing a wild taro stalk up and down the rasp-like surface of a piece of black palm. Then she mixed the lime green syrup with a carefully measured amount of water and sieved it through a piece of cloth. Peta sat outside with a bowl of the broth nestled in his lap and gazed skywards while he spoke to Taute. Once he'd finished asking the gods to empower the potion, he fell silent for about twenty seconds, then spat into the white froth floating on top of the slimy looking mixture. He repeated spitting into the brew and calling upon Taute five times, then he handed Gramma a huge coconut shell cup that was filled to the brim with the strong smelling concoction. Gramma mumbled a chant to Taute, then he wolfed down the potion in one swift hit. He put his head down, and clenched his trembling hands into fists as he fought the urge to vomit when a wave of nausea swept over him. Even the strongest of men normally throw up, lose control of their bowels, or slump to the ground unconscious. Thousands of goose bumps appeared on his malt skin, and his eyes became vague as they reddened and glazed over. For a few seconds he became temporarily detached from reality and was unable to speak until the initial rush subsided. When he tried to talk the burning in his throat was so intense that it reduced his speech to a faint rasp, but to his credit, he managed to remain upright and relatively composed throughout the whole of what was obviously a harrowing and painful ordeal.

The medication is repeated morning and night for five days, which requires a hardy disposition and strong nerves because those who've endured the painful ritual liken drinking the broth to chewing on *nangalat* leaves. It's not uncommon for most men to lose their voices completely for several weeks. If a *nangalat* leaf is brushed against the skin, the venomous vegetation is capable of reducing a grown man to tears when thousands of miniscule barbed hooks on the underside of the leaf release potent toxins into the system. While Taute was returning spiritual and physical strength to Gramma, to ensure the fleeing evil spirits didn't attack us, Peta sprayed everyone with a mouthful of water and made sure he coated both the back and front of those who were present during the ceremony. Once the five days of being medicated have passed, a *kastom* man performs a divination rite, and depending on the severity of the illness, the spirits can require a patient to abstain from eating meat for up to one year. Gramma was lucky as his supernatural guardians instructed him to refrain from dining on bullock for only two weeks to purify his damaged soul.

In Vanuatu's most vast and remote mountains there has always been few uninvited guests, and never any visiting tourists. With the speed that technology and humanity are rapidly diminishing wilderness areas, change was inevitable on an island the size of Santo. Time no longer stands still in the highlands. It is restless and anxious as it ticks into an uncertain era. During my absence several villagers invited a young American missionary who was affiliated with the Assembly of God church up to Middle Bush, but he left after staying for just one night. A group of Australians from the Protestant church did likewise. When all of them would only eat the food they'd carried up to Vanakanakarea, they inflicted a scathing insult upon their hosts. Several years ago, such despicable behaviour would never have been tolerated, yet nothing was said or done to the Christians. I was thankful when I was told that Winea still remains off limits to any outsiders.

Irrespective of his previous fears, Stephan Vavanaru has been ordered by the government to maintain his teaching position. Because Santo's mountains are filled with a goldmine of natural resources, I can't help but wonder if this is what has motivated the government to place a teacher in such an undesirable post. Now that so many highlanders hold education in such high esteem, the school boasts forty pupils. The very essence of the people's beliefs and their brutal charm seems exceedingly vulnerable, for the future of any culture lies with its children. The precarious survival of the highlander's traditional way of life is wholly dependant on an unquestioning belief in *kastom* during a time when it seems Christianity's dogma is here to stay.

The history of Middle Bush has never been peaceful, and up until now, no other culture in Vanuatu has guarded their beliefs so fervently and so well. Now that Peta is the paramount chief, he will still repel outsiders and injure or kill anyone who willingly or unknowingly breaches *kastom*. Any grievances the highlanders had with their traditional enemies have been settled, and as a consequence, outbreaks of intertribal conflict will be extremely rare. Warfare has lived and died in seclusion, away from the prying eyes and the morals of the outside world, but violence will still remain a vital part of *kastom* when *nakaimas* drink the warm blood and eat the twitching hearts of their victims. Up until the turn of the twentieth century, a human was seen as a vital sacrifice during the most *tabu* of rites, whereas nowadays, the blood of a pig is spilled. Peta acknowledges that the spirits demand an occasional brutal murder still occur, but the legacy of cannibalism due to conflict, which was once so firmly anchored in the history of Middle Bush, has ended abruptly. Unlike Busa, Peta isn't a blood-charged predator, and he has no desire to carrying on the inherent actions of his father by dining on the flesh of his victims. An air of peace might prevail throughout the mountains, but there definitely isn't an air of tranquillity. For instead of fighting against bows, *nul nuls,* and black magic, the highlanders are facing alien teachings, imported knowledge, and the bible—which can be potent and dangerous adversaries to an illiterate people.

Busa's death was both symbolic and significant. Not only did it mark the end of cannibalising victims who weren't being used for black magic, it signalled the rapid decay of a highly spirited culture which is older than recorded history. Three years must pass before I can visit his grave, and his funeral rite was so *tabu* that all I can mention is a *namele* palm and a border of stones mark his grave as a memorial to a great chief and warrior and that most of his remains were laid to rest at the site. When I was in Port Vila, I'd mentioned Busa's death, that he was a cannibal, and that the villagers still practice brutal rites to Ralph Regenvanu, the museum and cultural centres director. I could fully appreciate why he found it hard to believe that such a unique culture still flourished in the archipelago in this day and age and why he said there was no way that he could lend any credibility to my claims. Of course he couldn't, and he had every reason not to. If I was put in his position, I certainly wouldn't lend my name to the unknown. I didn't take the way he reacted as a personal insult, but without him having ventured into the region or having lived with the people, I felt it was unfair to pass any form of criticism or judgement.

Peta and Gramma were livid when I mentioned the cultural centre were dubious about the content of my studies. Their heated reaction surprised me, and once their initial rage subsided, they were almost sympathetic, as they knew I'd put myself completely at the mercy of the people and had endured unenviable hardships to document their beliefs. Peta shouted, "*Bastard! Necarcar tole garae!*" ("Bastard! White flying fox!") when I told him about Ralph's negative response. To be labelled a white flying fox is a huge insult throughout all of Vanuatu as it means you don't know about or appreciate your own culture. Gramma and Peta asked me why the cultural centre had never entered the region. If they didn't believe violent *kastom* still existed, then they must surely have nothing to fear. Both men calmly stated the next fieldworker, anyone associated with the cultural centre, or any uninvited outsider who entered the highlands would be killed on sight—and especially Ralph Regenvanu. In the past, I'd done everything within my power to try and enable academics that were better qualified than myself to enter Middle Bush and take over studying the highlanders. The last thing I'd wanted to do was jeopardise any future opportunities that might arise or, worst of all, to endanger Ralph's life. Peta told me I was the first person who wasn't born in the highlands to be gifted *kastom* and that I'd be the last. He sat down and after thinking quietly for several minutes, he asked me to draught a letter to give to Ralph Regenvanu. I carefully translated the message he dictated in Bislama into English so that it matched what he said, and the letter read as follows.

13 October, 2001
Nukurekum Village
Middle Bush, Santo

To whom it may concern.

This is to confirm that all information Tavua (Rick Williamson) has written in the article "The Stone Age Meets The Clone Age" and in his book is fact. Any man from the cultural centre is unwelcome. They will be killed. Any white man entering Middle Bush will be killed if he arrives uninvited. Chief Busa was the last cannibal chief. *Nakaimas* still perform cannibalism. The shooting of the proposed documentary isn't possible, as it has created a rift between the villages. There are those who believe they will lose their spirit and their physical form will change if they are captured on film. Blood will flow if the film is shot. Tavua would be killed. Lowland villagers will block any film crew as they are jealous of the material gains highlanders would reap if filming eventuated.

Signed: Chief Peta Loumei
Paramount Chief Middle Bush. X
Signed on behalf of Paramount Chief.

Son of Paramount Chief
Gramma Garae

Chief Peta Loumei has asked Tavua to forward this letter on his behalf, as it is not his wish to have to inflict injury upon outsiders. He and his people wish to be left alone. *Middle Bush, Santo, hemi tabu long ol man blong come tekem custom blong mifala. Sipus yu come yu died finis.* (It is forbidden for any man to enter Middle Bush, Santo, to document our customs. If you come here you will be killed.)

Signed: Gramma Garae
Son for Paramount Chief Peta Lumoei

Gramma was still fuming when I'd finished writing the letter and said I should mention to Ralph that because he has white blood running through his veins, if he or any other *disale* were killed, their bodies would be dragged down to the Jordan River, thrown in, and hopefully carried out to sea by the current because a repulsive *disale* would never be buried in sacred man bush ground. To do so would be the ultimate insult to Taute and the spirits of *bubu*, which he emphasized by saying, "even the sharks would shit big and vomit after eating a *disale*." After he finished venting his angerm I was surprised when he told me how lucky I was to still be alive. If my *kastom* family and several other friends had acted upon their initial instincts, I would've died at least a dozen brutal deaths. Apparently I'd been extremely fortunate and had narrowly cheated death numerous times while I lived amongst them. Peta agreed the spirits had been unusually kind to me, as he had wanted to shoot me with his bow or slit my throat three times. Ordinarily he would've without hesitation, but my supernatural bodyguards had intervened. Gramma had also come close to taking my life while we were bow fishing with Ravu, and on two other occasions. Garae had wanted to cut me up and smash a few bones, but said he would feel sorry if he had to kill me for I was a brother. There was no shortage of others who told me there were times when they were about to kill me but Taute and the spirits of *bubu* had intervened.

Chapter Twenty-Two

TABU BLONG BOW

Almost a century before my initiation, Felix Spieser, a Swiss anthropologist who was born in 1880, was the only other white man to have ever visited Winea. For just over two years, spanning from May of 1910 to July of 1912, Spieser made the most comprehensive study to date of Vanuatu's indigenous peoples and published his work in a book he titled *Ethnology of Vanuatu*. The oral history which is passed on to each successive generation is so efficient that despite the passage of time, Gramma recalled Spieser's visit as if it occurred yesterday. Once word spread throughout the highlands that the anthropologist wasn't a missionary, he was well received by Winea's inhabitants and the other pygmy clans that inhabited southwest Santo. In his book, *Two Years with the Natives in the Pacific* (published by Mills & Boon), he wrote this after he'd questioned villagers about the pygmies' existence: "Generally they stared at me without a sign of intelligence or else began to tell fairy-tales of dwarfs they had seen in the bush, of little men with tails and goat feet (probably derived from what they had heard of the devil from missionaries). All beings of whose existence they were perfectly convinced, whom they often see in the daytime and feel at night, so that it is very hard to separate truth from imagination" (page 161). Once he made contact with the region's diminutive natives, he wrote, "Pygmies laugh, chat, and are very hospitable. I always felt safer and more comfortable where the majority of inhabitants belonged to the smaller race." From the way he described his journey into the mountains, it seems when I first contacted the highlanders, little had changed since Spieser's visit. According to Gramma, small clans inhabited ridge top hamlets in about the same numbers as they do nowadays, but a lot more pygmies populated the highlands.

Unlike Spieser, who travelled with porters and his own supplies, not a single day went by where I felt safe and totally at ease. The privilege of being on the inside looking out, rather than trying to dissect a culture as an interested observer during a fleeting visit as Spieser had, was a mental and physical challenge. It became essential to learn to live in the moment because dwelling on past events, especially where my life had been threatened, was too disheartening, and projecting into the uncertain future was equally daunting. After some of the anxious moments I'd endured, to simply awake the next day with everything still intact was a joyous gift. There are the most *tabu* of rites which are forever destined to remain eternal secrets. These are safeguarded within an impenetrable reservoir of knowledge that's only accessible to those who have endured the necessary rites of passage. If I divulged everything I've experienced, in some cases, it would guarantee the informants and I suffered a brutal death.

Late one afternoon, when Gramma and Peta called me into the *nakamal* and solemnly informed me there was nothing else to learn and nothing more they could gift regarding *kastom*, I felt a gargantuan sense of relief. It meant I would no longer have to experience the feeling of making slow and sometimes painful advances along the *kastom* path, only to have to cautiously retreat until precious anthropological material was gifted to me. The biggest relief was knowing that the ebb and flow of the natives' and the spirits' mood swings would no longer regulate my life, and that at last, I could be my own man again. To be able to simply be and to just exist over my last few days in the highlands was sheer bliss. Not only was my frame of mind relaxed, so were some of the guidelines which regulated daily life. Inescapable change had gained so much momentum that since my last visit, many *tabus* weren't being enforced, and now men and women freely exited and entered through either door leading into the leaf huts.

Gramma and Peta told me that a people without *kastom* are a people without pride and purpose, and they're making plans to build another *nakamal* whose walls will be lined with sacred black palm. Christians will be banned from entering the *tabu* dwelling, which is destined to be a cultural sanctuary for youths who choose to follow the *kastom* road and study the teachings of their forefathers. Peta is concerned that if the next generation practices a form of church-friendly *kastom*, they will follow an uncertain path, and its teachings will be contrived and superficial. Gramma is disillusioned and uncertain of the benefits of Christianity, whereas without question he feels *kastom* offers solace from the daily rigours of etching out a frugal existence from Santo's mountains. He said the harsh environment demands respect and, more importantly, the highlanders must remain united if they are to survive in the bush and defend themselves from the onslaught of outside influences. Many villagers own land in the lowlands, and due to alien influences, they are starting to move down from Middle Bush permanently to work less demanding gardens and to enjoy an easier way of life. It's inevitable that the conflicting beliefs will divide the highlanders, and because of this, Gramma feels the energising sense of togetherness will be lost and no longer help them to combat the daily grind of living in the mountains.

After we'd finished talking in the *nakamal*, Gramma and I went and sat outside. As the sinking sun dimmed after making its daily life-giving journey across the planet, one by one, then by immeasurable numbers, sparkling celestial lights twinkled to life in the heavens. As I peered up into the cosmos I said to Gramma, "You know, some of those stars no longer exist but they still send light to the earth from thousands of light years away." He became lost in thought, and after a long but comfortable silence had passed, he said, "So the stars are so far away, they've exploded and the light is still reaching us?" I replied, "Yeah, that's right, mate." Then after he silently pondered again, Gramma looked at me intently and pointed to three stars forming a straight line. He told me they represent a male villager carrying taro back from the garden and are called *hauchich-alilmote*. The central star is his head and the two on either side are vegetables strung from a stick he's carrying across his shoulders. Then Gramma swung his arm across the horizon and picked out a cluster of stars in three vertical rows consisting of two, three, and two stars, which are flat across the bottom of the rows, but rise in the middle row to form the shape of a roof along the top. The third star of the middle row represents the ridge of a *rom* (leaf hut). When Gramma pointed directly overhead and I followed his outstretched arm, I picked out *machio saran*, a lone beacon that's used for navigation, which rises and falls in the universe without any real cultural significance or story attached to it.

There was a time in the distant past when the villagers used crude wooden pillows when they slept that were fashioned from a log. Just before daylight, *pateamachu*, the only star which is believed to possess a sacred spirit, dropped down to the earth and gently nudged every villager's head from their pillows. Up until several hundred years ago, the spirit was said to have acted as a silent and primitive alarm clock when it woke the villagers every morning. Before we left the bracing mountain air to go inside the hut and warm our chilled bodies around the fire, Gramma reached over, touched my arm, and said, "Tavua, giving *kastom* has been hard for both you and me. Inside my heart sometimes I feel heavy and no good sharing my beliefs, but in my mind I know *kastom* is nearly finished for the next generation. I want my son and his son to have a memory of how we once lived. To live with our people and understand our ways is hard for a *disale*. But now you aren't a *disale*. You are a true man bush. Peta and I have decided to give you the highest honour a man can receive. It beats gifting a pig, a mat, or a fowl. It beats everything. Tomorrow we will go to the jungle. I will make you a bow and a poisoned arrow."

The next morning, while we paused on a near vertical slope just short of the top of a *tabu* mountain called Reosara, I enjoyed the impressive scenery and was grateful that Gramma had slowed down to compensate for my burning middle-aged legs. Vanakanakarea and Nukurekum stood out below us like tropical islands set amidst a sea of sprawling green rainforest. I pondered over how many undiscovered mysteries the jungle still housed and how many secrets remained within the culture that it nourished. Without a doubt, living amongst these remarkable people had been one of the highlights of my life. It had been a privileged time of learning and of listening to enchanting stories, mostly in the sanctity of the sacred *nakamal*, whose walls have heard millennia of whispered secrets. And now once again, precious knowledge was about to be divulged on hallowed ground.

A huge white plastic water tank that was covered with a sheet of corrugated iron to catch the rain polluted the otherwise pristine landscape and looked like a festering pimple on the emerald face of the beautiful rainforest. Gramma had helped three others painstakingly haul the reservoir all the way up from the lowlands. Because of the swelling number of pupils attending Vanakanakarea's school, the tank nestled alongside the classroom had been a welcome addition. He looked at the tank and shook his head from side to side in disapproval, then he said, "I helped carry that up the mountains. It is good small. This is the way of the *disale*. Man bush enjoys walking through the jungle to gather fresh water. The *disale* must beat nature and bring the water to him." In the sultry midday heat, I struggled to keep up with his tireless stride, and as we climbed higher up the sacrosanct peak, I envied a shining cuckoo that flew effortlessly up to the crest of the mountain. I told Gramma I often hear the migratory birds' shrill and drawn out calls on the small farm I live on in New Zealand, and each time I did, it was a reminder never to forget my friends in Middle Bush. A smile spread across his face as he turned and looked back down at me.

He pointed to clusters of succulent shoots that sprouted like epiphytes from a coarsely barked tree and said, "*Yumi kai kai marere Tavua*" (We will eat *marere*, Tavua"). We cut a handful of sticks about six hundred millimetres long and sent them hissing through the air until we'd knocked several bunches of the stringy looking foliage to the ground. Then we rested and ate the pale green shoots that were in the core of each clump of leaves. Away in the distance, the great spiritual monolith, Mount Tambewessana, pierced the windblown clouds that were vainly trying to shroud its peak. Because it's believed to be a birthplace of evil spirits, and a favourite haunt of Damate, no one who is still alive from Middle Bush has ever conquered Vanuatu's highest peak. Only the highlanders' ancestors have, and the legend the villagers tell their children warns that those who stood on its crest felt the irate mountain shake with anger. Nowadays no one dares to emulate the feats of their adventurous forefathers, for to do so would require total silence during the climb, otherwise demons will cause a blinding cloud to descend to disorientate those who are striving to reach the summit. The superstitious villagers believe if they set foot on the crest of the mountain, it will unleash a devastating hurricane.

We climbed up a carpet of gnarled roots, reached the summit, and dropped down the other side into open jungle, where we sidled along the edge of a sharp ridge. Gramma pointed to a *tule garae* tree with a girth about the same size as a man's forearm. Because my totem is the flying fox, and the bow was to be purely ceremonial, the stave had to come from a *tule garae* tree. Although *wuluwulu garae*, a type of black palm, was the true mother of the flying fox lineage, during the creation of my bloodline, the *tule garae* also helped to spawn the flying fox. An old blaze that had been cut into the trunk indicated the tree had been previously selected from the maze of forest. The trunk was straight, free of disease and knots or any sprouting twigs, and appeared to be a good choice. Gramma rubbed his hands over the bark and fondled the trunk, then he stood back and gazed at the tree with uncertainty. He carefully scanned the surrounding jungle, nodded to himself, and then marked off the length of the stave and began felling the tree. Instead of hacking into the trunk, he almost apologetically and reluctantly began cutting and treated the gift from Taute with the utmost respect. Each swing of his machete sliced into the wood with the passion of an artist who was about to transform one of Taute's creations into a work of art.

Gramma was so engrossed in his craft that he was totally oblivious to me watching intently as millennia of accumulated skill and tradition unfolded before my inquisitive eyes. With slow and careful consideration, once he'd decided which section would provide the best back and belly, he patiently whittled the stave in half lengthwise and produced a white billet that was laden with moisture and had the bark left on its back. The crafting of a bow is shrouded in secrecy, and women are forbidden to view any part of the weapon's progress until it's completely finished, so we traipsed back down to Nukurekum with the stave carefully concealed in a wrap of *lap lap* leaves.

When we got back to the village, we were lucky because all of the women were meeting the demands of daily life down in the gardens. I sat on a log while Gramma got comfortable on a crude wooden stool outside his leaf hut and began transforming a rough piece of wood into a primal work of art. Nowadays a proficient Middle Bush bowyer can easily make a bow in a single day, but in the past when their ancestors used a stone axe called an *iasulu* to shape their weapons, it normally took about a month to complete a bow. They worked at their own leisure, and when a bow was almost finished, they smoothed off the limbs with a piece of fine coral or a block of sandstone. Unlike most primitive bowyers, the highlanders prefer to shape a bow from a freshly cut stave as the green timber is much easier to work with, but there are a few archers who prefer to season a billet in the firewood rack above the cooking fire before they start working with the wood. Sometimes a piece of broken glass or a pig tusk doubles as a primitive chisel and a spokeshave, but Gramma used the keen edge on his machete, which he'd honed on a sacred sharpening stone called Vinki. Before he started cutting, he gazed out into the crosshatch of unspoilt rainforest to draw inspiration from the mountains that had nurtured and provided the stave, then he cradled the wood in his arms as if he was lovingly holding his recently newborn child. His inherent patience and skill came from generations of expertise as he began to strip the bark from the back and removed generous amounts of sapwood while he carefully maintained the original contours of the grain. With the same fascination and joy of witnessing the birth of a child, I watched Gramma. His hands guided the machete as Vinki's sharp edge glided ever so gracefully back and forth, and the bow grew in his hands. Each cut was different as some were made visually by reading the timber and others were made by feeling and following the flow of the grain.

Two hours later, a pile of shavings covered the earth around Gramma's feet. He looked concerned. He constantly checked the progress of a tiny pin knot that was positioned mid limb, about a third of the weapon's length in from the tip of the bow. Now that the bow was ready for tillering, he looked troubled and shook his head from side to side at having been unable to work the small defect out of the timber. He stopped working, carefully concealed the bow, and headed to the rear of the hut for a snack of taro.

When we went back outside, Gramma was horrified to discover a small boy who'd returned to the village had errantly burnt the pile of shavings. The child had no idea the wood chips came from a bow and thought he was doing Tavua a favour by keeping the area around the hut clean. Instead of being angry, Gramma appeared deeply disappointed over the disastrous breach of *kastom*. Not only was all his patience and expertise doomed to destruction, he was equally saddened that the bow, which was an extension of his spirit and was embodied with his *rapee*, wouldn't follow me back to New Zealand. A fine defining line between success and failure always threatens the outcome when highlanders make a bow. Two out of every three newly crafted weapons break. And when you also take into account that if the bow doesn't secure a kill with its first shot to empower the weapon with an animal's *rapee*, it's rendered useless, a lasting bow that shoots well is a precious commodity.

Gramma became lost in his work again, and once he'd finished, I could feel his apprehension when he cautiously bent the bow. It didn't matter how carefully he stressed his creation, because he knew the gods had already sealed the weapon's fate. Slowly but steadily, he put opposing pressure on the top and middle of the bow with his hands, then with the same impact as booming thunder, there was a loud snap, and in a split second, the beautifully symmetrical lines were horribly distorted. I would've cherished the bow for the rest of my life, but I smiled at Gramma and told him that worse things have happened. When the boy burnt the wood chips, he'd disrupted the harmony between Gramma and his ancestral spirits, and the supernatural forces which empowered the stave had been insulted. The human detritus that is buried in the sacred land, the same ground that had nurtured the growth of the tree, had been gravely disrespected by mistakenly breaking the *tabu*. Even though the bow snapped right on the tiny harmless looking knot, Gramma wasn't surprised that Taute had found the weakest link in the bow's tightly knitted grain.

If the bow had survived, it would have been carefully tillered to a desired weight simply by observing the arc and symmetry of the limbs while another villager drew it back. Then, before it was used, it would've been stored in the firewood rack for at least a couple of months to season and smoke stain the timber. I would've treasured the bow, not as an artefact, but as a priceless gift that was alive with the spirit and the warmth of a valued friend and brother. Whereas the average bow measures around one and a half metres long, mine would've been shorter as we'd agreed it would be so precious that I'd never use it in the field. Although all bows are a basic D shape, the profile of their tips varies with each individual bowyer. Two types are preferred. If the bow is made from *tule garae*, a slightly rounded and wider tip keeps the string in alignment with the limbs. Most bows are fashioned from *natora*, which is stronger and more durable, and often have self nocks cut into the tips that are much thinner than a weapon which is crafted from *tule garae*.

We went back into the hut, where Gramma sat in silence for about ten minutes before he started making a poisoned arrow. Now that intertribal warfare is a rarity, Patevina, the deadly arrow whose sole purpose is to kill man, is never part of an archer's array of arrows. Not because an air of peace prevails, but because the arrow is considered so dangerous and so *tabu.* None are ever kept in the villages, and the few that do exist are stored in a well-hidden cave. The arrows are unique throughout Vanuatu, and possibly all of Melanesia, due to the attachment of two feathers just behind the arrowhead and are exclusive remnants of the pygmy's culture. Like the making of a bow, the manufacture of Patevina must remain shrouded in obscurity and an unseen mystery to females. From the time a wild cane arrow shaft is cut, it's seasoned in the hut for about one month before it's dry enough to use. After Gramma had selected a length of cane that was stored in the rafters of the hut, he sat next to a fire alongside his sleeping mat. Then he slowly drew the shaft through the glowing embers and made sure he kept it moving to avoid scorching its exterior. He squinted along its length, and pushed the shaft straight with a pad of folded *lap lap* leaf until he was satisfied with his handiwork, then he grabbed his machete and we headed down to one of his gardens.

After Gramma cast his eyes around the remote garden several times to make certain we were alone, he set to work and wrenched apart a *wuluwulu garae* windfall. Time and the tropical climate had rotted away portions of the black palm and left rock hard segments of wood that had remained impervious to the elements. He split a wide sliver with his machete, tested the strength of the hardwood by bending it in his hands, and sat on a log and began shaping an arrowhead. With the ease that comes from inherent expertise, it took him only minutes to make something that would last my entire lifetime. For Patevina to be efficient, it must have three vicious barbs spaced out over about 210 millimetres from the arrowhead's sharp tip to the bottom of the last barb. No less and no more barbs are ever used. The overall exposed length of the arrowhead from the end of the shaft measured 310 millimetres. It was twelve millimetres across the widest point of the barb and a streamlined five millimetres thick along the total length of the arrowhead. Once the arrowhead was finished, Gramma wrapped it in leaves and we climbed back up to the village.

The two feathers that are plucked from a village fowl to adorn the arrow are normally any colour, but Gramma chose one that was black and one that was white, to signify the brotherhood between himself, the ebony man bush, and Tavua, the white *disale*. He held the feathers together and said, "*Himi spirit blong yumi Tavua*" ("This is our joined spirit Tavua"), then started putting the arrow together by carefully smoothing off the stipules on the joints of the shaft with his machete. After he'd made sure the shaft tapered down towards the nock, he trimmed the end just behind a joint so that he could insert the arrowhead. Then he placed a moistened piece of dried inner bark from the banyan tree on his thigh, and to make it pliable, he scraped it with his machete before he expertly rolled a thin strip into cordage. With the feathers held on opposite sides of the shaft, he tightly bound them to the arrow, starting from the arrowhead end until the string was coiled around fifty millimetres of the cane. As well as holding the feathers in place, the cordage prevented the shaft from splitting when he slowly and carefully inserted the arrowhead. He pushed it in bit by bit, and kept stopping to check that everything was properly aligned. We went outside to where a *matoroa* tree only thirty metres away from the hut provided a handy source of glue, which was made by scraping the inner bark. It contains a sticky resin which Gramma squeezed from the bark over the binding to finish off the business end of the arrow. Then he counted off six spacings between the stipules to determine the length of the shaft, and to prevent the cane splitting, he cut a simplistic V shaped nock directly behind the last joint. Although the arrow was finished physically, it was far from complete. After it was wrapped in *lap lap* leaves, Gramma gave it to Peta.

The next day, after a strenuous walk through the mountains, Peta returned at dusk and disappeared into the *nakamal* with Patevina. Even without being empowered by the supernatural, if a wound is inflicted by a toxic black palm arrowhead, it's extremely painful and slow healing. But the hallowed projectile was now no longer just an arrow. It was alive with divine power and deadly poisonous. Only Peta possesses the wisdom and the *rapee* to perform the rite that embodied the arrow with the most potent of spirits. For over an hour he sang to the skulls of his forefathers and into a *tabu oktre* leaf. Then while he was submerged in a gripping but lucid trance, he crushed the leaf and milked its juice along the length of the arrow to empower it with Taute's revered spirit.

I knew that compared to receiving Patevina, all else pales, so I used tact and caution when I asked Peta if holding a simplistic ceremony when he gave me the arrow would breach *kastom*. The following morning we were both heading down to the lowlands at first light, and because of this, he readily agreed that only Gramma and himself would witness the huge honour that was being bestowed upon me.

Several hours later, when he placed Patevina in my hands, Peta told me to treat the ultimate gift with the utmost care and with the greatest respect. If ever I fired the arrow to kill an enemy, as it whistled through the air I would hear Taute singing from the two feathers. Because of its supreme spiritual guidance, it was highly unlikely the arrow would ever miss its mark, but if it did, the singing would guide me to its whereabouts. I was to do everything humanly possible to retrieve the wayward arrow, mainly to prevent the enemy from keeping Patevina, but also to prevent them from returning fire with the hallowed object. Never, under any circumstances was I to hold the arrowhead anywhere near my skin, as even a slight prick that draws blood guarantees an agonising death which is inflicted by the supernatural. If ever I needed to quickly remove the barbed arrowhead from an enemy's body so that I could use the arrow on my next foe, I must first position my body with the arrow at my back and look directly ahead. Then when I gave one swift pull, in spite of the barbs being encased in flesh, Taute would mysteriously allow the arrow to slip from the wound.

While I held Patevina, Peta said to me in a reverent tone, "Tavua, you are of the flying fox. Your brother the flying fox will carry your *rapee* on its back and soar effortlessly above the clouds, way up into the heavens, back to your country to become one with your spirit. Our master, Taute, will aim high with his bow and cast a spiritual arrow through the sky. Its flight will be true and fast and carry with it his immortal rapee. Listen for the singing of the arrow for its song will bring you great power. When you hear our master's music, don't be afraid, for he comes to become one with you. When our master's arrow strikes you and quivers to a halt, you will be a man of immense power. The most powerful spirit of Taute, all of the spirits of *bubu*, and the spirit of every man bush will stay with you for eternity." Peta's words were symbolic of his people's often-fragile and paradoxical existence in the highlands, as an arrow that was originally intended to kill an enemy would also bring me the most potent of *rapee* and give me added life force. We ended the simplistic rite by sharing a shell of kava. Now, even though I'd been initiated and I was no longer a *disale*, I would never be able to truly say goodbye to my friends in the highlands. They would always remain with my spirit and in my thoughts wherever I chose to call home, for in the eyes and minds of man bush, now that I'd received Patevina, Tavua was a man who was spawned from the most potent magic.

The next morning, when Gramma and I walked past Peta's leaf hut to the start of the trail that leads down to the Jordan River, almost everyone had left for a *lafaet* in the lowlands. Vetrivu and Vepeta stood at the top of the path gossiping, and both smiled and said, "*Bon tamamasa Tavua,*" ("Good morning, Tavua,") as we disappeared into the rainforest. There wasn't a huge *lafaet* or a huge send off in my honour, a simple "Good morning" sent me on my way. When I looked over my shoulder and bade them both farewell, I knew it would probably be for the last time. Over the past five years, I'd experienced incredible adventures, expanded my thinking, learnt valuable lessons about life and about myself, and had lived an explorer's dream come true. When I first made contact with the primitive highlanders, they had been a rarity in the modern world. I'm a realist not an idealist and never say never, but returning to witness the demise of my friend's culture could only turn the dream into a nightmare.

While Gramma and I walked below a hamlet nestled alongside the Jordan River, numerous voices called out, "*Tamamasa Tavua.*" I smiled and shouted back, "*Tamamasa,*" waving a greeting and a final goodbye. It took a long time for the smile to fade when I thought of the unique experiences that man bush had gifted me. I couldn't help but think that while I'd lived in what westerners would consider abject poverty, amidst the brutality of *kastom*, and amongst all of the discomfort and tribulations that come with life in the highlands, I'd been shown absolute selflessness and sincere kindness from a people who have the most brutal reputation throughout all of Vanuatu. Gramma skirted beneath the huts and didn't stop to join the *lafaet* because we had to reach the road before nightfall. As we headed towards civilization, Gramma told me that from now on he will revert back to a totally traditional way of life and will always follow the *kastom* road. One day he will be the paramount chief of Middle Bush, and no doubt a good one as he possesses the qualities of a great leader. He's adamant that when Peta dies, he will lie on top of his father's body to empower his *rapee*, then block an arrow that's fired at his heart with a *nul nul* or fend off a razor sharp spear, and even receive a brutal beating while

226 - RICK WILLIAMSON

he sleeps, simply because his father has died and simply because its *kastom*. With his people's indifference to hybridisation with the outside world already shaken, it would be futile to think that the other highlanders will share his stoic resolve and that their beliefs will remain unchanged amidst the struggle to greet and adapt to the forces of western civilization. When we went our separate ways, we never said goodbye. Gramma looked me in the eye and said, "It is hard, Tavua," then put his head down and walked away.

To expect to be able to ever fully understand the contradictions of man bush society, even after having undertaken a pagan apprenticeship, would be incredibly naïve, for their lives encompass the realm of life and death and what awaits beyond. While science is still coming to terms with everything from the natural and supernatural worlds being connected, even the most educated outsider can only speculate as to how the primitive mindset functions and how natural man is able to communicate with the spirits. To a *disale*, the very essence and the important truths of *kastom*, which stretch way beyond what we know to be fact, will never be crystal clear.

Chapter Twenty-Three

BARRACUDA AND BULLOCK

Vanuatu's northernmost islands are so remote that they only get one or two adventurous tourists who visit them each year. Once my friends in Luganville heard I was venturing up to Loh Island, which is one of the five sparsely populated islands in the isolated Torres group, their vivid imaginations sent a flood of incredulous gossip streaming my way. Because of a shortage of virile men on Loh, they all joked that I'd be ravaged by nubile and sex-starved women and married off to a local maiden before I'd even unpacked my bags. Missy, John Noel's wife, told me to stock up on food as cargo ships make infrequent stops in the far north. She never exaggerates so I took heed and crammed twenty kilos of rice and as much food as I could fit into my pack. Everyone warned that the ill placed islands seem to act as a magnet to passing cyclones and as soon as the gardens have recovered from a hurricane, another one strikes them. The general consensus in Luganville was to expect a people who were stricken with misery and deprivation.

Coming from Santo, when Van Air's twin otter touched down on tiny Linua Island, although no one said anything, the blank stares and unsmiling faces that greeted me when I exited the plane made it obvious my uninvited arrival wasn't overly welcome. With the Solomon Islands lying only 173 kilometres to the northwest, Loh's inhabitants appeared to have strong genetic links to the Tikopians, the Polynesian Solomon islanders that used to sail to Vanuatu to trade with the Torres and Banks islanders. As a consequence, the villagers lacked the sometimes-fierce looking Melanesian features that are so often belied by a Ni-Vanuatu's wide smile. I was unfazed by the indifferent reception and followed the villagers to the edge of a turquoise lagoon that separates uninhabited Linua Island from Loh Island. The blistering heat and my cheerful smile failed to thaw the frosty greeting, but I was undeterred and remained optimistic while I patiently sat on the edge of the lagoon.

When the only remaining group of villagers clambered into the last of the outrigger canoes that were ferrying everyone across to Loh, I thought I was about to be abandoned. Just before he pushed off, however, Woa Woteqo, a wiry and serious looking man who looked to be in his mid-thirties, shot several tentative glances in my direction, then made a hesitant approach. He explained that the last Europeans who'd visited the island had left a lasting and bad impression, and the bitter aftertaste from helping the marooned sailors still lingered in the villagers' mouths. When the yachties supplies had run out, they became abusive and constantly grumbled about the food the obliging locals had gifted them. I showed Woa a few photos of my initiation in Santo and the packets of rice and the other food that filled my swollen pack. Our edgy conversation became relaxed when I mentioned I hoped to stay for just one week, and when I said that I'd always eaten local food while I lived with primitive tribes, his stern mouth stretched into a welcoming smile.

After a short paddle across the one hundred metres wide lagoon, we entered an enchanted island idyll that reeked of simplicity and serenity. A short walk from the lagoon and not far from another glistening white sand beach, a smattering of leaf huts and a few western style buildings that were surrounded by tall coconut palms gave Lunghanglis village a peaceful atmosphere. Once Woa explained my intentions to the frigid looking villagers, they became warm and friendly. As well as being a tranquil paradise, Loh is a safe haven from malaria. And to ensure the island remained free of the parasite, the hospitable chief insisted that I head straight to the nearby clinic for a dose of Fansidar. When I explained I'd just recovered from a bout of the disease in Luganville's hospital and that my last tests were negative, it provided me with a welcome exemption as antimalarials wreak havoc on my system.

Woa told me that four months had passed since the last cargo ship had unloaded any provisions, but Van Air drops off supplies once a week when the plane picks up coconut crabs that are sold to restaurants in Port Vila. When basic goods are depleted, the resilient islanders, who already embrace a simplistic lifestyle, make soap from the *ngugua* vine and garnish their food with the salt residue the sun dries into granules in empty tidal pools. If crops that are already struggling to grow in the harsh climate and coral strewn soil are damaged by a cyclone, the islanders resort to making a starchy pudding with a flour that they grind from the plentiful and hurricane resistant *narava* plant. The ocean teems with an abundance of fish and seafood, and contrary to the widespread belief throughout Vanuatu that prompts many intending visitors to give the Torres a wide berth, no one endures perpetual hardship or dies of starvation.

Woa introduced me to Tunlera, a solidly built bachelor with a friendly face, who was in his mid-twenties. To reciprocate Tunlera's hospitality and the use of his spare bamboo slat bed, I gave him all of my food and asked him to share it out amongst the villagers. While I followed him through the village to his leaf hut, which was carpeted with white sand that squeaked beneath my feet, I wasn't ravaged by stampeding harems of topless and lust-filled women that I'd been warned about. Ever since the British evangelist Bishop Patterson first set foot on the island and successfully converted Loh's ancestors into English speaking, fully clothed Anglicans, they have religiously upheld the morals of the church.

That night, while I drank kava with the villagers, they told me how they've successfully blended their ancient traditions with Christianity and have managed to keep an important corridor to their age-old beliefs open by learning to compromise and to conserve. They said the turtle plays a crucial role in their beliefs. But when I asked, no one would say if the reptile was their totem. In the past, when turtles were hunted in the lagoon on moonlit nights, the expert fishermen silently cut through the clear water in a dugout canoe and easily spotted and harpooned the reptiles while they were engrossed in feeding on the abundant sea grass or they impaled the creatures while they gently propelled themselves along with their oar-like flippers. It was simple harvesting the meat they needed for the feasts they held twice a year, as was hunting the turtles every three months for a change of diet. Apart from wild fowl and flying foxes, Loh is devoid of any land dwelling game, and due to generations of unrestricted hunting pressure, the villagers noticed a sharp decline in the already perilously low numbers of turtles feeding in the lagoon. Because turtle meat provides an essential link to their ancestral beliefs, they realized that if the reptiles disappeared, as well as losing these beautiful animals, a vital part of the Torres Island's *kastom* would be lost forever.

The villagers all agreed that a strict conservation programme was the only hope they had of preserving their traditions and the reptiles. Female turtles, driven by maternal instinct, shuffle ashore during November and December to lay clutches of around one hundred eggs, which they bury on the beach. For the next two months, the eggs are incubated by the sand's natural warmth. With a dismal survival rate of an estimated one in one thousand, an alarming number of hatchlings fall victim to the ocean's predators, and because it takes fifteen years for a turtle to reach sexual maturity, the living fossils are easily hunted to extinction. The villagers keep a watchful eye on the eggs and harvest a small percentage of the emerging hatchlings, which they place in specially built pools. After they are hand reared for one year, the turtles are returned to their natural environment and are hopefully large enough to endure their previously lousy odds of survival. Nowadays between twenty to thirty turtles graze in the lagoon each night, but only when the villagers are fully satisfied that the number of reptiles has reached a sustainable level will the paramount chief once again allow traditional hunting to resume.

I spent the next two days relaxing on the peaceful island and effortlessly gained total acceptance from the amiable villagers. While the rest of the villagers were busy organizing a *lafaet* to honour the departure of a priest from the Solomon Islands who had lived and preached on Loh for the past year, Woa handed me a bowl of steaming coconut crab that was swimming in lemon juice and coconut milk. As I savoured each delectable morsel, my attention was quickly diverted from the mouth-watering meal when he told me that tomorrow morning, the fittest and strongest of the men were taking the big boat to hunt feral bulls on an outlying island and they'd invited me to join the hunt. I wasn't sure if he was joking when he said, "Here on Loh, when we hunt wild bullock in the traditional manner, we run them down and kill them with a knife." Woa looked surprised when I asked if they made a spear with the knife and used dogs. He then proudly stated that his forefather's have always chased wild bulls on foot and killed them with a machete or a knife.

Sometimes having a big ego and grim determination can put ambitious men in unenviable or stupid and dangerous positions. I always let sensibility make my decisions, but the more intimidating the task, the bigger my desire to succeed. If I ran in stifling heat and through the jungle with men half my age, it would be a great way to test my stamina after recently recovering from malaria, and it would also test the nerve of those who were pitting themselves against their dangerous quarry. The very thought of hunting an aggressive wild bull with a knife strikes most rational thinkers as an act of insanity. It's the type of lunacy that instantly conjures up mental images of reckless hunters being impaled on lethal horns and effortlessly tossed through the air like rag dolls that helplessly spin to the ground in a twisted heap. Although it's hardly the easiest way to grab a steak, without hesitating, I jumped at the offer to join the hunt.

Hunting is one of primitive man's most basic instincts and remains deeply ingrained in human nature. In civilized cultures, we often use hunting to forget about the stresses of modern life by getting back to nature and to satisfy our rudimentary instincts that are suppressed by living in a consumer society. Amongst primitive peoples, securing game is a deeply spiritual experience where the hunter becomes one with the animal, with the supernatural, and with every fundamental aspect of nature. When a triumphant hunter in Middle Bush, Santo, whoops and yells during the *bolo* dance, he's not jubilant because he's satisfied his ego by outwitting or overpowering a cunning animal. The surge of joyous emotion gives thanks to the gods, to nature, and to the slain animal, not as a worthy adversary, but as a kindred spirit who shares the same humbling connection with the earth and the spirits. Man bush loves the exhilaration of the hunt, his heightened sense of awareness when he becomes a predator, and the contentment of adequately providing for his family. But he never celebrates the death of an animal; instead, he welcomes its demise as a necessary part of the cycle of life. Of all the ingenious methods that natural man has devised to capture prey, successfully tracking, stalking, or running down an animal earns a hunter the most prestige. These means of filling the village pantry often help to preserve age-old traditions, but sometimes the brutal customs that are attached to a hunt blatantly contradict primitive man's close affinity with nature and the deep respect he has for his quarry.

The next morning when I followed the hunters to the lagoon, to my pygmy friends in Middle Bush, Santo, maybe the "big boat" that Woa had talked about would've been just that, but to a six foot one inch tall *disale* and seven other well-proportioned men, the five-metre long fibreglass dinghy was anything but big. Several sharp pulls on the starter chord and a chorus of obscenities failed to coax the temperamental fifteen horsepower engine to life. After ten minutes of tinkering and a liberal dose of much harsher swearing, on the first pull, the motor sent out a puff of blue smoke as it spluttered and coughed to life. We hooted and yelled while we clambered aboard, and as if to match our shouts, the engine roared into action and pushed us through the lagoon out towards the harbour. The blustery southeast trade winds that blow through Vanuatu in the dry season ensured we were in for an eventful ride. With perfect timing we surged through a lull in the waves that were crashing over the gap in the reef and raced over an unbroken swell into the open and turbulent ocean.

While a growing swell tossed our boat around, the way Silas handled the outboard and gave us some semblance of stability amidst a chaotic sea justified why throughout all of Vanuatu, the Torres Islanders are renowned as expert boatmen. Kara sat on top of the tiny canopy and, like the rest of the hunters, he was young and carefree and had a natural affinity with the ocean. Each time we were about to get hammered by a large wave, he yelled a warning above the din of the motor and the roar of the sea so that we had time to brace ourselves. When the waves pounded us, he laughed and shouted, then whenever there was a brief lull, he whistled to himself or sang custom songs without a care in the world.

Two hours later, when we pulled into the lee side of Tegua Island and entered Hestreux Passage, the contrast in the conditions was incredible. Not only had the weather abruptly changed, so did our luck. As we trolled through the silky waters, the nylon trailing from our handline snapped taught. About seventy meters away a protesting fish exploded from the surface and sent a plume of spray into the air. Tunlera casually wound the line in, and several minutes later, the shimmering silver belly of a barracuda flashed in the clear water alongside the boat. The struggling fish was full of fight, but its efforts to escape were in vain as it was well and truly hooked on a homemade lure Tunlera had made from a red plastic rice bag. Everyone was fearful of the barracuda's razor sharp teeth and lifted their bare feet when Tunlera flicked the violently flapping fish onto the plywood deck.

We cruised through the passage and headed towards Metoma Island, which is nestled midway between Tegua and Hiu Island, the northernmost island in Vanuatu. When we pulled up onto Metoma Island, apart from a few stands of tightly knitted *ngahoba* trees, the reasonably open jungle blanketing the six square kilometres atoll, and its reasonably flat terrain, gave a forgiving rather than foreboding first impression. In typical Ni-Vanuatu fashion, we received a warm and genuine welcome from the Makie family, who are the island's sole inhabitants. There was plenty of daylight left, so we went on a recce to see if there were any animals around. Late in the afternoon, we spotted a mob of cattle filtering down from the cover of the jungle, making a beeline across a large grove of coconut trees to quench their thirst from a well on the far side of the plantation. The lead bullock was extremely cautious and almost crept out from the rainforest with its ears pricked while its eyes searched for danger. Once they caught the first whiff of the breeze that wafted from behind us and cut our scent, they wheeled in fright and crashed off into the jungle. Even with the luxury of a high-powered rifle the fleeing cattle would've made an extremely difficult target. From the way the bullocks raced for cover, this wasn't going to be easy, and anyone who's easily discouraged couldn't help but think that trying to run down the animals was a futile exercise.

That night, Hamilton Makie and seven of her eleven children squeezed the eight of us into her leaf hut. Her husband was working on another island for several months, and because of this, she was especially anxious for us to target a bull that had been terrorizing her family. While they worked in the plantation, without provocation or warning, on numerous occasions a tan bull with a white patch on its forehead had charged and forced them to hurriedly claw up trees or take refuge inside their hut. To kill any large game animal with a knife is a big call in anyone's book, but to single out one particular bull, especially an aggro beast with a blatant disrespect for humans, sounded pretty daunting.

While we made small talk, the ground started shaking and a shudder ran up the sides of the creaking leaf hut as a mild earthquake rocked it from side to side. The children nervously looked at one another and remained silent until the tremor ceased, then they all burst out laughing. After that, Hamilton and her eldest daughter Vicki explained why so many coconut crabs abound on Metoma. They told me a mythical giant crab that originally gave birth to all of Vanuatu's coconut crabs lives on the island.

The coconut crab plays a vital role in supplying the Torres islanders with a source of income. Despite the crustacean's invincible appearance, with its imposing pinchers and an impenetrable looking armour plated shell, the creatures are extremely vulnerable. As you'd expect from its name, the crab's favourite food is the juicy flesh of the coconut. They climb the coconut palm with the efficiency of a lumberjack wearing crampons and wrench free clusters of nuts, which sometimes split when they hit the ground. Nature has provided the crustaceans with incredibly powerful claws that are capable of prising open a tough coconut husk, and when they do, they sometimes crawl inside the nut and feed for several days before they emerge. Once they digest the coconut meat, it's converted into coconut oil and is stored in a large body cavity which is protected by their tough shell. The creatures survive off of the stockpile of oil during periods of hibernation.

Their fondness for coconut meat and their predictable eating habits makes them easy to catch by staking a partially opened or halved coconut about ten meters from their burrow. The crabs are nocturnal and become so engrossed in their meal, that they're easily approached with a torch and captured by hand. During the day, they normally sleep in a burrow about three hundred millimetres long and are caught by probing the hole with a stick or a piece of wire. When the crab awakes, it gets agitated and grabs the intrusive object and gives it a good shake, which indicates their presence. Extracting them from their short burrow requires little effort, but their menacing claws must be treated with care and tied together as the powerful pincers are just as good at splitting fingers open as they are at opening coconuts. If one of them gets a hold of you, their grip is unrelenting and sometimes isn't relaxed for hours.

Coconut crabs mature extremely slowly and take about thirty years to grow to a harvestable weight of around two kilograms. The fragile balance between maintaining a sustainable population is easily disrupted as Hamilton's husband, Jean-Pierre, and his parents, Johnie and Anna Makie, discovered. Johnie decided pork would make a welcome addition to his family's subsistence diet and introduced pigs to the island. One particularly hot afternoon, after he and a friend from a neighbouring island had drank their way to the bottom of several bottles of wine, they fed the pigs.

Then the two inebriated men staggered away, leaving the gate to the pen open and errantly liberating the animals into the jungle.

Back then crabs were so numerous they could be seen at any time of the day. The pigs thrived on the abundant crustaceans and rapidly grew in numbers until they'd almost eradicated the entire crab population. Jean-Pierre was mortified by the dilapidated state of the crustacean's spiritual birthplace and declared Metoma a crab sanctuary. Then he purchased a rifle and two hunting dogs, and to appease the supernatural mother of all coconut crabs, in 1988, he hunted the very last pig off the island. To hasten the crabs' recovery, which had became his sole priority, he began restocking Metoma with crustaceans from the surrounding islands. Nowadays the creatures are so prolific that it's not unusual to see them during the day or to find them wandering about in the Makie's leaf hut, where they often make unwelcome houseguests.

We were up early the next morning, and without a cloud in the heavens to mar the sunrise, once the sun burst over the horizon, the island was enveloped in sweltering heat, which hardly provided the perfect conditions for running through the jungle. All of the hunters sharpened their machetes and caressed the edge of them with a file until they were satisfied their knives had a keen edge. To avoid the burden of running this early in the morning on full stomachs, we breakfasted on small helpings of rice and a few wild yams.

It was 7:00 a.m. when I glanced at my watch and we spread out in a wide line across the jungle. We stayed within earshot of each other, and although there was fresh signs everywhere, after we made several systematic sweeps from coast to coast, the wary cattle had managed to elude us. Once the sun hung above our shoulders and the atoll was swathed in blistering heat, the drinking holes that are dotted around the island were the obvious place to look, but each time we quietly crept up to them, all we found was freshly churned soil.

We fanned out again and walked in virtual silence across the island while we listened for a tell-tale bellow and tried to catch a fleeting glimpse of our elusive quarry. I was amazed at how a mob of cattle managed to move so quietly through the jungle and stay one step ahead of us. The sound of flies buzzing around steaming pats warned us that the bullocks were nearby, then seconds later someone shouted "Ahooo! Ahooo!" as they used the *lulau* call to let everyone know our prey had been sighted and the chase was on. As I followed in Rennell's swift footsteps, a chaotic racket of frenzied yelling and vegetation being noisily flattened with a sharp crack sounded way off to our right. The cattle moved with incredible speed and surprising agility in the fiery thirty-degrees-plus heat. We spent the next hour running around the island in hot pursuit, until the wily animals managed to outrun and outsmart us.

After a short rest, and revitalized by a new plan of attack, with a sense of urgency, we quickly set off across the island. There was no time to waste because we were heading back to Loh tonight with a boatload of coconut crabs that one of the Makie boys was picking up from Hiu Island. Woa had casually mentioned that no one has ever come back empty

234 — RICK WILLIAMSON

handed from a wild bull hunt, and if we did return without a boat full of beef, the hunters would lose face back at Loh. Rennell and I had only been walking for several minutes when a wild fowl exploded into flight from the undergrowth and settled in the lower branches of a nearby tree. The inquisitive bird cocked its head from side to side and was more curious than it was frightened as it peered down at us. I could see Rennell licking his lips at the thought of roast chicken while his machete flashed into action and he started hacking away at the lower branches to open up the vegetation. Then, by throwing a well-aimed stick, his first shot sent the bird flailing to the ground, and before it could gather its senses, he pounced on the stunned chicken with the speed of a seasoned bird dog.

The sun had reached its zenith and our weary muscles begged for rest when we regrouped again and gathered firewood to roast the fowl. While we chewed on the stringy chicken, everyone's envious eyes surveyed my boots. Except for Rennell, everyone else was barefoot and nursing raw feet from running over the sharp chunks of coral that are scattered across the whole of the island. After we washed down the chicken with a drink of sweet coconut milk and ate the flesh of the nut it was time to move again.

Even the shade beneath the canopy of trees offered little respite from the debilitating heat as we flailed through the forest after different groups of animals. We kept up the chase until late in the afternoon and stopped for a brief rest. The lengthening shadows crept across the forest floor and, like ravenous spirits, greedily consumed our precious light. All of us were teetering on the brink of exhaustion, but with dogged determination, we hobbled back to the plantation to make one final sweep. To the weak willed, our attempts would have appeared to be a discouraging fiasco, but with only an hour of daylight left, and after running for most of the day, the cattle were no doubt just as jaded as we were. Our persistence paid off when the sound of thundering hooves turned our heads and three bullocks unexpectedly charged past us across the open plantation. This was the last chance for the hunters to salvage their reputations and was time for some serious action. A sudden surge of adrenaline recharged our weary legs as we sprinted after the disappearing animals and screamed directions to one another. This time our plan worked to perfection as we channelled the fleeing cattle towards the northern tip of the island and drove them into a thick stand of *ngahoba* trees. We had to be careful, sidestepping the clusters of coconut crabs with menacing looking pincers that had crawled from their burrows to feed on a *ngawau* tree that was heavily laden with ripe fruit.

Hunting like this, in its most basic form, requires a combination of stamina, perseverance, and a big set of *cahones* with plenty of hair on them when it comes to facing off for the kill. Bill and I were first on the scene when all three of the exhausted bulls stopped, stood their ground, and took stock of the situation. One of the breathless animals was the aggro beast with the white forehead that had been harassing the Makies. Its stomach heaved violently and highlighted the sheen of sweat coating its glossy pelt. As the bull began pawing the ground, it stared at us with a look of hatred in its eyes, then steadied himself and gave his head a small shake while he decided which one of us to line up. All I had for protection was my wits, so I didn't wait for him to make up his mind and swung up the nearest tree. While the other two cattle crashed off in a blind panic into the sanctuary of the gloomy jungle, the bull never took its eyes off of Bill, and when it charged, the thundering mass of knotted muscles and sweeping horns were entirely focused on inflicting injury. Bill had nerves of steel and handled himself with the grace and skill of a seasoned matador. At the very last moment, with split second precision, just as the mountain of beef bore down on him, he sidestepped and slashed with his machete. As the bull thundered past, his wayward swipe with the razor sharp blade cut the animals tail clean off. The enraged beast vented its anger with a bellow as it spun around to launch another attack. When the infuriated bullock charged him again, Bill wisely bolted for cover behind a tree and took another quick swipe with his machete, but the bull was too quick for him and he missed completely. I jumped to the ground and was about to take a few action photos, but quickly changed my mind when I became the bull's centre of attention. Bill yelled a warning while I yelled a few choice lines of profanity and clawed up a perfectly positioned windfall to escape the charging animal. While it thrashed the windfall with its horns, Bill bravely dashed forward and hamstrung the bullock with one swift slash. By now the others had arrived on the scene and, just as the animal bellowed a gravely agonized bawl, Tulnera's machete took out its other hamstring and completely immobilised the hapless animal. Each time Bill tried to grab the bull by the horns, it raked its head towards his outstretched hands. The pit of my stomach swallowed up each of its pathetic cries when Tulnera and the others slammed sizeable lumps of coral into the anguished animal's forehead. The hardy bull was still full of fight and refused to submit to its fate peacefully until a hail of coral chunks finally dazed it long enough for Bill to wrestle with its horns while Lendi drove his knife into its heart and mercifully ended the hunt.

For a brief moment we all stood silent and gathered our thoughts while we stared at our fallen quarry. From the look on everyone's faces, it was obvious that no one had enjoyed watching the quivering bull suffer a cruel and barbaric death. It was as if Tunlera was reading my mind while I thought that the demise of any creature should be as quick and painless as possible. He looked at me and said, "It is hard and brutal but it is *kastom*, Rick." We quickly butchered the animal in the rapidly fading light and skewered the meat over the ends of sturdy saplings. A few of us paired off and shouldered the crippling loads of beef, while the others hacked a clear track ahead of us. Dusk had detonated an unbelievable explosion of cheeps and high pitched whines that pulsed through the jungle as the sound of every noisemaking insect united into a deafening symphony. Through the ear splitting din, we shouted out the *lulau* call so that those whose turn it was to carry the shoulder-bruising loads knew where the path was heading, until we reached the open plantation, which was bathed in bright moonlight.

Fireflies flickered and dived through the humid air as we loaded the beef and our aching bodies into the grossly overloaded boat. Even the passage where we were berthed looked uninviting and foamed with white caps. With two hundred and seventy five kilograms of coconut crabs, one bull, and eight men crammed into the dinghy, the little fifteen-horse motor was about to prove its worth. When we stripped down to our underpants and stowed our clothes under the canopy, I knew that once we were out in the open water, we were in for a soaking and one hell of a rough ride.

As the boat pushed through the turbulent passage effervescent algae glistened in the bow wave like millions of tiny moon drops. When an angry sea greeted our little craft, it did itself credit as it climbed up swells, then slammed into approaching waves that drenched us when plumes of spray showered the air. A pod of sleek dolphins that gracefully frolicked alongside us were totally oblivious to the tumultuous sea. When they torpedoed out of the water and momentarily glided across the turgid ocean, everyone started singing a *kastom* song in an attempt to bring the younger dolphins to the surface so they would bring us good luck. If I knew the words I would've screamed at the top of my voice, because we needed all the help we could get while the uncompromising ocean tossed us around.

Two hours into our journey, when the inevitable happened and a coconut crab escaped, the sound of its shell clattering against the wooden deck sent us scrambling to our feet. We held on tight to the side of the bucking boat and struggled to maintain our balance as we tried not to fall into the boiling sea until the menacing crustacean was captured. I was way out of my comfort zone, but everyone else seemed completely relaxed and laughed and hooted loudly each time the sea demanded respect by saturating us and our cargo.

After three and a half hours of constant bailing, lots of coarse language, and plenty of joking, our adventurous journey was over. The little dinghy knifed along the waves rolling towards Loh, surged through the break in the reef, and raced down the swell into the still waters of the moonlit lagoon. Several villagers sitting on the beach who'd been patiently waiting for us to return acknowledged our success with a reserved nod of their heads when they saw the boatload of meat. I jumped out of the boat and dug my toes into the soft white sand. Being back on land had never felt so good. We were shivering from the cold and limped up the beach with raw feet and aching limbs. To an outside observer with half an ounce of common sense, the whole trip might have seemed reckless and kamikaze, and in hindsight, it definitely was. But when you take into account that if an outboard motor or the dinghy isn't available, the hunters paddle their outrigger canoes all the way to Metoma, we'd travelled in relative comfort and safety.

Back at the village, after we'd finished shovelling mouthfuls of fire roasted heart, liver, and kidneys into our hungry mouths, we washed down the hard-earned meal with a shell of kava. No one bothered to tell the others how we'd braved wild bullocks and an angry sea. It wasn't because they were modest, everyone had expected a positive outcome because the hunters had made *kastom* before the hunt.

Chapter Twenty-Four

ANCESTRAL ARROWHEADS

It was easy to relax amongst peoples who live by the philosophy that life should never be hurried. I spent the next couple of days spear fishing with Rennell, flicking hordes of vibrantly coloured reef fish from amongst the coral crags with a bamboo fishing pole, and barbecuing the catch on the beach. Before we went reef fishing, Bretton, who was in his mid-fifties and wore a grizzled beard and a mop of curly grey hair, taught me how to walk across jagged reefs simply by removing a sun bleached coconut husk in two pieces and tying them to our feet with strips of bark from the banyan tree. Woa supplied our bait by stalking along the edge of the lagoon and shooting fish with his bow. Once Woa realized I had a keen interest in archery, I discovered that in the past, life on Loh wasn't so carefree, and contrary to popular belief, it was often fraught with danger.

Because I'd read several times that the Torres islanders were never cannibals, I was surprised to learn that before the introduction of Christianity, Loh's inhabitants were fierce warriors. No one ever ventured beyond their village boundaries unless they were heavily armed. The men always carried a bow, a *nul nul*, or a *ngakorung*, which is a type of spear that was used during combat. To what extent cannibalism occurred has been lost in the annals of time, but the villagers are adamant that their ancestors dined on human flesh, and of all the weapons that they used to slay their enemies, poisoned arrows were deemed the most potent. I was lucky because the villagers had recently discovered a cave called Villia in the heart of the island that houses ancestral skulls. Rennell offered to guide me to the cavern so that I could photograph the remains. Some of their bones were used to make lethal arrowheads.

Many primitive tribes believe they are virtually holding hands with their ancestors when they enter battle, which is an apt and nearly accurate description of how the Torres islanders used to face their foes. They weren't quite holding hands, but they literally carried body parts from the arms and legs of their forefathers. After we returned from Villia cave, we visited Loh's paramount chief at Rinuha village. He pulled a parcel of *lap lap* leaves from the soot-blackened rafters of his hut, then carefully unwrapped two ancient wild cane arrows that were tipped with long slender arrowheads fashioned from human bone. The arrows still contain a lethal ancestral spirit and at one time, were anointed with a deadly poison whose recipe is now unknown. While I carefully fondled and admired the artefacts, the chief warned that if I pricked myself with the arrowhead and drew blood, I was guaranteed to suffer an agonizing death.

A powerful *kastom* man called Dan Tatung made the last arrows that were tipped with human bone in the late 1800s. They were made from the bones of his own mother. Only fresh bones were ever used, and to ensure his mother's spirit empowered the arrowheads, Dan gave her a hallowed burial rite. He placed a *tabu* mat over a mound of burial rocks then laid the corpse on top of the mat. Branches from a sacred tree were staked around the body to ward off evil spirits and to show the site was *tabu*. Then to appease his mother's departing spirit, he hung a woven basket that was filled with food alongside her head.

On the fifth night, by which time the tropical climate had caused the body to start rotting, Dan sliced the flesh away from his mother's shins and forearms, then removed the *tabu* bones. He had to wait five days to give her spirit time to visit Marauhi, the *kastom* god. Only then would her spirit have returned and become embodied in the bones that Dan was about to fashion into arrowheads. Her decaying body was left on the burial mound to succumb to the humid elements, and once it had decomposed enough for the skull to be pulled away from the rest of the corpse, her head was stored in a sacred cavern alongside the bones of her ancestors.

While the arrowhead was being shaped, it required extreme care and patience for if blood was drawn with the bone, the villager died a horrific death. The bone was painstakingly rubbed over abrasive rock and coral to craft an arrowhead measuring 250 millimetres long that tapered from its base towards a fine point. Then the head was bound to a wooden insert with cordage that was made from the banyan tree, and when it was pushed into the wild cane shaft, one hundred millimetres of the insert was left projecting from the arrow, which is six segments long between the first and last stipules. Only two poisoned arrows remain on Loh, and so powerful is the respect and mana these artefacts command, that decades ago a major dispute with a neighbouring island was settled with the exchange of one of these arrows.

Although arguments are a rarity amongst Loh's laidback inhabitants, when problems do occur, they are also settled with an arrow. But nowadays no one evens the score when they have a bone to pick with someone by using a poisoned arrow that's made from a relative's body parts. After the paramount chief decides who is at fault, the offender makes a 350 millimetres long hardwood arrowhead in the same laborious manner as the bone arrowheads were crafted and gifts the arrow to the other party. Irrespective of what offence has occurred, the recipient harbours no malice towards the guilty party once they receive the arrow.

After we left the paramount chief, Rennell led me to a large cave that's used as a safe haven when Loh is bombarded by cyclones. It was massive and had a huge entrance that let in plenty of light, but it reeked from the sickly smell of centuries of bat excrement. Hundreds of the mammals were suspended from the cavern roof, and when our presence disturbed them, they became agitated and swooped and fluttered around our heads. They dive bombed us like miniature fighter planes, then expertly veered away from us at the last minute by using their acoustic radar.

In a sacred area of the cave, a circle of rocks and ancient seashells surrounded magic stones—some nature had created, others shaped by human hands—which are still used by the paramount chief and a few elders who are capable of evoking their ancestral spirits from the haphazard jumble of *tabu* relics. Black magic is still practised, and supernatural spirits are unleashed to cause death, to produce storms, to seduce women, and to create all manner of bedlam. Nowadays the sprits are mostly used to control the forces of nature and to manipulate the sun and the rain to help struggling crops flourish.

Rennell showed me where one of his ancestors had spat mouthfuls of red ochre over their hand and left an indelible handprint on the cave wall. He had no idea what the hand represented, so I gave its lost meaning a bit of thought. To me it was more than just a two dimensional piece of primitive rock art on a cave wall, and had a much deeper spiritual significance. After my initiation in Santo, I think that the hand of a man emblazoned on eternal rock symbolized the striking awareness Rennell's forefathers had of the unity between themselves and the land. The two were inseparable, and both left a permanent mark on each other. Because the cave is used to perform hallowed rituals with the magic stones, this would've heightened the eternal bond Rennell's ancestors had with the *tabu* site.

Like most good things, my time on Loh ended way to soon. As I was leaving, no one said a word as we silently waded across the lagoon at low tide so that I could catch a flight to Mota Lava Island. When we were halfway across and I asked Rennell why everyone was being so quiet, he said it was to avoid attracting the sharks and barracuda that abound in the waters, but not to worry as no one had been attacked yet.

Linua Island must arguably stake claim to the smallest restaurant in Vanuatu if not all of the Pacific. It seats three patrons if they keep their knees and elbows tucked in. The tiny thatched hut, which was built alongside the grass airstrip to welcome and feed visitors, reflects the mood and the sentiments of the Torres islanders. They've made an alliance with western culture, but on their own laid back and low-key terms.

Chapter Twenty-Five

SACRED LIASONS

After an enjoyable flight and a smooth landing at Ablow airfield on Mota Lava island, the plane shuddered to a stop and the pilot casually looked over his shoulder, and, to anyone who was on a tight schedule, he delivered "a blow." Without any prior warning, he apologetically announced that he had no idea when the next plane would return as the unkempt grass runway desperately needed cutting, and once he took off, the airstrip was officially closed. The driver of the mower was away visiting his relatives on another island, no one knew when he would be returning. It was so typical of carefree islanders who function at their own leisure and are still coming to grips with timetables and the routine of the western work ethic. I enjoyed the slow and relaxed pace of things happening at "island time" and didn't care about the airstrip being closed as I had months left on my visa and an open airline ticket. Worse things could happen than being marooned on beautiful Mota Lava. I looked forward to kicking back for a while on the long stretches of white sand beach that flank the thirty-five square kilometre paradise. Being the only European on the island didn't faze me either, because unlike the primitive and sometimes hostile forest based cultures I'd visited, I knew I wouldn't be eyed with deep suspicion, receive an aloof greeting, or be treated as if I was an uninvited alien species that had dropped from the skies. The small crowd of locals waiting for the plane were all friendly and had welcomed me with beaming smiles and genuine handshakes.

The soothing scenery and hospitable people had never been the island's initial drawcard. When I learned the swelling population was nudging the two thousand mark while there was barely enough fertile land left to sustain the natives' subsistence lifestyles, it didn't make sense. My intuition kept telling me that there must be an underlying reason for the poor land management and that maybe a veiled custom was responsible for the island being the most densely populated in the Banks group, if not all of Vanuatu. Instead of catching a ride on the back of a Toyota pickup that was taxying everyone back to their respective villages, I decided to take a leisurely eleven kilometres walk along the road to Avar village, which lies near the southwest tip of the island.

Fate's guiding hand provided me with good luck when only five hundred metres from the airstrip, I met a villager full of exuberance and good humour who was heading back to Avar. Seru was in his early twenties, and when he cheerfully fell into step alongside me, he offered to shoulder one of my packs. He looked worldly and down-to-earth so when I gave him the lighter of the two, I joked that a big guy like him could probably lift it with a hard-on. There was a good reason as to why he gave me a surprised and quizzical look before he burst out laughing. By the time we'd reached Avar, we were bouncing jokes off of one another, we'd become good friends, and Seru had proudly shared how he'd won first prize in the annual coconut lifting competition between Avar and nearby Rah Island. To claim first prize, he'd lifted two green coconuts off of the ground, which was a Herculean effort considering he'd used his erect penis. The way that he'd loosely talked about sex while we walked along, and his eye watering ability to power lift with his penis fuelled my suspicions as to why the island is overpopulated.

Throughout the Banks Islands, *kastom* is at its strongest on Mota Lava, and Avar village is the nucleus of tradition. Seru helped me find Skeva Bena, whose name I'd been given from a mutual acquaintance on another island. Skeva was in his mid-thirties, tall and lithe, and looked more Polynesian than Melanesian. He had a sharp mind and good nature, and from the moment we shook hands, we became good friends. When we first met, I had no idea he was the grandson of Japeth, who is the paramount chief of Mota Lava, and the most powerful *kastom* man in the Banks.

While we sat and talked, it came as no surprise to hear that Skeva had held an important position with the government, as his intelligent manner and profound thinking were evident. For two people who had just been introduced to each other, our conversation became deep, and once he knew I'd completed an initiation in Middle Bush, Santo, there was a mutual respect and a silent understanding between us. *Kastom* had left its indelible mark on Skeva and I could sense that he had succumbed to brutality and spiritual forces that are beyond the comprehension of most people. They bring to you a pain of their own that can only be understood through firsthand experience and can't be learnt from listening to the accounts of others. It was easy to pick a man who had walked the same painful walk and emerged with the same character. Within a couple of hours we were getting along like kindred spirits and were amazed when we discovered we literally were, as Skeva's bloodline traces back to Kakombona village in the Solomons. When I told him I was a *wantok* to Mathias, who is Kakambona's chief, we shook our heads in disbelief, as Skeva is also his distant relative.

I was welcome to stay in the village for as long as I liked, and while I walked around Avar with Skeva, two things quickly became apparent. There was an obvious feeling of unity between the sexes, and the women do most of the work while the men enjoy a relatively leisurely existence. Wherever we went, there were groups of hardworking and openly subservient women who were obviously at the bottom of the hierarchal scale, toiling away at routine tasks. Late in the afternoon, they returned from their gardens looking tired and dripping with sweat after carrying crippling loads of crops over their shoulders. They normally make the tiresome twenty-two kilometre return trek to their plantations at least three times a week. While we watched another group of women struggling to carry heavy pales of water from the nearby well, they looked dulled by the complacency of having to exist as a workhorse. Both sexes have their own *nakamals*, which are open only to those of the same gender, but despite the obvious divisions when it came to the different sexes practising certain customs, there was still a strong sense of social cohesion, of wellbeing, and of general happiness within the community.

Skeva treated me like a brother and told me I could sleep in a hut he no longer used, but invited me take my meals with his family. The first night that I dined with him, his wife submissively sat on the floor alongside us until we'd finished eating, because *kastom* forbade her dinning with a male guest or to be positioned higher than us. Although I was living in a patriarchal society, Skeva told me there were a few *tabus* that males have to observe. I had to avoid walking under any article of woman's clothing that was hanging out to dry, I couldn't mix my clothes with a female's, and males are forbidden to enter the women's *nakamal*.

Over the next few days I did very little except spend the nights in the men's *nakamal* drinking kava, and during the day I blended with the men while they carried out small and menial tasks. Although we'd grown close, it came as a complete surprise when Skeva took me aside and said he wanted to make me a *kastom* brother and a honorary chief. After the rigours of my initiation on Santo, I was fully aware of the hidden repercussions of agreeing and had to give it a lot of serious thought before I gave him an answer. Skeva probably wouldn't have thought any worse of me if I said no, and I felt he would fully understand if I chose to remain a guest rather than become entwined in his beliefs, but several hours later I bit the bullet and agreed to keep kindling the *kastom* flame by becoming a member of his clan.

That night, while I was bathed in subtle moonlight and sitting to the left of one-hundred-year-old Japeth, I questioned my sanity after having willingly agreed to blindly wander into uncharted territory again. My initiation began from beneath a basic thatch shelter while all of Skeva's extended family looked on. There hadn't been an intense build up, or the need to learn about *kastom* in the *nakamal*, and apart from wearing a necklace of flowers, there had been no preparation whatsoever. Personally I felt Japeth was closer to eighty than one hundred years old, but everyone relished the fact that their patriarch was still sprightly and alert at such a ripe old age. He wore a necklace of woven coconut leaves and called upon the spirits to bless three shells of kava that belonged to myself, to him, and to a chief who was seated to his right. Then he raised his shell, spoke to the heavens, and spilled a small portion of the brew on the ground. The other chief gave a short speech and also splashed kava at his feet. When Japeth motioned for me to speak, I reciprocated with a few words and tipped some of my kava onto the bare earth, and then the three of us guzzled down what was left of our kava. The brief formalities were over, and I'd made an effortless transition from being an outsider to being welcomed into Skeva's bloodline as one of the family. From now on I would be known as Rick Welegtabit instead of Rick Williamson. Welegtabit means gently flowing water and was my newfound totem. Throughout all of Vanuatu, water is an enviable element to be linked to, as it's the most potent totem, dousing the evil powers of *kastom* men who call upon spirits from a *tabu* fire. Water is revered because it heals, kills, can break down even the strongest rock, nurtures life, and can adapt to the shape of whatever vessel it's poured into, which is what I had learnt to do when I became a member of a different culture.

When I'd spilt the sanctified kava onto the ground, I'd opened my soul up to Quat, the *kastom* god, but I'd also paved the way for malicious devils to enter my being. Once we'd eaten our fill at a small *lafaet*, Skeva explained the *tabus* I had to observe now that I was one of the clan. Whenever I was alone at night in my hut, I was to keep my door locked at all times, and unless someone knocked and identified themself first, I wasn't to let them in. This precaution dates back millennia, to a time when Avar fought with neighbouring tribes and, contrary to what I'd read, when cannibalism occurred throughout the Banks Islands. I can understand why it's been documented that human flesh was never consumed, because it's highly unlikely that a visiting academic would ever get a true insight into a secret society or an honest answer from an informant regarding intimately shielded beliefs and rituals. With Skeva's bloodline tracing back to Kakambona in the Solomons, whose descendants were fierce headhunters and cannibals from Ullawa Island, it came as no surprise when I found out that cannibalism had existed.

If a screeching owl flew over the village, I was forbidden to leave my hut until the bird had flown away from the area. Anyone who fails to observe the *tabu* suffers from a terrible illness that's inflicted by evil spirits. The ghost of an old man who is believed to have been one of the island's first inhabitants protects us from evil and is often seen walking through the village at night. I was to embrace rather than fear his presence, as he is a guardian spirit who drives malevolent demons from Avar. Although the village is a stronghold for *kastom*, all of Avar's inhabitants don't believe in a single creator. They are practising Anglicans and worship Christianity in harmonious tandem with their ancestor's primordial beliefs. Even father Bretton Wopyet, the Anglican priest, is an esteemed *kastom* man. Skeva placed a lot of emphasis on treating the villagers with respect, especially Japeth, the other chiefs, and the *kastom* men.

Japeth led me back to my hut, placed a coconut leaf across the doorway, and told me it was crucial that I remained inside until daylight. He had sung into the leaf, which was now *tabu* and of vital importance to my initiation as it would repel the *kastom* devils who were seeking a new disciple, and while I slept, it ensured that only Quat would become embodied in my resting spirit.

The next morning, Skeva led me to a quiet stretch of beach that we had all to ourselves. While we sat and talked, he continued my cultural schooling and unravelled the tightly bound secret to Mota Lava's swelling population. Two bloodlines exist in Avar, and it's easy to distinguish which lineage a woman belongs to by the starlike tattoo she wears on either the left or right cheek of her face. The only visual way of telling which bloodline a man belongs to is by looking at his wife, which he must choose from outside of his own lineage.

The birth of a child is a special occasion in Melanesian society as the next generation guarantees the continuance of a bloodline and hopefully the preservation of *kastom*. For a first-time mother, childbirth can be a traumatic experience, and this is especially true for Avar's women, as an expectant mother must deliver her first child in total isolation. Once she's given birth, she severs the umbilical chord and eats the afterbirth and umbilical chord raw. The nutrients from the gruesome meal sustain her for the next five days, during which time she must remain in isolation with her infant. She is forbidden to wash, and cleans herself and her child with wild kava leaves which are believed to possess healing powers. While they remain in isolation, the mother catches her child's faeces and urine in a container woven from *tabu* leaves and keeps the foul smelling excrement in the corner of the hut.

At the end of her five days of solitary confinement, every woman from her bloodline joins her, and depending on the size of her family tree, sometimes up to thirty women come together. She leaves her newborn with one of her companions and heads to the nearby beach with the rest of the women in tow. First the mother bathes in the tepid ocean, then all of the women catch fish and gather enough seafood to feed themselves for just one day. By now the tropical heat has turned the infant's excrement into a stinking and vile mess. The mother washes the child's wastes into the sea, which casts a *tabu* over the ocean that prevents every male from harvesting any seafood.

The hungry mother leads the women back to the female *nakamal* and cooks the seafood for herself and the others. How many kinswomen reside in the *nakamal* determines the number of nights they stay together. They spend as many nights as there are women, and on her given day, each person chooses a food type. Nothing else is on offer once her choice is made, and everyone must dine on the same food.

There are seven villages on Mota Lava, but the most hallowed of rites are performed in one *nakamal* which is hidden in the depths of the jungle. Within that *nakamal* lies that answer to one of the island's biggest enigmas. Overpopulation is due to the Nataquat, a lifeless costume that's comprised of a woven headpiece from which a long veil of dried leaves hangs. All of the men from the proud father's bloodline gather in the secluded *nakamal*, but instead of celebrating the birth of his first child, they resurrect the fetish's dormant spirit to instil new life into the inanimate Nataquat. Only those who've attained the required rank in the *sukwe*, of which there are nine levels, has the ability to evoke the Nataquat's spirit, and anyone who divulges the more intricate details of the rite to outsiders is sentenced to death. Ordinary men place *tabu* leaves atop of their heads to become something extraordinary when overwhelming supernatural forces embalm their physical and spiritual being. When the wearer slides the fetish over his body and he's completely covered from head to toe by the guise, a dramatic transformation takes place, and his train of thought is no longer human. He is no longer in full control of his senses, and when the Nataquat arms itself with a stout stick, and is brimming with evil intent, it leaves the *nakamal* and goes in search of victims.

It's at this time that the women are gripped by a wave of fear. They know that when they leave the sanctity of the *nakamal* to gather food there's no safety in numbers. The Nataquat lurks in the shadows, stalking them, eagerly waiting, as it readies itself for the right moment to pounce and give them a brutal beating. They know that the Nataquat won't hold back and will show no mercy, and that their bones may shatter, and their blood will definitely flow. Some of them may end up in the nearby clinic with serious injuries, and although there is no love lost when the Nataquat pummels them, in a bizarre twist there's only love to be gained. Those who are brave enough can turn the tables by trying to beat the man spirit, but this very rarely happens. In such a patriarchal society if a man was overpowered while he wore the fetish he would be subjected to contempt and humiliation from his male peers and would vent his anger by inflicting terrible injuries on the women.

While the father of the newborn child wears the fetish, if there's more than one Nataquat roaming the village, he's always given the best opportunities to beat each and every one of the women. It's paramount that they all endure his wrath, because as well as raising welts and bloody bruises on the terrified women, he's gaining total control over a harem of submissive females. Once he's landed the last of his blows, all of the women from his wife's bloodline must show him absolute respect, answer his every beckon, and meet his every demand.

When the last of the women has chosen her food type and the final meal has been eaten, the onslaught of beatings cease and the fearful atmosphere subsides as the whole village gathers and starts preparing a *lafaet*. The men resume fishing and normally use a five hundred meters long *tabu* rope that's covered with leaves to encircle their prey. As they drive fish inside the closing ring of vegetation, they are forbidden to look over or let the rope touch their shoulders. While the fish are trying to escape, they beat the surface of the ocean into a boiling white froth. The men shoot the fish with bows, and they added to a smorgasbord of saltwater delicacies that are gathered for the feast. At the start of the *lafaet* the women lay their food out in a straight line, and then the men add their catch to the row of local cuisine. The child's aunt cradles the newborn infant in her arms and leads the women from the mother's bloodline around the food in single file while the mother trails at the rear. Then the parents express their gratitude to each of the women for enduring the severe beatings by gifting them a small amount of money.

The following day the newborn's father is confined to the men's *nakamal* for one month, and leaves its sanctity each day to gather food as the women did. Now the tables are turned and the aggressor becomes the aggrieved. The women's injuries are still healing, and they remember only too well the harsh injuries he inflicted on them without any scruples. They are eager to vent their revenge and don't need any help from the supernatural; oestrogen charged vengeance is the driving force behind the *nemvesi* rite when they hunt him down and brutally beat him for the next month.

The uncomplaining women use flaying fists and swinging sticks on the source of their contempt, and because they are condemned to a life of self-sacrifice to appease the men, they don't hold back when they express their pent-up frustrations.

At the end of a battering and bruising month, the rite ends and apart from one exception, life returns to normal. In most primitive societies, women are usually valued as an economic asset rather than being prized for purely sexual and social relationships. This isn't the case on Mota Lava, and now that he's empowered his wife's bloodline, her husband is now free to fornicate with as many women as he chooses from his wife's lineage, and as often as his libido will allow him. Although he enjoys a newfound sexual freedom and controls a harem of subservient slaves, he must maintain absolute respect for the women of his own lineage. He can never swear in front of them or joke with them in a sexual overtone. As well as serving up sexual favours on demand, his harem must provide him with labour for any task and without question. Although the women are treated like beasts of burden and a sexual commodity, the men are extremely protective, and any unwanted advances on the women from outsiders would receive quick and severe attention.

If a male treats a woman unfairly, beyond the realms of what's deemed socially acceptable, the women of her bloodline unite and mete out brutal punishment. The men are equally quick to put a rebellious woman in her place by giving her a severe beating, but the women can carry out the *nemvesi* rite at any time to pummel unreasonable men, and the men can evoke the Nataquat whenever they please to flay the women, which ensures both sexes maintain a healthy respect for each other.

To overcome the problem of paternity from having numerous sexual partners, children are divided out equally amongst the families of their respective bloodline. The infant has an intimate bond with the family who raise it, but instead of having just one godparent, the child enjoys the affection and attention from all of the parents within its lineage.

Skeva stopped talking, and while he stared at me, he looked uncomfortable and uncertain. It was as if he was trying to look past my superficial exterior, into my inner core, so that he could probe for some sort of a response to his own unanswered questions. I broke the silence and said, "You haven't finished, have you? But you're not sure if you want to carry on." He paused again, then said, "You are my brother. I must tell you." I soaked up his words and the totality of my acceptance when he picked up from where he left off. I was welcome to take my share of women from his wife's bloodline, but first I would have to submit to suffering and personal degradation. When I listened to what I would have to subject myself to, I graciously declined because my morals weren't that flexible, because of my sexuality, and because sexually transmitted diseases are rampant throughout Vanuatu and I had no desire to add one of them to the long list of tropical diseases I'd already suffered.

If a bachelor wants to satisfy his carnal desires by dominating all of the women from his opposite bloodline, he is taken to the hidden *nakamal*, where he places himself at the mercy of every man outside of his own bloodline. First the bachelor receives a severe beating from the Nataquat while the others chant and dance around him. The men start singing and their voices rise in a feverish pitch and keep increasing with an almost riotous intensity until they reach what must be a terrifying crescendo for the bachelor. To open up a world of sexual freedom, he must first lose his virginity, and while every man waits to take their turn to sodomize him, they shuffle and sing in a circle around the proceedings. Once he has endured the humiliation and unimaginable agony of pack rape, the bachelor can copulate with the women and has the same control over them as a married man.

Now I understood why Skeva had been so reluctant to share the ritual. He no doubt wondered and worried about how I'd react to knowing that the village men have engaged in homosexuality. To lighten his edgy mood I said, "Each to their own, Skeva. I know it's *kastom*, but, mate, my arse is still going to squeak when I walk after I leave the island. I've got all my hormones and love women, but nothing in this life will turn me into a moaning whore for a room full of men." Skeva laughed and nodded, as if to acknowledge that I understood the unquestionable motives behind the ceremony.

There are numerous types of Nataquat. Each plays a different role and is empowered by a different spirit. The villagers bring the Nataquat back to life during *kastom* dances, to change the weather, to promote a healthy crop, to catch fish, and for a multitude of other reasons which encompass most aspects of daily life. Although the Nataquat inflicts crippling injuries and sometimes even death, the spirit possesses healing powers and is used to treat illness. To banish the devils that inflict sickness, the Nataquat uses a gentle approach to drive out his spiritual adversaries and blows on a patient to exorcise their demons. Skeva felt I'd learnt enough for one day, and while he led us back to the village, he laughed aloud when I mimicked squeaking noises coming from my virginal rectum while I walked.

Chapter Twenty-Six

CULT OF THE DEAD

The way I'd so effortlessly become a member of a secret society had come as a huge and welcome surprise, but the way that I was gifted *kastom* so quickly and was allowed to share the people's beliefs with outsiders had amazed me. I immediately began questioning my own morals and wrestled with my conscience over making a shrouded cult translucent to those who would never understand how two opposing faiths could be smoothly blended or how Christianity could be embraced and moulded to suit the villager's sexual desires. Skeva and Japeth were adamant that I should write about their customs and had no qualms whatsoever about Avar's pagan rituals being published. Japeth told me that he'd been fore-warned by his spiritual bodyguards that I was coming to take photos and to uncover his people's hidden beliefs, and the spirits had told him I was a good man who could be entrusted with all of *kastom*.

The island's past is fascinating and contrary to the literature that covers Mota Lava. While Skeva shared his people's history, I learnt that long before the arrival of the first Europeans, it's inhabitants were fierce canni-balistic warriors. Death and deception shaped the brutal society during an era when intertribal warfare and cannibalism was rife. Neighbouring villages were viewed with contempt and always treated with suspicion. Quat, the almighty creator of the universe demanded appeasement, which the villagers did by eating human flesh. And because of this, *nakaimas* made sure that when a village wasn't at war and dining on their victims, that death remained a familiar. The society was so violent that even the preda-tory *kastom* men lived in a constant state of paranoia. Black magic was so prevalent that *nakaimas* were forced to live a solitary existence in the island's caves. To live in the village was to openly invite death from poi-soning, a rival's arrow, a swinging club, or from potent demonic forces. Every sorcerer had his own runner, who was normally a boy from his bloodline that was about ten years old. The child dutifully brought the *kastom* man food and whatever items he needed to perform evil deeds or to counter the malevolent spells of other *nakaimas*.

A minefield of hidden *tabu* stones surrounded the entrance to a sor-cerer's cave and acted as spiritual guardians that killed any mercenaries who tried to outwit and murder the *nakaimas*. The most potent rock that is embodied with a spirit is Natmale, and the stone is still used today by *kas-tom* men. It was wrapped in a *tabu* vine and whenever an attacker walked past the stone, once they disappeared from sight, the *nakaimas* chanted a spell into Natmale. Within a day, the victim perished.

Before a chief led his men into battle, he always called upon a *kastom* man to consult the supernatural. The sorcerer performed a ritual, then pointed in the direction of the enemy. If his wrist shook, it was an ominous sign that his people would be slaughtered. But if his shoulder began to shudder, sweet victory awaited the warriors, and the flesh of their victims would fill their cooking fires.

The most potent weapon that was used during combat was a poisoned arrow tipped with human bone. Before an archer entered battle, to empower himself and his weapon with supernatural might, he rubbed a sacred leaf over the arrowhead, then sung into the leaf while it was cupped in his hands. Anyone who was unfortunate enough to be on the receiving end of a well-placed arrow was said to have died standing. Many villagers claim to have watched Japeth shoot a dog with a poisoned arrow. The canine died instantly, but remained on its feet until Japeth walked up to it and pushed it over. When the small crowd of onlookers gathered around the dog, they were horrified. They had expected the dog to die suddenly, but were shocked when they saw the flesh surrounding the arrow wound was already rotten and seething with maggots.

Throughout Vanuatu, it's common knowledge that *nakaimas* kill one of their own relatives, drinks their warm blood, and eats their twitching heart. Sorcerers still practise cannibalism on Mota Lava, and as it is throughout the rest of the archipelago, a newborn's heart is the preferred organ as it contains the most potent mana. Dining on slain enemies ceased with the termination of intertribal warfare, but *talame*, the gruesome rite *nakaimas* use to empower themselves with the spirits of the dead, has yet to be laid to rest. The *talame* rite begins five days after a burial, when those who are devoted to the devil exhume a body. Because it's believed that the spirit has yet to leave the rotting corpse, the sorcerers tie the rank cadaver's limbs together, as they fear it's still capable of moving around by itself. Both sexes partake in the stomach-churning rite, and although the decaying flesh is normally writhing with maggots, the flesh is eaten raw. This is seen as a small sacrifice to be able to perform even stronger black magic by utilising the victim's spirit and to appease and nurture the devil by cannibalising the dead. I wasn't told why, but sometimes other *nakaimas* settle for fresher meat, and the bodies are exhumed and eaten immediately after a funeral.

Before the sorcerers dine on the dead, they always rub a *tabu* leaf over their bodies. When they consume the first horrific morsel of flesh, they are empowered by the spirit of the dead and a metamorphosis takes place which causes their skin to turn white. Once they've finished dining on the corpse, they rub another sacred leaf over their body that changes their skin back to its normal colour.

Whenever the villagers suspect the *talame* is being practiced, they take immediate steps to safeguard themselves and their water, which is the island's most precious commodity. Wild cane is staked around wells, tanks, and the drums that are used to catch runoff, as it's feared when the cannibals wash off the remnants of their heinous feast, the water supplies will be polluted. The corpse inflicts vengeance on the villagers for allowing the *nakaimas* to devour its flesh and steal its spirit by sending a gush of its oily body fluids from the cannibal into the water supply they use to cleanse themselves. Wild cane is used as a spiritual blockade to ward off incensed spirits and to ensure the water remains clean.

That afternoon, Skeva made arrangements for me to visit the remains of Vagagalgoigoi, Mota Lava's most famous and feared *kastom* man. The only way I could safely visit the bones of the *nakaimas* who strove for power and the highest rank in the afterlife by cannibalising hundreds of victims,was with the spiritual protection of two of Avar's most powerful *kastom* men. After two curious teenagers and I had finished listening to the *kastom* men telling us to do exactly as they said, we followed them down a bank covered with riotous vegetation just five minutes walk from the village. As we pushed through the wall of growth, the two youths looked absolutely terrified and no doubt the past events surrounding Vagagalgoigoi's remains still lingered in their anxious minds. A young boy had accidentally stumbled upon the bones and as he pushed through the vegetation blanketing a concave rock face, he unintentionally crushed Vagagalgoigoi's skull. The sorcerer's riled spirit retaliated by causing the terrified teenager's head to keep swelling like a slowly inflating balloon until the two *kastom* men we were with reversed his ailment with sacred leaves.

Vagagalgoigoi's reign of terror occurred around two hundred and fifty years ago, when he devoured the hearts and utilized the bones from his hundreds of victims to practice evil sorcery. He was so feared that simply mentioning his name was said to have instilled an overwhelming sense of dread into even the bravest of warriors. And when a *kastom* man residing on the other side of the island killed him with black magic, Mota Lava's inhabitants greeted Vagagalgoigoi's demise with a huge sigh of relief. Although most of his victims succumbed to poison, Vagagalgoigoi was an expert archer, and when he died, his bow was said to have instantly turned to stone. His insatiable craving for human flesh drove him to live like a solitary animal, stalking and slaying the villagers with arrows tipped with the bones of his previous victims.

The two *kastom* men rubbed protective *menmap* leaves over their hands before they parted the vegetation to give us a better view of the broken stone bow and the shattered skull. An eerie, almost ominous mood deepened as we silently peered at the only material remnants of the most despicable *nakaimas* in the island's history. The pieces of bone filled the air with a sense of utter evil, and once we'd satisfied our morbid curiosity, the *kastom* men flailed our bodies with wild kava leaves, starting at our heads until they'd hit every extremity. They worked down to our feet, and gave each foot an extra strong slap to exorcise any unwelcome presence, and then they did the same to each other before we quickly left the sinister shrine.

When something jolted me from my sleep the following morning, it was just after three a.m. when I glanced at my watch. I'd brushed aside the unnerving feeling that I was acutely aware of when we'd visited Vagagalgoigoi's bones, as the site had seemed more hazardous than haunted, but now I wasn't so sure. An inexplicable chill that started from the base of my neck and slowly spread to the base of my spine turned my back into a block of ice. It was as if my blood had frozen when my limbs felt numb and became paralysed. The spine chilling sensation completely overwhelmed me, and what felt like several minutes passed until it slowly subsided and I was able to move again.

The next day, I decided my initial reaction had been heightened by the drowsy state of my awakening consciousness, because when I fully awoke, the nerve-jangling sensation had abated. I was more curious than worried when I asked the two boys if they'd felt anything untoward in the middle of the night. When they both told me independently that they had been subjected to the same chilling experience, we instantly agreed to seek divine protection from the island's most powerful *kastom* man and underwent a further flaying with wild kava leaves.

Not far from Ablow airfield, there are sacred sites which reek of evil that are rigorously avoided by all of the island's inhabitants. Anyone who has foolishly ventured into the *tabu* areas has suffered an agonising death from a horrific and disfiguring ailment that's similar to leprosy. Because the supernatural plays such a vital role in the villager's lives, no one was alarmed to hear that we may have been touched by Vagagalgoigoi's angered spirit.

Chapter Twenty-Seven

THE LINE TO ETERNITY

Several days had passed when late one afternoon, Skeva ended our conversation by quietly telling me to go and grab my camera. Where we were headed was a mystery when Japeth slowly picked his way through the jungle, with Skeva and I silently following in single file. The way Japeth kept gazing over his shoulder to ensure we weren't being followed added an air of mystique to our secretive trek. Skeva also kept a vigilant watch and occasionally looked back down the path to check that we were still alone. Only a gentle evening breeze that made the leaves rustle softly and the vocal insects that were stirred by the approaching dusk uttered a sound. The lengthening shadows which threatened to rapidly merge the landscape into a darkened gloom enhanced the clandestine atmosphere. Skeva broke the silence when he quietly mentioned only the men from the Nataquat cult ever follow the sacred path. He motioned for me to stop and pointed to four lengths of wild cane that were staked around a *nakamal*, then he waved his hand around an imaginary line that defined a *tabu* border surrounding the sacred hut. He explained that although our brotherhood allowed him to share the most sacred of rites, it was only because I was an honorary chief that I had the right to cross the forbidden line which segregates outsiders from the initiated.

Skeva and I waited outside while Japeth went inside and prepared himself. Then from the real surroundings emerged an almost surreal phantom that seemed to glide across the ground in one precise and fluid motion. As the ghoulish fetish came towards me, only the feet and arms of the Nataquat's mortal courier were visible from beneath a woven headpiece and the light brown strips of rustling leaves that stretched to just short of the ground. When the paranormal predator raised a stout stick over its head, I readied myself to fend off a possible hail of bruising blows when slowly, with deliberate, menacing movements, the macabre deity bore down on me. Skeva motioned for me to raise my camera so that, for the first time, this type of Nataquat could be captured on film. The Nataquat vanished as quickly as it appeared and only gave me enough time to reel off a couple of grab shots.

That night, while we drank kava in the *nakamal*, Skeva told me how several years ago, an American tribal art collector had convinced a member of the Nataquat cult to allow him to steal a Nataquat fetish and a few other sacred items for twenty thousand vatu. The theft of *tabu* items from the *nakamal* incurs the death penalty, and once the villagers realized the goods had been taken, the American was extremely lucky to have escaped from Mota Lava with the help of another village who didn't fully understand his plight. If they had known he'd breached tribal law, they would never have radioed for a floatplane from Port Vila. Avar's inhabitants raced after him in a relentless pursuit to avenge Quat and the ancestral spirits with the art collector's life. He escaped at the last minute and wisely left the fetish and the other items behind as an angry crowd charged down the beach. If they'd caught him, there would have been no reasoning with the lynch mob. Skeva reinforced the severity of the crime by mentioning there isn't a currency strong enough to buy any aspect of Avar's *kastom* or for the American to have bought his way out of his impending death sentence. Even if a tourist errantly crosses the *tabu* line onto the sanctified ground surrounding the *nakamal*, they meet the same horrific fate—and for females, death doesn't come peacefully.

Because it's historical and has never before documented before, after a lot of soul searching, I decided to include the following story, which was shared in the utmost confidence. To be given the right to publish this barbaric act, so long as the name of the island and those who were involved in the savage rite remains anonymous, is extraordinary.

A twenty-five-year old wife and mother who was tired of living in habitual fear from existing in a violent and pitiless marriage couldn't take the torment anymore and spiralled into a deep depression. She was driven to despair and to her wit's end, and because she couldn't see any light at the end of her dark and ominous tunnel, she decided suicide was the only logical way to escape the incessant beatings from her cruel and equally disturbed husband. She purposefully waited for low tide and waded into an ocean teeming with sharks and life threatening currents and left her own beautiful islet. She crossed over to an equally spectacular but much larger island.

How the despondent woman knew where to find the path and how she knew that at the time the secret society was performing *kastom* in the carefully hidden *nakamal* is a mystery. All that matters is she did and that she knew once she set foot past the wild cane staked around the *nakamal*, there could be no turning back, ever. There wasn't even a remote chance of her outrunning or trying to outwit her aggressors once they were aware of her presence. She knew their relentless pursuit wouldn't end until she was captured and had faced her shocking fate.

In a gruesome twist, when she defiantly entered the *nakamal*, the way she sought solace from a life that had been filled with domestic violence incurred more brutality from her family. Although it had been decades since any of the older men had participated in the rite that was about to take place, the stringent schooling the young boys had received in the *nakamal* meant they were well prepared for what *kastom* demanded must happen. The poor woman was numbed by melancholy and desperation and willingly submitted to her fate when the men stripped her naked and prepared themselves for the necessary ritual.

They danced to a feverish beat and worked themselves into a frenzy as they moved in a circle around the tormented female while each of them took their turn to rape her. No one was exempt, even her father and brother preformed the act. If they failed to indulge in incest they knew all of the men would sodomize them. Although they could submit to pack rape, then face the men in a fight to the death to save the woman, they knew such actions were futile and they would die as well.

When the singing and dancing and the fornicating neared an ear-splitting crescendo, the paramount chief was the last to have intercourse with the woman. He held an ancient stone axe in his hand that had been empowered with the blood of other victims who had met the same terrifying fate, and after he finished raping her, he ended her suffering with a swift swing of the axe and repeatedly chopped the woman's skull until her brain spilled on to the ground.

Blood had flowed and avenged the angered spirits with the woman's spirit and her mana. Most of the men kept dancing and singing for several hours to appease Quat, while the others prepared a *lafaet* by killing a sacrificial pig and making *lap lap*. The paramount chief adorned himself with *tabu* leaves, then danced alone to reinforce the solidarity between mortals and the immortal and to stimulate the gods until they acknowledged that recompense had been provided after such a heinous breach of *kastom*. Although the woman's remains had been mutilated, humiliated, and spiritually emaciated, they were treated with respect and laid to rest in a grave.

The informant wasn't ashamed of what he'd done because it was *kastom*, but he was obviously trying to ease the psychological burden of feeling guilty by sharing the gruesome rite. His eyes welled with tears as he relived the ritual, which took place ten years before my travels around Vanuatu. Although it's a sad and horrific tale, to be able to share it is an exceptional privilege, for what happens in the *nakamal* must normally stay in the *nakamal*. If it was known that anyone had spoken about what had occurred within the hallowed hut, the informant would be committing suicide and die in the same horrific manner. For the villagers outside of the sect, how the woman died is open to conjecture. Some say she was taken by a shark, while others believe the sea claimed her life. Only the select few know her spirit belongs to the devil and has been damned to living in a world of eternal darkness.

On the last night that I stayed in the village, Skeva told me that when Quat created and placed the first man and woman in the Banks group, he gave them the gift of immortality. As they aged, they travelled to a sacred river and immersed themselves in the gentle current which peeled their old skins off and left them with a fresh and youthful appearance. The couple had a young daughter who cried the first time she saw her rejuvenated mother as she thought the younger looking woman was a total stranger. Her mother was filled with remorse at having upset her child and returned to the river, where she donned her old skin and became aged and withered again. This made her daughter happy, but by discarding her youthful outer shell into the *tabu* river she had also washed away the gift of eternal life.

Now that the time the humans spent on the physical world was measurable, Quat expanded his creativity and provided them with a window to the supernatural world that they could use when they passed away. When a villager dies, their spirit rises above the clouds, soars through the heavens to Gaua Island, and gently lands at the entrance of a gargantuan *kastom* cave. Worisris is the spirit devil and guardian of the catacomb, and his sole purpose is to unleash the deceased's spirit, which has been anchored to its earthly origins, so that it can pass through the cave to exist in a more exotic realm. If the relatives of the deceased want to visit their loved ones who reside in the other dimension, they can do so by walking around the shore of Lake Letas on Gaua. The lake is eight hundred metres above sea level, and is nestled in the lofty heart of the island beside an active volcano called Mount Garett. If Worisris accepts their offer of a live pig and a white fowl, they are mysteriously transported to the ethereal cave to visit their ancestral spirits. No one knows of the caves exact whereabouts, as it only exists in the supernatural realm.

Word kept filtering back to Avar each day that Ablow airstrip was still closed, and when the grass would be cut so the plane could land was anyone's guess. It was hard to leave such a friendly and relaxed atmosphere, but when the offer to catch a ride to Vanua Lava Island with the health department's dinghy came along, I decided to go. When I was made an honorary chief and a Welegtabit, I was also given a ready-made family. I had a *kastom* son living on Gaua Island that didn't know I existed, who I wanted to pay a visit. While I sat in the empty dinghy to secure a seat, my thoughts drifted into violent territory as I reflected on how such a gentle and kind natured people could be so ruthlessly brutal when it came to upholding their beliefs.

When a small amount of freight and ten adults squeezed into the five-metre boat, I figured the driver had a full fare. But when an unlucky thirteen of us wedged together, I questioned the skipper's common sense. I then asked myself what the hell I was doing when, with a bit of reshuffling, including the boat's operator, fifteen adults (one of whom was nine months pregnant) loaded the dinghy to the gunnels. There were just a few inches of freeboard left when we pushed off and waved our goodbyes. Once we were out in the open water, an angry wind-whipped sea constantly soaked our grossly overloaded craft. I joked to the guy sitting next to me that travelling in the health department's boat hardly seemed healthy and that the medical staff was short of organ donors and was trying to drum up a few body parts by drowning us all.

Midway through the sailing, if a wave swamped us this far out in the ocean, there wasn't much chance of surviving without a lifejacket. As we knifed through a turbulent but forgiving ocean, according to the cheerful captain, our human cargo hardly rated compared to the previous trips he'd made. While he constantly bailed the water that lapped around our feet, he proudly boasted that he'd once ferried twenty adult passengers across to Vanua Lava, and in a much more perilous sea. The middle-aged soccer coach that was jammed alongside me was obviously a landlubber. He shook his nerves off by constantly swearing throughout the one and a half hour journey and kept shaking his head in disbelief when water lapped over the sides or each time a barrage of small waves drenched us to the skin.

I was completely water logged and wondered if I must have already been suffering from water on the brain to have even considered sailing in such reckless and overcrowded conditions. When I waded ashore, I relished every coarse grain of Vanua Lava's auburn-coloured volcanic sand that rubbed between my toes.

Chapter Twenty-Eight

LIVE BAIT

While I strode up to Sola airport to check out when the next flight was to Gaua, the island's alluring jungle beckoned me to stay and explore the unruly looking utopia. A crowd of anxious onlookers, whose faces were creased by deep concern, were gathered around an elderly man who was stretched out on the floor of the ticketing office. The old man had been severely injured yet he remained remarkably calm and complacent. His accident had started with a freakish spate of bad luck when he was climbing a tree to harvest fruit, and his machete slipped from his hand and landed handle first in the soft mud with its well-honed blade pointing skyward. Then in a cruel quirk of fate, seconds later he lost his normally tenacious grip on the tree and plummeted to the ground. The point of the knife impaled the base of his bicep and sliced through the muscle until the tip of the blade exited through the top of his shoulder. He was more angry at having fallen than he was worried about his grotesque injury and gripped the handle, then with one swift pull, he wrenched the machete free. He was alone, and half an hour's walk from help, so he quickly stemmed the flow of gushing blood by crushing a vine and wringing its sap into the gaping wounds before he walked back to his village, where his shocked relatives raced him to the airport and radioed for an emergency flight to take him to the hospital at Luganville.

When I stepped outside, the scent of the local vegetation hanging in the salty air and the ramparts of crowded jungle wove an inviting tapestry that kept tugging at my instincts to stay and delve. I decided Gaua could wait while I spent a few days soaking up Vanua Lava's raw but tranquil beauty. I started walking across the island along a gently undulating road that eventually petered out into a well-trodden path. By late in the afternoon I'd reached Vetiboso village, where I met Chief Godfrey Manara, who cheerfully led me down the steep track which wound down to Nerr Bay on the western side of the island. He looked as if he was about to burst with excitement and tried his best to suppress his joy when, after waiting three years, I was about to be the first paying customer to stay in one of the two leaf hut bungalows he'd purposely built to promote tourism on the remote west coast. A visiting German photojournalist had implanted the idea when he promised to send a flood of tourists if Godfrey provided the accommodation. While the years slipped past, only a handful of travellers visited the island, and not one of them had bothered to check out Nerr bay.

Godfrey's simplistic bungalows are nestled on the fringe of a black sand beach in a tranquil setting. Apart from the two nearby waterfalls and a bit of fishing and pig hunting, these accommodations would only appeal to people who enjoy serenity and total seclusion. I loved them. And once Godfrey learnt that I was a photojournalist who sometimes wrote travel articles, he rolled out the red carpet and served succulent roast wild pork and freshly caught crayfish for dinner. Then he promised fish for breakfast, and some *kastom* dancing tomorrow afternoon.

The next morning I sat on the beach in the predawn stillness and watched faint envoys of light hopping from cloud to cloud, listening to a cacophony of beautiful bird song as the sun rose over the island. When I went back to the bungalows, Godfrey was equally vibrant and keen to revitalize his failed business venture. After a hearty breakfast, we traipsed up the path to visit Quatwan, a *kastom* rock where boisterous children with "strong heads" are cured of their delinquent behaviour. A parent pushes the child's head into a depression in the stone four times, then to completely cleanse any unsociable traits, the child is made to drink a handful of rainwater which gets trapped in a cavity in the rock.

We walked a short way up the track to where *tabu* stones which crudely resemble a fossilized coconut, yam, breadfruit, banana, and taro are used by *kastom* men, who combine them with a sacred leaf to improve crops if a poor yield looks imminent. Then we looked at two other rocks called Varam, which are rubbed four times by women who want to try and conceive twins. Several minutes' walk along the path, we came upon hand carved stone effigies of Quat, the supreme god. These used in the past to seek revenge during disputes by *nakaimas* who had the ability to offer a prayer to the fetishes and call upon Quat, who became embodied in a shark that devoured an unsuspecting adversary while they fished or swam in the sea.

Late in the afternoon, when the stifling heat that radiated off the black sand had started to languish, Godfrey led me to the *nasara*. Portly middle-aged women with bare flaccid breasts, wearing cloth wraparound skirts, performed the metre dance, a ritual where mourning women sing and dance around the body of a deceased relative. Because there were only five of us watching, to make up for the small audience, I clapped loudly and appreciatively when the brief dance finished. While we patiently waited for four men to prepare for the snake dance, Godfrey explained how it originated, and that it's a fertility rite which is used to bolster the potency of man.

Not long after Quat created the first man and woman on Vanua Lava, they produced a daughter who grew into a voluptuous girl. She fossicked near the ocean every day while she gathered seafood or playfully swam in the tepid water. A boy who lived in the ocean became hopelessly infatuated the instant he saw the stunning maiden, and each time she visited the ocean, the smitten boy yearned to tell the young beauty of his unrelenting love for her. He couldn't suppress his emotions any longer and decided to follow the girl back to her village, but when she looked over her shoulder as she waded from the ocean, the dazzling maiden was horrified to see a serpent marked with black and white bands following her. The boy was a spirit who was embodied in a sea snake. As she fled back to her village, she called for help from her father who was the chief and *kastom* man. He grabbed his *nul nul* and rushed to her aid, but stopped dead in his tracks. He was surprised to see the snake dancing alone on the *nasara*. Then miraculously, the snake turned into a handsome black boy who had white horizontal bands decorating his body. The gorgeous girl was mesmerised by his intoxicating dance and fell in love with the handsome man-snake. When the man-snake saw she had fallen for him, he said to the chief, "I will give you the body of a snake." To which the chief replied, "I will give you the body of a man so you can consummate your love for my daughter." Both men conjoined then divided to create a true man-snake with human qualities, so that the chief's daughter could marry the hybrid and have children.

When the four dancers appeared, bristling grass skirts covered their loins. A green, luminous grassy shrub that had been tightly bound at its roots to form a point was crudely fashioned into a macabre mask that completely concealed their faces and chests. Black and white banded effigies of snakes which had been carved from wood were coiled amongst the shroud of matted headgear, and three of the dancers held black and white–coloured serpentine sticks in each hand. All of the dancers were smeared from head to toe with striking white bands that symbolized the sea snake. One of them held a length of cane grass in each hand that had three bright orange spheres skewered and spaced equidistantly along them, which added a splash of distinctive colour.

As they wove their way through the nearby copra plantation to the *nasara*, the four men-snakes moved as one low crouching animal and eventually returned to the sea where they originated. I'm sure I never saw the true *kastom* snake dance. The brief performance seemed lacklustre and contrived and lacked conviction compared to the fervent, emotionally charged rituals I'd been involved in. I was grateful to have been shown it, and it was still enjoyable, as was my short and relaxing stay at Nerr Bay.

After sitting around for a few days, I was craving adventure, so when I got back to Sola I decided to track down a guide who'd been recommended to me. When I eventually found Kaleb, he was in his mid-twenties and had a staunch attitude that suggested he enjoyed a good argument and loved to fight. He was still friendly and easy to get along with, and to me, it was befitting that Kaleb was the island's most respected guide to a prehistoric creature with an equally formidable and intimidating manner, the crocodile.

Back in the 1860s, when bishop Patterson errantly released two crocodiles near the tannin-coloured Selva River, the evangelist proclaimed in the name of the Lord that the carnivorous predators would never attack humans. His request was a thoughtful gesture but unfortunately it wasn't answered, as since then there have been two nonfatal attacks on villagers. Animals as large as dogs, wild pigs, and bullocks have also fallen prey, which suggests the creatures may be the more aggressive saltwater species.

Kaleb had been bedridden for the last two weeks by ciguatera, which is contracted by eating poisoned fish. The sickness can be fatal, and although he was still recovering, he agreed to go croc spotting and set a quick pace as we followed the coastline. Once he learnt I was an adventurer who lived with remote and often inaccessible primitive tribes, he became more boisterous and started acting as if he had something to prove. We left the sweltering tan-coloured beach and squelched into a steamy, insect ridden, foreboding looking swamp that was filled with the constant drone of parched mosquitoes that were eagerly queuing up to drive their proboscises into the two lumps of profusely sweating human blood and protein. A slough of pungent smelling mud sucked at our feet as we twisted our way through a tangle of arching mangrove roots, which rose upwards to form a stilted and dishevelled looking forest. Distorted shadows that were cast from the gnarled mass of mangroves created a gloomy Jurassic atmosphere and provided the perfect backdrop to spotting living dinosaurs.

Kaleb slowed to a crawl, then cautiously crept to the edge of the morbid looking Selva River to try and sneak up on basking crocodiles. There were none around, and after he checked the muddy banks for slides or other telltale marks, it looked as though the reptiles were either submerged in the murky water or had moved elsewhere. When Kaleb scampered across a spindly log that was strewn across the river to get to the other bank and shimmied up a tree, I figured it was to get a better view of the river. After he fruitlessly scanned the area, he waved me towards the bank, then shook his head in disapproval and motioned for me to come closer when I stopped within what I felt was a safe distance from the tea-coloured water. He looked annoyed and kept silently gesturing me to move forward. I silently gestured that I was staying right where I was, whether there was fresh sign that the reptiles were around or no fresh sign. It didn't take the combined efforts of a rocket scientist and an eminent brain surgeon to figure out what Kaleb's game plan was when he cupped his hands and started barking wildly like a dog to attract the resident crocs. While he was safely perched up a tree, what used to be my trusted guide was ringing the dinner bell and using me as live bait. If I stood anywhere near the water's edge, I was teetering on the brink of either full-on excitement or potential disaster if a crocodile with a healthy appetite answered the call.

I smiled up at Kaleb, who was still baying like a sex-starved bloodhound that'd caught wind of a bitch in heat, and barked back with a liberal dose of harmless profanity that nothing in this life would make me stand near the riverbank. From the way he kept howling and barking, I wondered if the tainted fish had poisoned his brain and quickly deducted that he wasn't the sharpest tool in the shed. I burst out laughing and said, "All your dogs aren't barking; you're camped on the wrong side of the hill, mate." When he didn't answer, I added that I only wanted to look at a croc, not be dragged down one's throat, but my words were drowned out by his yapping.

He looked disappointed that nothing had surfaced and told me to cross over and follow him to the river mouth. When he waded into the water until it lapped his thighs, I waited on dry land and half expected him to wave his arms or start splashing while he squealed like a stuck pig or bellowed like a wounded bullock to attract the crocs. How he knew the coast was clear is beyond me, but he nonchalantly and noisily ploughed through the water as if there was a prize for getting to the other side first. While he grinned from ear to ear at having looked danger in the eye and won and told me to cross, I shook my head from side to side. It was more from what I'd just witnessed rather than as a reply to his goading "Come on. It's safe. Don't be a woman" when I decided to follow in his lunatic footsteps. I'd risked crossing croc-infested rivers numerous times. The reptiles possess a tiny brain about the size of a walnut and act instinctively, so moving quietly is paramount. After I had a good look around, with only twenty-five metres to cross, I took the plunge. When I was halfway across, it was Kaleb who seemingly had a brain the size of a peanut when he mimicked the calls of every tasty barnyard animal that would've had every croc within earshot smacking its lips. Then he tried to unsettle me by saying, "Look out. There they come. Look out Mr Adventurer! They look hungry." I remained calm, wondereding how stupid this would look on my epitaph if I did get eaten, and silently waded across to Kaleb. We looked at each other and both burst out laughing as I jokingly swore at him and his warped sense of humour.

As we followed the beach back to Sola so that I could catch a flight to Gaua, I asked Kaleb how he knew there weren't any crocs at the river mouth. He gave me a sideways glance as if to say I was the mad one, then said he didn't know if the reptiles were around or not. Although there was a remote chance they were back in the area, what he didn't know was that I knew the crocs hadn't been sighted for months since the river had flooded during a cyclone.

Chapter Twenty-Nine

KINDRED SPIRITS

Most westerners think of remote primitive tribes with a daunting reputation as being exotic, bizarre, barbaric, and have a tendency to be afraid of them. But imagine the traumatic impression we must have upon the previously quarantined minds of primitive peoples when a white man makes first contact with them. Even on some of Vanuatu's remote outer islands that are rarely visited by tourists but have what appear to be civilized inhabitants, Europeans are often treated with apprehension or a shy indifference. When I exited the plane and asked for directions from the affable and helpful locals, I wasn't surprised to hear that I was the only Caucasian on Gaua. They may have been dressed in clothes, but they still had a primitive mindset, and I was about to walk up to one of them and tell them I was his father. When I had less than a five-minute walk until I forged a new relationship with my unsuspecting *kastom* son, my thoughts drifted into unfamiliar territory, to having a family of my own. I wondered how I'd react if a total stranger who was a primitive black man knocked on my door, and then told me I was his newfound son.

I branched off the main and only coastal road and walked to the end of a forty-metre track, where tendrils of rising smoke leached through the thatch roof of a small square cookhouse. Directly beyond the mist of slowly evaporating smoke, a lone and humble looking leaf hut perched on top of sturdy poles was surrounded by gently rustling coconut palms and luscious fruit trees. A burble of cheerful chatter and hearty laughter suddenly stopped when someone noticed my presence. My *kastom* son, Jansen, was wearing black shorts and an apprehensive look on his mischievous features when he emerged from the cookhouse. He was tall and lithe, with tightly cropped hair, and carried his wiry twenty-nine-year-old body in an assertive but friendly manner. I introduced myself, and after we shook hands, I quickly handed him a letter that Skeva had addressed to him. Although I was unaware of its content, I let it do the rest of the talking. His head slowly followed each line, then when the realization of what I represented hit home, whenever he looked up and stared at me, his brow was creased by confusion. While he was reading, he kept glancing up at me as he tried to grasp the enormity of what the letter implied. He nodded to himself, then carefully folded the letter, and for a brief moment recomposed his stunned thoughts. Then he said in a respectful and subservient tone, "Welcome, father. Come. Please share a meal with us." There wasn't the slightest hint of scepticism, shock, indifference, or any offence taken once Jansen had quickly come to terms with the fact that I was his *kastom* father.

Although outside influences had stripped Mota Lava's inhabitants of their traditional dress and their superficial identity, *kastom* had remained the same, and whether Jansen liked it or not, my honorary chiefdom made us instant kindred spirits. *Kastom* had insisted he accept me with sincerity and affection. Because I was his father, he could never use foul language in my presence, never joke with me or question my decisions, and had to answer my every question without question. Above all else, he and his family had to show me absolute respect. They had to do all of this to a total stranger, a white stranger from a strange and distant land.

As I entered the cookhouse, my daughter-in-law, Emily, had a quick smile and a round Polynesian face framed by long straight black hair. She seemed dazed, and her daughters, twelve- year-old Franita and six-year-old Asnet, gaped in stunned silence when Jansen introduced me as his *kastom* father. Their ten-year-old son Lenny smiled sheepishly, while four-year-old Dan put his fingers in his mouth and didn't quite know what to make of me. Everyone hid their shocked response as best they could and called me either father or *bubu* before we all sat down to a meal of fire-roasted fish and *lap lap*.

While we sat and talked, Jansen told me why he'd left Mota Lava, what his new life was like on Gaua, and gave me a brief history lesson. At 330 square kilometres in size, the island is the second largest in the Banks group. Before the first Europeans made contact, Gaua was thought to have been inhabited by nearly twenty thousand natives. But introduced diseases created a wave of epidemics that kept reducing the once healthy population until in the early 1990s, only one thousand Gauans remained on the island. When Mota Lava's natural resources were stretched to the limit, Jansen joined an exodus of villagers who relocated on Gaua. Because there is an abundance of land for sale—a reasonable twenty thousand vatu plus a sacrificial pig to purchase a ten thousand square metre plot—people from the surrounding islands flocked to the fertile island. Throughout Vanuatu, many people believe that active volcanos are closely linked to black magic. Mount Garet's boiling cauldron of molten lava in the centre of the island is thought to lend power to the rampant sorcery which is practiced on Gaua.

The locals were quick to capitalize on selling off their undeveloped land, and in just a few years, the influx of immigrants had equalled the number of native Gauans. This created a tense and hostile atmosphere. Then a spate of inexplicable deaths became the catalyst that sent the mounting friction between the native residents and the new settlers to a dangerous high. When five immigrants died in the space of a month, the new settlers blamed the deaths on black magic, and their initial suspicions turned to anger and thoughts of retribution. The *nakaimas* from Mota Lava and Gaua are equally potent when it comes to spiritual warfare, so the new settlers called in a revered *kastom* man from Maewo Island, who declared the deaths weren't from natural causes. When the sorcerers from both sides cast a flurry of evil spells upon their adversaries, tempers became so flared that a civil war almost erupted. Both sides armed themselves to the teeth with bows, rifles, and traditional weapons, and during a tense meeting, the new settlers made it publicly known in no uncertain terms that if another inexplicable death occurred, bloodshed was inevitable.

While Jansen's wife and children went to work in the garden, we stayed behind and got properly acquainted by cramming nearly seventy years of combined living into several hours of easy conversation. As we quickly developed a firm friendship, I had every reason to approve of my ready-made son. His impish eyes sparkled and brimmed with life. He was full of self-restraint, but his relaxed mannerisms and sharp mind made it obvious that his quick sense of humour was bursting to unleash itself. There was something special about his combination of confidence, kindness, and wit that made him a natural leader and easy to confide in. Since his early childhood, for three months of every year, he'd ventured back to Mota Lava and lived in seclusion in the hidden *nakamal*, where he was taught every aspect of *kastom*. When he was an infant, Jansen had been the chosen one, as even during the initial stages of his life he'd portrayed the unique qualities of character that made him suitable for high chiefdom. Japeth was grooming him to be the next paramount chief and to become the most respected *kastom* man in the Banks group, which demands suffering and sacrifice. On the rare occasions that Jansen is allowed to leave the confines of the *nakamal* while he's undergoing his intensive cultural schooling, he ties a sacred leaf to his shoulder or drapes a branch sprouting the same *tabu* leaves down his back to warn the majority of villagers they must keep a healthy distance because approaching him is *tabu*. Of all the women, only the wife of a chief can approach him, but she must never touch him. The pagan apprenticeship requires abstinence from certain foods, and foodstuffs that are deemed as acceptable cuisine are roasted over a "*tabu* fire."

I knew it was a futile offer when I told him to feel free to swear and joke around me. For someone with his social standing, there could be no compromise when it came to *kastom*. He smiled and said, "You have followed the *kastom* road and already know the answer. You must be a special man, father. Japeth has never made *kastom* for any other white man. I want you to know that what's mine is yours." It seemed Rick Welegtabit would always be called father and would always be treated with the utmost respect by his son.

Jansen politely asked that I come outside so he could provide me with the spiritual protection I needed while I lived on Gaua. He handed me four leaves from a *nasara* tree, then I attentively followed his instructions to the letter and split them lengthways with the underside of the leaf facing the ground. I folded the left portion on top of the right, stacked them on top of each other, and rolled them into a tight ball. Then I circled the wad around my head four times, chewed the cud of sacred vegetation, and made sure that I swirled the tangy juices around my teeth. Of all the *nakaimas* throughout Vanuatu, the Banks islanders are most wary of those from Ambrym and Maewo. The leaves gave me an immunity that ensured

I would survive any spells that were directed at me by malevolent black magicians, and as an added bonus, I would also retain a full mouth of teeth until the day I died. But more importantly, two ancestral bodyguards had entered my soul, which prevented the Gauans from killing me with a welcome drink of kava that was laced with deadly toxins. With my supernatural subconscious on constant full alert, if any toxic brew passing my lips it would be involuntarily regurgitated. To try and poison my meals would be futile because the moment my hands came into contact with a tainted morsel, they would start shaking violently to forewarn me the food was contaminated.

The following day we walked to the nearby beach to meet Daniel, Jansen's genetic father, and to mingle with the locals. Everyone was attracted to Jansen's arresting manner and his boisterous enthusiasm for life. While the new settlers and the Gauans laughed and joked with my quick-witted son, there wasn't the slightest hint of any underlying social tension, as on the surface the Gauans were an extremely kind and affable people. By the end of the day, our unusual friendship was well and truly sealed, but I still found it hard not to be able to joke with my son.

There's an intimacy surrounding the dancing flames of a night time fire that sometimes drops people's guards and makes them more down to earth, more relaxed, and sometimes more talkative than they'd be in other situations. Late in the evening, when just the two of us were stoking the fire to cook a meal of fish, I felt the timing was right to probe for a firsthand account from a villager who'd witnessed or participated in a cannibal feast. While I was staying at Mota Lava, I knew if I asked, it could be dangerous to the informant and to myself and explained to Jansen that all previous literature has recorded that historically, two-legged meat was never a part of the Banks islanders' cuisine. I asked if he could verify that cannibalism ever occurred on Mota Lava, and after a brief but thoughtful silence, he took me back to his childhood.

In 1979, he was a carefree nine-year-old living on Mota Lava. The sudden death of an old man earlier in the day had saddened him, but as he'd already learnt a great deal about death in the hidden *nakamal*, he found solace in the thought that the deceased's departing spirit was about to join his ancestors in the supernatural world. That night, with his fear of ghosts dulled by the exuberance of his cocky youth, Jansen walked through the gloomy village alone. As he walked around the corner of a hut, he was horrified when he saw the old man's white bones glistening in the pale moonlight and scattered around the outside of the hut. An old crone that was sitting in the doorway wore a gruesome face-paint of blood, and there was mucous around her mouth as she noisily chewed on a mouthful of raw human flesh. The other *bubu* who were inside were too preoccupied with their grisly meal to care about the intrusion. All that mattered was the dead man's spirit was theirs and had empowered and enhanced their prowess as sorcerers. When Jansen questioned the old woman the following day, she had no qualms about telling him how they'd dined on their relative.

When I asked, "What about nowadays? Do *nakaimas* still eat the hearts of children?" his eyes squinted, not from the smoke of the fire but from contemplation. He seemed to be wrestling with his conscience, and paused for a while before he said, "In the past, this *kastom* was really strong. It is still used, but it follows strict—"

I cut him short mid-sentence, as taking advantage of my parental status was unfair, and enough had already been said to verify what I'd never doubted. To place us on even ground and maintain our mutual respect, I shared equally shocking rites I knew of from other islands to reciprocate the *kastom* knowledge he'd gifted me.

Chapter Thirty

CHILDREN OF THE SNAKE

Once you turn forty in Vanuatu, you're an "old fella" who's out to pasture and basically on the countdown to living out the last few good years of your life. Because I was single and nearing forty, a heartfelt "Oh, sorry" was a common response from inquisitive Ni-Vanuatu when I told them I didn't have a wife and children waiting for me at home while I satisfied my wanderlust and craving for adventure. If a villager with a sense of humour asked why I wasn't married, I often joked that back in New Zealand, I dressed my dog up, didn't mind fur balls, and planned to take my border collie to the lingerie factory when I returned home to really add spice to our already hot sex life. Most of the villagers shared my sense of humour and said if I wasn't fussy, they could offer me a village dog while I was away from my wife, but there were a few who thought I was serious and were disgusted. On Gaua, some of the people found my basic sense of humour cut a bit to close to the bone. Zoophilia, which is more commonly called bestiality, is practiced worldwide by many cultures, especially in remote rural areas. The sexual relationship between man and animals play an important role in fertility rites that a few primitive cultures deem as essential for their continued wellbeing. For several Gauans, the union of man with other species is simply for pleasure.

Sex isn't a *tabu* subject on Gaua because in the past, children weren't simply instructed on how to fornicate by their parents, they were shown. A mother copulated with her son once he reached puberty, and a daughter lost her virginity to her own father when he taught her how to pleasure a future husband. The relationships were seen to be purely educational and were never for pleasure or considered to be incestuous.

On an island this size, gossip races along the jungle grapevine at a blistering speed. Since Jansen has lived on Gaua, some of the natives' sexual liaisons with animals and objects have been hilarious, while others have been fatal. After a young boy had an encounter with a turtle, his penis became infected and fell off, and as the illness quickly spread, it claimed his life. Jansen kept a straight face to uphold the humourless respect he must show me, while his animated descriptions painted a vivid picture of how other youths were caught copulating with chickens, ducks, goats, and even a bullock. He'd only gotten as far as the duck, and I was rolling around on the ground in hysterics, tears streaming down my cheeks.

He still wore a serious look as we ambled down to the beach to visit some interesting settlers from Mere Island, and he told me about Banana

Tree, the most famous of the island's kinky inhabitants. Being forced to abstain from sex had driven the forty-year-old man to his wit's end. No matter what approach he used, his frigid wife steadfastly refused him all conjugal rights. While he was alone in his secluded garden, he came up with a novel way to release months of brewing sexual frustration, and used a machete to ream a hole at the appropriate height into the porous trunk of a banana tree. He cut a ripe pawpaw, then filled the void in the banana tree with the fruit's pulpy flesh to create the primal equivalent of a blow up doll. For several minutes, he shook the tree's leaves while he was locked in a passionate embrace with a beloved part of his crop. Just as the tree was literally about to bear the fruit of his loins, he was interrupted by a stunned group of friends who'd come to visit him. Within hours, he was the joke of the island, and even now young boys taunt him by calling out "Banana Tree," from a safe distance because he either cowers in shame or chases the bombastic youths away with a hail of swiftly thrown rocks. Jansen's lively narrative had me in stitches, and although I wasn't supposed to joke, I couldn't help myself and said that in New Zealand we use less offensive means of pollination and leave it to the birds and insects or other natural methods. By the end of the story, I'd laughed so hard my stomach hurt, and even Jansen couldn't keep up his straight-laced facade and burst into raucous laughter.

My string of ongoing jokes screeched to an abrupt halt when Jansen introduced me to the Wover family, who were living in a temporary and basic lean-to close to the beach. There was nothing even remotely funny about Joseph and Kathleen Wover's two sadly deformed children who had supposedly been created by the union of man and animal. The social dislocation they'd endured when they were treated as hybrid monsters was saddening. They originally came from Mere Island, which is a tiny islet not far from Mere Lava Island, and when Joseph told me about his children's condition, their story began with the very origins of time itself.

Humanity had yet to be created when the *kastom* god, Temetagangan, ruled the heavens. When he decided to place new life on earth, he chose Mere Island, and created five women, Lehona, Rosar, Rondu, Robere, and Rowere. They lived a happy and carefree existence. For years they were blissfully ignorant that man even existed, until Sagol sailed all the way from Makira in the Solomon Islands and beached his canoe on their shore. When Sagol married all of the women, Temetagangan looked down and could see that Sagol needed to be able to protect his wives and his inevitable offspring, so he provided him with two *kastom* rocks. One was on dry land, and the other was in the ocean. Sagol's totem was the shark, so Temetagangan gave him Lesura, the tabu shark stone. Like his distant clan in the Solomon's, Sagol used the stone to call *bager gengen*, the devil shark, who devoured any enemies that paddled their canoes or swam in the sea. Lesura was embodied with another demon, which Sagol used to kill his enemies when they were on dry land by causing them to fall from the top of a palm when they climbed for coconuts or perish from other unfortunate accidents that originated from a more sinister source. Sagol was the envy of every man that looked across from nearby Mere Lava

Island. He was the lord of his own island and served a harem of beautiful women, but the jealousy quickly faded when his wives fell pregnant and spawned the Wover clan, because the bloodline had been cursed for eternity.

The other *kastom* rock is called Votmot. This hallowed rock, which is about one hundred metre square with a two metre square pool in its centre, can be reached by wading through the shallows. Votmot is the most productive fishing spot around the island, but for the Wover women, it's also the most precarious. In the mystical depths of the pool that plunges through the core of the rock lurks a fiendish black and white banded *kastom* snake called Nemwe.

One of the Wover men from each successive generation inherited the powers to summon the devils from the two *kastom* stones. When Joseph lived on Mere, at Lesar village, he was the only one who could unleash the demonic forces from the rocks on command. Sometimes the supernatural snake appears of its own accord if it's provoked by the ignorance of mortals. If a male clambers onto its lair and errantly breaks off a piece of the rock, they suffer from an inexplicable illness or even a painful and lingering death. Before Christianity was introduced to the island, the Wover's slaughtered anyone who mistakenly disfigured the rock with a hail of poisoned arrows.

Whenever the Wover women fish from the rock, they must always perform a simplistic ritual, whereas other females enjoy the luxury of being immune to the snake's disfiguring curse. Kathleen often enjoyed fishing from Votmot, but before she did, she ran around the rock four times, then plunged into the pool four times to nullify the curse. One day, the teeming fish that swirled around the base of the rock distracted her as she ran around the perimeter of Votmot for the fourth time. She had a brood of hungry children waiting back at the village and became so preoccupied with providing the evening meal, she forgot to immerse herself into the pool and quickly cast her line into the water. The serpent devil immediately took advantage of the costly oversight and had the option of giving or taking life. Kathleen was lucky. The snake chose to create rather than to destroy. Otherwise Nemwe would've channelled his energy into drowning Kathleen with a gigantic tidal wave.

When Temetagangan first gifted Sagol the sacred rocks, he'd warned him that Nemwe could impregnate the Wover women to create his reptilian progeny if they ever disrespected the necessary *tabus*. Kathleen was ecstatic when she filled her fishing basket to the brim, but reeled back in horror when the *kastom* snake surfaced in the pool and looked her in the eyes. She was terrified that the unborn child she was carrying had been cursed and nervously waited for several unsettling months to pass before she gave birth. When Balam, the Wover's firstborn son, entered the world, Kathleen's deep concern had been justified. Five years later, when her daughter Annette was born, she was also disfigured by the reptilian devil. When her twin sister died at birth, the superstitious villagers were mortified and convinced that Nemwe had taken the infant's life to reclaim what they believed was the child of the *kastom* snake.

Balam and Annette were born with skin that was almost jet-black. Neither of them can speak as they're both mentally challenged. And even if they could talk, their thoughts remain trapped within in the confines of their own mute worlds because millennia of superstition had alienated them from any social contact with the anxious villagers. When both of the children reached puberty, Mere's inhabitants were terrified when the children's skin gradually lightened, then became mottled with white patches which gave them the same colouration as the snake. When both of the children developed the habit of flicking their tongues around their lips not long after they were born, the impressionable villagers thought Balam and Annette were tasting the air in the same manner as their supernatural sire. Then the superstitious natives' already emotive response to the two children exploded into one of sheer terror when the children's teeth fell out and left two fanglike incisors intact. Balam's eventually succumbed to decay, but Annette kept her two remaining teeth until she lost them when she accidentally fell over and smashed her face on a rock.

A dermatologist would probably confirm that the children were born with vitiligo, which is a skin disease that leads to the loss of pigmentation and causes dark skinned races to sometimes be covered in white spots or even completely change their skin tone. When the pigment cells are gradually destroyed, the skin loses its ability to produce melanin, which makes someone who sufferers from vitiligo extremely susceptible to sunburn. While the harsh rays from the tropical sun had little effect on the villagers' skins, Balam and Annette constantly endured sunburn. The villagers were adamant the children were shedding layers of skin just as a snake does, which proved beyond all doubt they were spawned from the devil serpent.

The dramatic impact the two children had on Mere's population was nothing short of incredible. Most of the natives were too terrified to reside on the cursed island, and shortly after Balam was born, a mass exodus of Mere's petrified inhabitants resettled on Gaua. The majority of those who had chosen to remain also fled when they witnessed Balam's snakelike metamorphous during the onset of puberty. The mental and social strain that was imposed on the Wover clan forced Joseph and Kathleen to leave their beloved home. They moved to Gaua and lifted their social status from living as total outcasts to being accepted as a part of a community.

Without the benefit of modern medicine's rationale, Nemwe, the mythical snake devil, continues to flourish as a reality in the pliable minds of the fourteen Mere islanders who still nervously call Lesar village home. The unflappable belief that a serpent spirit dwells in the nearby ocean has left the rest of the fertile island uninhabited. The traders who venture to Mere always anchor a healthy distance offshore, as nothing on this earth will make them go anywhere near the snake's lair. If the locals want to purchase goods or to sell their produce, they paddle out to the traders in their dugout canoes. As far as the superstitious natives are concerned, Balam and Annette have proved beyond all doubt that an opportune and sinister monster lingers beneath the ocean's surface and is waiting to uncoil and strike by impregnating its venomous and ruinous seed into the womb of its next unfortunate victim.

Chapter Thirty-One

BAT WOMEN

The rampant use of black magic and the belief in malevolent ghosts has instilled trepidation into the receptive minds of many of Gaua's inhabitants. A civilized observer would probably think that the natives are gullible and suffer from irrational phobias, but once the setting sun slips over the edge of the horizon, for many, the world becomes a frightening place, where mythical beasts and bloodthirsty devils are said to roam. Most villagers try to avoid travelling at night, especially through the jungle. Darkness belongs to the spirits, to dreams, to the nighthawk, and to the bat. Although the natives have an intimate relationship with nature, at night the haunted rainforest is a frightening and dangerous place for even the bravest of men, and it should definitely be an intimidating place for a lone woman.

Jansen and I were going fishing in the morning, so as the final glimmer of daylight faded and the rosy dusk slipped into an almost pitch-black darkness, we stayed behind while Emily and the children disappeared into the moonless night. They followed a trail leading deep into the rainforest to spend time at another village Jansen and his father had built up in the mountains. As I watched Franita's white T-shirt grow faint and then finally disappear out of sight, I said, "Emily's got big balls, mate. Most Ni-Vanuatu women living in this type of society would be too afraid to wander off into the night." When Jansen said, "She's got four tits as well as big balls, father," I figured he'd finally dropped his guard and was letting his sense of humour free, but he wasn't. I started joking about how lucky he was and that with his wife having two sets of breasts, he could double his pleasure when they made love. Then I remembered to keep the conversation humourless. My purely coincidental choice of words cut straight to the truth when I said an opossum or a bat must have fathered Emily.

Jansen told me how Emily's unique and fascinating heritage originated on Mere Lava Island, when Quat, the *kastom* god, had yet to make the mould for man but had populated the island with numerous women. The women craved male company and were so desperate to satisfy their carnal desires, they married fruit bats, who consummated the marriage by fornicating with the women's ears.

Word filtered across to nearby Mere Island that Mere Lava had a clan of women who yearned for male company. When a virile man paddled his canoe across to Mere Lava, the sky grew black with angry flying foxes who were insanely jealous of his sexual advances on their wives. He was armed with a *nul nul*, and his club sliced through the air until the last of the bats swooping at his head lay dead at his feet. The bloodlust from the kill had excited him and heightened his lust for the women, so he went and copulated with the whole harem and made every woman his wife.

Unbeknown to the man, one of the flying foxes had been a devil bat, and although he'd killed the *kastom* creature, before it died, it cast a curse over his wife who was pregnant with his hybrid child. Each successive generation from the Worsuru family gave birth to daughters that were spawned from the devil bat's seed. Emily Worsuru, who is Emily's mother, succumbed to the curse when she was two months pregnant. A bat silently flew into her hut and flapped its wings against her swelling torso, then fluttered off into the jungle. She was overcome by the sickening reality that the devil bat had just claimed her child and rushed outside and vomited from fear. When Jansen's wife entered the world as a healthy child, she bore no obvious deformities, only strange mannerisms that made it obvious she wasn't like her normal siblings.

Sorcery still abounds on Mere Lava, where *nakaimas* are said to exhume the bodies of the dead and dine on their raw flesh. Most Mere Lavans dread nighttime and are afraid of the sorcerer's mystical savvy and other sinister presences that might be lurking in the darkness. Since her early childhood, Emily has happily embraced a nocturnal environment, has had a ravenous appetite for fruit, and a penchant for biting her peers when they played together. A tiny freckle hidden near each of her armpits grew bigger with each passing year, and by the time she'd developed breasts, the two marks had grown into nipples that are positioned in the same place as those on a female fruit bat.

While Emily was pregnant with Franita and Asnet, she also fell prey to the curse. Jansen was startled when a large bat flew into the hut during the heat of the day, fluttered against his wife's bloated stomach, then escaped out the door. Both girls are growing an extra set of nipples, and like Emily, they fearlessly venture into the jungle at night. When Emily was breastfeeding Franita, the lactating nipples under her arms completely bewildered a visiting Australian doctor, but what he didn't witness was Franita's preference for suckling from the nipples near her mother's armpit.

When I mentioned my totem on Santo was the bat and asked Jansen if he had an affinity with any animal, he told me another captivating story. Emily may be the queen of darkness, but on Gaua, Jansen's realm extends from the coast to the mountains. The locals have dubbed him the king of the ocean and the lord of the jungle. Sharks have taken an unnerving number of divers from Gaua's waters, and whenever spearfisherman have failed to return from the ocean, Jansen is always the first person the concerned villagers look to. He's readily undertaken the unenviable task of finding, then dragging the grisly remains of half eaten bodies to the shore. There's a good reason as to why he exults in the dangerous realm of the lethal white pointers, the massive hammerheads, and the deadly tiger sharks that abound in the sea. With his father's totem tracing back to the shark in the Solomons, and to the turtle on his mothers side of the family, it's hardly surprising he's an expert waterman. Not long after Jansen was born, if his mother laid him on his back, his arms and legs flailed wildly and he shrieked and cried until he was turned over so he could sleep on his stomach as a turtle does. The strong link between his ancestors' mythical alliance with sea creatures has surfaced in his strange turtle-like mannerisms. Whether he's catching reef fish with a hook and line, trolling for tuna or barracuda, spear fishing, or being dragged around the lagoon at frightening speed in a small dugout by a thrashing shark that's as big as the tiny canoe, he's in his element.

The next day when I went fishing with Jansen, everyone I'd previously spoken with said the outcome would be predictable. He surfaced from the ocean floor with an octopus coiled around his arm, which we used for bait to catch a self-imposed quota of fish with clockwork precision. Every fisherman has jinxed days where the fish won't bite, but we didn't have any bad luck to dispel the myth of Jansen's affinity with the ocean.

While we were walking back to Jansen's hut to roast our catch, first I heard the pounding sound of running feet, then as a muscular man in his early twenties who was about six feet tall with broad shoulders noisily sprinted past, he said, "Shit! He's trying to kill me with a knife!" He literally dived into Jansen's hut, locked the door, and when he nervously peered out the window and saw the coast was clear, a huge smile split his worried face. Jansen shook his head from side to side, but not in disapproval, as he said, "Harold's been caught again." Then he casually looked back down the path for his brother-in-law's assailant, and chuckled away to himself as we put the fish in the cookhouse. Harold's good looks had landed him in strife before. This wasn't the only time he'd been caught in the act with a girl from the neighbouring village, but it was the first time he'd been interrupted by the girl's father. Harold and Jansen are handy boxers, and when the irate parent screamed and tried to commit blue murder, his wayward punches were no match for Harold's well-trained and lightning quick hands. When the enraged father was knocked to the ground with a swift punch, he dragged himself to his feet and figured a machete would even the unfair score and whittle a sensitive part of Harold's virile anatomy down to an unusable size. But when the old man grabbed his knife, his sluggish legs were no match for Harold's frantic and adrenaline charged getaway.

Harold was still catching his breath and oblivious to our presence when he performed an intense ritual, and called upon the spirit of his dead father to asked for two ancestral bodyguards to watch his back and keep the fuming, knife wielding, genital threatening villager at bay. Once the rite was over, he knew within himself that his prayers had been answered, but as an added precaution, he decided to follow us up to Wonmal village and lay low for a while at Jansen's bush retreat.

Jansen had an obvious affinity with the jungle when we climbed into the interior of the island a few hours later. No one else on Gaua lives this far inland because of the devils and mystical beasts who haunt the bush. When we hiked up to three primitive huts nestled on the side of a ridge, I relished the opportunity to spend time in a cool mountain rainforest again and escape the coastal heat.

Although Jansen has a tremendous love of nature and a deep respect for all its creatures, he despises the healthy population of wild pigs that relentlessly decimate Wonmal's crops. They are the bane of the island. And at a time when the villagers were already locked into an endless battle against the destructive animals, the greedy officialdom at Torba Province decided to capitalize on the people's plight by imposing a dog tax. Most of the villagers didn't have enough money to pay the tax so they were left with no other option but to dispose of their dogs. As soon as the hunting pressure was reduced, the already swelling numbers of pigs grew into a plague. We had two days to fill before another villager joined us with a team of hunting dogs, so we resorted to a less energetic means of culling the pigs. Personally I despise the use of sometimes cruel and indiscriminate snares unless they are used in a survival situation, but because the pigs were destroying the gardens and the jungle, Jansen had no qualms about using the primitive traps. The two types of noose we set on our first night near wallows and along pig runs captured a small, tasty boar. After the animal had sprung a sturdy sapling, the vine noose worked with the deadly efficiency of a tightening tourniquet and strangled the pig by its neck.

There was such an abundance of game in the area that we ate like royalty. Jansen showed me other means of trapping animals that were just as efficient but far more humane than snares. In the morning, he made several cuts into the broad trunk of a breadfruit tree, and by late in the afternoon, the bleeding resin had congealed and was ready to be chewed to the hardened consistency of chewing gum. He tightly coiled a mouthful of the sap around a six hundred millimetres long stake by feeding out the resin with his tongue while he slowly rotated the stick. Then he heated the sap with a naked flame, which transformed the gum into an extremely strong adhesive. We staked it into pieces of tempting fruit, and when flying foxes and other small creatures alighted on the adhesive sticks to feed on the bait, they became hopelessly glued to the perch. The villagers call the ingenious trap the *nubulbul*. A simplistic pyramid shaped Indian house made from wild cane also worked extremely well. We sat and waited, then gave a quick well-timed tug on a long length of vine that was attached to a spliced prop, acting as a trigger and causing the raised trap to fall. Or we let the birds, wild fowl, and other small game feeding on grated coconut trigger a trip wire to imprison themselves.

The next day, in spite of the atrocious weather, a twelve-year-old named Robert led his father's team of five pig dogs through a torrential downpour as he climbed up to Wonmal. Before we started hunting, we appeased Quat and the ancestral spirits by placing a *yotalel* leaf behind one of our ears, and Jansen asked his forefathers to give us their divine guidance during the hunt. Ordinarily the dogs would've found it impossible to scent game in the deluge, but because there were so many pigs in the area, they managed to grab an average sized boar just ten minutes' walk from the village. As soon as I tipped the hapless pig and stuck it through the heart with my knife, the dogs released their firm hold and tore off into the cross hatch of jungle in pursuit of another mob of fleeing pigs.

I ran after the dogs' frenzied trail of barking and flailed through the tightly packed rainforest at full gallop until an aggressive scoff and pained yelping drew me to the direction of the bail. When I pushed through a tangle of vegetation and vines, the others were cautiously positioned around a patch of fern and had every reason to hold back. So did the wary dogs as they waited for an opportune moment to rush in and grab their quarry. Then almost in unison, the frantic hounds gunned for blood and latched onto a massive black and white boar that sported huge menacing tusks. The irate hog chomped his impressive ivory, then with a violent shake of his head, he effortlessly sent two outmatched canine earrings somersaulting through the air. He was way too strong for the remaining dogs, who were merely antagonizing the powerful animal, and when it spun around with lightening speed, he easily shook off the rest of the struggling pack. Harold sensed the impending danger and swung his machete over his head to chop the stroppy boar on the back of its thick neck, but just as the pig spun around, his knife struck a vine, flicked out of his hand, and cut a deep gash in his bare foot. Luckily for Harold, the dogs regained their feet in time to divert the testy pig's attention. The angry mountain of pork gave a deep guttural grunt, then fled into the undergrowth with the hysterical canines in hot pursuit.

The machete had sliced to the bone, and with blood gushing from Harold's foot, stemming its flow took priority over tracking the dogs. Jansen used the back of his machete to pulp a length of *nuyuoel* vine, then wrung its sap into the wound. He held a wad of soft fibrous shavings from the *nobeolum* tree on the gash, which also acted as a coagulant. I always carry a bandage when I'm pig hunting because when a wild boar goes on the warpath, he can inflict serious injury. When I finished binding Harold's foot, he wanted to keep on hunting. But after an hour of searching, listening, and calling, we couldn't find the dogs, so we left the waterlogged jungle and returned to the comfort of Jansen's dry hut.

While we warmed our chilled bodies around the fire, I pulled a soaked two hundred vatu note from my pocket. Jansen explained that carrying money during a hunt is a breach of *kastom* and had no doubt brought us bad luck. Then Harold discovered he'd lost the *yotalel* leaf from behind his ear and was sure it was the reason why he'd cut his foot. When Emily mentioned she'd heard the dogs bailing in a valley way below the village, Robert didn't think his team was responsible. The Gauans believe the sacred *negatatau* vine can mimic animals, humans, and make numerous other sounds. Robert was adamant that if it wasn't the vine imitating the barking, then spirit dogs were chasing a gigantic white devil pig which is believed to roam the jungle. The mythical spirit pig leaves no footprints when it travels through the bush, and whenever Robert's caught a glimpse of the phantom boar, his terrified dogs have started yelping furiously and scampered to his side with their tails between their legs, hoping their master would protect them.

Although I offered to use modern medicines on Harold's cut, he chose to use traditional healing. When he dripped boiling water directly into the deep gash, it must have been absolute agony, but he endured the pain in total silence. From the way he threw his head back each time he doused the gaping wound with the piping hot remedy, it obviously was.

That night, while we dined on roast pork, Jansen's vivid description of gigantic eels which live in the pool below Lesaringi Falls made the slimy creatures sound both fascinating and repulsive. The massive fish grow to in excess of six feet long, and have no doubt inspired tales of horrific monsters which lurk beneath the surface of the murky water. When Jansen finished giving me a brief history lesson on how the huge eels came to live in the pool, I decided to take up his offer to see firsthand if the creatures lived up to their sizable reputation.

Not long after the dawn of creation, when man first inhabited Gaua, the paramount chief of Torba built a village in a lofty valley alongside the smouldering crater of Mount Garret. He told his warriors to build a huge canoe so that he could sail beyond the realm of his small dynasty. Once the canoe was finished, the powerful chief used black magic to create weeks of incessant rain to overcome the problem of portaging the bulky craft over the mountains. The deluge quickly filled the valley with water and created Lake Letas, but it also produced a massive flood which swept many villagers to their deaths. As the lake overflowed, it created an outlet for the canoe when the excess water spilled over the flanks of a huge rock face and formed Lesaringi falls. Quat took pity on an ill-fated husband and wife who were swept over the falls and were killed by the deadly torrent of water. He turned them into huge spirit eels and made them the eternal guardians of Mbe Salomul River.

When Quat answered the paramount chief's prayers, he also linked Lake Letas to the sea. Although it lies eight hundred metres above sea level, nowadays the lake mysteriously defies the laws of physics and logic by mirroring the ebb and flow of the ocean and rising and falling in sync with its tides. The elevated lake also emulates the different moods of the ocean by matching whatever conditions occur down on the coast. Many villagers who've climbed up to the lake claim to have seen the ghostly image of ships which have been sailing around the coast at the exact same time and to have seen ancestral spirits.

The next morning, when Lenny gave us a lingering can-I-come-too look, Jansen put him out of his misery by agreeing it was time his son paid his first visit to the sacred pool. Because Lenny and I had never entered the *tabu* area before, we had to perform a simplistic ritual when we were half an hour's walk from the falls. We dropped down a steep bank to Namakate, which are two *tabu* rocks that resemble the genitals of the guardian spirit eels. *Kastom* required us to strip naked and push a penis shaped stone into a cleft in a rock that resembles a vagina. The basic ritual is believed to cause the two spirit eels to copulate, then instantly spawn offspring, which ensures the pool always remains well stocked with fish.

Days of incessant rain in the heart of the island had transformed the river into a boiling torrent. By the time we'd rock hopped and waded to the base of the falls, the continual cloud of freezing mist that swirled around the waterfall had soaked us to the skin. Whenever the river is calm, Jansen sneaks along the bank and watches the shrewd eels that are floating belly up on the surface and playing possum. Insects fall for the ploy and mistakenly think the dead eels are about to provide them with an easy meal, then when *naura* (fresh water crayfish) start feeding on the smorgasbord of insects, the cunning eels quickly roll over and eat the crayfish.

As we slipped into the frigid water, goose bumps appeared on every bit of my skin. It only took a few minutes to find our first eel, and when Jansen gently tapped it on the snout with a shark hook that was tied to a wooden handle, the small fish slowly drifted back under the cover of a submerged windfall. While we glided along banks, through weed, and amongst the rocky bottom, we came face to face with numerous average sized eels, until Jansen calmly pointed into a gloomy rocky crag. I followed him to the surface, cleared the water from my goggles and dove back down after we filled our lungs with large gulps of fresh air. The visibility was so poor that I had to swim to within a metre of the beady black eyes of a gargantuan eel that was nestled between the rocks before it clearly came into view. I quietly back paddled while Jansen stealthily swam in from the side, then with blinding speed and brute force, he drove the hook into the eel's flesh. When I moved in for a closer look, the fish whipped Jansen's stomach with its tail, briefly wrapped its thick writhing body around his torso, and then released its unintentional hold as it desperately tried to escape. As Jansen kicked towards the surface, he had a firm grip on a piece of sturdy rope attached to the wooden handle. The six-foot-long eel coiled over and over as it thrashed the water into foam. Although no one has ever been bitten, I was mindful of the rows of sharp needle-like teeth when I helped him drag the eel up onto the bank, where a sharp blow with a sturdy stick ended its violent squirming.

The fish had a girth the size of a man's thigh and was more than big enough to satisfy our hunger, so we headed back to the village, where we roasted the succulent flesh in hot stones and washed down our tasty meal with several shells of strong kava. It was an enjoyable way to spend the last night with my newfound son. I saw a lot of myself in Jansen. Even though we were poles apart genetically, his carefree but responsible attitude and no nonsense approach to life helped us to become kindred spirits. So did his unflappable belief in *kastom*, which blinded him of all prejudice and demanded he embrace a total stranger who was a white man as his father.

Chapter Thirty-Two

SOVERIEGNTY BY SACRIFICE

Throughout all of Vanuatu, for millennia, both good and evil super-natural forces have been manipulated and appeased through the spilling of sacrificial blood. In the past, in Middle Bush, Santo, *kastom* feasts of great magnitude were considered irreverent and an insult to the gods and the spirits unless a human was sacrificed whenever village pigs were being slaughtered. Such sacrifices were the ultimate prayer, and during grade taking on other islands, or when a man became a chief on Santo, a pig kill was a demonstration of wealth. Nowadays, clans who are still firmly anchored to their primitive beliefs connect with the gods by sacrificing boars. Due to the Melanesians contempt for females, it seems logical that only male animals are deemed as worthy offerings to the supreme beings and that the killing of a pig, which for centuries was the largest animal in the archipelago, would replace human sacrifice.

Men who strive to achieve elevated status amongst their peers attain prestige and chiefdom by ritualistically slaughtering carefully reared pigs. The main objective of those who try to climb the social ladder is to pro-duce big-bodied boars which sport large curved tusks. To achieve this, male piglets are gagged, their upper tusks are struck with a rock, and the loosened teeth are prised out with a stick. Then the animal is castrated. And without any top grinders to impede their growth, if they don't grow back into its jaw, the barrow's bottom tusks grow into a full or—although it's extremely rare—second or even third circle. As the curvature of the tusks becomes more pronounced, the value of the boar increases.

Because a boar can take anywhere from five to seven years to grow its tusks into one full circle, and a lot of time is invested in hand rearing the animals to prevent their precious teeth from breaking, its hardly sur-prising the animals are held in such high esteem. To accumulate the required amount of pigs for each successive grade taking equates to hav-ing a hefty mortgage in western society. A man must borrow and buy pigs, breed from them, and pay back his loan over the years with the equivalent size and same number of animals. Once he becomes affluent, then he, in turn, will lend pigs to boys who will use them for future grade taking or rear as payment for bride price.

By becoming a patriarch, a man also properly prepares himself for death and, more importantly, ensures he will be well positioned in the afterlife. Great chiefs who are still alive and have slaughtered scores of boars are treated with the same reverence that is shown to the gods and to ancestral spirits. In total contrast to western values, the destruction of a man's most treasured possessions earns him immense respect, due to his generosity with his wealth, when he shares the animal's highly prized meat with everyone during *kastom* feasts.

The pig has made its most impressive mark on Vanuatu's traditional society on Ambae Island, at Atafola village, which is home to the archipelago's royal family. The head of the Melanesian monarchy is ninety-year-old Rupert Garaekoro, who is the Ratahigi, or paramount chief, for all of Vanuatu. To become the ultimate patriarch, he sacrificed an incredible one thousand pigs and one hundred roosters in a single day.

James A Michener immortalized Ambae after he gazed across the ocean to the tranquil isle while he was stationed on Santo during World War II. When he wrote the critically acclaimed Tales of the South Pacific, the fabled island Bali Ha'i, which blossomed from his fruitful imagination, was modelled on the distant islet. Unlike Michener, who never ventured to Ambae because he was afraid the reality would shatter the illusion his book had created, I had no qualms about chasing and catching his dream of a mythical island idyll. When I flew to Ambae, it was like most of Vanuatu's other outer islands and was a relatively untouched paradise devoid of commercial development which may well have lived up to Michener's enchanted vision had he stepped onto its shores.

I enjoyed a leisurely walk from Longana airfield and searched for a fieldworker from the cultural centre that lived on the island amidst a crowded carnival atmosphere of soccer games, volleyball, and numerous food stalls that were erected to celebrate the opening of new concrete block *nakamal* at Sarata Mata village. When I walked into a thatch kava bar, finding sixty-four-year-old Simon Garaelolo had been easy. The Polynesian looking chief was downing his third toe curling drink, which had dulled his smiling eyes and dripped off the end of his grizzled beard. After I introduced myself and struck up an easy conversation, to put us on common ground and the same wavelength, I quickly wolfed down two eye-watering shells. While we got acquainted, without being condescending or to gain respect, Simon casually mentioned that his father held the title of paramount chief for all of Vanuatu. When I'd asked the locals for directions to find a fieldworker, I had no idea that when the ailing Ratahigi passes away, Simon is next in line for the prestigious position or that he was the second highest-ranking chief in the land. I would never have picked that he held such a prominent and revered title. He was simply himself, his mannerisms were totally relaxed, and he had no hesitation welcoming me into the royal household.

Although Ambae remains a stronghold for sorcery, the church has influenced the majority of the islands inhabitants. They all wear western clothing. But the one thing Christianity hadn't curbed was chief Simon's insatiable thirst for strong kava. After four dizzying shells, as the lengthening shadows of dusk eerily merged the darkening landscape into one big blurred drab, I stumbled through the darkness in a drunken stupor and followed Simon's wavering footsteps back to his home at Alafoa village.

The two western style houses the government supplied to the royal families were hardly palatial. Time and the corrosive tropical elements had reduced both of the single storey homes to dishevelled looking dwellings that were in desperate need of urgent repair. I felt pretty ramshackle as well from the potent kava when I stretched out on the floor alongside Simon and got comfortable in the shabby surroundings. When our conversation flowed until around midnight, Simon was surprised and fascinated by my knowledge of secretive rites, while I found his honest outlook on life equally enlightening. He felt the more civilized and better educated Ni-Vanuatu became, the less intelligently they acted. He also felt that the invasive European culture was instilling a perverse and greedy mindset into the people and created a tumultuous conflict of values which was steadily breaking down traditional society. Without hesitating, he readily gave me his blessing to write a book that exposed never before documented rituals and beliefs and added that he would seek the opinion of chief Rupert. Everything started to spin when I staggered into bed, and from the sound of Simon noisily vomiting outside, I wasn't the only one who felt queasy.

A loud resonant sound reverberated through my head with the intensity of rolling thunder when I awoke to the dawn chorus of singing birds. I felt malaise and was half asleep when I wandered outside to see who was ringing a primitive alarm clock so early in the morning. Simon was going through the thrice-daily ritual of feeding his pigs halved coconuts by banging an axe on a hollow log to ring the breakfast bell. Huge pigs with voracious appetites burst from the nearby jungle in every direction and went into a feeding frenzy. Their ear piercing squeals and noisy scoffs went right through my hung over system while Simon explained why and how the gluttonous animals play such a vital role in his family's royal status. To become the paramount chief, he needs to complete the last two of the ten *nahunggwe* grades. Next year he plans to sacrifice ten boars with tusks which have grown into a full circle. Then when Rupert passes away, he will slaughter one hundred roosters and hundreds of pigs.

Although the pigs roam freely throughout the jungle, they never stray far from the village. Immediately after a piglet has endured the disgruntling surgery of having its testicles and teeth removed, a hallowed ritual prevents the free ranging animals from ever wandering off permanently. The owner blows across a grated rotten coconut, and then feeds a small portion of the sickly smelling fruit to the piglet while he chants to Tangaro, the *kastom* god.

For older men who've already attained prestige and power through pig kills, the *nahunggwe* offers them immense *manaki* (mana), but young men who are following the *kastom* road are guaranteed decades of struggle. Each grade taking becomes more complex and more demanding. The first grade, called the *moli*, requires only one boar to be sacrificed. Then five to ten are killed for the second step, until finally, to complete the tenth grade, the blood of one hundred to one thousand animals is spilled to become a chief. Of all the grades, it's the sixth which will never be repeated as this requires ten hermaphrodite pigs called *narave* to be slaughtered. Only three of the dual sexed genetic freaks remain on Ambae, and it's doubtful if ten exist throughout the whole of Vanuatu.

They're bred from an extremely rare bloodline and are the most highly prized of any type of pig.

To feed and rear one thousand animals is a gargantuan and physically impossible task for one man and his family. In order to accumulate this many pigs, many are purchased with intricately woven mats that are used as a form of currency. Others are borrowed, and when these are paid back, sometimes the lender requires interest in the form of additional animals. Although a high chief may possess great *manaki*, most of them remain indebted to others for the best part of their lives. Rupert's father held the title of paramount chief, as did his great great uncle, Vevineala, who also clubbed one thousand pigs to death. After years of careful farming and intense planning, when Rupert sacrificed one hundred and fifty roosters and fifteen hundred pigs to complete the *nahunggwe*, he was debt free.

Time has taken its toll on Rupert, and because he senses that he will soon reside in the spirit world, he's instructed Simon to prepare him a traditional grave. Massive rocks have been manhandled alongside his *nakamal* to form a circle with a five-metre diameter which will serve as a permanent memorial to the mighty chief. Rupert has resurrected the ancient tradition to ensure the road he follows to the supernatural paradise is properly paved. He performed a ritual to prepare the plot for his burial by drinking a portion of *tabu* red kava, then spilling the rest of the brew onto his sanctified grave. Because his health is so frail and he's too weak to swing a *nul nul*, he then touched the head of a sacrificial pig and got his grandson to club the animal to death. The sacrificial pork received the same treatment as the flesh of every other pig that's slaughtered during a *nahunggwe* and was cooked inside the *nakamal* in the *tavaru*, a sacred cooking pit surrounded by *tabu* stones. Then feasting and dancing continued through the night until dawn.

After the fifth *nahunggwe* is completed, a hunter who is pursuing pigs can always look forward to successfully securing game due to a supernatural link they form with their quarry. The night before a hunt, a shell of sacred red kava is prepared. While the hunter holds his spear, he blows across the kava, then chants to Tangaro to empower both his weapon and himself with *manaki*. Then during the night, he has a vivid dream that shows him exactly where to find the pig in the jungle. Simon had to go to Sarata Mata in the morning, and when he asked if I'd like to go hunting with his son, Oswo, instead of going to Sarata Mata, I jumped at the opportunity to go on a traditional hunt.

I was up before the sun the next day, but at 10:00 a.m., it still sounded as if Oswo was noisily cutting through a stack of wood as his discordant snoring resonated around the room like a badly tuned chainsaw with a hole in its muffler. When he finally woke up, he opened one eye, looked at me patiently waiting on the other bed, then rolled over and slept for another hour. When he awoke again, he reluctantly got up from his usual kava induced slumber, grabbed the dogs, and jumped over the back fence without a spear or a knife or having performed any type of ritual. I wondered what the hell was going on until he pointed to Simon's royal pigs and screamed, "*Sook! Sook!*" to get the dogs to attack the patriarch's prized animals.

Absolute mayhem exploded all around us as the dogs and the pigs went berserk and kicked up clouds of choking dust from the bare earth. A wire fence screeched as a mob of massive boars bulldozed through the stretching strands of wire to escape the fracas. A huge ginger boar went ballistic and spun around and scoffed as it slashed at the pack of mauling dogs with its long sweeping tusks. While I stood in the middle of the chaos, I laughed out aloud and shook my head in total disbelief. When I had to dodge a scoffing pig that galloped past, I decided to put an abrupt end to traumatising the monarchy's pigs. Although Oswo probably meant well, I had visions of Simon resurrecting the practice of human sacrifice if he got wind of what his son was up to. I muttered "Mad bastard" to myself, then told him I'd seen enough for one day of how the privileged hunt and asked him to call off the dogs.

The next morning, the type of heart wrenching sounds that normally follow the death of a loved one stirred me from my sleep. I could tell from the bloodcurdling wailing and the shrill shrieks that someone from within the family had suddenly died. As mourning relatives began to fill the house and expressed their sorrow, the heartbroken women seemed to lose all self-control when they held their hands over their heads and threw themselves against the walls while they cried and sobbed, whereas the stony-faced men showed little emotion. Oswo kept blissfully snoring away, and was completely unaware of the commotion in the next room. Such a poignant moment belonged to those who were in mourning. With death's dark aura hanging in the air, I offered everyone my condolences, thanked chief Simon for his kind hospitality, and so as not to intrude on the emotive scene, I bode him goodbye.

Although Rupert was gravely ill, he drank three shells of kava a day right up until he passed away several years after my visit. Before I left, he'd dressed in his royal regalia and allowed me to photograph him holding one of his precious pig jaws. When we'd finished taking the photos, his response to the content of my book was simply, "You have been chosen to write about all of the *kastom* that has been gifted to you. We Ni-Vanuatu are not ashamed of our secretive culture, no matter how barbaric the white man thinks some of our beliefs are. So you write your book." There will never be another Ratahigi like Rupert as his successors will never sacrifice a colossal one thousand pigs in a single day. And although they will be treated with the utmost respect, because of the impact Christianity has had on Ambae, it's doubtful that they will be revered as a living god.

Chapter Thirty-Three

HORRIFIC HARMONY

If an outsider who exposes the timeless secrets of the jungle and of its peoples becomes complacent, and errantly treats his discoveries with irreverence and ridicule, it can open the doorway to an underlying hell. Because to the tribes, who believe in the supernatural, the relationship they have with the spirits is sometimes as equally horrific as it is harmonious. While I was on Ambae, I'd heard tales about the brutal "hurters" on Maewo Island who supposedly inflict terrible injuries on the villagers, and any unlucky visitors, with sticks that are studded with nails. When I tried to research the origins of the custom and found the bizarre ritual has remained an undocumented enigma, I flew to the island to see if I could unearth the reason behind the vicious beatings.

Maewo has a reputation as being a stronghold for powerful black magic, yet there wasn't the slightest hint of a sinister atmosphere as I walked from the elevated airfield in the middle of the island down to the nearest coastal village. I revelled in the island's enchanting beauty as I traipsed through a lush rainforest, where stunning waterfalls flowed until they gently collided with the tepid ocean. The postcard image permeated an air of utter peace and tranquillity, and when I entered Naone village, I sensed the same serene atmosphere. Pigeons that should have instinctively erupted into flight on sighting a human happily picked amongst the grass for grubs, just metres away from a group of laughing and bright-eyed children who were wearing ragged clothes and playing soccer. A flying fox that was in a deep slumber hung unperturbed from a nearby ironwood tree. The unusual scene resembled a modern day garden of Eden, where normally distrustful creatures that would otherwise feature on most rural village menus were living in a safe haven. It turned out to be a wildlife sanctuary, as killing feral animals within the village boundaries is strictly forbidden. When the soccer ball rolled to my feet, I dribbled and swerved through the cheering crowd of children and pushed the ball past the grinning goalkeeper and scored a goal. The animated kids hooted and yelled and were devoid of inhibition as they hugged my body and screamed with delight.

Several men who heard the commotion casually wandered to their hut doorways, while a small boy who took it upon himself to be a messenger sprinted to the end of the village to forewarn the chief of my arrival. When I met the middle-aged patriarch, Wilson Lui possessed an almost indefinable aura that had a lasting and profound impact. His greying goatee exaggerated his slightly devilish features, which exuded both good and evil.

Yet from the time he first smiled and welcomed me with a handshake, the unassuming chief was one of the most kind hearted and affable human beings I have ever met. He glowed with a pronounced inner calm that cast a mood of utter serenity over me. His relaxed and humble manner made befriending him an uncomplicated privilege and belied his status as the most powerful *kastom* man on Maewo—possibly throughout the whole of Vanuatu. When I told him my work revolved around documenting *kastom* and that I'd heard about the island's "hurters" in the villages to the south, he laid down a few simplistic ground rules. As long as I shared his people's ethic of existing in peace and harmony with all of nature and with the other one 120 inhabitants, I was welcome to stay in the tiny leaf hut next to the thatch church.

While I rested in the hut and shook off an annoying fever, plates that were filled with gifts of food poured through the doorway. My jaws ached from chewing through a stringy leg of roast wild fowl and from smiling to the steady stream of villagers who offered me an affectionate welcome. Without a doubt, Naone's inhabitants were the friendliest and most cheerful people I'd met anywhere in Vanuatu. Even the most fearsome looking man in the village, who also had the meanest reputation, became my closest friend. Patrik Wesum was slightly chubby, thirty years old, and rarely stopped smiling. But when he did, his tough and contemptuous appearance gave me the impression he'd just as happily beat me up as he would befriend me. It didn't take long to realize that if I gave him half a reason to, he would—and in a heartbeat. From the moment we met, there were no false pretences between us, and there wasn't any unnecessary decorum. Yet within half an hour, his quick wit and foul mouth had me in hysterics and endeared me to his gruff, no-nonsense personality. When he left me to sweat out the last of my slowly subsiding fever, I told him I'd bounce back after a few hours of sleep, and accepted the offer of a customary welcoming drink of kava in the men's *nakamal*.

I awoke to the soothing sound of the women singing hymns next door. I then changed my clothes, which were soaked with sweat, and walked two hundred metres through the sultry night to the *nakamal*. Because I didn't know the correct protocol, and because Maewo's *kastom* men are some of the most revered and respected sorcerers throughout Vanuatu, I slowly entered the open walled *nakamal* and quietly sat down at the very front of the thatch dwelling. The building appeared to be segregated into three sections. Everyone gathered to socialize in the first, but the other areas were obviously reserved for those who'd achieved a higher rank through grade taking and were a dead giveaway that a secret society existed.

The mixing of kava was a ritual unto itself. To strengthen their already rock solid bonds of friendship, whenever anyone meticulously prepared a drink, it was gifted to a friend or to a guest. Patrik ground the root for my drink by twisting it in the palm of his hand against a coarse coral pestle. Then after he made a syrupy looking brew with the pulp, he expertly poured a thin stream of kava from a height of half a metre into a coconut shell cup without spilling a single drop. I thanked everyone for their kind welcome, then downed the sharp tasting brew in one quick hit. When Wilson gave Patrik a shell, he performed the next part of the ritual with his eyes closed because the fumes are believed to cause blindness. He held the kava under his nose and drew a deep breath, grunted like a pig while he swung his head from side to side over the top of his shell several times, and then he gulped down the acrid mixture in a single draught.

A well-travelled villager who was full of boundless curiosity swayed the conversation to my occupation and my previous experiences. When I mentioned my initiation in Middle Bush, Santo, and the honorary chiefdom I received on Mota Lava, it sparked a surge of deep interest. Especially when everyone learned that Rick Welegtabit's totem had been water and that we shared the same sacred bond with the highly revered element. Wilson told me that when Tangaro, the supreme *kastom* god, created Maewo, he gave it the country's highest rainfall and the archipelago's most spectacular waterfalls, and he also instructed Quato, the islands first man, to worship water as his totem. It was ironic that while one of the men was talking about our common affinity with water and how it enhanced our friendship, I looked up to see what was scuffling in the rafters and a rat with perfect aim directed a steady stream of urine right in my face. The solemn atmosphere surrounding the kava ceremony succumbed to instant hilarity as we all dropped our guard and burst out laughing. We relived the moment several times until Wilson put a dampener on our amusement and reminded everyone to respectfully return to a sombre mood. After another vision doubling shell of kava, I staggered back to my hut, where I lay in a pool of sweat and burnt off the rest off my lingering fever.

The next morning, a loud knock on the door stirred me from a feverish slumber that had been filled with hellish nightmares and left me feeling weak and sluggish. Patrik poked his head in the doorway, swore like a trooper when he told me I looked terrible, and asked me to join him for breakfast. After we'd eaten, we visited the pigs Patrik reared for grade taking. As we walked along, he made it clear in his own earthy way that he approved of our friendship when he said, "You're different from other white men. Some of them are bad-mannered. I could kill the bastards. The fuckers look down on us because of the way we live, but you eat our food and respect *kastom*. You're like a Ni-Van, and because you have made *kastom*, one day you'll be a special man Rick." His pigs were fenced inside deep coral crags that bordered a beach, and when the wild tempered boars scoffed and chomped as soon as they saw me, Patrik warned that if anyone other than himself foolishly entered the enclosure to feed them coconuts and fill their water troughs, they would probably be attacked by the fiery animals.

Later in the day when I offered to help Patrik carry some freshly cut planks back to the village, he seemed a little dumbfounded and said, "Most white men are bastards that take rather than give," then gratefully accepted the helping hand. As we climbed up through the jungle to get the lumber, the intense midday heat pumped a continual flow of perspiration from our bodies that seemed to sluice away the remnants of my fever. It was hard work climbing back down for several hours with the heavy weight of the lengths of green timber on our aching shoulders, yet we both stubbornly told each other there was no need to rest. I'm glad we didn't stop and that I decided to lend him a hand before I travelled down the coast in the afternoon to visit the "hurters" village, because it led to an unimaginable turn of events.

A faint shrill cry, unlike any bird or animal sound I'd ever heard, made me cock my head when we unloaded the timber alongside the *nakamal* and rubbed our throbbing muscles. Just as I was about to ask Patrik what the noise was, he looked to the rear of the sacred dwelling, then turned back to me and yelled, "Move your arse Rick! No bullshit, bro! Run!" His stern warning sent my jaded senses onto full alert, then into overdrive when I saw how the other villagers were reacting. A group of children who were playing nearby screamed and then exploded into flight with looks of sheer terror on their faces. A distraught mother reeled in horror, scooped her six-month-old baby into her arms and raced towards the sanctity of her hut. I sensed my world was about to be filled with danger, so I sprinted towards the running children. As I streaked past a few villagers, the sound of rustling leaves and pounding feet bore down on me, then it stopped abruptly and was replaced with a slapping noise and pained shrieks. When I glanced over my shoulder, I was shocked to see a small child, who'd stumbled in the stampede of escaping bodies, was being ruthlessly whipped with a switch of *nangalat* and mercilessly beaten with a wooden staff. The way that the serene atmosphere had been suddenly eclipsed with brutal violence took me completely by surprise, but my astonishment turned to sickness when I looked to my right and saw an old woman who'd fallen against the side of a hut screaming for mercy as lumps of coral were hurled into her frail body.

Although I desperately wanted to help the small boy that was being beaten, the terrified tone in the voices that were screaming at me to run and my self-preservation spurred me on. I swept a small girl into my arms and slipped through the door of a hut just as it was about to be slammed closed. While I peered through a crack in the door, it was easy to forget that mere mortals lurked beneath the swirling shroud of pandanus leaves and the elaborate black and red masks as four spirit fetishes similar to the Nataquat searched for victims. They went from hut to hut like predatory animals, and when one of the monstrosities zeroed in on our door, I whispered, "Here it comes" to several older boys who were holding the door fast. As the ghoulish spirit tried to vainly kick and push its way in, it became frustrated and slammed the side of the hut with its wooden staff. Several quivering children who were huddled in a corner let out a shriek and hugged one another. When the fetishes' shrill battle cries and the rustling of their leaves faded in the distance, only the sound of pained sobbing and horrible wailing remained.

Chapter Thirty-Four

THE RAWE AND MWAE

The illusion I had of Naone being an idyllic nirvana had just been shattered with a cataclysmic impact. As I cautiously exited the hut, I looked at the village through different eyes. Although my fresh outlook remained devoid of prejudice or judgement, and experience had conditioned my mind to physical and mental hardship, it was still hard not to think of the brutal rite that I'd just witnessed as being a massive blight on the people's morality. *Kastom* had survived the psychological pressures of embracing Christianity in tandem with its own brutal traditions. The different faiths had followed contradictory parallel lines which had somehow merged without any spiritual conflict. Anyone who lacked an intimate insight into *kastom* might feel betrayed by the hypocrisy of Wilson being so incredibly kind in such a peaceful setting, while he's the patriarch of villagers who inflict such brutal violence on one another.

Bloodied and bruised villagers lay on the ground nursing their injuries or were slowly dragging themselves to their feet. Tears streamed down the flushed face of a small boy whose tattered shirt and ragged shorts had offered him little protection when he'd been flayed with a branch of toxic *nangalat* leaves. His skin was on fire, and when Wilson started tending to the wounded, he applied a poultice of *wasawas* leaves to help subdue the child's unbearable pain, which normally lasts for days and sometimes for as long as one week. The traumatised child would endure several sleepless nights before the searing effects of the venomous vegetation subsided. When all of the injured had been taken care of and life returned to normal with a terseness that was equal to the sudden onslaught of violence, I decided the "hurters" could wait and that trying to document Naone's sadistic beliefs took precedence.

Several hours later, when Patrik and Wilson asked me to follow them to the *nakamal*, I could tell by the solemn tone of their voices that they were about to give me a deeper insight into the terror that I'd just witnessed. Patrik spoke first and said, "You are the only one, Rick. A few tourists have seen the Rawe and the Mwae, but no white man has ever heard what we are about to tell you." I was surprised that after I'd stayed in the village for just one night they were about to reveal the essence of their beliefs and make a ritual that had previously been swathed in secrecy suddenly transparent. When Wilson gave me permission to share the brutal rite with outsiders, I knew he would've communed with the spirits and that I must have met their godly approval.

Wilson started at the very beginning of Naone's history, with the legend of Quato, who was the first man to live on Maewo. While Quato was out checking the wild fowl traps he'd set in the depths of the jungle, he came across a dead Rawe (male devil spirit) hanging from a snare. Although Quato was renowned for his courage, he warily approached the evil spirit. Just as he was about to touch the Rawe, it began to slowly move, then gave a snort and started grunting and thrashing about. Quato was horrified when he saw that the spirit of a hermaphrodite pig had restored life to the Rawe. He bravely rushed in and delivered a fatal blow to the Rawe's forehead with one vicious swipe of his *nul nul*. That night, when Quato fell into a deep sleep, the Rawe entered his dreams and told him how to make and instil life into a Rawe, and also how to create a Mwae so that the spirit devil had a female mate. The devious spirit ensured he and the Mwae remained eternal by telling Quato that if he failed to resurrect both of the demons during certain rituals, his people would be plagued by sickness and cursed with misfortune for eternity.

The shrewd Rawe instructed Quato to evoke the evil spirits when a male child received its true *kastom* name, during times of sickness, and when a child requires extreme discipline. To ignore these inevitable events was to ignore the cycle of life and the natural order of creation. Quato knew if he disregarded the devil spirit's command, he was shunning *kastom's* destiny, its basis, and its outcome, and he would be flouting the fact that his people's wellbeing now lay in the Rawe's devilish hands. The devious Rawe left Quato with no other option than to become the patriarch of the Rawe and Mwae cult.

Anyone who joins the sect must obtain or rear sacrificial pigs. This is the reason why the men grunt like pigs before they drink kava, because emulating a boar is believed to produce large animals with huge tusks and also keeps their owners healthy and strong. Membership of the exclusively male cult starts at an incredibly early age. For the first grade taking, one- to three-year-old children are gifted a sacrificial pig from either a relative or from Wilson. The initiation rite begins when coconut leaves are wrapped around the centre post in the *nakamal* and a *tabu* shell is hung from the rafters. At that age, the children lack the strength to kill a pig, so they hold onto Wilson while he spears or clubs the animals to death in the *nakamal*. To conclude the simplistic rite, both the coconut leaf and the child's body are heavily anointed with the animal's blood. Once an initiate has completed the first three of eight grades, he has the right to create and wear the Rawe and Mwae fetishes and has secured himself a place in the first partition of the *nakamal*.

When the boys are christened with their true *kastom* name during their second grade taking, the villagers who aren't members of the cult are gripped by a mounting sense of dread and insecurity because they know that once the ritual is over, they will be subjected to terrible cruelty and suffer brutal beatings. A large sacrificial boar with curved tusks is roasted in hot stones in a *tabu* oven called the *cocona*, and for the next ten days, the children are forbidden to leave the confines of the sacred dwelling. *Kastom* demands that the boys must survive solely on the pork and that irrespective of how many of them there are, they must consume every edible part of the animal.

On the tenth day, after Wilson has dubbed the children with their tribal names, he leads them outside and they join the other members of the cult and perform the *bue* dance. Children who are barely able to walk, let alone dance, are held in the arms of men who shuffle in a circle in front of the *nakamal*. When the *bue* is being performed, the infants' mothers are jointly known as *horovtakpei*, and while they cradle cloths that are bundled full of fruit to symbolize their sons, the *horovtakpei* briefly join in the dance. They break away from the *bue* and place steaming parcels of *lap lap* in the centre of the dancing throng of bodies. Then they take their children from the men and lovingly cradle their sons while they perform the rest of the *bue* dance.

A shrill call from the supernatural realm announces the ceremony is almost over and sends a cold shiver down the mothers' spines when two Rawe emerge from the rear of the *nakamal*. Their long pandanus leaves rustle and clatter as they spin and twirl towards the women, then join in the *bue* dance. When the dancing ceases, all of the villagers nervously feast on the *lap lap*, because they know that when the *lafaet* is over, the Rawe and Mwae will go on the rampage and inflict an orgy of violence. The Rawe conclude the christening ritual by kicking away *lap lap* leaves that surround the food.

Although the beatings the Rawe will inflict are ritualistic, they are always severe and in the not so distant past, deaths occurred. The threat of being killed still lingers today, and serious injuries are always a probability. Several months before my arrival, a Rawe threw a green coconut at full force at the face of a small boy and shattered his jaw and teeth. The man who was wearing the fetish was devastated when he discovered he'd injured his own nephew, but claimed he had no recollection of inflicting the ruthless beating as the spirit of the Rawe had overwhelmed his senses and rationale. Wilson fined him one pig and ordered him to give it to his nephew as compensation.

The devil spirits arm themselves with a devastating array of weapons. They use switches of *nangalat*, lumps of coral, stones, sticks, and anything else they can find to wreak hurt. A club called the *solate* and a wooden fighting staff called the *kere* sometimes hospitalise unlucky victims. Nowadays Wilson uses the *kere* as a stamp of his authority during rituals, but in the past, when cannibalism was rife, his rock hard fighting stick, which is made from ironwood, had killed many enemies. Before Christianity mellowed the severity of the beatings, the Rawe and Mwae used the *kere* to club villagers to death or to spear them in the stomach. Whenever a victim had their torso impaled, the spirit fetish twisted the *kere's* star shaped head, then gave it a sharp pull and ripped out the victim's intestines. The *solate* is studded with fearsome looking *wala* thorns and also inflicts horrific injuries when unfortunate villagers are simultaneously raked and clubbed with the gruesome weapon.

Because females are forbidden to join the cult, the malicious demons will never run short of prey and the cycle of brutality will always continue. The moment feasting ceases at the *bue*, the Rawes launch a vicious attack, which instigates their two months' reign of terror over Naone. Nowhere is safe when, without warning and at any time, the Rawe and Mwae stalk the village, search the roads, and hunt the gardens for human prey. While Naone's inhabitants continue with their daily routines to provide for their subsistence lifestyle, they live in constant fear. Especially when the Mwae lurks nearby.

The female spirit is the devil the villagers fear the most. The Rawe has a hornlike spire that projects from the top of its headpiece. But the Mwae has none, which enables her to force her way into the huts more easily. When she does shove through the door, it's truly terrifying, as *kastom* demands that the villagers must submit to the violence without retaliating. Anyone who fights back or fends off the hail of blows is fined one fully-grown boar and a massive amount of vatu.

Seven weeks had passed since a previous christening ritual, and in the remaining week of the rite, I was witness to more ruthless brutality and terror. Two Mwae and a Rawe whipped and beat Wilson's mother, Ruth, until tears poured down her cheeks. When they turned on me while I captured the assault on film, I was amazed at how fast I had to sprint to outrun them to avoid being injured. On another occasion, I narrowly avoided an ambush from one of the spirit devils by escaping with a backwards roll, then springing to my feet and racing to safety. While I was crouching down to capture more of *kastom's* viciousness on camera, I failed to notice another Mwae rushing in and received a painful slap across the arm from a branch of *nangalat* as I rolled backwards then dived into a nearby hut.

By far the most ruthless beating I documented occurred in a nearby copra plantation when a Rawe and a Mwae used their supernatural stealth and cunning and seemed to almost eerily float between the trees like a silent breeze. When the Mwae slammed a *kere* into a middle-aged villager's back with vertebrae-cracking, leg-buckling intensity, he screamed and writhed in agony. The stunned man was transformed into a distraught knot of instinctive fear as he collapsed to the ground and curled up in the foetal position while a Rawe flogged him with nature's botanical barbed wire, a sturdy branch of venomous *nangalat*. Although he tried to contain his pain and anguish, he was so distressed that he openly wept like a child when Wilson soothed his wounds with medicinal leaves. I eased his woes with a bit of therapeutic humour, by making a derogatory remark about the spirit devils that included a fair amount of profanity. The small crowd of sympathetic villagers roared with laughter, and even Wilson grinned from ear to ear while he tried to mask his obvious amusement. Then as he took stock of his emotions, the laidback chief cast me a soul piercing glance and warned the sentence he was about to pass was extremely light considering my blatant disrespect of the spirits. He warned that next time there would be no lenience, and that tonight, I must pay penance by drinking two shells of three-year-old kava in the *nakamal*.

Whenever I immerse myself in the midst of primitive cultures to document unfamiliar customs, it usually means putting myself completely at the people's mercy. I accepted the punishment without question, and that night in the *nakamal* an absolute silence followed when the first chastising shell slid down my throat. The hut was filled with watchful eyes that were scrutinizing my every action as a listless apathy began to engulf my thoughts and movements. For the next ten minutes, I somehow managed to maintain a charade of composure and outwardly held everything together while Patrik mixed the second and much stronger shell. Just the vile smell of the potion almost made me vomit when my lips pursed around the rim of the coconut shell cup. After the volatile brew had collided with my already churning stomach, Patrik handed me a plate of food. I knew this was part of the punishment, as eating straight after you've drunk kava can sometimes turn a placid drink into a depth charger.

Not long after I'd eaten a generous helping of yam, as I looked into the pitch-black night sky, the stars began to distort and cast colourful flashing spotlights across the velvety cosmos. The buzzing insects that choked the humid air started sprinkling stardust into the inky heavens. I tried to speak but a dyslexic surge from the analgesic root ripped the jumbled mess of words from my mouth and threw them around the *nakamal*. When two Patriks looked me in the eye and said, "Oh shit, Rick," even his words seemed to waiver. While I lost all perception of time and sat in a trance, my tumultuous senses were lulled by the brew's archaic song ringing in my ears. Everything merged into a sickening blur, and when I became blinded with double vision, I watched my gyrating world and everything in it spin and cartwheel into a kaleidoscope of nauseating colour. Patrik offered to carry me back to my hut, but I stubbornly refused. As I tried to maintain some lame semblance of dignity, I fell flat on my face twice as fast as I stood up. Then I dragged myself up off the ground, slurred I was good to go, and staggered into the obscure darkness feeling completely disorientated.

The two hundred metres' walk back to my hut may as well have been an epic journey through a two hundred kilometre maze of impenetrable jungle. I was truly bamboozled and stumbled face-first into a tree, then slumped to the ground with a bloodied nose. After I pulled myself up the trunk, I blindly flailed through the darkness until I lurched into a wall of jungle and was forced to backtrack. I eventually bounced off the side of a leaf hut, groped for the door, then fell inside and staggered across the floor until I slammed into the back wall. My fantasy world erupted into a living nightmare when the hut's shocked sole occupant let rip with a blood-curdling scream. An old woman who thought I was a spirit kept up her hysterical shrieking until the beam of a torch pierced the darkness. I'd been barely functioning and just managed to tick over on the gaping edge of consciousness until two strong arms caught my slumping body as I spiralled into a black oblivion.

Patrik banged on the door the following morning, then swore, laughed, and jokingly gave me hell when he saw my kava-emaciated body. While I struggled to come to grips with reality again and groggily peered outside, a group of waiting villagers roared with intense laughter. For the next couple of days, I bore the brunt of their good-natured banter when they kept reminding me about my drunken midnight liaison with the terrified old widow.

By willingly accepting my punishment and adhering to *kastom*, I'd enhanced my already solid friendship with Patrik and gained Wilson's absolute respect. My kinship with Patrik and Wilson flourished from merely sharing the same totem into an offer to join the cult. Anthropologists have always faced the fundamental problem of describing and analysing a ritual from an observer's rather than a participant's point of view, which always leaves many perplexing questions unanswered. After I did a lot of deep and serious thinking, I decided I wasn't prepared to pledge my soul to the devil. To become his disciple so that I could seriously injure my friends held absolutely no appeal. If I wanted to wear the Rawe or the Mwae fetish, first I'd have to achieve the third grade by killing three sacrificial boars with curved tusks, and then dance in a sacred *nasara* in the jungle, which gave me the right to enter the third area in the rear of the *nakamal*. My gnawing conscience kept whispering that I should seize the opportunity to gain a rare and intimate insight into the cult, but my morals weren't flexible enough, and my abhorrence of violence ensured that I would remain an observer. Wilson and Patrik respected my decision and said they would share as much *kastom* as they could without me being a member of the sect.

Wilson told me that how the spirits are evoked to bring the Rawe and Mwae to life will always remain a mystery to outsiders. Both fetishes are prepared under a veil of secrecy, and the penalty for divulging the secrets to anyone outside of the cult is death at the merciless hands of the Rawe spirit. Those who create the physical aspects of a new fetish must adhere to a stringent ritual. Everyone that's been working on a costume never forgets to thoroughly wash their hands afterwards, because the consequences of overlooking such a simple task are dire. They believe their testicles and stomach will suddenly start to grow to an enormous size until they suffer an agonizing death.

During the two months after the *bue* dance, the devious devils steal food from vacant huts, and when the villagers return from their gardens laden with crops, they're beaten and their produce is stolen so that the members of the cult can consume it in the *nakamal*. The Rawe and Mwae not only steal for themselves, they also give to the needy. One of the cult goes from hut to hut wearing a mask that resembles the face of an old man and begs for food, money, mats, and other items that are taken back to the *nakamal* and distributed later. The rite originated when old widowers, elderly spinsters, and unmarried men who had no extended family to care for them needed help.

When the nerve-racking two months had thankfully drawn to an end, as dusk enveloped the village and lightning sheeted across an ominous looking sky, Wilson made *kastom* to stave off the gathering rain clouds that threatened to douse the closure of the *bue*. A measured and monotonous beat rang throughout the *nasara* to announce the start of the ritual. A line of drummers dripped with sweat as they pounded bamboo *tam tams* that were ornately decorated with clusters of flowers. Several men took turns to continually raise and slam a hollow log into the ground, which added what sounded like an unearthly echo to the already haunting music. The women moved with seemingly endless amounts of energy as they danced directly opposite the village men. They carried on through the night until dawn, and whenever they stopped to replenish their reserves with a quick snack, the men rested and drank kava. As the first shards of sunlight pierced the predawn darkness, the Rawe and Mwae emerged from the jungle and danced around Wilson as he stomped on lengths of wild cane that had been staked around the perimeter of the dancing throng of bodies. Although *kastom* forbade the spirit devils from attacking the women, an instinctive fear was etched into their features. After Wilson had flattened the last stalk of cane, the Rawe and Mwae disappeared to the rear of the *nakamal* and exited the villagers' lives until *kastom* demanded that their spirits be evoked again.

That night, while we were drinking kava in the *nakamal*, Patrik began swearing when I asked him about the "hurters" from central Maewo and muttered that if he ever laid eyes on an Ole again he would kill it. Between June and August, during the annual yam harvest, the Ole brandishes a stick that's studded with thorns and goes in search of victims. A few months before my arrival, the Ole had ventured up to Naone and committed a heinous and sacrilege assault by deliberately violating the sanctity of the *nakamal* when it beat the men while they were drinking kava. Patrik was enraged by the blatant disrespect and raced into the jungle, where he performed a quick rite and slipped on the Mwae fetish. He screamed a shrill war cry, and used a *kere* to beat the enemy Ole senseless with such savage and merciless fury that the Ole has never returned to Naone.

A few days after the *bue* had ended, a small boy suddenly became gravely ill and for a while, everyone was concerned he might die. Wilson uses the spirits and the pharmacy of herbs and plants from the jungle to cure numerous types of ailments. His healing powers are legendary, but during times of sickness, the Rawe and Mwae are also called upon to vanquish the evil spirits that are believed to be responsible for spreading illness. The members of the cult treat pain with pain and sometimes beat the villagers for a week before Wilson is satisfied the sickness bearing demons have been banished from Naone. During times of illness, even members of the sect are sometimes targeted. If the Rawe or Mwae approaches them, they stand with their arms at their sides. If they're lucky, they're overlooked, but sometimes they receive debilitating injuries. Fortunately the combination of Wilson's spiritual and herbal healing, and the Rawe and Mwae wounding healthy villagers, led to the boy's full recovery.

Of all the times that the devil spirits are evoked, one of the most ruthless beatings occurs when a child has committed an offence that is socially unacceptable. The headstrong infant's hands and feet are bound together, and then to deter any further antisocial behaviour, the Mwae uses brute force when it publicly flogs the child with a switch of *nangalat*. This very rarely happens, as only serious crimes or a blatant breach of the most sacred of customs warrants such a severe form of punishment.

Chapter Thirty-Five

PARADISE

The chance to spend some time in the jungle away from Naone's cruel traditions and sometimes menacing atmosphere was just what I needed when Patrik invited me hunting. When twelve of us noisily slashed our way through a wall of constricting jungle, I didn't hold much hope of securing a wild bullock that was to be sold to raise funds for the local school. We were making such a racket, and travelling through the tangle of rainforest was so slow and so laborious, that I figured the *tabu taplava* leaves we'd thrown behind us for good luck would have little effect. I was carrying my three-piece takedown recurve bow and had been given the honour of taking the first shot, while Wilson's younger brother, Hutchine, carried a dilapidated "musket" as a backup. The excuse for a twelve gauge shotgun was a death trap which was literally falling apart. Its split stock was bound together with a strip of rag, and the remains of the trigger mechanism had rusted beyond recognition and ceased to work decades ago. A crude homemade lead ball replaced the birdshot in the factory loaded cartridges, which were fired by pulling back and releasing the ancient hammer manually to send the projectile screaming down the treacherously pitted barrel. Because of my addiction to breathing, and the likelihood that the musket might blow apart in the courageous user's hands, I kept what I figured was a safe distance from Hutchine.

Our disorderly approach disturbed plenty of wild fowl that erupted into flight in a flash of colourful feathers. For a while, we quietly tracked some reasonably fresh pig sign to a recently used wallow, but without hunting dogs, in such thick jungle, it was a virtual waste of time. We dropped into a dry riverbed, and as we climbed towards the crest of the island, we walked past an ancient stone that Naone's first inhabitants had worshiped. The web of noisy and excited chatter that broke out as everyone started talking about the archaic deity suddenly stopped when steaming cowpats that were scattered around the jungle floor shed a dramatic change over the mood of the hunt.

The cluster of men fell into a deepening silence when Hutchine slowed from a quiet crawl to a halt and pointed directly ahead of us. While a favourable puff of wind whispered across the rugged landscape and blew directly into our alert faces, I could barely make out the faint sound of animals browsing on the lush vegetation. Although getting a clear shot with the bow through such dense vegetation seemed unlikely, Hutchine motioned for me to go first while he followed closely behind. I kept glimpsing over my shoulder and was more worried about him letting strip at close quarters with the suicidal musket than I was about facing a charging bull.

It was relatively easy to stalk to within twenty metres of our quarry by crouching down and using the cover of the riverbed. Just as I was about to take a partially obscured shot through a small opening in the vegetation, the browsing bullock moved forward so that I could only see its stomach. While I was letting the bowstring back down from full draw, without any warning a thunderous roar erupted over my shoulder and a small cloud of bluish grey smoke flashed past my ear. The unexpected explosion nearly turned me inside out, and the hot blast from the shotgun rattled my brains and pounded a painful tune on my ringing eardrums. I was still gathering my bewildered senses when I took off with the others in hot pursuit of the fleeing mob of cattle.

Strands of stretching wire screeched in protest when the animals eventually ploughed through a fence bordering the sprawling paddocks that have been carved from the jingle in the centre of the island. For the next forty-five minutes we ran after a wounded young bull through small stands of trees and across acres of open ground. When another shot rang out, the agonizing cries that were a prelude to the animal's lingering death brought our scattered group together. The exhausted bullock had been chased beyond the limits of its endurance, and teetered, then finally collapsed into a shuddering heap against the base of a wild apple tree, which sent a shower of purple blossom floating to the ground. We'd performed dismally and were disappointed in ourselves for failing to execute a quick and clean kill.

The following evening, when the meat was cooked and sold at a fundraising gala, it was obvious that trouble was brewing. I felt wiped out by several shells of strong kava and wasn't interested in witnessing petty squabbling, so I decided to have an early night. Before I headed back to my hut, I agreed to join Patrik in the morning and hunt the pigs we'd tracked while we were hunting for a wild bullock. Past animosities between traditional enemies still simmer beneath the surface, and when several youths from central Maewo who were hopelessly drunk on a cocktail of sugar, lemons, and pharmaceutical alcohol picked a fight they found themselves on the losing end of a one-sided battle. Patrik quickly curbed the unwanted violence by laying out the ringleader with a single punch.

I awoke to the first pale light of dawn with a pulsating headache and wondered if Patrik and Hutchine had also fallen victim to the potent kava until excited barking, a knock on the door, and Patrik's trademark swearing told me otherwise. As we wove and slashed our way through the dense jungle and followed the eleven keen dogs to the top of the island, it proved to be a fruitless but interesting exercise. We stumbled across pillars of rock that were covered in lichen, mute monuments that made us remember the slain warriors who were buried beneath them. They cast a sombre mood over Patrik and Hutchine because the primeval headstones were more than just sleeping memorials and eerie time capsules that marked a life that had been violently cut short. The rocks had been piled high to prevent the warrior's spirits from haunting their cannibalistic killers.

With the prospect of securing any pork looking increasingly slim, we decided to walk across to the other side of the island and put the bows we were carrying to good use. Wilson had granted me permission to visit Naolata beach and to bow fish in the lagoon. After he spoke with the village elders, he told me that no other white man had been allowed to set foot on the sacred stretch of white sand for at least forty years. A group of Europeans who visited the *tabu* region during the nineteenth century gained an unenviable place in the island's history. While their wooden sailing ship traversed Maewo's shores, it was caught in a sudden and violent storm and dashed to pieces on the treacherous reef that fringes Naolata beach. None of the crew managed to survive when the pounding surf dragged them over the coral and washed their limp bodies up onto the shore. The following day a group of villagers from Naone who'd decided to go fishing were overjoyed when they discovered fresh meat was strewn along the beach. A messenger was sent back to Naone, then the whole village marched across the island and indulged in an orgy of cannibalistic feasting. Like other cannibals that dined on the white man's flesh for the first time, they'd never seen a pair of boots before and complained about the Europeans tough feet when they tried to eat their footwear, which they thought was a part of the sailors' anatomy.

We dropped down from the heart of the island and followed an ancient trail called Waswasa, which means stone, that derived its name when Naone's ancestors used it to visit the beach to compete in stone throwing competitions. Along the side of the track we stopped and drank the cool tasty water that filtered down the face of a huge *tabu* rock called Liara. The sacred water not only quenched our thirst, it also cleansed any evil from our spirits and our souls. Since time immemorial, Naone's inhabitants have trekked through the rainforest to worship Liara and to use the stone to communicate with the supernatural. Numerous crab burrows pockmarked the ground, and when we dug up the crustaceans, Patrik snapped off one of their claws then released the creatures so that over time their tasty pincers would grow back again.

The enticing sound of crashing waves rumbling over the reef quickened our pace until we burst from the jungle onto a pristine beach whose white sand glistened in the bright sunshine. I stood on the seashore wearing a huge appreciative smile as I gazed at the turquoise lagoon and revelled in the tranquillity of the isolated paradise. Before I could relax and absorb the timeless beauty, anyone who sights the beach for the first time must perform an unusual and energetic ritual. A blistering sun soon had sweat bubbling from my every pore as I ran for several kilometres from one end of the beach to the other to appease the ancestral spirits who guard the spectacular stretch of sand.

An incoming tide and the still air provided the perfect conditions for bow fishing. Hutchine strung his basic D shaped bow that he'd made from the tight-grained wood of the *mamalac* tree. After he'd tied a topknot in a cordage bowstring made from the inner bark of a *bangwa* tree, he passed me a *walacoco* leaf. We rubbed the sacred vegetation over my aluminium and his wild cane arrows to empower them with *basi* (supernatural power or a spirit), to prevent the fish we arrowed from swimming away, and to stop the arrow from falling out. Just as it is in Middle Bush, Santo, unless a newly crafted bow secures a kill with its first shot and the slain animal's blood is rubbed over the limbs to gain the animal's *basi*, the weapon is deemed useless and ends up as firewood.

While Patrik gathered enough shellfish to fill a twenty litre pail, Hutchine and I quietly waded into the tepid lagoon. As we slowly stalked through the water, we took special care to pick our way around the massive heads of delicate coral. Stunning multicoloured fish that were banded with all of the rainbow's striking hues darted for cover amongst the coral gardens. The latticework of light that danced on the water as the sunlight shifted across the enamelled surface and the pacifying beauty of the marine haven swayed my interest from killing to observing the vast array of sea life. Half an hour of later, when my rumbling stomach transformed me into a hungry predator, five beautifully marked fish succumbed to my arrows, while Hutchine added another six to our photogenic tally. The rising tide brought more fish into the lagoon, and when a good-sized black tipped reef shark slowly cruised past, I decided it was time to quietly get out of the water.

We lit a blazing fire and roasted succulent crabmeat in the red-hot embers while bananas and fish simmered away in a broken metal fishing float that doubled as a cooking vessel. The good company and feasting on the local delicacies in such an unblemished and remote environment filled me with an unforgettable sense of serenity and of total freedom.

Although we hunted all the way back to Naone without success, it was hardly disappointing as it had been a fantastic day. As we hiked through the jungle, Patrik pointed to where his ancestors had slain a mythical gigantic butterfly. The insect was so monstrous that it had taken over one hundred men to drag it back to the village. By the time we got back to Naone and shared out the remaining seafood amongst the others, the flaming sun has almost sunk beneath the horizon.

Chapter Thirty-Six

DEVIL FROM THE BUSH

We rounded off our enjoyable day by relaxing in the *nakamal* with a shell of exceptionally strong kava. When the intoxicating brew sent my mind spiralling into an abstract world, I gazed up to the night sky, to its outer sphere of darkness, and tried to imagine what lay beyond the infinite cosmos. Patrik seemed to be on the same inebriated wavelength while he stared intensely at me, then asked why a white man would ever want to live with Ni-Vanuatu in primitive conditions. Instead of giving him a short answer, I swayed the conversation to my initiation in Middle Bush, Santo, and to how at times I'd felt the overwhelming reality of the supernatural. My belief in the sacredness of the departed, and their role as *tabu* couriers who mediated with mortals, had grown stronger with each new experience. We talked about the spirits that existed above us, all around us, and in a different reality and discussed how I sought to experience something unquestionably tangible from what many consider to be an unreal world.

I told him I wasn't interested in pitting science against superstition or in ignoring rationale in the hope of experiencing a miracle, but that I wanted to capture a hint of the essence of how spiritual primitive peoples think, and to feel what modern life in western civilisation had eroded and rigidly separated us from. Patrik went over and spoke to Wilson. He returned and solemnly stated that tomorrow night I would experience immense spiritual power, then we drank another shell and slipped into a silent stupor.

I greeted the new sunrise with mounting anticipation and was surprised when what I thought would be a long and expectant day quickly lapsed into night. Wilson and Patrik had cut down a six-foot length of bamboo and kept their eyes locked forward to observe the *tabu* of never looking behind while they carried it through the jungle to the rear of the *nakamal*. I was confined to the *nakamal* for the initial part of the rite, and for forty-five minutes, Wilson's monotone chanting pricked up my inquisitive ears. Then when he suddenly stopped and the night was filled with a jarring silence, Patrik appeared and said, "It is time, Rick. Baro is here." The centuries old spirit of chief Baro had been summoned with the evocative chant and asked to enter the bamboo. Of all the spirits I could feel physically, Baro is the most potent due to his ability to lift people from the ground. A subtle moon rode high in the sky and cast a pale glow over a natural amphitheatre in the trees at the rear of the *nakamal*, where Wilson, Patrik, and two others stood in a straight line with the pole lying on top of their open palms. While I crouched in front of the men, in the dim light I could clearly see the inanimate bamboo come to life as it moved from side to side and up and down. Wilson asked Baro if he approved of a white man participating in the ritual, while I questioned the reality of the amazing spectacle that I was beholding, especially when the answer was in my favour.

Wilson hardly settled my already racing mind when he said in a stern tone, "If you open your eyes or the bamboo strikes your head, you will die. No matter what happens, you must hold on with all your strength." While the others held the pole in a vertical position, I gripped the base and was astounded by the hefty weight of the hollow tube. As we walked to a patch of clear ground, I grimly held on and kept my eyes tightly shut. When the possessed bamboo suddenly leapt into action without any warning, it would have been easy to succumb to sheer terror as the crazed pole threatened to hit my forehead. Baro's overwhelming power dragged, jerked, and pulled us in all directions with frightening intensity. I swore out aloud when I was briefly pulled up onto the tips of my toes, even though I was the tallest and was holding the very base of the bamboo. As we were twisted around like rag dolls, I felt a searing pain shoot up my spine when a sudden change in direction wrenched my back. A surge of adrenaline numbed my discomfort while I grappled with the pole and desperately fought to keep my head out of harms way. Then, in a commanding voice, Wilson instructed Baro to return to the spirit world. At that same dramatic instant, the bamboo suddenly returned to its natural weight and became light again.

In that brief and vulnerable moment, extra dimensions had been added to my thinking but boundless questions raced through my stunned mind. The supernatural and its inexplicable forces had just defied logic and had confirmed my belief in the existence of the afterlife in such a tangible manner that I couldn't doubt what I'd just felt. As a calm fell over the restless scene and I looked at the other men, they casually returned to the *nakamal* with a matter-of-fact attitude for a few shells of kava. I experienced a strange surge of emotion which ended in a feeling of absolute bliss and contentment. It wasn't from receiving a startling revelation that had just been sledge hammered into my consciousness, it was from being gifted a warming confirmation that our mortality wasn't the end of our spiritual being.

I was bursting with curiosity and wanted to bombard Wilson with a whole host of questions when he sat beside me, but I remained composed and contented myself to listening to him unravel the mystery of how he became a *kastom* man. His true name, which must remain secretive, translates to "devil from the bush." Whereas other *kastom* men on the island attain their powers through a lengthy apprenticeship, the forty-seven-year-old sorcerer realised his ancestors had determined his fate when a bearded old man, who was the potent spirit of Quato, entered his dreams and started gifting him *kastom* when he was just twelve. Over time, the spirit of Maewo's first paramount chief empowered Wilson with the ability to heal, to kill, and to be able to safely cross the invisible divide into the spiritual realm.

Wilson controls the most potent of the totemic elements, and while water gives life, a malevolent sorcerer can misuse the fluid to cause mass destruction. Although Wilson has the ability to kill, he uses his skills to nurture life and to heal and has declared that taking a life out of hatred or spite is *tabu*. Because his legendary powers are the most potent on Maewo, *kastom* men from the other villages seek his guidance whenever modern pharmaceuticals or their traditional medicines fail to heal an ailment or when *nakaimas* are casting disruptive and deadly spells. Quato made it *tabu* for Wilson to share his knowledge with other sorcerers, so instead, he willingly provides them with already prepared medicinal potions or exorcises wayward demons and blocks curses with his potent *basi* and expertise.

The villages from north and south Maewo have been bitter enemies for centuries, and even nowadays they sometimes treat each other with obvious contempt and mistrust. Any sudden bouts of sickness are often believed to have stemmed from poisoning or from black magic. Wilson combats the attacks by placing a sacred leaf alongside ailing villagers. Then, as a warning, the *kastom* man who inflicted the sickness becomes violently ill five days later, but never dies.

Theft is rarely a problem within Naone's selfless society, but it occasionally occurs in the other villages. The chiefs from neighbouring clans pay Wilson one woven mat to apprehend a thief when they bring the prime suspects to Naone and make them stand before a length of bamboo. Wilson calls upon the divine guidance of an ancient spirit called Din Din and asks him to enter the bamboo, which moves by itself when the haunted bamboo points towards the guilty party.

From somewhere hidden deep in the jungle, Wilson manipulates the spirit of a sacred rock to create wind, rain, and to control the sun. He also uses leaves, bark, wood, herbs, stone, and *tabu* water to heal a wide array of illnesses. To empower the water with *basi*, he sings over a coconut or bamboo cup filled with the sacred fluid, which a patient drinks and then washes over the afflicted area. Sometimes he holds a sacred stone in one hand and heals the sick by touching them with his other hand. To ensure his special gift will help future generations, Wilson is sharing his knowledge with Vera, his eleven-year-old son.

When I told Wilson I planned to catch the next available flight to Ambrym Island, the muscles in his smiling face suddenly knotted with concern. He warned me that I was about to enter the heart of a demonic beast. Right throughout the archipelago, simply mentioning man Ambrym can send shockwaves of fear through superstitious villagers. Wilson has used his powers to render man Ambrym's black magic useless and to curb the ritualistic murders he so despises when family members or victims are killed and cannibalised. I gratefully accepted his offer to provide me with two ancestral bodyguards and took serious heed of his warning to always carry the small but incredibly potent talisman he was about to prepare for me.

He told me an ancient *kastom* story that explains why Maewo's magic is far more powerful than Ambrym's. After an evil spirit had tried to kill all of Maewo's inhabitants, a woman with her own son and her adopted son were the sole survivors. She favoured her own child more than her other son, who grew to hate his spoilt sibling. When she sensed that the adopted child was becoming spiteful, she only taught him a fraction of the island's customs. The adopted son became tired of living with the favouritism and moved to Ambrym with only a small amount of *kastom* knowledge, which he passed on to each successive generation. This is one of the reasons why Maewo's *kastom* men have the ability to quash and diffuse problems when *nakaimas* from Ambrym misuse their powers.

The day before I left Maewo, Patrik and Wilson donned their traditional dress and posed for me while I took their photos at a nearby waterfall. They looked impressive wearing a woven mat called an *emba*, *sasa* leaves, and *karisa* leaves that sprouted like bushy tails and reached halfway up their backs. Bright red *dali dali* berries that can only be worn by men who have achieved their fifth grade added a splash of vibrant colour against a cascading waterfall which provided a stunning backdrop. When I tried to bracket the first few shots, my camera went haywire. Then each time I pointed the lens away from the *tabu* waterfall, it functioned perfectly, but inexplicably became inoperable again whenever I tried to focus on Wilson. He seemed bemused and toyed with my astonishment until he told me to try again. Then the camera worked perfectly.

Despite the numerous warnings I was given, I flew towards Ambrym's allegedly profane realm loaded with more questions than answers and kept pressing ahead in my search for unique customs and their true meaning. The dramatic spiritual power I'd felt on Maewo and the immeasurable contrasts within their culture still left me puzzled. Naone's blurred belief system ensures humbleness will always combat harshness, and that friendliness will always face ferociousness.

Chapter Thirty-Seven

WALL OF SILENCE

No one managed to discourage me from undertaking what most people considered to be a reckless and hazardous journey. Vanuatu is full of exaggerated misnomers, and one of the biggest is that active volcanoes are thought to be closely linked to black magic. Their ominous presence supposedly enhances magical powers, whereas the reality is that some of the most powerful centres for sorcery are void of volcanic landscapes. Another fallacy is that Ambrym's inhabitants are always engaged in doing evil and murderous deeds and they should definitely be avoided. Everyone I'd met from Ambrym during my travels had been kind, good-natured people, who'd readily encouraged me to visit their island.

When I exited the plane at Craig Cove airfield, the first thing I noticed was a distinct sulphurous tang that the volcanoes had cast into the air. Several genial villagers who were returning to nearby Woru village were already burdened with their own luggage, yet they offered to help carry my packs and asked me to join them. My welcome couldn't have been warmer when I was introduced to Woru's chief. He invited me into his home and offered me a bed and to provide all of my meals for fee. We chatted and joked like old friends until I showed him an introductory letter from the cultural centre, then his good-humoured mood suddenly changed and he made it clear in no uncertain terms that there was no way anyone on Ambrym would share their secretive beliefs. His abrasive words painted a clear picture when he said, "We don't need probing outsiders here on Ambrym or care who or what you are. Even the prime minister comes here to do his business, then he must go." I lamely replied that I had no desire to document anything unless the *kastom* was willingly gifted, but it didn't help to restore his previously cheerful manner.

That night, while I was drinking kava with the locals in a *nakamal*, I found out that my honest and frank approach couldn't have come at a worse time as just a few days before my arrival, a *nakaimas* from another village had tried to kill the chief. Earlier in the year, two French filmmakers had persuaded a gullible boy to provide them with footage of a *tabu* ritual without realising the penalty for divulging guarded rites to an outsider is death. When the villagers found out that *kastom* had been breached, the boy was killed and the Frenchmen were extremely lucky to have escaped from the island unharmed. Once word of my occupation raced through the village, most of the inhabitants became indifferent, but in a friendly rather than obnoxious way. There were still plenty of villagers who couldn't have been more accommodating, and when I'd had enough kava and went to leave the *nakamal*, they warned me never to walk alone at night or to sleep by myself in an unlocked hut because of *nakaimas* who were using black magic.

Wilson had warned me that there would be elders who were so attuned to the paranormal, they would sense the presence of the two spiritual bodyguards he'd provided me with. The next day, when I met a weather beaten geriatric who looked to be in his eighties, it made me further appreciate the ability a mortal has to mediate with the supernatural. Our cheerful conversation flowed for the first couple of minutes, then when I slipped my hand into my pocket and started fondling my talisman, the old man's expression suddenly changed. It was as if he'd seen a ghost when first he looked to the left and then he glanced at my right shoulder. Then without provocation, he screamed, "Get away! You go! Now!" I apologised for upsetting the perceptive elder, and walked away thinking about how Wilson had mentioned the two ancestral spirits protecting my wellbeing would be perched on each of my shoulders.

Because the chief was already on edge, the last thing I wanted was for my presence to add to his problems. Although I'd arrived at a bad time, and anyone with my occupation would never be embraced, everyone still treated me extremely well. Apart from hitting an anticipated wall of silence whenever I spoke about *kastom*, I couldn't have hoped for a better reception. It was obvious that if I travelled to north Ambrym, where tradition is at its strongest, and I tried to document rituals, it would've been a futile and even dangerous exercise. In the north, where several pagan villages have resisted Christianity and most of modern society's trappings, a few old men still wear penis sheaths, but I had no desire to work where my mere presence as a photojournalist who was interested in *kastom* would antagonise people.

After I'd spent two days at Woru, I could sense it was definitely time to leave. And when I tried to take a leisurely fourteen kilometre walk along the coast to Sanesup village, an insistent taxi driver offered to drop me off seven kilometres up the road for free. Once I started walking, travelling incognito as a tourist was easy and enjoyable. Whenever I passed through a village, the locals shouted out the "Ambrym call" and yelled, "Come *kai kai*, friend" ("Come and eat, friend"). By the time I entered a small hamlet at Sanesup, which is renowned for its acts of dumbfounding black magic, the excessive hospitality left me feeling contented and bloated. Once again the welcome was overwhelming, and I was fed huge servings of local food and given my own hut, where I slept alone for several nights unharmed. The *nakaimas* who performs magic was visiting another village for a few days, so instead of waiting for him to return, I walked along the east coast to Lalinda to go hunting and to visit the active volcanoes.

When I left the main road and met chief Wilfred Backlulu as he was climbing up the track to Lalinda, he was so hospitable that I almost expected the rutted path we were following to turn into red carpet. Especially when I made it clear from the onset that I had no intentions of delving into *kastom*. He insisted I stay with his family in his leaf hut, and within an hour he'd organised the island's most experienced guide to take me hunting wild bullocks and had arranged a pig hunt when I returned.

Later that afternoon, Wilfred introduced me to my guide, thirty-year-old Jimmy Penuel, who is a veteran of numerous scientific expeditions where he helped French vulcanologists from ORSTOM to monitor the seismic activity while they studied erupting volcanoes. Jimmy had a skeletal build and high cheekbones that made his gaunt face look even thinner than it really was. In a modest tone he mentioned that he'd abseiled into Mount Benbow's boiling crater to take samples from the lake of molten lava and asked in a good-natured way if I was aware of the numerous dangers of climbing a volcano. I told him I was novice and asked him to give me the rundown.

The extreme landscape wasn't to be treated lightly, as over the last century, the brooding volcanoes have erupted with catastrophic force and caused numerous geological disasters. Pulsing flows of glowing magma have overflowed from the caldera wall, then raced down the valleys until they spilled onto the coast. Anything in the path of the red-hot lava, which has included several villages, has been annihilated with devastating effect. Clouds of ash and a toxic fog of noxious gases constantly belch from the sacred volcanoes. If strong ash falls are accompanied by a tropical downpour, it can create cataclysmic mudflows that sweep down the hillsides. As well as the obvious physical dangers, the volcanoes create a destructive acid rain that wreaks havoc on local crops and contaminates the villages' water supplies. After Jimmy gave me a thorough explanation of the numerous potential hazards, and said that realistically we'd have to be extremely unlucky to run into trouble, I was rearing to go.

As well as facing the potential dangers of the unique environment, everyone voiced their concern over me bow-hunting bulls that had an aggressive reputation. No one shared my confidence in the capabilities of my bow, especially those who'd had firsthand experience of trying to escape a charge from a wounded bullock when the landscape was treeless. From the stories I was told about narrow escapes, I knew there would be no margin for error and that good arrow placement was vital on such a large and dangerous animal.

Because I only hunt for sustenance and out of necessity, I asked Wilfred if a team of villagers would be prepared to climb up to the ash plains to help us carry back the meat. He readily agreed that sumptuous beefsteaks would be a welcome addition to the villagers' diet because a devastating cyclone had destroyed most of their bananas, which are the village staple, and the gardens were still in recovery mode. We made plans to leave at first light the next morning, then several boys would follow us later in the day.

Although a dreary looking sunrise greeted us the following morning, and billowing plumes of grey ash choked a bleak looking sky, I still relished every step of the amazing climb up to the caldera on the crown of the island. The landscape changed dramatically, from trekking through luscious jungle to dropping into the base of deep walled crevices where we followed prehistoric looking lava flows. We scaled a waterfall of solidified lava, then walked along a dormant river of ash that had swathed a serpentine path through the rainforest until nature's geological phenomena took my breath away. When we climbed up to the edge of a vast ash plain, I'd never seen anything like it. I imagined the desert wilderness had been created by cataclysmic forces that should have destroyed a world that had somehow managed to survive. It was as if the devil himself had created the lunar wasteland to spite the mythical Garden of Eden. We were about to enter the godforsaken gateway to a fiery hell of belching ash, molten misery, searing yellow sulphur, and corrosive beauty that held me utterly spellbound.

The heavy squalls of acidic rain that were blasted into our squinting eyes by gale force winds were typical of the region's sudden climatic change. While stifling fumes swirled around our heads, we followed a small creek that had been aptly named the ash river. Then we crossed a maze of volcanic gullies until we'd almost reached the base of Mount Neritaten. Jimmy stopped and asked me if I wanted to take a potentially dangerous shortcut. The air was thick with churning gases that gushed from the bowels of the earth. Crossing without facemasks was risky. But because there wasn't a bluish tinge to the swirling vapour, he explained, we should be ok. After I agreed to follow his every move, we decided to take the quickest option.

We were several hundred metres from the edge of the crater when Jimmy suddenly dropped to the ground and pressed his face into the ash-strewn earth, so I did the same and held my breath for as long as I could. Our luck had suddenly taken a turn for the worse when a deadly blue cloud of lung searing fumes engulfed us. The squally weather proved to be our saviour when a blast of strong wind blew away the volcano's rank breath. During the lung-bursting climb to reach the crater, we dived to the ground four times and waited for the pungent air to clear. Each time I saw Jimmy suddenly drop, a gnawing concern that was growing inside me faded when I felt a gust of wind come to our rescue and whip the fumes away.

As I stood on the far side of the crater, where the blustery weather safely dissipated the toxic gases, through red-rimmed and watering eyes, I watched the raw power of the earth's molten core humble me into insig-nificance. Neritaten was a living entity that slowly gasped for air before it noisily exhaled its vulgar breath. With each pulse of its heart, which beat with an eerie lifelike rhythm, blood red lava splattered and boiled deep within its bowels.

We climbed and leapt across a labyrinth of guts and ridges to reach the rim of the crater on Mount Mbwelesu. Jimmy threw all caution to the incessant wind and walked along the edge of the gaping chasm. I followed in his footsteps and balanced along the bladelike rim, but it put me on such a physical and mental knife-edge, that I dropped down several metres from the fragile looking lip. When Jimmy asked what I was afraid of, I told him flirting with death for the sake of a better view was way too reck-less for my sense of adventure.

I'd never seen anything that compared to the incredible spectacle we witnessed once we'd climbed to the top of the volcano. Mount Marum loomed way below us and was so beautiful, it almost seemed surreal. Right along the length of its vast crater, white puffy gases that looked like cottonwool gently rolled up and over the lip, then billowed into the valley as if they were flowing from a massive inverted waterfall. The whole landscape that swept to the north resembled a scene from some prehistoric fantasy world. A wandering cave man or a herd of grazing dinosaurs wouldn't have looked out of place. I was to mesmerised to even start to think about hunting, until Jimmy's keen eyes picked out a huge black and white bull down on a lava field about two kilometres away. Because of its sheer bulk, I was convinced it was a gigantic rock until it started moving and walked towards a forest of *lemanman* palms.

As we dropped over the side of Mount Mbwelesu and crossed another ash plain, it was obvious there was a healthy population of animals in the area. Numerous cattle had passed through the flat area we chose as a campsite and had churned the volcanic soil so that it resembled a well-used stockyard. We pitched Jimmy's three man tent, which offered us comfort and protection from a bitterly cold rain that had soaked us to the bone. When Jimmy returned from gathering water from a small creek one hundred metres away, he told me the others weren't coming from Lalinda to help us carry the beef back. He said he'd made *kastom* to prevent the precious meat from being wasted, then in an apologetic tone he said I wasn't to take his actions personally, and that there was no charge for being guided because no matter how hard I tried, the hunt would be unsuccessful.

Dusk was still several hours away so we took advantage of a brief break in the weather and stalked through a primeval palm forest filled with small undulating gullies. I stopped and nocked an arrow just five minutes walk from camp when I heard the distinct sound of an animal urinating. I slowly sidled along a bank and followed a trail of hoof prints around a sharp corner. I then inched forward and peered into a small depression, where no more than ten metres away stood the largest feral bull that I'd ever laid my eyes on. A red and white mountain of beef was standing broadside like the proverbial barn door and offered a perfect shot at its vitals. As I slowly pulled my bow to full draw, I was mindful of the warnings of how dangerous these bulls were if they're wounded, so I took careful aim and gently released the string. When I watched the arrow harmlessly pass between the animal's legs, I was dumbfounded as my subconscious had told me the easy shot had been well placed. The startled bull stumbled forward a short distance, then stopped to look back over his massive shoulder. I stretched the limbs of my bow to full draw a second time, and after a smooth release, I instinctively felt the shot was good from the instant the arrow left the bowstring. My head shook from side to side in utter disbelief as I watched the razor sharp broadhead fly over the bullock's back. The monstrous bull snorted in anger, shook his imposing looking horns, then lumbered along the gully, crashing away unscathed. There was no way I could provide a rational explanation for missing the easy shots, and I knew that if I shared the bizarre experience with anyone, I'd be open to ridicule. To make sure the toxic gases we'd breathed in hadn't rattled my brains or clouded my vision and judgment, as a double check, I fired two arrows into the middle of a hand-sized target from fifteen metres away.

The ancestral spirits Jimmy had called upon favoured the bulls for the rest of our luckless hunt, and we returned to our campsite just at dusk. When we took off our wet gear and stretched out in the tent, I noticed that most of the toes on Jimmy's left foot were missing. After I tactfully asked him how he'd lost them, he said he'd rolled into the fire when he was a child. A friend of mine in Port Vila who came from Ambrym was missing all the fingers on his left hand from where his own grandfather had cut them off and used them for black magic. Because there weren't any of the horrible scars that normally result from a burn, it looked like Jimmy's toes had been amputated with a blade.

Throughout the night a howling wind drove slanting sheets of rain into the tent with so much force that it was hard to drift off to sleep. Just after midnight, when I looked outside, the glow from the volcanoes had painted the underbellies of billowing clouds that were bunched together with a spectacular blood red hue. The slivers of cascading rain created an incredibly beautiful illusion that made it seem as if the heavens were aflame with a liquid fire that danced across the sky.

The next morning, when Jimmy asked me if I'd heard any screaming during the night, I told him I couldn't hear a thing above the sound of the wind and his snoring rattling around the tent. Before the introduction of Christianity, humans were sacrificed by throwing them into the molten lava to appease the guardian spirits of the volcanoes, and during the night, the terrible shrieks of those tortured ancestral souls had torn Jimmy from his sleep. An early morning hunt produced the same unsettling outcome when I missed the bigger of two gargantuan bulls that were grazing along the edge of the rainforest with three perfectly positioned, textbook shots. The area was a bow hunter's paradise, but I resigned myself to the fact that someone, or something, had decided it wasn't going to be my day.

Jimmy had never travelled across the eastern ash plains, and I was keen to try and arrow one of the pigs that inhabit the jungle flanking the eastern rim of the caldera. So instead of retracing our steps, we decided to take a different route back to Lalinda. As we leapt across a tangle of crevices and carefully wended our way through a jumble of clefts that had been scribed by millennia of violent eruptions, we were wary of steaming fumaroles and hidden vents. We moved at a quick pace but it still took us three and a half hours to cross the arid volcanic desert. There were plenty of massive footprints in the black sand, and when I first glanced at them, I mistook the marks for smallish cattle prints. On closer inspection, however, I was amazed to see that a gargantuan pig had passed by.

We hunted around the edge of the caldera, then headed towards Mount Otapanleplep without sighting any game. Several pigs cut our scent, then noisily crashed off through the jungle as we quietly walked back down through the rainforest towards Lalinda. I didn't care about our strange hunt being luckless. To be able to step off the only world I'd ever known, back into what felt like an archaic environment that was trapped in a primitive time warp, had been an incredible experience. I'd snow skied down beautiful volcanoes in New Zealand, but they lacked the intense and primal atmosphere of Ambrym's tormented interior. From the moment I set eyes on the hellish but enchanting landscape, bringing home the cursed beef had never really mattered.

Chapter Thirty-Eight

SPIRITUAL COMBAT

Christianity has had a superficial impact on the whole of the southern Ambrym. Most of the ministers who preach in the name of the white man's god have blended their Christian faiths with the island's pagan beliefs, so that they can serve the community with a heathen hand and with the hand of the Lord. Ambrym is full of striking contrasts, and like all of Vanuatu's traditional people's, the mystical island's *kastom* orientated society holds the pig in high esteem. Boars are ritualistically slaughtered during grade taking ceremonies called the *maghe*, but ironically, the highly prized creature that's reared to attain personal prestige and power is also deeply despised by the island's inhabitants, because wild pigs have reached plague proportions.

Although hunting feral pigs with dogs is hard work, it's pretty routine and really just a matter of going through the motions. In 1990, Wilfred's son, twenty-seven-year-old Joe Manuel, and another boy who was renowned for his prowess as a hunter were nominated by the villagers to try and reduce the rapidly growing pig population. For six months they slept on a beach below the gardens that were being raided and decimated with alarming regularity by the animals. Both hunters reverently attended church every Sunday, but during the rest of the week, they relentlessly hunted the marauding pigs.

The day before I'd arrived at Lalinda, Joe and his team of six dogs had managed to kill twelve pigs. Nowadays he still virtually hunts full time, and during a typical day in the jungle, he catches an average of five to seven pigs. When he agreed to take me hunting, I figured we'd have to wait for the atrocious weather that we were being bombarded with to pass over, but it failed to dampen his enthusiasm and he told me to be ready in the morning. After a fitful night's sleep that had been interrupted by rolling thunder and howling winds, I awoke to an equally miserable dawn and joined Joe to appease the spirits of the hunt by stomping on wild kava leaves which we'd thrown in front of us. Then we placed a wild kava flower behind our ear to keep the malevolent devil called Lesipsip at bay while he roams the jungle.

Torrents of blinding rain saturated us while we walked for two hours along the coast to reach our hunting ground. The monsoonal weather became so intense that even the shelter of the dense jungle offered us little protection from the elements. Although the trying conditions made it virtually impossible for the dogs to ground scent, Joe remained optimistic and hacked a track through the waterlogged vegetation to way above the gardens. Our sodden efforts proved fruitless until we found the water-filled mark of a huge black and white boar Joe had been chasing for months. Before we headed back down towards the garden where Joe figured the boar was sleeping, for added luck, we trampled more wild kava and asked for supernatural guidance. Instead of heading in a straight line, we took an erratic course and zigzagged away from the main trail to increase our chances of disturbing a dozing animal. While we crawled on our hands and knees through a highway of gloomy pig tunnels and slashed through impenetrable growth, somewhere along the way I lost my hat. As I followed behind Joe and his slashing machete, the rain washed the toxic sap from the freshly cut vines down my face and into my eyes. By the time a chorus of chaotic barking brought us to a sudden halt, the vision in my bloodshot left eye was so clouded that all I could see was a murky haze.

Joe casually leant against a tree and tried to listen through the din of the heavy rain as it muffled the dogs' trail barking. The fleeing pig scampered up a leading ridge with all of the frantic dogs in tow, then when it obviously ran out of steam, it did an about face and came charging back down the hill until the dogs hit it about fifty metres from where we were standing. We slid down a steep greasy bank, squelched along a small ravine, and then climbed back up to the forest floor using a thick vine. Our machete ended the piercing squeals of an average sized boar that was vainly trying to escape from the grip of the dogs' vicelike jaws. No one in their right mind would have considered carrying on hunting in such hideous conditions, so we called it a day. During the walk back to Lalinda, Joe stopped and carved a notch in the trunk of a coconut tree alongside the road, to chalk up another kill to his mind-boggling tally.

The following day, in kinder but still stormy weather, thirteen-year-old Randy and four younger boys led me into another area. Most of the dogs had had their tails removed at birth in the belief it would increase their endurance and hunting prowess. The young hunters compensated for their lack of strength with their speed and stamina, and as we sprinted from bail to bail, they prevented five pigs from ever digging up their gardens again. They're afraid to try and stick large ferocious boars, so they hack them across the spine with their machetes or spear aggressive animals from a safe distance. Although numerous pigs roam the jungle, the unrelenting hunting pressure has made the intelligent animals extremely wary. The combination of expert hunters and the finely honed skills of their talented dogs will never win the war to exterminate the rouge swine. Unbeknown to me, I was also about to enter into what has always been an eternal duel when I decided to head back to Sanesup to watch a *nakaimas* perform black magic.

Throughout the archipelago, where societies retain law and order solely with spiritual policing, the most important reason for performing inexplicable acts of black magic in public is to create social and cultural cohesion. If your whole morality is bound in worshiping the combined forces of the natural and supernatural, when commoners witness a sorcerer performing amazing feats that defy all logic, not only does it raise the mystical esteem of the *nakaimas*, it also encourages villagers to strictly adhere to *kastom's* guidelines. On Ambrym, magicians called *bungau* (*nakaimas*) manipulate the spirits to incite awe and trepidation, which in turn, produces an unquestioning faith in *kastom*. Because of this, most of Vanuatu's societies remain free of constricting prisons or the teams of disciplinary police that industrial civilizations require to maintain social harmony.

The ability to manipulate supernatural forces is undoubtedly Ambrym's most famous cultural phenomenon, and it's because of the *nakaimas* who blatantly abuse their powers that the island has gained such a fearsome reputation. To be able to handle dangerous spirits who are capable of doing both good and evil deeds requires immense care and the observance of strict *tabus*. When I arrived at Sanesup and met Joe Talin, he agreed to let me witness firsthand his mind-boggling sorcery, which I hoped would prove to me again that there wasn't a defining line that separated the worlds of the living and the dead. Joe was muscular, in his mid-twenties, and carried himself in a self-assured manner that made him look dignified and how you'd expect a sorcerer to be. He told me he needed time to carefully prepare both himself and his assistant, Joemai Aimibilujup. If extremely *tabu* magic is performed, sometimes weeks of abstinence and ritual are required, but Joe only needed to refrain from sex and twenty-four hours' grace to get ready.

Joe remained loyal to his secretive sect and offered all sorts of open-ended answers when I started talking about the secrets of black magic. He claimed that all of nature, the power of the sun, and inherent knowledge gave him his abilities. When I said that *nakaimas* on the other islands evoke spirits and conjure the powers of evil, he became increasingly agitated and snapped at me when he said that nature was solely responsible for his magic, mostly through the power of *tabu* leaves, which I would see with my own eyes. After he gave me a thorough interrogation, he reluctantly agreed to let me photograph and write about his powers on the condition I stayed at least ten metres away from him while he performed the magic.

In well documented cultural shows that were held at Port Vila, *nakaimas* have performed amazing feats to stunned audiences numbering in their thousands. Sorcerers who can defy gravity have levitated, wriggling fish dripping with saltwater have been caught after casting a line and a bare hook into a dusty patch of earth and grass, and shocked onlookers have witnessed plants miraculously growing and producing fruit in a matter of seconds. A length of wild cane that was placed inside the shell a *navele* nut inexplicably shrunk before an amazed audience, and assistants are killed and then brought back to life. The list of incredulous feats goes on and on. Acts that science deems impossible are possible, but the most *tabu* magic is never performed in public, like when a sorcerer supposedly decapitates a villager or slices off his tongue then restores the severed body parts without any ill effect.

The next day, I was excited at the prospect of witnessing feats that defy all the orthodox laws of science, defy the laws of nature, and defy the will of the white man's god—not as an advocate of the devil, but as a fascinated and unprejudiced observer. A group of villagers patiently milled around a *natsaro* (dance ground) under the sweltering midday sun while we waited for Joe and Joel to emerge from the jungle. The crowd of onlookers had devoutly merged at the *natsaro* with the same reverence that's attached to an uplifting religious pilgrimage. There wasn't any novelty factor attached to the magic. This was an opportunity for the villagers to find solace in their primal beliefs.

A hush fell over the murmuring crowd when Joel appeared from behind the trees with a large conch shell in his hand. He was adorned with a crude skirt of dried banana leaves that barely covered his shorts, and wore a light smear of almost invisible face paint made from the resin of a *tabu* tree. Joel walked in a full circle, placed the shell on the ground, then without any dramatic theatre, Joe materialized from the jungle holding a two metres long feather shaped *namele* leaf, which is similar in appearance to a coconut leaf. Joe waved nature's magic wand, then he gently stroked the top of the shell three times. I looked on in utter amazement through the viewfinder of my camera when I saw the shell jump up to the tip of the leaf. Joe briefly held his arm above his head to emphasize the dangling shell, before he slowly walked away and disappeared with the swaying shell into the backdrop of jungle. To have witnessed the sudden surge of divine energy that lifted the shell from the ground was truly astonishing.

Several minutes later, Joe reappeared from behind a rustling curtain of pandanus trees with the effigy of a black and white sea snake cradled in a *lap lap* leaf. Then Joel emerged holding a breadfruit leaf and left with the wooden snake mysteriously suspended from the tip of the leaf.

The gloomy jungle seemed to provide a corridor to the past, where the *nakaimas* mingled with ancient forces before they performed their equally astounding next act. Joe spat a mouthful of dark green leaf onto a wild kava leaf that he'd placed on the ground. Then he laid another one on top, with its long stalk facing in the opposite direction of the first leaf, and repeated the process until ten leaves were piled on top of one another. Joe plucked a wide-eyed, reluctant looking ten-year-old boy from the audience. The child lay face down with his stomach on top of the pile of leaves, arched his supple back, and reached behind and grabbed his ankles. The magicians stood on each side of the boy, gripped the stalks protruding from beneath his abdomen, and with the combined forces of nature and the paranormal, they lifted him from the ground and carried him thirty metres.

For their grand finale, the *nakaimas* led the crowd to the nearby road. Both of them wore woven coconut leaf baskets decorated with large yellow veined *tabu* leaves, and while they stood forty metres apart, Joe mimicked throwing twelve large *navele* nuts to Joel, who pretended to catch and put them in his basket. The faces of the watching crowd showed they perceived the enlightening magic as being perfectly normal, but that it was also to be held in the highest regard. When all of the nuts were gone Joe ripped open his empty basket, but when Joel did likewise the nuts spilled onto the ground in front of the captivated crowd. This stretched way beyond sleight of hand or clever trickery. I wallowed in the awe of the incredulous magic, but I needed something more concrete where I could experience and feel the raging energy of a supernatural spirit firsthand.

I doubted the sorcerers would accept my proposition to conjure up a more boisterous, more tangible spirit, but after a moment of deep thought, Joe agreed. By now only two villagers, the *nakaimas*, and myself remained. Joel ushered us to the edge of the *natsaro* and told us to wait while Joe vanished into the forest and prepared himself. He reappeared ten minutes later chewing a cud of dark green leaves as he carried a sturdy sapling and a *namele* leaf into the centre of the *natsaro*. He drove the stick into a bare patch of soft volcanic earth and created a hole about two hundred millimetres deep, and then he placed the slightly bulbous stem of the leaf into the hole. After he spat the mouthful of leaves into the hole, he gently tampered around the base of the *namele* stalk six times.

Joe pointed to a powerfully built villager in his mid-thirties and challenged him to pull the leaf from the soft ground. When he grit his teeth and tried his utmost to dislodge the leaf the dancing chords and striations in the startled man's straining muscles were no match for his spiritual adversary. It was incredible, as no matter how hard he tried, the leaf never budged.

To make sure I wasn't being hypnotized, I'd carefully avoided any eye contact with either of the *nakaimas*. Joe wore a stern look when he nodded his head and motioned with his hand for me to try and pull out the leaf. I spat into my palms, rubbed my hands together, and gripped the leaf at the height of my bent knees. Then I used my legs, my back, my biceps, and every other muscle that obeyed my command and pulled for all I was worth. When I couldn't shift the leaf, this went way beyond the sphere of anything I'd ever experienced. This was an intimate liaison with the supernatural. Although wrestling with a bamboo pole in the dark with my eyes closed on Maewo had been an amazing experience, it hardly compared to a one on one battle with a possessed unyielding leaf that was planted in porous soil.

When the ancestral spirit engaged in a spiritual tug of war, I was shocked, amazed, and determined. No matter how hard I tried, for the first few strenuous seconds I couldn't shift the leaf. By channelling every ounce of my energy, and with dogged determination, I slowly started to pull the leaf from the ground. The next instant threw me into sensory overdrive, when an unfathomable force reached up from the bowels of the earth, and with a violent jerk, it wrenched the *namele* leaf back into the soft soil. I felt as if I'd been on the receiving end of an unexpected snake-bite. To feel such a sudden surge of supernatural power was frightening and worsened the initial impact of being unable to pull out the leaf. I gave it everything I had, and then with one angry tug I ripped the *namele* leaf from the ground.

I looked at the leaf in my hand, then swore aloud and kept mouthing off a continual string of profanity. This went way beyond an honest person unwittingly deceiving himself or being deceived by having some hidden vortex in his subconscious manipulated. I'd just experienced an undeniable proof that spirits really existed and that the human consciousness is eternal. Even the strongest sceptic would've been unable to rationalize and debunk the sheer power of the spirit, whose impact would be ingrained in their mind forever. Joe shot me a wounded glance that said his ego had been shattered, and he looked astonished that his beliefs had betrayed him. Joel appeared slightly unnerved and looked at me as if I was some sort of demigod. While I slowly came to terms with what I'd just experienced, I kept swearing over and over. I'd radically defied the laws of Joe's forces of nature. This wasn't supposed to happen. No one has ever pulled the leaf from the ground. But then no one has ever been initiated into, or had divine alliances with, so many tribes throughout Vanuatu before. The less powerful had never beaten the masterful when they evoked spirits from the supernatural. Wilson's talisman had worked its own magic, and Maewo's water had just transformed the spirit who came from Ambrym's inferno from hell into a harmless, listless cloud of steam. A cloud that I was floating on in a suspended state of euphoria.

As a double check, I grabbed the stake, dug a deep hole, inserted the leaf, and compacted the earth for several minutes with the blunt end of the pole. Then using only my finger and thumb, I effortlessly pulled the leaf from the ground. I still struggled to come to terms with what I'd just experienced, so I walked over to a waist high shrub in the jungle, and although the tree had a good rooting system, ripping it from the volcanic soil was easy.

While the dumbfounded *nakaimas* did their best to hide their astonishment, I was grateful the crowd wasn't around to witness me undermining their mystical status. I knew that once word spread along the village grapevine, there could be serious repercussions, so I thanked the sorcerers, grabbed my packs, and walked back to Woru where I booked a seat on the first available flight off the island.

Chapter Thirty-Nine

MYSTERY BECOMES HISTORY

Unfortunately there are Ni-Vanuatu with misguided attitudes that for reasons of their own, despise the cultural centre and the very people who are trying their utmost to preserve the archipelago's diverse culture. I was given the right to publish the purpose of one of Ambrym's most sacred customs, but the informant insisted the rituals were to be included in this book rather than stored in the cultural centre's archives. Vanuatu's primitive secret societies are gradually vanishing. Now that the dazzling lights of mankind's foundation are dimming and flickering, and then burning out, after a lot of soul searching, I decided to write the following because unlike the diminishing lives and beliefs of those tribes who are contained within these pages, the images and words in this book will withstand the rigours of time.

Ambrym is host to a diverse array of well-known traditions. Around 180 sand drawings comprised of circular scribes and complex geometric designs form messages that depict numerous aspects of *kastom*. An experienced artist never lifts his finger from the sand once he's started drawing the complex pictures, which are also used to communicate with fellow villagers.

Slit drums that are made from the breadfruit tree called *tam tams*, which vary in size from being handheld to towering instruments that are six metres tall, are elaborately decorated with elongated faces with pronounced noses, protruding chins, and large circular eyes. A single *tam tam* may have many faces, and the number of these is dictated by the carver's rank. In the past, if a craftsman produced more faces than his grade allowed, the penalty was death. Tree fern carvings that are stylised with the same bizarre features keep watch over *natsaros*, are placed in gardens to induce fertility, and stand guard in the villages. Both the *tam tams* and tree fern carvings are believed to be occupied by ancestral spirits.

Ornate masks that are initially decorated with a smooth paste and then painted over in bright colours made from minerals, vegetable dyes, sap, and charred shells, are sold in the tribal art shops at Port Vila. These have been crafted under a special *tabu*, as any masks that are used during rituals are normally destroyed. Those that are worn during northern Ambrym's Ole Rom dance are always demolished. The spirit of the person wearing the mask is believed to become embodied in the fetish, and if they don't destroy the mask, their spirit becomes divided and renders them incomplete.

Nowadays several villages have bastardised the Rom by transforming it into a contrived tourist attraction. Outsiders will never get to experience the true Ole Rom and will always have to settle for the artificial version because like most of the archipelago's traditional dances, the real Rom is empowered by the supernatural. It also plays a vital role in a dark and sinister rite, where the dancers become aligned with the devil.

Every man that wears the Rom fetish during the dance is a *nakaimas*. Over the past few decades, the stringent ritual that is used to become a sorcerer has become dangerously relaxed, and anyone who possesses the knowledge can become a *nakaimas*. Initiates are taken into the jungle, where they survive for five to ten days on unhygienic, germ-infested food which is cooked over the flames of what is known as a *"tabu* fire." While they live off of a diet that would test the hardest of stomachs, the initiates' mental, physical, and spiritual endurance are pushed to their absolute limits.

Those who are respectful strive for the tenth and highest grade by following the correct protocol over a long period of time. In northern Ambrym, most of the elderly *nakaimas* reside with their wives and families, but they always dine alone after they've roasted their meals over the flames of a secretive *tabu* fire. There are those who recklessly ignore caution and blindly obey their demonic master for the sake of instant personal gratification. They worship death and destruction way too readily, because without the adequate knowledge and careful preparation, they usually die young. It's paramount that they fully understand both the good and evil aspects of their satanic apprenticeship, as the devil they embrace has no qualms about attacking and killing them. If a sorcerer is unable to counter a spiritual onslaught from their master, their death is guaranteed. *Nakaimas* also have worldly worries to contend with because the practitioners of black magic often target other sorcerers in a bid to gain supernatural supremacy and to become spiritual tyrants.

When an initiate pledges his allegiance to the *tabu* fire, learning to kill in order to nurture the devil with the blood, the spirit, and the soul of his sacrificial victims is first and foremost. The first time an aspiring *nakaimas* leaves the *tabu* fire, he must kill a relative, drink their warm blood, and eat their raw heart. It's imperative that this is done without remorse or repulsion as the devil is testing the initiate's resolve. To prepare themselves for the kill, sorcerers perform the *ambulip* rite, and for three days, they sing the victim's name into the smoke of their *tabu* fire. This is why the natives who worship a pagan religion throughout Vanuatu have two names and is why an individual will very rarely divulge their true *kastom* name to a stranger.

A *nakaimas* must physically kill his victims, which he does by burning the bones of a previously murdered villager over a *tabu* fire. Then he gathers the jet-black ash and uses it to poison his victim's food, or he sometimes sprinkles it on their head, but in most cases it's blown at the sacrificial villager. It's paramount the victim never sees the sorcerer when he blows the powder, especially if the victim's gut is going to be replaced with leaves. If this happens, after the *nakaimas* disembowels his prey's stomach, the wound will never heal properly and the victim won't be able to exist as a zombie for the next five days then suddenly die again.

Whenever a sorcerer plans a kill, absolutely nothing is left to chance, and the meticulous preparations are made with the precision of a military assassination. An experienced sorcerer always evokes demonic forces to help an initiate commit the murder for his first *ambulip*. *Nakaimas* are believed to be able to look into the future and to know the exact time and place to kill an unwary victim. Once the spirit of the devil is called, its hatred demands feeding and can be only nurtured through the spilling of blood. The demon is like a ticking time bomb that requires its sustenance within a given time, which is usually before daylight. If the premeditated murder is unsuccessful, another unfortunate villager has his life cut short, and if that fails, then one of the *nakaimas* must become the sacrifice. They turn upon themselves and kill another member of the cult, otherwise the sorcerer who evoked the devil will die. A high-ranking *nakaimas* with his own *natsaro*, who has made numerous sacrifices to the forces of evil, can feed the spirit at a much slower rate. As it is, on the other islands, the ultimate victim is a newborn child, as eating an infant's heart greatly increases a sorcerers powers.

When a *nakaimas* blows the powdered ash, his victim becomes completely disorientated, hopelessly weak, and walks around in a confused trance. Most sorcerers use a *nul nul* to put their victim to death, but those who have achieved higher grades have immense power and can fly, transform themselves into animals, open locked doors, and perform a multitude of physically impossible feats to make killing much easier. Whenever a woman is murdered, before she dies, *masing*, which is another satanic rite, is used to rape her. Powerful sorcerers can kill by using the power of the spirit, and in a multitude of ways. The preferred method is to place a *tabu* leaf over a container. The leaf begins to drip blood. And when the bowl is filled to the top, the victim suddenly dies. During an initiate's first nauseating taste of a relative's twitching heart, his eyes briefly widen as he literally becomes empowered by the spirit of one of his own flesh and blood.

The brutal history of the Rom dance has been forged through death, heartache, and terror. Its purpose is to evoke a malevolent ancestral spirit until all of the dancers have become possessed by the archaic demon. During the Rom, the most potent sorcerers lead the lines of dancers who diminish in authority until the lowest ranking *nakaimas* trails at the rear. All of them are completely shrouded with cloaks of dried banana leaves and wear beautifully decorated masks. When the dancing ceases, the dancers become crazed predators, and in a flurry of rustling dried banana leaves and rattling nutshell anklets, they ruthlessly attack the villagers with the clubs they carry during the dance. Blood must flow to provide an appetiser for the malicious spirit, and then when the ritualistic beatings cease, all of the *nakaimas* live together for one week in a *natsaro* hidden in the jungle. While they sit around the flames of a *tabu* fire, the fate of a sacrificial villager is decided. Then the unlucky victim is killed and cannibalised. The teeth on the Rom mask symbolise teeth that will tear into and eat human flesh, and the red colouration on the headdress represents blood that the sorcerers will drink.

It's crucial that a *nakaimas* washes his hands after he handles human ash or he will fall ill and possibly die. Once he has killed one of his relatives, he becomes the devil's eternal disciple, as there is no way to exorcise or cleanse his permanently tarnished spirit. Those who are akin to the devil live in a world of eternal darkness, where in order to survive, others must always die.

Chapter Forty

ANCESTRAL ARCHERS

While I was on a flight out of Ambrym, the aftereffects from my visit to the mystical island rippled through my body like a stone hitting water. I was as strong as an ox mentally, but physically, I suddenly fell apart at the seams without any warning. Concentric circles of searing pain radiated through the whole of my quivering body, then the agony slowly subsided until a strange feeling of listless wellbeing washed over me. By the time the plane had landed at Norsup airport, I'd recovered sufficiently from the short-lived ailment to explore Malakula Island.

The first wave of mariners who travelled from Europe to Vanuatu's second largest island also worried about their health. Malakula had such a fearsome reputation, that the sailors nicknamed the archipelago "The Cannibal Islands." Tales of men being mutilated beyond recognition and cannibalised by the Small and Big Nambas tribes who inhabit the rugged island failed to deter some of the archipelago's earliest and hardiest colonists from settling on Malekula. The two tribal groups derived their names from the respective sizes of their penis sheaths called *nambas* and deserved their formidable reputations. If a foreigner, a tribal enemy, or an unwelcome visitor entered the native's bloody territory, they usually suffered the same horrific fate and were instantly killed and cannibalised. Sometimes if an enemy's body wasn't eaten, it was treated with contempt and degradation and was hung upside down until it rotted.

Europeans and neighbouring clans never entered the dangerous Big Nambas territory in the north unless they were invited. The Big Nambas' unrelenting hostility quarantined them from the outside world and ensured they kept a scourge of depopulating epidemics at bay right up until the 1930s. Although they had an intimidating reputation when it came to confronting the colonials and warring clans, they quickly succumbed to an unstoppable and invisible enemy, the white man's disease. Catastrophic plagues of gonorrhoea, whooping cough, influenza, and other previously unknown ailments rapidly decimated them. Then they faced another blight when the gradual acceptance of outsiders encouraged an influx of zealous missionaries to push into the previously treacherous country, where they began to fervently erode millennia of tradition.

Nowadays the Big Nambas are renowned for their friendliness, and although their ravaged beliefs are undergoing a revival, they only wear their customary dress during important rituals and to entertain tourists. Their traditional stronghold used to be Amokh village, which was located on a lofty plateau, but this has been abandoned for the luxury of a less demanding lifestyle down on the coast. Even though Christianity has had a pacifying influence and their customs have been slowly destroyed, the last documented act of cannibalism occurred amongst the Big Nambas in 1969.

The Small Nambas live in remote hamlets dotted throughout central and southern Malakula and on Tomman Island, and unlike the Big Nambas, some of the clans have had limited contact with outsiders. Nowadays the tribes who used to be hostile enjoy a peaceful existence, but brutality is sometimes still an integral part of their tribal law. Just like the Big Nambas who were their traditional enemies, they have also become a casualty of alien beliefs and of modernization. Although outwardly they appear to be reasonably sophisticated, as traditional dress is only worn during rituals, beneath their civilized exterior, the Small Nambas are still clinging to their diminishing culture.

While I mingled with the locals at Norsup, I was told that Biten village was plagued with wild pigs, its people still adhered to *kastom*, and they were expert archers. I decided to pay them a visit, and an hour later, I was riding on the back of a pickup filled with bags of rice and sacks of flour. For several bone jarring hours we rattled along a crude road and called in at villages to drop off supplies to storekeepers and so the talkative driver could keep everyone up to date with the latest gossip. In dusk's closing light, we turned off the dusty road and headed inland for a few kilometres along a rough four-wheel drive track.

The Toyota clawed up a hill to where Biten is nestled on a slope near the fringe of the extremely rugged southeastern interior. In the gloomy light the primitive huts looked small and insignificant against the vast and verdant beauty of the mountains. I received an impassive welcome, and although no one grimaced, not one of the villagers smiled. Although I'd arrogantly arrived without an invitation, it's rare for most primitive cultures to turn away a respectful stranger. When I learnt that a white man had never stayed in the hamlet before, it explained why the villagers were indifferent and looked bewildered when I asked if I could live with them for a while. They seemed unsure of how I'd cope with their simplistic way of life, so I quickly waylaid the chief's apprehension by explaining how I'd lived with primitive tribes around the world while I documented their customs.

While we sat and talked, the chief's positive reaction to a few carefully worded questions I asked about Biten's traditions was encouraging. The dignified patriarch with grey hair and a deeply lined, tired looking face had no qualms about talking about *kastom* and told me that documenting his people's threatened beliefs was paramount. Like so many other indigenous peoples who'd suffered from the indiscriminate massacre of their culture by the church and outsiders, he appeared to be mourning the loss of his identity and yearned for the past. He warned me that black magic is so rampant throughout all of Malakula that some Ni-Vanuatu believe the island is where *nakaimas* first learnt their dark craft. Amongst the Small Nambas clans, both men and women take numerous grades called *nimangki*. They slaughter sacrificial pigs during the *nimangki* so that the men can become chiefs and to ensure both sexes have an affinity with the supernatural and are well placed in the afterlife. Because some of his peoples beliefs can be extremely brutal, the chief said that for my own safety, I must respect every *tabu*. But where *kastom* permitted, I was free to ask questions and to take photos. Then he called over a seventeen-year-old boy called Ramon, who looked impish and full of life, and told him to accommodate me in his hut and to help me with my work.

If I wanted to bridge the gulf from being an outside observer to a fully-fledged member of the tribe, it would take much more than a fleeting visit. To get a true insight into their fascinating and complex lives, first I'd have to feel the cutting edge of a bamboo knife. My biggest drawback was having a foreskin, because unless I undertook an initiation where I was painfully circumcised, even entering the *nakamal* was *tabu*. Anyone who recklessly or unconsciously violates *kastom* by entering the sacred dwelling without having first undertaken the necessary ritual faces dire consequences. The guardian spirits recognise women and uncircumcised men as being feminine trespassers in a strictly patriarchal domain, and for such a serious breach of tribal law, the maximum penalty is death. I discovered that no one had ever documented a traditional bow hunt or the significance of the beautifully crafted bow a boy uses during his initiation. Without hesitating, the chief granted me permission to gather information on both subjects. Ramon readily agreed to organise a traditional hunt, where all of the archers would wear a *nambas*.

That night, while I stretched out on a comfortable bamboo slat bed, I tossed and turned and was unable to sleep. The humid air was choked with an angry drone from a cloud of malarial mosquitoes that swarmed around my net. As I listened to their incessant whine, my mystery illness snuck up and pounced. It made me shake and groan for the next half an hour. When it slowly dissipated, I decided to ask Ramon in the morning if we could cover the initiation bow first, as I was exhausted and needed a day of rest before we went hunting.

The next morning I woke up feeling slightly groggy, and as soon as I pulled back my net, I was instantly bombarded by the hordes of mosquitoes. After a filling breakfast of fire roasted taro, Ramon and I headed up to the jungle, where he sat me down and explained the importance of his initiation bow. He started with an adolescent's transition to manhood, which is of immense significance and is indelibly etched into a young boy's mind when he undergoes his circumcision rite. The primitive surgery is performed in the *nakamal* without anaesthesia and takes five men to hold a child's arms, legs, and head, and one to hold the boy's penis while a *kastom* man cuts the foreskin. Throughout the operation, the initiate must show great bravery by remaining totally silent to prove to the gods he's strong and is worthy of being embraced by his ancestors' spirits. If he can endure the pain in silence, it's said to build character and inner strength and shows the elders he has the courage to face anything adulthood will throw at him.

For the next five days, he and his family survive solely on fire-roasted yams and are forbidden to drink any type of fluid. The initiate remains confined in a secluded *tabu* hut called the *nabaua* with other boys who also undertook the painful ritual. While they stay in the *nabaua*, they are harassed, humiliated, and subjected to numerous hardships. Although they are only five to eight years old, and the experience is both harrowing and demanding, they cope remarkably well, as *kastom* and the rigours of daily life have already instilled in them a resilience and maturity that stretches way beyond their years.

Rows of ancestral skulls are stored in the *nakamal*, and men who possess the ability to call upon their forefathers' supernatural powers, worship and manipulate the remains. Once the boy's have completely healed, they leave the *nabaua* and return to the *nakamal* to make a ceremonial bow. They may be young, but they are already accomplished bowyers and have fashioned weapons that they learnt to shoot and hunt with. But none will match the significance of the bow they are about to make, which plays a vital role in their first *nimangki* grade.

Under the watchful eyes of their male relatives and the mystical inner eyes of their ancestors' skulls, the young artisans create bows that are a true work of art. How and of what the weapon is made from is a closely guarded secret, and if anyone ever divulged the inherent techniques to outsiders, the village elders would sentence them to death. Before and after the young craftsmen work on the bows, they must carefully wash their hands, because if the *tabu* isn't observed, their testicles will keep growing to an enormous size until they suffer an agonizing death.

A basic D shaped bow, which is flat on its belly and rounded on its back, is covered with a black and white chequered weave made from dyed leaves. One hundred and fifty millimetres of the limbs are left bare from the end of each bow tip, then two faces that resemble a spirit are moulded onto the bow using a mixture of vegetable fibre and clay. The tusks from sacrificial pigs that were slaughtered in a previous *nimangki* are inlaid into the faces, and the effigies are painted with natural dyes. When the sacrificial blood of a pig is spilled, it feeds the spirits. The spirits reciprocate by empowering the tusks, which give the bow supernatural power. A completed bow will always remain an initiate's most hallowed possession and is stored in the *nakamal* with the hordes of ancestral skulls and other *tabu* objects. The esteemed bow is of such great importance that it determines the very purpose of his existence in the natural and supernatural realms.

Once the bow is finished, the initiates hold their ceremonial weapons while they dance in the *nakamal* to the primal throb of a *tam tam*, and to the resonant singing of their elders. It's a proud moment in the boy's life, and it's the first and last time he will ever shoot his bow. At what and why he fires an arrow must remain *tabu*. The twang of the bowstring sends an arrow into flight that shoots down the door which had previously blocked the archer from entering the spirit world. A sacrificial pig is killed, and from the moment the animal's blood flows onto the sanctified ground in the *nakamal*, the boy secures himself a place in the supernatural realm. At that instant, he's no longer considered a child nor will he be treated as one, and despite his youth, even his own mother must show him absolute respect and treat him as an adult.

During each successive *nimangki* rite, the bow is held while the villager performs a sacrificial dance before a pig is killed. A wild cane arrow which is tipped with a black palm arrowhead is nocked and carefully drawn, but it's never shot. If an arrow is accidentally released, it's believed the bow will break and the archer will die a horrific death from supernatural forces. The bow is so sacred that if a woman breaches *tabu* by even catching a glimpse of the ceremonial weapon, she suffers a similar fate. But her demise is physical, at the hands of the village men.

Chapter Forty-One

BOWHUNTER'S PARADISE

Late in the afternoon, while we were returning to the village, a chorus of frantic barking faded into the distance as the hunting dogs went through their daily routine of chasing feral pigs. The marauding swine were sneaking into the gardens under the cover of darkness and enjoying the fruits (and the vegetables) of the villagers' hard labour. A cyclone that ravaged the plantations earlier in the year with soul-destroying efficiency had made it difficult for the villagers to eke out a subsistence existence, and the last thing they needed was scavenging animals pillaging their remaining crops. From the sound of things, the elusive pigs had strapped on their running shoes, left the dogs in the starting blocks, and had once again won the daily race in their bid for freedom.

No one took any notice or bothered to chase after the barking. It would've been a wasted exercise because the wily pigs have run the hunting dogs ragged by memorising every available escape route. The battle-scarred dogs had been half starved to hone their hunting instincts, and most of them carried horrific injuries that were in various stages of healing which had been inflicted by ferocious boars. As well as being ravaged by their prey, the packs of savage wild dogs that roam the jungle also fight with the dishevelled canines if the two cross paths. The terrible brawls can cause horrendous and sometimes fatal injuries. When Ramon thought about the pigs destroying the gardens, he shook his head in disgust. Then when he asked if I was up to going for a hunt in the morning, I told him I was feeling a lot stronger and could hardly wait to help him wage war on the animals.

It wasn't very long ago that a different type of warfare was once a vital part of Biten's fascinating history. Caman Soum committed the last act of conflict related cannibalism in the early 1960s. Biten's oldest inhabitant, Tom, claims and looks to be one hundred years old, and his posture has been so stooped by time that he resembles a human question mark. He's proud to have killed many enemies with his bow and to have dined on their flesh when intertribal clashes were rife. In the past, some of the Small Nambas clans followed the strict custom of closing their eyes when they consumed their victims. While a warrior dined on a slain enemy and sank his teeth into a whole arm, he would sometimes bite into a tendon. This would caused the suddenly animated limb to slap him in the face. The horrified cannibal was convinced the victim's spirit had returned to seek revenge and threw down the arm, letting rip with a piercing scream as he sprinted into the nearby jungle. Nowadays, birds, fish, flying foxes, pigs, and feral bulls are the only animals that fall prey to the villagers wild cane arrows.

"The astounding accuracy of the natives" is probably one of the most misused misnomers when it comes to describing Vanuatu's primitive archers. Their inconsistent nocking and anchor points and the unpredictable aerodynamics of different sized, shaped, and weighted arrows provides way to many variables to maintain consistently tight grouping. They shoot off the top of the hand by grasping the bow where it instinctively feels right, which adds another variable to the accuracy equation. Because of the erratic flight of their primitive arrows, most archers find it extremely difficult to hit a small target beyond twenty metres. Ten metres is normally the maximum range where any type of consistent accuracy can be expected. If you take into account their simplistic equipment and the shooting techniques that are used, many of Vanuatu's primitive bow hunters are exceptional shots.

Ramon, Remo, Kaleb, and Itif were about to rely upon powers that transcend man's limited physical capabilities to improve their aim. Tomorrow morning they would call upon the spirits of ancestral archers and ask them to direct their arrows with divine guidance. Despite their youth, the sixteen- to eighteen-year-old boys had observed the *tabus* of abstaining from sex and refraining from drinking kava the night before a hunt numerous times. I was warned that carrying money and talking about snakes is also strictly forbidden and that even saying "snake" would guarantee a luckless hunt, as Demismara, the evil *kastom* devil, sometimes inhabits the reptiles.

While dawn crept through the darkness and slowly cast a misty paleness over the awakening landscape, I peered outside into an almost cloudless sky. I swatted and swore at the annoying clouds of mosquitoes that dive-bombed me from every angle like miniature kamikaze pilots. Ramon and the other boys' day had started much earlier. They were virtually naked and wore *lap lap* leaf penis sheaths that were held in place with a *talbengamous* vine that they tied around their waists. To stave off the biting predawn chill, they hugged their shoulders while they traipsed through the jungle to the *nakamal*, by following a well-hidden path that centuries of select tribal traffic had formed. The young hunters were lathered in sweat when they'd finished appeasing the spirits with an energetic dance, then they felt their way through the cavernous gloom of the dark jungle and headed back down to the village.

As we climbed up through the last of the upper gardens and the waking birds started to sing and chatter, every noisemaking creature in the rainforest stirred from its slumber and joined in nature's early morning chorus. When the boys stopped to inspect a patch of fresh pig rooting amongst their damaged crops, I really felt their anger when they shook their heads and swore in disgust. Although I was hoping to see what they could do by only using their bows, we were hunting with a pack of five dishevelled looking dogs. The whining finders were excited by the fresh sign and ploughed their noses along the recently turned soil, then raced towards the chaotic weave of forest. We were heading towards an area of jungle called Loweregh, which we hoped would be lousy with undisturbed game. No one had ventured into what the boys had described as being a bow hunter's paradise for the past six months, as the villagers had focused on hunting the marauding pigs that lived near the hamlet.

The previous cyclone had overpowered the geography of the hunter's oasis with catastrophic force, and turned what had previously been a four-hour slog over a well worn track to a prime hunting ground into a tangle of impenetrable vegetation. Our machetes hacked and slashed for hours, while the dogs kept barking and chasing numerous pigs in all directions without any success. When we climbed to the top of a calf-cramping ridge, a look of reverence spread across the boys' faces. We gave three half-buried rocks which marked the ruins of the ancient *nakamal* a wide berth, because beneath the stones lay the bodies of high chiefs. If we had walked on the *tabu* site, it would've been a heinous breach of *kastom*. By midday, we'd cut a track to the top of a wide and near vertical gully. I gazed across the canopy of a beautiful rainforest that blanketed the island's wild and virginal heartland with a mixture of vivid green colours. The succession of sharp ridges and abruptly tumbling valleys that lay ahead of us seemed endless.

Way below us, the Lewesainere River looked like a silver slash that snaked its way through a sea of emerald forest. While we hung onto small vines and saplings, and slid and vaulted towards the river, without warning, my stamina rapidly started to wane. At the bottom of the sheer face, we plummeted over a small drop and splashed into the clear shallow river. Its waters teemed with crayfish, which the boys arrowed with ease. Then we gathered *navele* nuts, and cut the tasty pith out of *nambagara* palms. After Ramon expertly started a fire by rubbing a stick over a shaved slab of dried wood, we roasted the succulent crayfish on the end of the black palm arrowheads and ate like ravenous kings.

Once we'd refuelled our bodies and felt refreshed, we followed the swathe the lazy flowing river cut through the jungle. Ramon pointed to a *nevenboatnats* tree, and then he exited the water and cut into its trunk with his machete. The other boys joined him and rubbed their cordage bow-strings, made from the bark of a banyan tree, across the oozing sap to keep them supple. The boys' bows were the same size and design as Vanuatu's other primitive bows, and I was surprised to learn that a ritual isn't per-formed when a hunting bow is crafted from the *nataroph* tree. Biten's arrows are easy to distinguish from the arrows that are used on other islands by the dried inner bark from a ground vine called the *natelevous*, which is wound around the top of the arrow shaft and glued in place with spots of blood-coloured resin from the *namalere* tree.

Twenty minutes later, we left the riverbed by clambering up a wind-fall and entered a flat expanse of reasonably open jungle. Fresh animal tracks were everywhere in the churned soil, so we waited for the luckless dogs to join us after they had gone on another drawn out and futile chase. As soon as the jaded canines found us and put their noses to the ground, they went berserk. Just a few minutes later, their hysterical trail barking echoed through the trees until their feverish tempo intensified when they'd obviously pulled up a fleeing pig. When the sound of rasping barks, pained yelping, and angry scoffing let us know they had the animal bailed, with a flurry of pumping arms and legs, the boys sprinted towards what sounded like a chaotic brawl.

I was suddenly besieged by my annoying illness and felt too weak to follow, so I sat down and patiently waited. Ramon was the first to return fifteen minutes later and was so ecstatic, he was unable to wipe the huge grin off his face when he clutched his testicles and said, "Ball pig. Himi big fella ball pig." The others weren't far behind him and climbed down to the riverbed with a massive boar swinging from a pole two of the boys carried between their shoulders. While Ramon relived the hunt for me, he was still pumped from the excitement. When the boys had arrived at the bail, the irate boar was furiously spinning and slashing with his menacing tusks. It tore one of the dogs' upper lip in half, then lifted its snout under another dog and gave it a deep jab in the ribs. As the rest of the wary dogs danced around the boar and waited for the right opportunity to latch onto an ear or to grab under a front leg, they prevented the archers from taking a safe shot. When the pig decided he'd had enough and broke from the dogs, two well-aimed arrows punched their way through its thick hide. The mortally wounded animal charged through the undergrowth with the dogs in hot pursuit and collapsed into a quivering heap fifty metres from where it had been arrowed.

Ramon and Kaleb lit a fire each, and while they waited for the flames to burn down, they extracted their black palm arrowheads which had snapped off in the boar's wounds. Then they doused the barely flickering fire, ground up pieces of charcoal with a rock, and made a viscous paste by mixing the powder with their spittle. They were bursting with pride when they moved to a clear patch of jungle and used the paste to anoint their faces and bodies with patterns that they spontaneously designed themselves. Ramon transformed a thick piece of green bamboo into a *tam tam*, then to show their ancestors the hunt had been a success, both of the hunters inserted the retrieved arrowheads into the back of their hair. Because the arrowheads had secured a kill, they were embodied with the boar's spirit and would be used again back at the village to empower new arrows for the next hunt.

While Kaleb pounded out a monotonous beat on the makeshift *tam tam* and sweat leached from his every pore, Ramon clasped his bow and tirelessly danced for over an hour until a sheen of perspiration glistened on his coffee-coloured skin. They traded places, then Kaleb took centre stage to appease the spirits and to thank them for their supernatural guidance during the hunt. Finally he stopped dancing, and the drawn out ritual was over.

Ramon breathed life back into a smouldering ember so that we could recharge our systems with the boar's roasted heart, liver, and kidneys. After we pulled off most of the large blood sucking lice from the pig, we divvied up the butchered pork, threaded it over sturdy saplings, and carried the meat over our shoulders in the traditional manner. When the dogs hit two average sized sows while we were following the river downstream, we cut back into the jungle and stuck them with our knives. We had more than enough meat to carry, so we kept the dogs with us and started the long trek home.

When the sun slipped beneath the canopy of the jungle and fireflies started flitting around our heads and formed dancing constellations in the twilight sky, they seemed to heighten the boy's already happy mood. An hour later, I felt violently ill and incredibly weak as we groped our way along a wide path in pitch-black darkness and was relieved when we eventually dropped down to the village. *Kastom* required us to give the chief a couple of legs of pork, and then the rest was divided out equally amongst the appreciative villagers.

To take a pig with a bow in thick jungle is a big call for any hunter, let alone for semi-naked adolescents who are armed with primitive bows. During subsequent hunts when the dogs weren't used, the expert hunters stalked with steps as light as air and moved as silently as falling rays of sunlight when they arrowed pigs. With the passing of each day, my fluctuating health went in and out with the tide. Still, one afternoon I agreed to join Ramon the following morning to go bow fishing in a nearby river. I'd arranged for a truck to take me back to Norsup the following day so that I could visit the hospital to make sure I wasn't suffering from malaria. The erratic symptoms differed from my previous bouts, but because the disease can attack the body in numerous ways, I didn't want to take any chances.

Chapter Forty-Two

SICKNESS OR SORCERY?

In dawns breaking light, we walked through the jungle for a leisurely hour, then we dropped down onto a gravel beach alongside the Nauwevis River. The crystal clear water looked like shimmering liquid silk as the rising sun sparkled on its surface and offered the perfect conditions for us to get our feet wet with some ancient angling techniques. To ensure the stunning stretch of water remains well stocked, tribal law safeguards the river's big eye (a type of fish), crayfish, and eels from being overexploited by only allowing a bow, a spear, or a line to be used.

When I slipped into the gentle current with Ramon, his instinctive movements were as fluid as the velvety water parting around our shins. We felt our way along the rough gravel bottom with bare feet and crouched low to the water as we slowly moved upstream. Ramon froze for a moment when he spotted several fish that were too busy feeding in the shallows to notice our presence. Then he moved with the stealth of a heron and crept forward ever so slowly to narrow the gap until he was sure of making a good shot. His bow stretched to full draw, the bowstring hissed through the air, then the arrow cut through the water with a hollow plopping sound. The wild cane shaft twitched violently from side to side when the barbed arrowhead sliced into a big eye's glistening silver belly. Ramon lifted the gasping fish from the water, then quickly pulled out the arrow. He looked ecstatic as he clamped his mouth over the big eye's full lips, bit down hard, and suffocated the flapping fish until it ceased to struggle. A look of reverence and appreciation had spread across his face while the fish was slowly dying. The brief ritual was an important part of his moral code, because the spirit of the dead fish that had been killed in the unhurried but customary manner had now empowered his bow for the rest of the hunt.

It took Ramon an hour to stalk through the shallows and arrow seven tasty looking big eye, and once the initial rite was over, the other fish died in a much more merciful manner. Ramon's teeth crunched down on the top of their heads, but he took special care not to rupture their bulbous eyes, which are full of a foul tasting fluid.

We had more than enough fish to eat and to share with Ramon's family back at the village, so we waded upstream towards a patch of wild cane growing alongside the bank. Ramon motioned for me to wait while he silently moved across the ankle deep water to the cluster of cane. Once the warming rays of the sun pierce the surface of the river, eels sometimes sunbathe amongst the weave of growth and provide an easy shot. As

Ramon stood motionless, only his eyes shifted while they meticulously scanned the water for his quarry. When he was satisfied that none of the fish were visible, he carefully parted the strands of cane with a nocked arrow, just as a mother would part a child's hair while she was looking for lice. Several minutes ticked by, then the supernatural guidance of his ancestral spirits helped his arrow find its mark. A slime covered eel writhed and squirmed as it coiled its snakelike body around the shaft of the arrow that had pinned it to the muddy riverbank.

It had been a textbook shot, and needed to be because eels are particularly hardy fish. If they're struck in the body or tail, they often flee downstream and are usually lost when they seek refuge under banks, beneath rocks, or amongst submerged logs. Although the eel was going to taste great when we roasted it in the embers of a cooking fire, by anyone's standards it was a bit of a tadpole. Ramon looked disappointed and was determined to try for something bigger.

Big eyes darted for cover in a shimmering blur when Ramon probed under rocks with an arrow to try and feel for eels. When his experienced eyes picked out a hole in the riverbed, he quietly told me to move a few metres upstream. Then with the diligence of an archaeologist unearthing a priceless artefact, he slowly and patiently dug away small portions of the entrance so as not to muddy the clear water. He painstakingly widened the hole bit by bit, then he stood back and waited. Several minutes later, the head of an inquisitive eel slithered forward to check out the intrusion, then it quickly retreated into the sanctity of its burrow. With endless amounts of patience, Ramon stood stock-still until a pair of lips, then a pair of beady eyes, slowly edged their way to the entrance of the burrow again. Only this time, the small eel was greeted with a black palm arrowhead that sliced through its gills.

While Ramon made a fire and started cleaning the fish, although I'd felt malaise and lingering tropical diseases can hit with frightening sudden intensity, I hadn't expected to collapse alongside the river. Ramon looked deeply concerned when he shook my shoulder, tried to coax me to my feet, and said, "Rick! Get up! Get up!" To put his mind at ease, I said, "I can't. Leave me for a while. I'll come right." The jungle began to waiver, and then it started doing a bizarre and nauseating psychedelic dance when the tips of the trees swept the sky's rippling belly. My senses roiled as my mind spiralled back to visions of my childhood. In a matter of minutes, I went from being really bad to worse and was unable to move, so I focused on the current of the river. As I listened to the soothing tune of the life-blood of the land, I could hear myself mentally humming to its timeless song and wondered if my time on earth was drawing to a close. For the first time in my life, I felt the jungle had become a green jail and that I was imprisoned by an unyielding cage of towering trees. I could hear myself moaning while my turgid mind transformed the calming effect of the babbling waters into nature's digestive juices, which began to corrode my sanity. Then I started drifting along the river through the bowels of the jungle and was convinced I was being embalmed in its acids and about to be turned into a stinking pile of fetid excrement. When the river contorted itself into a gigantic snake and the hiss of the wind ruffled leaves sounded the serpent's warning before it was about to sink its massive venomous fangs into my sweating flesh, I was sure I was about to die. I was vaguely aware of my surroundings while I floated in a surreal world, which was filled with bizarre hallucinations that slowly softened and finally faded. I swore out aloud, and then I told myself to move. I dragged my trembling body from the ground before my subconscious nightmare had a chance to revisit me. I can barely remember stumbling back to the village then collapsing into bed in an exhausted heap. During the night, when I shook from head to toe with a brain rattling fever, I downed four antimalarials which temporarily staved off the illness.

As I lay in bed and listened to a rooster stretch his wings, clear its throat with a short gurgling sound, and then herald the sunrise with a hearty crow outside my door, I wondered if something more sinister than microscopic protozoan's or bacteria were responsible for my illness. From the moment I'd pulled out the *namele* leaf during the black magic performance on Ambrym, I'd felt a little strange. In Pidgin English, the sorcerers are called *"man blong posen"* (man who uses poison), so I had every reason to be suspicious. Irrespective of what was responsible for my sickness, I needed to get to Norsup hospital straight away. During the night, the driver of the truck had sent a message to let me know his vehicle was going to be used to hunt wild bulls and he couldn't make it until the afternoon. My condition was symptomatic of having cerebral malaria, where twenty percent of sufferers die. The impaired consciousness, the delirium, and the weird neurological functions weren't to be taken lightly. I decided to try and make it to the main road, where there was a chance that I might be able to flag down a passing vehicle.

Just getting out of bed was a struggle. I was too weak to even lift my packs, let alone carry them, so Ramon and Kaleb shouldered my gear while I staggered towards the road. Each time I collapsed, I stubbornly picked myself back up, but toppled over again after several minutes of swaggering down the trail. I was grateful that this time there weren't any bizarre hallucinations whenever I was sprawled on the ground and slowly gathered my strength. Because the Small Nambas are a hardy people who are used to self-reliance, the boys didn't know how to react to seeing a white man in this condition and left me to cope in my own stubborn way. Time after time my legs buckled, and time after time I stood back up and refused to stay down like a boxer who'd taken too many blows but kept clawing back up the ropes as he refused to submit to defeat. I pushed my mind and body into an unfamiliar threshold, where I experienced an unbearable acidic pain that made it hard to think straight and crippled my movements. Ramon disappeared into the jungle when the end of the road was in sight, and returned with a ceremonial bow that was covered in a thick wrapping of *lap lap* leaves. When he said he'd made it for me as a gift, I jokingly told him to make an arrow as well and to put me out of my misery with a shot between my eyes. I was so exhausted and the agony was so intense that I couldn't take another step, so I crawled the final twenty metres to the main road, curled up into a ball, and slipped in and out of consciousness.

I was told later that for no reason, when Ramon had helped me onto the back of the pickup, I was abusive and swore at him. While I flopped around in a semiconscious state amongst a pile of blood soaked beef, one of the villagers who was riding to Norsup was afraid that I might fall off the back of the truck, so he banged on the roof and yelled at the driver to stop. When they sat me in the front seat, I collapsed face first into the driver's crotch. When I pulled myself back up, my limp head rolled from side to side and kept shifting from rattling against the door to slumping into the disgusted driver's lap. Although I must have looked like death warmed up, when we reached Norsup, any feelings of sympathy and concern about my condition were way down the driver's list of priorities. First he unloaded the meat, then he washed the blood off of his pickup. He took his time and stopped off at the local cooperative store to buy sacks of rice and flour. When a dresser from the hospital came out of the store and saw how seriously ill I was and told the insensitive driver to take me to the hospital immediately, there was a sudden sense of urgency.

By western standards, the hospital was a ramshackle collection of battered looking buildings that ran on a shoestring budget and could only afford basic and often unhygienic equipment. But for all of its shortcomings, it was still a welcome sight, and I was grateful that they had a doctor, as sometimes years can pass where a nurse or the matron are the only qualified professionals. Test after test came back negative. There was no stiff neck or locked jaw that lent towards cerebral malaria or overly dark urine to suggest kidney failure or black water fever. Because of the crude equipment, making an accurate diagnosis was extremely difficult and left the doctor with no other option but to treat me for malaria. When I was placed in my own room and I kept drifting in and out of a soul burning fever, hallucinating again, all that mattered to me was staying above ground and out of a coffin. My turbulent mind raced back to when I was an embryo, then my life began to flash before my bloodshot eyes. A neighbour from my childhood stood on our doorstep singing a Christmas carol while she held a burning candle under her chin which melted her flesh away until only her skull remained. I wanted to run but my eleven-year-old legs were rooted to the spot as the skull dripped with blood and laughed and taunted me until other haunting visions entered my mind. The last thing I saw was old Ni-Vanuatu men wearing *mul muls* made from beaten bark, and other natives from a more primitive era who were stark naked, standing over my body as they chanted and spat all over me.

Once my thoughts became lucid again, I woozily watched a man in his mid-thirties who was wearing a white coat read the chart hanging on the end of my bed. I obeyed his instructions and lifted my tongue while he looked down my throat, then I asked him what the prognosis was. According to him, I had tonsillitis. When I asked him who he was and told him I'd had my tonsils removed when I was five years old, he said he was the cook. Several hours later, another more convincing impersonator wearing a white smock walked in and read my notes. She told me to take four antimalarials immediately. Luckily I'd had the foresight to monitor how many pills I'd taken because if I'd followed her instructions, I would've overdosed and may well have died. Throughout Melanesia, for despondent youths who want to commit suicide, overdosing on antimalarials is the preferred method. When I asked her who she was, she said she was the cleaner.

For a while, when I became delirious again, I lost all track of space and time until the real doctor came and checked on me and wanted to put me on a drip. From the moment I was admitted, I'd steadfastly refused to be hooked up intravenously. Although I will always be extremely grateful of their help, the hygiene was so grim I was stubbornly emphatic about taking any medication I needed orally. When my temperature became dangerously high, I crawled out of bed and stood under a shower to lower my body heat, but when the mercury in the thermometer soared again, the concerned nurse called for a priest. A raging inferno that seared my pounding brain had started to subside when the pastor sat next to my bed and asked if I believed in Christ, if I was ready to embrace our saviour, and if I had any next of kin. I replied that I didn't worship Christianity or any other religion, and after what I'd experienced, I had to believe in certain facets of *kastom*. Science can refute many aspects of *kastom*, but while I remained impartial during my studies, I'd witnessed that what many would conceive as being humanly impossible was in fact possible with the aid of ancestral spirits. The priest became agitated when I told him that I simply exist and treat others with respect while I uphold my own morals and values and that I knew within myself I wasn't going to die.

His face soured, then he readily admitted to being a reformed *nakaimas* who'd turned to the white man's god for solace and salvation. All he needed was a pulpit when I listened to how I was playing with hell's fire, and that by opening up to *kastom*, I'd welcomed Satan into my heart. When I pulled the *namele* leaf from the ground at Ambrym, it had been extremely dangerous because *nakaimas* use the black ash from their victims powdered bones to perform the magic. If I hadn't washed my hands after I'd handled the leaf and eaten afterwards, I was incredibly lucky to still be alive. He warned that the repercussions from dabbling in *kastom* aren't always immediate. In the future, if ever I had children they could fall ill and die as a result of my previous experiences with *nakaimas* and their black magic. He finally finished telling me how miserable my future was going to be, and I asked him to help me by using *kastom*. He looked disgusted, then got up and walked out.

Over the next week I became so violently ill, I hypocritically used the Lord's Prayer as a holy balm, had faith in Wilson's prowess as a human elixir by placing his talisman on my forehead, and relied on self-belief to will myself to live, just in case the doctor should've prescribed spiritual healing. No one heard my groaning while I was wilting from a hellish fever, so I decided to help myself and grappled along the walls of the hospital towards the showers in the ablution block at the end of the building. A thin soup of urine and faeces that had been spread by a continually overflowing toilet covered the floor. I'd just about made it into the shower when I passed out and awoke to find myself wallowing in the repulsive sewage. The building contractors who were extending the hospital had turned the water off, so I sat there, overwhelmed by exhaustion and the rank smell, and waited for several hours for my energy to slowly return before the water was turned back on and I had enough strength to wash myself clean.

Even with the most sophisticated equipment and the best expertise, diagnosing an ailment can be extremely difficult. No one will ever know what type of sickness I succumbed to. For the record, the doctor wrote down that I had malaria, and although I agree with him, there are still numerous unanswered questions lingering in the back of my mind. While the articulate and well-educated physician gave me a through examination before I was discharged, a happy-natured nurse who was in the room suddenly became sullen and fell silent when I asked them if they treated many victims of black magic. They initially scoffed at the idea that people died from sorcery and became evasive and shrugged off my tactful questions. But when I showed them my photos of primitive peoples, and they listened intently to my inexplicable experiences with Vanuatu's pagan tribes, their sceptical attitudes completely turned around. Ordinarily I would never glorify my illness with an in-depth description, as sickness is part and parcel of my job description, but the stories they shared of patients suffering from terminal illness that were inflicted by black magic warranted it.

It was obvious that their fear of spiritual and professional retribution had initially stopped them from telling the truth. Both the doctor and the nurse hesitantly described how patients die in the hospital from inexplicable ailments that defy logic and science. The most common of the baffling deaths is caused by blood mysteriously haemorrhaging from a circular wound in the temple. Instead of congealing, the blood continually flows from the haemophilic wound for twenty-four hours after the patient has died and is believed to be caused by a *nakaimas* inserting a flower into the victim's ear. Even more startling are patients whose lungs have been eaten away. X-rays have revealed bizarre symptoms where lung tissue is replaced with an empty void or what remains of the organs is a terrible mess. Although it's physically impossible, the doctor likened the phenomenon to a human literally chewing away the patient's lungs. A young woman who was suffering from the complaint was recently transferred to Port Vila by plane, but she died during the flight. No one ever survives the puzzling sickness.

The victims of simultaneous gunshot wounds also challenge scientific rationale. In northwest Malekula, a group of local boys joined a *nakaimas* from Ambrym and spent two weeks making *kastom* around a *tabu* fire. After the rite was over and they supposedly turned into dogs, a terrified witness notified the police when she recognised them by the shape of their elbows, which pointed outwards like a human's instead of inwards like a dog's. The following night, when the police trailed the *nakaimas* through the jungle to where they were making *tabu* fire, the officers weren't taking any chances and waited for the sorcerers to fall asleep before they beat and arrested them, then took them to Lakatoro police station. While I travelled around Vanuatu, most forms of the media have reported tales of black magic, and the incident in northwest Malakula, which occurred in 1992, received a great deal of publicity. The young *nakaimas* had been extremely lucky to escape with their lives, because throughout the archipelago there are numerous reports of what are believed to be possessed dogs being shot and at the very same instant, *nakaimas* either fall over dead or are seriously injured from bullet wounds in exactly the same place as where the dogs were shot. When I asked the doctor if he'd ever seen leaves in a cadaver's gut during a post-mortem, it obviously struck a nerve. He told me I was free to go, then the apprehensive looking physician left the room.

Only by diligently keeping notes while I rode out my illness was I able to accurately recall and write about my affliction. Once I was well enough, I worked on another island, then returned to New Zealand where for three months, I suffered from dyslexia and chronic memory loss. There is a possibility that I may well have been suffering from some sort of a psychological block from having witnessed horrific events that were *tabu* to write about, but as I never sought professional help, I'll never know. It may have been a repercussion from cerebral malaria, which in medical terms is capable of clogging the cerebral microcirculation with parasitised red blood cells that have burst and stuck together to form a bloody sludge. Manifestations of neurological dysfunction can and do occur, but thankfully survivors of the disease rarely have permanent neurological damage. Open-minded people who believe in the supernatural might suppose that manifestations of a different kind were responsible. They might lay the blame with Ambrym's *nakaimas*, who sought revenge on a white man who'd been gifted the secrets of black magic and would be seen as a dangerous spiritual adversary because he somehow defied the power of their gods by pulling not only a sacred *namele* leaf, but the very essence of their *tabu* beliefs from the ground.

Chapter Forty-Three

DÉJÀ VU

From the broad spectrum of tumultuous emotions I experienced while I was in hospital, I was surprised that I never once felt afraid. Ignorance and a lack of understanding are potent catalysts that can cloud clear thinking and induce fear. As my physical body weakened, the wealth of knowledge I'd reaped from Vanuatu had expanded my thinking and made my mind more resilient and much stronger. My belief in the afterlife had changed my whole outlook on life and what lies beyond death. After everything I'd seen and experienced, adventure had become secondary but remained important while I searched for the true meaning of *kastom*. Now that I'd tested the foulest waters, diving headlong into the primitive pool of knowledge didn't faze me anymore. I still had to beware of submerged dangers and the denizens that lurked in the unexplored depths, but the previously murky waters were becoming increasingly clearer, and the grasp I sought on *kastom* was no longer out of arm's reach.

The next time I returned to Malakula, its inhospitable terrain and kilometres of dense jungle rolled beneath our small plane as it bucked and lurched in the thermals. A group of relieved American tourists who were carrying on to Port Vila cheered and clapped the pilot when the twin otter safely touched down on a grass airstrip at Wintua. I'd decided to explore the Small Nambas villages while I used Southwest Bay as a base and wondered if the geographical remoteness of the hamlets in the interior had preserved their culture.

This time I hoped that documenting *kastom* wouldn't be so exhausting and detrimental to my health. On the morning after my arrival, for just over a sweat-soaked hour, I climbed up a long-winded ridge into the mountains behind forty-year-old George, who was my guide and owned Alo lodge,where I was staying at Wintua. It had taken him years of patient negotiation to convince the wary chief of Venamabous village, which was where we were heading, to finally allow outsiders to visit the ridge-top hamlet.

An eye catching *tam tam* and brightly coloured fetishes that decorated the rear of a sacred dance ground gave Venamabous an untarnished and primitive atmosphere when we entered the remote village. The Small Nambas are renowned for making double-faced headdresses, puppets of mythological ancestors, effigies of birds and fish, and other stylised objects that are painted with vegetable dyes and ochres. Wild cane that had been staked into the ground denoted a *tabu* line in front of an area that was off-limits to visitors and only used during ritual. When several shabby looking natives exited the cluster of huts wearing ripped and threadbare clothing, the small hamlet lost its initial primeval air. I didn't have any expectations and wasn't disappointed, but I definitely had no desire to pay to watch them dress up and perform a contrived dance and *kastom* songs like other travellers did. All I wanted was to simply spend time with them.

Avong Lowane was tiny, a sprightly stub of a man with a grizzled beard and balding head who looked to be in his mid-fifties. His unwashed and ill-fitting ragged clothing gave him a miserable and impoverished look when he offered me a friendly but suspicious greeting. Although short visits were clearly welcomed, I could sense that he would rather be left alone by outsiders. After we made small talk about where I was from and what I did, I showed him my photos of other tribes. While he fingered through the prints, his craggy face suddenly lit up and glowed with pleasure. The old warrior looked up at me differently, almost respectfully, through hooded eyes that were starting to cloud with tears of nostalgia. A huge smile exposed the few crooked teeth he had left, and his welling tears of joy softened his coarse features. As I shared the precious moment with him, I felt the absolute bliss he expressed at seeing and hearing for the first time that other primitive cultures from faraway lands still existed in their original state, just as he had when he was a young man. The sad resignation in his misted eyes showed he knew that things would never be the same for his people and that he yearned for the past.

Once he realised my intentions were honest, and that I wasn't here to exploit but to help preserve his culture, Avong made it clear that the majority of his beliefs were *tabu* to outsiders. Even though I was a total stranger, my affinity with other tribes gave us something in common, and was no doubt what motivated him to share a never before documented and never to be repeated custom with me. When his wife, Latalsembai Lowane, died in 1979, she was given the village's last traditional funeral rite. For the first ten days after her death, Avong remained in his leaf hut and sat alongside her decomposing body. If an unmarried villager dies, the immediate family stay with the corpse in the *nakamal*. During the next twenty days, his relatives helped him to smoke her remains over a sacred fire, which they continually stoked because it must never burn out. From the time she died, her family mourned for one hundred days. A, and on the first day the fire was lit, her relatives coated their entire bodies with its hallowed ash and were forbidden to wash until the mourning period had ended. They reapplied a fresh layer of the ghoulish makeup every day to disguise themselves from any evil spirits that might be associated with her death.

After Latalsembai had been smoked for twenty days, her body was shifted to the *nakamal*. The whole village danced and feasted for one full day until daybreak, then she was laid to rest next to the *nakamal* in a specially built sacred hut, which was decorated with flowers and *tabu* leaves. One of her relatives used a bow and arrow to shoot a sacrificial boar with circular tusks, and then the pig was cooked and became a gargantuan meal that belonged solely to Latalsembai's grandfather. To appease the spirits, he set to eating the stomach-bloating feast single-handed and ate nothing else until he'd finished the last scrap of pork.

In the tropical heat, it didn't take long for the skull to rot away from the body. Avong removed his wife's head and stored it in a sacred *naka-mal* that's hidden deep in the rainforest. Time, scavenging dogs, and the carnivorous village pigs consumed the rest of her remains. The stones that were used to form a ring around the shelter that covered Latalsembai's body, which rotted away years ago, are the only material remnants that are left to remind the villagers the spot is *tabu*.

I was buzzing to have been gifted *kastom* so willingly and so quickly, as I knew it was a huge privilege. In the past, when a high-ranking chief died, his skull was coated with clay and plant fibres that were sculpted to resemble the patriarch's face. A weave of cobweb replaced his hair and was also used to make a beard, and a bamboo frame which was built to replace the rest of his body received the same symbolic flesh and was ornately painted with red, black, and white symbols. Then armbands, feathers, a *nambas*, and other artefacts completed the brightly decorated funeral effigy, which was called a *rambaramp*. The *rambaramp* was given its last rites during a *lafaet* and a *kastom* dance, then it was finally laid to rest in the hidden *nakamal*. Although several *rambaramp* have been pho-tographed and collected for prosperity, I knew beforehand that to try and capture Malakula's ancestral skulls on film would incur the wrath of the irate villagers and their seething gods. When I told Avong about the white man's morbid curiosity with his ancestors' skulls and with cannibalism, he looked into my eyes. Then what he said next took me completely by sur-prise. First, he needed time to prepare and to mediate with the spirits, then we could return in five days to photograph him wearing traditional dress while he held the skull of his brother, Ising Wilem.

George looked stunned, and said it had taken him years to get tourists accepted by a people who were once fierce cannibals. He couldn't believe it had only taken hours for me to gain the right to violate an ancient tribal law. While we hiked through the oppressive heat back down to Wintua, he kept emphasizing how lucky I was, as no outsider had ever taken photos of ancestral skulls from Venamabous before because they were considered way too *tabu*. I would definitely be the first, and those who'd foolishly tried to capture them on film in the past had died. He warned that tomor-row, when we visited Lawa village further up the coast, photographing any ancestral remains was definitely forbidden. Even though I'd been given the right, the spiritual and physical consequences of knowingly flouting a primitive people's beliefs kept invading my thoughts. The only way I could rationalize Avong's offer to break such a strong *tabu* was if the head didn't belong to a Small Nambas.

The next day, as we traipsed through the awakening rainforest, I rel-ished the sun's warmth and the rejuvenating rays that managed to filter through the cool early morning shadows. We hiked up through the jungle along a well-used path then dropped back down and followed the coast to Lawa village. At the end of our leisurely two and a half hour trek, I was overcome by a strange sensation that made me feel drained and nauseous.

Sarawoh Pahab, the paramount chief of Lawa, greeted us wearing a *lap lap* leaf *nambas* and a huge smile. He was genial man in his mid-fifties, with grey hair, a grizzled beard, and the look of a born leader. *Kastom* required him to replace his clothing with traditional dress so that he could show us through the sacrosanct ruins of Munlortoh, the ancient village where Lawa's inhabitants believe the Small Nambas originated from.

A ten minute walk up through the gloomy rainforest stepped us back through the ages into an epoch where cannibalism, warfare, and stringent rituals dictated how the villagers lived. After all of my experiences I still didn't consider myself to be a spiritual person, but I felt with equal clarity the same nervous awareness that had grabbed me at Winea when there was an unearthly presence. While Sarawoh stood in the centre of a path covered with broken coral, which was lined by crumbling stonewalls covered with lime green moss, I could literally feel the taught air throbbing with the energy of past lives. Before we followed the trail that would take us back millennia to a sacred burial ground where the exploits of ancient warriors still reverberated in the eerie atmosphere like a nerve jangling battle cry, I asked Sarawoh if I could take his photo. In a matter-of-fact tone, he told me I was welcome to try but it would be a waste of time. Then George casually said my camera wouldn't work and that when Polaroid shots developed themselves, the photos were always totally blank. Each time I focused on Sarawoh, a bizarre light show flashed on the camera's display panel, but whenever I pointed the viewfinder to a tree on the side of the trail, everything worked perfectly. After I tried and failed to take his photo five times, I gave up and put the camera back in my pack. Both of the men weren't the least bit surprised, and Sarawoh said I was lucky, as several cameras had suddenly broken when tourists had tried to take a photo without seeking his permission first.

We climbed up the path to an ancient site where time and the elements have reduced a once thriving village into a slumbering rubble of dishevelled looking foundation stones and tumbling coral walls that are being reclaimed by the encroaching rainforest. The remnants of centuries old headstones, small shrines, and stone burial mounds that were scattered around the silent jungle like primitive time capsules created a sombre mood that not only radiated a sense of loss, they also exuded a sense of life. Most of the larger trees had been fertilised with revered human detritus. The towering sentinels are memorials to warrior chiefs who had achieved greatness in life and would always remain prominent after death, as the names and the spirits of those men who are buried beneath the trees continue to live in the minds of the villagers that still worship the sacred vegetation. The skulls of the esteemed chiefs are stored in *nakamals* and hidden in other *tabu* places. Sarawoh told me that according to legend, the village had been built on the dawn of Malakulan creation.

Not far from the ruins, massive wooden *tam tams* that stand in the centre of an ancient *nasara* are still played during rituals. Whenever the villagers strike the instruments, ancestral voices are said to echo throughout the rainforest when the spirits of the dead who reside in the *tam tams* and in the huge evergreen trees and the palms encircling the dance ground respond to the music by calling out to their descendants.

Sarawoh took us to the tree of death, a *namele* palm that's used to kill enemies by pushing a *tabu* leaf inside a hole in a stone which is nestled at the base of the trunk. Then he showed me gravestones that are still used to manipulate the sun, induce rain, promote healthy crops, create a good catch when fishing, and to influence most aspects of daily life. While Sarawoh's grandfather held a hallowed vine, he'd stomped once on the war stone and asked the spirits to make his people victorious when he led them into battle.

Sarawoh carefully slid a flat slab of rock to one side and uncovered two small cherry sized stones. One was bright red and the other was yellow, and they were lying alongside the shattered remains of a human skull which had been damaged during a recent earthquake. The shards of broken bone belonged to Watamun, the wife of Bangakatuwoi, who was the demigod that created Munlortoh village.

When Sarawoh told me the tale of how life was first created on Malakula, he raced back through the ages to when Bangakatuwoi felt lonely from living a solitary existence at Munlortoh and yearned for the company of a wife and to have children. Early one morning, he hiked up to the top of the mountains to warm himself in the rising sun. While he looked across to Tomman Island, he saw a bright light glowing in the sky. And when curiosity got the better of him, he turned into an eagle and flew across to a place called Umran, on Tomman Island, where he spied a giant clam in the shallow water that lapped the shore. He was hungry, so he swooped down to feast on the flesh of the huge mollusc, but the wary shell saw him coming and clamped tight. The famished eagle spent the next four days trying to fill his belly with the clam's succulent meat, but each time he dived from the sky, the observant mollusc closed its shell. On the fifth day, he realized the clam was being warned by his shadow, so he flew as high as his wings would carry him towards the midday sun. This time the eagle was armed with a stick when he dived down, and he had no problem ambushing the clam so that he could feast on its tender flesh.

After he'd eaten his fill, he left half of the shell at Umran, then he flew back to Malakula and placed the other half of the shell in a pandanus tree at Wepia. From there he flew to Munlortoh and changed back to a man. Five days later, when he returned to Wepia to go fishing, he saw a beautiful maiden with a slender elongated skull standing on the beach. From the instant their eyes met, Wataman fell in love with Bangakatuwoi and asked him to take her to Munlortoh where she would live as his wife. He agreed, and after they were married, they had two sons, Ravi, and Melekello. When Wataman gave birth to the boys, she also delivered a yellow and a red stone. The family flourished and created the thriving population that used to inhabit Munlortoh. The villagers were envious of Wataman's beautifully elongated skull, but because throughout all of Vanuatu, a woman can never gift her *kastom* to her husband, and as she was from Tomman Island, they had to wait until a male introduced the practice of head binding to Malakula.

Bangakatuwoi turned into a god so that he could reside in the spirit world with Wataman when she died. Thousands of years later, Sarawoh holds the yellow and red *tabu* stones whenever he performs a *noho* rite (prays) at a sacred area called *loho* to commune directly with Bangakatuwoi when he seeks his guidance and asks for advice on chiefly matters.

We followed a coral strewn trail that scrunched beneath our feet until we stopped in front of a piece of wild cane that had been staked into the ground. While George and I waited, Sarawoh disappeared into the jungle to perform a ritual to lift the *tabu* from the path. A bizarre noise that started as an anxious murmur, then sounded like a growling wind, drifted through the trees. It rapidly grew in volume and kept rising and lowering in intensity as it made an unearthly whirring sound. If Sarawoh was speaking to his ancestors in the spirit world, it sounded as if they were answering back with an eerie hum. The familiar sound may have been a bullroarer, which is a small flat piece of wood shaped like a laurel leaf that's twirled around on a long thong. Other primitive peoples use the instrument to contact the supernatural, and although I was pretty sure that's what it was, *kastom* prevented Sarawoh from telling me what caused the strange sound.

When Sarawoh emerged from the trees and was about to remove the wild cane, which would allow us to visit a sacred burial ground called *nevetmoho*, he invited me to try and take a photo of him plucking out the cane. After the fourth time that I tried to focus on him and the camera went berserk, I gave up. Whenever he pulled out the cane and put it to one side, the camera functioned perfectly, but when he pushed the cane back into the ground, the camera was rendered useless. We were entering an area where an anthropologist who'd flouted the Small Nambas beliefs by trying to take photos was found lying dead alongside his shattered camera. Sarawoh instructed me to leave all of my photographic equipment at the base of a nearby tree before we followed him. When the path petered out, we made sure we walked in his footsteps so we didn't step on any *tabu* ground. All around us we could see where wild pigs had unearthed human skeletons and scattered the yellowed bones amongst the carpet of rotting detritus. After we carefully picked our way through the jungle and stood beneath *nevetmoho*, I could see skulls perched on ledges and wedged into crevices of the sacred cliff. Although the Small Nambas tribes have similar customs, each clan has it's own unique beliefs. Sarawoh's people believe in heaven and hell, and when they die, their head is placed at *nevetmoho*. If a bird flies down and pecks out the eyes, the villager's spirit is believed to soar to heaven, but if three days have passed and the eyes are still intact, their spirit is damned to hell.

Sarawoh is renowned for his healing powers, and when we walked back down to Lawa, he pinched the fleshy webs between my finger and thumbs and massaged pressure points all over my body to temporarily relieve my slightly feverish system. It was getting late in the day so George and I hitched a ride with a boat that was heading back to Wintua. The setting sun brushed the sky with a glorious red hue as we motored away from the shore and skimmed across a tranquil ocean. A small boy dangled his legs over the bow and serenaded us with a *kastom* song while the sky darkened and the moon sponged a shard of silver light across the perfectly smooth bay. I kicked back and basked in the idyllic scenery until the boat slid up onto the beach at Wintua. Sugran Alili, the tranquil faced and silver haired paramount chief of Tomman Island, was patiently waiting on the shore for George and greeted us with a warm smile.

Sugran may have looked docile but he didn't mince his words when I waited for him to finish speaking with George and asked if I could travel to his island. Without being unwelcoming or brusque, he invited me to sail with him in the morning on the condition that I only stayed for a few days. It was the same old sad story that ended with the ruinous seeds of mistrust being planted by westerners when Sugran told me the Tomman islanders are suspicious of outsiders and have no desire for tourists to overnight in their villages. Sugran's father, Ambonio Alilil, was the only surviving Tomman islander with an elongated skull, and if Ambonio agreed, I could take his photos, then I had to catch the next boat home.

The next morning, as we pulled away from the beach in a leaking five-meter long fibreglass canoe, a blustery southeast trade wind raced across the turgid ocean and unrelenting rain soaked us to the skin. The confident young boatman seemed unperturbed by the angry looking sea as he gripped the throttle of our fifteen horsepower motor. We rushed through a gap in the reef and surged into open water, where the conditions suddenly changed from drenching us in the wind-whipped bay, to us being swamped by a mountainous ocean. Sugran used an old plastic oil container to bail out a steady stream of water that was leaking into the boat and being blasted over us by the angry sea. If I was at the helm, we would've turned around and headed straight back for the safety of the bay. Our decrepit but stable little boat held its own as it slid down steep troughs, then clawed up to the foaming crests of enormous swells. As we pushed our way around the coast, huge waves rolled past us and crashed onto the nearby reef with a deafening roar. Sugran's ragged shirt fluttered like a tattered flag in the gale force wind, and when he caught a glimpse of a distant island from the top of a wave, he yelled out "Tomman" just as a stinging blast of salty spray ripped the words from his mouth and spread them across the turbulent ocean. It took us two and a half hours to complete our seventeen kilometre journey, which wasn't for the fainthearted. But to the young Tomman islander, reeling in a barracuda and several other smaller fish on a handline while he manoeuvred our boat amongst the intimidating waves, it was no big deal. When I saw a white sand beach where the dancing tops of coconut palms were waving furiously in the wind, it was almost as if they were beckoning us to get out of the water. I didn't need any coaxing when I leapt into the shallows and helped to pull the boat up onto the pristine shore.

Despite the initial air of mistrust, I was greeted by Vun'ai'amp village without prejudice or ill feeling. In the afternoon, copious amounts of kava flowed and the genuinely friendly villagers piled huge portions of food onto my plate when they gave me an official welcome. Without being paranoid, after my previous experiences, I'd taken every precaution to safeguard my health, yet I was still coming down with an energy sapping fever. Although it was still daylight, I excused myself and went to sleep in Sugran's hut.

I rested until the following afternoon, then Sugran led me one hundred metres across the beach to a neighbouring hamlet. Ambonio was hunched over and holding a walking stick while he sat on a bamboo seat in the cool interior of his hut. When he heard us approaching, he cocked his head, tentatively felt for the wall, and slowly pulled himself to his feet. I could tell from the way he moved that he was obviously blind. Age had robbed him of his sight, but when I was introduced to him, it was obvious that his eighty-year-old mind was still razor sharp. When I saw that Ambonio's bald forehead had been lengthened to twice its normal size, I stood and gawked at him like an excited and naïve schoolboy who was staring at his first naked woman. I knew he was the last of the Small Nambas to have such a pronounced skull, so I quickly shot two rolls of film and took as many photos as I could before he needed to rest his frail body.

When Ambonio was born, Christianity had just started to impact on the tiny atoll, but his parents were staunch traditionalists who refused to relinquish their Small Nambas beliefs. An elongated skull was considered exceptionally beautiful and was also functional when it came to wearing the elaborate double-faced headdresses that are still used during rituals and *kastom* dances. Deforming the skull was also believed to increase intelligence and cunning. The warriors' enhanced wisdom and the ability to outthink their shrewd enemies were highly prized weapons when skirmishes occurred with hostile tribes.

The lengthening of an infant's skull began on the day a child was born. Two to three *nimoli* nuts were roasted in a fire, then ground into a black paste called *nogoncon*. A liberal coating of the mixture was rubbed over the baby's head and was believed to promote quicker growth and to make the infant's skin more elastic. Then a headband called a *natar*, which was made from a piece of dried bark from a banana tree, was tightly bound around the child's forehead and a tight fitting woven basket called a *noonatar* was pulled over the baby's head. Every day during the next three years, the *natar* and *noonatar* were removed by the infant's mother and the child's head was washed and given a fresh coating of black *nogoncon* paste before the *natar* and *noonatar* were put back on. At the end of the three years, the child's uncle gifted the infant a boar with curved tusks to celebrate his nephew or his niece having an elongated skull.

Before I left the island a few days later, when I asked Sugran if I could photograph his ancestor's skulls, he answered me with an emphatic no and said they were so *tabu* that only their descendents could visit them. Several years after I'd visited Ambonio, I heard from the cultural centre that he'd passed away.

While I travelled back to Wintua on a much kinder sea, a storm raged inside my pounding head. That night, I had an excruciating headache and sharp spasms shook every one of my sweat soaked muscles until I was completely exhausted. Once the fever started to subside, bouts of chronic diarrhoea and vomiting added to my misery. When George heard my muffled groaning and came in and saw the state I was in, he rushed me to the nearby clinic where a nurse took blood samples and made slides so that she could send them on the next plane to Santo to be analysed. Before I fell into bed, I told George that I still wanted to leave at 6:00 a.m. to try and climb up to Venamabous and photograph Avong and his brother's skull.

From the moment I awoke, my reeling mind and weary body reared into defensive mode, and while sensibility told me the only sane option was to stay put, I drew on a mixture of bullheadedness and dogged determination and dragged myself out of bed. During the torturous walk up to Venamabous, the three enforced breathers I took while I recharged my ailing system with green coconut juice did little to alleviate the self-inflicted agony I suffered. When I swaggered into the village like a drunken wreck I tried my best to appear healthy and to stay composed.

Avong invited us into his leaf hut where the light from the quiet flicker of a cooking fire painted the soot-blackened rafters with a warm hue. A topless middle-aged woman wearing a short raffia grass skirt, woven armlets, and a stick through her pierced nasal septa shivered with fear. The poor woman had been told by the villagers to don her traditional dress and was horrified by the thought of having her photo taken. Avong had killed one of his precious fowl and prepared us a special meal. I gratefully accepted the steaming food but had to eat slowly until I was sure that I wouldn't vomit in front of our hosts. When we'd finished our meal, I went outside and took two quick photos of the shaking woman, only because the others insisted, and then I tried to put her mind at ease by reassuring her that the camera hadn't captured her spirit.

When Avong reached into a mouldy sack and pulled out a skull, the way everyone immediately scattered as if he was holding a lighted stick of dynamite aroused my suspicion. Avong's tiny frame didn't look so puny while he was wearing his traditional attire. A wooden nosepiece gave his splayed nostrils a fearsome appearance, and the sticks piercing his earlobes and an old pipe hanging from the corner of his mouth enhanced the primitive appearance of his *nambas*-clad body. He looked the proud warrior that he had once been when warfare and cannibalism were an integral part of his people's heritage. In the not so distant past, guiltless killing was carried out with passion and pride and was deemed to be a necessary part of Venamabous's complex religious and social structure. While Avong fondled the mottled skull, he seemed to caress it in a barbaric rather than an intimate way. To me he didn't seem like a man who yearned for his brother, whose skull he said it was. He came across as being a notorious cannibal who was reminiscing about past kills and was proudly showing off the skull as if it were a headhunting trophy, which is exactly what it was.

Avong's son confirmed my suspicions when I visited Gaua Island. He'd been living there for years and joined a small crowd of interested villagers that were pawing over my photos. When he saw the shots of his father, he looked stunned, so I apologised for allowing the others to see his uncle's sacred skull. He began smirking and confirmed my initial doubts were correct when he said, "It's okay. There isn't a *tabu*. This is the skull of the Big Nambas that murdered my mother." Then he said if I'd taken a photo of a Small Nambas skull, I'd probably be dead or, if I was lucky, at the very least I would've had to pay a massive amount of compensation. In the late 1970s, Avong grabbed his bow and hunted down and shot the Big Nambas to avenge his wife's death and, just as importantly, to appease his ancestral sprits with a payback killing. The vengeful murder had been ritualistic and had nothing do with proving his virility or his bravery. Only Avong knows if he cannibalised his victim, which in all probability he would have, to empower himself and defile the Big Nambas spirit because he'd murdered his wife.

After we hiked back down to Wintua, my health took a huge nosedive and required the type of professional help that wasn't available at the clinic. I curled up into the foetal position and was barely able to move while I waited at the airport for the plane to land. During the flight to Santo, I had visions of déjà vu and thought perverse spirits were attacking my soul when I started hallucinating. When I stepped off the plane, I was delirious and unable to walk properly and collapsed into the arms of a taxi driver who rushed me to Luganville hospital. All of my blood tests including the ones they'd received earlier came back negative. I'd played a dangerous and almost suicidal game, where I'd risked everything by holding off with any medication in order to seek the ultimate truth, to see if disease or spiritual unease was responsible for my sickness. None of the doctors could provide a rational explanation for my illness. Of course there's always the possibility that I was suffering from a disease that they couldn't diagnose or from an ailment that science has yet to identify. Once again they were left with no alternative but to treat me for malaria. Sometimes the microscopic bug is extremely hard to detect, so I'd purposely held off with taking any medicine to see if a more sinister parasite from another realm was responsible. I went to hell and back during my painful recovery and received alternative treatment from a *kastom* man as well as modern medicines until the doctors were satisfied that I was well enough to discharge myself.

A historian has an amusing tale of how Malakula derived its name from a group of French explorers who were arrogant and contemptuous towards the locals and their primitive beliefs. When one of the foreigners asked which was the best natural toilet paper to use, the natives decided to inflict some rough but humorous justice on their unwanted guests. He was given a handful of carefully folded *nangalat* leaves, and seconds after the Frenchman had parted them and replaced our paper work with the venomous vegetation, he screamed in agony from the intense pain and yelled out, "*Mal a cul*," which translates to "pain in the arse." The amused natives had heard him shout out "*mal a cul ahhh!*"

During another fleeting visit to explore Malakula, it proved to be a pain in the arse and to the rest of my body, but for me the consequences were much more severe than a red-hot rectum. I ended up in a shocking state and lay sprawled on the ground at Norsup airport while I suffered from another mysterious near-death condition. After I'd delved into dark and unexplored territory, it took me twelve months to recover and to return to full fitness. For me, setting foot on Malakula became synonymous with becoming the victim of an inexplicable illness. I could put becoming unwell once or twice down to bad luck, but after the third consecutive bout of sickness, although the sensible side of my rationale said I'd suffered from some type of undetectable ailment, I didn't discount that maybe I'd wrestled with something that was way beyond our comprehension and that maybe my intimate alliances with other tribes had given me partial immunity to what should've been a deadly affliction.

Chapter Forty-Four

THE ROOT OF ALL EVIL

To the weak willed, and to anyone who doesn't understand the rigours of being an adventurer in the tropics, enjoying my line of work would probably be a retrospective condition. I'd learnt to thrive on the hardships as well as the joys, which made the simplest of highs all the more heavenly. I was recovering from one of my bouts of sickness, and although my frail features looked gaunt, if I took my time, I could still carry my packs all day but without wining any prizes for being the first to the top of a mountain. Being pulverised and enlightened while I explored the mysteries of primitive man was much more interesting than recuperating back in New Zealand.

Without a doubt, Vanuatu's most famous cultural export is the *naghol*, which occurs on one or two days between April and May, when men and boys from southern Pentecost Island perform a land diving ritual to ensure a bountiful yam harvest. The *naghol* is the primeval prototype of the modern bungy jump and has become valuable cultural merchandise. Tourists flock from around the world and pay big money to watch virtually naked natives wearing penis sheaths dive from twenty to thirty metre high towers. As they arc through the air in a gigantic leap of faith, the death defying divers plunge to within inches of the ground, then with a sudden and violent jerk that looks capable of wrenching their kidneys to up around their ears, a springy liana vine that's tied to the tower and to the divers ankles hauls them safely upwards. This spectacular pinnacle of eco-tourism, and the customs of the island's primitive inhabitants, have been well documented. It was their uncanny affinity with the shark that had lured me to Pentecost.

I hiked along the southwest coast from Lonorore airfield and set my sights on the newly completed "white road," which is a twisting white-coloured thoroughfare that carves across the island's gnarled wilderness. Then when I was almost at the end of the road, I hoped to find the trail that leads to the previously remote but still primitive Bunlap village, nestled on the island's sheer eastern slopes. When bursts of bright sunlight seared through gathering rain clouds, they turned the already scorching grey sand beach into an oppressive stamina-robbing inferno. Every step that I took sunk into billions of minuscule grains of sand that sucked at my feet and was tiring enough without being roasted by a merciless and brazen sun. I left the flickering glaze of heat that bounced off the beach and headed back to the cool shadows of the tree-lined coastal road.

A woman who was returning from her garden saw the sweat pouring down my emaciated face and placed several over-ripe bananas in my hand, then offered me a drink of cool, refreshing water before I continued along the main road. Along the way, others who stopped for a friendly chat were curious as to where I was from and where I was going. This was the real Vanuatu that I'd grown to love when I visited the other outer islands. While I was walking along the road, I met John Mark, who had getting Vanuatu's most valuable asset, hospitality, down to a fine art. He was a stoutly built man, and his middle-aged, easygoing face was partially hidden beneath a wide-brimmed cowboy hat, but it was impossible not to see his infectious smile. Without being overbearing, he insisted I rest in his hut and have lunch with his family, then afterwards I could go with him to kill a bullock and catch a lift in his Toyota pickup to Pangi village.

Lunch was an intestine stretching five-course banquet of scrumptious local foods that John's wife prepared for me as a special treat. I was bursting at the seams from the stomach bloating kindness when I helped to push-start the rusted remains of the Toyota four-wheel drive. It was a death trap, whose broken instruments and vital components were tied together with a web of knotted wires. John's son, Martin, sat behind the wheel and used a skeleton key that had been ingeniously carved from a piece of bullock bone to turn on the ignition. I pushed on the pillar of the passenger's door, then clambered aboard halfway down a hill, when in a mechanical miracle, the bucking wreck coughed and defied all automotive logic by spluttering to life. We were engulfed by fumes that belched through a honeycomb of holes in the floor until we picked up enough speed to blow some of the toxic carbon dioxide out the windows. When we hit third gear along a straight, the dangerous and faulty steering box slewed us from one side of the road to the other. Our speed was grossly exaggerated by the rattling cab that shuddered as if it was punching through the sound barrier. I keeled over with laughter when right on cue, the sonic boom arrived as a deafening, ear-ringing backfire. While I sat in the cab in hysterics, the terrified boys who were hanging on the back slammed on the roof of the cab and screamed at Martin to slow down. He had to throttle off anyway, because without brakes it took us fifty metres to roll to a stop alongside a crude stockyard.

The tiny serrated knife John had in his hand looked as if it was better suited to peeling potatoes than to slaying the bull that was nervously thrashing about in a claustrophobic pen. One of the boys who was waiting to butcher the condemned bullock said, "Watch this. You'll be amazed." John carefully searched for the right spot, then with the precise and delicate touch of a Chinese acupuncturist, he gave an effortless short, sharp stab into the base of the hulking animal's neck. Its legs crumpled instantly, and the massive bull slumped to the ground in a shuddering heap.

I opted to ride to Pangi on the back of the pickup with the fly blackened meat and figured that if we were going to crash, at least I could jump to safety. Then to save my weak legs hours of toil, I caught a ride with another truck that clawed up and over the white road through an ocean of beautiful rainforest studded with tree ferns. My run of good luck continued when I met a young boy called Temakan, who stepped us off the white road and led me along a mountain trail that had been worn bare by centuries of barefooted villagers as they returned to Bunlap. It took a twenty-minute hike to go from one extreme to the other. We left the island's civilized inhabitants' overwhelming hospitality and entered a primitive world, where the paramount chief clearly resented my presence unless I was willing to pay ridiculously exorbitant amounts of money.

Over the years, the annual ebb and flow of tourists who'd paid to watch the *naghol* had left small cultural pools of alien affluence. The chief appeared to see them as money-filled wishing wells, where he didn't hope for, but demanded, more wealth from visiting travellers. Gramma and my other highland friends in Santo had taught me that criticism not only injures the source of your contempt, it also damages your own soul, but when it came to criticising Bunlap's chief, I couldn't help myself. He'd sacrificed the very core of *kastom* for material wealth and shared the mannerisms of a sleazy and cunning sewer rat that was equally happy to become an opportunist friend or a foe. Two friends from Port Vila who trade in tribal art had recently spent a month in the village, but for some strange reason the chief, who had a commanding physique, humourless eyes, and an arrogant personality, and Moses, his equally shady looking right-hand man, blatantly lied when they denied they ever knew them. When I offered to write a travel article to promote tourism, it bounced the decimal point around until we agreed on a more realistic fee for photography, and the greedy chief suddenly decided my accommodation and meals were free. Although the other villagers were extremely generous and incredibly welcoming, I didn't trust anyone.

The leaf huts that are perched on narrow ledges the villagers have built and are scattered along a steep rock-strewn hill that drops abruptly down to an indigo ocean, are filled with a friendly peoples who still adhere to their age-old beliefs. During the first night, when I was invited to the *nakamal*, men wearing penis sheaths called *pipis* sat at different levels while they socialised, ate their meals, and drank kava. Each section of floor was relative to the number of pigs they'd slaughtered during grade taking. High-ranking men slept, cooked, and ate together, away from their wives and families. I was given a warm welcome and sat at the bottom tier of the *nakamal* with those who were still striving to ascend through the hierarchal society.

On the second night, we danced around the *nasara* for an hour beneath gathering rain clouds, until the heavens opened up and torrents of rain sluiced down. Our feet scuffed and slid over the slippery bare earth until it was almost impossible to remain upright while we ran around in a mass of circling bodies. An old man with age-frosted hair screwed his wrinkled face into a smile and postponed the dance which was to celebrate his one hundredth pig kill for another week.

If I was going to write a travel article, I felt that I should be treated as a traveller and kept the strong alliance I have with other tribes to myself. When I mentioned to the chief and Moses that my photos would be kept in the archives at the cultural centre, they banned me from taking photos until the following afternoon, between 2:00 and 6:00 p.m. The next day, Moses followed me when I started taking photos, and when I pulled out two cameras, he insisted I either put one away or pay double the fee for photography. I was treated like a naïve tourist and knew I would only capture a brief, rather blurred glimpse of true village life. The contrived shots I took of villagers toiling amongst plots of taro and going about routine tasks were all I could expect and were all I received.

The following day I greeted the sunrise. While I stared at a beautiful golden sky, I decided that unless I had an open chequebook, I was wasting my time in an uncomfortable and expensive environment. The observed had picked up bad habits from their outside observers. As soon as I told Moses I was leaving, he asked me to wait while he went and spoke with the chief. I told him I wouldn't dream of leaving without first thanking him anyway and would do it now, but he insisted that he visit the chief alone. When Moses returned with the patriarch, the chief perched above me on a stonewall and gazed down with the piercing eyes of an eagle that was about to attack its hapless prey. He was obviously contemplating how he could fleece me. Several minutes later, he moved in for the kill. After he waved Moses over, they disappeared, then when they returned with thirteen other men and boys and surrounded me, I readied myself for the obvious.

The chief squinted his eyes to try and lend facial intimidation to his arrogant and unreasonable demands when he snarled, "You must pay for food, accommodation, and extra for the photos. If you don't, we won't let you leave." His threats didn't work, and I took my time and gave my answer and approach a lot of careful thought. The inherent blood of millennia of brave and cannibalistic warriors flowed through their veins, and I knew that if I underestimated the repercussions of not bowing to the patriarch, it could prove to be painful if the men still admired courage and honour—and liked a good fight. While I held a level but passive gaze and looked into everyone's eyes, it seemed that only Moses and the chief's morals had been ripped apart by hybridisation with the white man's greed for money. There didn't seem to be any resentment or hatred, and it didn't look as if anyone was about to burst from trying to suppress their aggression. From the way they carried themselves, it seemed unlikely the others meant me any harm. They were circled around me like cautious hunters who were afraid to move in for the kill on a wounded and dangerous animal.

I figured a comical approach would be wasted on the humourless chief, so I decided to hide my nervousness and to launch into an assertive attack. If this was Middle Bush, Santo, such a heinous act of greed and disrespect would most likely lead to a fight to the death. Although the patriarch tried to look intimidating, I couldn't help but treat his outlandish demands as pathetic. He reminded me of a money hungry village accountant who was throwing a tantrum, rather than a fierce warrior chief that was threatening my life when he broke the silence by saying, "We are many." I was outnumbered fifteen to one, alone, and in a remote village, but I called his bluff. It was time for an unflinching face off, and when I countered with, "its not going to be a fair fight, there aren't enough of you," I took the surly chief by surprise. A flaccid-faced elderly man smiled and gave me a mute nod of his head, to either admire my courage or marvel at my stupidity. Moses boldly puffed out his chest and said, "We don't care about what we do to you." There was a legitimate menace in his flurry of words, so I defied him in an aggressive tone with, "What makes you think I give a rat's arse about you?" Then I leant towards him so that only he could hear and whispered, "Before the others get hold of me, I'll rip your fucking head off and shit down your neck. Then I'll take out the chief, and the others can have what's left of me." From the way his body stiffened while he nervously looked away, each of my callous words had hit home with the intensity of a bone-crunching thud from a swinging club.

I pushed my luck to the limit when I brazenly but calmly ripped into the chief about his greed and said, "The white man has tainted your spirit. Barraculcul isn't your god anymore, money is. Instead of the *nakamal*, why don't you build a bank and worship that as a *tabu* shrine? You don't respect me, so why should I give a cold shit about you? I'll pay the agreed amount, then I'm leaving." Ordinarily there is no way in this life I would ever dream of speaking to a chief, or anyone, anywhere, in such a disrespectful manner, but the situation warranted it.

When half of the men followed me back to my hut without uttering a sound, the silence was piercing and uncomfortable. I was prepared to pay any amount to avoid violence, but maintained my poker face when I handed Moses his precious payment and said, "Here's your money. I'm leaving," His face soured, then he said, "You're not leaving." After I shouldered my pack, I said, "I'm not going to fall asleep waiting for you to carry out your pissant threats. I'm leaving now." Only the sound of the wind-ruffled leaves broke the silence as I casually walked towards the path exiting the village. Once I was out of sight, I ran as fast as I could and kept glancing over my shoulder, as I knew I wasn't out of the woods yet. I was about five minutes away from the white road, and on the threshold of neutral ground, when the sound of running feet set my heart thumping. One of Bunlap's lower ranking chiefs wiped sweat from his eyes, then began a sincere apology. "I'm sorry to you from everyone. We at Bunlap are good people. That was not our way. It is the fashion of Moses and the paramount chief." He shook my hand when we reached the white road, and before I walked across the island back to Pangi, he bade me farewell with another heartfelt request for forgiveness. When I told him I knew the people were kind hearted, which they had been, and that I would write that tourists should go and enjoy the *naghol*, it seemed to put his troubled mind at ease.

After my hard-hitting reaction to the paramount chief's debauch attitude, I decided that I'd been living in the jungle too long. As an adventurer who sometimes has to face confrontational and potentially dangerous situations, I'd grown a thick skin and had learnt to wear two faces. I needed to slip on a more sensible and more civilized look for a while and decided to rest and recover at Port Vila.

Several years later, Bunlap paid a high price for the chief's lust for money and from treating the sacred *naghol* rite as a business. A species of vine that's normally used to tie the towers together had been depleted through staging too many exhibition jumps. When a much weaker vine was used as a substitute, it proved disastrous when a tower collapsed in front of a crowd of horrified tourists and seriously injured several land divers.

Before I flew to Port Vila, I gathered sketchy information about the shark cult from a villager who lived at central Pentecost. When his close friend failed to return from diving for fish with a spear gun, he used a dugout canoe and frantically paddled throughout the night to try and find him. After a fruitless search, he was so exhausted that on daybreak he paddled back to the shore. He was unnerved by a huge shark whose swirling fin kept breaking the water around the canoe. It had been trailing him for most of the night, and when it followed him right up to the beach, he was suspicious that this wasn't a chance encounter so he ran up to the village. A weather-beaten elder gathered an armful of bullock bones and joined an excited crowd that was heading for the ocean.

The old man had no fear of the huge shark as it cruised in the shallows because he had a supernatural affinity with the savage-looking fish, which was embodied with his spirit. When he announced this, most of the onlookers, already amazed by the incredible scene, were stunned. An unruly youth tried to spear the shark but it retreated back into deeper water and swam out into the ocean. Everyone that I asked about the shark cult suggested I should travel to Paama Island, where *nakaimas* are famous for their affinity with the shark.

Chapter Forty-Five

ASSASSINS FROM THE DEEP

As each day passed, I slowly but steadily regained my health. I recuperated with Simeon Tovovur and his kind-hearted family who live at Freshwater, on the outskirts of Port Vila. Just as I was about to organize a visit to Paama, my plans screeched to an abrupt halt when I discovered the island's most knowledgeable *kastom* man is a close friend of Simeon and was living right under my nose. Sam Mahit, the paramount chief of Paama, owned the *nakamal* at the bottom of a steep and muddy track only several minutes' walk away. Sam had joined an exodus from his tiny thirty-two square kilometre island because of its scarce drinking water, overpopulation, and most of all because of a shortage of land. Only five hundred metres from where I was staying, he'd created an idyllic and secluded version of a much more bountiful Paama. When I walked into his private nirvana the impressive acreage brimmed with lush vegetation and healthy crops. Trees and plants that are indigenous to his home island, which are used for *kastom* and as alternative medicines, flourished around a traditional *nakamal* and a *tabu* dance ground.

Sam was still athletic for a man in his early forties, and his brash personality and proud nature made it obvious that he didn't suffer fools. I faced an expected barrage of questions when he queried what my motives were for wanting to explore Paama's beliefs. His terse but likeable manner didn't tolerate time wasting so I got straight to the point in a rapid but roundabout way, showing him my photos and articles which included shots of my initiation in Middle Bush, Santo. I gently threw everything I could muster at him, and modestly impressed him as best I could with tales of what life was like amongst the archipelagos most feared and volatile people. He listened intently and seemed to absorb then dissect every one of my carefully chosen words before he took his time to answer. At the end of my short-winded spiel, when I mentioned I was especially interested in Paama's supernatural affinity with the shark, there was a brief lull in the conversation. After he'd gathered his thoughts he said, "Come back tomorrow and we will talk again."

The next day, I returned to a deadly quiet. The normally lively hamlet resembled a deserted morgue, and apart from a few clucking chickens and squabbling ducks, not a hint of life stirred from within Sam's western style house. When I caught a whiff of pungent smoke, I headed towards a plantation several hundred metres away where a dark grey plume of smoke rose into the warm afternoon sky. Because Sam is the custodian of Paama's secretive beliefs and I was trying to delve into his *kastom*, his initial warmth and friendliness seemed to have smouldered, like the pile of debris he raked onto the bright orange flames. John Noel's wife, Missy, originates from Paama, so I mentioned that Santo's paramount chief and his wife were close friends who I always stayed with. It was enough to soften Sam's indifferent attitude and to keep us on common and convivial ground. I added how Missy had told me about her fifteen-year-old cousin, Maria Seto, who'd been swimming near Tahi village while her family was involved in a dispute. She suffered a horrific death when a shark devoured her legs and ate half of her stomach. I patiently waited in a curious silence until he said, "I will tell you everything." His mind had already been made up, because such *tabu* information is never gifted without first seeking the divine approval of the gods and of ancestral spirits.

Since the very beginning of the earth's creation, its oceans have remained mysterious realms. New discoveries lay hidden in its darkest depths, and when its enigmas are combined with the unexplored and dark domain of the *nakaimas*, the two create an environment that teems with unanswered questions and open-ended answers. Science can only speculate as to how, or if, the spirit of a man can become embodied in a shark. Sam told me to come back tomorrow at two o'clock in the afternoon. Then he would unravel the mysteries, and the myth of how a man could become one with a shark would become fact.

The following day, after Sam invited me into his house, he swore as he swatted aside several chickens that were scavenging for scraps of grated coconut on a table. They flew out open windows and darted for the door in a startled flurry of feathers. Then he muttered another string of profanity as he chased the last cackling fowl outside. He offered me a seat, reached inside an envelope and pulled out an anthropologist's dog-eared manuscript, which he rubbished by calling it "inaccurate bullshit" and a few other choice words. In a deadly serious tone he said, "No outsider, especially a white man, has ever heard this. You are the first. Even my friend here from Paama knows nothing of what I'm about to tell you." I looked at the plump islander who was hanging on every one of Sam's stern words and anxiously waiting to hear him share the secrets of the shark cult.

Sam bowed his head and seemed a bit hesitant, then he looked up and started talking about his father, Jimi Tulangi who was also the spiritual leader and paramount chief of Paama. When Jimi was on his deathbed at Tavie village, which is at the northwest tip of the island, he called his five sons and five daughters to his side. Although Sam was his fourth born son, Jimi chose to pass his profound knowledge of *kastom* on to him, as he had all of the attributes to become a great and respected chief. Everyone else was asked to leave the hut, then with his last words Jimi shared everything with Sam and started with the legend of how Ambrym, Paama, Epi, and Lapevi islands were once one land mass. The mythical volcanic island erupted and blasted massive pieces of land around the ocean to create the four islands. A *nakaimas* called Hari travelled to Paama, settled on the uninhabited island with his wife, and became the first paramount chief. He built a *nakamal* and called his village Tavie, which means "everything."

So from Tavie came everything that Hari and his wife needed to survive. Hari also named the area Senhari, which means the place that belongs to Hari.

Although Tavie met all of Hari's physical needs, he yearned for male company. So he decided to bring other men to the island by using black magic. At first he was unsure of how to use his *kastom* powers to transport a fully grown man across the ocean, until he made the *occak ten mato*, the woody canoe shaped sheath that grows on a coconut palm and produces flowers. Hari called his wife over and asked her what she thought of his beautiful creation. He told her it looked like a shark, and then he sent her to the garden to gather dried sugar cane leaves. When she returned, he wound the leaves around the *occak ten mato* to waterproof the pod so the man who was about to be carried inside his handiwork wouldn't drown. Hari was pleased with himself, and decided to turn the tightly bound pod into a shark. Then he told his wife the finished product resembled the nest of a rat and of a kingfisher, and like these creatures, his nest would also harbour life.

Hari used his supernatural power to instil his creation with *tocolkatie* (power) and gave it its true *kastom* name, *occak sen van*, which means the canoe (or shark) that will bring a stranger (van) from another island. Van, the stranger, was a potent *nakaimas* whose spirit embodied the first shark that Hari called to Paama. Nowadays Van's name still lives on in Tavie village, where his prowess as a *nakaimas* remains legendary.

Only a *nakaimas* has the ability to fuse his spirit with a shark, and to become powerful enough to perform the remarkable feat, they must first endure twenty months of hellish isolation and live solely from a physically emaciating and moral shredding *tabu* fire. The purpose of the drawn-out purification rite is to evoke and to nurture the spirit of the devil. It's *tabu* for a sorcerer to lay his eyes, let alone his manhood, on a woman until the brutal and demanding ritual is over. If the village women are menstruating, they know they must never walk anywhere near a *tabu* fire even if they remain out of sight because their soiled bodies will taint the sacred area. The *nakaimas* feed the demanding forces of darkness with the ultimate sacrifice, a human life, which enables their spirit to become personified in a shark and to control its physical form.

Between 1982 and 1986, sharks killed six people while they were swimming around the shores of Paama. Since then, whenever opposing clans have been involved in a heated dispute, there have been other fatalities from shark attacks, and enemies can and do pay a *nakaimas* to help them settle an argument with the aid of the sea's most feared predator.

Paama means "the biggest that beats everything," or "to conquer." When Hari named the tiny island, he knew that the fierce and cannibalistic warriors who originated from the shark would eventually leave Paama to go and search for other islands, which explains why nowadays "man Paama" can be found living throughout most of Vanuatu. This inherent thirst to travel and to conquer meant it wasn't shameful and was totally acceptable for the paramount chief to abandon his own island and create his own personal kingdom at Freshwater. When Sam reinforced how fortunate I was to be gifted an ancient secret that had been vigorously guarded by each successive generation of *nakaimas*, he laced with his words his usual liberal dose of profanity. Then he added that if I'd travelled to Paama, I would never have been given the keystone to the shark ritual. I'm mystified as to why the secret of the shark cult was gifted to me so easily. I was completely innocent of any profane act where I tried to pry the information from the chief, which would have been a futile exercise anyway as a paramount chief will never betray the spirits. Sam had stretched his chiefly rights, and the tolerance of his god and his ancestors, to their absolute limits. *Kastom* ordinarily decrees he should never have shared his wisdom with those who have never sat at the *tabu* fire and unveiled its mysteries through self-sacrifice and with the blood of others, yet for his own reasons, he gifted me what had remained an enigma for thousands of years.

Chapter Forty-Six

A SLIP OF THE TONGUE?

Vanuatu's primitive peoples are fantastic storytellers who have an incredibly rich oral history which, as a rule, is retold to each successive generation in an unvarying manner to ensure that their traditions are preserved in their original form. Amongst educated societies, the earliest written words remain unaffected by time, unlike the stories of illiterate primitive peoples that are woven from the past and passed through the ages. If each narrator suffers from the slightest slip of the tongue, the passing years and pliable minds can drastically alter a people's history. Even if over the centuries a clan's memoirs and beliefs are subjected to subtle change, one key factor has always remained constant with primitive peoples. Illiterate tribes that live on the other side of the world and are oblivious to each other's existence perform strikingly similar rituals.

Exactly where Vanuatu's first peoples migrated from will always remain an unsolvable enigma. Scientific opinion remains divided, but the commonly shared theory is that they first travelled down from South East Asia. Even the most educated of guesses place the time of the first arrivals at differing periods. The truth is no one will ever know, and the truth is no one will ever know if the roots of some of Vanuatu's peoples are more complex than historians could ever imagine.

Madagascar, the planet's fourth largest island, is situated four hundred kilometres off the south east coast of Africa. It has the same uncertainty as Vanuatu concerning when the first people arrived there, but the indigenous inhabitants believe their ancestors came from South East Asia. I've never been interested in documenting suspicious information that's more sensational than it is reliable. Historical records that academics thought were dubious which were later proved to be irrefutably true have proved that there might just be a slight element of truth to colourful tales and to seemingly far-fetched legends that have been bandied along the passage of time. While I was staying with Simeon in one of four attached home units, I met Ben Ishmael, who lives in the same block of houses. He's from Tongoa Island and is the son of chief John Kalotop, the patriarch of Meriu village. Ben told me the legend of how the people from Meriu and Rafenga villages immigrated to Tongoa Island thousands of years ago.

Many ancient voyages of discovery have become immortalized by what academics sometimes politely call debatable history. Long before Columbus, Cook, and the other legendary explorers pierced the distant horizon, the Tongoans fervently believe their ancestors sailed from Madagascar and that they have accurately preserved their fascinating history without their oral record evolving into a myth or being glorified by vivid imaginations over a long period of time.

Different driving forces may have spurred the Tongoans' adventurous forefathers to pit themselves against the uncompromising sea. Maybe they set off on a spiritual quest that was destined to shape their future or were on a ritualistic journey to appease the gods rather than being a curious peoples who were intent on exploring unchartered territories. Whatever their reason was, it required truly remarkable courage to face the rigours of an epic ocean voyage in the hope of chancing upon a distant world that might not even have existed.

The primitive mariners may have relied upon hope, the divine guidance of their gods and ancestral spirits, their seaworthy canoes, and their razor-sharp powers of observation to survive the rigours of their journey. Once the sun had dipped into the ocean, when the wheeling stars and the planets emerged from the horizon, they would've provided them with accurate navigation. They also had the ability to decipher the flight paths of migratory birds, to read swell patterns, cloud formations, and to use numerous other navigational indicators that would've enhanced their chances of surviving the massive challenges they faced. Sometimes a naked sailor slid into the ocean and held onto the side of the canoe, and when his sensitive testicles felt the flow of the current, it allowed them to make sure they were heading along the right liquid path.

Tongoa's historians tell of a huge flotilla of just over two hundred massive wooden canoes that caught the seasonal winds with sails that were made from a weave of fibrous leaves. The intrepid travellers were loaded with an enormous amount of provisions that they knew how to preserve and were blasted by howling hurricanes, battered by mountainous waves, and managed to elude the mythical monsters and malevolent demons that they thought were waiting to attack them when the sailed beyond the horizon. As the months slipped by, their food began to dwindle, and with the passing of each day, a painful hunger would've lingered in their bellies. When the long and hazardous voyage started to take its toll, anxiety must have invaded their desperate thoughts. Many of the exhausted crew were unable to endure the excruciating hunger, and when they couldn't satisfy their brutal thirst, they collapsed and died. All they could hope for was a speedy and merciful death to put an end to their misery or that their prayers of sighting land would be answered.

After months of living in a claustrophobic canoe amidst a vast ocean, a delirious sailor who was so weak he could barely move had just enough strength left to climb the mast to check out a cluster of dark clouds that were gathering in the distance. The weeks of despair, the hallucinating from thirst and starvation, and dreaming of sighting a lush paradise were over when he saw the peaks of a rugged mountain range scraping the base of the ominous looking clouds. The ecstatic sailor screamed out "*tu maori*" ("We are alive"), and when the canoes landed, some of the natives stayed in the land that was later called New Zealand and were so happy to be alive, they called themselves Maori.

Once they were rested and had restocked their supplies, the others were undeterred by the previous hazards they'd endured and decided to sail north and search for a sultrier, much kinder climate. After another adventurous journey, the lookout who was clinging to the top of the mast yelled out "*etanna*," which means "There's something down there," when he saw an island way in the distance. Some of the crew remained on the island and called it Tanna. The rest of the natives kept sailing north and into the unknown to began their colonization of Vanuatu.

In the predawn darkness, two men who were clinging to the top of the swaying mast scanned the ocean for the next unknown port of call. They were so surprised by the size of the next landfall they sighted that the chief named the new discovery Erromango, because *erro* means two, and *mango* means surprised. Once again, some of the natives settled on the island while the others set sail.

When the next tropical paradise came into view, flying foxes and birds filled the evening sky. The excited lookout shouted "*fete*" from his lofty perch, which means "nest of the birds" when he told the jubilant crew he could see the nesting place of the birds. After the canoes landed at Manuro point, they named the island Fete, which was later twisted to Efate. The flotilla carried on and settled its crew on Emao, Mataso, Makura, Tongoa, and the other islands in the Shepherds group.

Thousands of years later, the same adventurous spirits of the first Melanesian mariners are said to haunt *tabu* areas on Tongoa. Whenever the villagers enter the sacred ground, they are forbidden to fell the trees because this is where the spirits of the ancient sailors are believed to reside. During disputes, the Tongoans believe that by standing amongst the hallowed forest and shouting out an enemy's name, their intended victim will suddenly fall ill or even die. If these are the same ancestral spirits that called out the names of distant islands that saved their lives and were covered with a virginal empire of green rainforest, it's easy to understand why the trees are sacred to the descendants of the native sailors. Of course, unromantic scientific evidence and rationale would most likely blow the Tongoans' beliefs right out of the water, but if their remarkable voyage is in fact a part of Vanuatu's blurred history, it would be the longest journey that was ever successfully attempted by primitive native mariners.

Chapter Forty-Seven

CATASTROPHIC DISCOVERY

It's hardly surprising that the descendants of Vanuatu's earliest inhabitants find their intelligence insulted by the white man's distorted concept of having "discovered" the archipelago when they'd already settled the islands thousands of years prior to the arrival of the first European sailors. The early explorers' attempts to make peaceful contact with the Melanesians often ended in bloodshed. The mariners' approach was usually culturally insensitive and often authoritarian, which meant the cannibalistic natives had no other option but to appease their insulted gods with retribution. They were driven to retaliation, and their only means of defence against an alien culture they couldn't even start to identify with was violence. As far as they were concerned, all white men belonged to one despicable and never to be trusted tribe. Some of the worst atrocities that were ever inflicted on Vanuatu's peoples by Europeans occurred on Erromango Island.

Most islands depict their people's creation with a mystical *kastom* story, but Simeon Tovovur is adamant his ancestors travelled from an island near Africa. Later, when I visited Unpongkor, which is Simeon's home village on Erromango Island where he is a chief, no one came close to matching the twenty-eight-year-old's profound knowledge of his people's bloody history and of their beliefs. Before I left for the island, Simeon gave me the Erromangon perspective of his forefathers' turbulent past.

Captain James Cook first sighted the volatile island during a fierce epoch when cannibalism, warfare, and ritual dictated how the natives lived. Anyone who was in Cook's precarious situation had every reason to be apprehensive and to be constantly braced for an unprovoked attack. When a group of highly spirited natives waved his longboat ashore, they most probably enhanced the already wary explorer's feelings of mistrust. There wasn't a sinister motive behind the natives' boisterous welcome, and when Cook ordered his men to prepare for the worst, his instincts were horribly wrong. The astonished Erromangons were in absolute awe of the explorer and perceived the white man as being a sacred *nobu*, a god that had mysteriously arrived on his own floating village. The chief offered the demigods a welcoming gift of yams and called out, "*aremai ngo*" ("they are good to eat"), but instead of graciously accepting the vegetables as the natives had expected, Cook became increasingly wary. His growing suspicion overruled his sensibility, and he responded to the warm greeting with a volley of gunfire.

While Cook was safely onboard his ship which lay anchored off a prominent headland, he named the peninsula Traitors Point, but the only act of conspiracy had stemmed from within the explorer's suspicious mind. The Erromangons pronounce their words with a musical tone that almost sounds like Chinese. Cook misinterpreted "*aremai ngo*" and named the island Erromango. "They are good to eat" is exactly what the bewildered natives thought of the antagonistic white gods after they'd refused their hospitality, and they planned to find out if the next disrespectful white man that set foot on Erromango was "good to eat."

Whereas the earliest European adventurers were interested in colonisation and exploration, the next wave of foreign visitors were only interested in exploitation. Their arrival marked the beginning of a bloody epoch, which was instigated by unscrupulous whalers, ruthless blackbirders, and devious sandalwood traders. The seafaring whalers were mostly interested in plundering the ocean's bounty, and while they anchored offshore, they only paid an occasional visit to the coastal villages to replenish their supplies.

In 1825, the Irish merchant Peter Dillon published in the Australian paper *The Sydney Gazette* that he'd discovered vast quantities of sandalwood on Erromango. The perfumed wood, which was highly prized in China as a fragrant smelling incense, proved to be a catastrophic discovery. Erromango was suddenly besieged with an influx of feverish traders and became known throughout the Pacific as Sandalwood Island. Most of the merchants raced across the ocean towards inevitable conflict. After their deceitful bargaining, which usually cheated the islanders out of fair payment, the majority of traders took shameless advantage of the natives' primitive logic by totally ignoring their clan boundaries and greedily harvesting as much as their ships could carry. The waters surrounding Erromango quickly became Vanuatu's most dangerous destination when the dishonest merchants started to become the main course on a seething cannibal's menu.

Of all the missionaries who were trying to cast God's sterilizing light on what they thought were heathen savages, the Presbyterian minister, Reverend John Williams, was one of the most courageous and the most ardent. The famed member of The London Missionary Society had already made numerous converts around the pacific before he sailed into the archipelago on November of 1839. He was the first missionary to come to Vanuatu, and he wrote in his diary, "I consider the coming week as the most important in my life." When he arrived at Erromango on the twentieth of the same month to try and permeate the love of Jesus into the hearts of the primitive cannibals, it was also to be the last week of his life, because unbeknown to Williams, the well-meaning Christian was already dead on his feet.

A few days before Williams arrived, several Tongans and Cook islanders who were employed by blackbirders were ordered ashore at Unpongkor village. Three chiefs, Natigo, Tongtong, and Nompunare confronted them and asked them why the white man was so dishonourable, why he stole their sandalwood, and why he abused their initial hospitality.

Without any warning the slavers went berserk and indiscriminately slaughtered the villagers with their rifles.

Hostility and death were commonplace long before the arrival of the white man. For centuries, warring tribes had been well-versed in both spiritual and physical warfare. The *nakaimas* were incredibly potent and during astounding displays of metaphysical power, they absolutely terrified the natives by manipulating thunder. When a sorcerer performed the *kumwakoh ngi yowar* (to kill with thunder) rite, he induced deafening explosions from the skies that were capable of felling coconut trees and killing the villagers. The Erromangons naturally assumed the Tongans and Cook islanders were evoking the powers of the white man's gods and equated the cannonade of thunderous rifle shots and the fatally wounded villagers falling at their feet with their sorcerers' deadly magic. Everyone ran for their lives when the fearful warriors shouted out that their bows and axes were no match for the white man's rumbling death knoll. They fled into a nearby cave to escape the deadly din, but the blackbirders quickly lit a fire at the entrance and it wasn't long before smoke billowed into the cavern. Those who burst through the flames to escape the suffocating haze were slaughtered without mercy, and there was no motive when hundreds of Unpongkor inhabitants were brutally massacred with a hail of bullets.

The mindless act of violence shattered the already shaky relationship between the Erromangons' and outsiders. Now that the European's legacy of mistrust dripped with blood, their bloodlust demanded swift vengeance to appease the natives' irate gods. Kowiowo, the paramount chief, prepared his warriors and told them that next time they would do battle with the white man's *kumowakoh ngi yowar*. The ill-fated missionary came ashore on his longboat while the villagers were feasting. When Natigo, Tongtong, and Nompunare greeted him and his companion, James Harris, they somehow sensed the evangelists were different from the other despicable white men and decided to spare their lives. Natigo walked forward with a stick, placed it at Harris' feet and said "*nar*," which meant the stick was a *tabu* line that the missionaries were forbidden to cross. Williams' trust in God may have protected him in other volatile regions around the Pacific, but the instant Harris crossed the forbidden line, the native's pitiless retribution was swift. Natigo chased Williams to the nearby river and hacked him to death in front of the Christian's horrified crew. Williams' battered remains escaped the cooking fire because most of the natives believed he was a god and were afraid of spiritual retribution if they dined on his flesh. When some of Williams' predecessors suffered the same horrific fate, missionaries dubbed Erromango Martyrs' Island.

Evangelists may have deliberately decimated Erromango's culture, but religion's detrimental impact on *kastom* hardly compared to the premeditated deeds of the blackbirders and traders who were seeking revenge. The ruthless Europeans almost totally annihilated the natives by purposely introducing epidemics of dysentery, measles, and other fatal diseases, which wiped out two thirds of the island's population. Thou-

sands more died in a succession of plagues, and by the 1930s, only an estimated four hundred Erromangons had survived the biological genocide.

Although the Erromangons readily acknowledge that foreign diseases
claimed many lives, they believe jealousy, malice, and most of all, black
magic were responsible for the virtual eradication of their forefathers. For
centuries, the friction between enemy tribes had been to appease the gods
with payback killings, but when neighbouring clans or enemies profited
from sandalwood at the expense of islanders who'd succumbed to the
introduced diseases, the hostilities erupted into murderous hatred. Instead
of uniting to face their biggest threat, which was the Europeans, the Erromangons turned on each other.

Angered chiefs instructed their *nakaimas* to wage spiritual warfare on
their enemies by using *ndanum ngi nakave* (to kill with kava), which was
one of the sorcerer's most lethal weapons. What had once been a disciplinary measure became unimaginably destructive when thousands of
natives were ruthlessly massacred. Only *nakaimas* who'd eaten from the
tabu fire possessed the knowledge to save themselves. They began the
deadly ritual by encircling a small hole in the ground with sacred leaves,
then for the next four days, they filled the depression with water, sung out
the names of their victims, and spat chewed kava into the hole. On the
fifth day, when the water turned to blood, the hole was refilled using the
same soil and the victims died. Even nowadays, merely talking about the
murderous kava rite terrifies the villagers. *Ndanum ngi nakave* is considered so powerful, and so dangerous that no one on Erromango will even
mention the name of the ritual.

Equally deadly but less frightening ceremonies are also used to kill
enemies with kava. A live lizard is hung by a piece of *kastom* string that
has been made from a sacred vine, and the creature is sprayed with a
mouthful of kava. Then the *nakaimas* kills the writhing reptile and at that
same instant, his intended victim dies. If a screeching owl settles on a hut,
it's a sure sign that a sorcerer has targeted one of the inhabitants. By
throwing a lighted stick at the owl and screaming at the bird to return to
the *nakave* (kava), the curse is nullified and the bird is said to die. The villagers can safeguard themselves by drinking kava, then passing through a
tabu vine that has been shaped into an arch. This surrounds them with a
spiritual blockade against less potent black magic that uses kava, but only
a *nakaimas* can reverse a deadly curse.

Chapter Forty-Eight

THE WRATH OF GOD

Simeon warned me that when I travelled to Unpongkor village, I might witness firsthand that life often revolves around the dead when the deceased maintain an intimate and sometimes tumultuous bond with the living. Encounters with ancestral spirits are so commonplace that most of the villagers have listened to spirits talking in gibberish, shaking trees, cutting wood, and performing everyday tasks. To experience the inexplicable, and to even physically feel the supernatural, is considered normal and is almost an accepted part of daily life. A noisy apparition can be propelled back to the spirit world by confronting the ghost with a shout, but sometimes malevolent spirits appear in the guise of a white ghoul who is intent on overwhelming their earthly descendants.

If an infant constantly cries for the first few years of its life, it's believed that ghosts are terrifying the baby. The child's mother can usually banish the malicious apparitions with verbal abuse, but if this fails, the haunted infant is rechristened with the name of a deceased relative, several times if necessary, until it stops crying. When a child is born with body markings that are similar to one of its dead relatives, it's believed to have inherited their spirit and must become the deceased's namesake.

Whenever someone becomes unwell, dark forces from the supernatural are always thought to have caused the sickness. Three families at Unpongkor are revered for their ability to mediate with the spirits who tell them if an illness is of an earthbound or otherworldly origin. If ghouls are held responsible, then the person who performed the divination rite makes *kastom* with a *tabu* leaf and tells anyone but the patient that spirits are undermining the sufferer's health, which often results in an immediate recovery.

Domestic violence rarely occurs in the village, because the spirits of *abu* (ancestors) stem the flurry of household blows by causing one of the abused family members to become severely ill until the relationships within the family become harmonious. The dead are always keeping a constant vigil on their mortal descendants and demand they treat one another with respect.

Many Erromangons can recall inexplicable experiences during their childhood where they were unwillingly hauled through a spiralling void into a dream world that was so vivid and so authentic they returned to reality reeking of the afterlife's vile stench. Simeon was ten years old when he entered the uneasiness of another realm that was filled with both good and evil. His bizarre experience began when he and his older brother, Jacob, armed themselves with wild cane spears that were tipped with wire. They slipped into the cloudy waters of the Williams River, then waded towards the far bank. They were fishing for the shimmering schools of metallic-coloured sardines which darted around their feet, and it wasn't long before the baskets they carried were brimming with the tasty fish.

Simeon returned to the village and a few hours later he was overcome by a strange lethargy that quickly became an inexplicable and exhausting illness. His rapidly weakening body shook from a blistering fever, and after a ritual failed to exorcise any evil spirits, he was rushed to the nearby clinic. Western medicine was unable to offer him any respite, and over the next few weeks, his vitals began to wane, he couldn't talk, and he lost all control of his bowels. His father, Willy, knew Simeon was dying and that only a *nakaimas* could save his life, so he sent a message to his good friend Joe Kohwei. Joe was a revered sorcerer, and when he received a token payment of twenty vatu and a small bundle of kava from Willy, he raced to Simeon's side. After Joe circled the money around Simeon's head. He then departed and found somewhere private, where he entered the realities of the supernatural world. He fell into a deep trance and passed through the portal into the paranormal realm, beginning a frantic search for Simeon's misplaced spirit.

Joe crossed the Williams River, scrambled up the southern bank, and walked to the cemetery where the remains of his ancestors were buried alongside the bodies of murdered missionaries. The spirits of his *abu* told him to find a sacred burial ground that was hidden in a nearby stand of kwela trees, but before he tackled his ghostly adversaries, Joe's supernatural forefathers gave him a stern warning. These were true man bush spirits that were more potent and more evil than anything the *nakaimas* had ever faced, and if he dropped his guard, even for an instant, this time there might not be any handholds for him to climb back out of the spiritual abyss. He slipped further into the supernatural realm and was engulfed by a mystical presence when his spirit ventured to a heinous place filled with torment and death and despair, where dreams and reality collide.

He knew that if he didn't confront the demons, Simeon would die. Although Joe owned land at Dillon's Bay, none of the spirit men he met at the ancient cemetery recognised him as being one of their descendants. An elder who was stuffing tobacco into his bamboo pipe bellowed, "Get me stick fire" to Joe, then fierce looking men wearing *nambas* surrounded him and started hurling abuse and said that Simeon was theirs and he was about to die. Joe lunged past the devils, grabbed Simeon's spirit, and ran for his life with the boy's limp body under his arm. The primitive ghosts were no match for his powerful legs, and they gave up the chase when he swam across the river and ran back to the village.

While about twenty of Simeon's relatives were sitting at his bedside, they suddenly noticed the overwhelming odour of sardines wafting from his feverish body. Simeon's spirit had been captured while he carried the fish, and because of the strong smell, his kinfolk knew it had just returned. About an hour before dawn, Simeon uttered a moan and began to cry, and at the same instant the dogs that were milling around the leaf hut began to snarl and howl when they felt a terrifying presence with their uncanny sixth sense. The saddened relatives who'd gathered to watch Simeon die suddenly began to fear for their own lives. They knew they were about to succumb to a physical attack from the riled spirits unless they could call upon the powers of a *nakaimas*, so they locked the windows and doors and huddled together in a nervous silence.

When hordes of ghosts started charging around outside, the horrified villagers could hear the tinder dry leaves that had fallen from a nearby breadfruit tree and carpeted the ground around the hut being noisily crunched beneath the spirits' feet. The terrified dogs yelped and fled, and Simeon's relatives were so afraid that no one dared to venture outside until daylight. Joe returned just at daybreak and reassured Willy that his son would live now that he'd rescued Simeon's spirit. Before the bizarre event took place, no one had taken much notice of the shallow depressions amongst the stand of kwela trees that Joe visited in his dreams. A closer inspection revealed they were the resting place of their ancestors' bones, and to this day no one ever dares to enter the *tabu* graveyard.

On another occasion a ten-year-old girl was enticed to the profoundly sacred burial ground by her dead grandmother when she appeared as a pale ghost. The girl thought her *abu* was still alive and willingly followed the apparition. But when the child hugged her grandmother, the old crone said, "Don't eat our food or you will stay here forever."

The villagers were dismayed by the way the girl mysteriously disappeared and frantically searched for three days without finding her. On the fourth day, her father heard crying coming from the *tabu* cemetery, and when he peered through the trees, he was horrified to see his hungry and exhausted daughter sitting alongside her ashen grandmother. While the despondent girl watched the old woman eating bananas, tears rolled down the child's sullen cheeks. She was filled with so much sorrow, and fought so desperately to stay with the *abu* she'd loved so much, that her father had to drag the struggling child to safety.

It wasn't until they escaped across the river in his canoe that the relieved father noticed his daughter was covered from head to toe with pig lice and that she reeked of rotten human flesh. The spirit pigs that roamed freely amongst the village of the dead were infested with the parasites, and when the rotting *abu* had embraced her granddaughter, the putrid stench of death had clung to the child's body.

Sometimes the intimate relationship the Erromangons have with their ancestors has erupted into physical conflict between mortals and the spirits of the dead. The most famous clash occurred at what was once a thriving settlement called Ralifati village, which succumbed to an epidemic of introduced diseases and no longer exists. In the past, the villagers buried their dead in a canoe, and during the initial five-day mourning period, out of respect, all of the deceased's personal possessions, their property, and their gardens, were *tabu*.

A mourning woman, who was numbed by melancholy and had her mind clouded by grief, left her husband's body and without thinking, tore down his pig fence so that she could use the *tabu* wood back at the village to stoke a cooking fire. That evening, when the dogs outside her hut became nervous and started barking, her grieving family, who were eating an evening meal which had been cooked with the sacred wood, were stunned to see the dead man's angered spirit standing near the doorway. The breach of *kastom* made the ghoul so furious he declared *ndai noulet-ngon* (war) by slapping his *utvil* (stone axe) under his arm. His wife was to distressed to notice the pallid ghost's aggressive gesture, and she ran to her husband's spirit. But instead of being embraced, she was greeted with a hail of blows. When the terrified woman retreated into the hut and slammed the door, nothing was going to deter the persistent spirit from seeking revenge. He tried to climb through the window and take his young son back to the spirit world with him, but he was beaten back by the crowd of terrified mourners. Throughout the night, he desperately hacked at the hut with his stone axe, only to be driven away time and again by his relatives. The horrified natives breathed a sigh of relief and rejoiced when they saw the first rays of the rising sun drive the irate ghost back to the timeless world where he belonged. To ensure he remained with the dead, the mourners made *kastom* and apologised to the spirits of their *abu* for his wife's insensitive actions.

About four hundred people inhabit Unpongkor, and most of them are devout Christians who are seeking the Almighty's forgiveness in one of the village's eight churches. Presbyterian's boast the biggest flock from the different faiths, and although all of the Christians turn the pages of different bibles to worship the same deity, they share one common belief. They are convinced that when the blood of Vanuatu's first missionary, Reverend John Williams, turned the nearby river red, every Erromangon was cursed by the white man's god. Because one of their forefathers murdered the missionary, they are adamant God commanded their ancestral spirits to return for an eternity to drag their beloved children through the devil's portal, to keep them in their hellish world. The angels of death are always ready to strike and steal the children, who are constantly tempted to cross the threshold that leads to the land of the dead. They also believe that God and Jesus, their only saviours and their only means of redemption, cursed the island in a divine act of vengeance and turned the heathens' own savage customs against one another when the chiefs used *ndanum ngi nakava* (to kill with kava) to almost eradicate the entire population.

Chapter Forty-Nine

INVISIBLE BARRIERS

While Van Air's twin otter flew over Erromango, from the air I could see the Europeans' profane cruelty and arrogance hadn't only decimated the population, it had also drastically altered some of the landscape. What had once been a savannah covered in white sun-bleached grass was now smothered by a thick mantle of wattle trees that had been introduced by a foreigner. When I looked through a shimmering haze of heat, in the distance, the expanse of wattle forest had relinquished its invasive hold and submitted to gently rolling mountains that were sheathed in virginal rainforest. After the plane touched down on the grass airstrip, I caught a ride on the back of a Toyota Land Cruiser that slowly wound down a steep hill towards beautiful Dillon's Bay. The rusting pickup's brakes squeaked as it rocked and bucked over a road that was scarred with deep furrows that had been etched into the land by torrential rain.

Unpongkor was typical of the villages throughout Vanuatu that have succumbed to hybridisation. We drove past an assortment of tired looking houses and churches nestled alongside the Williams River that were constructed from a mottled mixture of traditional and modern materials that seemed to mirror the way the people had blended their pagan and Christian beliefs. I wasn't surprised when I received a lukewarm reception from a people who'd been disenfranchised of everything they once believed in by people with my skin tone. It was the same as everywhere else that had suffered at the hands of the white man. Once I made it known I was a close friend of Simeon's and that I was interested in documenting *kastom*, everyone's attitude changed markedly. Joe Tahumbri, a tall, lithe, and shy looking man who was about twenty years old, introduced himself and welcomed me to stay in his home. Although no one begrudged my presence because of the deplorable past, I could sense an invisible barrier that needed to be broken down if I was going to form any strong friendships.

The next day, while I slowly and patiently gained acceptance from the villagers, Joe told me that in the past, before his ancestors succumbed to introduced diseases and were annihilated by black magic, the equilibrium between man and the feral game living on the island had remained stable. The wild animals had been a welcome addition to the villagers' diet. But once the natives were decimated and the islands interior became devoid of people, the surviving Erromangons were beset with another curse when feral pigs quickly exploded into plague proportions. First the villagers lost their identity, and now their self-sufficiency is under attack from marauding pigs that constantly destroy their gardens. While Sundays belong to worship, Saturdays have been earmarked for wreaking havoc on the ever-increasing pig population. The hunters always return laden with meat, which has been detrimental to the villagers, who have never seen or heard of dental floss. Most of the elderly have lost their teeth from dining on excessive amounts of pork when they suffer from chronic gum disease due to their lack of dental hygiene. I asked Joe to tell the villagers that I would be happy to join them on a hunt, and if the chief was happy with the idea, to write a few articles to promote hunting on the island.

Late in the afternoon, while I was laying on my bed and resting, there was a knock on the door and a slim, fit looking man in his early twenties came in and introduced himself as a pig hunter. Tomkor Narai couldn't have made it more obvious that he didn't trust me and that he suffered my presence. After Tomkor fingered through the pages of a couple of my hunting articles, he bombarded my already aching head with a barrage of probing questions. Whenever I answered, Tomkor paused and glared at me in total silence. But despite his staunch attitude towards outsiders, he had the look of a likeable rouge that I couldn't help but like. When he said, "You look sick. Have you just taken the medicine for filariasis?" it gave me a chance to lighten up his serious mood. Everyone was undergoing a nationwide programme to eradicate the disease by taking free medication. The unwelcome side effects that most people were suffering from was the last thing I needed while I was slowly recovering so I'd given the drugs a miss. Filariasis is a horrible disfiguring disease that's transmitted by mosquitoes and leads to elephantiasis, which causes limbs and organs to irreversibly swell to unnatural and grotesque sizes. It often attacks the testicles and scrotum, so I said to Tomkor, "I didn't take the tablets because I want big, big balls." He smirked and said, "What did you just say?" I answered him with, "I said I want my balls to be huge. I want my balls to be so massive I have to carry the hefty mothers in front of me in a wheelbarrow or slump the monsters on the back of your Land Cruiser and run behind it." Then I emphasized the size of each testicle by pantomiming how I'd walk with my legs apart. Tomkor's serious eyes suddenly lit up, his lips puckered, and he dropped his tough facade and said, "Oh, shit. Oh, shit," then he burst out laughing.

Tomkor started to relax and told me how his father had recently died and left him a Toyota Land Cruiser, a boat, and a guesthouse at Elizabeth Bay, which is a remote area that's literally crawling with feral pigs, bullocks, and goats. Although it sounded like the perfect location for a hunting lodge, Tomkor wasn't an opportunist who was looking to plunder my photojournalistic skills. He kept asking questions and once he felt comfortable, our conversation became increasingly friendly. When I shifted the subject to the mutual friends we had in Port Vila, I struck an excruciatingly painful nerve that threw both of us into a stunned silence.

The first time I worked in Vanuatu, when I was in Port Vila, I met a Ni-Vanuatu from Ambrym who invited me to stay with his family. We became such good friends over the years that he freely admitted he was a *nakaimas*. He'd served a short apprenticeship, which gave him a scant understanding of black magic and left him vulnerable to an attack from the devil. Sometimes he'd disappear for days, then return in such a delusional and confused state that he was barely able to recognise his own family or who I was until his erratic mind slowly cleared. During the last time I stayed with his family, he warned me to leave, not because he wanted me to, but because he could feel the evil spirits he worshiped were turning on him. He felt defenceless against the devils that were snatching at his sanity and gnawing at his soul, so I took heed of his warning and left. When I returned from another island several months later, he'd gone stark raving mad. He talked incomprehensible gibberish, was chasing cars like a hyperactive dog, and terrorised his neighbours. None of the doctors at the hospital were able to help him, so they sent him to a *kastom* man, who prescribed drinking a broth made from the flowers of the paw paw tree three times a day. Six months later his sanity had returned, but so had his zest for black magic. Over the years, each time I briefly visited him, he'd gotten progressively worse until he eventually went completely insane.

When Tomkor spoke, his normally boisterous voice had softened to the sad tone of someone who was missing a loved one. He stared past my eyes, into my very core, with an unblinking almost punishing gaze while he solemnly said my *nakaimas* friend had killed his father with *kastom*. I was astonished by the bizarre twist of fate and tried to soften the bruising blow I'd just delivered, which I figured would end any chance of us ever becoming close friends, by mentioning the moment I realized he was a *nakaimas* who was dangerous and out of control, I'd severed our friendship. The last way I expected him to respond to hearing that I used to be a good friend of his father's killer was by saying, "Do you feel strong enough to go for a walk?" That was the last time we ever talked about the uncomfortable coincidence that gave me an indirect link to his father's death. After I laced up my boots, we slipped out the back of the house and cut along the edge of the jungle skirting the village. When I asked Tomkor why we were sneaking through the trees, he explained that he was supposed to be training with his soccer team for an upcoming tournament. It was easy to get to the bottom of the steep road that climbs away from Dillon's Bay without being detected. Whenever we were in full view of the village, Tomkor took off at a crouching run to stay out of sight and to purposely put my stamina to the test. While his tireless legs rippled with chords of powerful muscle and revealed his awesome fitness as we sprinted uphill, the rivulets of sweat soaking my clothing exposed my illness. Once we were safely out of view, his springy legs slowed to a walk and we hiked along the terracotta-coloured road for an hour to Unto village.

Just before we entered the village, Tomkor used a liberal dose of profanity when he said I was surprisingly strong for a white man who looked like hell, and then he asked me if I swore. I told him I never swear unless the other person does first and that I might seem fit, but after running up the hill, I felt as if I'd been fucked by twenty nymphomaniacs but still had enough kick left to go another round with twenty more. He said "Oh, shit" several times, and then he burst out laughing. It didn't take long for our down-to-earth banter and our similar irreverent sense of humour to break down any cultural barriers. By the time we'd walked back to Unpongkor later that afternoon, we were firm friends and had organized a hunting trip to Elizabeth Bay.

I loathe racial prejudice and any type of blatant cultural discrimination. That night, when I joined Tomkor and his close friend Thomas Lovo for an evening drink of kava with the village hooligans, I became the target of racist comments. Tomkor's older brother, Leibas Navie, went straight for the throat but purposely missed my jugular. He had that special knack of being able to deliver in a light-hearted tone what a more sensitive person would've thought was a scathing insult. While he reached out to shake my hand he said, "Hello, white maggot." When I matched his carefree tone and, without really thinking, I said "How's it going, black cockroach," a group of men who were leaning against a stonewall and chewing our kava nearly gagged. From the way he acted I could tell Leibas wasn't using me as a whipping post to vent his people's frustration at the way the early colonials had treated his forefathers; it was simply part of his wild and reckless personality. Leibas was the village hell raiser, brawler, drunk, and every other rebellious activity rolled into one inebriated package. He said, "Here, white maggot" as he passed me a shell of extra strong kava, which I chugged down in one hit. When I said, "Cheers, cockroach," he looked slightly edgy and eyed me up and down like a fighter who was trying to gauge his opponent's potential. Then he broke an uncomfortable and strained silence by slapping me on the back and telling everyone that white maggot was alright. Tomkor had warned me that Leibas had the "strongest head" in the village, but within ten minutes, and after several more shells of kava, we were bouncing jokes and friendly abuse off of one another like old friends.

The village thugs that I was drinking with weren't even remotely obnoxious, and for all of their social shortcomings, they were still decent people. The good-natured banter they dished out to make me feel welcome was devoid of any intimidation or malice. Leibas' bad reputation as the leader of a group of hardcore drinkers and substance abusers had preceded him long before we met, yet befriending him couldn't have been any easier. The European concept of being a drunkard differs from the village interpretation, where binge drinkers like Leibas are tarred with the same brush as a hopeless alcoholic is in western society. When he gets hammered with his friends, they normally drink dry bomb, but they sometimes boil tyres or torch batteries to make a potent brew. After it's left to stand for a week, the bitter sludge is sieved through a piece of cloth into a bowl of sugary water. Sugar masks the rank taste, but nothing can prevent the severe stomach ache that follows a heavy drinking session. They enjoy sniffing petrol and mixing meths, pharmaceutical alcohol, perfume, deodorant, aftershave, most aerosols, and whatever else works with a cocktail of water, fruit juice, and sugar.

When Leibas and his crew get drunk they always become violent and their first instinct is to stone people. Women, children, visitors, dogs, and whatever else moves runs the risk of being seriously injured. No one is exempt from being targeted with the deadly missiles, and when they shower the village with rocks, it always ends in a brawl when the angry villagers unite, storm the drunks, beat them to the ground, and then tie their hands and feet together until they sober up. I figured that small consolation is better than none when at the end of the night, Leibas said I was different to the other white maggots he'd met and that if he got me in his drunken sights while he was throwing rocks, he would aim for my arse instead of my head. While I walked alone in the pitch dark, I hoped to see or feel a ghost as I headed back for a good night's sleep, but none of the village ghouls were interested in showing themselves.

Chapter Fifty

VENGEFUL SPIRITS

The next day, instead of travelling by boat around the surf-scarred cliffs that skirt most of the northwest coastline, we decided to walk and hunt our way to Elizabeth Bay. We took the Land Cruiser and stopped half an hour's walk from the airport. With Tomkor and Thomas leading the way, I was in the company of Unpongkor's most respected huntsmen. And when eight of the village's best dogs spilled off the back of the Toyota, Tomkor promised fresh pork for dinner. Most of the dogs had their tails cut off in the belief it would make them stronger, more cunning, and more aggressive. Condom, whose named for what he safely does to pigs, led the impressive looking pack of mongrels through a tight plait of wattle trees. We kept our ears cocked while we ambled along a deeply rutted four-wheel drive track through an area called Souki bush. Within ten minutes, the sound of frantic barking sent us sliding down a greasy bank to the base of a stand of bamboo where we knifed an average sized sow. Before I'd finished hacking off the back legs for dinner, the dogs had taken off again and nailed a smaller but tastier looking boar.

Twenty minutes later, one of those deep guttural scoffs that tells you the pig's got a short temper, and conjures up the image of a massive boar sporting ivory like a warthog, stopped us dead in our tracks. A fracas of yapping, pained yelps, grunting, and the sharp crack of splintering vegetation being noisily flattened indicated the pig was just as mean as he sounded. All hell broke loose as the dogs charged from one ridge to another after the fleeing pig and barked themselves hoarse until the raucous pursuit faded into the distance. Both Tomkor and Thomas looked worried when the panting dogs returned from the futile chase. When I shrugged my shoulders and casually said worse things had happened, their creased frowns made it obvious they took their superstitious beliefs very seriously and that next time they came across the animal, worse things would definitely happen. If a hunter stands directly in front of a scoffing pig that manages to escape, it's an omen of impending doom. The elusive animal had just empowered the hunter's spirits, which meant the next time they crossed paths, they would be completely at the pig's mercy. Tomkor was adamant that the boar would seek revenge and would do so by goring the helpless and literally dispirited hunters to death.

As we dropped down towards remote Elizabeth Bay and I saw a beautiful and becalmed turquoise ocean, it made every step of the easy two-hour walk worthwhile. The newly built three-bedroom guesthouse was constructed from modern materials, and nestled fifty metres from the rocky shore, which offered the perfect location for the secluded but comfortable hunting lodge. I revelled in the serenity while we freshened up and washed off the day's blood and grime by stripping off and relaxing in cool freshwater pools that bubbled up alongside rocky tidal pools which were teeming with mullet. Before the arrival of Christianity, drinking the tasty spring water had been *tabu*, and it was believed that going to the toilet near the pools guaranteed you'd catch filariasis.

We had several hours of daylight left so Tomkor led us across a maze of jumbled boulders to the entrance of a sacred cave. A cluster of ancestral skulls were huddled together in a dark and musty recess and sat undisturbed, as they had done for centuries. A gaping fissure on the side of one skull that had been hacked open with a stone axe was a mute testimony to the island's violent past. Tomkor cradled one of the skulls in his cupped hands and while he looked up to the dripping roof, which had been carved into an elaborate gnarl by nature's artistic hand, he told his *abu* who were watching over their earthly remains that I was a brother and by taking photos I meant them no disrespect or harm. None of the deceased were camera shy, as no one from the paranormal protested when I cranked off several shots.

The skulls are treated with the utmost reverence, as are all of their ancestors' bones, which the villagers use for traditional healing. When Tomkor twisted his knee, a *kastom* man used a piece of his forefather's sharpened bone to make cuts around the kneecap. The remains of those who died from disease are never used for the primitive surgery, but the bones from those who were killed in battle or died of natural causes are ground into a fine powder, which is sprinkled into the cuts and then sealed into the wounds with the juice of a sacred leaf. Swollen tissue, bruises, broken bones, and numerous other ailments also receive the same treatment.

That night, while we wallowed in the afterglow of having eaten a hearty meal of roast pork that was washed down with a shell of kava, Tomkor and I sat opposite one another at the dinning room table while Thomas blissfully snored away in the next room. A flickering candle cast an eerie light across Tomkor's face and highlighted his features so that he looked like a ghoul and created the perfect eerie atmosphere for listening to ghost stories.

Tomkor told me about the recent visitations from the supernatural that have become a famous part of Erromangon folklore. After a hard day of cutting sandalwood at Swil Bay, Simeon's father and a group of his friends lit a blazing fire at a cave entrance, stretched out on a bed of *lap lap* leaves, and readied themselves for a much needed good night's sleep. Just as they began nodding off, a luminous sphere descended from the heavens and fell amongst them in a thunderous blast of blinding light. Glowing shards exploded in all directions, then a dazzling ball raced across the calm ocean, let rip with a hideous human scream, and vaporized into thin air. When the men got back to Unpongkor, they were told by an elder that the spirit appeared on the same day of each year to mark the anniversary of its death.

Simeon's stepbrother, David Natvuraka, derived his surname, which means to share, from when his ancestors generously gifted human flesh to the villagers during their frequent cannibal feasts. Whenever a captured enemy was spared from ending up in the cooking fire, they were normally tied to a pole and then flung from a cliff top into the ocean. While David and his father, Charlie, were fishing from a dugout canoe on a perfectly becalmed sea, two dim lights began looming up from the ocean floor. As the pair of lights rose up from the abyss, they kept growing brighter until they pierced the surface like a couple of blinding spotlights. The fishermen reeled back in horror when a spirit who was tied to a stick and had blazing eyes torpedoed out of the depths and glared at the trembling men. The glowing ghoul had been murdered by David's and Charlie's ancestors and had come back to haunt them. Their paddles were a blur, slicing through the water as the panicked men powered towards the shore and sprinted back to the village.

Before Tomkor started talking, to add drama to his next story, he widened his eyes then slowly looked over his shoulder. He had such an apprehensive look on his face that when I followed his nervous gaze, I half expected to see a ghostly apparition passing through the wall. While he pointed through the window he said, "Outside, less than one hundred metres away from here, live the spirits of thousands of angry *abu*." Just as the last word rolled off his tongue, an overhanging branch was nudged by the wind and screeched along the corrugated iron roof with the same nerve jangling impact as someone dragging their fingernails across a blackboard. Tomkor jumped, said "Oh, shit," and after he'd finished nervously laughing, he carried on with his story.

Within a minute's walk from where we were sitting, Tanwau village had thrived with the bustle and hum of thousands of villagers until a combination of foreign diseases and *kastom*-induced death decimated the entire settlement. The destructive forces of nature and time had reduced the once flourishing village to dormant piles of foundation stones and to a melancholy looking burial ground that was guarded by *tabu* trees whose growth had been nurtured by the bodies of revered chiefs. When a New Zealand logging company began milling timber in the area, there wasn't much left of the hallowed site. A middle aged local, Mathew Nelou, and Woris, another local who was employed by the loggers, were mortified when they were told that plans were being made to level the area with a bulldozer to clear a space for a portable sawmill. Their desperate pleas to not defile the *tabu* ground fell on unsympathetic ears and were answered by diesel fumes belching from the bulldozer's exhaust and their supervisor arrogantly yelling out that he didn't give a damn about *kastom*. He laughed off the superstitious mumbo jumbo and began destroying the esteemed ruins. By late in the afternoon, it had only taken several hours to disrespectfully decimate a sacred and historical site that had survived for millennia.

For decades, the spirits of *abu* had teased and disciplined visitors to the remains of the village with harmless supernatural "*play play*." Anyone who was wasteful and only partially ate the fruit and coconuts that still flourished at the ancient site was chastised by the angered ancestral ghosts. The gods despised such extravagant behaviour and made stones materialize from thin air, which they gently dropped on the offenders while they rained other rocks into the ground with such brute force that they shattered on impact. To pacify the irate ghosts, the villagers offered the spirits a genuine apology in their native tongue.

The New Zealanders' contempt for their beliefs literally sickened Mathew and Woris. Later in the day, they were overpowered by a strange lethargy that suddenly left them too weak and too queasy to eat. They tried to refurbish their despairing minds with a good night's sleep and stretched out in a *nakamal* alongside the vandalized ruins. Woris quickly succumbed to sleep while Mathew's mind went "cranky" as he wondered if his body and soul would remain intact for allowing the ancient relics and the *tabu* cemetery to be destroyed.

His worst nightmare became a harrowing reality when the hunting dogs that were outside began a chorus of unnerving howling. They didn't bark, they just cried out with drawn-out yowls, which were followed by the sound of the dogs frantically running around the *nakamal*. Mathew was terrified and felt certain the canine harbingers were announcing his death knoll, especially when the ghoulish chatter of centuries of deceased villagers started up outside. He'd never been so afraid in all of his life and ran to each end of the huge hut and barricaded the closed doors. The speaking suddenly stopped. Then without warning, a sudden blast of snarling wind ripped both the doors open. It was all too much for Mathew and an equally horrified Woris who'd been woken by the cyclonic wind. Mathew grabbed a burning lamp, tucked it under his arm, and both men sprinted into an empty caravan that belonged to the logging company and locked the door. Thousands of ghostly voices broke out into an eerie babble and while the spirits ran around the caravan, their feet scrunched a carpet of dry leaves littering the ground. The rattle of haunting chatter caused the two men's already quivering limbs to tremble uncontrollably, and when the pained wailing of an old woman cried out that the sacred graveyard had been desecrated and that their godly forces sought justice, the strapping natives were so scared they unashamedly hugged each other. Both of them were shaking from head to toe and were too aghast to speak, so they motioned with their eyes to what sounded like a stampede of approaching devils.

When the caravan jerked violently off the ground, the two distraught men suddenly found their vocal chords again and started screaming with fright and kept yelling when the caravan began bucking back and forwards. To save them from taking the brunt of the white man's arrogance, Mathew shouted out in a strong voice and apologized to the supernatural beings by telling the irate gods he'd been helpless to stop the destructive European. As the last remorseful words spilled from his lips, the disturbing commotion suddenly ceased, and apart from the trembling men's nervous chatter, the night fell deadly calm and eerily silent.

Later that night, when the two burly men went outside to go to the toilet, they were so traumatized they held each other's hands while they relieved themselves.

About a week later, two villagers who were gathering crabs for fishing bait reawakened the angered spirits. Pockets of fire mysteriously started to erupt in front of the men, who tried dousing the flames with a bucket of saltwater, but it did little to dampen the *abu's* rage. As soon as one fire was extinguished, flames sprung up from somewhere else on the bare ground until one of the men begged for forgiveness in his native tongue, which caused the bizarre fires to disappear.

I could see that Tomkor wasn't only telling the haunting tales, he was reliving them and becoming terrified by his own descriptive stories. Just as he finished the last tale, with perfect timing, a howling wind scraped the branches of the tree across the roof. While Tomkor nervously looked around the dark and now foreboding room, from the look on his face, he seemed to be imagining the screech had more sinister origins than a noisy puff of wind. Then as he turned and looked back at me, there was a startling bang and a high-pitched piercing squeal that sounded as if it came from the lungs of a demonic banshee. Tomkor threw his arms into the air with fright, let rip with a full-blooded scream, and cried out "Shit!" at the top of his voice. He nearly jumped out of his skin with such a sudden jolt that for a split second he seemed to momentarily levitate above his chair. A trap we'd set in the kitchen had made Tomkor's heart thump painfully hard when it snapped shut on a massive rat. I slumped onto the table, slapped it with my hand, and choked with laughter as my whole body shook hysterically while Tomkor said, "Oh, shit" about twenty times as tears of nervous laughter streamed down his cheeks.

For the next half an hour, while Tomkor lay in his bed, he kept swearing and laughing and reliving the heart-starting moment over and over until we dozed off and grabbed a few hours of sleep before we went hunting.

Chapter Fifty-One

PIG HUNTER'S HEAVEN

Long throaty bellows stirred us from our sleep as wild bullocks gruffly called to one another from above the guesthouse to herald the start of an already stifling day. The mobs of foraging cattle had grazed so extensively on the bush that there was little undergrowth, which made it easy for us to climb up from the coast into the vast and varied terrain of our hunting ground. To me, hunting has always been a mixture of adventure, pitting my wits against my quarry and following my primitive instincts to hunt for food. Right from the start it was obvious we were at war and that this had nothing to do with putting meat on the table. While we chased the barking dogs, there was little time to appreciate the stunning beauty of the island's wilderness. By midday we'd killed six pigs, but because there was such an abundance of game, Tomkor was disappointed with our low tally. When the dogs had accidentally split into two teams, Tomkor and I scrambled down a near vertical face to the Tanawau River, where we ran along the boulder-choked riverbed and followed four of the dogs from bail to bail. While we hunted along its banks, we had to bypass what Tomkor considered to be a prime hunting ground that's infested with game.

Thomas had his work cut out trying to stay within earshot of the other pack when his hunt became an exhausting chase through the rugged rainforest. The furiously barking dogs spent most of their time and energy chasing a wild bull, and it wasn't until he finally caught up to the persistent canines after running for miles through the jungle's endlessly varied terrain that he cautiously approached an arena of flattened vegetation. An evil-tempered knot of heavily built muscle and sinew frothed at the nostrils while it blithely charged the frenzied pack. The hulking giant of the forest had nothing but scorn for the dogs and its two-legged predator as it used its flaying hooves and its impressive sweeping horns to keep the dizzying circle of canines at bay. It treated the snarling dog's hysterical attack as more of a hindrance than a serious threat. Thomas has taken over one hundred feral cattle with a spear, and after he tied his machete to a strong sapling, he managed to courageously and expertly end the chase by thrusting his knife deep into the bullock's heart.

To replace our spent energy, we hacked freshwater crayfish with our machetes while they were walking on the bottom of shallow pools and ate them raw. After we heard a series of shouts, we eventually met up with Thomas, lit a fire, and roasted succulent slices of pork inside green bamboo while we crunched on nutritious *navele* nuts that we'd knocked from a nearby tree with well-aimed sticks. Tomkor decided to head for the airport to freight some of the pork to his relatives who were living on another island. He apologised for the small number of animals we'd taken, and then reassured me that tomorrow, when Thomas took me to "the dark bush" we would easily reach double figures.

While we walked back to the guesthouse, Thomas told me we'd hunted in a massive area called Sovu bush, where centuries ago a reclusive and mentally deficient tribe had lived. When one of the retarded natives and his wife visited Elizabeth bay for the first time, they'd never seen a pig before until they came across a villager who was walking a boar along the path they followed. The brainless man bush was fascinated by the animal as it rooted the soil with its snout and searched for food. He commented on how hard the villager's wife worked as she dug the earth, and then the idiot native asked if he could swap his lazy wife for the more industrious pig. Another member of the dense and unenlightened tribe discovered a blackbirder's barrel, which sent the whole of his clan into raptures. They thought they'd found the ultimate cooking pot and filled the flammable wooden barrel with taro, then placed it on a blazing fire. Nowadays if anyone acts in an unintelligent manner or does something dimwitted, throughout Erromango they are instantly called "man blong Sovu."

Early the next morning, as the sun burnt its way through a smattering of stationary clouds and the first glimmer of light lit up the sky, we knew it was going to be another hot and windless day. This time the dogs obediently stayed at our side for two and a half hours until we reached the Rabandamran River. The open and pristine rainforest was anything but "dark bush." It was a pig hunter's oasis of towering trees that formed a magnificent and undulating ocean of striking green jungle. I could see why the villagers deemed pursuing pigs as a vengeful quest rather than a sport, because without human intervention, Mother Nature was being thrown off balance and she was unable to find her feet. The bare earth at the base of the soaring trees was horribly scarred from mobs of roaming pigs that had destructively churned the soil in search of a meal. When Thomas muttered, "*sook sook, yeah yeah,*" it sent the eager dogs scampering along the river.

We'd only just started leaping from rock to rock along the riverbed when the dogs started bailing a pig. After we climbed up from the river and out of the jungle, I flailed behind Thomas for two hundred metres through a patch of coarse shoulder high *numnorong* grass. Thomas cautiously approached the shaking grass in front of us, then he leapt amongst a deafening fracas of mauling dogs, angry scoffs, and intense squeals. There was a look of contempt plastered across his sweating face when he drove his knife into the heart of a whippy little boar.

I'd just finished taking a photo of our first pig for the day when the dogs opened up about five hundred metres away. We bolted back down to the river, clambered across to the far bank, and raced back into the cool, damp jungle. An arc of mud sprayed me in the face when we arrived at a chaotic mud-spattered scene, as the hyped-up hounds bailed a black boar in a wallow at the end of a crevice. Thomas screamed *"yeah yeah"* to urge the dogs to lunge in and hold the feisty pig. They rushed in and clambered alongside each other to grab an ear, a leg, and a mouthful of sensitive testicles, which instantly sat the hapless animal on its haunches. Once they had a firm hold, Thomas waded into the small bog amongst the mud-caked dogs and ended the pig's piercing, high-pitched squeals.

Before Thomas had time to wipe the blood off his knife, a volley of barking one hundred metres upriver signalled the dogs had hit another pig. Then straight after we finished sticking the animal, the canines were in hot pursuit again. Sweat poured into our searing eyes and as we clawed our way up a steep three hundred metre long ridge, a nice fat looking sow flashed past with four determined dogs barking right behind her while another mob of pigs charged downhill about thirty metres away with two of the yapping dogs snapping hard at their heels. A harsh squeal and a pained yelp that rang out from above kept our protesting legs climbing. My drumming heart begged for rest so it could beat a more sedate tune, and I was gasping for breath when we dropped over the crest and slid into a small gut where the dogs and a mediocre boar were wedged in an uncomfortable and violent embrace. Thomas swore and slashed simultaneously with his machete when the irate boar came within a whisker of ripping him with its small but razor-sharp tusks. The keen edge of the knife hacked across the base of the pig's stocky neck, severed the animal's spine, and sent a fountain of bright red blood into the air.

We were both breathing heavily as we scrambled back up to the top of the ridge. We dropped over the side and flailed wildly down the sharp descent in a semi-controlled slide, and then raced back down to the river. I scooped up a handful of water and had a quick drink as we splashed across to the far bank and narrowed the two hundred metres separating us from the sow that had sped past us. By the time we arrived to end the chase the dogs' powerful jaws had clamped shut on their prey and held the helpless pig with the efficiency of a huge steel bear trap.

For the rest of the exhausting hunt it was more of the same. Right from the start until the exhausting finish we kept sprinting from one gruelling bail to another until we easily reached a double figure tally. None of the pigs were exceptionally big animals, but what they lacked in size they more than compensated for with their staggering numbers. We decided to walk back to Dillon's Bay and still had a long walk ahead of us so we finished hunting for the day.

Late in the afternoon we entered the jumbled remnants of Navoulu Village. During the early 1900s the settlement had pulsed with life, then every one of the thousands of inhabitants supposedly succumbed to a deadly curse that was inflicted with kava. Because it was Saturday, the normally abandoned village was a hive of activity. Pig carcasses hung from the limbs of trees, and the mouth-watering smell of roasting pork wafting in the air reminded us of our hunger. After the other hunters satisfied our grumbling stomachs by serving us a hearty meal, we gratefully accepted a ride with a Land Cruiser back to Dillon's Bay. The thirty plus dogs that streaked behind the four-wheel drive reminded me of a scene from a British foxhunt. If they had gotten wind of a pig, the poor animal would've been ripped apart, but the mass of jaded hounds were more intent on following us back to the village for a well-earned rest.

Chapter Fifty-Two

NALING

With the passing of each relaxing day, while I slipped into the restful pace of village life, Tomkor and I formed a bond as close as any brotherhood. Joe wanted me to stay with him forever and became emotional when I told him I planned to leave after the villagers had celebrated Vanuatu's twentieth anniversary for independence. Unfortunately not everyone had cause to revel in the upcoming festivities. A despondent woman with a three-day-old child threw herself from a cliff, but her attempt to kill herself was in vain when she landed headfirst and survived the horrific fall with a severely fractured skull. Although it's not a common occurrence, throughout Erromango, women who are tired of enduring miserable relationships have a tendency to commit suicide. The terrible incident put a dampener on the festive atmosphere leading up to the celebrations.

Further tension mounted when a group of greedy elders refused to pay Tomkor to supply the beef to feed the expected influx of visitors from the outlying villages. Everyone calls Tomkor "Natmono," which means strong heart. He lived up to his name when he decided he would provide the meat anyway, and five of us piled into his boat and motored around the reef-strewn coastline to Elizabeth Bay. We were armed with a light calibre .22 rifle which we used to shoot a massive wild bullock, a pig, and a goat that was clinging to the vertical cliffs rising out of the ocean.

After we sailed back around the coast on a calm and silvery sea to Unpongkor, that night, as we sat in a circle on Joe's concrete dinning room floor, Tomkor, Thomas, and a few others chewed kava. I was really looking forward to a relaxing drink after a hard day of lugging the meat through the jungle to the boat, until Tomkor started looking for something to sieve the kava through and pulled a rank smelling, mildew covered Canadian flag from the wall. He shook a pile of dried lizard droppings from the disgusting piece of cloth, and then he used it to prepare a large bowlful of kava. Everyone's attentive gaze was focused on me while I reluctantly helped them drink copious amounts of the revolting mould tainted brew. They were waiting to see if I'd commit a deplorable breach of etiquette by refusing the offer to drink the vile tasting concoction. Tomkor grinned, then said, "Even I didn't want to drink that shit. When you live with us, you aren't proud like most of the other white men. You are a brother. Tomorrow evening, on Independence Day, my family will make *kastom* for you. One day I will be a high chief. My middle name, Naling, is respected by everyone and was the name of one of Erromango's greatest chiefs. I want to give you this name. I want you to carry it and our spirits with you wherever you go."

Tomkor explained that each successive paramount chief from Elizabeth Bay had inherited the name and that Naling has several meanings: great warrior, great hunter, to unite, and to come together as one. Every Naling was revered as a powerful *nakaimas*. The black magic which is used to rape women or to secure a wife is known throughout most of Vanuatu as *masing*, but on Erromango, it's called *yangry mureau*. A sacred cave called Nepenti is the only place where the *tabu* soil which is the key ingredient for the ritual can be found. To perform the rite, a *nakaimas* fills a portion of bamboo with the sacred earth, sings to the devil, and then he must swim in one of the fresh water pools next to the ocean otherwise it's believed he will die.

The last chief Naling that resided at Elizabeth Bay used *yangry mureau*, which is the most lethal weapon in any *nakaimas's* mystical arsenal, to overwhelm and marry Tomkor's grandmother. When a sorcerer places the bamboo in the ground, he can use its daunting power to kill and to unleash unstoppable demonic forces. If a *nakaimas* holds a piece of the dirt in his mouth and says his victim's name while the wind carries his words in the direction of his target, their death is inevitable. Anyone who is cursed, can't stop crying until they eventually die. If a *nakaimas* secures his bride with *yangry mureau*, she is made to chew sugar cane that has been rubbed with a *tabu* leaf, which exorcises the devil's deadly spirit from her possessed body.

Once word raced along the village grapevine that Tomkor was about to make me his namesake, the smiles grew wider and the already warm greetings became even more genuine. At the opening of the Independence Day celebrations, I was unexpectedly invited to sit in front of the crowd alongside the chiefs and the other visiting dignitaries. My ear was literally inches away from the massive speakers that belted out the ear ringing speeches at a deafening, headache-inducing volume. Sambert Naritantop spoke of *ns'iesie* (respect), *nardmprom* (humbleness), and *nalcoiki* (to obey). He told the crowd these virtually nonexistent morals had been lost when Unpongkor's ancient traditions were eradicated and their cultural identity had faded away. Then he said that family values were rapidly decaying because the younger generation had become disjointed from *kastom* and that drunkenness and other introduced antisocial behaviour was steadily breaking down the values of traditional society.

Later in the day, a bigoted minister from one of the churches countered Sambert's desire for a resurgence of the belief in *kastom* by stating that the Lord had created all of the great chiefs and that only God could provide the people with salvation. Then he raced off on another unrelated tangent and accused several boys from the Kings soccer team of being disrespectful during one of his sermons. He launched into a fear-inducing lecture and warned that there was a *nakaimas* amongst us. After he finished breathing fire and brimstone, he roared, "The Kings soccer team will feel God's merciless wrath. All of them will be damned to hell," which ended his harsh and irrelevant words.

When the speeches were over, most of the villagers wandered up to the sports ground for the official opening of *kastom* dancing and the sporting competitions. Once the dancing started, I saw tears of joy streaming down an old man's face while he watched a group of children perform a vibrant dance that hadn't been seen for decades. The nostalgic elder kept saying "Number one. Number one," while he openly wept over the demise of his culture. I was honoured again when I was asked to present the winner's cup to the victors of women's volleyball. And Tomkor slotted a great goal into the back of the net and led his soccer team to a three one victory to clinch first place in the tournament.

At the end of what had been an extremely physical game, half of Tomkor's team limped off the field. They were bruised and bloodied from going into bone crunching tackles while they were barefooted against the opposition who were wearing sprigged boots. The wounded relieved their suffering by using razor-sharp bamboo and shards of broken glass to make numerous incisions to release the *"rabis blood"* (rubbish blood) from their injuries.

While Leibas was playing in a previous soccer tournament, he received the full force of a misplaced kick to his kneecap. As we watched Tomkor and his teammates slicing bloody lines into their flesh, Leibas said to me, "My knee looked about the same size as a man's baldhead." His serious injury failed to respond to the treatment he received at Unpongkor using human bone and western medicines, so he flew to neighbouring Tanna Island, and then travelled inland to primitive Yakel village for traditional surgery.

From there, he hobbled to a neighbouring hamlet five minutes' walk away and paid a round faced, grizzled *kastom* man, called Numaben, to operate on his damaged knee for the paltry fee of one fowl and a small bundle of kava. Four men pinned Leibas to the ground while Numaben used a bamboo knife to make a three centimetre long incision on each side of his knee that cut right to the bone. Numaben inserted a finger into each cut and scraped around the whole of Leibas's badly swollen kneecap to draw out the *"rabis blood."* Then he pulled the wounds apart and used a *tabu* leaf to wipe out what was left of the tainted blood. The pain was so excruciating that Leibas cried, urinated, and very nearly defecated himself.

Leibas was in agony as he lay on the floor of a leaf hut and willed away the pain-filled hours. The following morning, a poultice of leaves that covered his weeping wounds were removed and he underwent the same torturous operation to remove the blood again. Over the next week, the poultice of leaves was changed each day, and they dried out and almost completely healed the incisions. After seven days of recovering he was able to walk unaided. Two short puckered ridges on each side of his knee are the only unwanted remnants of his successful primitive surgery.

Impotence is also treated with a bamboo knife. While I was enjoying the festivities, Joe Walu, a seventy-three-year-old *kastom* man who is famous for his healing powers, said that for a miniscule twenty vatu, he could add spice to my sex life, as he'd done for the other Europeans who travelled from around Vanuatu to Unpongkor for his uplifting surgery. When I told him my penis is always up half an hour before I wake up every morning, the withered old man burst into hysterical laughter. Joe used his index finger to show me how he made cuts in the shaft, milked a leaf into the incisions, and rubbed the juice around the head of the organ. He guaranteed a successful operation and boasted that after ten days of abstinence to allow the wounds to heal, elderly men who even had trouble raising a smile were as virile as any adolescent with raging hormones.

That evening, while I sat alone back at the village and waited for Tomkor to return from the sports ground to give me his *kastom* name, a brusque villager, who only introduced himself as a pastor, sat beside me and gruffly interrupted my daydreaming. Before he told me his name, he said, "You are lucky. I used to hate and beat all white men before I became God's servant." As we shook hands, I said, "I'm Rick. Good to meet you. I guess we're lucky God found a place in your violent heart." The belligerent pastor said, "I'm Nemiah." Then he decided to share his life story with me and started with when he led Vietnam Two, who were a racist group of criminals that despised all whites. They were based at Freshwater on Efate Island, and expressed their prejudice and hatred by assaulting and robbing Europeans. Most of the victims were shot in the neck with a blowgun that fired darts which were made from umbrella wire. All of the stolen goods were hidden in a network of underground tunnels, similar to those that were used in the Vietnam War, until the lawless group was eventually disbanded and arrested by the police.

His already stern-looking face became even more serious when he said, "I'm from Ambrym. Before I found Jesus, I was a *nakaimas*. You have many devils within your tainted spirit. I can sense their evil presence. You are a man who has made *kastom* and welcomed darkness into your heart." He carried on his dismal sermon by proudly stating that he was a pastor with the NTM church, which originated when a self-styled Australian evangelist set up his ministry throughout the Pacific. Then the doom merchant really brightened my life up when he said the devil would eventually kill my family and me unless I welcomed the Lord and Jesus into my ill-fated life. Without God's salvation and a baptism, I was damned to hell. But if I was willing to seek redemption, he would happily take me to the Williams River to purify and save my imperilled soul.

After I'd been sweating all day, I figured my ripe armpits were due for a quick dip anyway, so I agreed to being dunked in the river and opened up my mind and made my spirit and soul vulnerable, just as I'd done whenever I participated in a ritual with a primitive tribe. Nemiah was brimming with religious fervour when he blessed the river and was armed with a bible as he looked skywards and defiantly shouted that all evil spirits must leave my soul in the name of the father, the son, and the Holy Ghost. As he threw me backwards into the river, murky water gushed up my nose. I came up for air sputtering and choking, and apart from having my sinuses irritated, I'd felt absolutely nothing. To me it was irrelevant that I was baptised without having a deep insight into the NTM church because Christians worship a universal creator. Although I'd treated the rite with respect and had taken it very seriously, I didn't experience an overwhelming feeling of being born again or an earth-shattering spiritual awakening that was about to change my life. None of the tangible power I'd felt and sensed during highly emotive primitive rituals enlightened my demon-infested soul. I don't have a desire to become Satan's disciple and, after the quick dousing, I felt equally positive that I wasn't about to become a Christian. I decided to continue living by my own principles. I've met numerous Ni-Vanuatu evangelists and reformed *nakaimas* who claim that the spirit of Jesus has the power to annihilate all *kastom* devils. Nemiah was adamant that the river whose waters had run red with the blood of Vanuatu's first missionary had flushed all of the evil from my soul. I felt contented when I heard his affirmation that after the baptism, my world would be filled with tranquillity. Then I walked down to Tomkor's house and waited to be named after one of the island's most potent devil worshipers.

Tomkor had sacrificed two of his finest fowl to make a *bunia*, which is a steaming package of yams, chicken, and onions that are cooked in *lap lap* leaves. All of his relatives crowded into the house and listened intently and quietly to Tomkor welcoming me into his home, his heart, and my new family. He spilt a small portion of kava onto the ground and called out "Naling," then I drank the remaining brew and bowed my head so that his mother could place a shell necklace called a *vanyone* around my neck. Tomkor ended his solemn speech by saying, "*Vanyone* means to unite. Now you are truly one of us." I used my pig-hunting knife to ceremoniously cut open the *lap lap* leaves encasing the *bunia*, which ended the simplistic rite. Then Tomkor took me aside and in a touching gesture that was in keeping with the oneness he spoke about, he offered me vast amounts of his hereditary land. I expressed a heartfelt thanks, then politely declined the generous offer, telling him he was the rightful guardian of the land which belonged to his unborn children, but that his name was something I would happily keep and treasure for eternity.

That night, while the Independence Day celebrations were in full swing, Tomkor got lost in the crowd of dancing bodies, and Joe and I got blind drunk on shell after shell of kava to officially christen me Naling. Leibas and the rest of the unruly village drunks swore and yelled abuse, stoned the villagers, and wreaked relatively harmless havoc throughout the night.

At about eight o'clock the next morning, when I wearily traipsed to Tomkor's house to bid his family farewell, Leibas and his friends were still partying. When he slobbered all over me and slurred, "White maggot, you are my best white friend," I returned his friendly greeting with, "Black cockroach. You take care, brother, and keep out of trouble." Several drunken men who were laughing and dancing to loud music surrounded us and thrust bowls filled with sugary aftershave under my nose. I drank a feigned farewell toast to Leibas and his inebriated friends from a huge aluminium washing dish, then we hugged and danced like lunatics, much to everyone's amusement. After we slapped each other on the back and shook hands, I was surprised when Leibas's smile faded into a grimaced, almost-wounded look that expressed genuine sadness when I walked away.

During my stay on Vanuatu's most haunted island, only the spirit of the living had reached out and touched me when I experienced kindness unto itself. At the airport, Tomkor lived up to his name of Natmono, when his strong heart overwhelmed his staunch exterior and any feelings of prejudice he had towards the white man. When we said our goodbyes at the back of the tiny terminal away from the small crowd, he was so saddened by my departure that he briefly wept like a grief-stricken child.

Chapter Fifty-Three

TANNA LAW

When I decided to fly to Erromango's neighbour, Tanna Island, I was warned that because of the legacy of its brutal past, Tanna bears the tarnished reputation of being the home of Vanuatu's most headstrong inhabitants. Before the arrival of the domineering missionaries and overbearing colonials, human sacrifice played an important role in Tannese society. Sacrificial blood was spilled into an indent in *tabu* rocks to quench the insatiable thirst of the native's ancestral spirits, and when the blood eventually vanished, it was thought to have been slowly consumed by devils. Death kept a constant vigil over the living during an era when life was valuable and the hazardous future was always uncertain. Life was precious in the sense that warriors gained formidable status and enhanced their mana by slaying and devouring their enemies. The genitals of both sexes were especially prized as an aphrodisiac, as dining on the organs was believed to improve a man's sexual prowess. Cannibalism was a regular dietary practise and chiefs and revered warriors were prime targets because their potent flesh instilled immense power into a man's spirit. Even if villagers died amongst friends it didn't guarantee them a reverential burial. Kinfolk who died from natural causes were often consumed, as human fresh was the ultimate meal, and sometimes the decaying remains of a friend or a foe that had been dead for weeks were eaten.

Everyone's existence revolved around appeasing the spirits to ensure they would be well placed in the afterlife. Tannese men who feared they would lead miserable and solitary lives in the spirit world ordered that after they died, their wives were to be strangled. A relative undertook the grisly task of killing the grieving widows, and then the strangled spouses were laid across their husband's body and buried with him to ensure he enjoyed female company in the hereafter.

Life on Tanna was brutally hard. Infanticide, strangulation, warfare, *kastom*, and suicide shaped what was a fearsome and barbaric society. Sometimes life was so cruel that weary and despondent wives often took their own lives. The ultimate expression of pent-up anger not only ended their misery, it was said to inflict the most scathing insult on a husband who had made their life a living hell. Rather than submitting to the merciless penalties that were meted out under tribal law, the women sometimes opted for a quicker, less painful, self-inflicted death. If they breached a *tabu* or were accused of having a strong head, females received horrible and ruthless forms of punishment. They were and still are chastised with what is known as Tanna law, or one law, and the legacy of that tribal justice is the very reason why nowadays many Ni-Vanuatu consider the Tannese as one of Vanuatu's most violent peoples.

While I was staying at Unpongkor, I developed a close friendship with Peter Kvaiou, who comes from Laukau village in northeastern Tanna. The affable eighteen-year-old had an easy smile, and his quick-witted banter kept me in fits of laughter. Peter always expressed amusement at the slightest opportunity, but his permanent grin faded when he shared his firsthand experiences with a totally humourless subject, Tanna law. His mother was an argumentative and domineering women with a strong head, whose constant squabbling drove her husband mad. Time and again she was warned to be quiet and to be subservient as a good Tannese wife should be, until her bull-headed defiance left her husband with no other option but to teach her an insufferably painful lesson using customary Tanna law.

Peter's grandfather passed sentence in the *nakamal* and decided to deliver the cruel punishment himself. A lynch mob grabbed Peter's bare breasted mother, slipped a rope around her chest and strung her from a tree. For two hellish days the rope cut deep and bloody tracks into her breasts and armpits while she hung without food or water, and wore only a grass skirt to stave off the cold subtropical nights. She was caked in blood from head to toe, and a crosshatch of ugly welts that were raised by whipping her with a stout stick oozed dripping blood down her wilting body. As the hours ticked by, she slipped in and out of consciousness and teetered between an agonizing life and a merciful but undignified death.

Peter felt every searing blow of the stick as it slammed into her body, every minute of her agony, and shared her lingering despair. Although he desperately wanted to intervene, no one ever does, because if he foolishly cut his mother down, it guaranteed he would receive the same barbaric treatment but with even less mercy. Whoever dishes out the punishment has total control over Tanna law, which is deemed as a reverent and *tabu* rite. Peter was completely powerless to help his beloved mother, and all he could do was shed a fountain of tears until her limp body was cut down and slumped to the ground. She was barely alive after her harrowing ordeal, but she slowly made a full recovery and became a dutiful and obedient wife.

Black magic is widespread throughout Tanna and of all the demonic rituals, the most potent is called *tamafa*, which uses kava as the key ingredient. *Nakaimas* perform the rite to induce spirits during festivals, to enhance everyday life, to kill, and for numerous other reasons. Once a sorcerer spits a mouthful of kava into the air and sings the victim's name out aloud, the only way to revoke the deadly curse is to pay the *nakaimas* a substantial amount of money. Whenever sickness, death, misfortune, and anything else disrupts the villager's lives, *tamafa* is always blamed.

Peter had just turned six when an unexpected death bought life in Laukau village to a sudden and violent halt. After one of the elders mediated with his ancestral spirits, he confirmed the villagers' suspicions and declared one of their own *nakaimas* was responsible for the death. All of the men and the boys who'd started sprouting facial hair were ordered to arm themselves with stout sticks, and Peter was told to join the other anxious villagers and become a reluctant witness to murderous Tanna law. Those who were told to inflict tribal justice slammed their sticks into the screaming sorcerer's body without remorse until they pounded the last breath from his pulverised body.

The *nakaimas's* body was battered and bloodied beyond recognition and laid to rest in an open grave for three days. None of the wailing relatives who were gathered at the graveside felt a hint of contempt or had any thoughts of vengeance. They accepted the sorcerer's death was a necessary part of *kastom* and remained with the body for the three days while they observed the *tabu* of not eating or drinking until the grave was filled.

Another *nakaimas* suffered a more merciful end when he was stuffed inside a copra sack then thrown off a towering cliff top. Peter watched the squirming sack sail over the edge and heard the muffled screams that begged for forgiveness fall silent when the sorcerer's body slammed into the jagged rocks. Other offenders who survived their punishment were made to endure a nightmare of unimaginable pain. A naked man who dangled from the rafters of the *nakamal* with a hangman's noose around his neck retched and gasped for air while the village men used their bare fists to beat their choking victim to within an inch of his life. When he recklessly broke a *tabu* for a second time, failing to take heed of his initial warning cost him his life when he was beaten and left to swing until he died.

Peter witnessed more cruelty in the first few years of his life than most westerners would ever want to see in their entire lifetime. He watched a middle-aged man endure the agony of being dragged by a rope that was tied around his wrists over a road made of abrasive coral. When the offender was raked over the coarse surface, his shredded flesh looked as if it had been mutilated by a cheese grater. Tanna law uses numerous barbaric methods to inflict its rough justice. While Peter watched the long lance-like spike that sprouts from the crown of the *nuiea* palm being speared through the hands and feet of a woman to pin her to the ground, it must have been gut wrenching.

Suicide is included in Tanna law's long list of harsh punishments. I could see Peter reliving the horrific memory when he told me how a middle-aged man who was tired of his wife's incessant arguing and infidelity, tied on a blindfold then hurled himself off a cliff. Peter was a small child and trembled with fear when he watched the mangled remains being scraped off the rocks and put piece by piece into a copra sack. If a despairing villager vents their rage by committing suicide, it's thought to punish the abusive partner by making them shoulder the unbearable burden of guilt, while death is an escape for those who were being abused so much that they were tired of living.

There are other cultures throughout the world whose time-honoured traditions frequently kill, maim, and brutalize their people to maintain social harmony, to vent prejudice, to punish, and to discipline those who bring shame upon their people or their beliefs. Tanna law still upholds its ruthless justice in the north of the island, but nowadays villagers who breach *kastom* in central and southern Tanna are fined or chastised by the chief who instructs a *nakaimas* to evoke a spirit that will dish out punishment. Like all Ni-Vanuatu, in general, the Tannese are regarded as a kind and good-natured people, but their first reaction during a fight is to flash the blade of a knife or to use whatever they can get their hands on—which includes their relatives, because irrespective of who or what caused the trouble, they won't tolerate one of their own being beaten up. If you take on one man from Tanna, you take on all of his clan. The Tannese have a bad reputation in Port Vila for having hot tempers and for instigating violence. With their genetic tendency to take the law into their own hands, it's hardly surprising they have no respect for the white man's judiciary, especially when *kastom* only recognises the brutalities of one law which has been used for millennia, Tanna law.

Chapter Fifty-Four

SELFLESS HOSPITALITY

It would be so easy for a civilised reader who learns about a barbaric ritual to instinctively form the sadly misguided opinion that spending time amongst those primitive peoples would be life threatening, but this couldn't be further from the truth. Tanna law will always remain secretive, and it will always only ever be administered in front of the members of a clan as it's *tabu* for outsiders to witness its horrors. From the instant I set foot on Tanna, I was offered nothing but selfless hospitality. And not one of Vanuatu's supposedly most aggressive people showed the slightest hint of having an abrasive or violent nature. These definitely weren't a people to be wary of or who should be avoided.

I spent my first night at Tanna Beach Resort, where I'd been given free accommodation on the condition I wrote a travel article. The next morning, although the unobtrusive thatch bungalows nestled alongside Embul Bay were a traveller's haven, I was happy to leave and make them part of a distant and materialistic world that I had no interest in. I joined a group of tourists taking a twenty minute ride through a pristine rainforest in the air-conditioned comfort of a four-wheel drive Toyota to visit Yakel *kastom* village. Whenever we bounced over the deeply rutted track, a league of nations giggled and laughed and clung to their seats each time the vehicle bucked. The thought of joining tourists who were on a photo safari so they could capture well-rehearsed images of Vanuatu's most accessible primitive tribe made it hard for me to share their mounting anticipation.

Yakel normally performs a *kastom* dance and walks visitors through its primitive world three times a day. While we sat and watched a dance and I heard a brash tourist talking about the "natives," who were within earshot, as if they were mute savages, it left me shaking my head in shame. The commercial fantasy world he so eagerly lapped up was great in that it gave him a quick taste of humanity's origins and allowed him to capture a glimpse of Vanuatu's rapidly diminishing culture, but following gawking visitors who peered at topless women in grass skirts and men wearing penis sheaths called *nagols* while they paraded about like anthropological curiosities definitely wasn't for me.

I stayed behind at the dance ground, which was flanked by massive sacred banyan trees, and introduced myself to Noaka. The tall, athletic twenty-two-year-old wore a mixed bag of hats and acted as the village business manager, the accountant, the official welcomer, and the interpreter. His almost perfect command of English and his polite and sociable manner helped our cheerful conversation flow and made it easy to ask him if I could stay in the village. At first, Noaka seemed surprised that a white man would want to live in primitive conditions, then he said, "It is good, but first we must ask the chief." He led me into the *nakamal* and introduced me to chief Kowia, who was drawing a lungful of smoke from his pipe which had been partly fashioned from an old .303 cartridge. Kowia scratched his aged scaly skin, which time had gnawed into the texture of wrinkled parchment, ran his fingers through his white bushy beard, and scratched his bouncy mop of hair while he listened to Noaka translating my request into his own language. The humble old patriarch laughed aloud, nodded his head in approval, and then clasped my hand in his gnarled fingers while he told Noaka to offer me all the help he could. When Kowia told me his people used to be brutal cannibals but they've replaced warfare with peace and that treating each other with boundless respect is the basis of his people's culture, his kind face screwed into a crinkled smile. Because the village markets itself as a sellable cultural commodity, I was surprised when Kowia said my food, accommodation, and having Noaka accompany me as a guide were free.

Later that afternoon, as the lengthening shadows crept across the dance ground and the sun started to set, the subtropical air became surprisingly cool, and although I was fully clothed, I still felt the cold. When virtually naked men wearing beards and penis sheaths wandered up to the *nasara* to chat and gossip, they squatted on their haunches and stretched their arms towards a blazing fire while they hugged its warmth. Several young boys who were similarly dressed leant against the outside wall of the *nakamal* while they chewed cuds of kava. Noaka told me only a male virgin can prepare kava, because once a boy loses his sexual innocence, if he chews kava for his elders they will fall ill and can only be cured with *kastom* medicine. White men obviously weren't treated with the same reverence. After Noaka spat out a pulpy wad of root and meticulously mixed my welcome drink, and I drank the saliva laced brew then chewed on the stringy pieces of pork which sizzled over the flames, it helped to ease any concerns the villagers had about feeding and accommodating a tourist.

Several hours later, when we walked down from the *nasara* to a tiny leaf hut which had been set aside for visitors, it had obviously been a long time since it had been used. Noaka shook his head in disgust as he brushed piles of fresh rat droppings from a foam squab that covered a bamboo-framed bed. Then he turned the grimy mattress over, but it didn't help to mask the impregnated stench of the rodents' sickly smelling urine. Despite the foul smell and the pungent tasting air, the extra strong shells of kava helped me sleep like a log.

The next morning I was up with the rising sun and couldn't get outside quick enough to draw long and deep breaths of cool fresh air. When I told Noaka I was busting and needed to empty my bowels, he pointed to a path that disappeared into the jungle and led to a small clearing which everyone uses as an open-aired toilet. Then he gave me a stout stick, smiled, and warned me "To watch my arse." As soon as I started heading down the trail, it was like ringing the breakfast bell. I felt like the pied piper. But instead of thousands of rats, a mob of squealing pigs trotted behind me, and instead of a flute, I was about to play an earthier tune with a flatulent human organ. As I squatted down and noisily emptied my bowels, my vocal efforts were echoed by the grunting and salivating pigs. The stick was to keep them at bay until I'd finished, because once I stood up, the mobile sewerage system rushed in and greedily consumed my excrement.

While we ate cold pork, which tasted like what the pig probably fed on every morning, and boiled *sushut* leaves, Noaka explained that ironically, if it wasn't for the tourists who have been visiting almost every day for the past eight years, Yakel, which is Tanna's traditional stronghold for *kastom*, would most likely have been another casualty of westernisation. Noaka was five when an American anthropologist the villagers respectfully called Mr Karl lived at Yakel and studied their customs for one year. At the time, most of Yakel's age-old traditions had been buried in the past, and apart from a few old men and women, everyone wore clothing. Mr Karl persuaded the chief to resurrect *kastom*, but over time the temptation to use modern goods and to wear warm clothes again virtually eliminated their pagan beliefs.

Then Mr Robert arrived from New Zealand to document what was left of Yakel's rapidly diminishing culture. But instead of remaining a passive and transitory observer, he motivated the villagers to follow the *kastom* road again. Whereas primitive man normally requires vigorous protection from the often traumatic impact of having contact with outsiders, Yakel has gone full circle and has become a refugee from the modern world but has managed to prosper both culturally and financially from their association with foreigners. Although it was Europeans who revived their waning beliefs, the bulk of *kastom* has remained *tabu* to outsiders.

We had a few hours to spare before the tourists arrived, so Noaka offered to pose for a few photos at a nearby waterfall. As we were walking through a field covered in sun-bleached grass to get to the edge of the jungle, the last thing I expected was for Noaka to scream, "Run," then see his nearly naked body turn about and streak across the paddock. When I saw a bad-tempered bull had me dead in his sights, I spun around with the speed of a startled cat. While I was eating Noaka's already settling dust, I could hear the bull's pounding feet getting closer until I could almost feel its snorting breath on the back of my neck. Then, according to Noaka, the sharp twang of a rope being stretched taut by the mountain of beef nearly jerked the charging animal off its feet. Noaka let rip with a string of what I guessed were obscenities in his native tongue. We looked at each other in shocked silence, and then we both laughed so hard and for so long that I fell over. I rolled around on the ground in hysterics until my shuddering stomach hurt. Once the adrenaline burned off, we dropped our previous politeness and didn't bother with any unnecessary courtesies. The photos I took of Noaka posing with his bow at the base of the waterfall while plumes of water cascaded over a jagged rock face made for priceless shots, but it was the solid friendship we'd formed that I really valued.

When we walked from Naoka's hut up to the dance ground to wait for the next influx of tourists, huge piles of taro, yams, and kava were being stored in the *nakamal* and around the *nasara*. Most of the village roosters that were fossicking for grubs made a hasty beeline for the jungle when we got too close to them. The remaining birds had been denuded of their tail feathers and partially plucked, which made them look ridiculously scrawny. They were wary of losing more iridescent plumage to the boys who were undergoing a circumcision ritual. The boys would emerge with feathers sprouting from their hair when their three months of living in seclusion behind a specially constructed fence that bordered the *nasara* was over. It had been eight years since the last circumcision rite, and twenty-seven boys aged from five to ten years old were preparing to leave the confines of the *tabu* area in several weeks'time.

Noaka told me if a smaller number of children had endured the painful rite, the two sacred huts perched high amongst the branches of the banyan trees are used. Throughout the ritual, women are forbidden to even look at the tree houses called *nimayatognivin* and carefully avoid going anywhere the *nasara*.

As a volley of flat blasts from what the villagers call the *ngayuk* shell reverberated from behind the crude fence, the haunting tone made all of the women scamper towards their huts or flee into the bush. The conch shell signalled that the initiates were about to leave the confines of the *tabu* area to go and bathe in the river, and another series of blasts on the shell also cleared the area when the boys were about to return. Noaka asked me to turn my back so I wouldn't catch a glimpse of the boys as they sprinted across the *nasara* and disappeared into the jungle. I knew a circumcision ritual is extremely *tabu*, but I still asked Noaka if I could document the rite. He went into the *nakamal* and returned several minutes later and said, "You are very, very, lucky. Chief Kowia has allowed me to share most of the *kastom* with you." Then he led me into the *nakamal* so that we were out of earshot from a huddle of gossiping women who had returned to carry on weaving a bundle of dried pandanus leaves into mats.

In the past, the intimidating ritual taught children to be tough, to be cruel, and not to have any empathy towards their enemies. Even today the small boys are bullied, terrorized, and humiliated so that they emerge from the rigours of a circumcision with the resolve of hardened men who have been conditioned to face life's hardships. The circumcision is one of the most important days in a boy's life, for it marks the transition from being a boy to being well on the way to adulthood. It's hard to imagine a five-year-old in a civilised society having the maturity to be able to fully come to terms with the importance and significance of not crying out when his foreskin is sliced off with a bamboo knife that's been tempered over a fire and is still smoking. If the child shows any sign of weakness by screaming or crying, he will never become a man. After he has spent the first month of his seclusion learning about manhood, the moment of truth arrives. Five men physically brace the child while another one holds the terrified boy's penis still so that the surgeon can begin cutting with the smouldering knife. As soon as the razor-sharp edge slices into the foreskin, a male member of the boy's family circles once around the wincing child, then when the operation is finished the boy's relative gifts the surgeon a kava plant and one fowl.

Throughout the next month, the child holds a *nagol* in front of his healing penis to symbolise that he is becoming a man. A *nagol* and a woman's skirt are both made from young *burau* stalks that have been submerged in a river for three weeks. The rotting outer bark is removed, then the inner bark is hung in the sun to dry for several days before it's sliced into fine strips and made into garments that almost have a silky texture. During the initiates' third month in isolation, their penises have healed enough for them to wear a *nagol*, whose tightly-bound top sits just below the navel then flares out in a tress that falls to just above the knee. Straps of bark that are dyed yellow with the juice of *tabu* berries are plaited into a rope called a *namas*, which is tied around the waist to hold the *nagol* in place when the boys finally emerge from behind the fence.

For the next three days, the initiates celebrate their newfound freedom with feasting and lively dancing. Copious amounts of food are cooked inside bark from the *nafa* tree, which emits a powerful odour that smells like liniment. Preheated stones are placed above and below the parcels of food, then a thick layer of fern is used to insulate the heat and dirt is shovelled over the feast. Ordinarily food is parcelled in *lap lap* leaves, and a wet sack replaces the bundles of fern, as the traditional oven called a *ngagwaneman* is only ever used during hallowed rituals.

My already extended visa left me with no other option than to leave for New Zealand several days before the celebratory feast was about to start. On the first day of feasting, the skin from the tips of taro and yams are removed in a symbolic circumcision. The following day, massive amounts of food are prepared and eaten. Then a huge feast is held on the last day, and the dancing starts in the evening and carries on throughout the night until daybreak to culminate the lengthy rite.

In Yakel's patriarchal society, a husband has total control over his wife but he must show absolute respect to other women. Although the young boys are no longer children and are treated with a newfound respect by their mothers, it's only when they shave for the first time that they are truly thought of as men. Their facial hair is cut away by an uncle with a bamboo razor, and then the uncle spills the blood of a sacrificial pig and spits a mouthful of kava onto the ground to show the ancestral spirits that the boy is now a man.

When I asked Noaka what happens to the foreskin, he shook his head from side to side and said, "Sorry. It's *tabu*." While I was on Erromango, Peter Kvaiou didn't have any reservations about sharing what happened to his foreskin after he was circumcised. His ceremony was as abrupt and as brutal as his people's tribal law. Peter's foreskin was cut away in four pieces with a smoking hot bamboo knife then hung from the rafters in the *nakamal*, where he and the other initiates were confined for only seven days. A sacred leaf was milked onto his bleeding penis as was the milk of grated coconut flesh, which, as well as being curative, is believed to enhance sexual performance and ensures the boys maintain a healthy libido well into their old age. There is no lengthy recovery period, and at the end of the week, the boys emerge from the *nakamal*, dig a hole, put in their foreskin, and then plant a tree on top of it. Whenever the child looks at the tree, he's reminded of his harrowing circumcision, of the pain and torment he endured, and to maintain the same strength and courage he showed during the barbaric surgery for the rest of his life.

For the young girls at Yakel, their pubescent transition to womanhood is equally traumatic as the boys' circumcision ritual. The biological development of a girl's body dictates when she must become an adult. When she menstruates for the first time, the initiate must endure an enforced one month stay in the *nemaemalaga*, which is a tiny hut where the girl must conceal herself as its *tabu* for her to be seen by a male. She doesn't use anything to stem her flow of blood, and during the night, under the veil of darkness, she sneaks into the jungle but carefully avoids the gardens so as she wont taint them with her menstruating body. Her female relatives are waiting for her in the jungle and give her food.

From the moment her menstrual blood begins to flow, during the day she quietly slips into the rainforest, where an old woman starts making two rows of vertical incisions in the girl's back with a bamboo knife. Each row consists of up to one hundred short intricate cuts, which start at the top of the shoulder blade and run down to the small of the girl's back. A horizontal row of vertical cuts runs beneath these and goes from one side of her waist to the other. Like her male counterparts, she must remain silent throughout the entire time-consuming operation. At the end of each session, the old woman rubs coconut milk into the wounds so that they heal into raised scars.

The girl must wait until nightfall, then she sneaks back to the edge of the village, and after she's sure no males are present, she sprints to the *nemaemalaga* and tries to sleep on her side or stomach for a while before she goes back and gets her food. After her menstrual flow has finished, her entire body is washed with coconut milk to cleanse her body and her spirit.

At the end of the harrowing month, all of her female relatives take her to a nearby river where they use the toxic stems of the taro plant and the rigid curved stalks from which bananas grow to give the girl a severe beating. The taro sears her skin with the same intensity as *nangalat* and the stalk leaves her bloodied and bruised. In the past, if a male errantly saw the girl being flayed, her brothers killed him, but nowadays the death penalty has been abolished and compensation of one pig is paid to her family.

The women escort the girl back to the village, then she leads them on a fierce and physical attack against her male relatives that can last for an hour once they get a victim and beat him with the taro and banana stalks. After a life of servitude, none of the women hold back. This is a rare and welcome opportunity for them to vent the frustrations of being or becoming a subservient workhorse and dominated wife in the patriarchal village. Apart from committing suicide, this is the only chance they have to get back at men who enjoy the unfair division of labour. Once the beatings have finished, her father slaughters a pig and celebrates his daughter's transition to womanhood with a *lafaet*. During the feast, he sprays a mouthful of kava onto the ground and from that instant the girl is treated as and takes on the unwelcome burden and numerous responsibilities of being a woman.

Before European laws were introduced, young girls who hadn't menstruated were betrothed to a husband who was picked by the chief. Kowia still pairs off partners who must get married, but he waits until the woman is sixteen which is the legal age for consensual sexual intercourse in Vanuatu. He chooses what he feels will be a suitable husband that's about the same age as his intended wife, and before they are married, the male must pay a bride price of five pigs, chickens, woven mats, and food to the bride's family.

There isn't a trial period to test the betrothed's compatibility with her arranged partner, and if the husband to be has an unwed sister, she must marry the bride's unwed brother to strengthen the alliance between the two families. The males from both families spit kava on the ground during the feast which is held to celebrate the union, and to make the marriage official, everyone dances throughout the night until dawn while the newlyweds consummate their marriage in one of the tree houses overlooking the *nasara*.

After the couple have their first child, they are forbidden to have sex for three years. This *tabu* is rarely broken because to do so incites the rage of ancestral spirits and endangers the child's life when it succumbs to an inevitable illness which is meted out by the supernatural. The only way for a husband who has breached the *tabu* to restore the health of his sick infant is to gift his wife a large bunch of kava and a pig. She must share the punishment by consuming the entire pig by herself, and the husband's uncle must also pay penance by mixing and drinking all of the brain rattling kava by himself in one mammoth session.

The villagers are given the opportunity to release any pent-up sexual frustrations during a spectacular three-day ceremony called the *nekowiar*. A flood of revellers arrives from other villages wearing bright face paint, feathers in their hair, and skirts that are dyed with striking colours to join an exhaustive orgy of pig kills, feasting, and highly spirited dancing. A *nakaimas* uses *tamafa* to evoke lively ancestral spirits, who empower the dancers with added strength to heighten their mood during the festivities. At the start of the second morning, the *toka*, which is the highlight of the celebrations, literally brings people together when groups of amorous men dance through the crowd and encircle and capture flamboyantly dressed women. Couples break away from the sexual dragnet and find somewhere private where they can indulge in gratuitous sex. The village elders police the lovemaking to ensure the infidelity doesn't last for too long, because the couples are only allowed to enjoy each other's bodies for a carefully regulated period of time and only during the *toka*.

Yakel has its own special charm, but it lacked the primitive aura and the remoteness of some of the other tribes I'd lived with. Anthropologists had already made extensive studies of their beliefs and the tourists flocking to view pre-ordered culture every day shaved the raw edges off the village. I doubted that I'd make any startling new discoveries, so that afternoon, I made plans to walk to Mount Yasur, which is one of the world's most accessible active volcanoes, and then to continue across the island to Port Resolution.

The next day, I followed Noaka through undulating terrain that was robed in luscious jungle until we burst out of the greenery into a grey lunar looking landscape. While we walked across a small desert, rocks that had been thrust from the bowels of the earth during violent eruptions floated above the volcanic sand and wavered in a mirage that was formed by the stifling heat waves on the shimmering horizon. A warm wind fanned our bodies as they instantly started to sweat, and it rustled the long hard leaves of the hardy palmlike pandanus that dotted the denuded wasteland.

Once we crossed the arid ash plain we climbed up a steep four-wheel drive track which stops ten minutes' walk from the barren volcano's glowing navel. Just as the sun was setting, we stood on the rim of the brooding and gaping crater and listened to, tasted, and smelt the fire-breathing dragon's fetid breath. The main vent gasped and roared with what sounded like a cannonade of booming thunder that sent a seething and molten mass of blood red magma through the sulphurous air in a hellish and unforgettable chaos of sight and sound.

We reached the coast the following afternoon and at the picturesque yacht anchorage at Port Resolution, I swam with the resident dugong, the sea mammal which sex-starved mariners mistook for a mermaid. A young boy from the yacht club slapped his cupped hands on the surface of the water, which sent a *thwok, thwok* resonating through the crystal clear ocean. Noaka pointed to the creature's graceful silhouette as it effortlessly slid through the water and came towards us. I was mesmerised as I swam alongside the playful dugong while it performed an elegant underwater dance by rolling its plump body over and over. It looked at me with its large radiant eyes, and gently nudged me with the bristly whiskers sprouting from its wide snout.

Just after dusk, we were walking along a road and were lucky to have avoided spending a night under the stars when we hitched a ride back to Tanna Beach Resort with a passing four-wheel drive that stopped for us in a cloud dust. When we were dropped off at Tanna Beach Resort, Noaka shot me a surprised look when I politely told Monica, the manageress, that if Noaka couldn't spend the night for free like I was for writing a travel article, then I wouldn't stay here either. Once I told her Noaka had guided me across the island to help reap material for a story to promote the resort, she agreed to let us stay. While Noaka marvelled at the flush toilets, an ice cold drink after walking all day, and compared his ridiculously plush bed to his simplistic sleeping mat back at the village, he said, "This isn't for the black man, Rick." His awe matched the massive rush of emotion I experienced whenever I made a startling new discovery amidst a remote jungle in a distant land, but the difference was this wasn't the unexplored end of the earth, it was only twenty minutes' drive from Yakel.

While we walked back up to Yakel the next morning and were laughing and joking, when Noaka said "You are different from other white men," it had a familiar ring. He asked why the Europeans always have to victimize Ni-Vanuatu, exploit everything they come into contact with, and had to alter his people's way. Then he said, "The white man has saved our *kastom*, but it was him who buggered us up in the first place. We might take his money from him every day, but we do it with a smile, and we respect him." When it was time for me to head back to Port Vila that afternoon, Noaka's voice was tinged with sadness when he said "My hut is small and dirty, and it isn't for the white man, but now it is our hut. Next time you come back, you stay with me and my wife."

Chapter Fifty-Five

A GODSEND

About a year later, after a hellish bout of malaria nearly sucked all of the life out of me, I was twenty-three pounds lighter than when I'd first arrived back in Vanuatu, and was so unwell I was barely able to stand. If I tried to walk without help, it left me feeling weak and exhausted. My plans to travel to Tanna were put on hold until I'd taken a well-earned rest and recuperated at Port Vila. The days slipped into a week while I rebuilt my stamina with slow walks, plenty of good nutrition, and by relaxing with a pile of books by the lagoon. As soon as I was strong enough to walk in a straight line while I carried my pack, I flew to Tanna and was rearing to go but at a subdued pace.

Weeks of incessant rain had transformed the road that winds up to Yakel into an impassable bog that was pockmarked with deep ruts. There were four hours of light left, so I pointed my bony body inland and started a slothful climb up the washed out track. An hour later, I realized my mind was a lot stronger than my weak legs, and when I reached the base of a long and tedious hill, I slumped to the side of the road for an enforced rest. It would've been easy to kick myself for not giving my protesting body a few more days' rest, but I'd sooner feel like hell and experience something new than be fresh-faced and doing nothing. Two men from Erromango who were heading in the same direction took turns carrying my pack until we parted company fifteen minutes' walk from Yakel.

Noaka was so mortified by my haggard body and gaunt cheeks when I entered the village that he swore in his native tongue, then said, "Shit! What happened to you, Rick? You look like hell." While we walked down to Noaka's hut and the ground started to tremble, I wondered if the rumbling tremor was a prelude to another violent eruption. Mount Yasur was in a hyperactive mood, and just a few weeks earlier an exodus of panicked villagers who feared the day of reckoning had arrived fled to the coast during a grade four eruption. That night I was so shattered that just the one shell of kava I had as an official welcome sent me spiralling into a deep sleep on a bamboo slat bed, while Noaka and his wife stretched out below me on sleeping mats they'd laid alongside the cooking fire in his cramped leaf hut.

I must have looked twice as bad as I felt the next morning because as soon as Noaka saw me, he grimaced and said I needed some *kastom* medicine. Ever since captain Cook and the other European explorers introduced the goat to Vanuatu, several superstitious tribes have believed the animal's flesh is a remedy for malaria. After we finished breakfast, we travelled down to a neighbouring hamlet, paid a *kastom* fee, then Noaka crept through a patch of jungle and caught a goat with his bare hands. When we got back to Yakel and lit a blazing fire, we decided when I felt strong enough, we would go hunting and try and arrow a wild pig. Noaka reassured me that eating the goat that sizzled over the flames would restore my sagging energy, then he sliced me off a huge portion of steaming meat.

I was chewing through my second helping of the strong tasting meat when a boy from the neighbouring village told us a New Zealander whose "legs had buggered up" was about to go under Numaben's bamboo knife. Noaka and I raced down to the old *kastom* man's hut to see if we could help. The astonishment was definitely mutual when we knocked on the door and were told to come in by a thin faced man with a thick mane of blond shoulder length hair, who was lying on a self inflating camping mattress. Jimmy looked about thirty years old and seemed pleasantly surprised when he greeted us with a huge smile. He pushed himself up to a sitting position, reached down and used both his arms to lift his atrophied legs into a more comfortable position, then he took a swig of green juice from a glass bottle and told us to sit down. When I saw Jimmy's wheelchair leaning against the thatch wall with his other belongings, the reason he was here was obvious.

Jimmy was one of life's good-natured cruisers and easy to get along with. When he was sixteen, he'd crashed through a skylight and lost the use of his legs when he landed on a concrete floor. Although I never complained about my health, recovering from malaria suddenly seemed pathetic compared to his plight. Here he was, alone, handicapped, and with the threat of a volcanic eruption noisily looming in the distance, and he was preparing himself for primitive surgery by drinking the lime green brew Numaben had concocted with *tabu* leaves. Numaben had held his hands over Jimmy's body and accurately diagnosed hidden problems which had already been picked up by doctors back in New Zealand. Unless you're put in a similar position, it's hard to fully understand how someone in a hopeless situation could hope for an improbable miracle. I tried to help Jimmy by answering his questions about how I'd experienced bizarre feats that science deemed as being physically impossible while I lived with primitive tribes, but I was also brutally honest about how I felt about him having an incision made in his back, through to his spinal chord, without anaesthesia. I said, "No offence, Noaka, but take a good look around you, Jimmy. Do you want Numaben prodding his fingers into your spine in these unhygienic conditions?" Noaka showed him the scar where Numaben had cut him with a bamboo knife and straightened out his broken collarbone. Then I told Jimmy that because Numaben could tie on bamboo splints, reset broken bones, and scrape out "*rabis blood*" from swollen limbs with his fingers, it hardly gave him the ideal recommendation as a back surgeon and that neither did the *kastom* he performed before each operation if a patient had Christian beliefs. In the days leading up to our hunt, we briefly visited Jimmy every day to make sure that he was okay and had everything he needed, but for the most part, I left him alone because I knew that if I didn't, I would try my best to talk him out of it.

In spite of the financial rewards ethnotourism yields for Yakel's inhabitants, they have chosen to live mainly on locally grown foods and very rarely eat rice and tinned goods to bolster their already adequate diet. Nowadays, although there are tribes who are trying to return to *kastom*, there isn't anywhere in Vanuatu that has preserved a truly traditional way of life by not using some type of western goods. Many clans rear introduced livestock and use their pigs as a source of meat, and as a consequence, the age-old art of hunting doesn't play the crucial role that it did in the past. But Noaka was taught at an early age to be a proficient archer and skilled huntsman.

The Tannese have a reputation for having cast iron stomachs and for eating anything. When I went on several hunts with Noaka during a previous visit and he shot a beautiful rooster with his bow, the head, feet, entrails, and offal were boiled into a fetid tasting brew the locals call "Tanna soup." Only the contents of the bird's intestines were discarded, and all of the feathers, except those from around the bird's rectum, which are considered dirty, were stored in a coconut shell to make a headdress for an upcoming *toka*. Wild fowl that are stunned with a blunt arrow are sometimes domesticated and used later as a sacrifice during rituals. The ultimate for any hunter is to return to the village with live game. When we caught an average sized boar with the dogs and then carried it back to the village alive, it elevated Noaka's status in the village for being such a skilled a hunter. He killed the pig with one vicious swing with a *nul nul*, then slit its throat and the dogs were made to drink its blood as it poured from the quivering boar to empower them with its spirit, which would enhance their strength and stamina for the next hunt. The night before the hunt, Noaka had chewed coconut flesh, laced it with the juice of a *tabu* leaf, and fed it to the dogs to boost their senses and to give them added power for the chase.

As each day passed, I slowly grew more energetic until I decided I was strong enough to go hunting. The evening before the hunt, a compulsory silence fell over the group of men sitting around a fire outside the *nakamal* while Noaka prepared a shell of kava, which only he was allowed to chew. Once the brew was mixed, he looked towards the heavens and spoke in his native tongue to call upon the divine guidance of his forefathers. After he drank most of the kava, he used the last mouthful to spit a fine spray onto the earth at his feet, then he told his ancestors that he was going to the jungle in the morning to hunt *puka* (pig). He scraped up a small portion of ash from the edge of a smouldering fire and placed the residue of a burnt coconut leaf into a small pouch, which he would tie to his penis sheath in the morning to empower him with mana during the hunt. Sometimes the ash from burnt wild cane leaves is used as a substitute for coconut leaves. I washed down a meal of medicinal goat meat with several strong shells of kava that the villagers offered me and felt so sluggish, I was forced to have an early night.

There are a few wild pigs that live in close proximity to Yakel but unless the animals are going to be used for ritualistic purposes, it's *tabu* to hunt them. About three hours' walk from the village, two types of feral pig inhabit an area of jungle called Yelgoin. Extremely low numbers of a captain cooker domestic cross and a more stunted relative roam the rainforest, which makes a successful hunt a rarity.

The next morning, several sharp tremors rattled our creaking leaf hut so violently that I was torn from a deep slumber just as dawn was breaking. As the rising sun vainly tried to burn through an angry looking sky, it was reduced to a dull glowing orb when darkening clouds of ash blocked the sunlight and cast an eerie twilight over the awakening village. Before we left the village, Noaka rubbed *manem* leaves over the hardwood limbs of his bow, which he'd made from a stave from a *namal* tree and was a similar size and shape as the hunting bows that are used by Vanuatu's other primitive tribes. Then he tied a *manem* leaf to the bow with a *tabu* vine in the belief it would help deliver his arrows with supernatural guidance. A cumbersome looking arrowhead he'd carved especially for the hunt from a piece of *namal* tree looked as though it would be better suited on the shaft of a spear than an arrow and closely resembled the large bamboo arrowheads I'd seen in Irian Jaya. In the past, the arrow would've been anointed with poison, but the venomous recipe was lost long ago when the missionaries curbed cannibalism and warfare.

As we followed an ancient trail that had been pounded into the landscape by the feet of numerous generations, an arid rain of fine gritty ash irritated our eyes and lungs. After we'd walked fifteen minutes, we stopped at Niben, the tree of death. The cowry shells imbedded in its gnarled limbs served as a grim reminder of the tree's gruesome past. Each shell represents a slain enemy who'd been cooked in the hollow bowels of the tree and then hung from its branches. Its massive roots are still charred from the fires that had roasted human flesh during cannibal feasts. Sometimes the corpses hung from the tree for three days before they were completely eaten, then after that, the grisly remains were considered too ripe to eat and were placed in another *tabu* banyan tree to rot or for scavenging animals to enjoy. Noaka licked his lips, squeezed my arm as if he was testing a side of beef, then his features took on the look of a half-starved, fully-demented cannibal when he looked towards the tree of death and said, "You better hope we kill a pig because I'm feeling hungry." Each time we walked past the tree, we bounced lame cannibal jokes off of one another so I said, "If I'm the best you can do in my sorry state, there's something wrong. With a bit of curry I might make a nice mystery mince once you get past the taste."

When I heard a thunderous roar in the distance and felt another tremor, I could imagine fireballs of ash and red-hot rocks belching from Mount Yasur's throat, while I wondered if the seismic activity and the mist of grey ash falling around us posed a real danger. Although there was the possible threat of a more vicious eruption hanging in the air, Noaka smiled and said, "That's good luck." Yakel's inhabitants worship Mount Yasur as a god, and Kapel, the supreme being, is embodied in an extremely *tabu* volcanic rock that has been worshiped since the beginning of time. As we walked along, Noaka told me special guardians keep other *tabu* rocks that are used to manipulate almost every aspect of life. If a villager wants a good crop of taro, he gifts a pig to the keeper of the taro rock, who then makes *kastom* by placing a *tabu* leaf on top of the stone and asks its spirit to provide a bountiful crop. There isn't a stone that's used to hunt pigs, but a rock is used to capture white-bellied rats, which are viewed as a delicacy, whereas the grey rat is despised and feared as a devil.

We threw all caution to the ash-choked wind, and with the volcanic grit stinging our eyes and rasping between our teeth, we noisily pushed towards our hunting ground. Our hurried approach startled pigeons and wild fowl that left small clouds of volcanic dust in their wake as they flew away. The weave of jungle was drenched in a sombre coating of thick grey ash, which made it look nothing like the pristine rainforest we'd ventured into during previous hunts. When we reached the fringe of our hunting ground, Noaka climbed a coconut palm and tossed down several green nuts. Their cool sweet juice oiled our parched throats and rinsed the grit from our mouths. After we finished eating the coconuts' succulent jelly-like flesh, we filled them with dirt before we threw them away. Lizards are the living embodiment of the devil, and if they eat any discarded food, their evil spirit causes the person who threw the food away to become violently ill.

While Noaka pushed through the vegetation, he flicked an annoying fog of ash into the air as we made our way down to a flat area of open jungle. He stopped when his keen eyes picked out a set of fresh sharp-edged marks and ran his hand over them. As we silently moved through the trees along a well-used pig run, watching him blend with his surroundings to become a finely honed predator was sheer bliss. We slowed to a virtual halt, then Noaka expertly and patiently stalked to within ten metres of a sow and piglets that were laid up in the twisted mass of aerial roots supporting a gigantic banyan tree. To arrow an animal from that distance would've been a formality, so we left the next generation of breeding stock undisturbed and dropped into a shallow creek that ran into a messy gully.

Thirty minutes later, we stood on the top of a ridge mantled with reasonably open jungle and wiped our perspiring brows and the grit from our eyes. Within minutes, Noaka put his intimate knowledge of the area and the habits of our quarry to good use when he led us to where it looked as if a medium sized captain cooker cross boar had recently churned the earth while it searched for worms and grubs before it moved on. I fell into silent step behind Noaka and revelled in his expert tracking ability and the way that he anticipated the animal's movements. Whenever the game trail disappeared into a thicket of vegetation that was more suited to hogs than two six-feet-tall hunters, we took the silent and easier option through open areas of jungle until we finally caught up with the boar while he was standing in his own enticing trail of footprints.

A gentle breeze drifted across the expanse of rainforest and wafted into our faces when we screeched to an immediate halt. Noaka nocked an arrow as the sound of muffled grunting and rustling vegetation sent our bodies into sensory overdrive. We crept forward with painstakingly slow movements and almost felt our way through a carpet of waist high fern by instinctive touch. When I emulated Noaka's intuitive movements step for step, we moved together as if we were performing a graceful synchronised dance. For a moment I could hear the pig rubbing himself against a tree, maybe to rid his bristly hide of the huge blood sucking lice that Vanuatu's pigs are infested with. Then apart from the ash filled breeze rusting through the leaves, it suddenly fell silent. We stood dead still with our heads cocked while we listened intently and waited for what seemed like an eternity, but in reality was no longer than a minute. I visualized the pig tasting the air with its twitching snout as it peered through the growth in search of danger, until a cloud of ash rose from about fifteen meters in front of us as the pig tilled the soft earth in search of an afternoon meal. The unmistakable rank odour of a boar drifted through the sulphurous air into our faces. Noaka was hunched over as he expertly narrowed the gap to about ten metres of the feeding animal. His supple muscles twitched and danced beneath his ebony skin when the bending limbs of the bow stretched to full draw, then the *manem* leaf worked its magic as the arrow hissed through the air and sliced through the startled animal's thick hide.

The boar scoffed and squealed in annoyance as it noisily ploughed through the fern and undergrowth until it vanished into the sanctuary of the jungle. For the next thirty minutes, we tracked the hog along a pig run that twisted around trees, ducked under windfalls, and went through more fern until the marks disappeared into a patch of wild cane. When Noaka cautiously peered into the thicket of cane, I tightened my grip on a bamboo spear that I'd cut myself and that Noaka had rubbed with a *manem* leaf. I could tell from his tense body language that he'd spotted the wounded pig. As he slowly bent down and carefully reached into the base of the cane, a deafening squeal assaulted our eardrums when he held onto a frantically kicking back leg and dragged the protesting boar clear of the vegetation. Although the arrow was back from the animal's front leg, I was still amazed when I saw that it had somehow managed to remain intact. Noaka quickly grabbed the shaft and thrust it deeper into the seriously injured pig to mercifully end the hunt.

We were both ecstatic, and while Noaka cheerfully sang *kastom* songs, he flashed a wide grin each time he turned around to see if my weak body was coping with carrying the boar while it swung from a sturdy sapling we carried across our shoulders. The day was rapidly drawing to a close, so we sped along the track to make sure that darkness didn't overtake us. And by the time we made it back to the village and slumped the pig to the ground, my malaria-ravaged body was completely shattered. After we butchered the pig, we divvied out equal portions of the meat and whatever else the native's hardened systems could digest.

We chewed coconut flesh and mixed it with crushed leaves to make a lather of natural soap to wash the grime and dust from our bodies. When the sun had almost finished blazing its way across the sky, we sat in the bowels of a sacred banyan tree whose roots had been hacked out to make a shelter and shared a meal of boiled pork, shells of kava, and a few more slices of curative goat meat with a family who was preparing to sleep in the hollowed-out tree. Noaka told everyone the volcano god had given us good luck. With the scarcity of game and the trying conditions, watching him take the pig with his bow had definitely been a godsend.

Chapter Fifty-Six

OUT OF THE BLUE

The next day when Noaka asked me if I felt like going for a walk, I didn't ask where we were going, and when we stopped at a nearby hamlet, I didn't ask what we were doing there. Apart from a few scrawny chickens fossicking for grubs and a couple of skinny dogs dozing in the pallid sun, the village was deserted. While we sat alongside each other with our backs against the sprawling roots of a colossal banyan tree that overshadowed a *nasara*, Noaka unexpectedly started to share the myth of how Yakel's peoples originated. When Kapel first created life, he made one black and one white man. The black man was blessed with a kind heart and had a reverence for all of nature, but the white man was evil and devious and had a cold heart that was filled with contempt for all of creation. Tanna was an idyllic unspoilt nirvana, which the black man loved and wanted to preserve as an enchanted kingdom. He was worried that his pale brother was intent on destroying Tanna's beauty, so he banished the white man for eternity and pushed him out into the ocean in a dugout canoe. But the resilient white man managed to survive and sailed around the world and populated every country that is inhabited by whites with his evil and ruinous seed. After Noaka told me the Tannese have prophesised that one day the white man will destroy all of humanity, I said to him, "So, do your people hate the white man?" His frown creased while he seemed to be thinking of a tactful answer then he said, "It is our *kastom* to be kind and to offer friendship. On the outside we are smiling, but in our hearts, we don't trust the white man." When I said, "It must be hard for your wife and your relatives to have me living in your hut if I'm considered evil," Noaka shook his head and said, "You are different, Rick. You're a true friend."

During the next hour, men slowly filtered into the *nasara* one by one until a dozen adults sat alongside us and chewed kava and listened and added to Noaka's conversation. For some reason, they touched on the very core of their beliefs, and the subject swung to death and sickness. They told me *tabu* rocks that are embodied with the rat and lizard spirit are used to inflict illness and create bad luck for their enemies. Of all the black magic that is used to wreak havoc and to hurt people, *tamafa* is the most potent and has various uses. But it's mostly used to cause death and destruction. When a villager passes away, their corpse is wrapped in banana leaves and is buried immediately. Once their spirit leaves the body, it transmigrates and is reborn in the deceased's surviving children. If the deceased doesn't have any offspring, their spirit is reincarnated in the progeny of a brother, a sister, or in any other relative. Everyone fell silent with the same hallowed hush that's normally reserved for rituals when Noaka placed a muddy looking shell of kava in my hand. Just looking at the brew made my ailing system shudder, so I said, "I feel like hell, mate. I don't want to offend you, but just this once, I think I'll pass." Noaka said, "Please, Rick. You must," then a few of the others urged me to take a drink, so I reluctantly gulped it down in one quick hit. One of the men who'd been holding a small piglet close to his chest used a rock to crack the animal's skull with a sharp blow. While he gutted the pig, a pile of smoking coconut leaves crackled to life and kindled a fire that Noaka used later to roast the piglet's tender flesh. Although I told him I'd lost my appetite, he insisted that I eat a small portion of the pork. After I swallowed a mouthful of the meat, smiles spread across the faces of the hopeful onlookers and Noaka said, "Because you have followed *kastom*, one day you will be a great and special man, Rick." Once Noaka had finished telling me how brilliant my future was going to be, he said it was important that I give a small amount of money to the next destitute woman that I saw, because showing her generosity would guarantee that I lived a long and happy life.

While we walked back to Yakel, I simply accepted without question that Noaka had obviously made *kastom* for me. I'll never know why he chose to perform the simple rite without my consent, and in the anonymity of another *nasara* with men from another village. What Noaka said next was so unexpected that I told him to repeat himself. He said that Yakel's peoples are staunch royalists who worship Prince Philip as a god. And Chief Kowia hopes that one day the patriarch of Britain's royal family will drive up in his range rover, but without Queen Elizabeth so that he can take a native wife. It had been a day that was full of surprises, and they kept coming when Noaka added that Yakel also belongs to the John Frum cult.

No one really knows exactly how the cargo cult originated, but it's thought that John Frum was a stranger from a faraway land who arrived on Tanna's shores around 1938. He promised all sorts of unrealistic happenings, such as the old becoming youthful again and the arrival of a treasure trove of modern goods if the Tannese returned to their pagan ways which had been decimated by the missionaries and the colonials. Like other cargo cults throughout Melanesia, the most important and common aspect of receiving European goods, which were believed to have been manufactured in the spirit world by the white man's god, was to hypocritically despise the European's living on Tanna and anything they were associated with despite the native's obsession with western possessions. The Tannese cleansed their contaminated culture by throwing away all of their foreign merchandise, repelling and defying the westerners, and returning to their age-old traditions. They suddenly stopped working for their white employers, and while most of them rid themselves of the Europeans' despicable money in an orgy of spending, some of the natives threw their hard-earned cash into the sea. Their children were withdrawn from the schools, the church was shunned, and everything that had been introduced by the white man was loathed. When the movement quickly spread through the villages, prophets who belonged to the cult suddenly started to appear and claimed to have had visitations from John Frum in their dreams, where he instructed them how to prepare for the massive influx of cargo.

During World War II, when Luganville suddenly swelled into a bustling military base, hundreds of primitive Tannese worked alongside black American soldiers, who had unimaginable wealth that the natives had never seen before. The Tannese saw material goods of inconceivable quantities and quality being delivered by the white man's god as they kept dropping from the skies and came from the distant horizon in aircraft and on ships. When they witnessed the coloured servicemen openly expressing their dislike of the way some of the colonials treated the natives and saw the Negroid soldiers who were of a higher rank giving orders to white soldiers, it reinforced the natives' prophecies that their saviour, John Frum, was about to return. The only logical explanation the Tannese had for the miraculous events was that the black Americans were brothers who'd been sent by John Frum. Word of the massive amount of goods that were awaiting the natives had already filtered back to Tanna, but when the Tannese who'd helped the military returned after the war and spread news of John Frum's imminent arrival, runways were cleared in the jungle and wharves were built to receive the precious cargo.

Nowadays the inhabitants of Ipeukal village, which is situated at Sulphur Bay, remain staunch disciples of the John Frum movement. Each year, on the fifteenth of February, the American flag is raised and mock soldiers with "USA" painted across their bare backs march with wooden rifles to celebrate John Frum day. The self-appointed Tannese Army pay tribute to John Frum by worshiping a large red wooden cross, and expectantly await his return even though over sixty years have passed since their mystical messiah first arrived on Tanna. The common belief is that the red cross symbolises the red cross that was worn by African American medics during the war who were seen to generously help the wounded without asking for anything in return. Some of the cult's prophets claim to have seen John Frum and an army of twenty thousand soldiers living in the boiling crater of Mount Yasur. It seems who John Frum was and where he originated from will always remain a mystery. His follower's obsession for cargo is as strong as it ever was, and the cult boasts a substantial following who are still patiently awaiting the arrival of their unprecedented wealth and their enigmatic saviour.

During my last day at Yakel before I few back to New Zealand, Noaka placed a beautiful antique bracelet that had been carved from a coconut shell in my hands and said, "This was gifted from father to son. I want you to have it." The artefact was at least one hundred years old and had belonged to his great grandfather. I politely refused the gift and said, "I'm not being disrespectful, but something this meaningful rightfully belongs to your children," then I handed him back the bracelet. When I accepted two highly prized pig tusks that had grown into a full circle,

Noaka smiled, then cheekily told me to wear two *nagol's* instead of the one that he'd also gifted me, to make my penis grow bigger and stronger, which is what the villagers believe a penis sheath does.

In the cool evening, after I shared a meal of boiled pork and roast yam with a chief that lived in a neighbouring hut, he unexpectedly gifted me an ornately carved walking stick, then said, "I have never met a white man like you. One day you will be special. This will be your memory of Yakel when you return to your country." Because I'd committed what most civilized travellers would consider hygiene suicide by sharing chewed kava and had lived in primitive conditions while I was recovering from malaria, it took its toll on my health. I never did find out if Numaben, whose mythical origins teach that the white man is a devil, sliced into Jimmy's pale skin with a bamboo knife. I said goodbye to a humble peoples who had the sensibility to place peace and respect above the very essence of their ancestral beliefs, which tell them to despise outsiders with fair skin. The ancestors of other remote tribes around the world who'd never seen a Caucasian passed on the same stunningly accurate prophecies that the white man will eventually lead to their demise.

Chapter Fifty-Seven

INTO THE HEART OF THE BEAST

While I was in recovery mode again in Port Vila after weeks of suffering from a self-inflicted illness I caught from dining on rotten meat in Middle Bush, Santo, my enthusiasm and resilience were at such a low ebb that I was ready to head back to New Zealand. The highlander's uncompromising tribal law had demanded I either jeopardise my health or face the violent consequences of flouting *kastom*. If I didn't eat the vile meat, I probably would've been beaten then forced to leave under a sentence of eternal banishment. When everything that was medically possible had been done to try and remedy my terrible sickness, the rest was up to the course of antibiotics I was taking and to time. The whites of my eyes were yellow, I was jaundiced, looked haggard, and I felt lethargic. Whenever I live in remote locations where self-reliance is a must, my health is a priceless commodity that I try to treat with the utmost respect. But crossing cultural divides means unwillingly abusing my body, and mine had taken a terrible beating from trying to roll with the flurry of punches Santo's primitive lifestyle had dished out. Anyone who doesn't think they're superhuman has a line which sensibility won't allow them to cross. I reached into that special place we look to from deep within ourselves when we're pushed to our limits, but self-preservation said enough was enough, I'd thrived on hardship for too long. My mental health had taken a battering that left me feeling a bit low and incomplete. It was as if the pipes that led to my clear thinking were clogged and my true self felt strangely hollow, like it was being consumed and replaced by something alien. The bizarre state of mind made me feel as if I needed to blow out years of accumulated internal grime and shed all of my unwanted spiritual baggage, yet in a strange way something positive was about to develop from the demoralizing situation.

Although I needed a break from the killing, the evil, and of the negative aspects of black magic and I sought a passive relaxing environment where I could thrive on the ordinary, be my own man, get well, and simply exist, Epi Island kept invading my thoughts. The island is a stronghold for sorcery, which gave me every reason to give it a wide berth, but because I'd covered something unique from every other province, I felt compelled to travel to Epi and complete my odyssey through Vanuatu's amazing archipelago.

I ignored my better judgement and my hunger for tranquillity and decided to bite the bullet and finish the final leg of my journey by boat. Whenever I went to the wharf and thought I was going to sail on a ragged

414 — RICK WILLIAMSON

looking cargo boat called the El Shaddi, I was told to come back tomorrow. It took three days for a welder to finally stem the flow of water seeping in through a crack in the hull. Once the captain was satisfied that the
boat was seaworthy, I joined a group of passengers patiently waiting for
the outgoing tide so that two Toyota pickups could be driven onboard.
Night had fallen when I sprawled out on the uncomfortable steel deck
between the vehicles and gazed up at the stars as the throbbing engine
built up speed and we pulled away from the twinkling lights Port Vila.
When the boom of the small cargo crane seemed to sway from side to
side, I thought that it had broken loose from its locked position until
someone shouted out that one of the steering chains had snapped. No one
seemed to worry and after sixteen hours of snaking from left to right
across a becalmed ocean, the following afternoon, we sighted Epi Island
and sailed into Lamen Bay.

A friend in Port Vila had arranged for me to live at Vela village with
Jack Noel and his relatives. As soon as I met Jack and he welcomed me to
stay in his hut, I knew that I'd arrived at a bad time. He looked tense and
claimed his entire family were recovering from malaria, but his animated
children looked fresh-faced and were exceptionally healthy. The edgy
tone in their voices and their poor attempt to disguise their nervousness
made it obvious that something was horribly wrong. My suspicion proved
to be correct when an hour before dusk I was invited to a small *lafaet* to
mark that five days had passed since a woman died and to celebrate her
departing spirit. While steaming parcels of food were being pulled from
amongst smoking hot stones, I had a nagging uneasiness that told me this
wasn't the right time to impose on the grieving villagers. When I thanked
them for their hospitality and told them I was going to move on, they were
equally happy to help me catch a ride across the bay to a small but enticing looking island called Lamen.

I wandered down to the beach and hitched a ride with sixty-five-year-
old Jake Taso, who paddled his outrigger canoe with the tireless energy of
a man half his age. His wiry muscles nudged us through a river of bubbling current that surges through the bay, then a brisk breeze made our sail
flutter and billow as it filled with a rising wind that pushed us past a line
of outriggers. In some of the tiny crafts, children were standing up and
holding up clusters of coconut leaves, which they used as crude sails to
catch the stiffening breeze. We skimmed across the ocean for two kilometres beneath a blood red sky and towards the sun as it set behind the tiny
island. The pallid light of a half moon shimmered across the still water of
the lagoon as we surged through a gap in the small breakers rolling over a
reef and sailed along a shoreline fringed by a white sand beach. Several
villagers who'd hung glowing lamps in a tree to act as a beacon for the
small flotilla of canoes that were still out in the middle of the bay helped
us to pull our outrigger onto the beach.

Even in the pale moonlight I could see that Lamen was one of the
most beautiful islands I'd ever visited. As we walked along immaculately
groomed roads that were bordered with low coral fences, lines of overhanging trees, and tall coconut palms, the spotless huts and gardens were

the best kept I'd seen anywhere in Vanuatu, but for all of its alluring beauty, I sensed the same brooding atmosphere I'd felt at Epi.

I had a letter Jack Noel had given me which asked his relative that lived at Fasaro village, who I only knew as Joel, if I could stay with him for a few days. Although Joel had been unexpectedly called away to another island, his wife Lizzie quickly read the note and told me I was welcome to stay for as long as I wanted. She apologised for having to rush away, made sure the four children she was taking to a prayer meeting were wearing clean clothes, then wandered off into the darkness. Her twelve-year-old son, Charlie, looked more than happy about missing church to keep me company. Half an hour later while we were making small talk to get to know one another, I heard a strange sound outside and said, "Did you hear that, Charlie? It sounds like someone's playing a flute." The musical sound suddenly stopped and for several minutes I could only hear the usual noises of the night. Then the faint, eerie tune started again. Charlie's eyes widened and his voice trembled when he shrieked, "It's Lorka! The devil! He's playing music with the bones of dead children."

When Lizzie and the children returned several hours later, they were terrified when Charlie told them Lorka had paid us a visit and that he might still be lurking outside in the shadows. Ten minutes later, when a dog barked as it chased a piglet that had been sleeping right outside the hut door and the pig let rip with a high pitched squeal, Lizzie and all the children screamed with fright. I grabbed my torch and went to go outside to the toilet, but Lizzie told me to wait and said if ever I ventured outside during the night, Sam, her eldest son was to always go with me because evil spirits and murderous devils roam the jungle and haunt the village.

The next morning, Lizzie was up an hour before the sun, and I could hear her in the next room feverishly blurting out passages from the bible and praying for all of us, probably to keep Lorka and the evil spirits at bay. When Charlie turned on his radio, a soccer team that was accused of using black magic to win the Torba provincial championship made the national news. Then Alex, the youngest of the boys, who looked to be about three years old, complained the weeping sores that covered most of his feet were painful. Lizzie grabbed a lighted stick from the cooking fire and kept passing the flame back and forth over the cluster of abscesses until the traditional healing was too much for Alex and he howled from the pain as tears streamed down his cheeks.

After I spent the morning chatting with some of the older locals, it was obvious there was something sinister lurking beneath the island's idyllic exterior. As soon as I mentioned I was waiting for Joel, who is a field worker for the cultural centre, and that I was interested in *kastom*, they suddenly became aloof and tried to avoid talking to me. In the afternoon, when I asked Lizzie if I could walk around the tiny island, which measures just over 1.25 square kilometres in size, she said that it was way too dangerous for me to travel alone and insisted that three teenaged boys guide me. We stuck to the beaches and to clearly defined paths, and when I mentioned to the boys I'd like to go for a walk through the jungle, they said it was *tabu* and too unsafe because the jungle belonged to the devils.

Some of the villagers had blatantly lied to me by saying there were no wild pigs on the island whereas I could see that Lamen clearly supported a healthy population of feral pigs. Apart from crops that were growing around the huts, it seemed strange that there weren't any plantations and that the villagers either have to paddle or sail across to Epi where they've purchased land and planted gardens.

We walked to the northern tip of the island, then left a beach that was so white it dazzled my eyes and headed to a leaf hut nestled alongside a church that was built from a mixture of modern and traditional materials. The pastor of the church, Kerry, was a placid looking man in his early thirties and had the humble nature of a man who'd dedicated his life to god. He was sitting next to a cooking fire and rose to his feet, then offered me a warm greeting. He grabbed a plate and a fork, then speared a nicely browned piece of meat that sizzled in his smoking frypan. When I asked him if it was wild pork he handed me on the plate, he said, "Yes, but only a few men hunt the pigs. You look unwell. Here eat this. Please take a seat." He gave the boys a few menial tasks to do around the church so we could speak alone. I couldn't help but think that Kerry had the ultimate lifestyle for an islander. He lived metres away from a lagoon teeming with fish, his small garden was laden with fruit and healthy crops, and he had a handy supply of wild pork on a paradise that's free of malaria.

After I'd finished my first mouthful of tender pork, I said, "This place is beautiful, but it reminds me of Ambrym and a few other islands where *kastom* is still strong. The people are friendly, but I keep getting the feeling it's crawling with *nakaimas*." Kerry put down his knife and fork then looked me in the eye as he said, "You're sick because you've made *kastom*. I can sense the spirits that are attacking your soul." I told him I was sick from eating rotten meat, and carried on talking without telling him I'd been initiated into several tribes. For a stranger I'd just met, he was incredibly open and didn't hesitate to tell me about his troubled life in the past. Before he found God, Kerry had dabbled in black magic with a sorcerer from Ambrym and did despicable things to innocent people that anyone with a conscience would be ashamed of let alone someone who's a pastor from The Assembly Of God church. Then he became a Christian, and before he left Efate, which is his home island, his family were shocked and worried when they heard the church was sending him to Lamen. Because of its formidable reputation, they feared he'd been granted a certain death sentence. When I told Kerry about my job, he creased the lines on his forehead into a deep frown and said, "You must be careful. If you ask about *kastom* here on Lamen, some of the people will try to kill you. The *nakaimas* wait until night to attack and have tried to murder me many times." While he's lived alone at the end of the island for the past three years, he's been a prime target for the sorcerers who despise the church. His vigilant guard dogs often bark at prowlers in the early hours of the morning. He arms himself with the bible and his unshakable faith, then runs outside, but he's only ever caught a glimpse of bearded men running off into the jungle. Every Tuesday and Thursday, members of the church who call themselves prayer warriors start at dusk and sometimes walk around the island until dawn to drive demonic forces back into the jungle.

Later in the afternoon, while I was back at Fasaro and had slipped into the netherworld between consciousness and slumber, I kept seeing flashes of the face of the devil that I'd dreamt about on Santo and all sorts of bizarre thoughts flooded my confused mind. I sat up with a jolt and felt that my world was no longer black or white, simply is or isn't. I wondered if I was paying the price for baring my soul and making myself vulnerable when I'd welcomed the spirits to enter my body during my initiations. Maybe it was psychosomatic and all I needed was to return to New Zealand where I simply existed without trying to document any type of spirituality. I decided to clear my head by going for a walk along the road that runs the length of the island and to pay pastor Kerry another visit.

Kerry was standing about forty meters from the church next to a pile of dirt, where arms that were glazed with sweat and flexed with taut muscles and tightened tendons sent shovel fulls of earth out of a deep hole. When Kerry flashed his toothy smile and called me over, the digging stopped and the back of a head with short silver-flecked hair rose up to ground level, slowly turned around, and then gave me a look that I'll never forget for as long as I live. Daniel Iolobu had a fixed, unnerving stare, but there was a strange intimacy in his cold eyes that entranced me. I could feel them burning through my body as if it was a translucent shell and looking into the very nucleus of my soul, into my mind, back to my past, and to what lay beyond. During my travels, I'd befriended many men who'd murdered loved ones and enemies for the sake of *kastom*, and although they could look ruthless, none of them had even come close to matching the marrow-chilling look in the middle-aged stranger's unsettling eyes as we gazed at each other. Without uttering a word, he looked away, then tilted his bowed head sideways as if he was listening to something. I'd never met anyone with such an overwhelming presence or felt such a strong and inexplicable connection with a total stranger. His sagging chest and overweight body made it obvious that he'd let himself go physically, but his profound gaze gave me the impression that beneath his flabby exterior, there was an incredibly powerful mind.

I don't know why but for some inexplicable reason I blurted out, "I need your help. I know you can help me," then I stood there dumbfounded and wondered why the hell I'd asked Daniel for his help once the words spilled from my mouth. In a deep and commanding voice he said, "I know why you're here. You're lucky. A few years ago, I would've used this shovel to kill you. I have listened to the spirits of my *bubu*," then he climbed out of the hole and said, "We need to talk." Kerry shot me a puzzled look which changed to an expression of understanding, then he excused himself and left us alone. I've never idolised anything or anyone in my life, but while I sat alongside Daniel on a log, he had a mesmerising aura that reeked of good and evil and a special charisma I was in absolute awe of.

The harsh look on Daniel's face softened when he told me there wasn't a doctor anywhere that could cure my illness and that he was amazed I'd managed to survive this long, because without his help I was going to die. While he was digging a toilet for the pastor, the spirits of his *bubu* had told him I was a good man who could be trusted. When he heard the most potent of all the ancestral spirits telling him to share the most hallowed secrets of *kastom* with me, it had stunned him, as no amount of riches or money could ever buy what he was about to tell me. Daniel said he'd worked as a dive master in Port Vila for seven years, so what I was about to learn didn't come from a primitive mind, but I knew superstition would still influence his thinking. Lamen's inhabitants are civilized in appearance, but Daniel had a hidden sophistication that belied his rugged and intimidating appearance and put him head and shoulders above the other villagers. He gave me one of his piercing looks and said, "You have entered the heart of the beast, and Lamen is its lifeblood and its dark demonic soul. Lizzie is my sister. Tomorrow you will come and live with me and my family. If you talk to anyone while you are on Lamen about what I'm going to teach you about *kastom*, you will probably be killed. No outsider has ever heard what I am going to tell you. Bring your things to my hut at Parua tomorrow morning, then we will go to church."

The next day, while I sat at the back of the packed church, when Kerry had finished giving a brief sermon, Daniel stood up and shouted, "Jesus, take me! Use me as your servant. Praise Jesus. Oooh! Oooh! Praise the Lord. Halleluiah. Please, dear God, forgive me for all my sins. Oh, sweet Jesus, take me." Daniel used to be a *nakaimas*, and empowering himself with the spirit of the devil had obviously placed a heavy psychological burden on his burly shoulders. He's a respected deacon and seemed to be trying to lighten the hefty weight of his guilt through praying aloud to the packed church. A flood of tears that were induced by the shame he felt from having been a *nakaimas* poured down his cheeks as he raised his outstretched arms to the heavens and burbled on non-stop, speaking in a bizarre, unintelligible gibberish. The rest of the flock rose to their feet and broke out into an unfathomable tangle of conversation as they looked to the heavens and talked in tongues. For the next two and a half hours, the excited congregation almost lifted the roof with their impassioned prayers, feverish shouting, and their loud, overzealous worship.

Every Saturday, the Christians sweep the road that leads to the isolated church clean of every single leaf and every piece of debris. Once the congregation started heading back to their villages, Daniel and I waited until we were the only ones walking along the spotless path. While I lived with primitive tribes around the world, I figured I would always be trying to find the answers to unanswerable questions. Up until I'd met Daniel I came to the realization that no matter how many pieces of the puzzle I slowly uncovered and put together, even after a lifetime I would never get a clear picture of tribal life or fully understand the primitive mindset, but Daniel was about to slot the last few vital missing pieces of the mystery into place.

As we ambled along the path, it cut through a cool, shaded jungle and Daniel said, "Those of us who are Christians have reached a compromise by practising the positive side of *kastom* as well. The Peace Corps, the teachers who are still working here, and the other aid agencies always feel they have to try and change our way of life. Some of what they do is good, but not much. We don't need them to tell us how to live. They talk about us becoming independent and self-reliant when we already have been for thousands of years. Many Europeans come to Vanuatu with a domineering attitude and ideas that aren't necessarily beneficial to our way of life. I see more defects in their way of thinking than the few positives they offer. You are different, Rick. I understand what you've put yourself through, mentally and physically, to document what is left of our customs. If the white man doesn't understand something, he mocks it. And sometimes he's so afraid of it, he destroys it to remove the source of his fear. Because you've followed the *kastom* road, one day you will be a great and special man. You could never understand us, yet you have shown great bravery. Your work is very dangerous, and from what I can see and what the spirits of my *bubu* have told me, you should be dead, but you have powerful spirits that are keeping you alive. First we must start by healing your mind and body, and then we will cleanse your spirit and your soul. This will take time. You have been poisoned physically and spiritually. You need to understand that this is a good thing, because now you've experienced all facets of Ni-Vanuatu life. Before we start healing you, first I want to share the history of our people, of my family, and tell you about myself. Then you can decide if you want my help."

When we got back to Daniel's hut, we sat under the shade of a thatch shelter and he travelled back to a time and place when history was still in the making and had yet to become legend, when on Efate Island, the most regal of the paramount chiefs, Roimata, ruled with a fair and just hand. Roimata was so powerful and so influential that he managed to unite tribes who'd been at war with one another so that his people could enjoy a relatively peaceful existence. Nowadays the keepers of his people's tradition tell of how Roimata was poisoned by his own brother and buried on Hat Island. One of his wives was killed and laid to rest with his body, as were eighteen of his chiefs, their wives, and the members of affiliated tribes who showed Roimata the ultimate act of respect by sacrificing their lives. Forty-six of his loyal followers and relatives shared his *tabu* grave, where it was said no tree or vegetation would ever grow.

Centuries later, a French archaeologist called Jose Garanger used the information he'd gathered from local orators and proved the origins of the myth were factual when he excavated a mass grave containing forty-seven skeletons, with the wives laid alongside the chiefs just as the elders had told each successive generation. The remains were unearthed in a natural clearing that was marked with two crude headstones, which proves the remarkable accuracy and reliability of some of Vanuatu's oral history.

Before Roimata's death, when life was cheap and was still extremely precarious, he instructed one of his chiefs to go and explore and determine if it was possible to resettle some of his people on the outer islands. Their journey was fraught with numerous dangers, as travelling through the anxiously guarded territory of hostile and cannibalistic tribes required extreme caution. An advance party of vigilant warriors scouted ahead of the chiefs as they headed north through the Sheppard Islands. Once the warriors ensured the route was safe, they returned from their reconnaissance, brought their leaders forward, and kept repeating the process for several legs of the voyage until they reached Purvanua village on Epi Island. When they saw Lamen Island, it looked enticing, but the wary travellers weren't sure if they could land on its shores without conflict. Once they were told the island was uninhabited and, more important, that it was safe to visit, ten natives who were comprised of three families paddled across the bay and staked claim to the deserted paradise.

Not long after they arrived on Lamen, the three families became involved in a heated and irreconcilable dispute. They were so furious that they went their separate ways and built their own *nakamals*, which created Parua, Lokumali, and Vasaro villages. This led to an inconceivable outcome. When the population increased, the natives' simmering hatred blossomed into savage warfare between the enemy clans. It only takes about eleven minutes to walk across the widest part of the tiny island, which must have made existing within the confines of such a volatile society a living nightmare.

As the years passed, the enforced isolation led to each tribe developing its own language and its own unique customs. Although the three villages were only several minutes' walk from each other, no one ever dared to visit a neighbouring clan because anyone who foolishly wandered into enemy territory unannounced was guaranteed a swift and violent death, and then their corpse was cannibalised. If a warrior managed to safely enter an enemy village, he usually did so as a complete stranger even though he only lived a short distance away. For centuries the constant threat of being killed from spiritual and physical warfare cast an ominous mood over the island. Both the men and women embraced an emerging religion which was based on devil worship, and over time they developed the powers to become *nakaimas*.

As their black magic became more potent, the sorcerers cursed their enemies with evil spells, and the fighting raged between the seething villages like an out of control epidemic. Society had grown so dangerous and life was so fragile that the women were forced to hide their pregnancies. They were afraid of the enemy *nakaimas* who secretly slipped into their village at night, dug a hole outside their hut, and then buried a *tabu* leaf that eventually killed their unborn child. Once their stomach started to swell and their pregnancy became obvious, a woman never ventured outside of her hut for fear of being struck by a well-aimed enemy arrow. Only her husband travelled to the garden to gather crops or went fishing or hunted for game. The fighting was so bad that a newborn child spent the first three years of its life in the sanctity of its parents' closely guarded hut. An infant's heart and blood were the ultimate for an enemy *nakaimas* to use as a sacrifice to the devil, so young boys were especially targeted, because killing them meant there would be one less potential warrior and one less archer to contend with when he was old enough to draw a bow.

A bow that was crafted from the *yandi* tree was the preferred weapon during battle and could send a wild cane arrow clean through an enemy. To empower the weapon, which is similar to other D shaped bows that are used throughout the archipelago, elders have suggested that blood from a slain enemy may have been rubbed into a notch in the bow. The archers tipped their arrows with human bone that possessed a deadly spirit, which ensured that even if an enemy wasn't mortally wounded, the supernatural spirit killed them. If the bones of family members were in short supply, barbed arrowheads were carved from black palm and anointed with a poison that was made from grinding a mixture of tree roots, herbs, and plants into a sticky paste.

When the island became so volatile that no one could be trusted, the loyalties of one clan became divided and caused a group of natives to move away and build a fourth village called Parawai. *Nakaimas* became so prevalent that a plague of death that was inflicted by black magic swept through the villages. The continual warfare between Parua and Parawai escalated into a terrible bloodbath when the warriors from Parua went on the rampage and destroyed Parawai village and slaughtered all of the inhabitants with a hail of arrows and swinging *nul nuls*. The jubilant victors stoked the cooking fires and celebrated the annihilation and extinction of Parawai's bloodline by eating every one of their slain victims.

The endless scourge of cannibalism, black magic, and bouts of sickness caused the remaining villages to depopulate so rapidly that they were forced to form an alliance with one another. It was the only means of ensuring the struggling natives would survive in such a hazardous society. Intermarriage followed, the chiefs shared customs to form one of Vanuatu's most powerful religions, warfare ceased, and a single language developed amidst a constant air of mistrust. The clans united at about the same time the first Europeans settled in Vanuatu. By the 1860s, recruiting slaves had become a major activity throughout Melanesia, but neither the missionaries nor the blackbirders were very successful when they came up against the volatile Lamen islanders, and only a few slaves were stolen and taken to Queensland.

When Thomas Mill, an ambitious Presbyterian minister, first arrived on Lamen, he was lucky he wasn't killed when he received a volatile reception from a group of warriors who were seeking vengeance after the previous actions of deceitful white men. The courageous missionary persevered and was eventually allowed to build a church on the low-lying crest of the island. Christianity failed to overwhelm *kastom*, but several chiefs who were seeking solace from the stresses of living under the constant threat of being killed by black magic embraced Presbyterianism. Thomas Mill may have paved the way for Christianity to become established on the island but his personal success was short-lived.

It seems incredible, but no one from Epi knew that Mill had been living on Lamen. The natives from Epi were too afraid to visit Lamen for fear of being killed and eaten by its fierce inhabitants. Not long after Mill first visited Epi, he offered to treat a woman who'd been injured in the groin. While Mill tended to a wound alongside the woman's genitals, a friend of her husband walked into the room. Mill had unintentionally committed a huge breach of *kastom* by looking at the woman's privates, and by the time a message had reached her husband, he was told that the white man had performed indecencies on his wife. Unfortunately for Mill, the woman's spouse was a *nakaimas*, and he tricked the evangelist into meeting him while they were alone. He used sorcery to decapitate the missionary, then he replaced his severed head. On Epi, a victim of black magic who is killed but still lives as the double of a man is called a *wawai*, which is what Mill became for the next five days until he died at Nuvenue village. His remains were laid to rest on Epi at Nakaura village, where a Presbyterian church was built in his memory.

A few of Mill's loyal converts upheld their pledge to the missionary's god. The natives who were afraid of being killed by a *nakaimas* saw something in Christianity that was akin to their own pagan beliefs and used the church as a safe haven from sorcery. Nowadays about nine hundred people live on Lamen, and of these, only about three hundred are Christians. Nearly all of the others worship the devil, which ensures the people will keep getting sick, have bad luck, and will die from black magic. Beneath the villagers' friendly smiles and carefree natures, most of them are living in fear because the same air of mistrust which prevailed centuries ago still exists today.

Chapter Fifty-Eight

THE MERLIN OF MELANESIA

The evening shadows were slowly creeping across the village when Daniel said, "Before I start with myself, I will tell you about my uncle, Avoi Koli, and share some of our customs with you" He looked around to make sure we were alone, then he began talking. In Lamen Island society, a son shares a more intimate and much more respectful bond with his uncle than he does with his own father. No one knows exactly why an uncle and his nephew form such a strong relationship, but there is no doubt that the custom has been practised for centuries, if not millennia.

Avio was born in 1912 and died at the ripe old age of eighty-two. His father, Kulyu, had been a great chief and an incredibly powerful *nakaimas* amongst a peoples who believe they have the strongest *kastom* in all of Vanuatu. On Ambrym, Lesipsip is feared as a supernatural devil, and although the Lamen islanders also treat him as a devil, they know for a fact that his spirit originated from a man rather than a supernatural demon, which is what the people from Ambrym believe he is. Lesipsip was a highly revered paramount chief and the most potent of all of the sorcerers. The Lamen islanders captured him on Epi, then they made him a prisoner on their island. Before Lesipsip was put to death, he told the villagers he worshiped Kesu, the supreme devil, and agreed to divulge all of the secrets of devil worship and to share his intimate knowledge of *kastom*.

Over the centuries, black magic evolved from what Lesipsip had taught the villagers and became even more potent and even more revered than when it first originated. Avio became an expert *nakaimas* at an early age, and when he lived from the *tabu* fire, the spirits of Kesu, the supreme devil, and Lesipsip entered his dreams to pass on their demonic knowledge and turned him into one of, if not the most, potent *kastom* man in postcolonial history. His kind and affable nature and his amazing healing powers endeared him to most people with a love/hate relationship. They loved him for his benevolence, but they also hated and feared him because like any *nakaimas*, he kept killing the villagers to nurture and appease the devil. Although it wasn't Avio's birthright, when the reigning chief died, the villagers were so afraid of Avio that instead of appointing the rightful heir, they made him the village patriarch for the last seventeen years that he lived on Lamen.

When the villagers chose a much younger patriarch as their paramount chief, Avio became insanely jealous and killed him. Although he'd already amassed an unacceptable tally of murders without being reprimanded, killing the paramount chief demanded retribution. The three highest-ranking chiefs passed judgement, and when they sentenced Avio to eternal banishment, he spent the last thirteen years of his life living at Port Vila. He'd outlived three wives, but the surviving fourth wife was so terrified of him that she remained on Lamen.

Avio had been revered as a demigod while he lived on Lamen, but when he started to perform mind-boggling magic and terrifying acts of sorcery while he lived at Port Vila, it quickly transformed him into a living legend. His name became synonymous with black magic when stunned Europeans and Ni-Vanuatu marvelled at his incredulous feats. He defied logic and science when he cut out and replaced a man's tongue for a private audience, pulled flapping fish from a grass lawn after casting a bare hook, and tied a thin thread between two trees and walked across the fragile strand as if it were a tightrope. He performed a long list of inexplicable feats that left well-educated expatriates shaking their heads in disbelief. Some of the Europeans began using his miraculous healing powers to cure their ailments and sought his advice when they required spiritual assistance.

Avio became so famous, and his daunting reputation had travelled so far, that a foreign film crew flew to Vanuatu and made a documentary on his remarkable life. When I returned to Port Vila, I watched the film at the cultural centre. Avio was a small elderly man with large bags under his eyes and was wearing a blue cap and a bushy white beard. He remained loyal to Kesu and lied to the camera when he said the spirits of his *bubu* had taught him to be a *cleva* in his dreams. *Clevas* do exist, and the peace-loving clairvoyants possess special healing powers and have the ability to exorcise evil spirits, but they never kill to enhance their powers. Avio said when he was a boy, he lived in the *nakamal* with *tabu* men and acted as their messenger while they taught him black magic, which is true. He added that the *nakaimas* taught him how to manipulate the weather with a sacred stone, by using one side for rain and the other to produce sunlight, and showed him how to part gathering clouds by parting two rocks. He also parted with a few more mistruths when he said his powers came from the mind and when he said, "I am the last of the high men. I followed the way of *bubu*. If I say 'yes' to something you must do it. No one can turn into an animal anymore." He was economical with the truth right to the end of the documentary, but was being honest when he said he'd gifted his chiefly powers back to the island. What he didn't say was that he'd passed his special powers onto Daniel. The only real secrets he revealed were that one form of killing a man is called *shu* and that when he was circumcised he was made to eat pig shit. I was surprised when he mentioned the secretive *tabu* fire when he said, "If you eat what I've eaten, you're no longer ordinary. My uncles made me eat pig shit after I was circumcised at the *tabu* fire." He omitted that he also drank human blood as if it was water and ate numerous human hearts.

The members of *shu* belong to an extremely exclusive secret society. The chaotic spirit of *shu* enslaves those who choose to become empowered with its evil, yet unlike a *nakaimas*, an exponent of *shu* can kill a victim without physical contact. If the demanding spirit isn't fed, however, the sorcerer becomes the sacrifice. But if he possesses the right knowledge, he can cast the spirit into a tree or any other living object so that it becomes the sacrifice and dies. *Shu* is so secretive that even though it was mentioned in the documentary, nowadays not many Ni-Vanuatu are aware of its existence.

When Vanuatu held its first cultural show at Port Vila in 1979 to celebrate the diversity of *kastom*, it attracted groups from throughout the archipelago who performed in front of huge crowds. Back then, Daniel was living on Efate, and the night before the festival, Avio said to him, "Tomorrow I want to kill you in front of thousands of people. I'll give you a few hours to make up your mind." Avio wasn't trying to shock the crowd. He wanted to portray the true meaning of becoming a *nakaimas* and to show that although Kesu had intended the chiefs to instruct their *nakaimas* to use their powers for good and evil, the main function was to control society, to teach respect, and to maintain harmony. Daniel was afraid to die until he heard the spirits of his *bubu* reassuring him that he would survive the performance, which was included in the documentary that was made about Avio.

Once the festival started, Tobur, who is the highest-ranking chief from north Ambrym, stunned thousands of onlookers when the famous sorcerer defied gravity by stomping and dancing on top of a twenty metre high platform that was made from fragile strips of bamboo. Because some of the performers were from islands that used to be traditional enemies and still viewed each other with suspicion, there was a lot of tension and competition between the *kastom* men during the festival. When Tobur finished performing, Avio said, "I can beat that. No problem. Quick. Let's go, Daniel." Then he took centre stage while the crowd was still coming to grips with Tobur's incredible feat.

Avio was holding his *tabu nul nul*, which everyone was afraid to touch after the arm of a curious native who'd handled the club instantly swelled up. He raised the *nul nul* above his head, then he pursed his lips and squeaked at Dick, who was pretending to be disrespectful and was walking away from a chief in the *nakamal*. In the past, the punishment for insolence was death, so Avio killed Daniel in front of the horrified crowd. Apart from being suddenly entombed by darkness, Daniel can't remember anything that happened while he lay dead on the ground. A *nakaimas* never reveals his true *kastom* name, so Daniel was called Natas in the documentary and was pronounced dead by a shocked European doctor off camera. Then Avio touched his chest and revived him with a *tabu* leaf.

After the show, when Daniel went back to where the performers were being accommodated, everybody gave him a wide berth. He was no longer considered to be a mere human being and was thought to be a dangerous immortal spirit who'd come back from the dead. The women were so terrified of Daniel that it took him three years to find a steady girlfriend, and then she refused to marry someone who'd been killed by Avio and had returned from the spirit world. Before a girl called Lina became Daniel's wife, she was already betrothed to another man, but Avio told her she had to marry his nephew. Like all of the other women, she was petrified of Avio and Daniel, but she bravely stood her ground and foolishly defied Avio's wishes. Avio made *kastom* to control Lina's mind and made her lose all self-control so that she kept welcoming Daniel's advances until the two were eventually married.

Daniel paused for a while and seemed to be deciding what to teach me next. Then he said, "I was one of the group of boys who had the last traditional circumcision. I was just nine years old when I had to withstand the type of pain and brutality that would break most grown men." Avio had forewarned Daniel's parents the night before the ritual that he would be coming for their son several hours after midnight. When Avio told Daniel they were going fishing for turtles, he became excited. But instead of going to the beach, they veered from the trail and walked through the jungle to a *nasara* hidden in the gloomy heart of the island. While Avio led Daniel through the forest, he'd kept such a tight grip on his nephew's hand that it throbbed when he was told in a harsh tone to sit down at the *nasara* with four other boys. The confused and frightened children were led inside the small *nakamal* and blindfolded. Then they sat in total darkness. When they listened to the piercing screams of the first boy to be taken outside, it made the already nervous children tremble with fear. Daniel's mind drifted back to the harrowing moment and he said, "Avio milked the juice of a *tabu* leaf onto the top of my head, then said to me, 'You must be strong! Do not shame me by screaming or crying out in pain.' I'll never forget how terrified I was when he led me out to the *nasara*." Throughout the traumatic surgery, he only had Avio to brace him when a *kastom* man placed Daniel's penis on a small slab of wood and used a razor edged bamboo knife to make a single lengthways cut along his foreskin. Then the surgeon slipped a flat piece of bamboo between the penis and foreskin and worked it around the head of the organ as he cut through the skin to prevent him from slicing into the flesh of the penis. After the foreskin was removed, Avio milked the juice from a curative leaf into the wound, then tied a leaf around the bleeding penis.

This was the hellish start to two months of remaining in seclusion in the *nakamal*. Each of the boys were given a personal cook who had to observe the *tabu* of never touching his own penis or looking at his wife until the ritual was over. When roast fowl, *lap lap*, and the very best of local foods were laid out on a woven mat for each of the initiates, their uncles became compassionate, and in sympathetic voices, they told the boys to eat the sumptuous looking meal and that it was to help soothe their wounds. Daniel was lulled into a false sense of security and thought the worst of his harrowing ordeal was over. But it hadn't even started. As soon as the boys had finished eating, Avio armed himself with a stout stick and flayed Daniel's back with such ferocity that blood poured from a crosshatch of gaping wounds.

Sleep didn't come easy to the boys on what was to be the first of many terrifying nights. They were told to lie on their bleeding backs and ordered to hold their swollen penises with their shaking hands. If they rolled onto their sides to alleviate the pain or let go of their tender genitals, they were given a beating that was much more callous than the first.

The constant intimidation and brutal whippings continued for the next four pain-filled days. By the fifth morning, an infection had turned Daniel's smarting penis into a vile-smelling pus-filled mess, and not long after midnight, he was horrified when the boys were ordered to swim in the ocean. Before the exhausted children entered the water, they were given a stern warning to suffer in silence when the saltwater seared and bit into their open wounds and were told that those who cried out would receive more brutal punishment. When none of the boys were able to bear the excruciating pain, their muffled screams and painful sobs ensured they would be greeted with more pain when they were back on the beach. While they listened to abuse and threatening taunts, and blood oozed from their wounds, the initiates were made to stay in the gloomy shark-filled waters until they were shaking from the cold. Daniel looked forward to hugging the flames of a huge fire that blazed on the beach. But when the shivering boys were eventually called ashore, their ruthless uncles extinguished the fire. As Daniel sat on the beach in a cool breeze and hugged his knees to his chest, he was made to suffer from his irrepressible shivering for about an hour until he was allowed to move around to make himself warm.

For the next five days the initiates were made to endure the agony of bathing in the ocean every night. It was a time of brief physical healing and a period of mental recovery. Avio tended to Daniel's numerous injuries by milking leaves onto his penis and into the tangle of cuts on his swollen back.

The temporary respite from the beatings allowed the boys to sufficiently recover so that they were strong enough to endure another wave of violence and cruelty. All of the men from the initiate's bloodline whipped them until blood flowed. Then when the uncles began preparing their nephews for the rigours of manhood, Avio told Daniel to harbour a grudge against his attackers, to never forget the pain, and to seek vengeance by inflicting a much more savage beating on his assailants and their family when his turn to inflict pain came around. Daniel was told that the pain was to teach him courage and to hate and how to hurt others without remorse or showing any mercy. He also learnt about love, about life, about respect, to be proud of tradition, and every piece of *kastom* knowledge his uncle was able to pass on to him. During what Daniel thought must surely be the most difficult time of his life, when he received Avio's words of wisdom and inherited *kastom* from the last of the high men, it was about to shape his daunting future.

At the beginning of the seventh week that the boys had been living in seclusion, their relatives started preparing for a huge feast back at the village. On the day that Daniel was finally about to leave the *nakamal*, Avio made him bend over and whipped him twice. Avio mustered all of his strength and flayed an X across Daniel's healing back, then he filled his hands with scented coconut oil and smeared a slick sheen over his nephew's quivering body. The boys' faces were painted with vegetable dyes. When they headed back to reality and the village *nakamal* for the conclusion of the ritual, which is still practiced nowadays, they kept their heads bowed in a submissive posture as they had for the whole of the two-months of isolation. Two men who were holding a bamboo *tam tam* walked in front of the line of initiates, while another man who followed at the rear performed a frenetic dance to a primal beat that was drummed out on the *tam tam* by a *kastom* man until the boys reached the *nakamal*. Daniel's father gifted him a large piece of cloth, a wooden *kastom* knife with a *tabu* leaf wrapped around its handle, and a yam that was wrapped in a sacred leaf. One of Daniel's sisters walked over and stood in front of him, then he placed the yam at her feet and cut it in half with the knife. Then his sister turned her back and Daniel gently flayed the back of her legs with the cloth, which he then gave to her. His sister had turned around and willingly accepted the placid punishment to symbolise that although Daniel was about to become a man in a patriarchal society and would dominate the women, having sex with his sister is strictly forbidden. She walked away, and then each initiate took his turn to complete the same simplistic rite with their sister.

Avio placed a pile of small rock-hard paw paws and stones at Daniel's feet, which he was about to use to vent two months of pent up frustration from being injured, humiliated, and angered. The initiates temporarily raised their bowed heads and pelted the villagers until blood flowed. In the past, people were killed, and nowadays serious injuries are still inflicted when the boys release their violent surge of suppressed emotions.

More blood is shed when all of the initiates' male relatives arm themselves with sticks and line both sides of a corridor that's two metres wide and twenty metres long, marked out with wild cane that's staked into the ground at one metre intervals. Avio held two sticks over his shoulder and made an X to try and protect his bare back. Then Daniel quickly led Avio along the corridor through a brutal gauntlet of hissing sticks that whipped Avio's back. The pain Avio suffered was cruel and intense, but despite his agony, it was *tabu* for him to run or to cry out when he was flayed. Enemies with personal grievances, and even close friends who are reluctant to draw blood, must swing the sticks with every ounce of their strength. Sometimes the sticks hit with so much force, they pierce the flesh and are left dangling from the mens' backs. A burly villager waits at the end of the corridor and catches the men, who are usually in a state of collapse after the horrific beating. If the initiate is mistakenly hit, whoever swung the wayward blow faces a massive fine and must compensate the boy with numerous pigs.

Years later, when Daniel became an uncle and his own nephew walked him through the hail of searing blows, Daniel was semiconscious and completely disorientated by the white-hot pain when he staggered to the end of the corridor. There is no shame attached to an uncle collapsing in a quivering heap, as this is what most men do when they stumble past the last stake of cane.

The frightening and exhaustive transition from childhood to manhood is almost over. Although the boys are still children physically, when they walk to the end of the corridor, they are allowed to raise their heads and view the world through the eyes of a man. After the initiates drink a *tabu* concoction that's made from the juice of sacred leaves, which is believed to make them virile and fertile right into their old age, the ruthless rite is over. But for the next three years, they are forbidden to have sex.

Nowadays circumcisions are performed under local anaesthetic at a clinic on Epi. The intimidation and the beatings that are meted out during the two months of seclusion are still harsh, but aren't as brutal as the torment Daniel endured. Other traditions and *tabus* that dictate social behaviour have been preserved in their original form, and of these, there were only a few to which I had to adhere. Men are forbidden to carry a stick over their shoulder with a bundle of firewood tied to the end of it, and they must never place firewood on top of their head and carry it like women do. Baskets that are woven from a coconut leaf are used solely by women, and if a man sees another male using one, the offender must give the villager who viewed the breach a fowl, a mat, a pig, or whatever is deemed as fair compensation.

Daniel said if I ever took a wife from Lamen, married life places numerous *tabus* on the members of the bride and groom's family. When a couple marry, the groom's unwed sister is automatically betrothed to the bride's unwed brother to strengthen the alliance between the two families. A father-in-law must never watch his son-in-law eat, and it's *tabu* for a son-in-law to enter a hut that belongs to his father-in-law. The groom can never joke with his in-laws or drink kava from his grandparents' coconut shell cup. If a nephew places a coconut in a bride's doorway, her own father must pay the nephew before he can enter her house. Any work the groom does for his relatives is always free of charge, even if it's a tiresome task like cutting copra or clearing a garden. Married life is both demanding and tiring for a husband, because as well as lending a helping hand to his in-laws, he also helps to provide for his parents while he raises his own family.

An aunt shares the same intimate relationship with her niece as an uncle does with his nephew. The bond is so close that when a niece is married off to another family, her aunts perform a ritual and express their grief by wearing soiled clothing and lying on top of a smouldering pile of *lap lap* that's being cooked by hot stones. Each aunt takes her turn and anxiously awaits for the bride's father to quickly gift her an item that she feels is acceptable before she can remove herself from the scorching mound of food. But before the equally apprehensive father can give the aunt a gift, he must fight his way through an angry mob of female relatives who are armed with burning logs, their fists, sticks, and stones.

On either the second or third day after a couple's first child is born, the infant's father slaughters a pig, then the animal's carcass is gifted to the grandparents. When the sacrificial blood spills from the pig onto the ground, it symbolizes when the mother's blood was spilt during childbirth and allows the ancestral spirits to recognise and to enter the child so they can empower its body. Newborn girls and boys become the namesake of the aunt or uncle that they are endeared to, and the parents seal the christening by paying one pig to the child's namesake.

After Daniel had filled my head with *kastom*, he said, "You see, Rick, it's impossible for the white man to ever understand the respect we have for one another. These are just a few of our customs. Our family relationships are so complex and our values are so contradictory that only a Ni-Van will ever be able to grasp the true essence of the meaning of our lives. I have shared all of this with you for good reason. Because without the small amount of understanding that you have of our people, you could never hope to comprehend what you are about to hear."

Chapter Fifty-Nine

THE MEANING OF LIFE

There was a subtle look of paranoia on Daniel's face when he slowly scanned everywhere within earshot again, then did another quick double check to make sure we were alone before he reached into a pocket in his shorts and said, "I could feel your bodyguards the first time we met. They are powerful spirits, but you must also carry this. Avio was the last of the high men who knew about its powers. This should keep you alive." He handed me the fleshy bulb of a small plant, which I put in my pocket alongside the talisman that Wilson Lui had given me just before I left Maewo. In a grave, hushed tone Daniel said, "You look like hell because you're on the brink of death, so listen very carefully. I'm not going to repeat myself. Don't breathe a word of what I'm about to tell you to anyone on Lamen except for Lina. Once you're off the island, and if this is published, there's a good chance that I might be killed. If I am, Lina or one of the family will contact you." The severity of his words and the possible repercussions of sharing his people's beliefs made me feel cold and tore at my conscience so much that I said, "If it's so dangerous, why the hell are you going to tell me? The last thing I want to do is endanger you and your family." Daniel gave me a stern look that I warned me not to question his judgement, then he said, "The last three white men who stayed with me died not long after they left Lamen. One of them was found dead in Vanuatu, and the other two died as soon as they returned to their country, even though they knew nothing. You see, Rick, I'm a chief, a deacon, and probably the most powerful *nakaimas* in Vanuatu. If a *nakaimas* kills me, he empowers himself with one of the strongest spirits and with immense mana. I'm always at risk so this won't change anything. And you know enough about *kastom* to know why I'm telling you. Lamen is seething with pure evil, and although you have protection, we still need to be careful. If you do exactly as I say, you'll live."

Ever since Lesipsip passed on his demonic knowledge generations of male and female *nakaimas* have taken numerous lives to feed Kesu's insatiable appetite. The spirits of those *nakaimas* reside in trees, at *tabu* sites, in stones, and are embodied in inanimate objects around the island. These evil forces from the past and the threat that sorcerers pose has placed the villagers under a siege that's lasted for centuries.

To haphazardly wander through the jungle and errantly walk over *tabu* ground is to invite death or an agonising illness. Only the feral pigs, other *nakaimas*, and those who know which paths to follow ever dare to enter the haunted rainforest. The dangers are so prevalent that tribal law stipulates that shortly after a woman's husband dies, she must marry her brother-in-law if he is single, or any other available male, to protect her from black magic.

Daniel reinforced how careful we needed to be when he said, "When I was made a chief, my brother-in-law became so jealous that he disputed my title. He tried to kill me with *kastom*, but his magic was hopeless against my powers. I had to sleep during the day and stay awake throughout the night to protect my family. This is how our *bubu* lived. When I was a child, my father never slept at night to make sure that no one killed us." There were a few things I'd noticed, which Daniel confirmed after I said, "So that's why a lot of the houses are surrounded by coral and your guard dog is called "Pillow." He lets you sleep at night, and no matter how lightfooted they are, no one can quietly sneak up without scrunching the coral and making a noise." Daniel nodded, then said, "That's very good, but don't get complacent. I have strong powers, but I couldn't prevent the death of my own father." Daniel's father, Apia, was the minister of a church, which made him a prime target for the *nakaimas* who bludgeoned his skull with a *nul nul*. Because of Daniel's unrivalled status as a powerful *nakaimas*, he's called to autopsies to determine if the deaths were from natural causes or if black magic was responsible. Both Daniel and the European doctor that examined Apia's body were repulsed by the excessively vile smell of his father's stomach contents and were shocked when they discovered that his kidneys had been replaced with sand.

Daniel began his demonic apprenticeship under Avio's expert tuition and became a *nakaimas* when he was just fifteen. While Avio lived on Lamen, only a few privileged people were ever allowed to sit and speak with him. He spent most of his time living as a recluse to guard the secrets of his *kastom*, but he always welcomed Daniel into the *nakamal* and started sharing the mysteries of his revered powers with him long before they lived like animals from a *tabu* fire. Daniel remained in seclusion for one full year during the initial part of his training, which is a must to become an expert *nakaimas*, because you need to fully understand the cycle of nature.

Tabu leaves are a vital and key ingredient to almost every aspect of black magic. The plants, the trees, and every type of vegetation is alive with divine power. Each of them has its own characteristics and are used to create different links to the supernatural. Death is most prevalent on Lamen during winter, from May to October, when the burst of new growth produces potent shoots. Because the vegetation is so lethal at this time of the year, at least six or seven villagers are murdered every winter. And it's rare for someone to be killed over summer. When modern man evolved, he tried to gain control over the forces of nature for his own means and has done this at a terrible cost to the planet and to humanity, whereas primitive man has learnt to manipulate and worship the spiritual forces nature.

When Daniel lived from the *tabu* fire, during the twelve months of isolation, any type of sexual gratification was forbidden. *Tabu* fire derives its name from the numerous restrictions it imposes and because only a *nakaimas* can eat the food that's roasted in its sacred flames. The *nakai-mas* live off yam, taro, and kumara, and these are never washed but are cleaned by rubbing the dirt off with a coconut husk. A leaf or sticks are used to eat the vegetables, as handling them is *tabu*. An initiate always drinks dirty water, which quickly takes its toll on his health, as does eating the excrement of animals and eating his own fetid shit. This is an absolute necessity, because eating their own vile wastes conditions their mind and body to be able to stomach anything. Daniel shook his head from side to side and seemed disgusted with himself as he recalled his appalling past and said, "At the end of my first year, I was emaciated and unclean. I'd lived like a stinking devil and was on the brink of insanity and close to death. I kept thinking like a mad man, like an angry vicious animal that was bursting to kill someone and lusted for human blood. Living from the *tabu* fire is just as hard mentally as it is physically."

When the first year of Daniel's intensive training was over, he returned to the village a haggard-looking emotional wreck. Although everyone knew he'd been with Avio and what they were doing, the villagers were so afraid of the old sorcerer that they said nothing about the shocking state of Daniel's health. There are several types of *nakaimas*. Some of them dig up bodies and favour babies that have been buried for a few days and are starting to decompose. They break open the chest, then eat the fetid heart. But this doesn't make a sorcerer a true *nakaimas* because it only gives him limited powers. Other *nakaimas* exhume the bones of the dead and use them to manipulate the spirits of their *bubu* and to cast evil spells. These are the lowest ranking black magicians. The first vital step to becoming a fully-fledged *nakaimas* after leaving the *tabu* fire is to murder a relative then eat their heart and drink their blood.

Human bones are one of the key ingredients that a sorcerer uses to kill a victim. They are ground into a white powder and, depending on what type of *tabu* leaf is milked into the residue, they are used to kill or to heal. When the powder is burnt down to a jet-black ash, this is also curative or deadly and is used to evoke spirits during displays of magic. Powder that's made from the bones of different body parts is used to kill in various ways. Some powders are used to poison food and others are blown from the palm of the hand and carried by the wind to render a victim weak and helpless before they are physically killed with a *nul nul*. If the concentrated powder blows back into the sorcerer's face, it's deadly. Both the black and white powders are ingested as a poison, but only the white is ever blown into a breeze. They can both be used to make a *tabu* paste, which is made by mixing the powders with the juice of a sacred leaf. This is used to anoint the face of a *nakaimas* by starting above one eye and drawing a line to below the opposite eye. Then the same is done to the other side of the face to make a cross, which shows Kesu that the sorcerer is no longer human, and has transformed himself into a living devil that's empowered by the spirit of his *bubu*.

There were so many parallels between becoming a *nakaimas* and our own evolution in industrial civilizations. Both cultures practise a deliberate cruelty that only mankind is capable of when newfound discoveries and unearthed secrets are unleashed to cause horrific destruction at the hands of men who are satisfying their uncontrollable lust for power and domination. Everything that Daniel told me next mirrored what I'd learnt about *nakaimas* on the other islands. Once the sorcerer has made *kastom* to Kesu, it's like a ticking time bomb, where someone must die within a given time, and if no one else can be killed to feed the spirit then a *nakaimas* is sacrificed. Just as we have nuclear arms that are capable of mass destruction, which are also ticking time bombs, the constant threat these weapons pose induces fear in all of humanity. They don't bring happiness to our existence or purpose, and the same is true once the evil fuse has been lit by a *nakaimas* to kill another native. A murder is always planned carefully. If a *nakaimas* is alone, he will only ever attempt to kill a child or the elderly or the frail. Sorcerers must always unite to murder the strong and healthy. The powdered bone only has the strength to weaken a target and can do so because it's empowered with the spirit of a *bubu*, which fights with them and overwhelms the victim's spirit. When Daniel left the *tabu* fire, he killed a close relative and performed the cannibalistic rite without showing any remorse to ensure he gained full acceptance into the realm of the all-persuasive devil. A *nakaimas* who has limited powers can kill a victim by himself, but this is normally considered too dangerous. Like one dictator of a country with nuclear arms, one *nakaimas* who possesses immense power that must be unleashed, not only terrifies his enemies, he terrifies his followers.

After Daniel cannibalised his relative, his spirit was no longer his own, he was enslaved for an eternity to the devil and became temporarily possessed by the spirit of his *bubu*. Throughout the horrific rite, he felt fearless and indestructible when Kesu gave him the ability to completely overpower and exploit the spirit and life of another human being. But the feeling of supremacy was short-lived when several days later, his own spirit returned and he was overwhelmed by guilt from having taken the life of a loved one. The realization that he wasn't only destroying himself but also his own people really hit home. The power that he'd strived to attain didn't bring happiness; instead, it filled him with hatred and changed the whole purpose of his existence. It wasn't long before the spirit of his *bubu* overpowered his sense of guilt and shame and instructed him to kill again.

By the time Daniel was eighteen, he'd eaten the hearts of ten victims over a three year period and had reached the tenth grade, which is the highest level a *nakaimas* can attain. Most sorcerers serve an incredibly complex apprenticeship to become an expert and take up to five years to complete their tenth grade. It's impossible for a *nakaimas* to expel the spirit of the devil from his body once he eats the heart of the first victim. Certain customs and powers can be exorcised or passed on to another sorcerer, or to a tree, or another part of nature, but Kesu will always keep invading their thoughts and constantly urging them to kill again. A high ranking sorcerer who has a profound knowledge of *kastom* can drink a broth made from *tabu* leaves to release a spirit. This spirit has the power to annihilate the evil spirits of his *bubu* if they turn on him because he's stopped feeding Kesu with human blood and body parts. When Daniel became a Christian, it didn't end his eternal torment, but it helped to curb the massive temptation he faces while Kesu keeps continually urging him to kill again. Daniel sat in silence for a while, then he said, "The power of *kastom* is immeasurable, but the power of goodness, which the white man calls God, is stronger. Man is both good and evil. Now I will tell you what man is made of."

Nakaimas are taught that the body is comprised of three key components: the flesh, the spirit, and the soul. Flesh is purely biological and is the unfeeling mechanical part of our body which simply keeps us alive and functioning. The spirit is the most vital of the three because it gives us desire, leads us, is our conscience, determines our actions, and is the very nucleus of mankind's being. The soul is a living entity that feels and then communicates with the spirit, which has total control over the soul. For example if you touched your arm, the soul feels the contact and relays the message to your more dominant spirit, which tells you your arm has been touched. Primitive tribes around the world who are completely unaware that each other exist yet practice similar rituals have known since prehistory that spiritual life is eternal. These primitive cultures worship and appease the spirits for good reason. It is the spirit, which is the very essence of man, that survives after death and travels to the next dimension in the other world or stays in this world.

The departing spirit can be good or evil because man is both. Uninterrupted nature has the potential to unleash unimaginable destruction, yet she provides us with medicines to heal and, in time, rectifies her own self-inflicted wounds. Primitive religions have a more intimate understanding of those forces than the dictators and the governments who rule powerful nations and define how the masses exist. Primitive cultures have realized for millennia that hatred and harmony in societies stem from the spirit of man. They have also realized the individual, his inner self, and his spirit are imperfect but must be revered and nurtured because in time, irrespective of what choices he makes while he's a mortal, man becomes the earth when his spirit lives on in nature. Instead of looking within ourselves for solace, tranquillity, humbleness, respect, and selflessness, in the civilized and what is deemed as a more sophisticated world, to a primitive man we overlook the true meaning of life. We look to science, to progress, and to economies to solve the immense problems we face. To primitive man, we are spiritually bankrupt in a tired and poisoned world filled with people who have no respect for each other or for the planet. They deem modern man as being spiritually bankrupt because many religions can only make an educated guess after they read a book as to what lies beyond death, whereas most illiterate primitive peoples have an unflappable certainty of where they are headed when they die. And to primitive man, life in the civilized world is a contrived illusion and a shadow of how man should naturally exist.

Although *kastom* is full of contradictions and confusing, while I listened carefully to every one of Daniel's words, he filled in the last few missing pieces of the puzzle, and the true significance of everything I'd learnt over the years became blatantly obvious. While we grope for the answers to mankind's survival and look to the past for the meaning of our existence, the answer may be with us here and now and could come from humanity's living heritage. The best prophecy for the future might be found by delving into our own past, and the elusive answer to the meaning of life might come from those who still live in what we see as the past. Many primitive tribes are threatened with extinction, and when they are unable to live in sync with the spirits, or can't live amidst pristine nature where they exist to simply fulfil the purpose and meaning of their lives, they either vanish or become a defective product of modern society. When they are able to adhere to their tribal laws in the natural realm, they adhere to one another, and more important, they form an inseparable bond with nature. So according to the laws of nature and the beliefs of natural man, there will never be total harmony in the world. Good and evil can coexist in a state of equilibrium by smoothing each other over, because the powers to stupefy and soothe come from within our own divine selves. Unless you've lived cheek to jowl with primitive peoples and have looked at their societies with an unbiased attitude while you've felt their hate, their love, and experienced the whole range of emotions as they do, the true essence of their existence will always remain a mystery. From what I've experienced firsthand, it seems that Vanuatu's pagan beliefs have numerous parallels with the doctrines of many other religions.

When Daniel said, "You know, Rick, some of Vanuatu's customs are practiced in the Solomons," I replied, Yeah, I know. I've been up there a few times. On Guadalcanal, they call a *nakaimas* a *vele*. Sometimes he murders his own relatives and uses their bones to kill." Then Daniel said, "In our hearts, we Lamen islanders know the people from Ambrym are generally good and kind. We will always be friendly and treat them with respect. But inside, we despise them for stealing our *kastom*. All of Ambrym's beliefs belong to Lamen. Not many people know what goes on here. Even the European teachers that live here are probably blind to the pure evil that exists around the island. If you ask Ni-Vans where black magic is strongest, most of them say Maewo or Ambrym. Most of us have abused *kastom*, but the people from Ambrym misuse it more than anyone else. Now is the time for death. The new shoots are coming through. Soon, while you are here, people will start to die. It has already begun on Epi."

The villagers were adamant that the woman who'd died five days before I first arrived at Epi had been killed with black magic. When her sudden death seemed suspicious, the chiefs held council. After a divination rite was performed, they decided that sorcery was to blame. They asked Daniel to help investigate the murder, and he discovered that two *nakaimas* had killed her. After they murdered her, they cut up her body with surgical precision, then mysteriously pieced her dissected corpse back together with the spiritual assistance of the devil. This is a complex ritual, and while the *nakaimas* realign the dismembered limbs, they sing to the spirits. As soon as Daniel saw the body, the lingering aroma from the juices of *tabu* leaves that were milked into the various body parts made it easy for him to ascertain that her death wasn't from natural causes. Any woman who is killed with *kastom* must first suffer the indignity of *masing*, when they are raped by the *nakaimas*. The spirit of *bubu* stifles a woman's screams into a silent gasp by overpowering her voice, which is controlled by a woman's soul. Daniel paused and looked away, maybe to clear his head of the horrific injuries he saw then he said, "The crotch of her panties had been torn out and her vagina was a pulverised mess. She'd been sexually mutilated with a piece of wood. A European doctor examined her body as well and was disgusted when he saw her genitals. This type of injury is common. I had all the evidence, but it doesn't stand up in the white man's court. British law doesn't cater for a man killing with black magic unless there is concrete proof that he committed the murder. Look at Avio. Everyone knew he'd killed scores of people. But the chiefs and the police knew a prison could never hold him, so we banished him from the island. Listen to how quiet it is. Not many people walk around at night alone because it's too dangerous." Apart from a few howling and barking dogs and the normal noises of the night, there was an eerie silence. There wasn't any laughter or the sound of children playing like there normally is in a village of this size.

A *nakaimas* can't become embodied in the flesh of an animal unless he wears a beard. They disguise themselves by inhabiting an animal to kill, or to protect their loved ones by following them if they are travelling alone at night. This is why the villagers who own a rifle try to keep it a closely guarded secret. There are several well publicised stories that tell of dogs that had elbows which faced outwards like a human's being shot, then a *nakaimas* died somewhere else of gunshot wounds at the same time the dog was killed. If a sorcerer plans to murder someone while he's masquerading as an animal and knows that his victim owns a firearm, he renders the weapon useless with black magic. Daniel warned that if I heard an owl screeching outside, never under any circumstances was I to leave the hut because the bird is also a devil.

When I told Daniel I had an unbearable headache and needed to end what had been a fascinating night, he said, "So now that I have shared all of this with you, do you want my help?" Without hesitating I said, "Yeah. I'd really appreciate it. I know it's going to involve *kastom*. So that I can feel your power and the power of your *bubu*, tomorrow, can I try and pull a *namele* leaf from the ground?" Daniel agreed to evoke a spirit, and then he went and slept in a separate hut with Lina, while I slept alone in a room next door to Leta, his eldest daughter. At about two o'clock the next morning, I crept across the coral that surrounds the huts, rubbed Pillow behind the ears to stop him growling, and walked forty meters to the communal leaf hut toilet where I was violently ill with vomiting and diarrhoea. When I got up just on sunrise, Daniel was waiting outside my hut and read me the riot act when he asked if I was on a death wish. He said I hadn't been listening to a word he'd said last night, and that if he wasn't watching over me when I went to the toilet, I could've been killed because a *nakaimas* can disable a victim with powdered bone from about twenty meters away.

That afternoon, when I followed Daniel to a clear patch of ground to try and wrench a *namele* leaf from the ground, I'd decided to leave my talisman from Maewo in my pack. I got a tight grip on the long stalk, pulled for all I was worth, and ripped the leaf from the ground with so much force that I toppled over backwards and ended up sitting on my throbbing arse. Daniel had been toying with me and quietly chuckled away to himself while I picked myself up and brushed the dirt off of my elbows and pants. He threw me a pointed stick and told me to dig another hole and partially bury the leaf. Then I stomped the earth so that it was compacted around the base of the stalk. I felt the same massive surge of emotion I'd experienced on Ambrym when no matter how hard I tried, I couldn't budge the leaf. A burly middle-aged villager grunted and groaned but his vocal attempt to shift the leaf was unsuccessful. When Daniel said, "Now try it," I braced myself again but I needn't have bothered because as soon as I gripped the stalk, it was enough to loosen it, and I effortlessly pulled it from the soft ground. Daniel plucked a ripe *pablemous* from a nearby tree and said, "You look hungry. Here eat this." I'd just started peeling the skin when he walked over and grabbed the fruit from my hands, then hurled it over the treetops into the surrounding jungle. He shook his head from side to side and said, "You've still got a lot to learn. This is why most *nakaimas* die when they're young. A single grain, even the smallest speck of the poisonous powder that's used to prepare the *namele* leaf for this *kastom* is enough to kill you if it passes your lips. You must wash your hands thoroughly, then we will eat." We returned to Daniel's hut, and as each hour passed by, I could feel my body getting progressively weaker. It was as if Daniel had been reading my mind when he said, "This afternoon we will visit a *kastom* man and begin your exorcism."

Chapter Sixty

VANQUISHING THE DEVIL

An hour before sunset we walked a few hundred metres to where Halpy Talso, the husband of Avio's firstborn daughter, lived so that he could perform a divination rite to see who it was from the supernatural that was invading my soul and why they were doing it. Although I felt disjointed from my true self, I hadn't suddenly gained superhuman strength and the ability to talk in foreign languages or started rotating my head three hundred and sixty degrees around my shoulders. I was a physical wreck and emotionally drained, but I hadn't developed any of the classic symptoms that Hollywood movies associate with an exorcism, and Halpy certainly didn't look like a mystical healer. He was a quiet-spoken, silver-haired man with tranquil eyes and a wide smile. Halpy opened a piece of *lap lap* leaf that had been folded into a small parcel which contained a wad of chewed leaves. Then he poured water over the pulpy cud and sieved the lime-coloured mixture through a piece of cloth into a coconut shell. He repeated the whole process, but this time he filtered the brew through the cloth into another shell. He tucked my hair behind my ears, gently pressed the tips of his fingers into my neck, then took a sip from the shell and spat a fine spray into both of my ears and over the rest of my body. When Halpy wiped across the top of my head then across my forehead with the cloth that he'd used to sieve the potion, he nodded as if to say the initial part of the simplistic rite had ended. I carefully followed Halpy's instructions and used my right hand to give him a paltry payment of four hundred vatu while he handed me the wad of leaves. In a soft almost melodious voice he said, "It will be dark soon. Now you must go and place the leaves under your head while you sleep."

That night, while I drifted off to sleep, Halpy entered the other realm to follow my footsteps back into my past and to pay off the ancestral spirits with the vatu I'd given him to save my life. When I slipped into a dream, it was so incredibly real and so vivid that I woke up lathered in sweat with a heaving chest and a dry mouth. The gaunt-faced devil from Santo, Wilson Lui from Maewo, Japeth from Mota Lava, a striking warrior called Naling from Erromango, and the other *kastom* men I saw were so real that I felt I could reach into my subconscious and touch them. The whole bizarre scenario was just as Daniel had said it would be. He'd told me before I went to sleep that I would awake to the sound of a rooster crowing in the middle of the night, which I had, and that I would feel a strange sensation like I'd never experienced before.

The next morning, Daniel and I visited Halpy again. I'd kept the bulk of my previous travels to myself so that Halpy had no idea of what I'd done and where my footsteps would lead him. He told us his subliminal journey began at Santo, where a *nakaimas* who was disguised as a snake had attacked my spirit, but luckily a bearded man who was the perfect description of Ravu had nullified the black magic. When I'd eaten rotten meat with the villagers, it had poisoned my body, but it was a *kastom* man that had called upon the spirits of his *bubu* who'd unwittingly created my problems. His ancestral spirits were holding me tight and wanted to make me a chief in the supernatural realm. On Maewo, the benevolent spirits of the people's forefathers wanted to keep my spirit with them in their mystical world for an eternity. The same thing had happened to me on the other islands, and according to Halpy, I was literally being loved to death. He told me his involvement was over and that I had to go and take the wad of chewed leaves from under my pillow and throw them onto the roof of my hut.

While Daniel and I walked back to my hut, I felt a strange sense of déjà vu when I told him about life in Middle Bush, Santo, and my previous initiations. Especially when he said, "I already know what you've been through and how difficult it has been, but it's good that you're no stranger to hardship because the *kastom* you are about to make is extremely dangerous. Come, we must go." We spent the rest of the day visiting his *nakamal* and the graves of great chiefs that were entombed beneath stone cairns. Then we visited Avio's headstone and met Avio's sons. In the last of dusk's fading light, Avio's great grandson, Joseph, shimmied to the top of a coconut palm and twisted off a young green coconut. As he slid down the trunk, he held the stalk of the nut in his teeth, then carefully handed the nut to Daniel because throwing down or errantly dropping the coconut is *tabu*.

When I stepped outside the next morning and rubbed the remnants of a fitful night's sleep from my eyes, a cheery looking grey-haired woman wearing a brightly coloured dress that was emblazoned with a gaudy floral print was patiently waiting for me. Lomasigia Jake looked to be in her mid-fifties and had the green coconut tucked under her arm as she motioned for me to follow her to the cooking hut. After the numerous warnings I'd been given about taking the dangerous rite seriously, I figured getting my spirit cleansed for a thousand vatu was a bargain when I gave Lomasigia the money, and although she would've been happy with half as much, I didn't have any smaller notes and felt that upping her small payment wouldn't do any harm. She smiled, then thanked me and sat down. Her leathery hands worked back and forwards as she scraped a knife along a clump of ginger-coloured roots. Then with a sharp slash, she sliced away the top of the coconut and left a hole that was just big enough for me to fit my lips into. She placed the grated roots in a cloth, then carefully poured the milk from the coconut over them and caught the tan-coloured mixture in a bowl. She smiled again and told me to sit on the ground with my back against the centre pole of the hut while she poured the dirty looking milk back into the coconut.

After I sat down, she held the coconut in both hands, circled it around my head four times, then she spilt four small portions of the milk onto the top of my head. As she placed the nut to my lips and poured a small mouthful of the bitter-tasting fluid down my throat, she said, "You must hold it now and keep your mouth over the hole. Breathe in and out with your mouth and don't use your nose. It's *tabu*. Don't stop until I return. Not for anything." The first ten minutes weren't so bad, then it felt as if something suddenly snuck up and overwhelmed my senses. My mind drifted into a bizarre trance, maybe because of the intense concentration, maybe because I was drawing deep laborious breaths from inside the shell. This would increase the carbon dioxide in my blood in the same way that breathing into a paper bag does, and might explain why I slipped into a strange stupor. During the next fifty minutes, I felt light-headed and was continually on the verge of vomiting. I had three attacks that lasted several minutes where my whole body convulsed and shook more violently than it ever had during my worst bout of malaria. It took all of my self-control not to breath through my nose and not to pull my mouth away and gulp down a huge lungful of fresh air.

When Lomasigia returned and lifted the coconut from my quivering hands, she handed me a coconut shell cup filled with a potion that had a sweet leafy taste and told me to drink it to wash away the bitter aftertaste of the coconut juice. Then she placed a leaf over the hole in the nut and pushed the top of the coconut back into place to seal the contents and said, "You must go and rest." After she put the coconut at the base of the pole I'd been sitting against and covered it with a much larger leaf, she waved her hand towards my hut and said, "You will sleep for a few hours." I was exhausted and felt so drained and vacant that I collapsed onto my mattress and fell into a deep uninterrupted sleep.

I awoke several hours later and walked outside just as Lomasigia was coming out of the cooking hut holding the coconut and a wild taro leaf. A small crowd of curious villagers followed us to the edge of the jungle, where Lomasigia pressed the leaf into a shallow depression in the ground and placed a rock on each side of the small hollow. When she slashed the coconut in half and poured a muddy-coloured, fetid-looking mess into the taro leaf, the anxious onlookers reeled back in horror and cried out, "Sweet Jesus. My God what a stink. Holy Jesus! Hmmmph! What a smell." They all complained of a vile stench and covered their mouths and noses by pulling up the necks of their T-shirts or using their cupped hands. It was strange, because no matter how hard I sniffed, even when I put my nose only inches away from the leaf, I couldn't smell a thing. Daniel took me aside and said, "Sometimes if the *makas* (dirty coconut milk) is really black there is no hope. Because yours is so dirty, you're lucky to be alive. For the next three full days, it's *tabu* for you to go near the ocean. Don't eat bush cabbage, bananas, or take salt. They will react with the *tabu* leaves that were used during the ritual. This is a time for you to sit and think and for you to show respect to the spirits."

There has never been a clinic on Lamen, so the self-reliant villagers heal most of their ailments with alternative plant remedies or other forms of traditional healing. Daniel sometimes uses the same methods that Numaben uses on Tanna and cuts injuries with bamboo and uses the juice of *tabu* leaves. He taught me how to treat yaws by using part of the porous trunk from a banana plant as a poultice and to heal cuts by rolling manioc leaves between my hands, then milking the antiseptic juice into the wound, which also helps to stem the flow of blood. A manioc leaf is then used to bandage the cut and helps to speed up healing. I had a massive headache when I woke up after breathing into the coconut, and although it was slowly starting to fade, there was no way of hiding that I was unwell. Daniel placed his index finger between my eyes and said, "You have a headache. An old woman called Makiman can fix this for you and so can I. I'll do it for you now." When he disappeared into his hut and returned with a miniature bow and an arrow that was tipped with a shard of glass, before he started plugging me full of holes, I said, "Thanks, Daniel, but I'll take a few Panadol instead. It's staring to go away, and in another half an hour, I'll probably feel so fit, I'll be dangerous." Lina was suffering from a terrible bout of sinusitis, so he decided to treat her instead. The tiny bow reached full draw numerous times and each twang of the thin bowstring thrust the razor sharp arrowhead between her eyes until blood was pouring down her face and dripping off the end of her nose to bleed out the evil spirits that were making her unwell.

During my three day purification rite, I started to awake feeling more fresh-faced and greeted the first rays of each new day with a renewed energy that filled my mind with optimistic thoughts. Daniel told me I was looking and feeling better because my soul was healing and my spirit was growing stronger. I drank a tonic made from male flowers from the paw paw tree once a day, which seemed to help revitalize and flush out my system. Lamen islanders believe the energizing brew breaks down the fat in clogged arteries, is a diuretic, helps with weight loss, and repels evil spirits. While I rested in the village during my purification rite and sat and talked with Lina while she wove mats from pandanus leaves, Daniel paddled across to Epi and worked in his garden every day.

Late one afternoon, when Lina commented on how my appearance had shocked her when we'd first met, she said, "Look at you now. Your eyes are coming clear, and your face is looking young again. The *kastom* medicine is making you strong." When one of Lina's relatives paid us a brief visit and told us someone had just died and that the seasonal killings had started again, it made Lina edgy. She looked worried and said, "If any *nakaimas* find out you know about *kastom*, they will try to kill you. You are lucky this isn't 1998. Back then, four *nakaimas* were killed about this time of the year. Things were really bad." The villagers were so terrified that children rarely played on the beach and they never went anywhere without an adult. Once darkness fell, no one ventured out of their huts unless it was absolutely necessary. Many of the villagers that fell victim to a plague of black magic were cured with *tabu* leaves and when *kastom* men performed exorcisms.

Lomasigia was called across to Epi to perform more healing rituals and exorcisms, which extended my *tabu* by another day. The afternoon that she returned from Epi, Daniel gave me a semi-ripe banana to eat. I noticed it had been cut lengthways, and when I split the fruit apart, I immediately thought the worst when I saw it was filled with jet-black powder. There was no way that my morals were flexible enough for me to eat human bone so I said to Daniel, "I have every reason to trust you. You've gifted me knowledge that could cost you your life, but I wouldn't eat someone's burnt bones unless I was dying of hunger." His face soured and he said. "You are dying, and you will die if you don't eat this to complete the healing." I knew better than to ask but I still enquired, "Is this human bone?" There was a silent rage building in Daniel's eyes when he said in a grim tone, "It is *tabu*. If you trust me, then don't question the help I'm giving you." My instincts and conscience were screaming at me to give the banana back to him, but I ignored all of my squirming morals, and because there was only one way to complete my exorcism, I ate the bland banana and tasteless powder as quickly as I could.

Five days later another villager died unexpectedly under suspicious circumstances. Now that my *tabu* was lifted, when Daniel asked me early one morning if I'd like to go spear fishing with him, I offered to paddle his canoe while he dived for fish. We walked past a family who were midway through skinning a cat that they were about to cook for breakfast, then we cut through a row of houses and followed the main road that heads towards the ocean. I noticed a sheet of corrugated iron lying on top of a fresh grave that had been dug alongside one of the houses and a lamp hanging from a stick that had been pushed into the ground next to the grave. Daniel told me at least one family member keeps a vigilant watch for the first five nights after a burial to try and stop the *nakaimas* from digging up the body and using it for black magic.

We followed the road for a few minutes, then we cut into the jungle and visited the grave of Avio's wife. As soon as Daniel saw that something had tried to unearth her body he said, "The bastards. Now we really have to be careful." He looked worried when he told me he could tell from the way that the grave had been disturbed that *nakaimas* had exhumed her bones. At first I thought wild pigs were responsible, but when I had a closer look, there weren't any footprints in the loose soil that was scattered around the grave. Daniel said that her bones possessed great power and that maybe the sorcerers who were responsible would use her remains to counter his powers and kill us because they suspected he was sharing *kastom* with me.

We walked to the church at the end of the island and while Daniel and one of his friends whose name was Tomson caulked a small leak in their canoe, pastor Kerry called me into the church. He gave me an impromptu sermon and warned me that my exorcism was a satanic rite because even the good spirits of *bubu* were the devil in disguise. When I agreed to let him place the bible on my head to cleanse my soul, he looked to the heavens and shouted, "This is more than just a book. The spirits of *bubu* will be driven from your tainted soul. With the blood of Jesus, all evil with leave brother Rick."

As I watched Daniel finish making the canoe watertight, he told me each family has their own private portion of reef to fish from, but beyond the reef is open to everyone. His totem is the turtle and has given him such an intimate relationship with the ocean that whenever he's asked to catch a turtle for a *kastom* feast, he never fails. He developed the uncanny bond with his totem by drinking the blood and eating the heart of the first turtle he ever captured. While he's still out diving, Avio's sister, who also shares the same close affinity with the turtle, tells the villagers how many of the creatures Daniel will capture and what sex and how big they will be. So far she's never been wrong. Daniel waded into the ocean and swam over the reef while Tomson and I continuously paddled for two hours against a buffeting wind to hold the canoe steady, so that whenever Daniel speared a beautiful multi-coloured fish, he could throw it in the canoe before one of the numerous sharks that were swimming around the reef darted in and grabbed it.

The following day I was invited to a feast which celebrated five days had passed since a woman died and to release her spirit. Men who were wearing stubble on their chins carried the bodies of sacrificial pigs and an assortment of food which they placed on the twelve piles of offerings which represented each *nasara* on the island. They also put a razor on top of each pile to signify their grief. When the *lafaet* was over, most of the men were allowed to shave, but for the immediate family, many *tabus* remained in place. Male relatives are forbidden to shave until one month after the death, and if a nephew farts in front of his grieving uncle, the nephew must remain with his uncle until he farts, then he compensates his uncle with one pig. The same law that regulates flatulence applies to a niece and aunt. It's *tabu* for all of the kinfolk to clean the inside and around the outside of their huts, and they must wear the same clothes until the end of the one-month mourning period. A small *lafaet* is held at the end of the month and lifts all of the *tabus* except for the one which prevents the family from fishing in their section of reef. The *tabu* is enforced for one year, then at the end of the twelve months, a nephew from the grieving clan receives a small payment from the rest of the family. Then he goes fishing, and once he catches the first fish, this ends the *tabu*.

Whenever I joked and talked with the friendly villagers, it was easy to forget that these kind and affable people were killing one another to nurture the devil and satisfy their own egos. It was obvious that when they greeted Daniel with wide smiles, everyone both feared and respected him. I could tell from their mannerisms that because he'd inherited Avio's immense power, it would make him a social liability for the rest of his life.

When I left the island and was paddling across Lamen Bay with Daniel and another villager to catch a flight back to Port Vila, I felt incredibly weak and lethargic. Daniel explained that I felt unwell because he and his family were embracing my spirit because they loved me and were reluctant to let me leave, but after we said our final goodbyes, I would feel healthy and refreshed again. While we sat outside the small airport terminal by ourselves, although I already knew the answer, I asked him why he'd shared the most sacred aspects of his beliefs, especially with a white man, when he knew he would be putting his family's lives at risk. He said, "Ambae's paramount chief, the highest chief in the land, has given you the right to publish your book. So has Avio's spirit. The Ratahigi who gave you his blessing on Ambae had a superiority which he gained from quantity when he sacrificed over one thousand pigs. That isn't to say he wasn't also a special man, because he was a great chief. Avio's blessing was different. It had another quality. His spirit possesses an immeasurable awareness and immense supernatural power. When you lived with different clans around Vanuatu, no amount of money could ever have bought the knowledge that was gifted to you. The gift of understanding hasn't come from powerful chiefs or wise *kastom* men. It wasn't me or any other individual that had the right to teach you *kastom*. We only shared our customs with you because our forefathers approved of you and it's what they wanted us to do."

Chapter Sixty-One

COLONIAL CONQUEST

The first time I visited Port Vila, it was like any other developing third world town that was still experiencing growing pains. Many of the Ni-Vanuatu were trying to acclimatise to the uniform development of a modern society. They being were forced into an unbalanced existence as they tried to take the best from both worlds while their transition from a traditional way of life to westernisation was still slowly levelling itself out. Whenever I returned from an adventure on an outer island, I loved what must be one of the Pacific's most picturesque ports. I enjoyed the company of its friendly people and soaked up the creature comforts the town offered. But now that my travels around Vanuatu were over, I looked at the town through eyes that were worldlier and had seen and learned more than I could ever have hoped for. Port Vila screamed of colonial conquest. The modest main street seemed to inflate itself into a kaleidoscope of impatient activity that was choked with traffic and foul-tasting fumes and hordes of jostling people. The locals who live in ragged dwellings on the outskirts of town where I normally stayed have been reduced to impoverished squatters who are living in the backwash of a civilization that has collided with their own culture with a traumatic and devastating impact.

The first European explorers who landed on Efate were initially treated as gods because of their white skin. When their ships disappeared into the horizon, they were thought to fly off into the sky, and the general opinion of those who have been forced to live in squalid conditions while they adapt to modernization and western standardization is that the white man should have kept going on a one-way flight. Especially the old people who long for a paradise that was once familiar to them but is now part of a withering dream that will never become a reality again. That traditional life is a world away for the next disillusioned generation who wander around aimlessly without any chance of gaining meaningful employment or getting any type of welfare. These despondent youths face an uphill battle against poverty and face a newly introduced disease, low self-esteem. Their lives no longer revolve around tradition which was always meant to be the very core of a Ni-Vanuatu's existence. The unemployed *"spearem publik road"* or work for "the big fella company." These are the terms that are used to describe the locals who hang around the roads while they aimlessly kill time with the rest of the jobless.

After I lived with the most primitive tribes and then lived in the slums, the crux of Vanuatu's social problems appear to stem from the need for self-sufficiency being replaced with the white man's ideals which teach that success is based on creating an efficient economy. The rush to build a vibrant and prosperous future has made the unemployed people become dependant on their working relatives while they are left feeling worthless at being unable to contribute towards their own and their family's welfares. That's not to say we should bulldoze down all of the western buildings, replace them with leaf huts, and turn back the clock, because improved healthcare and some of the other modern services are obviously beneficial. Introducing a foreign culture has led to the rapid decay of primitive man's most basic instinct, self-reliance. To be able to be self-reliant, the people need individual and cultural freedom within a well-defined set of rules. Because westernisation has replaced the need to actively participate in a traditional lifestyle by making Ni-Vans dependant on a consumer society, it's bewildered a people who worshiped not only all aspects of daily life, but life itself. That life will always be a hollow existence unless you can freely express who and what you are. The need to embrace a traditional life has been replaced with a rebellious attitude against a foreign existence. For those who have no other choice than to become passive spectators instead of being key contributors to that existence, their lost sense of purpose has inevitably led to a discontented society. Any culture that makes an inventory of its ill-treated past and is left feeling frustrated, emotionally stressed, jealous, angry, and depressed has the potential to become antisocial and lawless. With the exception of Middle Bush, Santo, where uninvited guests are greeted with an instinctive antagonism, Vanuatu is by far the safest country I have ever lived or travelled in. The tourists who visit and the expatriates who have lived there for decades will rarely and most likely never be witness to the brutalities of secretive customs. They will usually only get to enjoy its friendly people and stunning beauty.

Petty and malicious crime is on the rise in Port Vila due to the breakdown of traditional society. I found it incredible that as a goodwill gesture on the eve of the new millennium, the government decided to grant every criminal who was in prison a pardon. Habitual rapists, murderers, and other unruly citizens were released by an introduced system that isn't fully compatible with the wants and needs of its own people. To let criminals free, whether it's on a whim or because of a date or because the Melanesians won't tolerate their country being ruled by British law, is unimaginable in a western country. As a result, a prisoner who was released on New Year's Day killed an expatriate, and because murdering a European is such an improbable crime, it led to a huge public outcry. I decided to pay the police a visit to see how black magic has influenced the judicial system and the rest of Vanuatu's modern society.

I was staying at Freshwater, and as I walked into town, I stopped for a meal of rice and stewed beef at a roadside stall that was dwarfed by a construction site next door. Two unemployed youths were sitting at my table, so I said to them, "What does this new hotel mean to you guys?" The better educated of the two felt it was great for tourism and would bring more money into Vanuatu, but the less sophisticated one griped, "We were here first, but we always seem to be the last to get anything. All of the best buildings cater for the needs of rich tourists, not for us poor Ni-Vans."

A lanky policeman who was milling around outside the police station looked bewildered when I asked him about grave robbers and *nakaimas*. He seemed shocked that a white man wanted to discuss and delve into a sensitive and highly secretive aspect of his culture and said, "I don't know anything about it, but you can try inside. Ask for private Simons." When I tracked down the private, the same question was greeted with an equally astounded but more cooperative response. I followed him into a backroom where he shut the door, slouched back in his chair, and willingly revealed the secrets of sorcery in civilized Vanuatu.

According to private Simons, black magic is rampant throughout all levels of society and is a prime suspect in most of the crimes he deals with. He stretched back in his chair, and then he put his hands behind his head and said, "The judiciary has no means of prosecuting a *nakaimas* because British law doesn't cater to black magic. We are very afraid of *nakaimas* who perform ritualistic murders. I know for a fact that some of our own officers practice sorcery. Look at the barbed wire fence around the cemetery. We had to put that up years ago and provide security to stop *kastom* men from digging up the bodies. Here on Efate this was done before the white man arrived. Some tribes traded the bodies of slain enemies to other cannibalistic clans in exchange for pigs. They used to rob graves back then for human flesh and to use the bones for *kastom*. Whoever would've thought that this type of thing would still be happening now."

While I was staying with John Noel at Luganville, two men from Ambrym hamstrung two young girls, repeatedly raped them, and then tied them up with a rope and dragged them behind a car until they died. Despite the horrific nature of the crime, after the offenders had been in prison for just two weeks, they were granted total freedom. This is common and happens when the accused lies to the judge with the aid of black magic, which is known as sweet mouthing. Before he's jailed, a *nakaimas* inserts *tabu* leaves into his rectum, then during the night the leaves are removed, cleaned, and used to make *kastom*. When a defendant stands before a judge, he usually has a leaf under his tongue or concealed elsewhere so that the moment he speaks his words completely confuse the judge's train of thought. What should ordinarily be harsh sentences are reduced to a pittance or completely quashed.

When I asked Simons if he thought sweet mouthing had anything to do with the government releasing prisoners on the eve of the new millennium, he shook his head in disgust and said, "It was a real kick in the teeth to us. Sweet mouthing had everything to do with it. We place messages over national radio to warn people to be careful at night if we know *nakaimas* are active in Port Vila or in Luganville. It poses a huge problem for us. No offence but the white man is to blame. Because we have to exist by using his money, it has led to an increase in black magic. People abuse *kastom* during disputes on the outer islands, but here in Port Vila, they also use it out of greed to get money or because they're jealous of the affluence others have. Here in Vanuatu the constitution allows the freedom of worship. Man bush still worships stones, plants, bats, and all sorts of things. Now I'm getting reports about a group of expatriates who are starting up a demonic cult on the outskirts of Vila. Even if this is true, unless we catch them breaking the law, we're powerless to do anything. Black magic is even used to manipulate sport. Most soccer teams rub salt on their legs, or if they're playing near the coast, they swim in the ocean before a game and let the salt dry on their bodies. Salt buggers up the power of the leaves that are used for *kastom*." When I said, "What about politics? Is black magic used to sway the balance of political power?" Simons thought long and hard before he said, "You didn't hear this from me. Each political party employs a full-time *nakaimas*. They give politicians directives as to how the opposition are thinking or going to act. I believe this is why there is so much political instability and corruption in Vanuatu. Before we became westernised, our primitive forefathers used black magic as a form of discipline. They did my job. Now the *nakaimas* are like mercenaries. People pay them to kill or to disrupt their enemIES' lives."

Before I returned to New Zealand, I convalesced while I stayed at Freshwater with Simeon Tovovur for a few days. My body had been subjected to so much unwanted abuse over the years that regaining full health was a slow and gradual process. Simeon suggested I go and see Nari, who's a *cleva* from Erromango. Nari lives on the outskirts of town, so I took a slow walk and visited her that afternoon. She looked about sixty years old, and was a lovely natured woman with a plump build, a quick wit, and bright eyes. Nari told me that her forefathers had first arrived on Erromango after they sailed across the ocean with Pokurvi, who's Erromango's most powerful devil. Because the ocean let them survive their epic voyage from an island close to Africa, Nari's clan made their totem saltwater. Pokurvi lurks beneath the waters of the Tumpmbu River on Erromango, and in 1977, the potent spirit entered Nari's dreams and told her what flowers, leaves, and fruits to use for healing. Her healing powers are legendry, but she is unable to tell who was responsible for stealing an item, who poisoned someone, and she can't look into the future as she only received the ability to cure sickness. She travels around Efate every day to tend to her patients, and the villagers fly her to Erromango to perform a healing ritual if other treatments have failed to remedy an illness.

Nari told me she'd never treated a white man before and said, "There's a first time for everything," as she walked with a slight waddle and led me to the bottom of her garden. She said if a *kastom* man asks for an exorbitant amount of money to cure an ailment, they aren't a traditional healer. She insists on only ever receiving a token payment of one hundred vatu, of which she keeps half for herself and donates the other half to the church to thank god for her gift. The rite was incredibly short and simplistic. After I gave her a coin, she circled it around my head twice, then told me to return in the morning. That night, after Nari placed the money under her pillow, she slipped into the dream world to try and find out why I was unwell.

The next day, while I listened to her recall her subconscious journey, I was in total awe of the humorous old woman. Although she didn't name the island, her description of Lamen painted an incredibly accurate picture. She described rows of canoes parked on a dazzling white sand beach on a tiny low lying island, and dead flat roads that were bordered by coral fences and rows of trees. It was a beautiful place, but the idyllic island with immaculately groomed villages housed numerous secrets and had an overwhelming evil presence that was stronger than anything she'd felt anywhere else in Vanuatu. Nari said, "Nothing has ever matched the power of the demonic forces I sensed on the island. The families you lived with were good people. There was one man in his mid-thirties who was your good friend that looked evil when he wasn't smiling, but he had a kind heart." Then she described with amazing exactness his tall wiry physique, thin face, chiselled features, and his goatee beard, as she painted a perfect portrait in my mind of someone I'd befriended while I lived on Lamen. Nari gave me a smile that said I had nothing to worry about and said, "When I saw you with this man in my dream, the head of a snake rose from out of the ground alongside him. I paid him the one hundred vatu and he released your spirit. While I paddled a canoe across a large bay to take your spirit to another island, the sea was so rough we were lucky not to drown. The bodyguard that you carry is good. It has saved your life many times." I was stunned, and when Nari pointed to my pocket, I pulled the talisman from my shorts and told her it had come from Maewo.

Nari always feels tired after she awakes from a dream. When she travelled into the supernatural realm to capture my spirit, it had left her dazed and exhausted. She said, "I was so slack that I burnt my husband's breakfast this morning. You are very, very, lucky. If you'd left Vanuatu without healing your spirit, you would've died. I can feel that you have made *kastom* with people with different beliefs. *Kastom* belongs to each island. What you have done isn't wrong or a bad thing, but if the people don't want to release your spirit, it can be extremely dangerous. You see, Rick, we Ni-Vanuatu are tied to the land, and we believe the land and our spirit are one. Your body is very tough. It looks like you have worked in a plantation all your life, but it will take the strongest leaf to cleanse your spirit." She blew a gentle puff of breath into two glasses that were filled to the top with a lime-green fluid, then she reassured me that because I was about to drink a double dose of *kastom* medicine, it would purify my tainted spirit. When it was time to leave, she shook my hand, leant across, and kissed me on both cheeks, then she said, "Because you have made *kastom* and lived like a Ni-Van, one day you'll be a special man."

While I flew back to New Zealand, I thought about what I'd been through and the significance of my travels. I'd never intended to go on a bold quest to seek the ultimate meaning of life or to try and discover the intricate blueprint for humanity. I'd hoped to learn about some of the most enchanting places and some of the most captivating people on earth, and then share the knowledge I was gifted. The paranormal is interesting, but while I live in New Zealand, no amount of money could get me to dabble in the occult. When I was told what a primitive man thinks it is to be truly human, and when I explored the supernatural, these were inevitable consequences of living amongst deeply spiritual primitive peoples. To be able to fulfil my lust for adventure and my burning desire to explore remote jungles is a huge privilege. I decided from the moment I became a photojournalist that unless I shared my experiences with brutal honesty so as to give the reader an intimate insight into my experiences and into the lives of the peoples I visited, there was no point in sharing my travels. I feel like I've only been a medium, who has hopefully helped to express primitive people's values, their thoughts, and how they see their world. Although I've done the best I can, this book will no doubt have its faults because, in reality, it is not me but the people who can tell their true story and understand the true essence of their beliefs.

There are numerous aspects of humanity's condition that we will never be able to completely grasp or fathom. It's a sad reflection on the way that some of us have been conditioned to think in modern society when the things that we don't fully understand are often scorned and ridiculed or destroyed by narrow minded people. While I was going through customs at the airport in New Zealand, the woman stamping my passport said, "You've been to Vanuatu. From what I've heard, it sounds really nice, but you look as though you need another holiday to get over your holiday." I didn't care about how unwell I looked. I'd put my mind and body through hell but fortunately, several months later, I was fit and well again. I don't regret for a minute what I've been through because to have had such an incredible experience, and then to be able to share images and thoughts which not only make us think about different ethnic groups, but also makes us think about ourselves, is something I really value.

Chapter Sixty-Two

EPILOGUE

Although I've been given an unprecedented insight into *kastom*, and the most powerful men in Vanuatu have given me the right to strip away the mysteries surrounding the archipelago's primitive religions, there will always be people who argue that it doesn't give me the right to make a previously veiled culture transparent. I don't look upon the *kastom* that was gifted to me as a much-coveted prize or a trophy that I get to proudly display in the pages of a book. The knowledge is a treasured gift that I've been allowed to share with everyone—and, more important, with future generations. I've chosen to expose those closely guarded beliefs that have remained obscure for millennia because unless we try to understand the best and worst aspects of any culture and learn to appreciate other races and cultural differences irrespective of how barbaric they seem, not only won't we fully understand other racial groups, we won't fully understand humanity at a time when we're becoming more and more removed from each other, at a time when we seem to be rushing towards a goal that modern man is unable to define and has no idea where it will lead us.

It's so hypocritical and self-defeating to develop science and technology so that mankind can climb to the top of the evolutionary tree to get a better look at the world if the human race destroys what remains of the evolutionary tree's living roots. That tree will eventually come crashing down, like the rich and complex primitive cultures that we've devastated in the past and will destroy in the future. We could learn so much from these people, but it's doubtful that these cultures will ever enrich our thinking as much as they should because our morals, our ideals, and our purpose are contradictory and, in some respects, our thinking couldn't be more diametrically opposed. Some of these societies have a profound knowledge of nature that puts our scientific understanding of the earth to shame. If we aren't big enough to accept criticism about how we've systematically destroyed primitive societies, then we're too small to accept praise for the way we're shaping our own precarious future.

It's ironic that the stresses of living in a modern society make us look to natural man, to his mysticism, and to his environment to escape civilization's pressurized lifestyle. There are those who seek solace, spiritual rebirth, re-enchantment, and tranquillity by escaping to wilderness settings to get away from it all, the "it all" being the sometimes inhospitable way of life that we've created for ourselves. Instead of defining the strength of a nation by its material wealth, maybe we'd be better off by taking pride in a nation that measures its worth by the richness of its culture and by the happiness and wellbeing of the people who nurture that culture.

Before I left Vanuatu, Simeon Tovovur's final words were, "You've run the gauntlet and survived when you should've been hacked to pieces." The captives of American Indians that managed to survive running through two lines of braves who delivered a hail of deadly blows with knives, clubs, and tomahawks were held in high esteem and believed to possess great spiritual power. Simeon told me I'd "won" when I should be dead but I still have much to learn, and because I'd followed the *kastom* road that one day I'd be a special man. Only now do I think I understand the significance of being a special man. It's not in the eyes of others. Maybe the Ni-Vanuatu's concept of special is being able to truly appreciate our individual worth, our individual freedom, and most of all our relationship with nature and with each other. I've followed the *kastom* road and discovered its destination was understanding and forming a better relationship with all of creation to become a special man. It wasn't about looking within myself and feeling confident with my own conclusions or looking to others for their awe inspiring answers. It was about looking all around myself and looking beyond the words of those wise *kastom* men until I got a clearer view of nature and learnt to savour even her most insignificant aspects. It was about turning those years of puzzlement into sheer pleasure once I found the insight I'd been looking for. And it was about accepting people for who they are irrespective of what they believe in. It took me nearly a decade to realize the futility of trying to rationalize a culture's irrational beliefs or their bizarre behaviour in the hope of gaining a true insight into the mindset of primitive man.

Despite all of my privileged experiences, I'm still not a deeply spiritual person. After everything I've been through, my outlook on life can never be black or white, simply is or isn't. While I live in New Zealand, I don't worship any form of religion or don a loincloth, dance around a fire or sacrifices pigs. I simply exist with the peace of mind that I've been given from my unwavering certainty that spiritual life continues after death. Once I personally felt the power of the supernatural, it made me look at nature differently, with a spiritual reverence. Like man bush and the other primitive peoples I've lived with, now that I have a much more heightened awareness of life and what waits beyond, I enjoy a much closer bond with the natural realm. Not with a New Age, touchy-feely, tree hugging, leaf fondling intimacy, but with a much deeper respect and understanding.

THE NARRATIVE PRESS

TRUE FIRST-PERSON HISTORICAL ACCOUNTS

THE HISTORICAL ADVENTURE AND EXPLORATION SERIES

The *Historical Adventure and Exploration Series* from The Narrative Press are all first-hand reports written by the explorers, pioneers, scientists, mountain men, prospectors, spies, lawmen, and fortune hunters themselves.

Most of these adventures are classics, about people and places now long gone. They take place all over the world – in Africa, South America, the Arctic and Antarctic, in America (in the Old West and before), on islands, and on the open seas.

Some of our authors are famous – Ernest Shackleton, Kit Carson, Henry Stanley, David Livingston, William Bligh, John Muir, Richard Burton, Elizabeth Custer, Teddy Roosevelt, Charles Darwin, Osborne Russell, John Fremont, Joshua Slocum, William Manley, Tom Horn, Philip St. George Cooke, Apsley Cherry-Garrard, Richard Henry Dana, Jack London, and Buffalo Bill, to name a few.

One thread binds all of our books: every one is historically important, and every one of them is fascinating.

Visit our website today. You can also call or write to us for a free copy of our printed catalogue.

THE NARRATIVE PRESS

P.O.Box 2487
SANTA BARBARA, CALIFORNIA 93120 U.S.A.
(800) 315-9005
www.narrativepress.com